THE FIGHTING NEVER STOPPED

THE FIGHTING NEVER STOPPED

A Comprehensive Guide to World Conflict Since 1945

Originally published under the title *World Conflicts*

PATRICK BROGAN

VINTAGE BOOKS

A Division of Random House, Inc.   New York

Vintage Books Edition, February 1990
First American Edition

Library of Congress Cataloging-in-Publication Data
Brogan, Patrick.
    The fighting never stopped.
    "A Vintage original."
    Includes bibliographical references.
    1. Military history, Modern—20th century.
2. Revolutions—History—20th century.   3. Terrorism
—History—20th century.   I. Brogan, Patrick. World
conflicts.   II. Title.
D842.B69   1989   909.82   89-22472
ISBN 0-679-72033-2

Manufactured in the United States of America
10 9 8 7 6 5 4 3 2 1

CONTENTS

INTRODUCTION

The world has never been at peace since the victory celebrations of 1945. The great wars that have shaken Asia and Africa and the lesser conflicts that have afflicted the rest of the world have sometimes subsided and have sometimes flared up into monstrous conflagration. They have never ceased. In 1988, foreign powers declared that they would withdraw from the wars in Afghanistan, Angola and Cambodia, to leave the native peoples of those countries to continue their civil wars on their own; there was no hope for peace in any of them. Iran and Iraq agreed to a ceasefire, to end the largest conflict since the Korean war, though not the most costly. However, the bitter animosities between the two countries persist, and both are frantically preparing for a new war.

About 40 countries in the world are in the unshaking grip of war, rebellion, foreign infiltration, terrorism or endemic banditry. Another score maintain a fragile peace that could shatter at any moment. The bloodiest of recent conflicts were the war between Iran and Iraq and the Soviet intervention in Afghanistan. One lasted eight years, the other nine, and both accomplished nothing decisive, at enormous cost. Political and military considerations finally brought them to an end, without resolving the problems that precipitated them.

At the opposite extreme was the relatively low level of terrorism in such places as Northern Ireland or the Basque country in Spain, each provoked by the separatist demands of a minority population. For these intractable and inherited problems there appeared to be no possible solution. Other contemporary conflicts include the armed truce between Israel and her neighbours; the endemic tribal wars of Africa; the peasant insurgencies of Central America; and the Communist rebellion in the Philippines.

There have been at least 80 wars since 1945, resulting in the deaths of between 15 and 30 million people. Millions more have been driven from their homes. There are well over 30 million refugees in the world today – probably as many as there were during the mass movements of people after World War II. At the end of 1988, the US Committee for Refugees calculated that approximately 13 million people were refugees in foreign lands, and that there were about 16 million 'internal refugees' – that is, people who had fled their homes to escape danger.

Most of the conflicts in the world today are between peoples and races. Only a few are between nations, and even fewer are ideological. That pattern might change: Iran and Iraq showed that national animosities can still erupt into full-scale war, and the miseries of the Third World may well produce a revival of ideological struggle in the next generation. Today, however, the bleak prospects for peace in the world reflect chiefly the bitter quarrels between peoples in the Middle East, the whole of Africa, India, the Soviet Union, South-east Asia and the Balkans. The rest of this frightful century, and the next, will continue on the violent path set over the past 75 years.

If anything, the world has become more violent with each succeeding decade since the murderous '40s. In Africa, only the Biafra war was more deadly than the civil wars of the 1980s in Uganda, Mozambique and Angola. At a very rough estimate, 450,000 people were killed in the Iran–Iraq war between 1980 and 1988, far more than in all the other wars in the Middle East. The Afghan war has, so far, probably resulted in the deaths of half a million people by violence, disease or starvation. These five contemporary conflicts have uprooted at least 17 million people, over 7 million of them into foreign countries. The proliferation of arms in the Middle East and Africa and the aggravation of tribal hatreds and ideological violence have destroyed Lebanon and Uganda, and brought a number of other countries to the verge of dissolution, among them Angola, Mozambique, Sudan, Cambodia and Ethiopia. Several other countries are so fragile that they could easily go the way of Lebanon. What is going to happen to Iran without the ayatollah or to Afghanistan without the Soviet army?

There was one consummated ceasefire in 1988 – between Iran and Iraq – and the Soviet Union's withdrawal from Afghanistan at least changed the nature of that conflict. There were also prospects of an end to the war in Namibia and a settlement in the Western Sahara. On the other side of the ledger was the possibility of the return of the Khmers Rouges to Phnom Penh, the outbreak of civil war in Somalia and the resumption of tribal massacres in Burundi. The Philippine government was strengthened, but those of Colombia, Peru and El Salvador were further weakened, and Burma, after a series of upheavals, hesitated on the brink of anarchy.

Humanity is still adapting to the disappearance of the empires that kept the peace before 1945 – a tranquillity imposed at the point of a bayonet, intended to permit the exploitation of brown, black and yellow peoples by white men. However, the world outside Europe is a much less peaceful place than it was when five or six European capitals governed all Africa, the Middle East, India and Central and South-east Asia – and, before 1821, South America as well.

The decline of the empires was inevitable. It required merely that a relatively small class in any colony should ask itself why it should be governed by foreigners, and the advance of education produced that class everywhere. The empires were built by force: the British conquered India with the musket and Africa with the Gatling gun. Once modern weapons became freely available to rebels, who vastly outnumbered the colonial garrisons, the balance of force shifted and the empires were defeated. The Soviet Union has discovered in Afghanistan that the same principle applies to the Soviet 'bloc' as well as to the old-fashioned capitalist empires that Marx and Lenin denounced so vigorously.

However, once the secret that power grows out of the barrel of a gun was revealed to the tribes of the Middle East, of Africa and of India, not to mention its rediscovery by European terrorists, the fissiparous tendencies that had destroyed the empires came to threaten the emerging countries of the Third World. India, Nigeria and Lebanon are less nations than geographical expressions. The Sikhs and the Ibo, as well as all the peoples and sects of Lebanon, consider themselves nations, and have fought or are fighting for their independence. Their defeat is never permanent, as the Sikhs have shown.

There have been few all-out national wars since 1945. The most costly were the Korean, the Vietnam and the Iran–Iraq wars. Europe, hitherto the most bellicose of continents, is conspicuously missing from this list. It remains obsessed by more than three decades of frightful carnage, from 1914 to 1945: the French lost 300,000 dead in four months during the Battle of Verdun; the British lost over 20,000 dead on 1 July 1916, the first day of the Battle of the Somme, and nearly a million during the four years of World War I; the Soviet Union's losses between 1941 and 1945 exceeded 20 million. By comparison, the losses of the United States during the Vietnam war – 55,000 dead – were inconsiderable. Europe still mourns the slaughter of the Great War and the Soviet Union is daily reminded of the losses of the Great Patriotic War, but in the past 20 years, Vietnam, Cambodia, Uganda, Nigeria, Mozambique and half a dozen other countries have suffered, proportionately, just as heavily and sometimes far more.

Wars between nations are usually caused by territorial disputes, ideological rivalry, a lust for conquest or, occasionally, by diplomatic incompetence. There have been wars of all these kinds since 1945, and the threat of more hangs over a good part of the globe. The fact that there are, at the moment, so few national quarrels on the verge of explosion does not mean that humanity has changed its ways.

There have been several territorial wars in the past 20 years, including the Falklands war between Argentina and Britain, the Ogaden war between Ethiopia and Somalia, and the Iran–Iraq war, which ostensibly concerned the question of whether the frontier between the two lay in the middle of a river or on its east bank. There are many other territorial claims outstanding, among them the latent animosities in the Balkans that have been suppressed since 1945 by the Red Army. Most of the countries in Africa are vulnerable to irredentist claims, as are many nations in Asia; China, for instance, has a long-standing frontier dispute with the Soviet Union. Nearly every nation in South America has a claim on at least one of its neighbours.

As for ideological wars, they have much diminished in recent years. The United States entered the Vietnam war for ideological reasons, and the Soviet Union intervened in Afghanistan to prop up a disintegrating Communist regime. They both bit off far more than they could chew. Otherwise, and despite many melodramatic promises to 'roll back' Communism or to 'bury' the West, both have been exceedingly cautious in the exercise of their own military power. It was notable that President Reagan never actually sent the Marines into Nicaragua. That sensible example has been followed by lesser nations.

Marxist revolutionary zeal is a declining force in the world, 70 years after the Bolshevik revolution, and it is likely that, in the short term at least, there will be fewer massacres of the innocents in the name of that future Utopia. The post-colonial wars in Africa, which often proclaimed themselves to be 'people's revolutions', have all turned into straightforward power struggles. Old-fashioned ideological wars continue in El Salvador and the Philippines; and the Shining Path in Peru, like the Khmers Rouges in Cambodia, have demonstrated that, in some places at least, ideological fury retains all its powers of destruction.

Wars of conquest have been out of fashion since Hitler, but they still occur. President Saddam Hussein of Iraq thought he could conquer the Arab-speaking and oil-rich provinces of Iran (that famous river dispute was merely a pretext). On three occasions, the Arabs thought they could conquer Israel. They were all mistaken.

Diplomatic incompetence remains one of the greatest dangers to the peace of the world. The ineptitude of a handful of men in Berlin, Vienna, St Petersburg, London and Paris brought down upon the world the horrors of World War I and all the catastrophes that followed. It might easily have happened again in the days of Molotov and Dulles if it had not been for the nuclear deterrent, which protected East and West alike from their leaders' aggression, and also from their stupidity. The nearest that they approached disaster was during the Cuban missile crisis of 1962. The Falklands war was a result of diplomatic misjudgment in London and Buenos Aires, and the Six Day War of 1967 was the result of Nasser's folly: he thought he could humiliate Israel without fighting.

There were many 'wars of national liberation', or colonial wars, between 1945 and 1975. Indochina and Algeria were the bloodiest, but there were many others in Africa and Asia. Of all modern European empires, Portugal's was the most squalid and indefensible, its decolonization the most brutal and incompetent, and the ensuing fighting the most savage.

Now there are hardly any colonies left, and there are only three continuing colonial wars: the SWAPO insurgency in Namibia; the Eritreans' war against Ethiopia; and the Polisario Front's attempt to liberate the Western Sahara from Morocco. In 1988, South Africa promised Namibia its independence, and Morocco tentatively offered the Western Sahara the right to decide its own future.

Civil wars have become much more frequent since the end of the colonial era, as societies have torn themselves to pieces on ideological, sectarian or ethnic lines. The first and most calamitous since 1945 was the civil war in China, in which millions of people were killed. The Communist victory was one of the great disasters in history, inflicting untold sufferings and further millions of deaths upon the Chinese people. China only began to recover in the late 1970s, after the defeat of the Gang of Four who had submitted the country to a last spasm of ideological frenzy.

Civil wars have been particularly frequent in recently liberated colonies, as their peoples' belligerent inclinations, whetted by confrontation with the colonial powers, turned inwards. There has been immense, continuous bloodletting from Guatemala to Biafra and from Lebanon to Cambodia, and there is no sign that it will abate.

Terrorism remains a major preoccupation, particularly in the West. Some acts of terrorism have changed history – among them, the assassinations of Julius Caesar, Abraham Lincoln and the Archduke Franz Ferdinand. (Appendix III provides a list of post-war assassinations, some of which had a profound effect on the countries involved.) However, most terrorists have conspicuously failed to achieve their ends. The Israelis have not been moved by all the murderous attacks they have endured; the British are still in Northern Ireland after 20 years of terrorism; the Basque provinces remain a part of Spain; and the French, Italian and West German republics have not been shaken by the terrorist assaults upon them. The terrorists' greatest achievement has been their contribution to the destruction of Lebanon, but in that case, terrorism became a weapon in a civil war.

None of these conflicts can be understood without some knowledge of their historical background. Americans, in particular, often underestimate the force of history on the actions of people. Argentina went to war with Britain in 1982 to revenge a trivial incident that had occurred in 1833. The origins of the tribal warfare in Belfast can be traced back to events of 1689, or earlier. The Greeks and Turks have been enemies for over 900 years, and the Vietnamese and Cambodians for almost as long. The most extreme case of historical memory is the revival of Israel.

There are a few instances of a conscious rejection of past hatreds. In the 1950s, France and West Germany decided, consciously and deliberately, to end a quarrel reaching back centuries, one that had caused three wars within 70 years. That decision, which had its origins most prosaically in the setting up of the European Coal and Steel Community in 1949, still stands as the greatest achievement of post-war diplomacy.

This achievement is particularly admirable because the engine that powers most of the wars in today's world is ethnic hostility. Of that, apparently, there is no end. If no longer the French and the Germans, it is now the Sikhs and the Hindus in India, Catholics and Protestants in Northern Ireland, Tamil and Sinhalese in Sri Lanka, Vietnamese and Cambodians, Palestinians and Israelis. When President Sadat made peace with Israel, the event was extraordinary because such deeds are so rare. The Nigerian government under General Gowon pursued a policy of reconciliation after the Biafra war. There was no persecution of the vanquished, no reparations were exacted and no medals were issued to the victorious soldiery. Gowon's example has not often been emulated, and Sadat was murdered.

The latent conflicts that might burst into flames at any moment cover the whole spectrum. In some countries, such as Cyprus, there is an uneasy truce. In others – Uganda, for example, now enjoying a moment of tranquillity between coups – over 20 years of pogroms, massacres, civil wars and violent revolutions almost guarantee further troubles. The governments of a dozen nations, including Burma, Somalia, Ivory Coast, Guatemala and Peru, might collapse at any moment, while some long-lasting tyrannies, such as Libya, Syria and Chile, may at last follow them. Other countries, such as Saudi Arabia, have been relatively calm for years but are showing signs of stress. Still others, where ethnic disputes are frequent and increasing, may be in the first stages of dissolution: the most important are India and the Soviet Union. In Eastern Europe, the Communist governments imposed after 1945 are on the verge of collapse.

A further danger to the peace of the world comes from the antagonisms between some heavily armed and belligerent Third World countries. India has nuclear weapons and so, probably, does Pakistan, and they are both actively seeking long-range missiles that could deliver them. It is also highly likely that both Israel and South Africa now have nuclear capabilities.

Each of the Middle East wars has been more violent than the last because of the increase in the quantity and quality of armaments. Israelis and Arabs now have long-range surface-to-surface missiles, and another Arab–Israeli war is only too likely. Iraq has not learned moderation from its war with Iran, and its use of poison gas in that conflict might very well be imitated. Libya and Chad, Ethiopia and Somalia seem bound to resume fighting at the first opportunity, and that opportunity will be soon. Some time before the century ends, the real war will start in South Africa if the whites there do not agree to cede power to the blacks.

Running through a great number of these conflicts is the theme of outside interference. The Soviet Union has sown murder and disaster across the Third World for 30 years in the name of liberation and socialism. Young Africans, Latin Americans and Asians were taken to Moscow by the thousands, to study the dialectic and the Kalashnikov. They are now back at home, slaughtering each other.

The largest interventions in foreign wars have been in Korea, Vietnam and Afghanistan. Only the first was to any degree successful, and both sides claimed victory: the Western alliance, led by the United States, saved South Korea, and China saved the North. In fact, both had wanted to reunify Korea under their patronage, and both failed, leaving the Korean problem, which was caused by outside interference, to future generations.

If they do not send armies, outside powers send 'advisers' into foreign conflicts or they arm their clients. The Soviet Union sent large quantities of arms and financed Cuban mercenary armies in Angola in 1975 and in Ethiopia in 1977, saving the new regimes there from collapse. While Cuban soldiers and Soviet advisers were keeping the Angolan government and military afloat, South African intervention on behalf of the Unita rebels did the same for them. The South Africans have aided the Renamo rebels in Mozambique, as Tanzania helped Frelimo during the war against Portugal. Colonel Moammar Khadafy of Libya has sent his armies to Chad and Uganda, and he supplies weapons and money to a variety of resistance and terrorist organizations. The United States has intervened vigorously – with weapons, money and advisers – in a dozen conflicts.

One of the key events of the past few years was the Soviet decision (or series of decisions) to stop interfering in a number of foreign struggles. First, the Soviets decided to get out of Afghanistan. Then they ordered the Cubans home from Angola and urged the Vietnamese to pull out of Cambodia. There has been no general Soviet retreat; they have merely ended the most costly of their adventures. However, as other imperial powers have discovered in the past, a retreat begun is not easy to stop, and it is quite possible that the Soviets will soon also abandon Ethiopia, South Yemen and others that have recently become their client states. Fidel Castro has also been told that the USSR can no longer afford subsidies of $3–5 billion a year. That will leave the Soviets with only Eastern Europe to worry about.

Other countries also reduced their meddling abroad in 1988. South Africa pulled its troops out of Angola, and agreed to give Namibia its independence, and the United States abandoned its attempt to overthrow the government of Nicaragua. However, the US was still deeply involved in El Salvador, and South Africa evidently intended to retain its dominant position in southern Africa.

The great majority of the millions who have died in the past decades have not been killed by bombs, tanks or fighter aircraft. They have been killed by rifles, pistols and rocket-propelled grenades. The Kalashnikov is the most popular automatic rifle in the world because of its reliability and simplicity. Sam Cummings, the Anglo-American arms dealer, calculated that, by 1982, the 30 or so factories throughout the world that produce Kalashnikovs had made over 30 million between them. This number has greatly increased since then, and now light arms are made, and well made, in a score of Third World countries. The Chinese, North Koreans, Brazilians, Mexicans and Indians all have large armaments industries, and all vigorously export their wares. The proliferation of small arms means that starting a war or an insurrection is relatively cheap and easy. There are guns everywhere, and the death toll among combatants and civilians is appalling.

The United States and its Western allies also supply arms and training to insurgents, though not on the same lavish scale as the USSR. Stinger and Redeye anti-aircraft missiles or the British Blowpipe, carried by one or two soldiers, changed the nature of the wars in Afghanistan and Angola. Once the Soviet Union gets its production lines working with comparable weapons, they will have the same effect on different battlefields – in the Middle East, for instance. One civilian airliner was shot down by Soviet missiles supplied to the guerrillas of what was then Rhodesia, and another was downed by a missile acquired by Sudanese rebels. On 9 December 1988, the Polisario Front army shot down an American DC7 over the Western Sahara with a Soviet missile; the crew of five were all killed. The plane had been spraying locust swarms in Senegal and was returning to base in Morocco. It had evidently been mistaken for a Moroccan bomber.

Even if all foreign intervention were suddenly to cease, and if the world's sword factories were all converted to the manufacture of ploughshares, the fighting would still continue. The Philippine guerrillas and the Shining Path in Peru have done without outside assistance from the beginning. Despite Rajiv Gandhi's fantasies, the Sikh insurrection in India is not the result of a Pakistani plot. Jonas Savimbi and Unita in Angola and the anonymous terrorists of Renamo in Mozambique are not going to end their wars if South Africa abandons them. The slaughter in Uganda has been driven by native animosities, not outside interference, and there is a terrible possibility that, when the Vietnamese withdraw from Cambodia, the Khmers Rouges will return to Phnom Penh.

Humanity's capacity for hatred, not the plots of foreigners, will ensure that the blood of innocents will continue to flow. Hatred is not new. The Old Testament is full of it. That most beautiful of lamentations in exile, the 137th Psalm, ends with a cry for vengeance that still chills the blood:

By the rivers of Babylon, there we sat down, yea, we wept, when we remembered Zion. We hanged our harps upon the willows in the midst thereof . . . O daughter of Babylon, who art to be destroyed; happy shall he be that rewardeth thee as thou hast served us. Happy shall he be that taketh and dasheth thy little ones against the stones.

Hatred can be manifested in many different ways and many different places. In the spring of 1988, Zola Budd, a 23-year-old South African runner, who had become a British citizen in order to compete in the Olympics, was suddenly promoted as a symbol of all the evil in the world. Whenever she appeared in Britain, there were violent demonstrations against her. Crowds of British pacifists turned into lynch mobs, and television reports showed their delight at their shared hatred. In their eyes, Zola Budd was transformed from a scared young woman into

South Africa personified, and therefore, it was morally right to attack her. This transformation of people into objects (which are much easier to disregard) was also seen when the US navy shot down an Iranian airliner, killing 290 people. American public reaction was generally callous. Although the dead included 60 children under the age of 10, they were all perceived as 'just Iranians' and therefore enemies, and no sympathy was felt for them at all.

Hatred can be inspired by ideology, like that of the Khmers Rouges or the Shining Path in Peru; by ancestral ethnic or religious animosities, like the Hindus and Muslims who slaughtered each other in India in 1947, or the Protestants and Catholics in Belfast; by racism, like the Americans in the South who, in the 1960s, beat up and sometimes murdered black 'Freedom Riders'; by tribal rivalry, like the Tutsi and Hutu of Burundi and Rwanda; even by crazed historicism, like Armenians from California and Lebanon who murder Turkish diplomats to avenge crimes committed 70 years ago.

The Holocaust was the extreme modern example of the lengths to which hatred can go. It was exceptional not because of its cruelty but because it was so cold-blooded, a matter of government decision and careful planning. There are plenty of examples of equal cruelty. In 1978, for instance, Cambodian soldiers raided across the border into Vietnam to massacre Vietnamese children in their villages. In Rwanda, in 1963, 10,000 Tutsi were massacred by the Hutu. Two years later, a further 2000 Tutsi were killed in Burundi, and in retaliation, the Tutsis, who rule there, slaughtered 200,000 Hutu. The massacres resumed in 1988. Today and every day, the civil wars in Mozambique, Sudan and Ethiopia provide examples of the systematic slaughter of civilians, including woman and children. Most notoriously, between 1975 and 1979, the government of Cambodia deliberately killed hundreds of thousands of its own people.

The Holocaust was a warning: this is what can happen. The Holocaust memorials now being built in Washington and New York should include, next to the photographs of Treblinka and Auschwitz, photographs of the killing fields of Cambodia, where the Vietnamese found tens of thousands of skulls, or the rivers choked with the bodies of the Tutsi and the Hutu. It could also include a memorial to the Soviet peasants, particularly the Ukrainians, who were massacred or starved to death during Stalin's collectivization of agriculture in 1931–3.

Whole libraries have been written on the question of strategic balance between East and West, and there is still a thriving industry, in the United States and Europe and in Moscow, devoted to analysing the problem. Fortunately, whatever their public utterances, political leaders on both sides have usually been too sensible to listen to their military advisers or to pay any attention to the frenetic speculations of the think-tanks.

When they did listen in 1962, the world teetered on the brink of disaster. Nikita Khrushchev fell victim to the cartographic delusion that has so afflicted the world this century. The Americans, perpetually deluded by the tidy world of the map-makers, had tried to 'surround' the Soviet Union and its allies. The concept was meaningless: the USSR and China are far too big to be surrounded in any real sense. It was also pointless: what on earth could be achieved by surrounding them? But for a moment, Khrushchev fell for the delusion himself and sent missiles to Cuba to escape his supposed encirclement. For a chess-playing nation, it was a remarkably stupid move. The Soviets evidently had not thought what the next move would be. Missiles in Cuba did not change the real balance of power, but they so provoked the Americans that a nuclear war became a real possibility – which would have destroyed the USSR, not the USA.

The cartographic delusion continues. When the Soviets invaded Afghanistan, Washington think-tanks proclaimed that the Red Army was clearly aiming at the Persian Gulf, as though a 1000-mile detour through the Himalayas made any sense to a nation that already controls the passes into Iran from the north. Maps were published with fierce red arrows driving through Africa to surround Europe. In the early 1980s, the notion was once again advanced that, if the Sandinistas were allowed to establish themselves in Nicaragua, they would be in Texas the following year. It looked so close and easy on the map, so it must be true.

In fact, what is happening in the world is almost exactly the reverse of those menacing arrows on the map. The Soviet Union vastly overcommitted itself in the 1970s, setting up client states in Vietnam, Cambodia, Afghanistan, South Yemen, Angola, Ethiopia, Mozambique and Nicaragua. The US State Department contends that the USSR spends $500 million a year in Nicaragua alone. Added to the enormous expenditure in Afghanistan and the cost of subsidizing Cuba ($3–5 billion a year) and $1–2 billion each in Angola, Ethiopia and Vietnam, the USSR was probably spending $20–30 billion outside Europe in 1988. The cost of its garrisons in Eastern Europe might be twice that, and further prodigious sums support the arms industries and the Red Army itself at home.

As far as anyone can tell, the Soviet people gain no practical advantage whatever from these expenditures. On the contrary, the need to maintain the impressive array of Soviet power in the world means that Soviet citizens have to stand in line to buy items that Westerners take for granted. The country with the greatest acreage of trees in the world cannot produce and distribute enough paper for its population, and the Soviet people are deprived of other creature comforts that a more efficient economic system and a less imperialist national ambition would have provided long ago. Delegates to the Moscow party conference in June 1988 observed bitterly that life is better in South Korea and Taiwan than it is in the Socialist Motherland.

In addition, being the vanguard of the world revolutionary movement for the past 70 years has meant a level of domestic political oppression that cannot be maintained indefinitely. As happened with the other European empires, the moment comes when the citizens suddenly realize that they do not have to put up with it anymore, and the government discovers that it no longer has the nerve and the authority to impose its will. The Soviet Union is crumbling from within at the same time that its leaders have lost their faith in their revolutionary mission and are preparing to withdraw from the outposts of empire.

In the long view of history, the Soviet Union's collapse is perhaps inevitable, but among the proximate causes of that event, if it does occur, would undoubtedly be the Soviet 'victories' in the 1970s, which American hawks had so deplored. Like the British empire before it, the Soviet empire has grown far too large for the home economy to support, and it must now retreat.

The retreat of Soviet power, and perhaps the dissolution of the Soviet Union itself, may be welcomed by many in the West, but it will also promote great instability in the world, and entail high costs that the West will have to pay. The Soviet Union has found the burdens of hegemony intolerable, and may be preparing to transfer them to the United States. If the USSR withdraws from Mozambique and Angola, Afghanistan and Nicaragua, the Americans will suddenly be presented with very considerable bills by their allies. Unita, the Contras, the Mujaheddin and whatever government emerges in Maputo will all want American help to clear up the mess they will inherit. As the Soviets have discovered, it costs much more to defend an empire than to subvert it from outside. The West may also be about to relearn the related thesis that it costs much more to restore a ruined nation to stability and health than it costs to destroy it.

The most serious consequences of the Soviet retreat will be felt in Europe. The essential deal struck between Stalin and the Western allies during World War II was that Germany would be divided and Eastern Europe would be a Soviet sphere of influence; in return, Stalin promised not to subvert the governments of Western Europe. By and large, both sides have kept their promises. But what will happen if the USSR withdraws or is expelled from Eastern Europe?

Will Germany reunite? And if it does, what effect will it have on the balance of power in the rest of Europe? Hitler killed himself in his bunker over 40 years ago, but he is not forgotten. Even that admirable reconciliation between France and West Germany might be seriously strained if Prussia and Saxony were restored to the Fatherland, and its capital moved back to Berlin.

That would be the extreme test for rationality and diplomacy. In the nuclear age, there is no possibility that a reunited Germany could ever endanger Europe and the world as the Third Reich once did – the Soviet Union will survive in some form and will always be capable of overwhelming Germany. But it is all a matter of perception: the USSR has fantasized about revanchist Germans for more than four decades, even as it has built itself into a superpower. Will *glasnost* be sufficient to change the lessons of two generations, to show the Soviets that, in fact, there is no danger from the West? The matter was settled when a Red Army soldier hung the red flag from the Brandenburg Gate. The question is, will the Soviets recognize the fact and admit their own victory?

It is by no means certain. In the early 1960s, John F. Kennedy, Richard Nixon and other level-headed people endlessly fulminated against Communist Cuba '60 miles off the coast of Florida', which they claimed was a mortal danger to US security. That was almost 30 years ago, and the nation has survived; the only people who still lose sleep over Castro are Cuban refugees in Miami. But the United States has learned absolutely nothing from the lesson: throughout the Reagan years, apparently intelligent people endlessly denounced 'a Communist presence on the American mainland', as though Nicaragua were a threat to the United States. If Americans can so delude themselves, is it surprising that the Soviets feel threatened by the Germans – who are far more numerous and considerably richer than the Nicaraguans?

Europe remains the most dangerous place on the planet, but not because Nato and the Warsaw Pact have any desire or intention of fighting each other. The danger comes from the imminent collapse of the Soviet empire. If all of Eastern Europe rises up against its oppressor, it is entirely possible that the Soviet Union will revert to Stalinist savagery to restore its authority, as it did in Budapest in

1956. The Cold War would then revive with a vengeance. Conversely, if Gorbachev lacks the will to grind down any resistance from the Poles, Hungarians and East Germans, and those countries recover their independence, the tide of revolt might very well spread to the subject nations of the USSR: the Ukrainians and Uzbeks, Azerbaijanis and Khirgiz.

Gorbachev may be the Kerensky of a new revolution, but this time, the government commands enormous armies, which are disciplined and heavily armed, unlike the rabble of 1917. The fall of empires is always dangerous and seldom leads to the tranquil prosperity that their enemies anticipate. It is most unlikely that the dissolution of the greatest of all 20th-century empires will be accomplished peacefully.

Patrick Brogan

AUTHOR'S NOTE

SOURCES

A bibliography of sources is given at the end of each chapter. I have found three series of publications particularly useful. First, the *Country Studies* published by American University, Washington, orginally prepared for the Pentagon. Each volume includes a comprehensive bibliography. Second, reports by Amnesty International on violations of human rights, and third, reports by the Minority Rights Group.

I have also made copious use of reports by foreign correspondents of *The New York Times, The Washington Post, The New Yorker, The Times, Guardian, Observer* and *Independent* (London), and various other publications.

The figures for population and GNP are the World Bank's, where available and are for 1986. In countries like Cambodia or Afghanistan, GNP figures are exceedingly speculative. Changes in the exchange rate for the dollar since 1986 have induced book-keeping differences, but the figures remain useful as an indication of comparative incomes.

The refugee statistics come from the US Committee for Refugees, 1989. The committee uses a strict definition of refugee, namely someone in need of protection and assistance. The figures, therefore, do not include people who have been absorbed into the host country's citizenry, like the Indochinese and Cuban refugees in the United States. Those figures marked with a star (*) are disputed by the host government, usually for political reasons.

Appendix I provides a list of wars since 1945, together with estimates of the numbers killed in each of them. The speculative nature of the estimates is discussed in a note to that appendix. Appendix II lists *coups d'état* and Appendix III assassinations during the same period.

I have described the wars afflicting the world today, and have also described a number of past wars and rebellions whose effects linger: I have not described the Algerian war, because it is over and done with and it is now part of Algerian and French history. On the other hand, I have described the Korean War briefly, because the issues that caused it remain unresolved. I have included chapters on a few of the countries that seem most likely to suffer serious conflicts in the near future (East Europe, for instance), but not all of them. There are separate chapters on the 'drug wars' and on terrorism.

While I have tried to get all the names, dates and facts right and I will be grateful to any reader who corrects any of my mistakes.

NAMES

The names of great numbers of nations, cities and natural features have been changed in the 20th century, some more than once. The reasons are usually political: Russia became the Union of Soviet Socialist Republics, a change of extreme political significance. Saigon became Ho Chi Minh City, as St Petersburg had become Petrograd and then Leningrad. Colonial names were changed throughout Africa: Leopoldville became Kinshasa, Lourenço Marques became Maputo and so on.

Sometimes the reasons are linguistic: the Chinese, attempting to introduce a uniform system of transliteration from their own ideographs into Latin characters changed the accepted Latin spelling of most proper names by decree in 1975. Under the new Pinyin system, Mao Tse-tung became Mao Zedong, Peking became Beijing.

In the contemporary world, using names often reflects a political choice. Between 1975 and 1978, the government of Cambodia called the country Democratic Kampuchea. Using that name now implies at least some tacit recognition of the continued existence of Pol Pot's regime. The United Nations refers to Namibia, but South Africa, which controls the territory, calls it South-West Africa. Turkish Cypriots call their part of the island the Republic of North Kibris. The territory the British call Northern Ireland is referred to by Protestants as Ulster and by Catholics as the Six Counties. For decades, Arabs refused to use the word Israel, preferring 'Occupied Palestine'.

When writing about past events it is necessary to use the names appropriate to the period to avoid anachronism and confusion, particularly when the names are politically significant. Thus Zimbabwe was Southern Rhodesia before 1965, Rhodesia from 1965 to 1980, and very briefly Zimbabwe-Rhodesia. The Central African Republic became the Central African Empire for a while, and Cuidad Domingo became Cuidad Trujillo. When using those names, the writer is referring to the reigns of the Emperor Bokassa I and Generalissimo Rafael Leonidas Trujillo respectively.

AFRICA

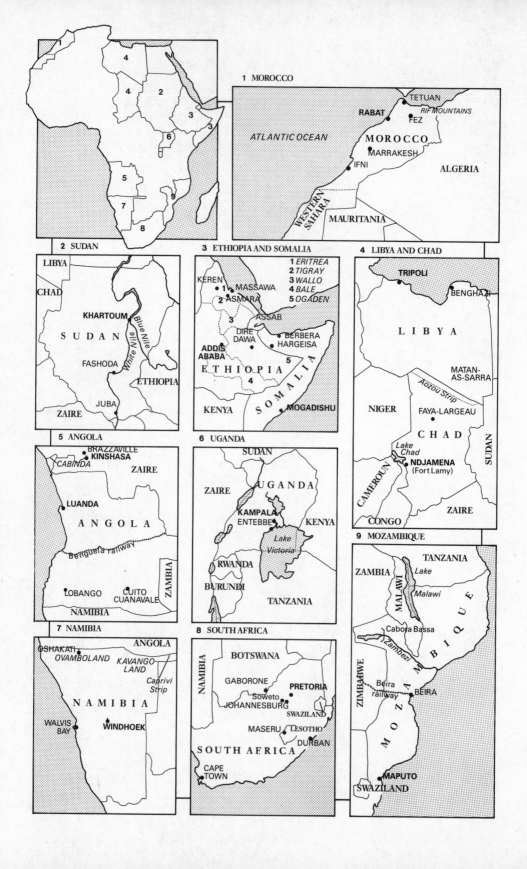

1 MOROCCO

TETUAN
RIF MOUNTAINS
RABAT
FEZ
ATLANTIC OCEAN
MOROCCO
MARRAKESH
ALGERIA
IFNI
WESTERN SAHARA
MAURITANIA

2 SUDAN

LIBYA
CHAD
KHARTOUM
Blue Nile
S U D A N
White Nile
FASHODA
ETHIOPIA
JUBA
ZAIRE

3 ETHIOPIA AND SOMALIA

1 *ERITREA*
2 *TIGRAY*
3 *WALLO*
4 *BALE*
5 *OGADEN*

KEREN
1 MASSAWA
2 ASMARA
3
ASSAB
DIRE DAWA
BERBERA
ADDIS ABABA
HARGEISA
5
E T H I O P I A
4
KENYA
S O M A L I A
MOGADISHU

4 LIBYA AND CHAD

TRIPOLI
BENGHAZI
L I B Y A
MATAN-AS-SARRA
Aozou Strip
NIGER
FAYA-LARGEAU
C H A D
SUDAN
Lake Chad
NDJAMENA
(Fort Lamy)
CAMEROUN
CONGO
ZAIRE

5 ANGOLA

BRAZZAVILLE
KINSHASA
CABINDA
ZAIRE
LUANDA
A N G O L A
Benguela railway
ZAMBIA
LOBANGO
CUITO CUANAVALE
NAMIBIA

6 UGANDA

SUDAN
ZAIRE
U G A N D A
KAMPALA
ENTEBBE
KENYA
Lake Victoria
RWANDA
BURUNDI
TANZANIA

7 NAMIBIA

ANGOLA
OSHAKATI
OVAMBOLAND
KAVANGO-LAND
Caprivi Strip
N A M I B I A
WALVIS BAY
WINDHOEK

8 SOUTH AFRICA

BOTSWANA
NAMIBIA
GABORONE
PRETORIA
Soweto
JOHANNESBURG
SWAZILAND
MASERU
Lesotho
DURBAN
S O U T H   A F R I C A
CAPE TOWN

9 MOZAMBIQUE

TANZANIA
ZAMBIA
Lake Malawi
MALAWI
M O Z A M B I Q U E
Cabora Bassa
Zambezi
ZIMBABWE
Beira railway
BEIRA
MAPUTO
SWAZILAND

ANGOLA

Geography	481,351 sq. miles (1,246,694 sq. km). Larger than the total area of Spain, Portugal, France and the Benelux countries. Cabinda, a small Angolan enclave north of the Zaïre (Congo) River, supplies most of Angola's oil.
Population	8.9 million. Of these, about 2 million are Ovimbundu, in central and southern Angola; 1.5 million Kimbundu in the north-west, around the capital (Luanda); and 700,000 Bakongo in the north (most of the Bakongo live in Zaïre and the Congo Republic).
Resources	Oil, diamonds, coffee, iron ore, forest products, sisal, maize.
Refugees	In Angola: 74,000 from Namibia, 12,300 from Zaïre, 9400 from South Africa. From Angola: 310,000 in Zaïre, 94,000 in Zambia.
Parties	● MPLA: *Movimento Popular de Libertacão de Angola* (People's Movement for the Liberation of Angola). Marxist party based on the Kimbundu tribe of north-central Angola. Founded in 1956. The MPLA won the 1975–6 civil war and now forms the government. Supported by the USSR and Cuba.
	● FNLA: *Frente Nacional de Libertacão de Angola* (National Front for the Liberation of Angola). Founded in 1960 by Holden Roberto. Split along tribal lines in 1961. Its rump is based on the Bakongo tribe of northern Angola and Zaïre. Supported by Zaïre.
	● Unita: *União Nacional para a Independencia Total de Angola* (National Union for the Total Independence of Angola). Founded by Jonas Savimbi in a breakaway from the FNLA, in 1966. Based on the Ovimbundu tribe (the largest in Angola), of central and southern Angola. Defeated in 1975–6, Savimbi has since continued to lead a rebellion based on his tribal homeland and supported by South Africa and the US.
Casualties	About 90,000 people were killed during the colonial war, 1961–75. About 50,000 were killed in the civil war and foreign intervention, 1975–6, and 150,000 people have been killed since 1976. These are all very approximate totals.

Angola, like Mozambique, went directly from 15 years of revolutionary war against Portuguese colonialism (1961–75), to a civil and tribal war that has lasted ever since. The MPLA government, supported by between 30,000 and 55,000 Cuban troops and heavy investment by the USSR, has been fighting Jonas Savimbi's Unita, which is supported by South Africa and the US. Under the

3

provisions of a ceasefire agreement, approved in principle by Angola, Cuba and South Africa in August 1988 and completed in December, South Africa withdrew its forces from Angola, and Cuba promised to bring all its troops home progressively by July 1991. In the meantime, there was a *de facto* ceasefire between Cuba and Unita, but not between the latter and the MPLA. The agreement settled, at least for the moment, the dispute between Cuba and South Africa but left most of the other questions unanswered.

As in Mozambique, the mass exodus of Portuguese settlers, the war and the government's Marxist-inspired incompetence have all reduced the economy to ruin, except for the oil industry. In economic and social terms, the regime benefited little from its association with the Soviet Union. It received minimal economic aid, and was constrained to devote all the revenues from its oil fields to paying its Cuban mercenaries and buying Soviet arms. (The war now consumes 70 per cent of the national budget.) If the Cubans do indeed withdraw, the government might well collapse completely.

In the 1980s, Angola became the chosen battlefield of the competing ideologies of the Soviet Union and the United States. However, neither country has any real interest in Angola, commercial, strategic or political. If Cuba pulls out, it will be because the Soviets have washed their hands of the place. They have invested billions in the MPLA, far more than the US has in Unita, to no perceptible advantage.

HISTORY

Angola was first colonized by the Portuguese in 1575, when they established a coastal fort that became Luanda. They ruled the country with a mixture of incompetence and cruelty for four centuries. Before the slave trade was stopped by the British navy, Portugal had sent about 3 million slaves from Angola to Brazil.

From that point until the 1950s, Portugal neglected its African colonies completely. Then, as the rest of black Africa moved towards independence, Portugal increased its investment in Angola and Mozambique, hoping to build new Brazils there by exporting Portuguese peasants to Africa; about 300,000 eventually settled in Angola.

Independence movements developed in Angola, as elsewhere in Africa, led by members of the tiny educated class of Africans. The first was the MPLA, established in 1956; the FNLA was founded in 1960. The war against Portugal came closer to reality in 1961, after the independence of the Belgian Congo (Zaïre) in 1960 provided a base for the FNLA, which was composed chiefly of the same tribe that is dominant in Zaïre, the Bakongo. The uprising began in March 1961. About 700 whites were killed, including large numbers of civilians massacred on their farms. The Portuguese army and settler militias put down the rising in six months, with great brutality, killing about 20,000 black Angolans.

The events of 1961 shocked the Portuguese government of Dr Antonio Salazar, and led to a number of reforms. However, there was no question of Portugal abandoning its colonies like the other colonial powers. In 1963, guerrilla warfare started in Portuguese Guinea and, a year later, Mozambique.

The FNLA was supported by the Congolese government, and also by the CIA. However, its leader Holden Roberto was never an effective guerrilla commander (for one thing, he preferred the comforts of life in Leopoldville). One of his deputies, Jonas Savimbi, broke away from the FNLA in 1966 and formed Unita, based on the Ovimbundu tribe. Unita then started a guerrilla insurrection in east-central Angola.

The other rebel group, the Marxist MPLA, was formed in 1956 among exiled Angolan intellectuals. Its leader, Dr Agostinho Neto, was a physician and poet, and his greatest contribution was to meet Che Guevara in 1965 and win Cuban support for a Marxist revolution in Angola. However, even though the Cubans trained some MPLA guerrillas, it was an ineffective and unsuccessful fighting force. It was based in Zaïre and could not break through the Bakongo areas in the north, which were thoroughly policed by the Portuguese, to reach the Kimbundu tribe around Luanda, which was its main support. The MPLA then tried an offensive from Zambia in 1966, with a notable lack of success.

The Portuguese army fought against the rebels with great ferocity, aided by South Africa and Ian Smith's regime in Rhodesia. Portugal won the war in Angola: the three divided and ineffectual guerrilla movements were no serious threat. However, the war in Guinea went badly, and by 1974, the war in Mozambique was also proving an intolerable drain upon Portugal's resources. It became apparent to the junior ranks in the army that the wars could not be won, and on 25 April 1974, young officers of the Portuguese army seized power in a bloodless coup in Lisbon. They immediately announced that they would give all Portuguese colonies their independence.

In Angola, the rebels came out of the bush and staked their competing claims for the future. The Portuguese attempted to set up a coalition government of the three revolutionary parties. Roberto, Neto and Savimbi were brought to Portugal, and signed the Alvor agreement on 15 January 1975. It provided that the three would form a coalition government, that there would be elections for a constituent assembly in October, and that independence would be on Armistice Day, 11 November 1975, 400 years after the Portuguese first arrived (and ten years to the day after Ian Smith's declaration of independence in Rhodesia). The three agreed to freeze their military positions, and to contribute 8000 men each to a new national army.

The new government took office on 31 January 1975, and fighting broke out between the MPLA and FNLA the next day. None of the three parties showed any serious willingness to cooperate with the others. Holden Roberto had been building up his army with the help of President Mobutu of Zaïre and had obtained help from the Chinese the previous summer, while continuing his earlier contacts with the Americans. By the beginning of 1975, he had about 15,000 troops. The MPLA, which had only 3000 men at the time of the Portuguese revolution, asked for help from their Cuban friends. The USSR, seeing an opportunity to thwart both the Chinese and the Americans at the same time, started sending arms at once. The MPLA also had the support of a force of exiled Katangese gendarmes, expelled from the Congolese province of Katanga after the failure of Moise Tshombe's attempt to make it independent, and who harboured a lasting detestation of Zaïre and its president. As for Savimbi, he enjoyed the widest support because his tribe was the biggest in Angola, but he had the smallest army, only about 1000 men. He was supported by Zambia and Tanzania, and now set about wooing the remaining Portuguese settlers and, later, the Americans and South Africans.

The civil war got under way quickly. Early in 1975, the Cubans sent 250 instructors, who set up camps in Angola to train the MPLA. The party had the inestimable advantage that its main support came from the Kimbundu tribe which dominated Luanda and its hinterland. In July, the MPLA drove the FNLA and Unita out of Luanda, and the coalition government collapsed. About 20,000 people were killed in the fighting; the Portuguese settlers fled, all 300,000 of them, in six months; and Angola seemed in a state of complete anarchy.

The Americans had not been seriously involved so far, and although Cuba and the USSR had helped the MPLA, theirs had not been a vast investment. After the events of July, however, both sides plunged into the fray.

The United States had just seen 20 years' effort in Vietnam collapse. The secretary of state, Dr Henry Kissinger, conceived that the establishment of a Communist government in Angola could be construed as another defeat for the US, and was determined to prevent it. The CIA began sending large quantities of arms to the FNLA and Unita through Zaïre and Zambia. The USSR retaliated by shipping arms to the MPLA, with the advantage that it could do so directly by sea into Luanda.

As Independence Day approached, the FNLA mounted an attack on the MPLA from the north and east. Unita, aided by a South African armoured column, attacked from the south and got as far as Novo Redondo, 120 miles (186 km) south of Luanda. In addition, President Mobutu of Zaïre unsuccessfully attacked Cabinda.

The FNLA and Unita were defeated by a mixed force of MPLA fighters and Cuban troops, under Soviet command. As their enemies closed in on Luanda, Cuba flew in 15,000 troops and the USSR supplied massive quantities of arms, including heavy artillery – notably 'Stalin Organs', multiple rocket launchers. American aid had been on an altogether more modest scale (Congress had no intention of starting a new war so quickly after Vietnam), and the South Africans were not ready to take on the Soviet Union. The South African Defence Minister, P. W. Botha, for ever after swore that he had been robbed of victory by US duplicity, and vowed vengeance. He later became president of South Africa.

The attacking armies disintegrated. The last FNLA position was occupied on 11 February 1976, and on the same day, Savimbi's capital, Huambo in the centre of the country, fell to the MPLA. The South Africans beat a hasty retreat. The MPLA victory appeared to be complete.

During the débâcle, the commander of a group of white mercenaries, a Cyprus-born British soldier called Costas Georgiou, using the *nom de guerre* 'Colonel Callan', summarily executed 14 of his troops for cowardice. He was later captured and executed, along with an American and two other British mercenaries. Belgian, Portuguese and French mercenaries, including Colonel Bob Denard, also took part in the fighting, to no effect.

THE GUERRILLA WAR SINCE 1976

While the FNLA disintegrated, Jonas Savimbi and Unita retreated in good order into the bush to continue the war. However, in December 1975, the US Congress passed a law forbidding the president from sending any covert assistance to Unita, and Savimbi's former allies in Zambia and Tanzania abandoned him, recognizing the MPLA regime in Luanda. He therefore turned for support to the white regimes in Rhodesia and South Africa.

This alliance brought much contumely upon his head, but it proved its worth in military terms. He established a permanent base at Jamba, in the extreme south-east of Angola, near the frontier with Namibia (South-west Africa). Jamba, protected by the South African Air Force, expanded into a vast city-camp, with hospitals, factories and extensive training facilities, all carefully camouflaged. Savimbi's armies have grown to nearly 30,000 regular troops, and 35,000 guerrillas. Apart from the aid sent by South Africa and, later, by the United States, Unita controls a large enough part of the country to generate its own revenues; in particular, it controls some of Angola's diamond mines.

Savimbi pursued the same tactics he had used against the Portuguese, sending small forces of guerrillas to harass government positions, to cut communications, to attack isolated government units and to sabotage economic targets. To begin with, the war was on a small scale – the MPLA was busy establishing itself in Luanda and the Cubans were training an army, while Savimbi was building up his forces in the bush. As the latter's operations expanded, and the government's ability to fight improved, the war soon established a regular pattern. Every year, during the dry season, Angolan troops would launch an offensive towards Jamba, only to be defeated by Unita and the South Africans.

At the same time, Unita progressively extended its operations in central Angola, the homeland of the Ovimbundu tribe that is its principal support. A key economic target in the region is the Benguela railway, which runs from the copper belt in Zaïre to the Angolan coast at Benguela. In an offensive in January 1988, Unita claimed to have occupied the entire length of the railway, from the mountains behind Benguela to the frontier with Zaïre (but not the major towns). If it succeeded in consolidating these victories, it would control most of the country, leaving the MPLA entrenched along the coast and in the north.

That would look very impressive on the map, but Unita was not ready to fight a conventional war of position and heavy equipment against the MPLA, let alone the Cubans. If it captured and tried to hold cities, they would have to be defended against the government's counter-offensive, and the military advantage would then swing to the far better equipped government army.

From the time that Unita first became a serious threat to the government, in the late 1970s, until mid-1988, the situation on the ground was at a permanent stalemate. The MPLA, backed by Cuba, might mount offensives against Jamba, but they could not take it. Nor could they eliminate Unita guerrillas in the endless bush of eastern and central Angola. Conversely, Savimbi and his allies might succeed in extending their control over much of the country, but they could not win the war without occupying Luanda, and they could not do that as long as the Soviet Union backed the MPLA.

FOREIGN INTERVENTION
The Cubans provided training and logistical and technical support for the Angolans, including 9000 teachers, doctors and other professionals. However, until the battles of early 1988, Cuban troops did not normally join the fighting. None the less, service in Angola was considered hard and became increasingly unpopular.　　7

This has been Castro's contribution to Soviet foreign policy. Although the Angolans have been obliged to pay Castro for the services of his mercenary army, in dollars earned from their oil exports, it has not been a profitable endeavour. A Cuban defector, Air Force General Rafaél del Piño, who flew to the United States in May 1987, claimed that there had been 10,000 Cuban casualties in Angola, including several thousand dead. He said that the war was deeply unpopular, and that only Castro and his brother Raoúl believed that victory was possible.

As for the Soviets, they became involved in Angola and elsewhere in Africa in the mid-1970s without a proper calculation of the costs and advantages of the enterprise. The first have turned out to be enormous, and the second non-existent.

For the past 25 years, the South Africans have been conducting a secondary war against SWAPO, the South-West Africa People's Organization, which is fighting for the independence of Namibia. At the same time, they have been fighting the African National Congress (ANC), the main guerrilla group in South Africa. SWAPO is based in Lobango, in southern Angola, and the ANC has bases among the 9000 or so South African refugees living in Angola. The South Africans established a security zone in southern Angola, which they policed with Unita's assistance. They did this because the area includes a major hydroelectric complex that they built during the Portuguese period, and also because they want a free-fire zone along the border. The South Africans also provided the essential air cover and artillery to defeat the successive Angolan offensives against Jamba, and in November 1987, President Botha paid a formal and much publicized visit to Savimbi there.

The United States started backing Unita soon after President Reagan took office in January 1981 and obtained the repeal of the 1975 Congressional ban. It was a crucial decision: South Africa had agreed in 1978 to give Namibia its independence, and the last details were to be settled in a conference in Geneva in January 1981. But in the previous November, Reagan had won the American presidential election, partly because of his promises to roll back the Communist conquests of the previous five years. South Africa decided to scuttle the agreement on Namibia, and Angola and Namibia have suffered a further eight years of war as a consequence.

American support for Unita was at first clandestine, but soon it was openly avowed. Savimbi visited Washington in January 1986, and was received as a hero. On 30 January, he paid a formal call upon President Reagan in the White House – the final accolade. Unita got about $15 million a year in weapons from the US, including Stinger anti-aircraft and TOW anti-tank missiles. As in Afghanistan and Nicaragua, this small American investment caused an enormous expenditure by the Soviet Union to keep the Cubans and the Angolan army in the field: by the mid-1980s, the USSR was sending Angola $1 billion in weapons every year. For the United States, it was an exceedingly cost-effective way of putting pressure on the Soviets, the reverse of what happened in Vietnam.

Not all Americans see it that way. Savimbi returned to the US in June 1988, in the midst of the presidential campaign. He again visited President Reagan, on 27 June, but was chiefly concerned to put his case to the Democrats. For all his pains, he was roundly attacked by the black Democratic leader Jesse Jackson as a tool of the South Africans.

Although the United States does not recognize the Angolan government, it is Angola's main trading partner. The American oil companies Chevron (Gulf) and Texaco, protected by Cuban soldiers, do flourishing business, and Angola had a trade surplus of $642 million with the US in 1986, which it could spend on arms or industrial imports. This situation is one of the oddities of the modern world. South African commandos attacked the Chevron oil installations in Cabinda in May 1985, were repulsed by the Cubans and two of the commandos were killed and one captured.

The United Nations tried continuously to mediate, to arrange for the independence of Namibia and the simultaneous withdrawal of the Cubans from Angola. For years, it met with no success. The US assistant secretary of state for Africa in the Reagan administration, Chester Crocker, also devoted himself to the cause of arranging a peace agreement in southern Africa. His efforts were constantly unsuccessful until the late spring of 1988.

THE BREAK-THROUGH

In 1987, the MPLA launched another offensive against Mavinga, a key position defending Savimbi's capital at Jamba. For the first time since 1975, South Africa sent large numbers of troops and artillery north to bolster Unita's defences. The Angolan army was defeated in a major battle at the Lomba River in September, and Savimbi's forces then counter-attacked the MPLA and Cubans in their last base in the south-east, at Cuito Cuanavale. For a while, it looked as though Unita was going to sweep its enemies completely out of southern Angola.

Savimbi laid siege to Cuito Cuanavale for several months, helped by long-range South African artillery – and even claimed to have captured it – but the Angolans and their Cuban allies rushed in reinforcements and held the place. Castro sent an extra 12,000 troops, and in March 1988, the siege of Cuito Cuanavale was lifted and the South Africans withdrew their troops from Angola, leaving only a small number to police the 'security zone' along the border.

The Cubans then advanced their troops to the border with Namibia, and for the first time, there were serious clashes between Cuban and South African forces in the frontier zone. On 27 June 1988, 12 South African soldiers were killed in a fight with Angolans and Cubans. The Cubans were then building major military and air bases in southern Angola facing South African bases in Namibia, and it appeared entirely possible that there might be a major war between the two armies.

The casualties that both Cuba and South Africa suffered in these battles and the prospect of further and more serious fighting were important elements in their decision to sign the August ceasefire. However, the decision to withdraw Cuban troops was not taken in Havana; it was taken in Moscow. The Soviet Union (which, at the time of the ceasefire, had about 1000 military advisers in Angola) was then pulling its own troops out of Afghanistan and urging its Vietnamese allies to get out of Cambodia. It evidently decided to cut its losses in Angola as well.

Mikhail Gorbachev had asked the key question: what was the point, for the Soviet Union, in spending $1 billion or more a year on a perpetual stalemate in southern Africa? The Soviet leadership found the answer in the spring of 1988, after the abrupt escalation in the fighting in Angola. At the December 1987 summit   9 meeting between President Reagan and Gorbachev in Washington, the Soviet spokesman was asked whether the retreat from Afghanistan indicated that Angola would be next. He insisted that there was no connection – beside the coincidence that both countries' names began with 'A'. That statement was disingenuous: the Soviets had had a far greater investment, morally and physically, in Afghanistan, and if they could abandon Kabul, they could certainly abandon Luanda. However, the decision had not been taken then. In early June, Reagan went to Moscow for his fourth summit with Gorbachev. They agreed, in a statement buried in their final communiqué, that efforts should be made to reach a settlement of the Angola question by 29 September, the tenth anniversary of the UN Security Council Resolution 435 which called on South Africa to leave Namibia.

The diplomatic effort to end the war had already resumed. After meeting in London in May, representatives of Angola, Cuba, South Africa and the United States met in Cairo, in New York and finally in Geneva. In New York, an outline agreement was reached on 12 June, which provided that Cuba would withdraw from Angola and that South Africa would pull out of Namibia. On 26 July, Fidel Castro announced that Cuba would withdraw all its troops from Angola 'gradually and totally'.

The agreement was signed on 5 August in Geneva, and ratified by the governments of South Africa, Cuba and Angola three days later. It laid down a timetable for ending the wars in Angola and Namibia:

● A ceasefire between Cuban and South African troops came into force immediately, and South Africa withdrew its 600 remaining troops in Angola by the end of August.

● Further negotiations were to be held on the remaining issues, which included the precise timetable for Cuban withdrawal, future American and South African aid to Unita, and Soviet and Cuban aid to the MPLA, Angolan aid to the ANC, and how to pay for the proposed UN peacekeeping force.

● The UN plan for the independence of Namibia was to be put into operation on 1 November. The process was to lead to elections for a constituent assembly in Namibia by 1 June 1989. This assembly would draw up a constitution and set a date for independence.

● The Cubans were to withdraw from Angola, but the timetable was not settled. Cuba had proposed four years, but South Africa demanded that the withdrawal be concluded before Namibia's independence. Finding an acceptable compromise took another four months.

● The South Africans were to withdraw their 50,000 troops from Namibia, except for a 1500-man force in two southern bases. A UN force of 7500 would be sent to Namibia to keep the peace.

It was an ambitious plan, and it would not be at all surprising if it failed. Its chief weakness was not the timetable: if Cuba were really determined to leave Angola, and the South Africans to leave Namibia, the details did not matter. The real questions were whether Cuba and South Africa were sincere, and to what extent would aid be given to Unita and the Angolan government in the future. There was no magic in the various dates (and the first, the 1 November deadline, was soon abandoned). The main, immediate concern was to settle Cuba's withdrawal from its advanced positions along the border and to ensure that, after they had left, the South Africans did not cross into Angola again. These details were settled, in principle, at Geneva on 15 November and approved by the three governments.

As for Angola, despite its assent to the agreement, the MPLA has no wish to see the Cubans depart, fearing that Unita will then win the war. However, Cuba and the USSR will not necessarily take the Angolans' wishes any more seriously than the Soviets have taken the wishes of the Afghan government, or President Nixon and Dr Henry Kissinger took the wishes of the South Vietnamese government in 1972. Angola flatly refused to negotiate directly with Unita, despite Soviet pressure, just as the South Vietnamese government refused to negotiate with the Vietcong.

South Africa's sincerity in abandoning Namibia is also open to doubt. The escalation of the fighting in 1987–8 brought the costs of the war to a rate of over $1 billion a year, so Pretoria's interest in inducing the Cubans to depart was obvious. But Namibia is a most valuable colony. It may not be worth what it is costing now, but South Africa has no intention of losing what it has already invested, and still less of permitting a hostile regime set up there. Its long-term strategy for its neighbours – the 'front-line states' – is to make them all economically and politically dependent upon South Africa, to reduce them once again to the status of colonies without South Africa itself having to undertake all the obligations and odium of a colonial power.

The official American position after the Geneva agreement was signed, was that the United States had the right to continue to aid Savimbi, and would do so for as long as the USSR and Cuba continued to arm the MPLA. Both the United States and the USSR continually urged the Luanda government to open negotiations with Unita – and it obdurately refused. The prospect, therefore, was that the civil war would continue after the Namibia settlement and Cuba's withdrawal. Savimbi would face certain logistical problems, without the easy access from Namibia, but his alliance with President Mobutu of Zaïre holds firm and his supplies would come from the east instead of from the south.

One of the unstated terms of the August ceasefire agreement between South Africa and Cuba was that there would also be a ceasefire between Cuba and Unita. Savimbi was left alone in Jamba and, in turn, Unita troops left the Cubans undisturbed. The final details were settled in a meeting in Brazzaville in November, but the agreement was not signed then. There was a last-minute hitch in Pretoria, and a further session was required before the agreement was finally signed, in Brazzaville, on 13 December. It was formally confirmed in a ceremony at the UN on 22 December.

The agreement provided that the process leading to Namibian independence would begin on 1 April 1989. In the following four months, 3000 Cuban troops would leave Angola and all Cuban troops would move north of the 15th parallel (about 190 miles/300 km north of the border). The Namibian elections are to be held on 1 November 1989. By then, according to the Brazzaville agreement, half of the Cuban troops in Angola would have been withdrawn completely, and the remainder would be withdrawn north of the 13th parallel (roughly the Benguela railway). There will be further reductions by 1 April 1990, leaving only a third of 11 the original number of Cubans in Angola, and by 1 August 1990, the remainder would be reduced to 13,000. This last contingent would leave by July 1991.

MODERN ANGOLA

The Angolan currency is worthless, but because of the oil – revenue was $2.5 billion in 1985 – the economy is considered viable by the World Bank and other international organizations. Angola is one of the few bankrupt nations with a credit line.

Immediately after independence in 1975, and the abrupt departure of the 300,000 Portuguese settlers, the government collectivized agriculture and national-ized all industry, except oil. The results were catastrophic. Agriculture and industry have both collapsed, and Angola has to import food from Europe and the United States to feed half its people. There was once an elegant promenade along the waterfront at Luanda, modelled on the Copacabana in Rio de Janeiro or the Promenade des Anglais in Nice. Now it is deserted, its shops, hotels and offices boarded up. The MPLA followed the advice of Soviet planners who knew nothing about Africa and tried to impose there a system not notably successful at home in Europe. Private enterprise was abolished and state companies were set up to replace them.

In 1988, the Soviet Union blandly admitted that the economic model that it had imposed upon its African clients was wholly unsuited to their needs. Anatoly Adamishin, the deputy foreign minister for African affairs, who conducted the negotiations with the US and South Africa on the future of Angola and Namibia, was asked at a press conference whether he thought SWAPO should adopt socialism. 'I personally don't think they are going to build socialism in this part of the world,' he replied. 'There are few people in the Soviet Union who would advise them to build a socialist society in these particular conditions of Africa.' For 20 years or more, the Soviet Union had peddled 'scientific socialism' as the solution to all Africa's woes, and had even set up a Patrice Lumumba University in Moscow to train the future *aparatchiks* of a Communist Africa. Thousands of Africans had devoted their lives to furthering a Communist revolution, and hundreds of thousands of people had been killed in the effort, or had died of starvation or disease because of the revolution's failure. Now the Soviets have dropped Marxism into the dustheap of history, at least as far as Africa is concerned. The future suddenly looks very bleak for Third World Marxists.

Exchange rates in Angola are so unrealistic and price controls so erratic that the few foreign companies still operating in Luanda pay their local employees in consumer goods. A visiting American journalist found, in December 1987, that the favoured unit of exchange was a case of beer. Two cases could be sold for enough local currency to pay for a round-trip flight to Rio or Lisbon.

The standard of living, life expectancy, infant mortality rates, medical provision and public safety are probably worse now for the Angolans than at any time since the abolition of the slave trade in the early 19th century. According to Unicef, 45 per cent of Angolan children suffer from malnutrition, and the amount spent on health care has dropped from $10.30 a head in 1981 to $0.90 in 1987 (these figures are expressed in dollars because the local currency is worthless). The *International Index of Human Suffering*, prepared by the Population Crisis Committee in

Washington, puts Angola second on the list of suffering countries; only Mozambique is more unfortunate.

The failure of Marxism is so flagrant that, in 1987, the government reversed course and proposed to revive the private sector. State shops, farms, service companies and so on were to be sold off. In addition, the government announced a month in advance that the currency (the kwanza) would be devalued by nearly 100 per cent – in other words, it recognized that the kwanza was completely valueless and would have to be replaced. These extreme measures have been welcomed by international organizations and by the European Community, which will now resume aid to Angola.

The security situation is almost as bad as in Mozambique. By one calculation, only 400 miles (640 km) of paved road are still safe, out of the 4400 miles (7040 km) bequeathed by Portugal. Foreign embassies recommended that their staff not travel more than 25 miles (40 km) outside the capital after three Swedish aid workers were kidnapped by Unita guerrillas in September 1987, 30 miles (48 km) outside Luanda, and one of them was killed. Even the coast road is not safe, and travel is now restricted to heavy convoys, or to the air. Government-controlled territory comprises a series of islands in a hostile sea, like Cambodia in the last days of Lon Nol. The parallel will be closer still if the Cubans leave. Discipline among Angolan soldiers is an increasing problem, as it was in Uganda, with many taking to banditry.

On 24 July 1989, at a summit meeting in Zaire which was attended by a number of African heads of state, President dos Santos and Jonas Savimbi met for the first time since 1975 and agreed to a ceasefire. No details of the agreement were published, and it soon broke down. Dos Santos claimed that Savimbi had agreed to leave the country, and Savimbi asserted that dos Santos had agreed to share power with Unita. The war continued.

Further negotiations between the two sides were arranged in Kinshasa but the only reasons for hope were that the outside powers, Cuba, the Soviet Union and South Africa all appeared determined to extract themselves from the Angolan imbroglio.

FURTHER READING

American University, *Angola: A Country Study*, Washington, 1979.

Bridgland, Fred, *Jonas Savimbi: A Key to Africa*, New York, Paragon House, 1987.

Henderson, Lawrence W., *Angola: Five Centuries of Conflict*, Ithaca, New York, Cornell University Press, 1979.

Klinghoffer, Arthur J., *The Angola War: A Study in Soviet Policy in the Third World*, Boulder, Colo., Westview Press, 1980.

Somerville, Keith, *Angola: Politics, Economics and Society*, London, Frances Pinter, 1986.

Stockwell, John, *In Search of Enemies: A CIA Story*, New York, W. W. Norton, 1978.

Wolfers, Michael, *Angola in the Frontline*, London, Zed Press, 1983.

BURUNDI AND RWANDA

BURUNDI

Area	10,707 sq. miles (27,731 sq. km).
Population	4.8 million. At independence, in 1962, 83% of the people were Hutu, 16% Tutsi and 1% Twa (pygmy). There have been no ethnic censuses since.
GNP per capita	$240

RWANDA

Area	10,169 sq. miles (26,338 sq. km).
Population	6.2 million. At independence, about 10 % of the population was Tutsi, 1% Twa and the rest Hutu.
GNP per capita	$290
Refugees	(Before the events of August 1988) From Burundi: 20,600 in Rwanda, 156,000 in Tanzania, 9600 in Zaïre. From Rwanda: 65,800* in Burundi, 11,000 in Zaïre, 118,000 in Uganda, 21,000 in Tanzania, 2000 in Kenya.
Casualties	20,000 Tutsi murdered in Rwanda, 1959–62; 100,000 Hutu murdered in Burundi, 1972; 1000–4000 Tutsi and up to 20,000 Hutu killed in Burundi, 1988.

In August 1988, without warning, the Hutu in northern Burundi started to massacre the minority Tutsi there. Between 1000 and 4000 Tutsi were killed, and then the army, which is almost entirely Tutsi, came to wreak vengeance on the Hutu. As many as 20,000 people were killed, and a wave of refugees – about 50,000 people – fled over the border into Rwanda. Many of them were wounded: European doctors in hospitals near the border reported scores of cases of women and children who had bayonet wounds in their backs. The people of entire villages had been ordered to lie face-down on the ground, and were bayoneted. A few escaped. By the end of the year, all but 1500 of the refugees had returned home.

The Tutsi have ruled Burundi for four centuries, apart from a 60-year colonial interlude (when it was known as Urundi). They originally came from the north, perhaps from Ethiopia: they are conspicuously tall and endowed with what Europeans used to call a classical profile. They have maintained their rule over the majority tribe in Burundi, the Hutu, in the only way possible: by force. The two tribes now speak the same language, and often intermarry, but despite this, their separation remains extreme. They are like the tribes of Northern Ireland, with the difference that the more recent arrivals, the Tutsi, are in a small minority, comprising only one-sixth of the population. The only other African state with a similar system of government is South Africa.

The Tutsi also used to rule neighbouring Rwanda (which under colonial rule was called Ruanda), but in a series of uprisings in 1959–62, the Hutu majority of Rwanda overthrew the Tutsi monarchy and domination. In the process, up to 20,000 Tutsi were murdered and 100,000 fled to Burundi. In 1972, in the worst pogrom in post-colonial Africa, about 100,000 Hutu in Burundi were murdered by the Tutsi. The troubles returned in 1988.

HISTORY

Ruanda–Urundi was part of German East Africa from 1899 until it was conquered by the British in 1916. It was a remote and neglected province: the Germans, who concentrated on developing the more accessible areas of Tanganyika, only established themselves early in the new century and were not there long enough to make much of an impression. Then, in the peace settlement after World War I, the territory was ceded to Belgium, as some compensation for its sufferings, and because it was contiguous with the Belgian Congo.

The peace-makers had been misreading the maps again. Ruanda–Urundi was even more remote from Leopoldville than from Dar-es-Salaam and, of course, its people were not consulted. It would have made much more sense to integrate it with Tanganyika. Belgium was given a mandate under the League of Nations to administer Ruanda–Urundi, and the Hutu and the Tutsi, after a few years of administration in German, had to adapt themselves to French and Flemish.

Ruanda and Urundi, though administered as a single colony, were kept separate because each had been an independent kingdom for generations. They were not merged as the British merged the kingdoms of Uganda. The Belgians anticipated that eventually there would be Hutu-dominated governments in both countries, but the matter was taken out of their hands.

First, in Ruanda, when the Tutsi king died in July 1959, the Hutu rose against his successor. There were massacres throughout the country and the bodies of hundreds of Tutsi were thrown in the river and floated down into Lake Tanganyika in Urundi. By the time the Hutu had established their control, as many as 20,000 Tutsi had been killed and 100,000 Tutsi refugees driven south into Urundi or north into Uganda (these figures are disputed by the government of Rwanda). There are now about 200,000 Rwandan refugees in neighbouring countries.

With the Hutu now in control of Ruanda, the Belgians, who had by then abruptly abandoned the Congo, made as graceful an exit as circumstances permitted, and in 1962, left behind the new Hutu government of Rwanda, headed by President Grégoire Kayibanda. The Tutsi retained power in Burundi, under their hereditary monarch, the Mwami Mwambutsa. His eldest son, Prince Rwagasore, was assassinated in October 1961, during the preparations for independence, and the Mwami then exercised absolute power during the last months of Belgian rule, and this continued after they left. In May 1965, there were legislative elections which Hutu parties won overwhelmingly, but the Mwami refused to recognize the results, 15 and appointed a Tutsi prime minister. The first Hutu revolt occurred in October; before it was suppressed, between 2500 and 5000 Hutu had been killed, including over 100 prominent government officials and officers. The Mwami fled the country, and his second son, Charles Ndizeye, was put on the throne, taking the name Ntare V, in September 1966. In November, he was deposed by his own prime minister, Captain Michel Micombero, who became president.

In September 1969, Micombero discovered a Hutu plot and summarily executed about 20 prominent Hutu, including one minister and two former ministers; others were jailed. In July 1971, Micombero discovered a Tutsi plot, and executed a number of prominent Tutsis.

On 29 April 1972, there was a Hutu uprising in Bujumbura, the capital, and in the southern parts of the country. The rebels, numbering perhaps 10,000, were aided by a small army of Hutu exiles, and by some of the surviving troops of Pierre Mulele, who had played a role in the Congo civil wars. The Burundi government at the time claimed that 50,000 Tutsi were killed, but the real total was probably nearer 2000, most of them Hutu. The invaders, who attacked the Bujumbura radio station, were easily defeated. President Mobutu of Zaïre sent a small contingent to the capital to keep the peace, allowing the Burundi army to concentrate on the Hutu.

Then the reprisals began. One of the first victims was the former Mwami, Ntare V. He had been visiting Uganda on business in March 1972, and Micombero asked Idi Amin to deliver him to Bujumbura, under promise of safe-conduct: 'Just like you, I believe in God ... Your Excellency can be assured that as soon as Mr Charles Ndizeye returns back to my country, he will be considered as an ordinary citizen and that as such his life and security will be assured.' Ntare was then summarily bundled into Micombero's presidential plane, much against his will, and flown to Bujumbura. He was murdered shortly after the rebellion broke out on 29 April.

Then the Tutsi embarked on a massacre of the Hutu. On 30 April, the government imposed a dawn-to-dusk curfew. The army and the Tutsi youth movement sought out and killed all Hutu with secondary education, all politicians, teachers, businessmen and tens of thousands of peasants. At the Official University at Bujumbura, one-third of the students were murdered, and at the capital's *lycée* (high school) 300 of 700 students enrolled were killed, as were 60 per cent of Protestant clergy (all Hutu). It was a deliberate attempt to wipe out all Hutu who might ever take the lead in opposition to the Tutsi. There is no precise estimate of the number who lost their lives, but the generally accepted figure is 100,000. Reginald Kay writes that conservative estimates put the number, including those killed in the brief Hutu rebellion, between 80,000 and 100,000. He goes on: 'By no means fanciful reports have suggested that the figure was closer to 150,000, or almost 5 per cent of the population.' About 150,000 Hutu fled abroad. There were no protests, either from the Organization of African Unity (OAU), the United Nations or from Western countries which, according to Kay, suffer from 'a deeply rooted and guilt-based fear of censuring the conduct of nations in the developing world'.

MODERN BURUNDI

Burundi has never escaped from the shadow of those terrible events. Micombero was deposed in a coup in 1976 by his cousin, Colonel Jean-Baptiste Bagaza. The two men had been watching a soccer match together in the presidential box, when Bagaza informed Micombero that the large number of troops around the stadium had switched their allegiance, and he was now president. Micombero was put on a plane and sent into exile.

Bagaza had been out of the country during the 1972 massacres and therefore escaped any personal blame, but he too pursued a policy of relentless persecution of the Hutu. In 1987, there were four Hutu ministers out of a total of 20 in the government, one of 15 provincial governors, seven Hutus in the National Assembly and two in the governing party's 65-strong central committee. Very few Hutu children go to high school, and only one-third of the students at university level are Hutu. Since the Hutu are mostly Catholic, persecution extended to the Church: foreign missionaries and priests were expelled, including the Bishop of Bururui who had worked in Burundi for 50 years; church schools were closed and church land was expropriated. The governing was a nasty and friendless dictatorship, and the country stagnated economically. Its only resource was the export of coffee, chiefly grown by Hutu peasants in the northern provinces (much of it was smuggled over the border to Rwanda). Its only international support came from France, which sustains all French-speaking countries – even though French had been suppressed as the language of education in the schools.

In September 1987, a bloodless army coup overthrew the government and a new president, Major Pierre Buyoya, took office. He had been in Brussels during the 1972 massacre, was less paranoid than Bagaza, and began to improve relations between Tutsi and Hutu. He released all political prisoners, restored church property, jailed some Tutsis on corruption charges, and urged his fellow Tutsis to allow the Hutus to enjoy equal rights with them.

In the relatively affluent north, the Hutu began to act on Buyoya's promises, but the local Tutsi administration did not. Word spread around the district of troubles to come. According to one account, the Tutsi mayor of Marangara, a northern town, told the local Hutu on 28 June 1988, 'You are preparing your knives, but ours are already sharp and they cut more than yours.' Then the national army, which is almost exclusively Tutsi, came north for manoeuvres and to attempt to stop coffee smuggling. The Hutu thought that the soldiers intended to kill them, and some of them began sabotaging bridges or blocking roads with tree trunks to delay the army's movements. On 14 August, panic swept the small Tutsi population of Marangara. They fled north, to the village of Ntega, where some of them took refuge in a church. In the next few days, there was widespread killing of Tutsi by Hutu: 2000 to 3000 died, including the people in the church.

The army arrived on 18 August and immediately began taking its revenge. The estimate of 20,000 killed came from doctors in a hospital near the border with Rwanda, and from relief workers. Refugees were crossing at a rate of 5000 a day, and over 50,000 had reached Rwanda by the end of August. Journalists who visited the country reported that the once heavily populated northern districts were empty. A month earlier, there had been 150,000 people living peacefully in their hill-top villages. Now there was none. The people had hidden in the bush, fled the country or had been killed.

The government claimed that the troubles were caused by Hutu exiles from Rwanda and Zaïre and played down the massacres, just as their predecessors had   17 done in 1972. In October, President Buyoya established the position of prime minister, and appointed a Hutu, Adrien Sibomana. The number of Hutu cabinet ministers, already raised to seven since the massacre, was increased to 11. The government's measures restored security to the north, and most of the refugees returned home. Real power remained with the Tutsi, however, and both tribes feared troubles yet to come.

FURTHER READING

American University, *Rwanda, A Country Study*, Washington, 1969.
Kay, Reginald, *Burundi Since the Genocide*, London, Minority Rights Group, 1987.
Lemarchand, René, *Rwanda and Burundi*, New York, Praeger, 1970.
Melady, Thomas Patrick, *Burundi: The Tragic Years*, Maryknoll, N.Y., Orbis Books, 1974.

CHAD

Size	490,733 sq. miles (1,270,994 sq. km).
Population	5.1 million.
GNP per capita	NA
Refugees	150,000–300,000 internal refugees; 40,000 refugees in other countries, including 25,000 in Sudan
Casualties	About 50,000 Chadians and Libyans have been killed in the civil wars and foreign interventions since 1965.

Chad suffers from all the woes of Africa. It is utterly impoverished. There are rumours of oil and uranium, but they have never been substantiated; and the last estimate of per capita income (in 1982) was $88 a year. There are no more than two or three other nations on Earth so completely destitute. And like many other African states, it is wracked by hatred, between the Arab north and the Christian and animist south. The northern tribes are bitterly divided among themselves and have fought constantly for supremacy – and there has been a ceaseless struggle for power among the leaders of the major southern tribe, the Sara. In 1979, the government disintegrated completely and had to be replaced by a bewildering sequence of African 'peace-keeping forces'.

France, the former colonial power, has had to come to the rescue of the government on four occasions, and Libya has invaded twice, in 1980–81 occupying the capital for a year. The United States, too, has intervened twice. Finally, Chad, which is largely desert, suffered frightfully from the great drought of the early 1970s, which returned in 1984 and again in 1988.

HISTORY
The only reason for Chad's existence is that the French did not occupy Tripolitania and Cyrenaica (now combined to form Libya) in the 19th century. They annexed the rest of the north and most of west and central Africa, but the Italians took Libya and, in due course, laid claim to the Fezzan, the desert to the south of Libya. France by then controlled the western Sudan, the Sahel region stretching from the Atlantic to the Anglo-Egyptian Sudan in the east. Therefore the French and Italians drew some lines on the map to delimit their zones in the Sahara, and in the   **19**

process, the wild Tibesti, one of the most inhospitable places on Earth, and populated by black Muslim nomads, was arbitrarily added to French Equatorial Africa (AEF). The only history that the two regions shared was that, for centuries, the nomads had raided south for slaves and had driven their unfortunate victims across the desert to the slave markets of Tripoli.

It was well into the 1930s before the French finally conquered the Tibesti, and when they abandoned the AEF in 1960, dividing it into four separate countries, the nomads found themselves amalgamated with southerners, of whom they knew little. The Sara, who were partially converted to Christianity, were the dominant tribe in the new state. Remembering the slave trade, they were deeply suspicious of the Muslim north.

The northern provinces – Borkou, Ennedi and Tibesti, referred to as the BET – were administered by the French until 1965, when the Chadian government thought itself ready to take over. The new president, François Tombalbaye, an autocratic, incompetent and corrupt man, sent his fellow-tribesmen north to rule the BET. The tribes there promptly rose in revolt. Tombalbaye tried to repress them, and as a result, part of the Toubou tribe, under their traditional chief, the Derde, took refuge in Libya.

THE FIRST CIVIL WAR

The rebellion soon went out of control, and in 1968, Tombalbaye had to appeal to the French for help. The Foreign Legion therefore returned to Fort Lamy, the capital, and defeated the rebels. The Frence insisted that Tombalbaye institute reforms, restoring the privileges of the Muslim chiefs and appointing Muslim ministers. Most French troops were recalled in 1971.

The troubles continued, and Tombalbaye reacted by reviving animist customs among the Sara, making the cult of the Yondo – which involved particularly strenuous and unpleasant initiation rites – into a national religion. Tombalbaye persecuted Christian Sara who refused to participate – and resumed the persecution of the Muslims. He changed the capital's name to Ndjamena, and abandoned his Christian name, renaming himself Ngarta. In 1975, the army, which chiefly comprised Sara, deposed and killed him.

By then the north was in open revolt, and it was beyond the force of Tombalbaye's successor, General Félix Malloum, to defeat it. A loose coalition of exiled and rebel groups, called the *Front pour la Libération du Tchad* – Frolinat for short – had two armies in the field: the *Forces Armées du Nord* (FAN) and the First Liberation Army, in the east. In 1976, the FAN split between two leaders of the Toubou tribe: Goukouni Oueddei, son of the Derde of Tibesti who had fled to Libya; and Hissène Habré. This was chiefly the result of a clash of personal ambitions, which was brought out into the open by the annexation by Libya of a strip of Chadian territory, the Aozou. Goukouni acquiesced in the annexation; Habré opposed it. In the years that have followed, their dispute has nearly destroyed the country.

Goukouni was a traditional Toubou leader, an illiterate fighter with no interests beyond his native Tibesti. Habré had studied in France, and achieved worldwide notice when, in April 1974, he kidnapped a French anthropologist, Françoise Claustre, and held her prisoner in the Tibesti for almost three years, demanding arms from France as her ransom. It became a *cause célèbre* in France, like other hostage affairs would become later, and much preoccupied the government of President Valéry Giscard d'Estaing. A French officer was murdered by Habré's men when negotiating with them, and Claustre's husband, Pierre, was detained when he tried to visit his wife in August 1975. The following month, Giscard sent another emissary to negotiate a ransom. The French offered 4 million francs ($880,000) and promised a further 6 million francs' worth of equipment. When the French dropped a radio transmitter into the Tibesti to facilitate negotiations, General Malloum accused them of arming the rebels and demanded that the last French troops be evacuated from the south. They moved over the border into the Central African Empire, conveniently placed to return to Chad when needed, and also to depose Emperor Bokassa, which they did in 1979.

The Claustres were released on 30 January 1977, thanks to the intercession of Colonel Khadafy. Later that year, in the first round of fighting between Goukouni and Habré, Habré was defeated and driven out of the BET. He took refuge with a few followers in the east. Goukouni, turning to Libya for help against Malloum, soon controlled most of the BET and, in March 1978, occupied its principal town, Faya-Largeau. He then sent his armies south, in conjunction with another rebel group, the Volcan (also supported by Libya), which attacked from the east. In this extremity, Malloum called for French help, and for the second time, France came to the rescue: 1500 troops were flown to defend the capital Ndjamena, and the air force was used to defeat the Volcan army.

Habré, meanwhile, had built up a powerful army of his own, with support from Sudan, and now Malloum invited him to join the government. Habré became prime minister in a Government of National Unity (GUNT), but the government collapsed in February 1979. Fierce fighting between Habré's and Malloum's armies devastated Ndjamena, and soon deteriorated into a series of massacres in which southern troops slaughtered Muslims in the capital. Habré's forces drove Malloum and his army south, where they continued to massacre Muslims. Goukouni's troops moved into Ndjamena and started killing the Sara. Between 10,000 and 20,000 people died during these events.

THE FIRST INTERREGNUM

By now, Chad had no government. The Nigerians briefly sent an army to Ndjamena to keep the peace, and troops from a variety of other African countries, sponsored by the Organization of African Unity (OAU), put in fleeting appearances. In November 1979, after a series of international mediation efforts, a new government was put together with Goukouni as president, Habré as minister of defence, and the new leader of the Sara, Lieutenant Colonel Widal Kamougue, as vice-president. All three kept their private armies in Ndjamena, and soon Goukouni and Kamougue allied themselves against Habré.

The government again collapsed in March 1980. In April, France withdrew its last 1100 troops, and fighting immediately flared up between the rival potentates. It was during this period that the former CIA agent, Edwin Wilson, organized bands of European and American mercenaries to fly Libyan planes making deliveries to Goukouni's forces.

Habré was driven out of the government, but kept his troops in Ndjamena. Sporadic fighting continued throughout the year, and deteriorated into full-scale civil war again in December. Goukouni then called on Libya for help, and Khadafy sent tanks, planes and troops to Ndjamena. Habré was defeated, and took refuge in Cameroun, immediately to the south. In January 1981, Khadafy announced a union between Libya and Chad.

THE LIBYAN INTERVENTION

It is customary to denounce Libyan imperialism and Khadafy's megalomania, but in the case of Chad, he has a case worth considering. There is, first, the dispute over the Aozou strip in north-west Chad, a stretch of territory whose boundaries were first determined in 1935, in a moment of relative French weakness and Italian strength. France was then courting Italy as an ally against Hitler, and the border was drawn to Libya's advantage, but the French never ratified the agreement. Then Mussolini was evicted, first from Libya, then from Rome. When General de Gaulle took power in Paris, a new border was drawn, incorporating Aozou into French Africa, and the agreement was ratified by the British, who then controlled Libya. Colonel Khadafy professes to see no reason why a line drawn by the French and the British has greater validity than one drawn by the French and the Italians. On neither occasion, of course, were the region's inhabitants consulted.

Khadafy considers that the Tibesti has far more in common with the Fezzan than with Equatorial Africa, and it is quite possible that if the tribesmen were asked to choose between citizenship of Muslim and Arab Libya (annual income $7500 per capita) or citizenship of Chad, with a Christian-animist and non-Arab majority (annual income $88), they might choose Libya. That was the view taken by Goukouni, who controlled the BET from 1965 until 1988.

However, Khadafy did not just covet the barren BET. He wanted all of Chad. As for Habré, he would rather be president of impoverished Chad than a provincial leader of wealthy Libya. Goukouni, apparently, wanted both the economic advantages of the Libyan connection and the privileges of the presidency.

The southerners, now led by Colonel Kamougue, opposed the merger with Libya, and Habré sought support in Sudan, Egypt and, eventually, the United States to defeat it. Khadafy found himself in a difficult position, under bitter attack by the OAU which accused him of imperialism. Instead of brazening it out, like King Hassan of Morocco in the former Spanish Sahara, Khadafy abruptly abandoned Chad in October 1981. The civil war promptly resumed.

THE SECOND CIVIL WAR

Habré had by then built up his army again, with support from Khadafy's numerous enemies, most notably Sudan. He crossed the border early in 1982 and soon occupied the east and most of the north. On 6 June, his armies entered Ndjamena, and then it was Goukouni's turn to flee across the border to Cameroun. Habré proclaimed himself president and then set about conquering the south, defeating Kamougue and occupying the latter's headquarters at Moundou. Kamougue fled the country and, in October, joined Goukouni in Libya to set up a government in exile.

THE THIRD CIVIL WAR

Chad was at peace for almost a year, an unusual experience. Then in June 1983, Goukouni raised the northern tribes, and seized Faya-Largeau on 24 June, and the eastern city of Abéché on 6 July. Habré counterattacked and recaptured the two cities at the end of July – and then Libya again intervened.

Habré was besieged in Faya-Largeau, and once more called for help. The United States became involved for the first time, sending two AWAC planes and eight F-15s to Chad to control Libyan air activities, as well as $10 million in other types of military aid. France, for the third time, sent troops and planes to Ndjamena. They rescued Habré from Faya (he was brought out on a Red Cross plane) shortly before Goukouni and the Libyans recaptured the place on 11 August. The French then sent troops to defend Abéché, and drew a 'Red Line' across Chad, on the 16th parallel, effectively partitioning the country. Habré controlled everything to the south, and Goukouni held the north, with Libyan help (though Khadafy strenuously denied that any Libyan forces were in Chad).

There was now a stalemate, and it lasted for a year. There were more than 3000 French troops and a squadron of Jaguars at Ndjamena, and Libyan troops in Faya-Largeau. A mediation attempted by the OAU in Addis Ababa collapsed in January 1984, when the rivals each insisted on his exclusive right to fly the Chadian flag. The drought drove the nomads into the towns, where an international effort was needed to keep them alive. Meanwhile, secret negotiations took place between Libya and France, and on 17 September 1984, Khadafy announced that the two governments had agreed to withdraw their forces from Chad within two months.

On 10 November 1984, the two countries announced that the withdrawal was complete (even though Libya had never admitted to having any troops there in the first place), but the US State Department declared that there were still 5500 Libyan troops in Chad. On 16 November, President Mitterrand met Khadafy in Crete, with the Greek prime minister, Andreas Papandreou, as mediator, and accepted Khadafy's repeated assurances that all Libyan troops had withdrawn. The next day, back in Paris and with considerable embarrassment, Mitterrand had to admit that Khadafy had lied to him. (Presumably, the Americans had provided the relevant satellite photographs.) However, France declined to send its troops back to Ndjamena.

Chad then enjoyed two years of unparalleled tranquillity, with the beginnings of reconstruction in Ndjamena and efforts to revive the economy. However, at the same time, the French and Americans were building up Habré's forces, while the Libyans were contructing roads and air bases in southern Libya and northern Chad – both sides preparing for a renewal of the civil war.

THE FOURTH CIVIL WAR

It came in February 1986, with an attack by Goukouni and the Libyans across the 'Red Line'. The French sent their Jaguars into action and beat off the attackers. After much threatening and manoeuvring, the *status quo ante* was restored. Then in October occurred one of the more remarkable episodes of the protracted war. Goukouni Oueddei apparently decided that he had had enough of dependency on Libya, and tried to make his peace with Habré. He was shot and wounded in Tripoli – 'while resisting arrest' – on 30 October. The Toubou of the Tibesti, who

23

had followed him for 20 years, promptly changed sides and invited Habré to come to their rescue. It was the signal he had been waiting for, and he immediately began moving his troops north.

In the meantime, there was a renewal of the air war between France and Libya. On 11 December, Libyan jets crossed the 'Red Line' in an attempt to attack Ndjamena, and on 7 January 1987, French jets struck a Libyan air base in northern Chad. Five days earlier, Hissène Habré had launched his attack.

It was a remarkable campaign. Habré equipped his troops with small Toyota four-wheel-drive trucks, descendants of World War II Jeeps, each mounted with a heavy machine-gun or an anti-tank gun. The tribesmen rode their trucks like the cavalry of the caliphs, attacking Libyan columns from every direction. They were joined by troops loyal to Goukouni, natives of the region, who brought their Libyan-supplied arms with them when they changed sides.

On 2 January, Habré's troops took Fada, a crossroads in the desert. Among the booty they captured were dozens of Soviet T-55 tanks and six Italian anti-aircraft guns. On 19 March, a Libyan armoured column set out from an air base in north-central Chad, at Wadi Doum, to recapture Fada. The column was ambushed and destroyed, and when a second convoy set out to rescue it, from Faya-Largeau, it too was ambushed and destroyed. Habré's men claimed to have killed 800 Libyans in the two battles. Then they moved on to capture Wadi Doum on 21 March and, six days later, Faya-Largeau. The French and Americans provided arms for the offensive, and the French also gave considerable logistical support, moving equipment and weapons up from depots in Ndjamena to the northern front.

The Chadians killed 1200 Libyans at Faya, attacking over the sand dunes in their Toyotas, taking the Libyans completely by surprise. They took an immense booty, including scores of Tupolev fighter-bombers, MiG-21s, helicopters, three complete batteries of the latest Soviet SAM 13s and the latest Soviet radar, and over 100 tanks. They calculated that the value of all this was between $500 million and $1 billion.

By the end of March, Chad claimed to have killed 3603 Libyans and captured 1165, with losses of 35 Chadians killed. Many of those Libyans killed and captured turned out to be mercenaries. Some were Sudanese, who had no clear idea where they were, and 1700 were Druse militiamen from Lebanon, hired out by their leader Walid Jumblatt at a monthly rate of $500 to $2300 per mercenary; their families were assured of $50,000 if they were killed.

Habré's forces then proceeded to clear the Libyans out of the rest of the country. In June, the Chadian leader visited the United States and saw President Reagan. He was promised $32 million in aid, including Stinger anti-aircraft missiles. In exchange, the Americans were permitted to buy a selection of the captured Soviet military equipment, which much interested Pentagon specialists.

In August, Habré's men drove the Libyans out of the Aozou strip, but this last victory proved only temporary. The French had refused to provide air cover, and the battle was too far from Habré's bases. On 28 August, the Libyans retook Aozou and, for the first time, flew foreign journalists down into the desert to prove their victory. Habré avenged his defeat by sending a column across the border more than 60 miles (100 km) into Libya and destroying the major Libyan air base in the region, at Matan as-Sarra. The Chadians claimed to have killed 1700 Libyans, taken 312 prisoners (including an East German and two Yugoslavs), while losing 65 men themselves.

The OAU organized a ceasefire, which took effect on 11 September 1987. By American calculations, Khadafy had lost one-tenth of his army, 7500 men killed and $1.5 billion in equipment captured or destroyed.

CEASEFIRE

Both sides are preparing for the next war. The Libyans are building bases and airstrips in the Aozou strip, while Chad is improving communications with the north, and re-equipping its armed forces. The US has delivered Stinger surface-to-air missiles. The French continue to aid Chad to the tune of $70 million a year, and keep a small force in Abéché to deter attacks from the east, and a squadron of Jaguars at Ndjamena. They have also been endeavouring to persuade Chad and Libya to submit the Aozou strip dispute to arbitration.

Habré's old friend President Nimeiri of Sudan was overthrown in a coup in April 1985, and the Sudan now gives Libya a measure of support in its conflict with Chad. Khadafy has also been courting the government of Niger, to the west, and as a result, there has been a resurgence of small-scale guerrilla attacks into Chad from both Sudan and Niger. On 8 March 1988, a Libyan attack on a Chadian border post on the Sudan frontier was repulsed with the loss of 20 killed and ten captured. The attackers were members of the 'Islamic Legion', a mercenary army formed by Khadafy of men recruited in west Africa, chiefly in Benin, Mali and Nigeria. Still more mercenaries, from other Arab countries, are serving in the Libyan armed forces. After the frontier skirmish, there was a large anti-Libyan demonstration in Khartoum, a reminder that the new alliance with Libya was not necessarily popular.

Meanwhile, Goukouni moved to Algiers and resumed negotiations with Habré. They have not succeeded, so it is entirely possible that the Toubou will once again change sides. Diplomatic skirmishing continues between Chad and Libya. In May 1988, Khadafy refused to attend the 25th anniversary of the OAU in Addis Ababa, where other heads of government planned to urge him to make his peace with Hissène Habré. Then as the conference opened on 25 May, Khadafy abruptly announced that the war was over, and that he would recognize Habré as the legitimate president of Chad – 'as a gift to Africa'. He said nothing, however, about renouncing his claim to the Aozou strip.

In the course of 1988, Khadafy tried to mend his fences with a number of his former enemies in the Arab world and in Africa, and in October, Chad and Libya resumed diplomatic relations. Habré treated the Libyans with great caution: he urged the French to keep their garrison and air contingent in Ndjamena, although the French were anxious to recall them; he also kept the 2000 or so Libyan prisoners of war he had captured in 1987. He continued to insist that Libya must give up its claim to the Aozou strip before he would return the PoWs and send the French home. Khadafy remained as unpredictable as ever. However, during the war with Chad and the confrontation with the United States, he had discovered the inconvenience of his international isolation, and was now trying to end it. Habré still does not trust him, and even if Libya abandons its claim to the Aozou strip, he will always expect the worst.

It seems probable that the conflict will continue, at least as long as Hissène Habré rules in Chad and Moammar Khadafy in Libya. The Libyans' enormous oil wealth gives them a decided advantage: however much military equipment they may lose, they can always buy more. Also, they can build roads and air bases and establish depots of weapons and material near the frontier, and thus fight the next war with short lines of communication, while the Chadians have to move their scanty forces over a 1000 miles (1600 km) of desert. Another Libyan advantage was reported early in 1989. Khadafy was said by the Americans to have built a factory capable of producing poison gas. It was not difficult to guess which of Libya's neighbours was most likely to be its first victim.

The Chadian advantage is in morale. Libyans have no wish at all to fight and die for the Aozou strip, and Khadafy has therefore had to hire mercenaries – who are also disinclined to die for Khadafy and Aozou. Habré showed in 1987 how effective his desert warriors were. They were defeated in the Aozou strip only because they were over-extended and they lacked air cover. Now that the US has supplied them with Stinger missiles, that deficiency may have been remedied.

FURTHER READING

American University, *Chad, A Country Study*, Washington, 1972.
Kelley, Michael, *A State in Disarray: Conditions of Chad's Survival*, Boulder, Colo., Westview Press, 1986.
Thompson, Virginia McLean, *Conflict in Chad*, Institute of International Studies, University of California, 1981.

ETHIOPIA

Size	471,776 sq. miles (1,221,875 sq. km), the size of Spain, Portugal and France together.
Population	43.4 million: including about 9 million Amhara, 15 million Oromo, 4 million Eritreans, and 5 million Tigreans. Over 70 languages and over 200 dialects are spoken.
GNP per capita	$120
Refugees	Internal: 750,000–1.5 million Ethiopians*; 330,000 from Sudan. From Ethiopia: 430,000* in Somalia; 660,000 in Sudan; 2200 in Kenya. In the summer of 1988, 205,000 refugees from Somalia poured across the border into Ethiopia.
Casualties	The revolution, the four secessionist wars and the famines have killed up to 2 million people between 1972 and 1988, 300,000–350,000 in the fighting in Eritrea.

In the mid-1970s, there were four full-scale revolts under way against the Republic of Ethiopia – in Eritrea, Tigray and the Ogaden, and among the Oromo in central and southern Ethiopia – and a smaller revolt among the Afars in the north-east. The government survived, thanks to massive support by the Soviet Union and Cuba.

A Somali invasion was defeated and the revolts were contained. There are now low-level guerrilla conflicts in the Ogaden and the Oromo provinces. However, the guerrilla war in Tigray and, above all, the Eritrean wars are bleeding Ethiopia to death.

The regime survived the famine of 1984 that followed the great drought of the early 1980s, though 1 million people starved. A new famine threatened in 1988, after a further drought afflicted East Africa in 1987–8, but its worst effects were averted by international efforts and heavy rains in the summer of 1988. At the same time, however, Ethiopia suffered serious defeats in its war in Eritrea. The Soviet Union still supports Ethiopia militarily, but the Gorbachev regime is conspicuously less enthusiastic about African adventures than were its predecessors. Ethiopia must be accounted one of the states least likely to survive.

HISTORY
Ethiopia is a mountainous country, with high plateaux and inaccessible valleys.   27

Until the 1950s, it was known as Abyssinia. Its dominant tribe, the Amhara, were converted to Christianity in the 4th century and have adhered ever since to the Coptic Church, which also survives in Egypt. The Islamic conquests of the 7th century cut Ethiopia off from the rest of the Christendom, and throughout the Middle Ages, Europeans heard legends of the wondrous kingdom of Prester John, lost somewhere beyond the horizon.

The reality was less glorious. Ethiopia was remote and poor, and its rulers fought constantly against other tribes. Their empire sometimes extended to roughly Ethiopia's present extent, and was sometimes restricted to the Amhara homelands in the mountains. Explorers of the 19th century discovered a land of extreme poverty and ignorance, whose paranoid rulers imprisoned their sons for fear they would rise in revolt. Among the explorers was the French poet Rimbaud, who travelled throughout Somalia, the Ogaden and Abyssinia from 1882 to 1891. He lived in Harar and sold guns to Emperor Menelik (who never paid him); he died of an infection contracted there.

Because it was so inaccessible, Abyssinia was left alone by European powers until late in the century. In 1868, the British in India, incensed by Abyssinian mistreatment of British subjects, mounted a punitive expedition against the Emperor Theodore. It was commanded by General Lord Napier, who conducted it like an excursion into Afghanistan. He loaded his guns on to elephants, and marched into the heart of the empire, building bridges and roads as he went, and laid siege to Theodore's last fortress. The emperor committed suicide rather than surrender. Their honour satisfied, the British then marched back to the coast and sailed away, leaving the Abyssinians to fight among themselves for the succession.

The eventual victor was Menelik II, King of Shoa (1844–1913), who crowned himself emperor in 1889 after his predecessor had been killed in battle in the Sudan. Menelik doubled the size of the empire by conquering fertile provinces to the south and south-west, and the desert Ogaden, peopled by nomadic Somalis, to the south-east. By that time, the Italians had seized Eritrea, and the French, British and Italians had established themselves along the coasts of the Horn of Africa. Abyssinia therefore remained cut off from the sea.

In 1895, in a moment of imperial *folie de grandeur*, the Italians tried to conquer Abyssinia. They were resoundingly defeated in the battle of Adowa in February 1897 – the only decisive defeat that the Europeans encountered in the scramble for Africa. The victorious Menelik signed treaties with his European neighbours, and Abyssinia was left to its own devices for the next 37 years.

Menelik died in 1913 and, after a period of considerable turbulence and international intrigue, was succeeded by his cousin Ras Lej Tafari Makonnen, who proclaimed himself crown prince and effective ruler of the country in 1916. He eventually crowned himself as the Emperor Haile Selassie in 1930. Evelyn Waugh reported the event for the London *Daily Mail*, and it later provided the basis for his African novels, *Scoop* and *Black Mischief*. One of Selassie's titles was Lion of Judah: he claimed descent from King Solomon and the Queen of Sheba.

In 1934, the Italians under Mussolini concocted a border incident as *causus belli* and again invaded Abyssinia. This time, they had bombs and poison gas to defeat the Abyssinians, and they occupied Addis Ababa in May 1936. Then they set up Italian East Africa, which consisted of Eritrea, Abyssinia and Somalia.

Haile Selassie went to the headquarters of the League of Nations in Geneva to denounce its members for allowing one of their number to be annexed by an aggressor. However, the British and French, wanting to keep Mussolini in the alliance against Hitler, recognized the conquest in 1938. Their perfidy was rewarded two years later when Italy joined Hitler, stabbed France in the back and occupied British Somaliland.

In due course, Mussolini met his just desserts. The British conquered Italian East Africa in a six-month campaign, taking 200,000 prisoners. After the war, feeling guilty about the way they had treated Haile Selassie, and influenced by the fact that the United States was now his ally, they handed Eritrea over to him in 1952, and also returned the Ogaden, which had been briefly reunited with the rest of Somalia. Ethiopia was then officially awarded Eritrea as a mandate by the UN. John Foster Dulles, the new US secretary of state, remarked, 'From the point of view of justice, the opinions of the Eritrean people must receive consideration. Nevertheless, the strategic interest of the United States . . . [make] it necessary that the country has to be linked with our ally, Ethiopia.' (Ethiopia had sent troops to Korea and offered the United States bases, notably a communications base at Kagnew, in the mountains near Asmara.)

In 1962, Haile Selassie summarily annexed Eritrea. Ethiopia had at last reached the sea. All its subsequent sorrows, including the 1974 revolution and the deposition of the emperor, derive from this success.

THE REVOLUTION

Haile Selassie's empire was a feudal relic in the late 20th century. The country's only exports were coffee and oil-seed, not nearly enough to sustain a large and developing country. The social regime, if not the monarchy, might have survived and modernized itself if the government had not been so corrupt and inefficient. As the emperor aged, he progressively lost control of his family and officials, who left the administration of the country to look after itself while they enriched themselves. A few reforms were decreed, but most of them remained paper enactments. Ethiopia was like Shah Mohammed Reza's Persia, only far poorer. It had no oil and only a tiny educated class.

Haile Selassie was sinking into senility, but refused to allow any competent prince or minister to run the government. One of his sons was killed in a car crash, another had a stroke and retired to Switzerland, and Haile Selassie, who was born in July 1892, never designated a successor.

The spark that ignited the revolution was a drought in 1972–3, followed by the 'Wollo famine' in which over 200,000 people were left to starve to death in Wollo and Tigray provinces. The government was quite incapable of helping them, and denied that there was any problem. In fact, grain exports from areas not affected by the drought doubled during the famine. The truth of the disaster was only known abroad when Jonathan Dimbleby revealed it in a BBC television programme.

In January 1974, a series of mutinies shook the army. The rebels in Eritrea had defeated it, forcing it to retreat into its few surviving bases, and the junior ranks were demoralized and resentful of their officers' incompetence. The government, unable to assert any sort of authority, gave in to every demand made by the 29 mutineers. In March, there was a general strike, and by spring, the mutineers had arrested their senior officers. In June, they set up a coordinating committee with up to 126 members, representing all the units of the army. It was called the Dergue, the Amharic word for 'committee', and it progressively took control of the whole country in a 'creeping *coup d'état*'. Its chairman was Major Mengistu (or Mangistu) Haile Mariam, then aged 30. He was chosen because he was neither Amhara nor Eritrean, but Oromo.

Haile Selassie, then 82 years old and in his dotage, lost all his authority to the Dergue, which arrested his ministers. The Dergue then broadcast the BBC film on the Wallo famine to the Ethiopian people, to prove the emperor's unworthiness. On 12 September 1974, the Dergue deposed him, and he was driven away from his palace in a Volkswagen and imprisoned. He died, or was murdered, on 27 August 1975.

THE NEW ETHIOPIA

The new regime had much in common with the old. It was secretive, dictatorial, brutal and incompetent. In November 1974, the head of the armed forces and *de facto* head of state, General Aman Michael Andom, an Eritrean, recommended that the Eritrean war be ended and that country abandoned. The other leading members of the Dergue, notably Mengistu (now promoted to lieutenant colonel), rejected this proposal and Aman was summarily shot. Two days later, on 23 November, Mengistu ordered the execution of 59 people (some reports say it was as many as 82). The massacre was presented as a settling of accounts with the *ancien régime* and the defeat of a counter-revolutionary plot – and thus, retroactively, justifying Aman's murder. Most of those shot were the ministers, princes, generals and other notables imprisoned since the revolution, among them Haile Selassie's grandson. (In May 1988, the Dergue released seven surviving princesses, including the emperor's 79-year-old daughter and the murdered grandson's widow. Three others remained imprisoned.)

In July 1976, after further reverses in Eritrea, there was another attempt in the Dergue to change course and come to terms with the Eritreans, but Mengistu once again reacted by having his dissident colleagues shot. In September, surviving members of the Dergue voted to strip Mengistu of most of his powers. Unfortunately, they neglected to have him arrested, and on 2 February 1977, he reasserted himself in a shootout at a Dergue meeting at which all his opponents were killed, including the head of state, General Teferi Banti.

Several political parties were formed in the wake of the revolution, among them the Ethiopian People's Revolutionary Party (EPRP). The Dergue itself only formed its own party, the SEDED (Workers' Party), two years later. After the February coup, Mengistu launched a 'red terror' against his enemies, and urban militia squads hunted down members of the EPRP. Eventually, at least 5000 youths, aged between 12 and 25, were killed in Addis Ababa. Another revolutionary party, the All-Ethiopian Socialist Movement – known by its Amharic acronym of MEISON – attempted a coup in 1977, lost and was slaughtered by Mengistu's security police. The terror reached a peak in December 1977 and January 1978, and in the end, the EPRP and MEISON had been wiped out.

Immediately after the 'creeping *coup d'état*' had been successfully concluded, 30   Ethiopia proclaimed itself a Marxist state and nationalized industries and collectivized agriculture on the Bolshevik model. The United States no longer had a use for its satellite communications centre and the new Carter administration, appalled at the regime's human rights abuses, suspended arms shipments in February 1977. In May 1977, Mengistu flew to Moscow and signed treaties of friendship with the USSR and other Communist states.

The regime's chief concern was survival. The Eritrean People's Liberation Front (EPLF), supported by Sudan and Saudi Arabia even though it too proclaimed itself Marxist, had proved a highly successful guerrilla organization and had extended its control to the whole of the province, with the exception of two or three major towns. Between August 1977 and July 1979, the Dergue lost one-third of its army in Eritrea, and had simultaneously to fight off an invasion from Somalia, which attempted to conquer the Ogaden. (See below for the Eritrea war, and the article on Somalia for the war with that country.)

At the same time, the Tigray People's Liberation Front (TPLF) was formed, and it rapidly took control of the province, which is in the north of Ethiopia, between the plateau and Eritrea on the Red Sea. Since all routes to Eritrea pass through Tigray, this was a serious loss. However, unlike Eritrea, Tigray was not necessarily bent on dismembering the state: the Tigreans had been part of the Ethiopian empire for generations and were not committed to secession.

The fourth revolt was uncompromisingly secessionist. The Oromo, who number about 15 million, one-third of the population of Ethiopia, made a bid for freedom with the Oromo Liberation Front. Potentially, that was the most dangerous of all the secession movements. Ethiopia's far greater population can, in theory, hold Eritrea and the Ogaden indefinitely, and should a change of government in Addis call for a retreat, the country would survive their loss. Eritrea and the Ogaden have no resources and do nothing to strengthen Ethiopia. The Oromo provinces, however, are Ethiopia's richest. If they were to secede, Ethiopia would be restricted to the high, poverty-stricken plateau from which the Amhara had emerged in the 19th century.

Ethiopia would not have survived these threats without the unstinting material help of the Soviet Union, and without Cuban troops. At the height of the war with Somalia, in the autumn of 1977, Cuba supplied 17,000 troops and the USSR airlifted enormous quantities of military supplies to Addis Ababa. The Ethiopians were thus able to turn the tide and defeat the Somali invasion, and recover most of Eritrea.

ERITREA

Eritrea has suffered constant war for the past 15 years, and small-scale guerrilla war for a decade before that. The Eritrean People's Liberation Front has developed into an efficient and powerful army, with about 35,000 regular troops, many of them women, supported by the majority of the population. It has won permanent control of about one-third of the province, in the north-west, protected by a fortified front 220 miles (350 km) long which the Ethiopian army has been unable to cross. In this protected zone, the EPLF has factories, schools, hospitals and workshops to repair weapons, all dug into the hills for protection from the Ethiopian air force.

Eritrea covers about 46,000 sq. miles (120,000 sq. km) – about the size of Pennsylvania and rather smaller than England – and has a population of 4 million. Half of the people are Christian, and the remainder are Muslim. The Christians occupy the mountains to the west and speak Tigrinya, the language spoken in Tigray, which is related to Amharic. The Muslims speak Arabic and various other languages, and live on the Red Sea coast. Eritrea thus is no more homogeneous than Ethiopia itself, and its nationalism is largely the result of the Italian occupation and of continued opposition to the government in Addis Ababa. The EPLF controls most of the countryside, leaving the Ethiopians in the principal towns, although in a major offensive in March/April 1988, the EPLF seized several cities in the mountains in the west and south. There are about 120,000 Ethiopian troops in the province.

Casualty figures are impossible to verify. In 1983, Colin Legum estimated that up to 250,000 people had been killed in the fighting since 1974, and another 50,000–100,000 have been killed since then. The 660,000 refugees in Sudan are almost all Eritreans and Tigreans, and counting the internal refugees, and those deported by the Dergue, it is probable that over half the Eritreans have been driven from their homes.

THE WAR

The rebellion began in 1961, even before Haile Selassie annexed Eritrea formally. The Eritrean Liberation Front (ELF) was formed in that year, and launched its guerrilla campaign in September. It was a primarily Arab-speaking Muslim organization, its militants coming from the educated classes in Asmara and Massawa, and from among those who had travelled or studied in Saudi Arabia or Cairo. From the start, the ELF was supported by radical Arab regimes, and as a consequence, suffered from the varying fortunes of Nasserites and Iraqi and Syrian Ba'athists, and was frequently split and reconstituted.

In 1970 came the formation of a rival organization, the EPLF, whose members are chiefly Tigrinya-speaking Christians drawn from the highlands. Its leader is Isaias Aferworki. Both the ELF and the EPLF professed a Marxist philosophy, and they soon started fighting among themselves. Between 1970 and 1975, about 3000 Eritreans were killed in this war within a war, in which the EPLF prevailed. Various efforts in the late 1970s and early 1980s to unite the guerrilla movements all failed, partly because of the question of relations with the Arab world, partly because of the suggestion, promoted by the Soviet Union, that the Eritreans should negotiate a federal agreement with the Ethiopians.

During the early years of the rebellion, before the Ethiopian revolution, the Soviet Union armed the rebels and sent Cuban advisers to train them, as part of their effort to destabilize Haile Selassie. The United States and Israel, which wanted to keep the Arabs away from the southern shore of the Red Sea, helped Haile Selassie. Israel continues to support the Ethiopian government, for the same reasons of *realpolitik*.

There was a brief moment after the 1974 Ethiopian revolution when the Eritreans could hope that the new government would allow them self-determination. It ended with the assassination of the head of state, General Aman Michael Andom, who was Eritrean. Eritrean police and army units deserted to the rebels *en masse*, and Eritrean guerrillas infiltrated the provincial capital, Asmara, and almost captured it. They were only defeated after savage fighting with Ethiopian troops. The Dergue's decision to suppress the Eritrean independence movement, and its vicious methods, hugely stimulated the EPLF's recruitment drive: in early 1975, it had 6000 guerrillas, but within two years, that had grown to over 40,000.

Mengistu's first weapon was famine. The drought continued, and the Dergue used it ruthlessly against the Eritreans. However, the general confusion in Ethiopia was so great that the rebels were able to take over most of Eritrea, besieging Ethiopian troops in Asmara and in the two ports of Assab and Massawa, and controlling practically the whole of the rest of the province.

In May 1976, in desperation, the Dergue summarily rounded up 40,000 peasants and marched them against the Eritrean positions. They were slaughtered. In 1977, it seemed to the Eritreans that victory was imminent: Ethiopia was barely hanging on to Asmara and Massawa; the Somalis were preparing to invade the Ogaden; and the regime in Addis Ababa seemed on the verge of collapse. The Soviet Union was faced with an unpalatable choice. It had supported both Somalia and Eritrea for years, and with Ethiopia proclaiming its sudden conversion to Marxism, the USSR strongly urged a federation of the three nations, a sort of Soviet Union of the Horn of Africa. Even Aden, across the Strait of Bab el Mandeb, might join. None of the principals showed the least interest in these Soviet fantasies. Eritrea wanted freedom, Somalia wanted the Ogaden, and Marxist Ethiopia wanted to hang on to all the conquests of the emperors.

The Soviet Union therefore changed sides. It abruptly stopped arming the Eritreans and Somalis, and instead swung its support behind Mengistu. The Soviet navy shelled EPLF positions besieging Massawa, and by the end of 1978, Ethiopia had recovered most of its lost territory.

It did so on its own, with only material help, not troops, from the Soviets and the Cubans. Fidel Castro, who had been denouncing Haile Selassie for years and proclaiming the Eritreans' inalienable right to self-determination, refused to send his men to fight with the Ethiopians in the north. The 14,000 Cuban troops who had fought in the Ogaden war stayed out of Eritrea. However, the USSR had delivered so much equipment that the Ethiopians, fresh from their victory over Somalia, were able to raise the siege of Massawa in July 1978, and reoccupy most of the rest of Eritrea by the end of November.

The EPLF withdrew into the north, abandoning its positions in the rest of the country, and prepared for the long haul. In 1981, there was a flare-up of fighting between the EPLF and the ELF, which ended in the destruction of the ELF.

The Ethiopian army has mounted eight general offensives against the Eritreans since 1973, the latest in 1988. Each has been defeated. After re-establishing its positions and expanding and retraining its armies, the regime launched Operation Red Star in February 1982, with 140,000 troops. Ethiopian losses were very high (Robert Kaplan reports 40,000 dead and wounded), and despite all the assistance provided by the Soviets and Cubans, the Ethiopians were unable to occupy the EPLF's northern fortress. Subsequent offensives suffered the same fate.

In the winter of 1987/8, the EPLF launched a series of attacks on the Ethiopian army, inflicting heavy casualties and breaking through the Ethiopian front. In a tour of inspection, Mengistu arrested a number of officers, and had the commanding general, Brigadier General Taiku Taye, shot in front of his troops – *pour encourager les autres*. It had a disastrous effect on morale.

On 17 March, the EPLF mounted a general offensive. In a series of battles – during which it claims to have killed 18,000 and captured over 6000 Ethiopian troops, and wiped out an entire armoured brigade – it captured several cities, notably Af Abet, a garrison town and the main Ethiopian military depot in the north. The EPLF also captured enormous stocks of munitions, including 50 Soviet tanks. Among its prisoners were the Ethiopian army's chief political commissar in Eritrea and three Soviet officers – two colonels and a lieutenant (a fourth was killed). The EPLF now claims to have as many as 16,000 Ethiopian PoWs (in 1982, it released 3000 to Sudan). It was the biggest EPLF victory in nearly a decade.

At the same time, the Tigrean rebels made major advances. The Ethiopians counter-attacked in May, and were repulsed. An élite airborne commando unit was wiped out and its commander killed. Mengistu called for volunteers throughout Ethiopia to fight in the north, and demanded that every Ethiopian 'voluntarily' contribute one month's wages or pension to the government to pay for the war. After signing an agreement with Somalia to restore diplomatic relations, he began to airlift troops to the north from the Ogaden, where, since the end of the Ogaden war, Ethiopia had permanently stationed 150,000 troops.

Except for Af Abet, the EPLF did not keep the towns it occupied: that would have invited the Ethiopian air force to bomb them. Instead, it returned to its northern stronghold with its booty, and further reinforced its control of the countryside. By late summer 1988, the Ethiopians had their backs to the wall. Their demoralized army had a precarious hold on Keren, north-west of Asmara, but the EPLF had bypassed the town. The Ethiopians' last line of defence ran from Asmara in the hills down to Massawa on the Red Sea.

The regime has decreed that a band of territory along the coast north of Massawa is a free-fire zone – that is, anything moving there will be attacked from the air. Since this district is a principal grazing area for Eritrean nomads, the regime clearly intends to starve them into submission. It is following the same policy by other means in the territory between Massawa and Keren. Its troops have systematically devastated that part of the country, and Eritrean relief authorities estimated that between 350,000 and 500,000 people fled their homes in the district between March and August 1988. The Ethiopians will do nothing to help them: on the contrary, it is they who have caused the problem.

The war is now inextricably linked with famine relief. During the 1984–5 famine, while 1 million people died in Ethiopia, Mengistu forbade foreign relief agencies to work in Eritrea and prevented the Ethiopian relief agency from operating there. The EPLF brought in supplies from Sudan and moved 100,000 people to camps on the border, where they could be fed. It was during those terrible years that Israel, aided by the United States and Sudan, rescued 10,000 Ethiopian Jews, the Falasha, from Tigray and Gondar – and starvation and destruction. Famine returned in 1988, and this time about 7 million people were affected throughout Ethiopia, 3.5 million in Tigray and Eritrea. The government will feed only those in areas under its own direct control, and tries to prevent supplies reaching areas controlled by the EPLF. The latter, too, uses food as a weapon. It retains the support of starving Eritrean peasants by feeding them, but despite this, in October 1987, EPLF guerrillas shot up a government food convoy outside Asmara: 23 UN trucks, carrying enough American wheat to feed 45,000 people for a month, were destroyed.

The US and international relief organizations protested vehemently, and the EPLF promised to leave food convoys alone in future. However, in the next five months, a further 106 relief vehicles were destroyed, including many supplied by Live Aid, the relief agency set up by the Irish rock singer Bob Geldof. In March 1988, the Tigray rebels destroyed two of the three government-run food distribution centres in the province; when they captured the third, at Wukro, the Ethiopian air force promptly bombed it. At the same time, the government was trying to resettle 1.5 million peasants from Tigray and Eritrea in southern Ethiopia. Ostensibly, this is supposed to save their lives; it will also take them out of the reach of the guerrillas.

In April 1988, Mengistu expelled all foreign aid workers from the northern provinces, allegedly on security grounds and claiming that Ethiopian relief organizations were quite capable of handling the crisis. Western governments disagreed, and urged him to permit a resumption of international relief. Mengistu also declared a six-mile (10 km) wide area along the border with Sudan to be a war zone, and promised to bomb any vehicles seen there. Later, he relented to some extent, announcing that the ban on foreign workers would not include those representing the UN. During the 1984 famine, the US had permitted the delivery of some food supplies directly to the EPLF through Sudan, and in the summer of 1988, the US State Department intimated that it would now do so again, despite the danger from the Ethiopian air force.

The EPLF was initially a staunchly Marxist organization. However, since the USSR has given unstinting support to Ethiopia, and Sudan and Saudi Arabia have supported the Eritreans, its politics have become less dogmatic. Besides, the failure of Marxism in other parts of Africa has been a dreadful warning. The EPLF's chief characteristic is now independence: it has at various times been supported and opposed by Sudan, the Arab states and the Soviet Union, and has learned to distrust them all. Its one steadfast ally has been Somalia.

The United States has not supported the EPLF, partly because of its professions of Marxism, partly because it has its hands full supporting rebels in Nicaragua, Angola and Afghanistan. This unusual moderation has not helped limit the damage. The EPLF gets all the weapons it needs from other donors and via booty captured from the Ethiopian army.

The war is going badly for the Ethiopians. However, since the Soviets began aiding the regime, the army has increased from 65,000 men to over 300,000, and at one point, there were 2000 Soviet advisers in Ethiopia. If this army holds together, it can defeat the EPLF in open warfare, and hold the cities. On the other hand, the past decade has shown that Mengistu has no hope of crushing the EPLF, and the debilitating effects of constant defeat and frustration may yet destroy the regime.

TIGRAY

Tigray province, in the northern part of Ethiopia proper, has a population of about 5 million, 70 per cent of whom are Christians, the rest Muslim. The Tigreans were the chief rivals to the Amhara of Shoa, to their south, to whom they are closely 35 related. The Emperor Theodore and his successor John IV were Tigreans, and Tigray only reluctantly accepted the rule of the Shoan king, Menelik, when he made himself emperor in 1889. When Menelik marched his army of 100,000 conscripted peasants through Tigray to meet the Italians at Adowa, they lived off the land; as a consequence, they left seven years of famine behind them. The Tigreans rebelled against Haile Selassie in 1943, and were put down with the help of the British, who bombed the capital, Makelle.

In 1972–3, there was famine in Tigray and the neighbouring province, Wollo, and over 200,000 Tigreans starved to death. It was the imperial government's incompetence and callousness during this disaster that precipitated the 1974 revolution.

In February 1975, opposition forces in Tigray formed the Tigray People's Liberation Front, which began a guerrilla war against the Ethiopians. It had a strongly Marxist charter, proclaiming itself to be 'anti-imperialist, anti-Zionist, anti-feudal, anti-national oppression, and anti-Fascist'. It asserted that its goal was national self-determination, which was not necessarily secessionist.

The TPLF was opposed by a conservative party, the Ethiopian Democratic Union, and from 1976 to 1978, the two fought a violent civil war in Tigray, which ended with the complete victory of the TPLF. At the same time, the TPLF fought and defeated the Ethiopian People's Revolutionary Party (EPRP), a radical Communist party that was also fighting the Dergue in Addis Ababa. Many thousands of people were killed in these civil wars.

During the early years after the revolution, the Dergue was distracted by the war with Somalia. In the summer of 1978, the victorious TPLF joined forces with the Eritrean EPLF, and defeated an attempt by the Dergue to reconquer the two provinces.

In 1979, the TPLF captured several towns in Tigray and cut the road connecting Addis Ababa to Eritrea. With the support of the USSR and Cuba, the Ethiopians retook the towns, but have never retaken the countryside, which remains firmly under the control of the TPLF. In a major offensive in 1980/81, the Ethiopians ravaged central Tigray, driving the population from their farms and burning crops in an attempt to starve the peasantry into submission. The country was devastated, scores of thousands of people were killed or starved to death, but the Ethiopians failed to reconquer western Tigray. When Mengistu's offensive failed, the TPLF reoccupied the areas it had abandoned.

The same thing happened during the next Ethiopian offensive in 1983: the armies advanced from Addis Ababa, laying the country waste, but later in the year withdrew again.

The next year, 1984, was the time of the great famine, in which a million Ethiopians starved to death. Tigray suffered heavily, and those people who survived did so because of international relief operations.

The war continued to wash across Tigray. The TPLF controlled most of the country, while the Dergue held the principal towns and concentrated its efforts on the war with Eritrea – Tigray was always secondary. The TPLF applied its socialistic doctrines by redistributing the land in the areas under its control, trying to ensure the survival of the peasantry in time of war. When famine returned to northern Ethiopia in 1987, the war flared up with massacres and ambushes and a constant battle over food supplies. Some food for the starving peasantry comes in from Sudan to areas controlled by the TPLF, but the Ethiopian government's attempts to bring relief and to extend its control have all failed.

In the spring of 1988, as the EPLF defeated the Ethiopian army in battle in northern Eritrea, the TPLF mounted an offensive of its own. It captured Axum, the ancient capital of Ethiopia, as well as several other towns and laid siege to Makelle. It claimed to control the whole province except for Makelle and two other towns in the south. Its success meant that a great part of the Ethiopian army is now needed to keep open the road through Tigray to Asmara, and from there down to Massawa on the coast.

OROMO

Population estimates of the Oromo, also known as the Galla, range from 15 to 18 million. They are by far the largest national group in Ethiopia, and one of the largest in sub-Saharan Africa, and they dominate central, southern and western Ethiopia. They were conquered by Menelik in the late 19th century, and the emperor advanced a policy of converting the Oromo to Christianity and teaching them to speak Amharic. He was partially successful, at least with the richer classes. The present head of the Ethiopian government, Mengistu, is Oromo.

In the 1960s, there was an uprising in one of the Oromo provinces, Bale, that lasted for seven years. It required a large part of Haile Selassie's army to suppress. The Oromo Liberation Front was founded in October 1974, a month after Haile Selassie was deposed. It proclaimed the usual Marxist objectives, and announced its intention of establishing a People's Democratic Republic of Oromia. It was, to begin with, an essentially urban movement, drawing its support from students and the lower middle classes. Unlike the TPLF, it had little contact with the peasantry, but it hoped that it would soon develop a base in the countryside, where at least 90 per cent of the Oromo live.

So far, it has been less successful than the EPLF and the TPLF, and has to face the antagonism of the Somalis as well as fight the Amhara. However, the government's control in many provinces is at best tenuous, and support for the OLF is growing.

MODERN ETHIOPIA

By 1980, with the help of the USSR and Cuba, the government of Ethiopia had re-established its control over the national territory, except for the disputed areas of Eritrea. The wars in the Ogaden, Tigray and Oromo provinces had degenerated into minor guerrilla actions, and Mengistu's government could attempt to put its house in order.

It most conspicuously failed to do so. In 1984, the regime celebrated its tenth anniversary with much public fanfare, just as the outside world, appalled, learned that there was mass starvation in the countryside, one of the worst famines of the century. Belatedly, the Ethiopian government appealed for help. Soon seven million people were being fed by international relief organizations. The US (but not the USSR) sent large quantities of food, and Bob Geldof organized a series of concerts to raise funds for famine relief. However, despite all this effort, and although competent relief organizations were set up in Addis Ababa and in the areas controlled by the TPLF and the EPLF, one million people died.

37

The war continued to go badly for the government in 1988 and 1989, though heavy rains averted famine. The rebels' spring offensive of 1988 cost the government most of Tigray and drove its armies back onto its bases in Eritrea. The spring offensive in 1989 completed the liberation of Tigray: government troops in Eritrea could no longer be supplied by road. This disaster was followed, on 17 May, by an attempted military coup against Mengistu, when he was visiting East Germany. The revolt was put down with great brutality (nine generals were shot).

The Soviet Union evidently decided to cut its losses in Ethiopia. It had supported Mengistu loyally since 1974, at enormous cost, and had nothing whatsoever to show for its investment. The last 3,000 Cuban troops went home in September 1989, and the Soviets let it be known that they would cut their military aid to Ethiopia.

In September 1989, first, tentative negotiations between the government and the ELF opened in Atlanta, Georgia, sponsored by the former American President Jimmy Carter. The most significant factor was that Carter's efforts were enthusiastically supported by the Soviet Union, which publicly urged Mengistu to abandon Eritrea.

FURTHER READING

American University, *Ethiopia: A Country Study*, Washington D.C., 1981.

Bereket, Habte Selassie, *Conflict and Intervention in the Horn of Africa*, New York, Monthly Review Press, 1982.

Erlick, Haggai. *The Struggle over Eritrea*, Stanford, Calif., Hoover Institute Press, 1983.

Farrer, Tom J., *War Clouds on the Horn of Africa.*

Kaplan, Robert D., 'The Loneliest War', *Atlantic Monthly*, July 1988.

Lefort, René, *Ethiopia – An Heretical Revolution*, translated by A. M. Berrett, London, Zed Press, 1983.

Legum, Colin and Firebrace, James, *Eritrea and Tigray*, Minority Rights Group, 1983.

Moorehead, Alan, *The Blue Nile*, New York/London, Harper and Row.

Moseley, Leonard, *Haile Selassie, the Conquering Lion*, Englewood Cliffs, New Jersey, Prentice-Hall, 1965.

Sherman, Richard, *Eritrea, the Unfinished Revolution*, New York, Praegar, 1980.

Waugh, Evelyn, *Scoop* and *Black Mischief*, London, Penguin Books.

LIBYA

Geography	679,358 sq. miles (1,759,350 sq. km). About the size of Western Europe. It is almost entirely desert.
Population	3.9 million.
GNP per capita	$7170.
Resources	Libya has oil reserves of 21.1 billion barrels.

This vast desert was one of the poorest countries in the Middle East until the discovery of oil. Then in the latter half of the 1970s and in the early 1980s, until the collapse of oil prices, it enjoyed one of the highest *per capita* incomes in the world. By any standards, it is still rich, with a *per capita* income of over $7000 a year.

HISTORY

The relics of past civilizations are scattered along the coast, reminders that prosperity and glories do not last for ever. In the western capital, Tripoli, there is a small cemetery where some of the US Marines who stormed ashore in 1804 in pursuit of the Barbary pirates are buried. There are more substantial traces of the desert battles of World War II: the Italians, Germans and British fought back and forth across the country, particularly in the eastern province, Cyrenaica, before Rommel was finally defeated in 1943.

Libya was Turkey's last possession in North Africa, until 1911, when Italy seized it. The Italians fought a savage war against the Libyan tribes, driving the recalcitrant among them into the desert to starve. Mussolini, who hoped to recreate the Roman empire, completed the conquest, and excavated Roman cities buried in the sand, restored irrigation systems and built a triumphal arch (larger than Napoleon's) halfway between Tripoli and Benghazi: passing British soldiers later called it 'Marble Arch'. Mussolini also settled 300,000 Italian peasants in Libya, and its cities were for a while as Italian as Palermo or Naples.

By losing the war, the Italians lost their African empire. The British occupied Libya until 1951, when they installed as king the Amir Sayyid Mohammed Idris, the leader of the Senussi Islamic movement, who had led the resistance to the Italians in the 1920s. Mussolini had missed Libya's real wealth: oil was discovered in 1958, and rapidly developed. The British presence in Libya was progressively   39 reduced, but the United States maintained a huge air base near Tripoli, Wheelus Field, which served the USAF admirably for training purposes.

As Libyan prosperity rose by leaps and bounds, and as the number of young educated Libyans increased, the conservative Arab monarchy in Libya became increasingly anomalous, bordered as it was by Nasser's Egypt and Boumedienne's Algeria. It is surprising that King Idris lasted so long. He barely survived riots that broke out after Egypt's defeat by Israel in June 1967: a number of Libyan Jews were murdered, and the remainder, about 4500, fled the country. Idris was finally deposed on 1 September 1969 while visiting Athens, and replaced by a group of young officers, whose principal leader was Colonel Moammar Khadafy.

The new regime pulled down 'Marble Arch', closed Wheelus Field and ended Libya's Western alliances; the Italians lost their property and were expelled. Khadafy's first great coup was to nationalize the Western oil companies, and to force a substantial price rise. This example was enthusiastically followed by other Arabs and by the Iranians after the 1973 Middle East war, and Libya was suddenly rich beyond the dreams of avarice.

The price of Libyan oil had risen from $2.23 a barrel in 1961 to $2.71 in 1971. Khadafy was considered wildly extortionate in forcing the price to $3.42 in July that year and to $4.00 a barrel in April 1973. In the aftermath of the Yom Kippur War, when Saudi Arabia suspended shipments, Libya put the price up to $16.00 on 1 January 1974, and to $21.00 in May. After the Iranian revolution in 1979, the price rose to $34.00 in January 1980 and reached its peak, $41.00, in 1981.

Not only did the price increase rapidly, so did Libyan production. As a result, Libyan revenues from oil rose from $3 million in 1961 to $1.17 billion in 1969 (the year Khadafy seized power), to $2.2 billion in 1973, $8 billion in 1978 and $22 billion in 1980.

KHADAFY'S LIBYA

Khadafy sees himself as the heir to Nasser but has been constantly frustrated in his ambitions. His foreign adventures have been uniformly unsuccessful, and although other Arab leaders have always been ready to take his money, they are not ready to take him seriously. At various times, Khadafy has signed treaties of union with Egypt, Syria, Tunisia, Chad, Sudan, Algeria and (the latest) Morocco, and treaties of eternal friendship with most of them. None of these treaties has ever lasted: King Hassan cancelled the union with Morocco in August 1986. In 1987, Khadafy began wooing Niger, an impoverished nation across the Sahara to the south-west.

Khadafy provoked a minor border war with Egypt in 1977. He later invaded Tunisia, which was far less able to defend itself, and the French had to send their navy to the rescue. He sent his armies into Chad, where they were defeated, and sent troops to the aid of Idi Amin in Uganda where, again, they were overcome. (These episodes are described in the sections on Chad and Uganda.) He has repeatedly intervened in the various revolts and wars in Sudan.

Libya has been allied with the Soviet Union for some time, but has constantly refused to allow the USSR to set up naval or air bases. Khadafy's dreams of military glory have led him to spend billions on Soviet weaponry, far more than his armies can possibly use, and the Soviets made him pay in dollars, and in cash. His only close ally has been Malta, which has accepted Libyan largesse with delight and proclaimed its deep hostility to the West, while maintaining an incorrigibly Western society. Khadafy also professed undying admiration for Khomeini's Iran, although, as a devout Sunni, he deplores the Ayatollah's Shiite heresy.

Khadafy considers himself a political theorist of the highest order, and wrote a 'Green Book' to prove it, modelled on Mao Tse-tung's Red Book. Green is the colour of Islam, and Khadafy's theories attempt to reconcile Islam with Marxism. He has imposed strict Islamic laws upon Libya, including the laws against alcohol. In 1973, during negotiations for a federation with Egypt, he mobilized the population for an 'Arab Unity March' on Egypt, to force President Sadat's hand. The Libyans fell enthusiastically into the spirit of the thing, and by scores of thousands, they drove their cars, trucks and Land Rovers to the Egyptian frontier. The Egyptians were prepared for them, with huge stocks of every sort of alcohol, which they sold to the Libyans for hard cash. Khadafy called off the invasion and the Libyans went happily home.

He once summoned an international conference to discuss the theories contained in his Green Book, and the serious problems facing the world. One of the first items on the agenda was the need to restore to Islam the Great Mosque at Grenada, unjustly occupied by Spain since 1492.

Libyan socialism has been an abject failure. Khadafy has abolished private enterprise, including the private ownership of real estate, and instead of the traditional Arab markets, there are huge state stores where it is frequently impossible to find basic necessities. Because private market gardens are banned, there is fresh produce only when the state companies have imported it from Europe. These failures are the result of incompetence and doctrine, not poverty. However, grandiose plans for new cities in the desert and for an industrial centre and port at Mizurata, on the Gulf of Sirte, have been abandoned or suspended since the fall in oil revenues.

TERRORISM

Khadafy would be merely an unimportant, eccentric figure on the world scene except that he has espoused terrorism as a means of furthering his policies. He has arranged for Libyan exiles to be assassinated in the Middle East, Europe and the United States. When a dignitary from Lebanon, the Shiite leader Imam Musa Sadr, was visiting Libya in 1978, he was murdered in flagrant violation of the Arab duty of hospitality. Khadafy has also sent truck bombs into Egypt to blow up the American embassy, and hired American terrorists, led by the former CIA operative Edwin Wilson, to train Libyans in the trade. He has subsidized and supported the IRA and various Arab terrorist organizations, and has attempted to foment coups in Egypt, Sudan, Chad and Tunisia, and the governments of the latter three countries had to be rescued by their allies.

In 1973, during the putative union with Egypt, a group of American Jews chartered the *Queen Elizabeth II* to tour the Mediterranean and visit Israel on the occasion of its 25th anniversary. Khadafy ordered a submarine in his navy, with Egyptian officers, to sink the *QEII*. The captain promptly took his boat to Alexandria and reported to President Sadat.

Relations between Libya and Egypt deteriorated rapidly after the failure of the union. In 1977, Khadafy sent a series of saboteurs into Egypt, some of whom were   41 arrested on 12 July. A week later, there was a skirmish on the border, in which, according to the Egyptians, 20 Libyan armoured cars and their crews were destroyed. Sadat decided that it was time to teach Khadafy a lesson, and he sent an armoured column to a Libyan base at Masaad, 5 miles (8 km) inside the border: 40 Libyan tanks were destroyed and 42 prisoners were taken; Egyptian planes also shot down two Libyan fighters. The next day, the Egyptian air force mounted a full-scale attack on a major Libyan air base, at El Adem, near Tobruk; three Soviet advisers were reportedly killed. Sadat blamed 'That very strange person', Khadafy, and said, 'Yesterday and today our armed forces gave him a lesson he should never forget.' There were further Egyptian air attacks on 23 and 24 July, in which a large number of Libyan planes were destroyed, with an admitted Egyptian loss of two planes. Libya mobilized 30,000 reservists, and Egypt moved an armoured division up to the border. However, on the 24th, Sadat announced a unilateral ceasefire.

After his troubles with Egypt, Khadafy united Libya with Tunisia. This union collapsed in 1978 and on 27 January 1980, a raid was mounted against Gafsa in southern Tunisia, carried out by 50 commandos, either Libyans or exiled Tunisians trained in Libya. The attack was well-planned and skilfully executed. The raiders came over the border from Algeria and attacked the police station, an army barracks, and a militia barracks, killing 41 people, mostly military men; then they escaped back into Libya. The French sent a small naval squadron to Tunis, in case Libya planned further hostilities, and on 4 February, a Libyan mob burned the French embassy in Tripoli and the consulate in Benghazi. In the event, possibly because of the French presence, there was no repeat of the raid.

Libya's reaction was standard operating procedure. Whenever there is a dispute with a foreign government, a mob is called out to burn its embassy in Tripoli – the British and American embassies were both burned before those countries broke off diplomatic relations with Libya. Khadafy has used his own embassies for nefarious purposes: he turned the one in London into a base for terrorists, and when a group of Libyan exiles mounted a demonstration outside on 17 April 1984, protesting against the public hanging of two Libyan students in Tripoli, a gunman inside the embassy shot and killed a London policewoman, who had been simply keeping the peace, and wounded 11 other people.

In July 1984, a number of mines were found in the Red Sea. They did a certain amount of damage to shipping, and had to be laboriously cleared by an international fleet of mine-sweepers including American, British, Soviet and French vessels. A Libyan ship had passed through the Red Sea just before the first mine had been found, and it seems most likely that the mining was Khadafy's doing, another anti-Egyptian gesture.

Khadafy assumed that he led a charmed life, and was oblivious to the geographic and political realities of his situation. However, Libya is one of the most strategically vulnerable countries of the world, with all its cities and resources strung out along a 1500-mile (2415-km) coastline, and with an army and air force quite inadequate to defend them. The other states most strongly suspected of promoting terrorism – Syria and Iran – are geographically and militarily far better protected, as the United States has discovered. Furthermore, none of Khadafy's expensively bought allies would lift a finger to help him.

In 1981, in a moment of slightly comic panic, the Reagan administration announced that Khadafy was sending hit squads to assassinate American politicians. Trucks filled with sand were hastily drawn up around the White House and Capitol, later to be replaced by hideous concrete barriers, all to protect those buildings against phantom bombers. There was never any real evidence that Khadafy had organized the sending of hit squads to the United States, although he had certainly done so in Tunisia and Egypt. He also helped and applauded Abu Nidal, the most ruthless of Palestinian terrorists.

The United States expelled the Libyan embassy in Washington in May 1981, alleging that it was harbouring terrorists. Later, President Reagan, on three occasions, sent the Sixth Fleet into the Gulf of Sirte as a warning to Khadafy. On 19 August 1981, fighters from a US aircraft carrier shot down two Libyan planes that had attacked them (unsuccessfully) with air-to-air missiles. There was a further encounter between American and Libyan planes in the Gulf in February 1983, and the US then sent AWACs to Egypt to give early warning of any attacks by Colonel Khadafy against his neighbour.

In March 1986, the Americans sent an enormous fleet into the Gulf, including three aircraft carriers. Khadafy proclaimed a 'line of death' across the Gulf, which he claims is Libyan territory, and with remarkable foolhardiness sent several small ships of his navy to attack the US fleet. The Americans sank at least two Libyan vessels and took out a Libyan SAM missile base at Sirte after the Libyans fired six SAMs at them. There were reportedly 72 Libyans killed.

On 5 April 1986, a bomb exploded in a bar frequented by American soldiers in West Berlin, killing one of them and a Turkish woman. The Americans announced that they had evidence that the attack had been planned by Libya – evidence that, apparently, consisted of radio messages between Tripoli and the Libyan embassy in East Berlin which were read as orders to attack the American bar, and then congratulations at the attack's success. Subsequently, it emerged that the attack had been the work of Lebanese terrorists, possibly under Syrian control.

However, because of these allegations of complicity in the West Berlin bombing, President Reagan ordered an attack on Libya on 14 April. For reasons that have never been adequately explained, the Sixth Fleet was considered insufficient for the task. (If a complete carrier group cannot take on as insubstantial an enemy as Libya, it can hardly serve any useful purpose in a real war with a real enemy.) Aircraft from the fleet were therefore reinforced with F-111s based in England. France and Spain, both Nato allies, refused to permit them to cross their territory, and as a result, they had to fly 2800 miles (4500 km), down the Atlantic and through the Mediterranean, to their targets. They had to be refuelled in the air several times during the raid, and were in the air for 14 hours.

The attacks wiped out a number of Libyan military installations in and around Tripoli and Benghazi, with the loss of one F-111 and its two-man crew. One of the chosen targets was Colonel Khadafy's personal headquarters in the El Azziziya barracks in Tripoli. A great deal of damage was done, and one of Khadafy's children was among those killed and two others were wounded, but his personal tent, pitched in the middle of the barracks, escaped. The Pentagon denied that it had targeted Khadafy personally, a denial that should not be taken too seriously.

The raid also demolished the French embassy, and damaged Roumanian, Austrian, Swiss and Japanese diplomatic residences, to the considerable embarrassment of the Pentagon, which had boasted of the precision of its 'smart bombs', and which at first scornfully denied French reports of the damage. Afterwards, it emerged that five of the 18 F-111s on the raid and two of the 15 A-6s had not dropped their bombs, being unsure of their targets, despite all the elaborate electronics they carried. Within a few weeks of the raid, the Libyans had replaced the radar and SAM batteries they had lost.

Militarily, while the raid proved that the United States Air Force could hit a target far from its bases, it also showed that its accuracy was not nearly so great as it had claimed. No one who remembered the claims of various air forces in World War II and in Vietnam was in the least surprised.

Politically, the raid was considered to be a great success in the United States. Colonel Khadafy was apparently seriously shaken by his near-escape and played little part in world politics for the next 18 months. He did launch two missiles at an American Coast Guard base on the island of Lampedusa, off the coast of Sicily (they missed); an American technician in the US embassy in Khartoum was shot and seriously wounded; and Khadafy's Lebanese allies retaliated for the US raid by murdering three of the hostages they held, two British and one American. However, Mrs Thatcher's popularity survived Labour party criticism of the use to which British air bases had been put, and American resentment at France's unhelpfulness was smoothed over later that year during celebrations of the centenary of the Statue of Liberty.

On 4 January 1989, two Libyan MiGs approached too close to an air patrol of the US Sixth Fleet and were shot down. The incident coincided with an international debate over an American report that Libya had built a factory capable of producing poison gas. For a few days, it appeared that there would be another serious conflict between the US and Libya, but for once, both sides decided that caution was the wisest course. It was two weeks before the change of administration in Washington, and Khadafy perhaps preferred to wait to see how President Bush would react.

LIBYA TODAY

There have been many attempts to assassinate Colonel Khadafy, and at least one full-fledged coup attempt, on 8 May 1984: a group of commandos tried to storm the El Azziziya barracks, but were detected; they took refuge in a building in Tripoli, where they were all killed or captured. The Colonel's repeated failures to extend Libya's influence to its neighbours and, in particular, his humiliating defeat in Chad in 1987 have presumably caused much resentment in the army. Perhaps one day he will go the way of so many other Arab potentates, though it should be remembered that Egypt and the rest of the countries of North Africa do not have a tradition of resolving political disputes by coups or assassinations. Libya is not Lebanon, Syria or Iraq.

In the meantime, it must be assumed that Colonel Khadafy will recover his courage and take up his habit of interfering abroad. Already in 1987, he resumed sending large consignments of arms to the IRA. On 30 October, the French navy intercepted a coaster, the *Eksund*, off the coast of Brittany, which contained 150 tons of arms destined for the Irish terrorists, including 20 SAM-7s, 10 12.77-mm machine-guns, anti-tank launchers and 1000 Kalashnikov AK-47s.

The US raid does not seem to have modified Khadafy's more bizarre personality traits. At an Arab summit meeting in Algeria in June 1988, he wore one white glove, like the pop star Michael Jackson, so that he would never have to soil his hand by contact with King Hassan of Morocco who had met the Israeli prime minister, Shimon Peres, to discuss the Middle East situation. The Libyan leader also pulled a hood over his head when King Hussein of Jordan spoke, and blew cigar smoke at King Fahd, who was sitting next to him. At a previous summit, at Addis Ababa, Khadafy had managed to offend the conservative Arab leaders by parading around town with a bodyguard of shapely female soldiers, who officiously protected him from the (male) bodyguards of the more traditional rulers.

In the course of 1988, Khadafy tried to improve relations with some of his adversaries. He reopened the border with Tunisia, and used the ceasefire in the Gulf War as a pretext to mend his fences with Iraq. He restored diplomatic relations with Chad in October (but did not abandon the Aozou strip). He also tried to reopen contact with Europe: he sent his deputy, Major Abdul Salaam Jalloud, to Rome in November to make peace there, in the hopes that, if Italy could forgive him for launching missiles against Lampedusa, the rest of Europe would resume normal trade relations. Perhaps he intended eventually to try to patch up his relations with Britain and the United States. Neither country showed any interest in such a prospect.

FURTHER READING

Blundy, David and Lycett, Andrew, *Qaddafi and the Libyan Revolution*, Boston, Little, Brown, 1987.

El-Kaiwas, Mohamed, *Qaddafi: His ideology in Theory and Practice*, Brattleboro, Vermont, Amara Books, 1986.

Cooley, John, *Libyan Sandstorm,* New York, Holt, Rinehart & Winston, 1982.

Goulden, Joseph with Raffio, Alexander, *The Death Merchant*, New York, Simon and Schuster, 1984.

Harris, Lillian Craig, *Libya: Qadhafi's Revolution and the Modern State*, Boulder, Colo., Westview Press, 1986.

Maas, Peter, *Manhunt*, New York: Random House, 1986.

Wright, John L., *Libya, a Modern History*, Baltimore, Johns Hopkins University Press, 1982.

MOROCCO

Geography	240,160 sq. miles (622,012 sq. km). About the size of France plus Benelux. The disputed territory of the Western Sahara covers 102,676 sq. miles (266,000 sq. km), about the size of Great Britain.
Population	Morocco: 22.4 million. In 1974, the Western Sahara had 95,019 people, of whom 74,000 were indigenous Saharawis, the rest Spanish. The Spanish left in 1975 and over half the Saharawis fled from the Moroccan invasion.
GNP per capita	$590.
Refugees	From Morocco: 165,000* from the Western Sahara and southern Moroccans in Algeria.
Casualties	About 10,000 dead since 1975.

From 1975 to 1988, Morocco fought a continuous war to control the Western Sahara (formerly Spanish Sahara), a territory along the Atlantic immediately south of Morocco itself. Morocco had seized it after Spain withdrew, in flagrant violation of UN resolutions and the wishes of the territory's inhabitants. After the Moroccan occupation, a large part of the population fled to Algeria, and their political organization, the Polisario Front, formed an army to fight the invaders. The Front was supported by Algeria. There was soon a permanent stalemate between the two sides: the Moroccans held the towns and the territory's mineral resources; Polisario guerrillas patrolled the desert.

In May 1988, Algeria abruptly abandoned the Front and resumed diplomatic relations with Morocco. The UN proposed a ceasefire, to be followed by a referendum on the Western Sahara's future, to be organized and supervised by a 2000-man UN peacekeeping force. The proposal was accepted by the two sides in August.

HISTORY
The Mediterranean and Atlantic coastal plains of Morocco have been urbanized since antiquity: Morocco was a Roman province. The interior was a different matter. The Atlas mountains and the Sahara desert were only occasionally controlled by the sultans in Marrakesh or Fez, and the settled cities were constantly threatened by the tribesmen of desert and mountain.

In the 17th century, the Alawite dynasty originating in the southern desert conquered Morocco and extended its rule as far as Timbuctoo on the Niger and to most of what is now Mauritania. The empire did not last long: the Alawites were soon restricted to the Atlantic coast of Morocco and the principal cities. However, the modern Alawite sultans (now kings) of Morocco have used their ancestors' conquests as a basis for their claims on the whole of the Western Sahara.

Over the centuries, Moroccan rulers had constantly to resist encroachments from Europeans and from the Turks. In 1415, Portugal occupied Ceuta, the southern of the twin Pillars of Hercules marking the entrance to the Mediterranean (the northern is Gibraltar). Spain took over Ceuta in 1578 and has ruled it ever since. The other Spanish *presidio*, further east, is Melilla, which has been under Spanish rule since 1496.

Otherwise, Morocco maintained its independence until the late 19th century. By then, France had colonized Algeria, and France, Spain, Britain and Germany all coveted Morocco. France and Britain agreed to exclude Germany, and Morocco was then partitioned between France and Spain. Spain did badly out of the negotiations, with its sector restricted to three small areas: a narrow strip along the north coast, dominated by the Rif mountains, with its capital at Tetuan; a small enclave on the Atlantic coast, called Ifni, on the site of a short-lived 16th-century Spanish colony; and Rio de Oro, a strip of desert in south Morocco next to Spain's already existing colony, the Spanish Sahara. Tangiers, in the extreme north-west, was made an international zone, and for half a century enjoyed its reputation as the smugglers' capital of the world.

In the early 1920s, Mohammed Abd el-Krim rose in revolt in the Rif, and it took Spain half a million soldiers to defeat him. The Spanish army rebellion in 1936 was launched from Morocco by its commander, General Francisco Franco. During that conflict, Franco took Moorish troops across to fight in Spain, in what was the only substantial contribution that Spain's Moroccan empire ever made to the motherland.

France established the frontiers between Algeria and Morocco, much to the advantage of Algeria, which was considered part of France, while Morocco was only a protectorate. France also conquered the Sahara and established the frontiers between Spanish West Africa and Mauritania, which was part of French West Africa. Since Spain's colony, Rio de Oro, consisted of only one impoverished village on the coast (Villa Cisneros), France did not have to attend much to Spanish susceptibilities, and so was generous in awarding the Sahara desert to itself.

In 1926, a visitor found Villa Cisneros to comprise 20 houses and 28 tents. Its population was 150 natives and 35 soldiers, together with a captain-governor, a lieutenant, a doctor, a policeman, a chaplain and a representative of the TransAtlantic shipping line. Spain had come out last in the 'scramble for Africa'.

The desert was richer than anyone suspected. Under the French allocation, Algeria got oil and the iron ore at Tindouf, and Mauritania got the iron at Zouarte: Spanish Sahara got the enormous phosphate deposits at Bou-Craa. Morocco was to covet all these riches, despite the fact that it already possessed the world's largest phosphate reserves.

One resource of the Western Sahara has been known for centuries: some of the world's richest fisheries are off its coast, with a possible catch of 2 million tons a year. In the Spanish period, the catch was limited to fleets from the Canaries and Europe.

THE POST-COLONIAL PERIOD

After World War II, France was faced with serious trouble in its North African empire. The Algerian National Liberation Front (FLN) started its war in November 1954, and in Morocco, an anti-French and anti-royalist Army of Liberation was formed in the Atlas mountains and in the desert to the south and began operations against French positions. The French deposed the sultan of Morocco, Mohammed V, in August 1953, and replaced him with a more compliant monarch. However, the country quickly became ungovernable, and in October 1955, the puppet sultan was himself deposed, and Mohammed returned to his throne on 6 November. Disturbances in Morocco and Tunisia were distractions from the main event – the battle for Algeria – and in 1956, France gave Morocco and Tunisia their independence.

Spain was obliged to follow France's example, and abandoned its territory in Morocco. It left the north immediately, except for Ceuta and Melilla, and also agreed to leave the south as soon as independent Morocco could take over. The Army of Liberation then extended its operations against Ifni, Spanish South Morocco and Spanish Sahara, across the wholly artificial international frontier. The Spanish army abandoned all its positions in the interior of those territories, remaining only in Ifni, in a 12-mile (20 km) strip around the village of Sidi Ifni, which had a population of 24,000.

To begin with, the newly independent kingdom of Morocco was unable to assert its authority in the south, where the Army of Liberation was as much a menace to the royal government as it was to Spain and France. It attacked French positions in Algeria and Mauritania, and in February 1957, France launched Operation Hurricane to destroy the Army of Liberation in its bases in Mauritania and the Spanish Sahara. The operation was completely successful.

In 1958, when the Moroccan army was strong enough to replace it, Spain withdrew from southern Morocco. It abandoned its central African colonies, Rio Muni and the island of Fernando Po in 1968 (they became Equatorial Guinea), and ceded Ifni to Morocco in 1969. Morocco had already reclaimed Tangiers and reoccupied it in April 1960. Spain retained the Spanish Sahara and began to develop the phosphate deposits, which had been discovered in 1945.

When France gave Mauritania its independence in 1960, its new president, Mokhtar Ould-Daddah, claimed the Spanish Sahara. Morocco mounted a vigorous diplomatic campaign to assert its own claim to the same territory (which it called South Morocco) as well as to all Mauritania. It opposed Mauritania's admission to the United Nations and, later, to the Organization of African Unity (OAU), not recognizing it until 1969. The Arab League supported Morocco, but France's other former colonies in Africa all backed Mauritania.

Morocco was also embroiled in a dispute with Algeria, which became independent in 1962. Morocco laid claim to a substantial area of western Algeria, around Tindouf, which has some of the richest iron ore deposits in the world. Furthermore, King Hassan was concerned that Algeria's radical Nasserite regime was a danger to the Moroccan monarchy. Hassan sent troops to occupy Algerian border posts immediately after the French departed, but the new Algerian army pushed them out. In September 1963, Hassan tried again, sending his army across the border into the disputed territories. The Moroccan advance got within a few miles of Tindouf before it was stopped.

48

After mediation by the OAU, a demilitarized zone was established along the border. Eventually, Morocco recognized the frontier established by the French, but relations remained cool.

In the 1960s, there was heavy investment in mining in both Mauritania and the Spanish Sahara. In Mauritania, the mines at Zouarte (near the frontier with the Spanish Sahara) were developed and a 420-mile (650 km) railway was built to carry the ore to the coast. It runs due south, and then west, parallel to the frontier. The phosphate deposits at Bou-Craa in the Spanish Sahara were opened up by a state-owned company, which built a 60-mile (100 km) conveyor-belt to take the ore to a new port on the coast. The first shipments went out in 1972, at a rate of 2.6 million tons a year, and the company anticipated exports of 10 million tons annually by 1980.

THE FOUNDING OF THE POLISARIO FRONT

Morocco's claim to Spanish Sahara remained latent until 1974. By then, an anti-colonial movement had been founded by young Saharawis who had studied in Moroccan schools and universities and had imbibed the revolutionary notions of the radical Arabs. They formed the Polisario Front in 1972, the name being an acronym for the *Frente Popular para la Liberatión de Saguia el-Hamra y Río de Oro*. (The Saguia el-Hamra is a river which has given its name to the northern part of Spanish Sahara; Rio de Oro is the southern part.) Polisario launched its guerrilla war in 1973, with the help of a small consignment of arms from Libya, and in October 1974, it sabotaged the Bou-Craa conveyor belt.

Franco was in his dotage. He had seen the Portuguese Fascist regime overthrown in April, and the collapse of the Portuguese empire. He and Spain decided that their interests would be best served by giving Spanish Sahara its independence, following the neo-colonial example that France had established in West Africa. Spain expected that an independent Sahara would continue to protect Spanish investments and follow its lead, as France's former colonies were doing. Therefore, in August 1974, Spain proposed a referendum on the future of the Spanish Sahara.

The proposal galvanized King Hassan into action. He badly needed a success: he had barely survived two military coups in 1971 and 1972. In the first, rebel soldiers had attacked a royal garden party and slaughtered the guests. The king had hidden in a pavilion, where he had overheard soldiers discussing those evil plotters who had killed the king; he emerged, introduced himself and persuaded the deluded soldiers to arrest their officers. Then, on 16 August 1972, two air force fighters had tried to shoot down King Hassan's plane, on the orders of the Minister of the Interior, General Mohammed Oufkir. They had missed. Oufkir was permitted to shoot himself.

KING HASSAN'S GREEN MARCH

The king was still suspicious of his army and of the opposition. He appealed to their chauvinism and rallied them all behind his claim to the Spanish Sahara. He successfully bought time by submitting the claim to the International Court of Justice at The Hague. He thus persuaded Spain to postpone its proposed referendum and, eventually, to abandon it. He also sought support from his two principal allies, the United States and France.

49

These two countries wanted stability in Morocco above all. After King Hassan had committed all his prestige to the Spanish Sahara project, they feared that he would lose his throne if he were defeated. Furthermore, Dr Henry Kissinger and President Valéry Giscard d'Estaing opposed Polisario on principle, because of its leftist tendencies.

Spain, still under a Fascist government, reached the opposite conclusion. It wanted to protect its investments from the Moroccans and, after secret talks with Polisario, decided that it could easily work with a Polisario regime. Simultaneously, Algeria threw its weight behind the Front. The United Nations sent a mission to the Spanish Sahara, to gauge its inhabitants' wishes, and was everywhere met by demonstrations in favour of Polisario.

Morocco massed 20,000 troops on the border in the summer of 1975. Then, on 15 October, the UN mission announced its findings: 'The majority of the population within the Spanish Sahara was manifestly in favour of independence.' Polisario was clearly the territory's choice. The next day, the International Court of Justice ruled that there was no 'tie of territorial sovereignty between the Territory of Western Sahara and the Kingdom of Morocco or the Mauritanian entity'.

King Hassan reacted to these defeats with one of the more extraordinary modern examples of the Big Lie. He simply announced that the court had ruled in his favour. Then he called on 320,000 volunteers to join in a 'Green March' across the border to recover the Western Sahara. Moroccans responded with enthusiasm, and by 21 October, there were 524,000 of them in camps on the border.

At the height of the crisis, on 17 October 1975, Franco collapsed during a cabinet meeting. He was evidently dying, and the Madrid government was far more concerned to ensure a smooth transition at home than it was with the fate of the Spanish Sahara. The United States and France supported Hassan, and Spain broke its commitments to Polisario. It opened negotiations with Morocco on 21 October, and began evacuating the territory seven days later.

All civilians were evacuated; the Spanish cemetery at Villa Cisneros was cleared and the 1000 bodies moved to the Canaries; the animals in the Al-Ayoun zoo were sent to Spain. Spanish troops began withdrawing from outlying posts, and were replaced by Polisario units or the Moroccan army, which were soon fighting each other for control.

The Green March finally began on 6 November 1975. About 200,000 people crossed the border at several points, advanced 6 miles (10 km) and stopped. On 8 November Spain finally capitulated and agreed to abandon the territory to Morocco and Mauritania; in exchange, those two governments guaranteed Spain's economic interests. The marchers were then sent home. Negotiations with Spain were resumed on 12 November, and on the 14th an agreement was reached between Spain, Morocco and Mauritania, under which Spain would withdraw by the end of February, handing over the administration of the colony (but without renouncing sovereignty) to Morocco and Mauritania.

Franco died on 20 November. The Moroccans reached Al-Ayoun on 11 December, and by mid-January, Spain had completed the evacuation. By then, 40,000 Saharawis had fled their homes.

THE WAR

King Hassan and President Ould-Daddah had apparently won. However, Morocco got all the valuable parts of the Spanish Sahara, while Mauritania had to settle for the Tiris al-Gharbia, valueless desert in the south of the territory, and Villa Cisneros, renamed Dakhla.

Both Morocco and Mauritania had underestimated the Polisario Front and failed to take account of Algerian intentions. President Houari Boumedienne had warned Ould-Daddah that he would support Polisario. The inhabitants of the Spanish Sahara fled the Moroccans. Over half the population were soon refugees in Algeria, where they were settled around Tindouf, to whose population they were closely related.

Polisario stepped up its guerrilla attacks, concentrating on Mauritania as the weaker target. Polisario's military forces – the Saharawi People's Liberation Army (SPLA) – conducted raids across hundreds of miles of wasteland, just like the tribes of old, or like the British Long-range Desert Group which had operated behind German lines in World War II. The SPLA even attacked Nouakchott, Mauritania's capital, 900 miles across the desert. The founder and secretary-general of Polisario, El-Ouali Mustapha Sayed, was killed on the first of those raids in June 1976. He was succeeded by Mohammed Abdelazziz, who remains Polisario's secretary-general.

The SPLA soon mobilized virtually all the adult men of the Saharawi refugees – 20,000 in all – and these were armed and equipped by the Algerians. They attacked the iron mines at Zouarte and the railway linking it to the coast, hitting the latter almost every month, and in May 1977 occupying Zouarte itself. Mining was soon brought to a halt, and Mauritania's economy, already suffering seriously from the effects of the great drought in the Sahel, was brought to the verge of collapse.

The Moroccans sent troops to help, occupying Dakhla to protect it from SPLA raids, and the French despatched their air force. French Jaguars attacked SPLA columns with lethal effect, causing the rebels to split into much smaller groups, and to travel only at night.

Mauritania's situation continued to deteriorate, and on 9 July 1978, the army overthrew Ould-Daddah in a bloodless coup. Polisario declared a ceasefire the next day. The new military regime wanted to end the war, but was unable to do so: it was afraid of Morocco. Its hesitations continued until Polisario broke the ceasefire a year after it began, on 12 July 1979. It once again hit the ore railway. The Mauritanian regime then abandoned the Tiris al-Gharbia and signed a peace treaty with Polisario on 5 August. Morocco reinforced its garrisons in the territory, including Dakhla and, on 14 August, announced that it had annexed the Tiris al-Gharbia.

THE POLISARIO FRONT V. MOROCCO

For the first two or three years after the coup in Mauritania, the war went badly for the Moroccans. The SPLA won a series of important victories by means of sudden attacks on isolated garrisons. On one occasion, in August 1979, they seized a base in southern Morocco and captured an immense haul of equipment, including 37 T-54 tanks.

SPLA units were soon armed with modern equipment by Algeria. They carried rockets, including Stalin Organs, in trucks, and attacked at will; Moroccan casualties were so heavy that the army soon abandoned over 80 per cent of the contested territory. By 1980, Morocco had established a defence perimeter around the 'useful triangle' of the Western Sahara, including Al-Ayoun, the phosphate mines at Bou-Craa and a short stretch of coast including the new port of El-Ayoun Playa. A separate enclave included Dakhla in the south.

The defences consisted of sand barriers, two or three metres high and eventually about 1000 miles (1600 km) long, protected by minefields and barbed wire, with electronic listening devices and mobile forces patrolling to prevent any incursions. Morocco has an army of 150,000 defending the barrier. Behind it, the phosphate mines and the conveyor belt were finally reopened in 1982. Everything else was left to the SPLA.

Polisario's primary strength was (and is) its support among the desert people of the Western Sahara. Like the Kurds in the Middle East, the Saharawis lived in all four states of the region, while considering themselves one nation. By the time the war began, a majority had abandoned their nomadic existence, but the tradition remained strong, and they called themselves 'sons of the clouds'. The refugees around Tindouf, coming from Morocco as well as the Western Sahara, soon numbered over 100,000, considerably more than the remaining indigenous population in Morocco's 'useful triangle'. Those who had left were replaced by Moroccans, who moved south to benefit from the large inducements offered by the government, and to work the phosphate mines.

Polisario also depended upon Algeria's constant support. Algeria was too powerful for Morocco to attack, so the Front had a safe base across the border. Algeria, whose economy is two-and-a-half times larger than Morocco's, is quite rich enough to arm the guerrillas and feed and educate their families.

Finally, Polisario enjoyed widespread diplomatic support. On 27 February 1976, it proclaimed the Saharan Arab Democratic Republic (SADR), and set about a vigorous diplomatic offensive against Morocco. Soon, a majority of the members of the OAU recognized the SADR, and voted to give it a seat in the organization. In 1981, in an attempt to hold the line in the OAU, Hassan promised to hold a referendum. It never took place. In February 1983, the SADR took its seat in an OAU summit, but 34 other members walked out, in protest, and the meeting collapsed.

Morocco has been able to maintain its diplomatic position in the OAU and the UN with the support of an unusual alliance of Arab and Western powers. With the notable exception of Algeria, most Arabs upheld Morocco, out of a spirit of Arab solidarity. In 1984, Libya, which had previously opposed Morocco, suddenly swung around, and Colonel Khadafy and King Hassan signed a treaty uniting the two countries. (Libya was going through an anti-Algerian phase at the time.) Two years later, after Khadafy had swung the other way, Hassan abrogated the treaty.

The cost of maintaining over 100,000 troops in the Western Sahara, as well as building the barrier and maintaining it, is far greater than the income that Morocco earns from phosphates. By the early 1980s, it had become one of the most heavily indebted nations in the world for its size. The International Monetary Fund (IMF) imposed stringent conditions on Morocco for further credit, obliging the government to cut food subsidies. In June 1981, there were violent riots in Casablanca in protest, in which over 600 people were killed, and more riots in early 1984, in

Marrakesh. Generous US aid has helped Morocco survive since then, but it still pays a heavy price for the Western Sahara. There have also been constant rumours of disaffection in the army, and in January 1983, its most senior officer, General Ahmed Dlimi, was killed in suspicious circumstances. In the official version, he died in a car crash.

DIPLOMACY

In May 1988, Morocco and Algeria resumed diplomatic relations, which had been broken 12 years before, when Morocco first annexed the Western Sahara. Algerian President Chadli Benjedid wanted to ensure King Hassan's presence at an Arab summit in Algiers in June. Colonel Khadafy wore a white glove at that meeting, so that he would not soil his hand by touching, among others, King Hassan.

Although Hassan once again promised to hold a referendum in the Western Sahara, the agreement between Morocco and Algeria was a serious blow to Polisario, and suggested, at the very least, a sharp decrease in Algerian support for the Front. And if, this time, King Hassan actually held a referendum, the fairness of the poll could be called into question: there are now more Moroccans than Saharawis living in the Western Sahara, and Hassan said nothing about readmitting the refugees. However, Morocco was under continuous pressure from its Western allies to resolve the conflict.

The stalemate in the war had lasted for years. The SNLA was unable to penetrate the sand barrier, but Morocco could never relax, could never reduce the size of its garrisons – who detested the heat and tedium of guarding a gigantic sandtrap in the inhospitable desert. Both sides were war-weary, but it remained to be seen whether either was ready to make the compromises necessary for peace.

In August 1988, the secretary-general of the UN, Javier Pérez de Cuellar, proposed an immediate truce between Morocco and the SNLA, to be followed by a plebiscite in the Western Sahara. There remained a whole series of procedural difficulties to overcome, and the basic dispute – independence for the Western Sahara or recognition of its integration with Morocco – could only be attained if one side or the other surrendered. There was no sign that either was ready to do so.

The procedural questions concerned a Polisario demand that Moroccan troops withdraw from the Western Sahara before the plebiscite, and its further demand for direct talks with Morocco. The UN suggested that it should send a 2000-man peace-keeping force to police the territory during the plebiscite. The Moroccan army would remain in its barracks and the SNLA would remain behind the sand barrier. At the end of the year, on 27 December 1988, King Hassan announced that he would open talks with the Polisario Front – an announcement that signalled the end of his refusal to recognize the Front, a policy that had lasted 13 years. He received a Polisario delegation the following month.

The UN peace proposal was based on the hope that Morocco and the Polisario Front could agree on a form of limited autonomy for the Western Sahara, something less than full independence that would also amount to less than full integration with Morocco. The refugees in Tindouf, and the Moroccan conscripts manning the sand barrier, waited fatalistically to hear the results of the latest manoeuvres.

FURTHER READING

American University, *Mauritania: A Country Study*, Washington D.C., 1972.
Amnesty International, *Torture in Morocco*, London, 1986.
Hodges, Tony, *Western Sahara: The Roots of a Desert War*, London, Croom Helm, 1984 and *The Western Saharans*, Minority Rights Group, 1984.

MOZAMBIQUE

Geography	303,000 sq. miles (784,961 sq. km). As large as Turkey.
Population	14 million
GNP per capita	$95.00
Refugees	Internal: 3.5 million. External: more than 1,137,000. There were over 640,000 Mozambican refugees in Malawi, in August 1988, and they continued to arrive at a rate of 10,000–20,000 a month. There are also 72,000 in Tanzania, 180,000* in South Africa, 171,000 in Zimbabwe, 30,000 in Zambia and 64,000* in Swaziland.
Casualties	Wars and famines since 1975 have killed 400,000 people. Infant mortality rate is 35%, the highest in the world.

The *International Index of Human Suffering*, published by the Population Crisis Committee in Washington, rates Mozambique as the most unhappy nation on Earth. Its nearest competitors in this lamentable rivalry are Angola, Afghanistan and Chad. The miseries of Ethiopia, Lebanon and Uganda – genocide, famine, civil war and terrorism – are better known to the world, but they are all surpassed by those of Mozambique.

Mozambique is now in the last stages of national disintegration. The government controls the main towns, after a fashion, but provides few or none of the services that people elsewhere take for granted. The capital, Maputo, was previously known as Lourenço Marques, when it was the seedy, raffish centre for minor international intrigue encountered by Malcolm Muggeridge in World War II. For a while, it became or aspired to become the Las Vegas of the Indian Ocean, frequented by South Africans looking for multi-racial solace from the Puritan rigours of apartheid.

Since independence in 1975, it has become a ghost town. The supply of drinking water and electricity is infrequent, inadequate and unpredictable. Hospitals can only offer rudimentary care for a fraction of their patients, and heavily armed convoys can offer only approximate security for 30 miles (50 km) beyond the city limits.

In 1987, the Mozambican government, in desperation, abandoned its commitment to Marxism and permitted a degree of free enterprise. The International Monetary Fund (IMF) and Western countries started supplying economic aid, for the first time since independence, and food, drink and clothing reappeared in some

55

of Maputo's shops. However, these commodities are only within reach of the small affluent class, those who had done well out of the revolution. For the rest, the hotels remain closed and the shops boarded up, and the population subsists by barter.

Mozambican farmers can now provide only 6 per cent of the grain needed to feed city-dwellers – including 2 million refugees. Since 1981, 2518 schools (two-thirds of all educational facilities in the country) have been destroyed according to the Ministry of Education, but the real number is probably far higher. Nearly 600 rural clinics and health posts have been destroyed or abandoned. Plantations, mines and factories have been destroyed. Railways, bridges, powerlines and the whole infrastructure of the country have been damaged or destroyed. *Per capita* income has dropped by half between 1986 and 1988, from $210 p.a. to $95. Mozambique was exceedingly poor when Portugal gave it its independence; it has now lost every economic gain of the past century.

Foreign relief agencies have taken over the burden of keeping about 6.5 million of Mozambique's people alive – either half or two-thirds of the total, depending on whichever of the unreliable population figures is preferred. At the beginning of 1988, 3.2 million people depended wholly on international relief organizations, another 3.3 million did so partially – but the collapse of security throughout the country has meant that the situation is destined to get much worse. Mozambique faces a famine as severe as Ethiopia in 1984.

HISTORY

In the early 16th century, Portugal established bases along the East African coast, at Lourenço Marques and Beira. These holdings survived the loss of Portugal's Asian empire, and when the European powers carved up Africa in the late 19th century, Portugal was allowed to claim a territory twice the size of California. Superimposed upon a map of the United States, Mozambique would stretch from Portland, Maine to Tampa, Florida. On a map of Europe, it would stretch from Stockholm to Rome.

For most of its history as a Portuguese colony, Mozambique was utterly neglected. The Portuguese claimed to be colour-blind, unlike the British or French, but in 1975, in all Mozambique, only 4500 black people legally qualified for Portuguese citizenship. There were a further 30,000 of mixed blood, and perhaps 250,000 in the cities with some degree of education.

After World War II, the Salazar government had visions of a new Brazil in East Africa and encouraged large-scale settlement by Portuguese peasants: there were 50,000 settlers in 1955, and the number increased by another 200,000 in the following 20 years. The centrepiece of the colony's economic development was to be an enormous dam at Cabora Bassa on the Zambezi river near the frontier with Nyasaland (now Malawi). (Upon independence, the name was changed to Cahora Bassa.) The other elements of the colony's prosperity were a rail link from Beira to Salisbury (now Harare), in Southern Rhodesia, and trade with South Africa. Mozambique's ports served as outlets for Rhodesian and South African exports.

It was all delusion. The notion that Portugal, with a population of 8 million, could export a million peasants to Mozambique was pure fantasy, and the thought that the Portuguese empire could survive was lunacy. A 'wind of change' started to blow through Africa in the late 1950s, as the British, French and Belgians dismantled their colonial empires. Resistance movements started in all Portuguese colonies. The *Frente Libertacão de Moçambique* – Frelimo (Front for the Liberation of Mozambique) – was founded in 1962 and began its guerrilla campaign in 1964.

It was based in Tanzania and attacked and ambushed army posts, convoys and other economic targets. Its chief support was among the Makonde tribe of northern Mozambique, but for several years it failed to make any progress in the rest of the country, partly because of the traditional hostility between the Makonde and the Makua tribe, the largest in Mozambique, whose territory is in the centre of the country. Most of the Portuguese army was African, and to begin with, it had great success in building fortified villages to protect loyal Africans against the guerrillas. The Portuguese retained the initiative in Mozambique until 1972. In that year, the army mounted Operation Gordian Knot, which drove Frelimo back to the Tanzanian frontier.

Portugal was assisted in Mozambique and Angola by South Africa and by the white Rhodesian government, which had declared its independence in 1965, but the tide turned after 'Gordian Knot'. Frelimo opened a second front, by moving troops south through Zambia, Malawi and the wild border country between Rhodesia and Mozambique, and attacking Tete province. That was where the Cabora Bassa dam was nearing completion, where the Beira railway carried Rhodesian exports to the sea and where most of the recently arrived Portuguese settlers were becoming established.

The Portuguese had by then won the war in Angola, driving the fragmented and disputatious guerrilla movements to the frontiers or over the border. Things were different in Portuguese Guinea (now Guinea-Bissau) in West Africa, where the guerrillas controlled most of the country, and Portuguese garrisons had to be supplied by air. Now the war in Mozambique grew steadily more savage, and Portugal progressively lost control of the territory. With Tanzanian and Zambian help, Frelimo dominated the north of the country, and the Portuguese army withdrew from the border provinces. However, Portugal still controlled the south, where there were no Frelimo bands, and, with Rhodesian help, held Tete and the Beira corridor. They were not defeated militarily, any more than the French were defeated in Algeria, or the Americans in Vietnam.

The chief factor in the sudden collapse of the Portuguese empire was the resistance of the Portuguese army itself, reflecting the war weariness of the Portuguese people. Conscripted peasants from the motherland felt no pride in empire, and had no wish to suffer and die for a new Brazil on the Indian Ocean. Portugal had 140,000 soldiers in Africa, proportionately seven times as many men as the United States sent to Vietnam, and was spending 40 per cent of its national budget on colonial wars. By 1974, the Portuguese military concluded that it could not preserve the empire, and soldiers from the colonial armies overthrew the government in Lisbon in April. Within a year, they had abandoned Portuguese Guinea, Angola and Mozambique to their own devices.

Mozambique became independent on 25 June 1975. The Portuguese colonists fled – 200,000 at once and the remaining 40,000 within the next few years – leaving Mozambique destitute. When Frelimo marched south to Laurenço Marques, there were no engineers to keep the essential public works functioning, no teachers, no professional people. The plantations, mines, factories and power plants were all abandoned. The great dam was finished and useless: there was no one to service its generators.

57

INDEPENDENT MOZAMBIQUE

Frelimo, like the MPLA in Angola, turned to the Soviet Union for help. The Soviets provided minimal services as well as weapons for the new army, but it was not nearly enough. The Soviet Union was barely able to keep Angola and Ethiopia afloat, and while it wanted Mozambique as an ally, it was unable or unwilling to provide enough aid to restore its economy.

Frelimo, in gratitude for these few crumbs, and following the disastrous examples of other African countries, such as Tanzania and Zambia, proclaimed itself a Marxist state. It nationalized the bankrupt and abandoned Portuguese industries and businesses, and tried to collectivize agriculture on the best Soviet model: industrial and agricultural production dropped by 50 per cent. The country's difficulties were compounded by the drought that afflicted southern Africa in the late 1970s.

Instead of trying to develop into a mass party, Frelimo remained a small, tightly organized cabal, based largely on the northern tribes. It called itself a 'vanguard' party, in quite inappropriate imitation of Lenin's Bolsheviks. The president, Samora Machel, tried to set up a Marxist dictatorship, complete with 're-education camps' for disaffected citizens. At one time, 10,000 prisoners were reported to be languishing in them, and they proved an admirable recruiting ground for Renamo.

The Soviet Union provided training for the Mozambican armed forces, and in the mid-1980s, it was calculated that about 600 Soviets and East Germans and about 1000 Cubans were stationed in the country on training missions; Mozambican pilots have also been trained in East Germany and the Soviet Union. The Soviet Union also supplied great quantities of military equipment, including tanks and jet fighters, which served little useful purposes in a guerrilla war. However, this was not the Soviets' plan; rather, they conscientiously set about training the Mozambicans to fight a conventional war with South Africa. They failed, and anyway, there was never any likelihood of such a conflict.

THE BEGINNING OF THE WAR

Upon independence, the Frelimo government proclaimed its hostility to South Africa and Rhodesia, cutting off Rhodesia's railway to Beira, and allowing the Rhodesian resistance to establish bases near the frontier. Rhodesia retaliated by supporting the fight against Frelimo waged by white Portuguese who had stayed and by black former soldiers in the Portuguese army, particularly those who were not members of the Makonde tribe.

The Mozambique National Resistance Organization (Renamo) was set up in 1976 by the Rhodesian Central Intelligence Organization. Its mission was to harass the Mozambican armed forces and to spy on the Zimbabwe African National Union (Zanu), whose forces (the Zimbabwe African National Liberation Army) had moved from Tanzania to Mozambique after the latter's independence and started attacking Rhodesia across the border.

Among the Portuguese who founded Renamo were: Jorge Jardim, a businessman; Orlando Christina, a former secret policeman; and Domingos Arouca, a plantation owner. Former Frelimo guerrillas also joined, including André Matzangaissa and Alfonso Dhlakama, who became the principal leaders of Renamo; according to the Mozambicans, they had both been cashiered by the Mozambican army on charges of theft. They set up bases in Rhodesia and across the border in Mozambique, and the Rhodesians established a radio station for them.

In this initial period of its operations, Renamo was not notably successful. In October 1979, the Mozambique army managed a successful attack on the main Renamo base inside the country, in the Gorongosa game reserve, and killed Matzangaissa. There followed a bloody dispute over the command of Renamo, which was eventually won by Dhlakama, and his deputy was Lieutenant Adriano Bomba, a former Mozambique air force pilot.

Renamo has an international office. Its first secretary-general was Orlando Christina who was assassinated at his home outside Pretoria in 1983. He was succeeded by Evo Fernandes, who was based in Lisbon, and who, in turn, was kidnapped and murdered there in April 1988.

Zimbabwe became independent in April 1980, and Renamo had to move its bases to South Africa. The African National Congress (ANC) was beginning guerrilla operations against South Africa from bases in Mozambique, and as a result, South Africa greatly expanded its support for Renamo. The latter began to raid deep into Mozambique, its commandos often transported by South African planes, helicopters or ships, and Mozambique armed forces proved quite unable to contain the attacks. Renamo then set up bases inside Mozambique and in Malawi. The Malawi government now hotly denies that it ever offered Renamo any assistance, denials not taken too seriously by other African states. When President Samora Machel was killed in a plane crash in South Africa, the South Africans found in the wreckage notes of a meeting of African leaders that he had just attended, at which they discussed attacking Malawi because of the help it gave Renamo. However, by most reports, all such assistance has now ended.

From the day of its independence, Mozambique had announced its support for the ANC, which has been fighting against apartheid in South Africa since the 1960s. As well as increasing its support for Renamo, the South Africans responded by applying economic sanctions, immediately cutting the number of Mozambicans employed in the mines from 100,000 to 40,000, and stopping direct payments in gold to Mozambique. The cost of these measures to Mozambique was $2.5 billion a year.

South African security forces then carried the war to Mozambique, by raiding ANC offices in Maputo, which is close to the border and very vulnerable. In the first of these raids, in January 1981, South African commandos wearing Mozambican uniforms killed 11 members of the ANC and were then picked up by helicopter. There were further bombing raids on ANC positions, which the Mozambicans were quite unable to prevent, and in December 1982, another commando raid destroyed the oil storage tanks at Beira. In 1982, Ruth First, a South African Communist, and wife of the ANC commander Joe Slovo, was killed by a letter bomb in Maputo.

THE CIVIL WAR

In 1984, Renamo had at least 12,000 guerrillas under arms, and by 1988, this number had increased to 15,000–20,000, to fight a Mozambican army reduced from 40,000 to 30,000, aided by an equal number of troops from Tanzania and Zimbabwe.

Renamo caused such disruption that, on 16 March 1984, President Machel signed an agreement with P. W. Botha, prime minister (and subsequently president) of South Africa, at Nkomati on the border between the two countries. The Nkomati accord provided that Mozambique would end all support for the ANC and South Africa would end its support for Renamo.

Mozambique promptly closed the ANC offices, and raids were carried out in refugee camps in search of weapons. It was a major victory for South Africa: now none of the 'front-line states' except Angola was prepared to allow its territory to be used against South Africa. However, for Mozambique, conditions have steadily and rapidly deteriorated ever since. It is widely believed in southern Africa that, despite the treaty, South Africa continues to support Renamo. In March 1988, a Renamo defector, Paulo Oliveira, who had been the group's representative in Europe, gave a detailed description of links between Renamo and the South Africans. He described Renamo bases in South Africa, notably one at Phalaborwa in the northern Transvaal, and told how the South African army trained and supplied the Renamo guerrillas.

Renamo commandos and armed bandits, mostly deserters fom Frelimo armies, now dominate most of the country. Their tactics consist of conducting hit-and-run raids on economic targets, including railways, pipelines and powerlines. They follow a scorched earth policy, burning crops, destroying food stores and intimidating villagers, driving them into refugee centres. They ambush vehicles on highways and burn state farms and communal villages. They destroy clinics, government buildings, schools and factories, as though they were waging total war in enemy territory. There have been many well-authenticated cases of massacres. In the early days, Renamo attacked development projects and kidnapped Europeans who were directing them. There are now few development projects left.

They usually travel on foot, but use advanced radio equipment, supplied by the South Africans. (At least until 1984, and perhaps afterwards, South African air reconnaissance reported targets and kept track of the movement of Mozambique troops.) When the army counter-attacks, and clears Renamo out of one district, it simply moves to another, and resumes its campaign of destruction. It has made little effort to establish permanent bases or areas that may be described as 'liberated', as Unita has 'liberated' south-east Angola.

Renamo's chief economic targets are the railways, and the powerlines from the Cabora Bassa dam. Twelve thousand troops from Zimbabwe, trained by the British, patrol the Beira corridor, the railway linking Zimbabwe to the coast. Other contingents of Tanzanian and Zambian troops, aided by a small British unit, are having less success keeping open the northern railway, which runs from Malawi to Nacala. Renamo now also harasses the line that runs from Zimbabwe into Maputo. Other foreign troops protect the hundreds of miles of powerlines that run through territory controlled by Renamo.

At least 100,000 people were killed between 1984 and 1988, a further 300,000 died of starvation and the death toll is rising rapidly. Renamo's tactics seem to be aimed at reducing Mozambique to total poverty and its government to helplessness. In August 1988, there were over 640,000 refugees from Mozambique in Malawi, and hundreds more crossed the border every day: in May and June, 130,000 refugees arrived. By then, there was a total of well over 1.4 million Mozambican refugees in neighbouring countries and 3.5 million inside Mozambique, crowding into inadequate refugee centres and into the towns.

Renamo intends to isolate Maputo completely from the rest of the country, and that might well be achieved. Maputo is at the extreme south of the country, and Frelimo's chief base of support is in the far north among the Makonde. It is thus the reverse of the situation in Angola, where the MPLA government's chief strength is among the Mbundu tribe, which occupies the north of the country and the capital, Luanda. Renamo hopes that the government will then collapse, and then it will inherit power. This is what happened in similar circumstances in Chad in 1982 and in Uganda 1986.

However, isolating Maputo is one thing, capturing it is another. Frelimo's army may be incapable of defeating Renamo and sweeping the country clear of bandits, but it can defend the capital against Renamo as long as foreign powers keep it supplied. These supplies come by sea.

In July 1988, four American journalists were taken to visit Alfonso Dhlakama, the Renamo leader, at a base deep in central Mozambique. John Battersby of the *New York Times* wrote:

An atmosphere of the surreal dominated the rebels' leafy hide-out. Print-outs of incoming messages from commanders arrived from a new laptop computer linked to the field radio. Traditional dancers entertained rebel officials in a small clearing in the forest, and the high-pitched sounds of a women's choir rang out through the majestic panga-panga trees.

William Boot, celebrated correspondent of *The Daily Beast* (in Evelyn Waugh's *Scoop*), could not have said it better.

Dhlakama assured his visitors that all the tales of massacres and atrocities were lies, and that 'We are waging a war to demoralize and lower the profile of the enemy.' On tactics, he said, 'Our aim is not to win the war militarily, but to force the Frelimo government to accept our conditions. The Western countries are dreaming if they think the ruling Frelimo government will change its Communist ideology.'

Renamo claims that all its weapons are captured from the Mozambican armed forces, and maintains that it receives no direct support from South Africa. It does admit to receiving help from a number of American groups, made up of wealthy businessmen and some Baptist missionaries (the journalists' trip was financed by an American group called Freedom Inc.) and similar people in Europe and South Africa.

THE PRESENT SITUATION

On 19 October 1986, Samora Machel was killed in a plane crash on a flight from Lusaka to Maputo. The plane came down in South Africa, and Africans suspected sabotage or even that the South African Air Force had shot the plane down. However, an international team of investigators concluded that the crash was the result of error by the Soviet pilot, possibly compounded by bad maintenance of the plane by the Soviet crew. Machel was succeeded as president by Joaquim Chissano.

The Soviet Union has obtained no political, commercial or economic advantage whatsoever from its huge investment in Mozambique. It continues to give support in the form of arms and some economic assistance, but Frelimo is increasingly turning to the West. As early as 1980, Machel started to denounce 'ultra-leftism' and to revive private enterprise. It is now entirely possible that the USSR may decide to abandon its African adventures because they are too costly and interfere with improving relations with the West.

The South Africans deny that they provide any assistance to Renamo, insisting that they have kept to the terms of the Nkomati agreement. In May 1988, they announced plans to start training units of the Mozambican army, being particularly concerned with the defence of the powerlines from Cabora Bassa to South Africa.

The Reagan administration steadfastly refused to offer any support for Renamo, despite aggressive lobbying on its behalf by the right wing of the Republican party, who argue that because Frelimo calls itself Marxist and is supported by the USSR, it should therefore be opposed by the United States, while Renamo professes to practise free enterprise and is therefore worthy of American support. For 11 months in 1987, Republican senators – led by Senator Jesse Helms but supported by many more moderate figures, including Senator Bob Dole, the minority leader – blocked the appointment of a new American ambassador to Maputo, seeking to use the issue to swing administration policy in Renamo's favour. Finally, President Reagan managed to win the appointment. The new ambassador, Melissa Wells, makes no bones about her opposition to Renamo. In April 1988, the State Department issued a devastating report on Mozambique, asserting that Renamo has murdered at least 100,000 people.

Frelimo is trying to improve relations with the West and begging for aid to prevent its people from starving. A deal seems to have been struck with Washington in which it will provide humanitarian aid, but further Western assistance will depend upon Mozambique abandoning Marxism. Since Mozambican Marxism has been catastrophically unsuccessful (and the political tide all over Africa is now running against socialism), it is quite possible that Washington will succeed in persuading Frelimo to change its allegiance.

On 12 September 1988, the president of South Africa, P. W. Botha, paid an official visit to Mozambique, his first to an African state, apart from a visit to Swaziland. He met President Chissano at the Cabora Bassa dam. South Africa had agreed to restore the 560-mile (900 km) powerline running from the dam into South Africa, which had been destroyed by Renamo in 1982. To protect it against Renamo, South African troops will be employed. The hydroelectric plant at the dam will provide enough electricity for all Mozambique (and 10 per cent of South Africa's needs), but only if the powerlines can be protected.

Botha used the occasion to urge Renamo to accept an amnesty offered by the Mozambican government: 'We stand for cooperation and good will among our neighbours,' he said. Chissano was equally conciliatory. He not only welcomed Botha, but he abandoned the charge that South Africa had been responsible for Machel's death, and stated frequently and publicly that he intended continued cooperation with South Africa.

In August, 1989, the Renamo leader Alfonso Dhlakama went to Nairobi to meet church leaders from Mozambique, as a first step towards peace negotiations. The talks were sponsored by President Daniel arap Moi of Kenya and President Robert Mugabe, of Zimbabwe. Dhlakama demanded elections and a coalition government, including Renamo ministers, and also insisted that Frelimo abandon socialism, restore a market economy and respect the position of tribal chiefs. By then, the

Frelimo government had abandoned most of its Marxist principles, and had apparently concluded, like the government of Angola and perhaps also Ethiopia, that it could no longer count on Soviet support. The Nairobi negotiations produced no significant break-through, but they were the first sign of hope for Mozambique for many years.

FURTHER READING

American University, *Mozambique: A Country Study*, Washington D.C.
Cambridge History of Africa, Vol. VIII, Cambridge University Press.
Fauvet, Paul and Gomez, Alves, *The So-Called Mozambique National Resistance*, London, Sechaba, 1982.
Hanlon, Joseph, *Mozambique, the Revolution under Fire*, London, Zed Press, 1984.
Henriksen, Thomas A., *Mozambique, A History*, London, Collins, 1978.
Isaacman, Allan F. and Isaacman, Barbara, *Mozambique, from Colonialism to Revolution*, Boulder, Colorado, Westview Press, 1983.

NAMIBIA

Geography	318,261 sq. miles (824,293 sq. km). About the size of France and West Germany combined. It is in south-west Africa and borders on the south with South Africa, to the east with Botswana and to the north with Angola. A narrow extension to the north-east, the Caprivi strip, gives it a frontier with Zambia and a point of contact with Zimbabwe.
Population	1.16 million, including about 100,000 whites. 50% of the Africans are Ovambo, 10% Kavango.
GNP per capita	$1020. This figure (from the World Bank) gives no indication of the disparity between white and black incomes. In 1965, an official survey showed white incomes to average R1602, and non-white incomes ranging from R229 in the more prosperous south to R61 in the most backward northern reserves. These proportions are probably still valid.
Refugees	From Namibia: 70,000 in Angola, and 7500 in Zambia. About 70,000 people from Angola now live in Namibia, but are not considered refugees.
Casualties	The SWAPO insurrection has resulted in the deaths of between 20,000 and 25,000 people since 1966.

Parties and other organizations

- SWAPO (South-West Africa People's Organization): founded 1960, political organization of black opposition. Mainly Ovambo.
- PLAN (People's Liberation Army of Namibia): SWAPO's military arm.
- SWANU (South-West Africa National Union): founded in 1959. Mainly Herero. It is split between pro-SWAPO and anti-SWAPO factions.
- DTA (Democratic Turnhalle Alliance): founded 1978. Alliance of non-SWAPO ethnic parties and tribal leaders represented at the Turnhalle conference, including the white Republican Party, led by Dirk Mudge.
- MPC (Multi-Party Conference): founded 1983. An alliance of DTA, SWANU and other democratic non-SWAPO organizations.
- National Party of South West Africa: conservative Afrikaaner party.
- MPLA (People's Movement for the Liberation of Angola): Marxist government of Angola.
- Unita (National Union for the Total Independence of Angola): non-Marxist rebels in Angola, fighting MPLA.

The SWAPO insurrection in Namibia (South-west Africa) is one of the longest-running wars in Africa. It has persisted for over 20 years as a steady, low-intensity conflict at the margins of the much more violent civil war in Angola, and there seemed to be no hope of a settlement in Namibia without an end to the Angolan conflict. However, in August 1988, changing policies in Moscow, Washington and Pretoria finally brought the prospect of peace to both Angola and Namibia. Cuba, at Moscow's urging, agreed to withdraw its troops from Angola, and South Africa agreed to give Namibia its independence in a process beginning in 1989.

THE LAND AND ITS PEOPLE

Namibia is largely desert. It takes its name from the Namib desert, which runs along the coast for the entire length of the country. There is a belt of savannah behind the Namib, and beyond that the Kalahari desert.

Namibia has great mineral wealth – including the largest deposits of gem diamonds in the world, as well as uranium, beryllium, lithium, tungsten, copper and vanadium – and is the principal non-Communist source of some of these rare and strategically important minerals. The enormous income that South Africa derives from mining operations there was one of its two principal reasons for retaining Namibia against the unanimous vote of the United Nations; the other was to keep guerrilla operations as far from the white heartlands as possible. Until the last year of the war in Angola, which South Africa had entered in order to protect its position in Namibia, it remained a highly profitable colony. Then the costs escalated to $1 billion a year, and South Africa sought a diplomatic solution to the stalemate.

The principal African tribe in Namibia is the Ovambo in the north, making up slightly more than half the population. The Kavango, who are related to the Ovambo, comprise another 10 per cent. The other tribes are much smaller, the best known being the Hereros, who were decimated by the Germans in one of the most brutal of colonial wars in the early 20th century.

Now that it is much too late, the South Africans must regret that it never occurred to them, 50 years ago, to amend the irrational northern frontier, which cuts the Ovambo tribe in half, by ceding Ovamboland to Portugal: a strip 100 miles (160 km) wide would have excluded half of Namibia's black population, guaranteeing South Africa's retention of the rest.

HISTORY

South-west Africa was allocated to Germany when the European powers carved up Africa in the 1880s, because the British did not want it. The frontiers bore no relation to tribal divisions or to topography: they were drawn by map-makers in Berlin who had never been to Africa and knew very little about the place. A late 19th-century German chancellor, Leo von Caprivi, demanded access to the Zambezi, and the Caprivi strip was therefore added to the territory; five African countries meet at its tip. The German governor who began the persecution of the Nama (Hottentots) and Hereros, which ended with the deaths of half the Hereros and three-quarters of the Nama, was Heinrich Goering. His son Hermann was to exceed his achievements.

The British retained the only port in the territory, Walvis Bay, which they had occupied earlier in the century. During World War I, they used it as a base for their successful invasion and occupation of the colony.

65

In 1920, the League of Nations proclaimed South-west Africa a trust territory, ratifying one of the proposals of President Woodrow Wilson at the Conference of Versailles, and South Africa was given the mandate to administer it on behalf of its inhabitants. It was therefore not legally a South African colony, nor was South Africa entitled to annex it. The mandate, part of the charter of the League, provided that 'there shall be applied the principle that the well-being and development of such people form a sacred trust of civilization'.

The United Nations, as heir to the League, withdrew the mandate in 1947, an act that South Africa ignored. In October 1966, the UN General Assembly passed a resolution terminating the mandate; in 1969, the Security Council declared the occupation of Namibia illegal and called for an immediate withdrawal of all South African personnel; in December 1974 it ruled that Namibia should become independent by the end of the following May; and finally, in September 1978, in Resolution 435, it ordered South Africa to give the territory its independence and set out a detailed plan for it to follow. The International Court of Justice at The Hague has ruled that the UN decisions are legal and binding on South Africa. South Africa has refused to obey them.

THE ORIGINS OF THE WAR

The laws of apartheid were never applied so strictly in Namibia as in South Africa proper, but nevertheless, black Namibians have been denied all political rights and their social and economic freedoms have been severely restricted. Most of the territory's land has been taken by whites, who exploit all its enormous mineral riches for their own exclusive benefit.

When most of black Africa won its independence in the 1960s, the liberation movement soon reached Namibia. SWAPO was founded in 1964, a political movement dedicated to Marxist revolution. Its leader, Sam Nujoma, and most other members were Ovambo, though there were at first a few white radicals. Peter Fraenkel and Roger Murray, in their Minority Rights Group report on Namibia, insist that SWAPO is supported by other tribes, beside the Ovambo, while the South African authorities claim that 95 per cent of the members belong to that one tribe. (The South Africans are naturally concerned to incite the other tribes against the Ovambo, on the old principle of divide and rule.)

In 1967, South Africa tried 37 Namibians for supporting terrorism. One of them was Herman Toivo ja Toivo, one of the founders of SWAPO. He was sentenced to 20 years' imprisonment on Robben Island, and after his release in 1989, he joined Njoma who had escaped to Angola.

The central fact of the situation in Namibia is the civil war in Angola. When Portugal abandoned its African colonies in 1975, the Marxist MPLA, which drew most of its support from one of the northern tribes of Angola, seized the capital, Luanda. The Soviets rushed in arms and economic aid, and the MPLA government beat off attacks by its rivals, the most important of which was Unita, led by Jonas Savimbi and based on the Ovimbundu tribe in southern and eastern Angola. The MPLA has never defeated Unita and the civil war has continued, with South Africa supporting Unita and the Soviets and Cuba supporting the MPLA. The United States does not recognize the MPLA government and now supplies arms to Unita. (For more information on Angola, see pp. 3–13).

SWAPO is recognized by most of black Africa and by the UN as the legal representative of Namibia. It professes a loosely Marxist ideology, like other 'liberation movements', and remains closely allied to the MPLA government of Angola, which is notionally Communist and has depended on the Soviet Union and Cuba for its survival. Up to the time of the August 1988 ceasefire, more SWAPO troops were used in the fight against Unita than in incursions into Namibia. The frontier between Angola and Namibia has no military importance: the war between Unita and South Africa, on one side, and Angola, Cuba and SWAPO, on the other, has been chiefly conducted inside Angola, although SWAPO still managed to infiltrate a trickle of guerrillas into Namibia. In addition, when Cubans moved down to the Angolan frontier, there was serious fighting in the Namibian border zone.

Because of constant South African raids into Angola, and because Unita controls most of southern Angola, SWAPO moved its headquarters to Lubango, 180 miles (290 km) north of the border. This greatly reduced its effectiveness as a military force and did not guarantee security: in February 1988, in retaliation for a bomb attack on a bank in Namibia, the South Africans sent their Mirage fighter-bombers to attack SWAPO headquarters. SWAPO's leader, Sam Nujoma, lives in Luanda, capital of Angola, as far as possible from the battlefield and South African commando raids.

THE WAR

SWAPO established the People's Liberation Army of Namibia (PLAN) in 1966, and began the armed revolt. Because Angola was still a Portuguese colony and Rhodesia (now Zimbabwe) was then controlled by a white government, SWAPO's lines of communication back to sympathetic black governments were too long to permit any serious guerrilla warfare against the South African forces in Namibia. Therefore, in its early years, it concentrated on political work among the Ovambo and carried out some acts of small-scale terrorism.

After Portugal left Angola in 1975, SWAPO was able to mount a proper guerrilla war. It built up its forces rapidly: the South Africans calculate that, by 1978, SWAPO had 18,000 men under arms in Angola, and could put 800 guerrillas at a time into action in Namibia. In that year, Pretoria began a policy of attacking across the borders, striking at SWAPO's bases in Angola. In retaliation for a SWAPO rocket attack in the Caprivi Strip from across the border in Zambia, which killed ten South African troops, the South Africans raided Zambia, reaching the outskirts of Lusaka and doing great damage. Zambia has been most circumspect in supporting SWAPO since then.

In a series of raids into Angola, South Africa broke up SWAPO's bases and drove it back 200 miles (320 km). These actions brought the South Africans into conflict with the Angolan army. They fought their first battle in 1981, and the South Africans claim to have destroyed two Angolan brigades and killed two Soviet generals and their wives.

About 10,600 SWAPO guerrillas have been killed since 1966, by the South Africans' count, and an unknown number of civilians, both in Namibia and in Angola. If the estimate of guerrillas killed is approximately correct, the total number who have lost their lives is probably considerably higher than the 20,000 usually admitted. The South African security forces do not publish their own casualty figures, but the number is probably about 600–800, the great majority of them black. Security forces were losing at about 60 men a year until the sudden escalation in the fighting in 1987–8.

SWAPO was soon reduced to conducting hit-and-run raids against targets in northern Namibia, principally in Ovamboland and Kavangoland, both tribal territories along the northern border. In 1980, the South Africans reported 1175 incidents of 'terrorism', including intimidation of civilians; this number dropped to 476 in 1986, in a much more restricted area. South Africans claim that, in 1983, there were 64 cases of civilians, chiefly Ovambo, bringing information to the security forces, which led to the killing or capture of guerrillas; three years later, that number had risen to 1211. The South Africans say that they killed 694 SWAPO guerrillas in Namibia in 1986, increasing to nearly 800 in 1987.

These incidents were all small-scale, with individual guerrillas or bands of two or three men moving through the countryside. This was quite a change from 1980, at the height of the SWAPO war, when bands of up to 200 men ranged far south into Namibia, attacking villages and police posts, and laying mines and mounting ambushes. South African incursions into Angola had effectively broken up the SWAPO infrastructure there and ended large-scale SWAPO raids.

In 1980, according to the South Africans, SWAPO had an army of about 16,000 men. By 1988, the number was down to 8700, of whom no more than 800 were stationed close to the border. The South Africans had 10,000–12,000 men in the South-west Africa Territorial Force in northern Namibia, 80 per cent of them black. (Late in 1987, midsummer in the southern hemisphere, one of the black regiments briefly refused to fight, but the mutiny was soon suppressed.) There were also special police forces – the Koevoet, locally recruited and with a sinister reputation – and a home guard: the grand total may have been as large as 30,000, quite enough to cope with any possible SWAPO incursion from across the border – but not if the Cubans were to mount a full-scale attack.

The South African army introduced the usual anti-guerrilla tactic of forming fortified villages in Ovamboland, in which the Ovambo peasants were obliged to live. The idea was to make contact between guerrillas and local people impossible. It was effective, but it also alienated people who had no wish to be locked up permanently in these villages. As a result, about 75,000 refugees, mostly Ovambo, now live in Angola.

South Africa had succeeded in reducing the war to a minor nuisance on its northern border, but at a continuing cost of perhaps $1.5 million a day. Until the 1988 escalation of the fighting, the cost in white lives was small.

In July 1987, a South African unit operating in Angola was ambushed by the Angolan army. In the ensuing firefight, the South Africans killed at least 190 soldiers, most of them Angolan. On 1 November, South Africa announced that its forces had crossed into Angola and had killed more than 150 SWAPO guerrillas in a pre-emptive strike against one of their bases. Eleven South Africans were killed, and although their race was not announced, presumably most or all of them were black.

The protracted civil war in Angola reached a crisis late in 1987. Unita, with South African assistance, then inflicted a serious defeat on the MPLA army, which had been attacking towards Unita's main base in the south-east. Unita then counter-attacked and laid siege to the government's main base in that part of the country, at Cuito Cuanavale. The South Africans sent artillery to help in the siege, which developed into a major artillery battle between South Africa and Cuba. The Cubans rushed reinforcements into place and, for the first time in several years, took a direct part in the fighting. The siege was eventually abandoned in early 1988, and then the Cubans sent an extra 10,000 heavily armed troops and, for the first time, moved large units of their army to the border. There was suddenly a serious possibility of a direct conflict between Cuban and South African troops.

On 19 February 1988, a SWAPO bomb in a bank in Oshakati, a small town in Ovamboland, killed 21 people, mostly Ovambo cashing their pay cheques – the most serious terrorist incident in several years. The next day, South Africa's air force raided SWAPO bases in Angola near Lubango, the main Angolan military base in the southern part of the country, while helicopter gunships raided SWAPO bases near the frontier.

By August, the tide had turned. There was a heavy Cuban presence on the Angolan side of the border, and guerrillas were regularly attacking South African bases and installations in Namibia. The South Africans refrained from retaliating in their usual manner, for fear of provoking a full-scale battle with the Cubans, who have a formidably well-equipped army in Angola.

DIPLOMATIC MANOEUVRING

South Africa has made various plans for the future of Namibia. The first was known as the Odendaal Report, produced by a commission that examined the situation in the 1960s. It recommended partitioning the territory into 'Bantustans' and white areas, on the South African model. In December 1974, when the UN Security Council ruled that Namibia should become independent by 30 May 1975, South Africa reacted by summoning the Turnhalle conference to discuss the future. It opened on 1 September, taking its name from a former German drill hall in Windhoek, the Namibian capital, where it held its meetings. SWAPO was not invited to the conference. While the parties that did attend spent nearly two years discussing methods for attaining independence, by way of an interim government, the Vorster government continued to set up a number of homelands – starting with the Caprivi strip, the Bushmen and the Nama – which were even less independent than South Africa's own Bantustans. In June 1977, Vorster abandoned the Turnhalle concept of an interim government, and appointed an administrator-general for South-west Africa. Progressively, the various government functions that had been exercised from Pretoria were transferred to the administrator-general in Windhoek.

Elections for a constituent assembly for Namibia were held in December 1978, on a highly restrictive franchise. They were won by the Democratic Turnhalle Alliance (DTA), under the leadership of Dirk Mudge, head of the white Republican Party. A local administration was set up in 1980, under Mudge, to run Namibia under the tutelage of the administrator-general. Mudge had no authority over defence, security or foreign affairs, and the administrator had the power of veto over all the local government's actions. There was a white national assembly, as well as 'second-tier' assemblies that represented five of the 11 ethnic groups in Namibia. In November 1980, elections for the assemblies were held, but most 69

Namibian parties boycotted them. The DTA won three of them, but were defeated in the white assembly by the Nationalists. Mudge resigned in January 1983, and the administrator dissolved the national assembly.

In the 1980s, in response to UN pressure, a 'contact group' of Western powers was formed, including the United States and Britain, with a mission to persuade the South Africans to give Namibia its independence. The United States took the lead in these negotiations, in the person of Chester Crocker, assistant secretary of state for Africa, and very soon the issue became one of linking the departure of Cuban troops from Angola to independence for Namibia. Angola professed its willingness to see the Cubans leave, but only after a protracted transitional period, and South Africa insisted that it would eventually give Namibia its independence – but not while the Cubans remained in Angola. They were both being equally hypocritical: the MPLA government feared that it would not survive a Cuban withdrawal, and South Africa had no wish to give Namibia its independence. The situation appeared to be a permanent and mutually advantageous stalemate.

In 1985, another conference was held on Namibia, which led, in June, to the setting up of a constitutional council, which was meant to draft a new constitution. An eight-member transitional government was appointed by the administrator-general, with a black chairman, Andrew Matjila, and Dirk Mudge as finance minister, and it spent three years attempting to win general agreement to a new constitution. The essential dispute between the administrator and the transitional government was the question of whether elections should be held on an ethnic basis or on a common roll.

The idea of a common roll is anathema to the South African government; so is the multi-racial character of the Namibia interim government. However, the racial laws and even the political laws were much less rigorous in Namibia than the emergency measures introduced in South Africa proper after the riots in 1986: SWAPO remained a legal party, and the press enjoyed far greater freedom than in South Africa.

In April 1988, President Botha announced that South Africa would reassert more direct control of Namibia. The administrator-general's powers would be greatly increased, and he would have authority to censor the press and impose emergency regulations, like those in effect in South Africa. The chief target of the press censorship was destined to be *The Namibian*, a weekly tabloid that regularly attacked the government. In June 1988, when black trade union leaders called a general strike, the administration seized the opportunity to arrest *The Namibian*'s editor, Gwen Lister. She was accused of publishing an article suggesting that South African emergency legislation would be extended to Namibia.

THE CEASEFIRE

Negotiations between South Africa, Angola and Cuba, under the aegis of the United States, suddenly accelerated in early 1988. There were a number of factors at play. On the Communist side, the chief one was undoubtedly Soviet pressure. The USSR had been spending at least $1 billion a year to support the MPLA and there was no end in sight. The Soviet Union derived no perceptible advantage from the continuing war, and the new government in Moscow was inclined to consider the cost-effectiveness of foreign entanglements. The United States was spending $15 million a year on Unita. Clearly, the US was winning that exchange.

On the other side, South Africa's expenses had risen sharply as a result of the escalation in the fighting in Angola. More important, its international isolation was increasing: in 1987, the United States Congress had voted sanctions against South Africa, which eventually passed into law over President Reagan's veto, and even more stringent sanctions were to be voted in August 1988. Getting out of Namibia would relieve some of the pressure, and South Africa could hope to set the terms for its independence, including the preservation of South African business interests, and then ensure that it would be able to enforce them. In this way, independent Namibia would remain inextricably linked economically to South Africa. Furthermore, South Africa intends to keep Walvis Bay, which has never been legally integrated with Namibia. The British, whose colony it was, ceded it to South Africa in 1920. It is the only port in the territory, and by retaining it, South Africa would ensure that it controlled all independent Namibia's access to the outside world.

The agreement was finally approved and was announced on 8 August 1988, in Geneva. It provided for an immediate ceasefire between Cuba, Angola and SWAPO on the one side, and South Africa on the other. South Africa promised to remove all its troops from Angola (variously estimated at between 600 and 2000) by 1 November. The next step, setting a date for Namibia's independence, depended upon an agreement on a timetable for Cuba's withdrawal from Angola.

There were further negotiations between South Africa, Cuba and Angola mediated by the US, which culminated on 15 November with a draft agreement on Cuban withdrawal from Angola. There remained some details to be settled but that was the crucial decision. It was finally confirmed at Brazzaville on 13 December, and a formal signing took place at the UN on 22 December. The implementation of the agreement was set for 1 April 1989: South Africa would then set in motion the process of giving Namibia its independence, and Cuba would begin to withdraw from Angola. Three thousand Cuban troops would leave immediately, and the Cuban forces along the border would be pulled back to the 15th parallel by 1 August; they would withdraw further, to the 13th parallel, by 1 November 1989.

As for Namibia, South Africa agreed to begin moving its troops out of the country on 1 April 1989, leaving no more than 1500 men in two garrisons in bases at Grootfontein and Otjiwarango, between Windhoek and the Angolan border. The UN would send in a peace-keeping force to supervise elections that will be held on 1 November. Independence would follow a year later.

Immediately the Geneva agreement was approved, the parties in Namibia resumed their manoeuvring. SWAPO and the other opposition parties remained deeply sceptical of South Africa's intentions, suspecting that South Africa would either wriggle out of its promise to leave Namibia, or would ensure that SWAPO was excluded from power.

The US and the USSR both objected to the cost of the proposed UN operation in Namibia, so the UN peace-keeping force, originally set at 7500, was reduced to 360 and the number of poll-watchers to supervise the election was cut to 800. South Africa would continue to provide security during the transition. Koevoet was disbanded, but its members joined the regular police force, which remained under South African control. Evidently, South Africa intended to remain the dominant voice in Namibia during the transition and afterwards.

The SWAPO refugees were airlifted back from Angola by the UN. They were 71 received with much joy and celebration, under the unfriendly eyes of the South Africans. SWAPO leaders took to issuing reassuring statements to the effect that they would not interfere with the property or rights of the white Namibians, and manoeuvring for membership in the new government went on apace.

SWAPO guerrillas declined the UN's offer to regroup in camps near the border, on the grounds that the camps were controlled by the South Africans, and the future of the South African-led paramilitary forces, the Koevoet, was a matter of hot dispute. SWAPO and its supporters feared that the Koevoet would remain in being, under another name, and serve as a South African proxy army in Namibia.

The South Africans allowed the UN commissioner to establish himself in Windhoek and the territory entered into an uneasy period with three competing authorities, in preparation for the elections and the eventual transfer of power. South Africa was evidently sincere in its professed intention to leave Namibia, but it was equally obvious that it intended to remain the dominant force in the region.

FURTHER READING

Fraenkel, Peter and Murray, Roger, *The Namibians*, Minority Rights Group.
Green, Reginald, H. (et alia), *Namibia, the last Colony*, Burnt Hill, Harlow, Essex, Longmans, 1981.
Pomeroy, William J., *Apartheid, Imperialism and African Freedom*, New York, International Publishers, 1986.
See also suggestions for further reading at the end of the section on South Africa.

SOMALIA

Geography	246,155 sq. miles (637,539 sq. km). The size of France and Benelux together, but its frontiers are disputed. It is on the Horn of Africa, commanding the entrance to the Red Sea and the north-western sector of the Indian Ocean.
Population	5.6 million
GNP per capita	$280
Refugees	600,000 internal refugees; 430,000* refugees from Ethiopia. 300,000 Somali refugees fled to Ethiopia in the summer of 1988.

Somalia is a poor desert country on the Horn of Africa. In 1977–8, it fought and lost a war with Ethiopia for the Ogaden (an area of Ethiopia inhabited by Somalis). Its claims on that region, and similar irredentist claims on parts of Kenya and Djibouti, are now in abeyance but may be revived at any time. Somalia was allied to the USSR when the United States supported Emperor Haile Selassie of Ethiopia, but switched its allegiance when Ethiopia turned Communist and joined the Soviet bloc. There was an uprising against the government in northern Somalia in May 1988, and there are now about 400,000 Somali refugees living in Ethiopia. The United States suspended aid to the country because of its flagrant violations of human rights. President Siad Barre's regime is near the top of all lists of regimes that may be overthrown at any time.

HISTORY

The tribes of the wild and arid interior of the Horn of Africa grazed their flocks and fought their clan wars undisturbed by outside interference until the late 19th century. Arabs built trading posts along the coasts and raided the hinterland for slaves, but never established their hegemony.

In the 1870s, Egypt extended its control along the north coast, but withdrew at the time of the Mahdi's revolt in Sudan in 1881. The British, concerned about the safety of their colony of Aden on the other side of the Red Sea, and following the usual 19th-century imperial practice of expanding into vacuums, established a protectorate in the areas Egypt had left. In 1883, France, vexed by the British 73 presence in Aden, established a small colony on the Somali Red Sea coast at Djibouti, as a coaling station. The Italians, meanwhile, had annexed Eritrea, a non-Somali territory to the north of Djibouti, and progressively took over the east coast of the Horn, facing the Indian Ocean, which eventually became Italian Somaliland.

These were the usual European manoeuvres in the scramble for Africa. What made the situation in the Horn different was Abyssinia. (*See also* Ethiopia section.) The Emperor Menelik II doubled the size of his empire in the 1870s and 1880s, expanding Abyssinian control into areas inhabited by Somalis in the Ogaden, a largely desert area populated by nomads to the south-east of the Abyssinian heartlands. In due course, he came into conflict with the Europeans. In 1896, the Italians in Eritrea went to war with him, and were soundly beaten at the Battle of Adowa.

Afterwards, Italy, France and Britain all concluded treaties with Menelik, settling the frontiers of their colonies much to Abyssinia's advantage. This meant that the Somali people were now under five separate foreign governments: in French, British and Italian Somaliland, in Abyssinia, and also in the British colony of Kenya which had a large nomadic Somali population in the Northern Frontier District (NFD).

In 1899, the Imam Mohammed ibn Abdallah Hassan raised some of the desert tribes in revolt against the British, but this was a civil war as much as it was an anti-colonial conflict. Mohammed Abdallah, like many other Islamic reformers before and since, wanted to purify the cities of the plain. Only a minority of the Somalis followed him; the rest supported the British. The latter contemptuously referred to him as the 'Mad Mullah', but four punitive expeditions between 1901 and 1910 failed to defeat him. The British then abandoned the interior of British Somalia to Mohammed Abdallah, who fought a ferocious war to control the tribes: it is thought that about one-third of all male Somalis lost their lives during the fighting.

After World War I, the British reasserted their control and finally defeated Mohammed Abdallah; they ceded half of Kenya's NFD to Italy. In the 1930s, Mussolini, wanting to expand the meagre territories of the Italian empire, pushed Italian Somaliland's frontiers into Abyssinia in the Ogaden. There was a brief skirmish at the water wells of Wal Wal, well inside Abyssinia, in November 1934, and Mussolini used the incident as a *causus belli*. He launched an invasion of Abyssinia from Eritrea and Somalia in October 1935, and captured Addis Ababa in April of the following year. Abyssinia was then annexed, and became part of Italian East Africa.

During World War II, the British liberated Abyssinia and conquered Italian Somaliland and Eritrea. In 1948, they proposed to unite British and Italian Somalilands with the Ogaden, but were opposed by the United States, which had become the protector of Abyssinia (by now renamed Ethiopia), and also by the Soviet Union, which defended Italy's interests in the belief that the Italian Communist Party was about to take power in Rome.

Britain weakly agreed to its allies' demands. The Ogaden was returned to Ethiopia, together with an area of British Somaliland called the Haud. Italy was given ten years to prepare Italian Somaliland (now renamed Somalia) for independence in 1960. In due course, Britain also ruled that the NFD would stay in Kenya. The French remained in Djibouti.

Somalia duly became independent on 1 July 1960 – a union between (Italian) Somalia and British Somaliland. Despite the rivalries of the tribes and clans of the indigenous population, it is a homogeneous nation, unlike most others in Africa. However, half the area occupied by Somalis and perhaps one-third of the people now live under foreign rule, and independent Somalia has been pressing its irredentist claims on its neighbours ever since.

INDEPENDENT SOMALIA

Somalia started life as a multi-party democracy but, like many other African countries, the regime soon degenerated into corruption and inefficiency. In 1969, the president was assassinated by a disgruntled policeman, and a week later, the army, armed and trained by the Soviet Union, took the opportunity to seize power. Its leaders set up a revolutionary government, proclaimed a new, Marxist policy and began vigorously tackling the many problems they had inherited.

Their links with the USSR had more to do with the close alliance between Ethiopia and the United States than any serious ideological preference. When Ethiopia went Communist after Haile Selassie was deposed in 1974, and allied itself with the Soviet Union in the midst of the war with Somalia, Somalia smartly reversed its alliances and became staunchly pro-Western.

THE SOMALI QUESTION

Irredentism is anathema to modern African states because almost all of them could assert claims against their neighbours. Somalia therefore has little support for its claims on Ethiopia, Kenya and Djibouti.

Even before independence, Somali tribesmen in the NFD started agitating to join their compatriots to the north, and soon an extensive guerrilla war developed. The Kenyans called the guerrillas *shiftas* ('bandits') who raided across the deserts and mounted small-scale attacks on Kenyan police. When Kenya became independent in 1963, there was an immediate escalation of fighting. The war came to an end in 1964, and since then, Somalia has insisted that it is making no claim on the NFD. Kenya does not believe the disclaimer and, as a consequence, supported Ethiopia during the 1977–8 war, fearing that, if Somalia won, it would then turn its armies south. In 1980, there was an upsurge of guerrilla activity in the NFD (now the north-eastern province of Kenya), and the *shiftas* formed a NFD Liberation Front. Somalia denies that it gives any support to this movement.

Djibouti became independent in 1977 after a referendum organized by the French, and Somalia recognized its new neighbour. About half the 220,000 population of the new state are Somalis, concentrated in the city of Djibouti. At the time of Djibouti's independence, Somalia was deeply enmeshed in its war with Ethiopia and was disinclined to confront France as well. When it lost the Ethiopian war, a period of retrenchment and waiting began, but Djibouti remains justifiably nervous of Somalia's ambitions, and depends on an alliance with Ethiopia to guarantee its independence.

THE OGADEN WAR

Somalis in the Ogaden began small-scale guerrilla warfare in the early 1960s, and there were short border wars between Somalia and Ethiopia in 1961 and 1964,   75 which Ethiopia won without difficulty. After that, Somalia refrained from challenging Ethiopia until its 1974 revolution greatly weakened the central government in Addis Ababa. Somali President Mohammed Siad Barre proposed to the new regime in Ethiopia that it should permit self-determination in the Ogaden. When that was refused in 1975, he began to offer active support to the Western Somali Liberation Front (WSLF).

Plentifully supplied with Soviet-made equipment and 'volunteers' from the regular Somali army, the WSLF soon overran most of the Ogaden. In the summer of 1977, the Somalis cut the railway from Djibouti to Addis Ababa, the main land route into Ethiopia. The railway runs north of a mountain range that extends from central Ethiopia eastwards towards the sea. In July, judging the time ripe, Siad Barre ordered a full-scale armoured invasion of Ethiopia, and his armies attacked simultaneously north of the mountains, towards Dire Dawa, and south of them towards Harar, the Ethiopians' base in the east. The two cities stand at either end of the main pass through the mountains, and if they had fallen, Ethiopia would have been cut off from the whole south and east.

The Somalis, who committed 50,000 troops to the war, were repulsed at Dire Dawa, which is a major air base as well as a key town on the railway. However, south of the mountains, they captured Jijiga in September, after a major tank battle. It was less than 60 miles (100 km) from Harar, and they pushed resolutely towards that city. Ethiopia was reeling from the effects of military defeat, revolution and insurgencies in Eritrea and elsewhere, and by mid-September, the Somalis controlled 90 per cent of the Ogaden. However, Siad Barre had already over-extended himself. He needed new arms and munitions to resume the offensive, and urgently appealed to his ally, the USSR, for supplies.

The Soviets were faced with a dilemma. Their long-standing ally, Somalia, was at war with their new friends in Addis Ababa, who had evicted the Americans from their bases in Ethiopia and had turned to Moscow for assistance. The Soviets had to make a choice, and they chose the larger and richer ally. They suspended all military deliveries to Somalia, recalled their 4000 advisers, and sent them straight back to Ethiopia, where they also rushed huge quantities of arms. In November, Somalia abrogated its treaty with the USSR and expelled all remaining Soviets.

Since the Djibouti railway was closed, and the road from Massawa and Assab was blocked by Eritrean guerrillas, the Soviets airlifted the arms and armour for the Ethiopians directly into Addis Ababa. They re-equipped new Ethiopian armoured divisions, and padded them out with 17,000 Cuban troops.

The Somalis pressed their attack on Harar and then on Dire Dawa until January, but failed to take either city. Then the Soviets airlifted an entire Ethiopian armoured division over the mountains and landed them behind the Somalis besieging Harar, in a most impressive demonstration of the power of the Soviet airlift forces. The Somalis were trapped. In February 1978, the Ethiopians and their Cuban allies counterattacked and inflicted a resounding defeat on the Somalis. Siad Barre announced on 9 March that all Somali troops would be pulled out of the Ogaden.

THE AFTERMATH

The Somalis lost 8000 men, three-quarters of their tanks and half their planes.

However, the WSLF continued its guerrilla war, and despite Siad's announcement, regular Somali troops continued to help them. For the next two years, the irregulars continued to control the countryside, while the Ethiopians were distracted by the war in Eritrea, but in 1980, the Ethiopians gained the upper hand, defeating the Somalis again, who finally pulled their last troops out of the Ogaden. During the fighting, about 650,000 Somali refugees fled the Ogaden and settled in camps in Somalia, which appealed to the United Nations for help.

THE CURRENT SITUATION

Ethiopia has far larger and better-equipped armed forces than Somalia, perhaps 320,000 men in all. Its population is 44 million, compared to Somalia's 5.6 million. Furthermore, since 1977, the USSR has given the Ethiopian regime all the military support it needs, while budgetry constraints in Washington have precluded any large-scale military help for the Somalis.

So, they wait and hope. The Ethiopian government remains very fragile. Its inefficiency and doctrinaire Marxism, as well as the continual debilitating effects of the rebellions in Eritrea and elsewhere, suggest that the regime will not last for ever. Well over half the population are of different tribes and speak different languages to the dominant Amhara, and have revolted against them at various times. The Soviets derive no particular benefits from their investment in Ethiopia, except the pleasure of replacing the United States, and therefore they may cut back their aid programme.

Somalia's own economic and political situation deteriorated steadily through the 1980s, as Siad became more tyrannical and unpredictable. His government's economic policies seemed to have no beneficial effects for the population at large, and the American aid programme was quite insufficient to meet the country's needs. The US occupied the former Soviet (and originally British) naval base at Berbera but otherwise played little part in the life of the country. Foreign visitors were discouraged, and journalists were rigorously excluded. Somalia was faced with a depressing future as a perpetually impoverished Third World country with very few natural resources, constantly burdened by drought and the refugees from Ethiopia.

Although Somalia has a homogeneous population, the different clans remain as suspicious of each other and as resentful of the central government as they were in colonial days. The Mengistu government discovered the delights of playing off one clan against the other and, in 1982, established a Somali National Movement (SNM) based on the Issak clans of what was formerly British Somaliland. Siad and most of his government are members of the Marehan clan.

Siad Barre, reputedly 80 years old, was clearly coming to the end of his long presidency. An Amnesty International report in June 1988 stated that the government had been torturing its opponents and supposed opponents since 1981, and that there had been 'widespread arbitrary arrests, ill-treatment and summary executions' of civilians suspected of collaborating with the SNM.

In April 1988, after suffering severe losses in Eritrea and Tigray, Ethiopia agreed to restore diplomatic relations with Somalia without first signing a peace treaty demarcating the border. The Ethiopians were then able to move troops out of the Ogaden and send them to Eritrea. Siad presumably calculated that, if Ethiopia   77 recovered in the north, the Somalis would at least have obtained *de facto* peace without conceding their irredentist claims on the Ogaden. However, the WSLF continued small-scale guerrilla actions in the Ogaden, and if Ethiopia loses in Eritrea and disintegrates, Somalia will be well placed to resume the offensive.

One of the clauses of the agreement between Ethiopia and Somalia provided that the exiles of the SNM could return home. As they did so, they brought with them quantities of modern weapons, supplied by Ethiopia, and, on 26 May 1988, attacked the government garrisons in the north, defeating two weak Somali divisions. They then attacked Hargeisa and Burao, the two main cities of the northern interior; they captured Burao, but the government managed to hold Hargeisa and later retook Burao. News filtering out of Somalia spoke of mass executions of Issak clansmen in Hargeisa, and that the SNM forces had almost reached Berbera. Some reports claimed that 10,000 people were killed in the fighting in late May and June, and the civil war was continuing with great ferocity. Hargeisa and Burao are said to be ghost towns, abandoned by their inhabitants.

At the beginning of June, 167 foreign relief workers were evacuated from the region by air, and no further foreigners were allowed into the war zone. Refugees started pouring across the border into Ethiopia at the rate of 4000 or 5000 a day, and by mid-August, there were 300,000 in Ethiopia, most of them in camps near Jijiga but at least 100,000 in remote parts of the Ogaden. The number rose to 400,000 by the end of the year.

Siad Barre managed to re-establish his authority, but the divisions in the country could not be contained for ever. The United States suspended its aid to Somalia ($55 million in 1988) because of the serious human rights violations reported by such organizations as Amnesty International.

FURTHER READING

American University, *Somalia: A Country Study*, Washington D.C., 1977.
Bereket, Habte Selassie, *Conflict and Intervention in the Horn of Africa*, New York, Monthly Review Press, 1982.
Laitin, David D., *Somalia: A Nation in Search of a State*, Boulder, Colo., Westview Press, 1987.
Lewis, Ioan Myrddin, *A Modern History of Somalia*, London/New York, Longman, 1980.

SOUTH AFRICA

Geography	471,445 sq. miles (1,221,038 sq. km). Five times the size of the United Kingdom.
Population	26,700,000

Blacks:	18,200,000
Whites:	4,800,000
Coloureds:	2,800,000
Asians:	880,000

The black population includes the 4.5 million inhabitants of the four nominally independent Bantustans, and the six other homelands. It does not include the 1.15 million inhabitants of Namibia (South-west Africa). The black population is increasing at 2.7% p.a., the coloured at 2%, Asians at 2.4% and the whites at 1.7%.

Resources	Has the world's largest-known reserves of gold, chromium, platinum, vanadium, manganese and andalusite, as well as large deposits of other minerals including diamonds, asbestos and antimony. It produces about 670 tons of gold a year, half the world's supply.
GNP per capita	$1800

South Africa plays a special role in contemporary demonology. It has come to represent all the past evils of colonialism and exploitive capitalism and, by extension, all the supposed failings of the predominantly conservative societies of the West. It is a catalyst that can unite the Third World, minorities in the United States and Europe, and the left wing generally. Because it is so unpopular, it has few defenders, so 'anti-apartheid coalitions' can be formed in universities or Congress or the streets and impose defeats upon university administrations or the president or govenment which could not otherwise be achieved. These victories may have no effect on the situation in South Africa itself, but they may change the balance of power on the campus or in Washington.

Bayard Rustin, an American civil rights leader, once described a visit he had made to the campus of the University of Iowa at Des Moines at the height of the agitation for 'divestiture'. The whole place was in an uproar, demanding that the university sell any stock it owned in companies doing business in South Africa.   79

The university capitulated, and the anti-apartheid coalition won a great victory. A few months later, Rustin returned to Des Moines to give a lecture on social problems in South African townships, and addressed a nearly empty lecture hall.

Sixty-nine people were killed in the Sharpeville massacre in 1960, 575 in Soweto in 1976 and about 3000 in riots in 1985–8 – in all, perhaps 4000 or 5000 in 30 years. South Africans point out that the death tolls in other African states have been far worse: hundreds of thousands killed in civil wars in Nigeria, Ethiopia and Sudan; 100,000 Hutu massacred in Burundi in 1972. A textbook for British university students, *Modern Africa* by Basil Davidson, gives much more space to the Sharpeville massacre (69 dead) than to the Biafra war (2 million dead), and barely mentions the 1972 Hutu massacres. In August 1988, in Burundi again, the Tutsi slaughtered a further 20,000 Hutu after Hutu killed perhaps 2000 Tutsi, and the world scarcely noted. The United States continued its aid programme. There were no demonstrations outside the Burundi embassy in Washington, no Congressmen got themselves arrested for obstruction. White South Africans protest, plaintively, that there is a double standard.

They are obviously right, and equally obviously, no one feels the least sympathy. They carry the weight of their history, which is also the long and shameful history of European exploitation of Africa and the Africans. More important still, white Europeans and Americans feel a vicarious guilt for the misdeeds of white South Africans, and want to atone – symbolically, of course. They feel no guilt about black Africans killing each other. South Africans should understand the point: is not their entire system of government based on the doctrine of racial solidarity?

HISTORY

The first European colony in South Africa was set up at Cape Town by the Dutch East India Company in 1652. It was an unimportant post on the route to the Indies: if the winds were fair, the fleets passed the Cape without stopping. For 150 years, the colony was small and isolated, forgotten by the Dutch government and barely subsisting on the fringes of a vast and unexplored continent. The British annexed it during the Napoleonic wars and the Dutch scarcely protested: they were much more concerned to recover their colony in Java.

There was very little immigration, apart from an influx of Huguenot refugees in the late 17th century, escaping the persecutions of Louis XIV. In their isolation, the settlers preserved and intensified their Calvinist faith. They were intolerant fundamentalists who encountered no social or theological alternatives from the 17th to the 19th centuries, and for very many of them, the hard carapace of their world-view survived unchallenged and unchanged into the late 20th century.

They also preserved their language: it is called Afrikaans now, but is easily understood by modern Dutchmen or Flemings. They called themselves Afrikaners just as the English living in North America called themselves Americans. They were no longer Europeans; they were as much Africans as the Bantu tribes that reached South Africa at about the same time. Afrikaners and Bantu (which include the Zulu and Xhosa tribes) both came into conflict with the indigenous tribes, whom the Afrikaners called Hottentots and Bushmen.

During the 19th century, the history of South Africa was defined by conflicts
80   between English and Afrikaner, between white and black, and between blacks.

Early in the century, Shaka, king of the Zulus, one of the most bloodthirsty tyrants in history and also one of the most remarkable conquerors, built an empire based on what is now Natal and the Transvaal. In 12 years, he may have killed a million people before he was himself assassinated, an African achievement to hold against Genghiz Khan's or Tamburlaine's. The Zulus drove the Xhosa people before them, who in turn came into conflict with the small white colony in the Cape. The rivalry between Zulu and Xhosa remains a key to contemporary South African politics.

The British expanded the colony to protect it from the Xhosa, and also sought to dilute the Afrikaners by encouraging settlers from England. They were not notably successful: Afrikaners remained a majority and resented the anglicization of the colony. To this day, their descendants are taught horror stories of the persecutions of 160 years ago, often pure fiction. In 1834, the British abolished slavery throughout their empire, and the Afrikaners, who had enslaved local blacks and brought in others from West Africa and the Indies, were outraged. Slaves were property and it was God's law that blacks should serve whites.

The most determined among the Afrikaners packed up and left, in the Great Trek, abandoning their farms in the Cape Province and crossing the empty veld as far as the Orange and Vaal rivers, passing through country emptied by Shaka's massacres. The movement was on a much smaller scale than the American wagon trails westward, and the distances shorter. About 5000 people went in the first wave, in the 1830s, and the distance was a few hundred miles, compared to the 1500 miles (2415 km) of the American migration. However, the Trek was far more dangerous than the Oregon trail, the land much less hospitable and the Zulus incomparably more to be feared than the Sioux.

Fortunately for the Boers (the term means 'farmer'), the Zulus had no firearms, but despite this, over 700 Boers were massacred by Dingaan, who had succeeded Shaka as king of the Zulus. The crisis of the Great Trek occurred on 16 December 1838, at the Battle of Blood River. A party of Trekkers lashed their ox wagons together in a ring and held off a full-scale attack by the Zulu army. The Zulus, with matchless bravery, charged the Afrikaners' muzzle loaders all day, and lost 3000 killed, compared to the Afrikaners' three wounded. The anniversary has been celebrated by the Afrikaners ever since: it is known as the Day of the Covenant.

First, the Trekkers established a new colony in Natal. The British annexed it, and eventually the Trekkers established two small Boer republics for themselves, the Orange Free State and the South African Republic (Transvaal). The British meanwhile expanded the Cape Colony eastwards and extended Natal beyond its capital, Durban. These four territories expanded slowly: there was little immigration and no industry, and constant conflict with the black Africans. Then, in 1857, diamonds were found in Kimberley and, in 1887, gold on the Witwatersrand. The diamond fields were north of the Cape Colony and to the west of the Orange Free State, and the British promptly annexed them. The Rand, in the heart of the Transvaal, turned out to be the largest gold deposit in the world, and like San Francisco before it, the mining camp at Johannesburg soon developed into a major city.

Ten years earlier, the British had annexed the Transvaal, and had then been persuaded to restore its independence after the skirmishes that came to be known as the First Boer War. There was a continuing debate in London between those who   81 wanted to expand the empire, and those who thought it was quite big enough. In the late 19th century, the imperialists usually won the argument, and it was now evident to them that the Boer republics, and their gold fields, must be incorporated into British Africa.

Cecil Rhodes, an adventurer and financier who had won control of the diamond fields, had already established British colonies north of the Boer republics, which he modestly named Rhodesia. His immediate purpose was to cut off further Boer expansion northwards, and he succeeded. South Africa's northern frontier is still where he set it, along the 'great, grey-green, greasy Limpopo River, all set about with fever trees'. His wider purpose was to make Africa British from the Cape to Cairo. This was not a mere cartographic fantasy; it was megalomania pure – Rhodes also wanted to bring the United States back into the empire, and then to incorporate Germany, too.

The British government, even in its most imperialistic flights of fancy, never indulged in such lunacies, but it allowed Rhodes and his representatives to push a 'forward policy' in southern Africa. The Zulus were no longer a problem: they had finally been brought under control in 1879 (after they first wiped out a British army at Isandhlwana). In 1896, Rhodes, backed by Joseph Chamberlain, the colonial secretary, tried to provoke a rebellion by the large non-Dutch community in Johannesburg. This was the Jameson Raid, a notable fiasco. Three years later, convinced (probably correctly) that the British were intent on annexing the republics (and the gold fields), the Boers attacked first. They invaded Natal and the northern Cape on 11 October 1899 (spring in the southern hemisphere), and laid siege to Ladysmith on the road to Durban, and to Kimberley and Mafeking in the northern Cape Province. Rhodes was besieged in Kimberley (he emerged afterwards, safe and sound, but died in 1902).

The British, after suffering humiliating reverses in the first months, rushed 200,000 reinforcements to South Africa. Kimberley was relieved in February 1900, Ladysmith at the end of March (Winston Churchill rode in with the first squadron), Mafeking on 17 May. When news reached London, there was an amazing outburst of public rejoicing. The commanding general of Mafeking, Robert Baden-Powell, returned a national hero and invented the Boy Scouts.

The Orange Free State was annexed on 28 May, Johannesburg was captured on the 30th and Pretoria a week later – Churchill, once again, arriving first (he had been held prisoner there for a few weeks six months earlier). The annexation of the Transvaal was proclaimed on 25 October. The British thought the war was over. The Boers unsportingly continued the fight until 31 May 1902.

They formed 'commandos' (raiding parties) and carried out a strenuous guerrilla war against the occupiers. They raided deep into the Cape and Natal, and their generals – Botha, Hertzog, Smuts and De Wet – proved to be soldiers of genius. The British tried to defeat them by rounding up the civilian population of the veld into concentration camps. Between 18,000 and 28,000 Afrikaner civilians died of disease in the camps before proper facilities were provided. Many more would have succumbed but for a remarkable Englishwoman, Emily Hobhouse, who visited the camps and sent descriptions of them to England – in one letter, she wrote of 'crass male ignorance, stupidity, helplessness and muddling' – all of which provoked a storm of indignation. In a debate in the House of Commons, Lloyd George, the

Liberal politician, denounced the government for making war on women and children, and observed: 'It will always be remembered that this is the way British rule started there, and this is the method by which it was brought about.' Indeed. Over 80 years later, the British are still accused of having invented concentration camps.

The Boers were eventually ground down by the British, but it had been the latter's most costly war since the Napoleonic wars: 5774 British soldiers killed by enemy action; 16,168 dead from wounds or disease. Proportionately, this was twice the American losses in Vietnam. However, like the Vietnamese, Boers suffered far worse: about 7000 killed in action; between 18,000 and 28,000 civilians dead, and their farms devastated. About 20,000 black Africans were also killed.

In 1910, the Union of South Africa was established by federating the two Afrikaner and the two British territories. The federation was approved at a convention of the four states and ratified in London. It was a self-governing dominion, like Canada and Australia, and for generations afterwards the British prided themselves on the magnanimity they had shown their defeated enemies. Churchill was by then Under-Secretary for the Colonies and played a large part in the transaction. He also persuaded Edward VII to accept the Cullinan diamond when it was offered to him by Botha, by then prime minister of the Transvaal, as a symbol of the new colony's loyalty.

In the past 20 years or so, much less has been heard of that splendid British achievement. The union was at first governed by an alliance between the British and pro-British Afrikaners, of whom the most prominent were Botha and Smuts (who was later made a field-marshal and played a large role in imperial affairs in both world wars). However, in 1948, the conservative Afrikaners, represented by the National party, who had never made peace with the British, won a general election. They have ruled South Africa ever since.

THE OTHER SOUTH AFRICANS

In the early years of the Dutch settlement in the Cape, when white men largely outnumbered white women, those stern Calvinists took native concubines. Their children were neither white nor black, and their descendants are today South Africa's nearly 3 million 'coloureds'. They remained in the Cape Province, speaking Afrikaans.

From the beginning, the white settlers in South Africa established themselves at the expense of the blacks. First the Hottentots and then the Bantu (the term applied to the majority of black tribes in southern Africa) were pushed out of the way during the colony's expansion from Cape Town. White farmers took slaves and, later, farm workers from among the Bantu, who lived on the white farms in their own *kraals*, but the great majority of the black population remained in the tribal homelands, which were steadily diminished by the whites.

In the middle of the 19th century, believing the Africans unsuited to regular labour on plantations, the British brought in Indians to work in Natal, and their 800,000 descendants are still there. In the first decade of this century, an Indian lawyer, Mohandras K. Gandhi, came to do battle on their behalf.

The discovery of the diamond mines and the goldfields changed everything. Scores of thousands of workers were needed immediately for the diggings, and to build houses, roads and railways, and white businessmen quickly discovered that 83 the Bantu were just as capable of steady work as anyone else. In the last quarter of the 19th century, South Africa acquired a network of railways stretching as far north as Salisbury in Southern Rhodesia and east to Lourenço Marques in Portuguese East Africa. Therefore, by the time the Union was established, all the essential infrastructure was in place, paid with gold and built with black labour.

This has been the pattern ever since. There has been an endless supply of cheap black labour, and with it, the white South Africans have built a modern state, the only one in Africa. Until the panic of the 1980s, they enjoyed the highest standard of living in the world (except for that in a few oil states), built on the backs of African workers. It was an extreme example of the class basis of Western society, fitting all the Marxist descriptions of the division of labour, but with one difference: the class barrier was defined by race. No one could ever cross it. American or British workers are, perhaps, exploited by capitalists, but they can all, in theory, escape from their condition. Their votes can change the government and bring legal and legislative remedies to economic oppression. Black South Africans were forever deprived of all hope of personal progress. They were hewers of wood and drawers of water from the cradle to the grave – and if ever they rebelled, and refused to work for their white masters, they would be replaced by the hungry masses from the north.

The whites note that African standards of living are far higher in South Africa than anywhere else in black Africa, that black South Africans are in general better educated than their cousins to the north, and that health care is far more comprehensive. All this is true – but black South Africans compare their condition not with remote and impoverished people to the far north, but to the rich and comfortable white communities of their own country, people whose comforts depend upon black labour. Furthermore, in absolute terms, black Africans are lamentably poor: a study by the Carnegie Corporation in 1984 discovered that one-third of all black South African children under the age of 14 are stunted in their growth because of malnutrition, and in some rural areas, nearly half of them suffer from tuberculosis. Overall, South Africa probably 'has one of the most unequal distributions of national wealth in the world'.

APARTHEID

The word is pronounced 'apart-hate', which is appropriate – keep them separate and hate them. The National party government elected in 1948 set out to establish complete separation between the races, under the direction of a series of grim and fanatically racist prime ministers. English-speaking South Africans have blamed the Afrikaners ever since, but it is important to note that racial separation goes all the way back to South Africa's colonial origins. And for 30 years after the Nationalists' victory, while English-speaking South Africans tut-tutted about the excesses of 'petty apartheid' and explained to their foreign friends that they themselves were not racist at all, it was the Afrikaners who had unfortunately won control of the government, they did nothing about it. They accepted apartheid and all the benefits it brought them without protest, while patronizing the Afrikaners in the best British manner.

The Government of South Africa Act, 1909, which set up the Union, was passed
84 by a Liberal British government and included provisions guaranteeing the voting

rights of the Cape coloureds. They could vote in elections, but they lost the right to serve in the legislature themselves. Some blacks, too, won the vote, through a strict property franchise. However, the Act was a flimsy barrier to the coming racist onslaught, and the British did nothing more to protect the interests of the millions of subjects whom they then handed over to local white control.

In 1931, in the Statute of Westminster, Parliament in London renounced all claim to legislate for the white dominions (a right that had, in fact, lapsed in the previous century as far as the older dominions were concerned), and also recognized that they could all conduct their own defence and foreign affairs. South Africa took the opportunity to move those Cape blacks who had acquired the vote off the common electoral roll; in future, they would vote, separately, for white representatives in Parliament. In 1951, the Nationalist government also removed the Cape coloureds from the common rolls, allocating them four white representatives elected on a separate roll. (It was this violation of the 1909 constitution that provoked the formation of the Black Sash movement – black in mourning for the constitution. Members of the organization devote themselves to helping black, coloured and Asian South Africans cope with the apartheid laws.) Those blacks in Cape Province who still had the right to elect three white Members of Parliament lost it in 1954, and finally, in 1969, the coloureds lost their last four (white) representatives in the Assembly.

Under the theory of apartheid, the population of South Africa was deemed to consist of ten separate black nations, one white, one Indian and one coloured. The ten black and one white nations each had its own territory – white South Africa, of course, comprising over 80 per cent of the total, including all the best farmland, the mines and the cities. Any blacks who happened to live in white areas were permitted to remain on sufferance, but in practice, they were merely guest-workers, like the Algerians in France or the Turks in West Germany. Under the 'pass laws' (the Influx Control Acts), they had to carry passes to permit them to enter white areas to work, and while they were there, they were kept entirely separate from the whites. Under the 1953 Reservation of Separate Amenities Act, blacks went to different shops, beaches, cinemas, even drive-in movie theatres; white taxi drivers did not take black passengers or vice versa; park benches were segregated; and in office buildings, there were separate lifts for whites and non-whites. Public transport was also segregated: in the most extreme case, an entire suburban railway out of Johannesburg was set up to take blacks to and from their jobs in the white districts and their homes in the townships.

A vast bureaucracy was set up to maintain the system, and one of its main concerns was to establish who was white and who was not. The Population Registration Act of 1950 asserted: 'A white is a person who in appearance obviously is, or is generally accepted as, a white person, but does not include a person who, although in appearance obviously a white person, is generally accepted as a coloured person.' Enforcing the Act was the source of much misery. People were obliged to prove their racial origins, and sometimes members of the same family were classified as members of different races. Mixed marriages were made illegal in 1949, and sexual relations between blacks and whites became a crime in 1950. The state needed no more coloured people.

Blacks, Indians and coloureds were not allowed to own land or take out leases in white South Africa, under the terms of the 1950 Group Areas Act and the 1954   85

Resettlement of Natives Act. The Cape coloureds, who had lived around Cape Town for three centuries, were moved away from white neighbourhoods: 70,000 of them were evicted from 'District 6', where they had lived for generations; today, it remains a wasteland in a 'white' area, where nobody will build for fear of some later vengeance. As for the blacks, the ideal was the system employed by the mines. Young men from the homelands (*see below*) or from black states to the north were housed in dormitories for the year or two they worked down the mines, and then they went home. They were all transients, and of course, the mining companies and the state did not have to concern themselves with pensions and family allowances. The black workers' wages remained unchanged for decades. That fine leader of liberal South Africa, Harry Oppenheimer, chairman of the Anglo-American Corporation, presided over this system of ruthless exploitation that was unmatched among the advanced nations of the world.

Although the government tries its best, such a system could never be imposed in the cities; the need for labour was too great. Johannesburg could not function without hundreds of thousands of black workers – not just the house servants, though that is an enormous industry, but all the unskilled and most of the semi-skilled workers required by any modern society. The government was obliged to allow them to remain, and to recognize their townships, despite the fact that, in theory, they were all temporary and their inhabitants were citizens of the homelands. The largest was Johannesburg's South-west Township, given the African-sounding acronym Soweto. It now has a population of well over 1 million, perhaps as many as 2 million; no one knows for sure since most of its people are there illegally. It is probably bigger than Johannesburg, and therefore the largest city in South Africa.

Blacks living in Johannesburg itself were progressively cleared out of their homes: in Sophiatown, over 60,000 were evicted and sent to the townships; a new white district was built there and tactfully named Triumph. There are varying estimates of how many people were 'resettled' between 1960 and 1970, ranging from 600,000 to 3.5 million. The vagueness in the statistics is due to the fact that most of the black and coloured people who were moved from 'white' areas were 'illegals' and therefore were not officially there in the first place.

The government set up ten tribal homelands, known derisively as 'Bantustans', starting in 1963. They cover 13.7 per cent of the country's land area. Four of them consist of a single parcel of territory, the others of fragments – for example, KwaZulu has eight sections. Of the ten homelands, four have been proclaimed independent (though none of them is recognized by any nation in the world except South Africa and the other three): Transkei, set up in 1976; Bophuthatswana (1977); Venda (1979); Ciskei (1981). The other six are self-governing but have declined the honour of independence. Three independent states in southern Africa – formerly British protectorates that were never ceded to South Africa – have many of the characteristics of Bantustans. They are: Lesotho (formerly Basutoland), which is entirely surrounded by South African territory; Swaziland, between South Africa and Mozambique; and Botswana (formerly Bechuanaland) to the north-west. Botswana is the only democracy in Africa, and the most independent of the three former protectorates: it has considerable mineral resources and is thus not wholly dependent on the South African economy, like the other two and all ten true

Bantustans. South Africa plans to set up Namibia as another Bantustan.

The four 'independent' Bantustans are travesties of real nations. The first, Transkei, a Xhosa state, is as corrupt and tyrannical as any other African dictatorship. In 1987, there were two army coups there. Earlier, Transkei had been in a state of virtual war with another Bantustan, Ciskei: a group of white mercenaries from Transkei was sent into Ciskei to break into a prison to rescue the brother of Ciskei's president. The South African army intervened in Bophuthatswana in February 1988, to reverse a military coup there. One of the scattered fragments of Bophuthatswana, 60 miles (96 km) north of Johannesburg, has achieved a measure of prosperity by building Sun City, a sort of South African Las Vegas within easy reach of the white metropolis, free from all the Calvinistic restraints of South Africa proper.

THE AFRIKANERS
The popular image of Afrikaners in the outside world is dominated by the blatantly Nazi groups, whose militias wear brown shirts and wave red and black flags decorated with a symbol that is first cousin to the swastika. Reality is more complicated than that. The majority of Afrikaners may indeed be what liberal Americans and Europeans would call racist, but there is no longer a solid, Afrikaner monolith. President Pieter W. Botha has led a retreat from many of the principles of apartheid (and has been repudiated by the extremists in his own community for doing so), and there are now plenty of Afrikaners among South African reformers.

They once accepted the title 'Boer' – farmer – because that was what they were. They were Calvinist farmers of the most reactionary description: Paul Kruger, their pre-eminent 19th-century leader, claimed to believe the Earth was flat – presumably a joke meant to tease the British. However, nowadays, Afrikaners are as well educated and cosmopolitan as the English-speaking South Africans, as well represented in boardrooms and on university faculties. There is a flourishing Afrikaner literature, and the government can no longer take it for granted that Afrikaner newspapers will offer unconditional support.

It has been a considerable evolution. For half a century after the Boer wars, Afrikaner politics consisted of a battle between those who wanted to cooperate with the British, and accepted the Crown and the Commonwealth, and those who wanted to recover Afrikaner independence. In both world wars, extremist Afrikaners sided with Germany, not because the Nazis were racist but because 'the enemy of my enemy is my friend.' John Vorster, later prime minister, was interned during the war because of his pro-Nazi activities.

The 'liberal' Afrikaners, led by Botha and Smuts, who ran the country from 1910 to 1948 (co-opting the 'nationalist' opposition party, led by J. B. M. Hertzog on the way), never disagreed with the 'extremists' on the basic principle that South Africa was a white man's country. Their differences were over the questions of relations with Britain and the extent to which the blacks should be allowed to participate in South Africa's economy. When the new Nationalist party, led by D. F. Malan, won the 1948 election, they showed considerable moderation in dealing with the British. After all, English-speaking South Africans were a large block of white South Africa, and English-speaking capitalists dominated the economy. Furthermore, a viciously anti-British policy, however gratifying to survivors of the Boer wars and their children, would alienate American and British investors, whose allegiance was essential for the country. **87**

In the event, the problem solved itself. English-speaking South Africans accepted the new dispensation without demur, but the Commonwealth made it clear that it could not tolerate South Africa any more. The climactic year was 1960, the year of the Congo's independence and disasters.

On 2 February, the British prime minister, Harold Macmillan, concluded a tour of Africa with a visit to Pretoria, where he made a memorable speech to the legislature, informing them that a 'wind of change' was sweeping over the continent: all the colonies to the north would soon be independent, and South Africa must expect rough times. The speech was ill received. South Africans do not like being lectured by foreigners, least of all when the foreigners are telling them unpalatable truths. Then on 20 March 1960, 69 blacks were killed in the Sharpeville massacre (*see below*). The economy briefly collapsed, and for the first time, South Africa suffered the severe consequences of foreign censure: it felt besieged. In October, the government of Hendrik Verwoerd seized the opportunity to hold a referendum on the monarchy: those still wanting Queen Elizabeth to remain head of state lost by about 70,000 votes (out of a total of 1.63 million) to those who wanted a republic. In March 1961, Verwoerd attended his last Commonwealth Prime Ministers' Conference in London. The Commonwealth was no longer a white man's club, and Verwoerd pulled South Africa out rather than wait to be expelled.

Verwoerd was the third Nationalist prime minister, succeeding Malan (1948–54) and J. C. Strijom (1954–8); he was also the most extreme racist. He was an ardent supporter of the Nazis during World War II and, after it, opposed Jewish immigration (there are now about 120,000 Jews in South Africa, although some have taken refuge in London, Israel and New York); he had been minister for native affairs when the various apartheid laws were enacted. When he returned from London after leaving the Commonwealth, he was received like a hero by the Afrikaners: the Boer defeat of 1902 had at last been overturned. It was notable, however, that he also enjoyed considerable support among the English-speaking community: his party won 126 of the 166 seats in Parliament in the 1966 elections. Shortly afterwards, he was assassinated by a demented Parliamentary messenger, on the floor of the House of Assembly.

He was succeeded by Balthazar Johannes (John) Vorster, who pursued the policy of reconciliation with the British. That led to the first split in the party. The two trends were known as *verligtes* (enlightened) and *verkramptes* (narrow-minded). The minister of posts, Albert Hertzog, son of the Boer general, who kept television out of South Africa until 1976 because it was degenerate and subversive, now denounced the English-speaking part of the population as being too liberal. He formed a break-away party, the Reconstituted National party (Herstigte Nasional party), but the HNP never made an electoral break-through: Vorster won 134 of the seats in the 1977 election.

Vorster was prime minister at the time of the Soweto riots in 1976, and made the first tentative moves away from apartheid. He also pushed Ian Smith of Rhodesia towards a settlement, believing that the white Rhodesians were bound to be defeated in the end, and opened a dialogue with several black states, notably Banda's Malawi and Mobutu's Zaïre. Vorster's career ended abruptly in 1978 in a scandal involving secret service funds, and he was succeeded by P. W. Botha.

THE 'WIND OF CHANGE'

The white South Africans ran their own affairs, including 'native affairs', without much outside criticism or interference and also without sustained and effective black opposition well into the 1950s. During the 1919 peace negotiations in Paris, Smuts failed to persuade Woodrow Wilson and Lloyd George to permit him to annex German South-west Africa (now Namibia; *see* p. 66), and had to settle for a League of Nations mandate. He also failed to persuade the British to transfer the three 'High Commission Territories' (Basutoland, Bechuanaland and Swaziland) to South Africa, and to induce the white settlers in Southern Rhodesia to join the Union, but otherwise South Africa's diplomacy was consistently successful. It was one of the seven countries that declared war on Germany in 1939, without waiting to be attacked, and was a founder member of the United Nations.

By 1960, as Macmillan observed, a 'wind of change' was blowing through Africa. British West Africa (including Nigeria) was being prepared for independence in the 1950s. After De Gaulle took power in France in 1958, the French possessions in Africa (except for Algeria and Djibouti) were all given self-government and soon moved to full independence. In 1960, with Nigeria about to become independent, riots in the Belgian Congo led the Belgians abruptly to abandon it, as well as their other African colony Ruanda-Urundi (now Rwanda and Burundi). The British decided that their possessions in East and Central Africa would inevitably follow suit far more quickly than anyone had anticipated.

The reason for this sudden abandonment of the European empires was that the Africans demanded it and the Europeans were no longer imbued with the imperial spirit. The great majority of the British and French people did not want an empire any more. There were a few die-hards (there always are), but it was notable that the basic decisions to get out of Africa were taken by Conservative governments in Britain and by General de Gaulle in France. There was a wind of change in Europe, too.

The Portuguese resisted until 1975, and the 220,000 British settlers in Southern Rhodesia defied the world in 1965, proclaiming their independence and their undying commitment to white supremacy. Ian Smith chose 11 November, Armistice Day, for his unilateral declaration of independence (UDI). He intended to remind the world that Rhodesians had played their part in both world wars (Smith himself had been a fighter pilot in the RAF and was seriously wounded in action). He also chose to quote liberally from the American Declaration of Independence, though he conspicuously left out the phrase about all men being created equal.

The British organized an elaborate blockade of Rhodesia, imposed sanctions and even sent the navy to patrol the Indian Ocean to prevent oil for Rhodesia reaching Beira in Mozambique. The Rhodesians resisted all these measures successfully, supported by the South Africans. As long as Pretoria allowed oil and other supplies to go north, the Rhodesians could survive sanctions.

There were two guerrilla movements in Rhodesia: the Zimbabwean African National Union (ZANU), based on the Shona tribe in the north and east of the country and led by Robert Mugabe; and the Zimbabwean African People's Union (ZAPU), based on the Matabele in the south-west and led by Joshua Nkomo. They steadily built up their forces, armed and supplied by Tanzania and Zambia, who were in turn helped by the Soviet Union and China. The Rhodesians fought

89

back, but after Mozambique's independence, which allowed the guerrillas to operate throughout the east of Rhodesia, it became apparent that they were destined to lose. South Africa encouraged a settlement, which was eventually reached in London in 1980, and Rhodesia became Zimbabwe. Since then, black Africans have anticipated, and white South Africans have feared, that the Rhodesian story will prove a precedent for South Africa.

THE AFRICAN NATIONAL CONGRESS

These were external events that had serious repercussions in South Africa, but the main challenge to white supremacy came from inside the country. It was the same phenomenon that had appeared all over Africa: the Africans had never accepted colonialism with any enthusiasm, and as soon as they saw that it was not the natural order of things (or was no longer so), they demanded that it must end.

By then, South Africa had become a major industrial power, the economic motor for the whole of southern Africa. Hundreds of thousands of Africans moved to the cities during World War II to meet the enormous needs of the war economy, and still more flooded in during the years of (relative) prosperity that followed. South Africa was one of those fortunate countries that did well out of the war (the others include the US and Canada). Its prosperity depended upon black unskilled and semi-skilled labour, but as a modern industrial society, it also needed educated workers. It now reaped the benefits of the schools and colleges that had been established for blacks over the years. These were very inadequate, considering the need, poor and underequipped compared with white schools, but a vast improvement on what had gone before, or compared with the lands to the north.

South Africa was the Mecca for ambitious and intelligent students from other countries, too: in the 1920s, Hastings Banda, an ambitious boy from Nyasaland, walked to South Africa to get an education; in due course, he became president of Malawi. The same schools produced the future leaders of black South Africa. From the start, there had been those who had opposed white supremacy, who had demanded their rights, and by the 1950s, just as Verwoerd was erecting apartheid into a comprehensive system of oppression, the first serious opposition movement got under way among the blacks.

The African National Congress (ANC) was founded in 1912 and for 50 years was the leading advocate of African advancement. In the 1950s, its chairman was Chief Albert Luthuli, who personified the African demand for peaceful change based on Christian principles. His autobiography states: 'May God's will, holy and perfect, be done in South Africa, the dearly loved land, whose children we all are.' He won the Nobel Peace Prize in 1960, a gesture that focused the world's attention on South Africa just as the disasters in the Congo were demonstrating the dangers of the situation.

Luthuli was 'banned' by the government, meaning he could not take part in politics and had to live in isolation in a remote part of the country, where he died. By then, the ANC was already moving into a more militant phase.

In 1955, Luthuli had presided over a meeting that issued the Freedom Charter. Another ANC leader who helped draft it was Nelson Mandela (born 1918), a Xhosa lawyer who had set up in partnership with Oliver Tambo (now the exiled chairman of the ANC). Mandela had joined the ANC in 1944. He established its youth wing, and organized one of its first big campaigns in 1952, for which he was banned for three years.

The Freedom Charter's preamble states:

● We, the people of South Africa, declare for all our country and the world to know:
● That South Africa belongs to all who live in it, black and white, and that no government can justly claim authority unless it is based on the will of the people.
● That our people have been robbed of their birthright to land, liberty and peace by a form of government founded on injustice and inequality.
● That our country will never be prosperous and free until all our people live in brotherhood, enjoying equal rights and opportunities.
● That only a democratic state, based on the will of all the people, can secure to all their birthright without distinction of color, race, sex or belief.

In 1956, Mandela and 155 other members of the ANC were charged with treason. They were acquitted, and Mandela and others went underground and founded the 'Spear of the Nation', the military wing of the ANC, whose mission it was to sabotage government buildings – it specifically rejected all attacks on civilians. In 1957, Mandela was arrested and charged with inciting strikes. He was sentenced to five years' in prison. In June 1963, police raided an ANC secret headquarters in Rivona, a suburb of Johannesburg, where they found evidence that the Spear of the Nation was planning a campaign of sabotage. Mandela was tried again, with eight others (five blacks, two whites and one Indian); all but one were convicted and sentenced to life imprisonment. Mandela was kept in a prison on Robben Island, off Cape Town, until 1982 and was then moved to Pollsmoor Prison on the mainland. In August 1988, after contracting tuberculosis, he was transferred to a clinic in a suburb of Cape Town.

Luthuli and Mandela consistently advocated cooperation between black and white in South Africa. There was, however, another trend in black politics, and in 1959, radical members of the ANC broke away to form the Pan-African Congress. The PAC distrusted all whites, and thought that the liberation struggle should be an 'African' struggle. It later came to be dominated by Stephen Biko's 'Black Consciousness' movement, heavily influenced by Black Power in the United States. Biko appealed to black intellectuals – teachers, journalists, publicists – but never supplanted the ANC as the chosen representative of the black people. He died in police custody in 1977.

SHARPEVILLE AND BEYOND
The Sharpeville massacre, in which 69 blacks were shot by security men, took place on 21 March 1960. There had been a series of black demonstrations against the pass laws. A large crowd (organized by the PAC) gathered in front of a police station at Sharpeville, a township outside Vereeniging, 40 miles (65 km) south of Johannesburg, where there were about 150 police. The crowd taunted them, threw stones and became progressively more unruly. One of the police officers panicked and opened fire, and his example was followed by others. It was not a cold-blooded, deliberate massacre, but it might as well have been as far as public opinion, both in South Africa and abroad, was concerned. It was seen as a declaration of war.

91

As panic among the whites spread, the economy was seriously affected: house prices collapsed; many people emigrated; there was a mass flight of capital out of the country, which was only stopped when the government imposed stringent exchange controls. This was the year of the Congo's independence and all the horrors that had followed: the wind of change had blown up into a hurricane.

But then it subsided, and South Africa entered a period of sustained economic growth, its 'First World' urban economy expanding by 6 per cent a year. There was large-scale white immigration, reinforced in the 1970s by Rhodesians escaping first the war and, later, the black government of Zimbabwe. (These recent arrivals are among the most extreme racists in South Africa today.) South Africa's 'Third World' black, rural economy, on the other hand, did not do so well, but the difference was obscured by the great general prosperity of the times. Much of this was due to the insatiable demand for South African minerals. In 1971, when President Nixon took the United States (and therefore the rest of the world) off the gold standard, the price of gold shot up from the $35 an ounce it had held since 1933 to a price that varied, in the inflationary 1970s, between $400 and $800 an ounce. South Africa was the leading producer of gold, and did even better than the oil countries as the value of its major export increased 15 or 20 times. Its economy expanded faster than that of any other country in the world except Japan.

Prosperity was, however, a two-edged weapon for white South Africa. The boom produced a never-ending demand for labour, and blacks poured into the townships. Verwoerd's government made energetic efforts to keep them out, but every time a shantytown near Cape Town was bulldozed, another sprang up a few miles away, and when the authorities turned their attention to that, blacks returned to the first.

Furthermore, the black population was rising fast, with hundreds of thousands of young people joining the workforce every year. The black population of South Africa (including coloured and Asian people) was 7.5 million in 1952, 15 million in 1972, and has almost doubled again since then. Soweto, originally conceived to hold 50,000 people, soon had ten times that number. It is now as big as Johannesburg, if not bigger, and other black townships are increasing rapidly. The whole notion of apartheid was being overwhelmed by numbers, and by the needs of industry. Only in the gold mines were the old rules maintained, because the bulk of the workers came from abroad, and could be shipped home at the end of their one- or two-year stints down the mines.

After Verwoerd's assassination in 1966, the new prime minister, John Vorster, saw the need to form a united front with English-speaking South Africans (a move that led to the first split in the ranks of the Nationalist party) and began to look for ways to lessen South Africa's international isolation. At the same time, however, the republic continued to give every support to Portugal's wars in Angola and Mozambique, and to Ian Smith's resistance in Rhodesia. All this came apart in 1975 and 1976. First, Portugal precipitously abandoned its colonies, and South Africa suffered a humiliating defeat in the 1975 Angola civil war. It therefore became evident to Vorster that Rhodesia would eventually be defeated, and he began to prepare for that evil day. Lastly, there were the Soweto riots in 1976.

SOWETO

92 Vorster, beset on all sides, tried to appease the Afrikaners by appointing one of the

most rigid *verkrampte* leaders, Andries Treurnicht, as deputy minister of Bantu affairs (the ministry was later renamed 'cooperation and development'), and put him in charge of Bantu education. Two years earlier, a rule had been introduced that, in black secondary schools, science and practical subjects were to be taught in English and mathematics and social studies in Afrikaans. The rule was deeply unpopular: Afrikaans was seen by blacks as the language of oppression; and besides, there were not nearly enough teachers proficient in it. Treurnicht insisted that the rule be applied, despite numerous warnings by his officials and others. The official response was that, if black children did not like it, they could move to the homelands; since whites were paying for black education, it was their right to decide what was taught, and in what language.

There were demonstrations of protest in many schools, and on 16 June 1976, a big march of schoolchildren took place in Soweto. The demonstrators were aggressive and threw stones at police. By mid-morning, there were 5000 or 6000 students gathered, facing 48 police – 40 of whom were black. The police colonel in charge ordered the demonstrators to disperse (such gatherings were illegal); the crowd responded by throwing stones at him. The police were surrounded and clearly in danger. In the ensuing shooting, two students were killed and 11 wounded. Rioting then spread throughout Soweto.

In Soweto, 15 people were killed on 16 June, and another 247 between 17 June and the end of February 1978, when the troubles finally died down. There were riots throughout the country, except in Durban, where the Zulus kept the peace. Altogether, 495 blacks, 75 coloureds, 5 whites and 1 Indian were killed.

Two years later, Vorster was succeeded as prime minister by P. W. Botha, who set about the cautious process of reform.

REFORM

The fundamental question is whether these reforms are genuine, and how far they will lead. Will the whites give power, real power, to the blacks without a fight? Or will there be a long, bitter civil war, ending with black victory and the ruin of South Africa?

There are plenty of white South Africans ready to charge Botha with treason. Treurnicht broke away from the National party in 1982, to form the Conservative party, which is now the largest opposition party in the Legislative Assembly. A yet more extreme party, the Afrikaner Weerstandsbeweging (Afrikaner Resistance Movement), led by Eugene Terre' Blanche, is openly Nazi; they are still a small minority among Afrikaners, but they probably have many more sympathizers than opinion polls show. The riots that began in 1985 have had the usual effect of pushing some people towards the extreme, while others (including the government) have taken the opposite position, saying that the riots showed that reform is essential. Botha's reforms came to a halt in 1987, after the troubles had temporarily been repressed, but the debate continued.

The smoke from burning buildings, the tear gas, the sight of troops in armoured cars patrolling the townships have all obscured the extent of the reforms that Botha has introduced, at least for most foreigners. The reforms are worth noting:

● Abolition of restrictions on black trade unions (1981).   93

- Complete integration of all sports (1982).
- Uniform income tax laws (1984).
- Admission of non-whites to state universities (1984). The reform is not complete: they are admitted on a quota basis.
- The introduction of mixed business districts in previously white-only areas (1984). There are still extensive restrictions on non-white businesses.
- The repeal of laws banning mixed marriages and sexual intercourse between people of different races (1985).
- Granting permanent residency rights to 'illegal' blacks who have lived in 'white' areas since birth or who have lived or been employed there for more than ten years (1985).
- The repeal of the ban on mixed political parties (1985).
- Abolition of all race restrictions on the sale of liquor (1986).
- Granting residential rights to coloureds and Indians in the Orange Free State and northern Natal (1986).
- Abolition of Influx Control Acts (1986).
- Abolition of the pass laws (1986).
- Restoration of full South African citizenship to people who had been declared citizens of the four 'independent' Bantustans (1986).
- Ending all compulsory resettlements (1986).
- Repeal of laws against blacks acquiring freeholds in townships (1986). Previously they had been allowed to buy 99-year leases only.
- Relaxation of the laws governing non-whites' residence in 'white' areas (1986).
- Repeal of segregation laws covering hotels and restaurants. Cinemas and theatres permitted to desegregate on application (1986).
- Repeal of restrictions on black access to some 'white' recreational facilities, such as beaches (1986).
- Partial integration of public transport.

These reforms swept away most of the 'petty' apartheid legislation and also several of the props holding up the whole edifice: the repeal of the pass laws, the abandonment of the pretence that people living in the townships were foreigners, the ending of 'resettlement' under which millions of people had been evicted from their homes, repeal of the ban on mixed marriages and sexual relations – and these are all fundamental matters. There are now black students in the universities and over 1.5 million black trade unionists. However, in June 1988, under pressure from white conservatives, Botha started to back away from some of these reforms (*see below*).

Another important reform was the establishment of elected local councils to administer the townships – black, coloured and Indian. The councils were one of the chief targets of the rioters in 1985–6 but have since been re-established – many of them by adopting a policy of uncompromising hostility to the government.

CONSTITUTIONAL REFORM

The riots were provoked by Botha's most substantial reform measure so far, the constitutional amendment that gave a measure of power to the coloured and Indian communities, while excluding the blacks. The reforms were announced in 1984.

The exclusively white assembly was dissolved, to be replaced by three separate bodies: the white Legislative Assembly, with 178 members; a House of Representatives for coloured people, with 85 members; and a House of Deputies, to represent the Indians, with 45 members.

Each house would be exclusively responsible for its community's 'own' affairs, a term that has been much debated, but which includes social welfare, health and education. Each chamber elects a Ministers' Council to supervise these matters. 'General' affairs, including defence, foreign relations and police matters, are supervised by joint committees of the three houses. Since the proportions have been set at 4:2:1, whites will always be in a majority under this system. Furthermore, a new office – executive president – was created. The president is elected by the three houses (meaning that he will be elected by the whites). Botha took the job, which, because it is less subject to legislative control, is far more powerful than that of prime minister under the old constitution. Among other things, the president defines what is 'own' and what is 'general' and thus effectively decides which powers the three houses will enjoy. No legislation passes into law without his consent, so the coloured and Asian houses have no real independence. There is also a President's Council, also divided on the 4:2:1 ratio – a 'body of last resort' that is meant to resolve differences that cannot otherwise be settled. The theory is that the three communities will reach agreement by consensus. It has not worked like that.

The new constitution was submitted to a whites-only referendum on 2 November 1983. It was vigorously opposed by the conservative Afrikaners as well as by liberals and by the great majority of coloureds and Asians who were meant to benefit from the proposal. The conservatives rejected any concession at all, and the liberals objected to the continued subjection of non-Europeans. Indians bitterly opposed to the new constitution argued that, in the long term, it would be disastrous for South African Indians to side with the whites against the blacks. The government insisted that, on the one hand, it was maintaining white supremacy, while on the other hand, it was firmly committed to reform. The vote was 65.95 per cent in favour and 33.53 per cent opposed (the remaining 0.52 per cent comprised spoiled papers).

The government did not propose a referendum for coloureds and Asians, certain that the proposal would be defeated. The battle was therefore fought in the elections to the new parliament. The government used every possible inducement to get people to vote, and leaders of the coloured, Asian and liberal white communities advocated a boycott.

There was not a united front. The Labour party, the dominant political party of the coloured community led by The Reverend Allan Hendrickse, took Botha at his word. Hendrickse, whose church had been demolished under the Group Areas Act because it was in a district designated for whites (though it had stood for 50 years), was no patsy for the government – he had been jailed for opposition activities and had steadfastly opposed apartheid all his life. However, he believed that this time the government was moving in the right direction. His decision led to a violent dispute with other coloured leaders, the most prominent of whom was The Reverend Allan Boesak, president of the World Alliance of Reformed Churches. He and his followers argue that the coloured community must throw in its lot with the blacks, and therefore they support a common electoral roll for all South Africa.   95

The coloured elections were on 22 August 1984, the Indian elections a week later. The boycott was most effective in the Cape (where the great majority of coloureds live). Overall, about 30 per cent of the coloured and 20 per cent of the Indian electorate voted, enough for Botha to claim victory. The opposition pointed out that since only two-thirds of coloureds and Indians were registered, the turn-out had been, in fact, less than 20 per cent. Hendrickse took office as leader of the coloured deputies.

THE RIOTS

There had been steadily increasing trouble in the townships in the early 1980s, and it accelerated as the debate on the new constitution engulfed the country. In the course of 1983, there were repeated demonstrations at black schools against inadequate facilities. The first death occurred in February 1984: police came to break up a student demonstration at a school in Atteridgeville township outside Pretoria; in the scuffle, a 15-year-old schoolgirl was run over by a police Land Rover, and killed. In the months that followed, the fights between police and students grew more frequent and more violent. Students took an active part in the campaign to boycott the coloured elections, and when these took place in August, there was an active campaign of harassment to prevent people from voting.

On 3 September 1984, there were 12 hours of rioting in Sharpeville. Fourteen people were killed, including several blacks burned to death by black rioters, who accused them of collaborating with the government. Indian shops were sacked and their homes burned. The riots resumed the following day, and spread across the country. It was a long, hot summer, and soon troops were called in to control the situation. By the time the government declared a state of emergency on 20 July 1985, over 600 people had been killed.

The state of emergency was lifted at the end of the year, but reimposed in June 1986, and it was further extended in 1987 and 1988. Between September 1985 and the end of 1986, when the rioting died down, a total of 2291 people had been killed. Half of them had been black 'collaborators' who were 'executed' by other blacks. One favoured method was 'necklacing': a car tyre filled with petrol was placed around the victim's neck and set on fire. Winnie Mandela, the wife of the ANC leader, expressed her approval of this barbarity.

THE BLACK OPPOSITION

The Zulu are the largest tribe in South Africa, about 7 million strong, and whatever the country's future, they will clearly play a large part. There are two Zulu factions: the Inkatha, the traditional party led by Chief Mangosuthu Gatsha Buthelezi, chief minister of KwaZulu, the Zulu homeland; and the Natal wing of the United Democratic Front. The national UDF was founded by The Reverend Allan Boesak (*see below*), but in Natal, it is largely an opposition Zulu organization, based on the cities. Buthelezi has produced a plan for the future of Natal, under which political control would be transferred to the blacks (meaning to him), but leaving the whites a power of veto over such matters as property rights, education and language. Many whites see the proposals as a possible way out of the country's predicament. The UDF accuses Buthelezi of selling out to the government; it rejects all special provision for the whites and demands an immediate move to majority rule.

However, the dispute between Inkatha and the UDF is less about relations with the whites than it is a straightforward power dispute between Zulus. Hundreds of people – over 200 in the last two months of 1987 alone – have been killed in what seems sometimes to be a near civil war in the townships around Durban and Pietermaritzburg, and because the UDF is closely allied to the ANC, the fighting is relevant to the whole country. In 1987 and 1988, Inkatha appeared to be losing the fight, largely because it was seen as a supporter of the white government. However, Buthelezi recovered some credibility by refusing to participate in meetings on constitutional matters convened by President Botha as long as Mandela and other ANC leaders were excluded.

Opposition to the apartheid system comes in various forms. In 1983, Allan Boesak formed the UDF, an alliance of some 400 organizations with a total membership of 2.5 million people. It was meant to fight the constitutional reforms that Botha had proposed, but went on to proclaim that it cherished 'the vision of a united, democratic South Africa based on the will of the people'. Its programme was 'united action against the evils of apartheid, economic and all other forms of exploitation'. The UDF included many white organizations, as well as blacks, but excluded Buthelezi's Inkatha and the Progressive Federal party, the rump liberal white opposition party, because they had both participated in the undemocratic political process.

Another opposition group is the National Forum, organized by survivors of Steve Biko's Black Consciousness movement. Its most influential component is the Azanian People's Organization (AZAPO), a militant, socialist party which advocates the exclusion of all whites from any political role in the future 'Azania', the name they propose to give to South Africa.

Another centre of opposition is provided by the churches, of which the most important is the Anglican church, now headed by Archbishop Desmond Tutu, who became black South Africa's leading spokesman (apart from Mandela) after winning the Nobel Peace Prize in 1984. Four years later, in March 1988, he set up a Committee for the Defence of Democracy, which was immediately banned by the government. Tutu, because of his international reputation and his church position, has escaped the political and physical intimidation meted out to other opposition leaders, but there are clearly limits to his freedom.

AZAPO, the National Forum and the UDF were all banned in February 1988, under the provisions of the state of emergency. The decree forbade them, and 14 other opposition groups, to 'carry on or perform any acts whatever'. The Congress of South African Trade Unions (COSATU) was not banned, but its activities were severely restricted: it was forbidden to support sanctions or divestiture or to call for the release of detainees.

Since black unions were legalized in 1981, they have rapidly expanded into some of the country's leading institutions, with at least 1.5 million members. They have met with mixed success. A prolonged strike in the mines was defeated in September 1987 by the traditional methods of force and the importation of strike-breakers from outside. Leading South African businessmen who had long demanded an end to apartheid suddenly found themselves face to face with the economic consequences of the policy they proposed. Blacks would no longer accept starvation wages and demanded other rights as well. Granting these demands would severely reduce the profitability of the mines and other industries, reduce the living standards of   **97** whites, increase inflation and doubtless lead to further demands by the blacks. So, casting their capitalist liberalism aside, the mine owners reacted as fiercely as the most obdurate Afrikaner farmer. They defeated the mine union, without resolving the dilemma: the South African economy cannot expand sufficiently to meet the demands of its rapidly increasing black population, at even their present levels of income, unless economic apartheid is ended; but if it is, the economy will suffer in the short run, and the long-term prospects of capitalists and managers (all white) will be much reduced.

The parliamentary opposition in the white Legislative Assembly is inconsequential (the Progressive Federal party even lost control of Johannesburg City Council in 1988). However, the coloured House of Delegates achieved an important symbolic victory when it obliged Botha to withdraw his proposed legislation to tighten the Group Areas Act: he apparently decided that the votes to be won from the conservatives by strengthening apartheid were less important than the troubles he would encounter.

Although there has been little rioting since the end of 1986, the state of emergency was extended for another year in June 1988. A three-day general strike that month had wide support and the government's control of the townships remains precarious.

THE GUERRILLA WAR

The chief opposition force in South Africa remains the ANC. It was crippled by the arrests of Mandela and his friends in the early 1960s, but revived after the Soweto riots in 1976. Each time the government banned a moderate black opposition group, there was a surge of new recruits to the ANC. It is undoubtedly active in townships throughout the country, and the popularity of Nelson Mandela is sufficient evidence of its influence.

In 1980, its first successful bombing campaign began with simultaneous attacks on three of South Africa's most important economic facilities: the plants manufacturing oil from coal. In December 1982, South African raiders killed 42 members of the ANC in Maseru, Lesotho. In May 1983, a car bomb outside the Ministry of Defence in Pretoria killed 19 people and injured over 200, including many black civilians. That episode provoked a great debate inside the ANC, between the heirs to Albert Luthuli, who vehemently opposed killing civilians, and the hardliners who favoured terrorism as a legitimate military tactic. The split mirrored the political divisions in the ANC: the movement is divided between dedicated Communists, obedient to commands from Moscow, and more pragmatic and moderate groups.

ANC headquarters are in Lusaka, the capital of Zambia, but its members are still at risk of South African terror even thousands of miles from its borders. South African commandos have attacked its offices in Maputo in Mozambique, in Gaborone in Botswana, and in Maseru in Lesotho. In March 1988, its representative in Paris was assassinated, and in April, a car bomb injured a prominent white member of the ANC in Maputo.

The ANC's bombing campaign against South Africa increased sharply after the 1984–6 riots. There were scores of attacks, killing many people, throughout South Africa, many of them clearly intended to inflict casualties on civilians. In August 1988, the ANC's 35-member executive committee issued a statement saying, 'It is contrary to our policy to select targets whose sole objective is to strike at civilians.

Our morality as revolutionaries dictates that we respect the values underpinning the humane conduct of war.' The committee recognized its responsibility for a number of civilian casualties, and then dismissed the commander of its military wing.

These worthy sentiments may have been a sincere statement of intent by the more moderate faction, but it had little effect on events. The terrorists continued their work: 13 people were killed in a dozen bombing attacks in June; there were more than 90 bombings in the first six months of the year. On 2 July, a car bomb exploded outside a football stadium in Johannesburg, killing two people, and in the month before the local elections in October, there were many more attacks, including a car bomb in a coal-mining town near Johannesburg on 24 October, which killed another two people. By the government's count, there was a total of 900 bombings and other acts of terrorism between 1980 and June 1988.

The Conservative party won control of a number of local city councils in the October local elections, and immediately reimposed all the rules of 'petty apartheid' that had previously been dismantled. The result was a surprising political victory for the government, which was able to present itself as the new, main-line, centrist party. President Botha and his government denounced the return to apartheid.

Botha suffered a stroke in February 1989 and was replaced, first as leader of the National Party and, in August, as president, by F. W. de Klerk. One of Botha's last acts as president was to invite Nelson Mandela to tea, and de Klerk's first act was to visit Kenneth Kaunda in Zambia. Parliamentary elections were held on 7 September 1989. The Nationalists won 47 per cent of the white vote and dropped from 123 to 93 seats in the Assembly. The Conservatives went from 22 to 39 (the Resistance Movement collapsed after a particularly ludicrous sex scandal involving Eugene Terre' Blanche) and the new Democratic party, replacing various liberal groups that had held 21 seats, won 33. De Klerk campaigned on a vague platform of reform but continued to refuse to recognize the ANC. He correctly claimed that there was a large white majority in favour of change. There was a derisory turn out in the elections for the Asian and Coloured houses and over 20 black and Asian people were killed in demonstrations protesting against the elections.

Immediately after the elections, de Klerk permitted a series of opposition demonstrations. For the first time in decades, mass rallies were held in Johannesburg and Cape Town at which the ANC flag was openly displayed, without police interference. De Klerk met Archbishop Tutu and the Rev. Allan Boesak, who described their role as 'facilitators'. They wanted to open the way to formal negotiations between the government and the ANC. Then de Klerk released Walter Sisulu and six other senior leaders of the ANC, and a leader of the PAC. Sisulu had been in jail for over 25 years. Only Mandela remained imprisoned, and de Klerk evidently intended to release him too, and then to open negotiations with him on the country's future.

FOREIGN POLICY

In August 1988, South Africa announced that it had accepted a ceasefire in Angola and would proceed to grant independence to Namibia, provided that Cuba agreed to withdraw its troops from Angola within a short period. The government had evidently decided that it could no longer afford the costs of the conflict: $1 billion a year on the defence budget and incalculable political difficulties. The South Africans were out of Angola a few weeks later, leaving Jonas Savimbi to face the 99

Cubans and the Angolan government alone, or at least apparently alone. No doubt he continued to receive substantial secret help via Zaïre. Final agreement was reached in December (*see* 'Angola', pp. 9–13 and 'Namibia', pp. 70–72), and the process leading to Namibia's independence was due to begin in 1989.

The agreement followed the non-aggression pact with Mozambique that Botha had signed in March 1983. That agreement obliged Mozambique to expel the ANC, and committed South Africa to end its support for the Mozambique rebels, Renamo. (*See* 'Mozambique', pp. 58–63.) In September 1988, Botha visited President Mobutu in his native village in Zaïre, and was received with all the pomp due to a head of state, and then he paid a call on President Houphouët-Boigny of the Ivory Coast. Once again, South Africa was leapfrogging the 'front-line states' and establishing trade and political relations with the rest of Africa.

The reasons for South Africa's success in this endeavour are largely economic. The front-line states, despite their loathing for apartheid, depend on South Africa's transport network for their economic survival, and upon South Africa's food exports to save their people from starvation. Zimbabwe, Zambia, Malawi, Mozambique, Zaïre and Tanzania are all heavily dependent upon South Africa in this way. If Cuba pulls its troops out of Angola and the Soviet Union reduces its presence, Angola, too, will fall into South Africa's orbit, whether or not Savimbi wins his civil war.

The price South Africa will extort will be an end to all support for the ANC, a condition already enforced on Mozambique. The new dispensation will not reduce South Africa's international isolation, but it will give the white South Africans a breathing space. They will have a few more years to try to make President Botha's constitutional reforms work, and to try to come to an agreement with the black majority, before the next upheaval. The Soweto riots in 1976 were much more serious than the disturbances that had followed the Sharpeville massacre in 1960. The uprising in 1984–6 was much more serious than Soweto.

FURTHER READING

American University, *South Africa: A Country Study*, Washington, D.C., 1981.

Butts, Kent Hughes, and Thomas, Paul R., *The Geopolitics of Southern Africa: South Africa as Regional Superpower*.

Carter, Gwendolen, and O'Meara, Patrick, *International Politics in Southern Africa*, Bloomington, Indiana University Press, 1982.

Davis, Stephen M., *Apartheid's Rebels: Inside South Africa's Hidden War*, New Haven, Conn., Yale University Press, 1988.

Luthuli, Albert, *Let My People Go*, London, Fontana, 1962.

Mandy, Nigel, *A City Divided – Johannesburg and Soweto*, New York, St Martin's Press, 1984.

Mermelstein, David (ed.), *The Anti-Apartheid Reader*, New York, Grove Press, 1987.

Pakenham, Thomas, *The Boer War*, London, Weidenfeld & Nicolson, 1979.

Seidman, Ann, *The Roots of the Crisis in Southern Africa*, Trenton, New Jersey, African World Press, 1985.

Unger, Sanford, *Africa – The People and Politics of an Emerging Continent*, New York, Simon and Schuster, 1985.

Villet, Barbara, *Blood River*, New York, Everest House, 1982.

SUDAN

Geography	967,491 sq. miles (2,505,792 sq. km). About half the size of Europe, or as big as the US east of the Mississippi.
Population	22,569,000: 14 million in the north are Muslims and speak Arabic; 8 million in the south are animists or Christian, belong to many different tribes and speak a great variety of languages.
GNP per capita	$320
Refugees	2 million 'internal' refugees: 667,000* from Ethiopia, 90,000 from Uganda, 25,000 from Chad, 5000 from Zaïre. There were 330,000 refugees from Sudan in Ethiopia in 1988; a further 8000 to 10,000 people cross the border every month.
Casualties	First civil war (1963–72): about 400,000 people were killed. Second civil war (1983–): 400,000 people are reported dead so far, including 250,000 of starvation in 1988.

HISTORY

Sudan is an immense country, split by the great fault-line of Africa. Two-thirds of the population live to the north. They are Muslims by religion and Arab by culture, and they look north to Egypt and east to Mecca. Their land is dry, hot, partly desert, and they have a written history stretching back to classical times.

The south is pagan or Christian. It is a green, fertile land, larger than Texas, a part of black, equatorial Africa, and its population looks to Central and East Africa. The two disparate parts of the country are united today because, at the end of the 19th century, the French coveted and the British conquered the territory then designated the eastern Sudan. It was an episode that marked the high tide of European imperialism. Neither France nor Britain had any rational use for the endless expanse of deserts and swamps (let alone any moral right to annex it), but each determined to seize it because the other wanted it.

The Sudan was conquered by the Egyptians in 1819, who ruled it from Khartoum and permitted the continuance of the slave trade in the south. In the 1870s, Egypt itself was occupied and controlled by Britain. A British general, Charles Gordon, was seconded to the Egyptian army to suppress the slave trade, which he accomplished with great zeal. Then the Sudanese rose in revolt. They followed a religious leader, Mohammed Ahmed, who proclaimed himself the 'Mahdi', and a military leader of genius, Abdullah ibn Mohammed, who proclaimed himself 'Khalifa', ruler of the Sudan. His army, known to the British as the Dervishes, swept out the intruders, and the British decided in 1883 that the Egyptians would be prudent to withdraw completely. In January 1884, Gordon was sent to direct the withdrawal but, as soon as he reached Khartoum, refused to leave. He was besieged from 15 March 1884 and held the place against enormous odds for ten months. In December, the British belatedly sent a relief expedition up the Nile, but it only reached the outskirts of Khartoum on 27 January 1885 – two days after Gordon's garrison had been overwhelmed. He had been killed on the steps of his palace and entered imperial legend.

In 1898, the British sent a large expedition up the Nile to avenge Gordon and conquer the Sudan – and frustrate the French. The last was the chief objective. The Khalifa was killed, and the Sudanese were defeated at the Battle of Omdurman on 2 September, the last battle that was decided in a cavalry charge. Lieutenant Winston Churchill, then of the 21st Lancers, took part in the war and the charge and later wrote an exuberant account of the business.

After Omdurman, the commander of the British expeditionary force, General Kitchener, sailed up the White Nile to Fashoda, far to the south. A French expedition that had marched across the width of Africa from the Atlantic had just established itself there. Kitchener and his large and powerful army reached Fashoda on 19 September. The French expedition, led by Major Jean-Baptiste Marchand, consisted of only eight French officers and 120 African soldiers. It had taken them two years to march to Fashoda and they were now told, politely but firmly, to go home. This resulted in a crisis in which the two countries almost went to war, and which was finally resolved when the French backed down. On the second page of his memoirs, General de Gaulle listed the disasters that had afflicted France in his youth and that had led him to devote himself to France's greatness: the first on the list was the Fashoda incident. He got his revenge 65 years later when he vetoed Britain's request to join the European Community.

The British set up a new regime, calling the country the Anglo-Egyptian Sudan, but there was never any doubt that Britain was senior partner in that enterprise. Over the next 50 years, there was considerable economic development, particularly the introduction of cotton and sugar plantations. The north was administered in Arabic from Khartoum, and the south was kept entirely separate and was administered in English from Juba.

INDEPENDENCE

In 1953, as the British were reluctantly beginning to evacuate the Middle East, they decided to compel the Egyptians to abandon Sudan. The last British administrators left in 1954 and the country became formally independent in 1956, but by then, the disasters had already begun. In July 1955, a labour dispute in the southern city of Nzara had developed into riots that had to be put down by the police, killing 20 people. In August, the southern corps of the army had mutinied and seized control of the equatorial provinces, except for the capital, Juba, which was held by loyal northern troops. Hundreds of northern traders and officials had been slaughtered before order was restored and the mutineers defeated.

In 1958, the civilian government that the British had set up was overthrown by a military coup. General Ibrahim Abboud made himself president, and set about crushing all opposition, particularly in the south. He actively promoted Arabic as the national language, decreed that Friday, not Sunday, should be the day of rest in the south, expelled Christian missionaries in 1962 and exiled southern politicians.

THE FIRST CIVIL WAR

In 1963, some of the exiles formed a resistance movement, which they named Anya Nya, 'snake venom' in one of the southern languages. The movement won the support of the Dinka tribes and was armed by rebels in the Congo, by the Ethiopians (who objected to the support that the Sudanese had offered the Eritrean rebels), and by Israel which, on general principle, always supported any movement that might divide and divert the Arabs.

The war soon deteriorated into a merciless struggle between Arabs and Africans, like the slave wars of old. No prisoners were ever taken, and the usual estimate of the numbers killed is 400,000. Most of them, of course, were civilians.

The Anya Nya soon controlled most of the southern provinces and periodically occupied small towns and laid siege to government garrisons. In this unequal war, the northerners had access to all the weapons they needed, were far better trained and educated than the southerners, and had also inherited the martial traditions of the Mahdi. However, in so enormous a territory, they could never patrol every village and every forest. The war could not be won, by either side.

On 25 May 1969, there was a new coup. Abboud was summarily removed and replaced by another general, Jaafar Nimeiri. During his subsequent long term in office, he was to prove to be one of the more remarkable African leaders. He liked to wander through the markets of Khartoum early in the morning, listening to the workers there and exhorting them to industry. He was closely allied to Egypt, particularly to Anwar Sadat, and resolutely defended him for making peace with Israel. He was also an implacable enemy of Moammar Khadafy of Libya, who was forever plotting against him, inciting coups, even on one occasion sending a plane to bomb Khartoum. Khadafy's main object was the north-western province of Sudan, the northern Darfur, which he wanted as a base of operations against Chad.

Nimeiri decided to put an end to the war in the south. In 1972, he convoked a conference in Khartoum, to which he invited the southern rebel leaders, and there proposed sweeping concessions to them. The three southern provinces were amalgamated into one, with a regional assembly in Juba that would enjoy almost complete autonomy. The central government reserved defence and foreign affairs to itself, but otherwise left the southerners to their own destiny. The rebels were granted a general amnesty and the Anya Nya troops were incorporated into the regular army.

It was one of the most statesman-like and successful manoeuvres that any African leader has ever accomplished, comparable to the general reconciliation in Nigeria after the Biafran war. Unfortunately, the settlement did not last. Political and economic developments in Khartoum, and the deterioration of Nimeiri's regime, provoked a resumption of the rebellion.

In the years following the end of the civil war, there were repeated attempted coups in Khartoum, fomented by Libya or the opposition. In 1975, a coup attempt by mercenaries hired by Libya was suppressed with great severity: Nimeiri executed

98 people. His principal political opponent, Saddiq el-Mahdi – at one time Nimeiri's prime minister, and great-grandson of the Mahdi, a name to conjure with – led two plots in 1975 and 1976 and was exiled. Later, he was pardoned and, for a number of years, lived peacefully in Khartoum, frequently playing tennis with Nimeiri.

However wise Nimeiri's handling of the southern question at the outset, his government was a failure in all other respects. In particular, he presided over a steady decline in the economy. At independence, Sudan was relatively prosperous, had a sufficiently large educated class to govern the country efficiently, and had enormous potential. It was one of the world's leading producers of cotton and was self-sufficient in grain and sugar. All that has been lost.

Sudan suffers from all the woes of post-colonial Africa but in an extreme degree, exacerbated by the country's vast size and the antagonism between north and south. The government imposes farm prices so low that no farmer can ever benefit from selling his crops. Government resources are devoted to subsidizing city dwellers while the peasants starve. The cotton industry has collapsed, and Sudan now imports sugar.

Nimeiri became increasingly autocratic as the years passed. He also became an extreme Muslim fundamentalist, imposing the *sharia*, the Koranic law code, upon the country. Adulterers were stoned to death, thieves had their hands amputated, and the prohibition against alcohol was extended to medical alcohol in hospitals. In January 1985, Mahmoud Mohammed Taha, a leader of one of the secular parties, the Republican Brotherhood, was publicly hanged in Khartoum for questioning the wisdom of Nimeiri's religious fanaticism.

Nimeiri's authority was flouted in the south, which insisted on maintaining the autonomy he had promised in 1972, and soon there was fighting between dissident tribesmen and northern troops. The drought that afflicted all East Africa and the Sahel (the area just south of the Sahara desert) was particularly severe in Sudan. Millions of starving people crowded into refugee camps, and protested that the central government was doing nothing to save them.

The civil war resumed in 1983. A new organization – the Sudan People's Liberation Army – came into existence, led by Colonel John Garang, an American-educated Christian Dinka. The SPLA began attacks on relief workers, and in February 1985, most foreign relief workers fled the south.

The United States poured hundreds of millions of aid into Sudan to ensure its loyalty – economic aid to the tune of $67 million in 1988 and $77.4 million in 1989, and much larger sums in military aid. The money was enough to keep the government afloat, but not enough to rescue the people. Early in 1985, the United States, Britain, West Germany and Saudi Arabia all suspended their aid programmes and insisted that they would not resume payments unless Nimeiri introduced extensive reforms. The International Monetary Fund (IMF) set harsh terms for its assistance, starting with the demand that food subsidies be ended. There was no hope for the country's economy unless the rural sector revived.

Nimeiri agreed and ended the subsidies in March 1985. He then set out on a foreign tour, culminating in a visit to President Reagan in Washington on 1 April. The Americans then released $67 million in emergency aid. It was too late. During Nimeiri's absence, there were riots against the increase in the price of bread, a general strike and mass demonstrations against the regime. Nimeiri continued his tour. On 6 April, the army high command announced that he had been deposed.

THE NEW SUDAN

The new regime restored the food subsidies. Sudan's economy therefore continues on the same disastrous course, kept afloat by foreign aid, destined to collapse. The government does not dare introduce economic reforms for fear that it would then suffer Nimeiri's fate.

The army called elections in April 1986, a year after the coup, and handed over power to Saddiq el-Mahdi whose Umma party won the largest number of seats in parliament. He has ruled ever since, in a series of unstable coalitions with other parties. The new government at first relaxed Nimeiri's Muslim severity: Mahdi did not have to prove his religious orthodoxy to anyone, his own name was enough. Furthermore, he encouraged freedom of the press and rival political parties. With Botswana far to the south, Sudan was briefly the nearest thing to a real democracy on the continent.

Immediately after the 1985 coup, Sudan resumed diplomatic relations with Libya and Ethiopia, and now accepts large-scale assistance from Khadafy. There is a price: Khadafy, with his usual lack of restraint, meddles ceaselessly in Sudanese affairs. After a border incident, in which Libyan troops attacked Sudanese border guards, there were riots in Khartoum against the Libyans. Sudan has no intention of becoming Khadafy's puppet.

Relations with the United States and Egypt are less cordial than they were under Nimieri. In April 1986, a radio man from the American embassy was shot and severely wounded, apparently in retaliation for the American attack on Libya. The United States promptly withdrew 200 dependants of its embassy personnel. There were no further incidents until May 1988, when Arabs carrying Lebanese passports attacked a hotel and club in Khartoum, killing seven people. The attack was deliberately aimed at foreigners: the dead were a British family of four (the children were aged 3 and 1), a 32-year-old British teacher and two Sudanese. The culprits were arrested.

THE WAR

The war continues. There have been various attempts at negotiations between the government and the SPLA, without success. In July 1986, Mahdi met Garang in Addis Ababa, but broke off the talks the following month, after the shooting down of a civilian airliner by the SPLA. A further round of negotiations was held in London in December 1987, but without result. Garang's army – said to number between 20,000 and 30,000 men – has infiltrated within 200 miles of Khartoum and has threatened the capital's electricity supplies, which come from the Roseires dam on the Blue Nile to the south-east. The government intermittently claims successes against the SPLA: in December 1987, for example, the army claimed a great victory, saying it had killed over 3000 rebels. The following April, however, the SPLA attacked Juba.

Garang has steadily expanded his base beyond his own Dinka tribe. In 1987, he persuaded leaders of the Nuer tribe to join him. Their organization is called Anya Nya II, and is heir to the movement that directed the 1963–72 civil war. In   105 subsequent months, Garang won the support of other southern tribes and, with their aid, in January 1988, occupied a major city, Kapoeta in the far south-west, near the border with Uganda.

The Sudanese army generally stays in the north or safely in garrison towns, and sends Arab militias to fight the SPLA. The militias are based on northern Arab tribes, whose ancestors used to raid south for slaves a century ago. The difference now is that, in their attacks on Dinka and Nuer villages, the raiders are armed with automatic rifles and mortars, and drive in trucks: the Dinka and Nuer men are killed, the women taken away.

According to the Sudanese government in the summer of 1988, there were 3 million people in danger of dying by starvation. Over 300,000 Sudanese had crossed the border into south-western Ethiopia – of all countries in the world, the one least able to help them. They survive thanks only to the efforts of international relief organizations.

If there were no wars in Sudan and Ethiopia, the starving could be fed. As it is, relief organizations are often helpless. In August 1986, the SPLA shot down a Sudan Airways airliner with a Soviet-made SAM-7, killing 60 people; the Red Cross then suspended its airlift into Juba. That meant disaster for the refugees: the roads are so bad, the railway network so decayed, that the only way to move food is often by air. In vast areas of southern Sudan, there is no possibility of sending relief because of the war and the breakdown of communications. Even though the drought broke in the highlands of Ethiopia in July 1988 (and led to severe flooding down the Nile, as far away as Khartoum), its after-effects persist: millions are still in danger of death, and their fate will be decided by the rains of 1989.

People flee the drought and the war. The few thousand who can make it to the camps in Ethiopia are in the last stages of emaciation: 'When they come into the camps, they're not even able to stand. They're walking skeletons,' one refugee official said in April 1988. According to another, 'They compare poorly with pictures of Nazi concentration camp victims and are as bad as or worse than anything seen in Ethiopia during the 1984–5 famine.'

By the end of the year, the situation in southern Sudan was worse than it had been in Ethiopia in 1984. The United States was restrained in its criticism of the Khartoum government, for fear of alienating Mahdi and driving him into the arms of Colonel Khadafy. American relief specialists were less restrained, however, accusing the Sudanese government of following a policy of genocide in the south. Journalists brought back frightful stories and photographs of starvation. They discovered that, as the SPLA maintained its siege of the towns, hoping to starve them out, the army was flying in food to feed its garrisons in the south, but leaving the civilian population in the grip of famine. As for the US State Department's fear of offending Mahdi, as usual it failed in its purpose. The Sudan government sought out Khadafy and was soon one of his most faithful allies.

In 1988, Mahdi reversed himself and started to apply the Koranic code – the *sharia* – and in May, he brought the Islamic Front into the government. It is headed by Hassan al-Turabi, who led the attempt to impose the *sharia* under President Nimeiri. Mahdi was walking the difficult path between Islamic extremism and the need to settle the war, and outside observers were unable to decide on his real intentions. In November, in negotiations in Addis Ababa between representatives of the government and the SPLA, a ceasefire was agreed, on condition that the imposition of the *sharia* be postponed. Simultaneously, Mahdi visited Libya and signed an agreement to merge the two countries.

The agreement with Libya was deeply unpopular with the Sudan army and negotiations with Garang ran into the sands. Mahdi refused to suspend the imposition of the *sharia*, the one essential condition for reconciliation with the south. The economy continued to deteriorate and the war and the famine in the south persisted. The army issued a number of warnings that it could not indefinitely tolerate the continuing disintegration of the country, and on 30 June took power again. The coup was welcomed by Egypt and, discreetly by the United States and Britain.

By then, two million southerners had fled their homes and an equal number were starving. In February 1989, the US State Department reported that between 100,000 and 250,000 people had died of starvation in southern Sudan 'after elements of the armed forces on each side interfered or failed to cooperate with efforts to deliver food supplies to regions controlled by the other side'. It is one of the great disasters of a disastrous decade, and there was not too much hope that the army would be any more successful in ending it than the civilians.

FURTHER READING

American University, *Sudan: A Country Study*, Washington D.C., 1982.
Collins, Robert O., *Egypt and the Sudan*, Englewood Cliff, N. J., Prentice Hall, 1967.
Beshir, Mohammed Omer, *The Southern Sudan, from Conflict to Peace*, London, Hurst, 1975.
Betts, Tristam, *The Southern Sudan, the Cease-fire and After*, London, Africa Publications Trust, 1974.
Lewis, David Levering, *The Race to Fashoda*, London, Bloomsbury, 1988.
Manson, Andrew, *Southern Sudan, a Growing Conflict*, London, The World Today, December, 1984.
Moorehead, Alan, *The Blue Nile*, New York/London, Harper and Row.
Voli, John Obert, *The Sudan: Unity and Diversity in a Multicultural State*, Boulder, Colo., Westview Press, 1985.

UGANDA

Geography	91,134 sq. miles (236,036 sq. km). The size of Great Britain.
Population	15.1 million
GNP per capita	$230 (1984)
Refugees	250,000 'internal refugees' in Uganda, and 96,900 Ugandan refugees in other countries. There are 124,000 refugees from other countries in Uganda (118,000 from Rwanda).
Casualties	About 2000 people were killed in 1966, when Obote suppressed the Baganda. 250,000 to 350,000 people were killed during Idi Amin's presidency. 4000 were killed in the war with Tanzania in 1978–9. Between 1979 and 1986, when Yoweni Musaveni took power, a further 100,000 to 300,000 people were killed. According to a US State Department report in 1989, up to 10,000 people have been killed since then.

Uganda has the unusual distinction of having been destroyed by one man: Field-Marshal President for Life Dr Idi Amin Dada VC. The other countries in the world that have suffered most greatly from wars domestic and foreign, from famines, massacres, pogroms and corruption are usually the victims of ideologies, ethnic rivalries, outside interference and the ambitions and greed of many men. Although Amin's predecessor, Milton Obote, tried to set up a personal dictatorship, and inflicted considerable damage to the country's institutions and economy, the ruin that followed was Idi Amin's personal achievement.

Between 1971 and 1979, while he was president, about 250,000 Ugandans were killed; the entire 80,000-strong community of Asians, who made up the country's commercial class, was expelled; the country's economy was ruined; and the fabric of society was so totally destroyed that it has never recovered.

After Amin was deposed by the Tanzanians, a state of endemic civil war and banditry ensued. Estimates of the numbers killed range from 100,000 to 300,000. Out of this carnage, a new regime finally emerged in 1986, led by the guerrilla leader Yoweni Musaveni. The fighting continued, but in the summer of 1988, the last guerrilla organization surrendered. It is too early to say whether Musaveni will succeed in rebuilding the nation. Sixteen years of disasters have left him very little to build on.

HISTORY

Uganda in the 19th century consisted of a number of tribal kingdoms, of which by far the most important was Buganda, in the south. British explorers, looking for the sources of the Nile, visited Uganda in the middle of the century, and during the scramble for Africa in the 1880s, the British asserted their claims to Kenya, Uganda and Sudan. Uganda became a protectorate in 1894.

The entire period from the first British encroachments in Kenya to independence for Kenya, Uganda and Tanganyika (Tanzania) was shorter than one man's life: Jomo Kenyatta was born in 1889, before the arrival of the British, and for a decade after they left, he presided over independent Kenya until his death in 1978.

The constitution that the British left behind in Uganda in 1963 provided for a ceremonial presidency and an executive prime minister. The first president was the Kabaka (king) of Buganda and the first prime minister was Milton Obote, who was from the Langi tribe. The new nation's first crisis was the mutiny in the army, in January 1964, following mutinies in the Tanzanian and Kenyan armies. They were all put down by British troops. In 1966, Obote deposed the Kabaka, sending Lieutenant Colonel Amin to occupy Kampala; about 2000 Baganda were killed in that operation. Obote needed the army to make him president, but afterwards failed to control it. Amin, by now a major general, staged a coup while Obote was abroad, proclaiming himself president on 21 January 1971.

THE AMIN YEARS

Amin had been recruited into the British East African army from the Kakwa, a small tribe in the easternmost part of the country near the Sudan border. He was a heavyweight boxing champion in the King's East African Rifles, a huge, imposing man who made an excellent drill sergeant. The British recognized some of his abilities and made him an officer, but for many years, they, and Milton Obote, underestimated the ambition and cunning of the large, genial soldier.

Amin realized, from the first, that power grew out of the barrel of a gun, and determined that he would control the guns. His criterion of loyalty was tribal: he recruited his fellow-tribesmen into the army, and also men from other West Nile Province tribes and from neighbouring districts of Sudan and Zaïre. When he made himself president, he consolidated his power by disposing of the soldiers who were members of other tribes, many of them Langi and Acholi. He did so in the most straightforward way possible: he had them killed. By July 1971, he had rid himself of 5000 soldiers, half the army; the rest were killed later. The new army was 40 per cent Muslim, in a nation that was at most 5 per cent Muslim. Half the 25,000 soldiers came from Sudan, a quarter from Zaïre and the remainder were Ugandans from West Nile.

In 1972, Amin abruptly expelled all the East African Asians living in Uganda. They were mostly Indians and had been allowed to retain British citizenship when Uganda became independent. Kenya followed Uganda's example, though far less brutally, and Britain, most reluctantly, allowed most of the expelled Asians to settle there.

The effect on the Ugandan economy was catastrophic. Amin allowed his soldiers to loot the Asians' property, and rewarded his supporters with the jobs and contracts that the Asians had left behind. Few of them were capable of taking over the business and commerce of the Asians, and Uganda, therefore, had to do without. Meanwhile, Amin had established close relations with Moammar Khadafy in Libya, who supplied his fellow Muslim anti-imperialist with arms, training for his special forces, and equipment for his terror apparatus.

Amin, aided by an Englishman, Bob Astles, set up the State Research Bureau (SRB), which conducted sophisticated counter-intelligence operations against opposition groups. It also tortured and murdered people by the thousands. The American terrorist Frank Terpil supplied equipment to the SRB. In 1977, Amnesty International calculated that 300,000 people had died during Amin's reign of terror – which then had a further two years to run.

In June 1975, a British teacher living in Uganda, Denis Hills, was charged with treason and sentenced to death for describing Amin as a 'village tyrant' in an unpublished manuscript. The British government sent Lieutenant General Sir Charles Blair, who had commanded the King's African Rifles when Amin had served in it, and Major Iain Grahame, Amin's former batallion commander, to plead for Hills' life. Amin postponed the execution, and on 20 July, the British foreign secretary, James Callaghan, flew to Kampala to collect Hills. Amin announced: 'This proves that I am not mad, as British newspapers said.' The field-marshal then claimed that this incident made him victor over the British empire, and he awarded himself the Victoria Cross.

On 27 June 1976, Palestinian and West German terrorists hijacked an Air France plane flying from Tel Aviv to Paris, via Athens, and took it to Entebbe airport in Uganda. The Germans – a man and a woman – were members of the Baader–Meinhof gang, the two Arabs members of the Popular Front for the Liberation of Palestine. There were 256 passengers and a 12-man crew on board. Shortly after arriving in Entebbe, the non-Israeli (and non-Jewish) passengers were freed, and sent on to France. The plane's captain stayed with the remaining 89 Israeli passengers and one elderly British lady, Dora Bloch, who was Jewish. Amin welcomed the hijackers, and allowed them to leave the aircraft and move their prisoners into a hangar at the airport; the Ugandan army stood guard while the hijackers negotiated with Israel, France and Britain; other terrorists were permitted to join the original gang. The Ugandans were clearly fully assisting the terrorists.

The Israelis rescued the prisoners on the night of 4 July, with the cooperation of various other governments, notably Kenya, which allowed the three planes on the rescue flight to land and refuel at Nairobi airport on the way back. The four hijackers, nine other terrorists, 35 Ugandan soldiers and one hostage were killed during the Israeli assault. While they were in Entebbe, the Israelis destroyed 11 Ugandan MiGs parked at the airport. It was one of the most skilful, daring and successful military operations in modern times.

Dora Bloch, who was sick, had been taken to hospital in Kampala. She was the only passenger left. Amin sent his troops to find her: they murdered her in the hospital grounds.

Amin killed off everyone who might oppose him who had not already escaped abroad, and that meant a large part of the educated and commercial classes. He killed the chief justice and the chief of staff of the army together. One technique he employed was to chain a score of men together, and hand a club to the second in line. He would be told to kill the first man. The club would be passed to the third, who would kill the second, and so on down the line. The survivor was then shot.

Production dropped by 50 per cent between 1971 and 1978, and the tea, coffee, cotton and sugar plantations have still not recovered. Amin set up a 'Stansted shuttle' between Entebbe and Stansted airport near London, exporting coffee and importing expensive cars, drink, cameras and other luxury goods for himself and his cronies – and for his soldiers who were thus spared the privations and, ultimately, the starvation that afflicted other Ugandans. The planes often stopped at Benghazi in Libya to pick up arms.

Amin's relations with his neighbours were usually bad. Milton Obote had settled in Tanzania and tried to start a guerrilla operation against Amin, but with little success. Amin detested Julius Nyerere, president of Tanzania, and once challenged him to a boxing match to settle their differences, proposing Muhammad Ali as referee, and saying that he would fight with one arm tied behind his back. The challenge was ignored.

On 16 February 1977, the Anglican archbishop of Uganda, Janane Luwum, was murdered on Amin's orders. In May 1978, the Ugandan president had a prominent former Kenyan minister, Bruce McKenzie, assassinated by having a bomb put in his plane. He killed his own wife in 1974. Late in 1977, there was a purge of Amin's inner circle, culminating in the murder of his minister of defence. Frank Terpil later claimed that the man's head had been delivered to Amin on a salver during an official dinner.

THE WAR WITH TANZANIA

Despite Amin's best efforts, there was considerable disaffection in the army – perhaps officers were afraid their turn would come next. In September 1978, possibly to distract them, possibly out of mere blind folly, Amin invaded Tanzania.

He laid claim to a small packet of territory in the extreme north-west of Tanzania, west of Lake Victoria: the Kagera salient. There were various border incidents, all provoked by Uganda, and on 30 September, Amin sent his army across the frontier in force. They advanced 20 miles (32 km) and killed about 1500 civilians.

Tanzania was quite unprepared for war. There was one brigade of the Tanzanian army capable of action, but it had to be moved 1500 miles (2400 km) by rail and road to reach the front. Despite this poor beginning, the Tanzanians managed to expand their armed forces to 75,000 men in four months, train and equip them adequately, and conduct a proper military campaign that ended with the occupation of Uganda. The fact that the Ugandans never showed any willingness to fight should not diminish the Tanzanians' considerable achievement. Their only serious failure occurred when Tanzanian anti-aircraft batteries shot down three of their own MiGs by mistake.

The Kagera salient was liberated in November. On 21 January 1979, the Tanzanians crossed the border into Uganda, and began the march on Kampala. Their main difficulties turned out to be communications and supplies but the latter problem was solved by the huge quantities of weaponry and material that they captured from the Ugandans, everything from trucks to tanks. They also shot down 19 Ugandan planes in January–February, and after that the Ugandan air force abandoned the fight.

The Tanzanians were joined in the invasion by a small army of Obote's supporters, headed by Titus Okello, and by an independent guerrilla force headed by Yoweni Musaveni.

Colonel Khadafy sent a contingent of 2000 Libyan troops (mostly militia, not regular army) to Amin's rescue, and they joined a small contingent of PLO terrorists who had been training in Uganda. In March, in the only considerable battle of the war, the Libyans counter-attacked against the Tanzanians. Of the 1000 Libyans involved, 200 were killed and one was taken prisoner: the Tanzanian political officers had told their troops that the Arabs were returning to Africa to restore the slave trade. A further 300 Libyans were killed in the capture of Entebbe.

Entebbe fell on 7 April 1979 and Kampala on 10 April. The city was then looted by its citizens, with Tanzanian assistance. Every shop, every office, every empty house (and many inhabited ones that were inadequately defended) were stripped bare. (The Tanzanians had great difficulty finding even a dozen or so chairs for the official party when they swore in the new government on 13 April.) When they examined the State Research Bureau, they discovered that the basement was filled with corpses and the offices packed with expensive electronic equipment and endless reports on opposition activities, much of it exceedingly accurate.

Ugandan exiles had formed a National Liberation Front, and agreed to appoint as president Yusufu Lule, a distinguished academic, believed to be acceptable to the various tribes and factions. He arrived in Kampala in the Tanzanians' baggage and was set up in office. However, he never exercised any authority: there was none to exercise. The government was a phantom. Lule tried to make appointments without consulting the Liberation Front, which deposed him on 19 June 1979. He was replaced by Godfrey Binaisa, with Yoweni Musaveni as minister of defence. The new president was as powerless as the old.

The Tanzanians, meanwhile, completed the occupation of Uganda. They proceeded cautiously, fearing that Amin would make a last stand somewhere, perhaps in his home village, but in fact, he had fled the country as the Tanzanians reached Kampala. He eventually took refuge in Saudi Arabia.

During the war, approximately 4000 people were killed: 373 Tanzanian soldiers; 150 Ugandan rebels fighting alongside the Tanzanians; 600 Libyans; 1000 of Amin's troops; 1500 Tanzanian civilians massacred by Ugandan troops; and about 500 Ugandan civilians.

AFTER AMIN

A reign of terror began immediately after the end of the war. Amin's army disintegrated, but the soldiers remained heavily armed and took to banditry. The opposing guerrilla armies were incapable of imposing order, so there was none. Amin's soldiers, based in Sudan and Zaïre, organized raids across the border, slaughtering civilians and any unarmed soldiers they could find.

The victors began to fight among themselves: Binaisa was deposed by the army on 12 May 1980. The following December, there were elections that were blatantly fraudulent; despite this, Milton Obote claimed to have won and was proclaimed president. The most competent Ugandan guerrilla leader, Yoweni Musaveni, took to the bush, where he formed the National Resistance Army and began a civil war. The Ugandan army, led by the elderly general Titus Okello, proved quite incapable of defeating Musaveni or suppressing the Amin bandits. The Tanzanians pulled their last troops out of Uganda in June 1981, Nyerere insisting that it was not his job to police neighbouring countries.

Obote hung on to power, spending his time wreaking revenge on his many enemies, and trying to rebuild his power on the basis of his own tribe. As a result, Uganda succumbed to total anarchy. Musaveni's NRA extended its control over most of the south and west of the country, and fought a brutal war against Okello's troops north of Kampala. In 1985 there were student riots which Obote suppressed with great brutality. The final straw was a split in the army between Obote's Langi tribesmen and the Acholi.

Obote was deposed by Okello on 27 July 1985, and fled back to Tanzania. Okello's army immediately disintegrated, just as Amin's army had six years earlier. His troops took to the bush, carrying their weapons, and a new round of banditry and civil war began. After six months of fruitless negotiation between Okello and Musaveni, the government collapsed and Musaveni proclaimed a government of national unity, making himself president on 29 January 1986.

Musaveni was able to bring some semblance of order to the southern part of the country, but the north and west were abandoned to the bandits, who now called themselves the Uganda People's Democratic Army and may have numbered 40,000. Between the overthrow of Amin and Musaveni's victory, at least 100,000 people were killed, although one estimate has put the deaths as high as 600,000.

A new contributor to the general confusion was Alice Lakwena, the prophetess and leader of a sect called the Holy Spirit Movement, based on the Acholi tribe in northern Uganda. In 1985, it sallied forth to fight the government. Lakwena assured her followers invincibility, but in August 1987, government troops killed 400 Holy Spirit warriors in one battle. By the end of the year, Lakwena's movement had been broken up, her army, which had numbered about 7000 at the height of its power, reduced to about 500. Lakwena took refuge in Kenya, where she was imprisoned for three months, and then released.

Relations between Uganda and its neighbours have continued to be difficult. In December 1987, at least 15 people were killed in fighting along the border with Kenya, and the border was closed for a few days.

In the spring of 1988, Musaveni's troops returned to northern Uganda, and induced 8000 members of the Uganda People's Democratic Army to accept an amnesty and to surrender. Other UPDA leaders refused to recognize the ceasefire and fighting continued, particularly in the east.

The government established a commission into past atrocities, which began to hold public hearings in Kampala. The evidence offered to the commission was as grisly as anything in Pol Pot's Cambodia, or in Zaïre immediately after independence. Government agents started collecting the bones of tens of thousands of people who had been murdered and whose bodies had been left in the killing fields. Normal life resumed in Kampala, and gradually spread to the countryside, but Uganda's polity remains exceedingly fragile, suffering as it does from an extreme form of two of Africa's curses: corruption and tribalism. Government officials who survived the repeated wars, massacres, purges and revolutions have lost all respect for the public good, and steal everything they can lay their hands on. The tribal animosities, which had been stirred up by Obote and Amin, and which led to the worst of the massacres, have not been appeased. Musaveni may have won the battle, but winning the peace will be far more difficult.

FURTHER READING

American University, *Uganda: A Country Study*, Washington D.C., 1969.
Avirgan, Tony and Honey, Martha, *War in Uganda: The Legacy of Idi Amin*, Westport, Conn, L. Hill, 1982.
Jorgenson, Jan Jelmert, *Uganda: A Modern History*, New York, St Martin's Press, 1981.
Mamdani, Mahmoud, *Imperialism and Fascism in Uganda*, Trenton, N.J., African World Press, 1984.
Minority Rights Group, *Uganda and Sudan*, London, 1984.
Mittleman, James H., *Ideology and Politics in Uganda from Obote to Amin*, Ithaca, N.Y., Cornell University Press, 1975.
Moorehead, Alan, *The White Nile*, New York/London, Harper and Row, 1960.
Smith, George Ivan, *Ghosts of Kampala*, New York, St Martin's Press, 1980.

ASIA

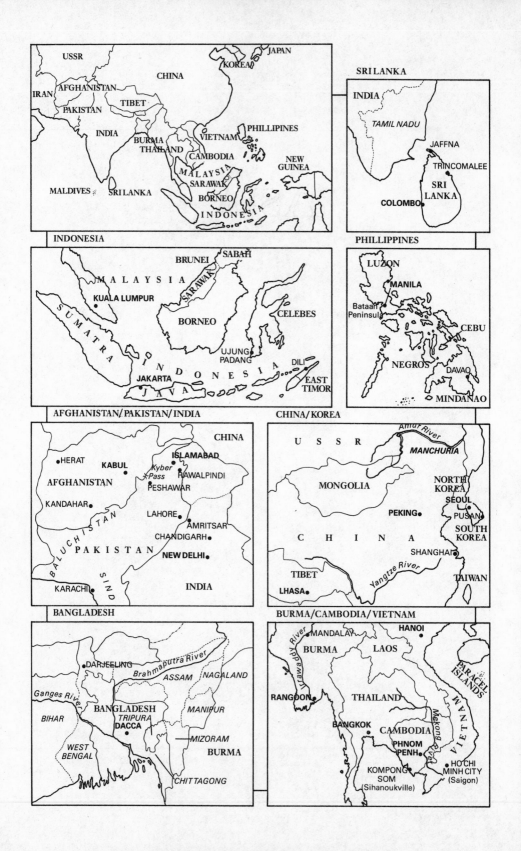

AFGHANISTAN

Geography	251,000 sq. miles (637,000 sq. km). The same size as Texas, and twice the size of Italy.Half the country is at an altitude of over 6000 ft (1800 m); one-fifth of it is desert. The mountains of the Hindu Kush ('Killer of Hindus'), an extension of the Himalayas, run 600 miles (960 km) from east to west, cutting the country in half; their average height is 13,500 ft (4000 m). In the north-east is the Pamir Knot, among the highest mountains in the world, with over 100 peaks between 20,000 and 25,000 ft (6000–7500 m) high.
Population	Estimates range from 8 million to 19 million. In 1979, the population was computed at 15.5 million, and the most numerous tribes were:

Pushtun (Pathan)	6,500,000
Tadzhik	3,500,000
Uzbek	1,000,000
Hazara	870,000
Aimaq	800,000
Farsiwan	600,000
Baluchi	100,000

	There are also a dozen less numerous tribes. The Tadzhik and Uzbek are cousins to major nations in Soviet Central Asia, the Pushtun are equally divided between Afghanistan and Pakistan, while the Baluchi extend into Pakistan and Iran. There are also numerous languages, the two principal ones being·Pushtu and Dari, a dialect of Persian.
GNP per capita	$160
Refugees	At the end of 1988, the US Committee for Refugees counted 7.6 million Afghan refugees. Internal: 2 million. External: 2.35 million in Iran; 3,272,000 in Pakistan; 5200 in India.
Casualties	The USSR lost about 15,000 killed. In May 1988, it counted 311 missing and 35,478 wounded. Estimates of the number of Afghans killed differ wildly, running from 100,000 to 1 million. The latter figure is favoured by the US government, and is certainly too high, even if it is taken to include those who have died of famine or preventable disease in either Afghanistan or the refugee camps. Even before the war, one in five Afghan children died before the age of 5.

Afghanistan had the misfortune to mark the high tide of Soviet expansionism. It was the last place where a small band of revolutionaries, with Soviet aid, overthrew the government and established a Communist state, and it was the last to which the Soviets applied the 'Brezhnev Doctrine'. This stated that once a country had adopted Communism, the Socialist Motherland would guarantee that it would always remain Communist (*see* Eastern Europe [Czechoslovakia] pp. 364–65).

History will credit the Afghans with being the first people to defeat a Soviet army of occupation and drive it out. The Communist coup occurred in April 1978, and was followed by a general uprising against the new government. It soon became apparent that the regime could not sustain itself without Soviet help, so for 18 months, the Soviets poured money, arms and advisers into Afghanistan, but still the government was losing the civil war. Furthermore, Afghan Communists were bitterly divided into two factions which fought a murderous war against each other. Finally, in December 1979, the Soviets invaded Afghanistan, set up a puppet government in Kabul and went to war with the rebels. They were never able to dominate the countryside and put down the rebellion. A succession of elderly Soviet leaders was faced with the fact that they had embarked upon a pointless war that was unpopular at home and had a disastrous effect upon their international image. In 1988, Mikhail Gorbachev cut the Gordian knot and simply withdrew. The last Soviet soldier crossed the border back to the USSR on 15 February 1989.

The country was left desolate, and was faced with the problem of resettling over 5 million refugees, most of whose homes have been destroyed. In the short run, Afghanistan will, like Lebanon, continue to suffer all the horrors of civil war, and it is not clear whether outside powers, starting with the Soviet Union, will leave the Afghans to fight it out alone. The world will probably turn to other concerns, the chief of which is whether the Soviets have learned their lesson and will now retreat freely from their other unwilling colonies, or wait until they are pushed out.

HISTORY

Afghanistan, like many other countries in the world, is a wholly artificial creation. It is a geographical expression, an area on the map with arbitrary boundaries, inhabited by peoples who have spent most of history fighting each other. The largest tribe of the Afghans are the Pushtun, known to the British as the Pathan, who make up about one-third of the population of Afghanistan. However, half the Pushtun live in Pakistan, and none of the tribe in either country recognizes the frontier. Hillmen do not consider the high mountains to be barriers: that is a plainsman's delusion. And the Oxus river, which now separates Afghanistan from the Soviet Union, only became a frontier dividing cousins living on opposite sides when the Russians arrived 100 years ago.

The territory that is now Afghanistan has usually been part of some larger empire. Those empires included areas of Central Asia that are now in the Soviet Union, part or all of Iran, and the Punjab, most of which is now in Pakistan. In ancient times, Afghanistan was part of the Persian empire; it was then conquered by Alexander, and later its tribes conquered all of Persia and Mesopotamia, and the Punjab as well. The Mongols passed that way, as did Tamburlaine, the lame shepherd from Samarkand who conquered everything from Delhi to Anatolia and put the Turkish sultan in a cage. In the 16th century, Babur the Tiger, a descendant of both Genghiz Khan and Tamburlaine conquered north India and established the Moghul empire at Delhi. He chose to be buried in Kabul, and one of his descendants built the Taj Mahal at Agra as a tomb for his wife.

In the 18th and 19th centuries, the British conquered India but never seriously attempted to extend their empire beyond the Khyber Pass. They did invade Afghanistan twice, in 1838 and in 1878. The first war ended in one of the great disasters of British imperial history: the expeditionary force was wiped out during its retreat from Kabul, and the king they had installed in Kabul was murdered. In 1878, when the British occupied Afghanistan again, they again discovered that they could not hold it, and therefore withdrew – this time successfully. One of the many errors of the Soviet leaders was that they never studied the history of Afghanistan.

The British designated it a buffer state between Russia and India, and the Russians accepted the designation. The frontiers were drawn to separate the two empires, even though that involved adding a finger of territory in the east which now joins Afghanistan to China through some of the highest mountains in the world. A dynasty that had established a kingdom in Kabul south of the Hindu Kush in the 18th century was allowed to extend its territory to the north, as far as the Oxus river, and became the rulers of the new kingdom.

After the Russian Revolution in 1917, the new Soviet government continued the policy of the tsars – to leave well enough alone. Until the British left India, Afghanistan was a British client state that maintained good relations with the Soviet Union. Its time of troubles began with India's independence in 1947.

British India was partitioned, and Pakistan inherited the frontiers that the British had established. The Afghan government, which had acquiesced in the British cutting the Pushtun territories in two, promptly raised an irredentist claim against Pakistan. It demanded that the Northwest Frontier Province be given the right of self-determination – which Afghanistan believed would mean its annexation to Afghanistan. Pakistan adamantly refused to consider the frontier question, and as a result, there has been constant hostility between the two countries. Afghanistan turned for support to its neighbour in the north. The United States was already allied to Pakistan, and therefore supported its retention of Pashtunistan, and so the Soviets agreed to support the Afghans.

They became the major suppliers of aid to Afghanistan, including military aid, although the United States contributed to the building of the road network that opened up the country. The most remarkable feat of engineering was accomplished by the Soviets: they built a road through the Hindu Kush, including the mile-long (1.6 km) Salang tunnel at 10,000 feet (3000 m), which connected Kabul to the Soviet frontier.

A group of radical intellectuals founded the People's Democratic Party of Afghanistan (PDPA) on 1 January 1965; its principal leaders were Nur Mohammed Taraki and Babrak Karmal. Four years later, the party split between two factions: Khalq ('The Masses') led by Taraki; and Parcham ('The Banner') led by Babrak – the names for the factions originating with those of newspapers that the two men had edited. The Khalqis were Leninists who aimed to build a small, tightly knit and militant party that would form the vanguard of the proletariat, seize power as soon as possible and force Communism upon the country. Parcham believed that Afghanistan was not ready for Communism, and advocated a gradualist approach.

119

There was another reason for the split. Khalq members were mostly sons of Pushtu-speaking peasants and nomads. Parcham's supporters and leaders, on the other hand, mostly came from the cities, and spoke Dari, a form of Persian. Taraki's father was a herdsman, Babrak's was a general. Taraki was for a while press attaché at the embassy in Washington. Hafizullah Amin, the most extreme of Khalq leaders, had studied at Teachers' College of Columbia University in New York during the turbulent 1960s.

The Soviet Union, despite its own Leninist antecedents, considered that Afghanistan was not ripe for Communism – for a start, it had no proletariat. Therefore, the USSR supported the Parchamis. Unfortunately, Khalq was better led and more successful, particularly in recruiting from among the armed forces.

From 1953 to 1963, the Afghan government was headed by Sardar Mohammed Daoud Khan, a cousin and brother-in-law of King Zahir Shah. He strenuously campaigned against Pakistan on the Pushtun issue and expanded relations with the Soviet Union; he also encouraged cautious economic and political development. In 1963, the king asserted himself, dismissed Daoud and took over. His subsequent rule was unremarkable: he was as authoritarian as Daoud but less competent. A famine in 1972 killed 100,000 people, and the following year, when Zahir Shah was out of the country, Daoud staged a *coup d'état* and established a republic.

He did so with the aid of the Parcham faction of the PDPA, presumably with the connivance of the Soviet Union. However, during his second period in office, he moved away from previous dependence on the USSR and improved relations with Pakistan, at the urging of the shah of Iran who had ambitions of leading an alliance of the three countries. The reconciliation with Pakistan was not easy. Both President Bhutto and President Zia aided Pushtun guerrillas who were fighting Daoud, and Zia showed particular affection for the Muslim extremists among them who considered Daoud a dangerous Communist because of his reform measures.

In the mid-1970s, Daoud tried to purge the Parchamis, but by then, the PDPA had become well established in the army. In April 1978, after a mass PDPA demonstration in Kabul, Daoud arrested the leading leftists. On 27 April, their allies in the armed forces staged a coup against the president. He was killed defending his palace, and most of his family massacred.

The PDPA leaders were released from jail and took over the government. Taraki, the Khalq leader, became president and his closest associate, Hafizullah Amin, quickly became the dominant figure in the regime. In July, ten leading members of the Parcham faction, including Babrak Karmal, were sent abroad as ambassadors. Babrak was sent to Prague. In August, the remaining Parcham leaders were arrested, some of them tortured and killed, and the ambassadors were all summoned home. They wisely refused, and went to Moscow.

Taraki and Amin now set about Communizing Afghanistan at full tilt. They reformed the system of land tenure, the status of women and the usury laws. The first of their decrees began with the ritual words 'In the Name of God the Compassionate' but that formula was soon dropped. The first signs of disaffection occurred as early as May 1978, a month after the revolution, and the first full-scale insurrection broke out in the east in September and soon spread across the whole country. On 12 March 1979, one of the resistance groups, the National Liberation Front, declared a *jihad* – a holy war – against the godless government in Kabul.

The Soviets attempted to persuade the Khalq to conciliate the opposition, to work with traditional leaders. That was how they had established their control over Central Asia after the Revolution, and they believed that it was the only way to convert fanatic and backward Muslim peasants to the merits of Communism.

Taraki and Amin went to Moscow in December 1978 to sign a treaty of friendship, good neighbourliness and cooperation, which contained a clause promising military assistance. Under this clause, a year later, the Soviets killed Amin.

Amin, increasingly influential in the government, was determined to push ahead with the revolution. He grew suspicious of the Soviets, and there were also some signs that he wanted a reconciliation with the United States to counterbalance Soviet influence. He saw a great deal of the American ambassador, Adolph Dubs, but on 14 February 1979, Dubs was kidnapped, apparently by Maoist extremists, who held him prisoner and demanded the release of some of their comrades from jail. Instead of negotiating with them, security forces stormed the hotel room where Dubs was held and he was killed. The regime offered the United States no condolences and no apologies for the incident. That ended American interest in Afghanistan. The Americans were also preoccupied by events in Iran (the Shah had fled the previous month).

In March 1979, an uprising of Shiites (under the influence of revolutionary Iran) in Herat, capital of west Afghanistan, resulted in the killing of over 100 Soviets, some of whom were also tortured horribly. Although government forces recaptured the city, killing 3000 to 5000 people, it was clear that the country was progressively sliding into anarchy.

The Soviets greatly increased their presence during the year, taking over security in the cities and administrating many government departments. In July, they deployed their first combat unit in Afghanistan, north of Kabul. They also looked for ways to replace Amin. They persuaded Taraki that Amin was a danger to him. Taraki had been progressively excluded from all authority (he was reputedly in an alcoholic daze most of the time), and on 14 September 1979, he tried to assassinate his prime minister. He invited Amin to a meeting, and his guards tried to shoot him as he mounted the steps of the presidential palace. Amin rolled down the steps and escaped, called up the tanks, and had Taraki arrested. Two days later, the government announced that he had resigned all his posts – 'for health reason'. On 10 October, the *Kabul Times* published a short article on the back page stating that 'Taraki died yesterday morning of a serious illness, which he had been suffering for some time.' The illness, according to one well-informed observer, 'was lack of oxygen, brought on by the application of fingers to the neck and pillows over the nose and mouth, by three members of the palace guard.'

Amin made himself president. He controlled very little of the government, however, and the government controlled very little of the country. General Ivan Pavlovsky, the Soviet officer who had organized the invasion of Czechoslovakia in 1968, paid a two-month visit to Afghanistan in August–September. Feeling the noose tightening around him, Amin tried to play the Pakistani card, and talked about reconciliation with Pakistan and the United States. However, when Zia hesitated to welcome the prodigal, he swung around completely and announced that he would arm anti-Pakistani and anti-Khomeini guerrillas.

121

By one account, the Soviets tried to kidnap Amin on 26 December 1979, by drugging his food and arresting him. The plot failed. On 27 December, Soviet troops occupied military bases, radio stations and government buildings in Kabul and elsewhere. They went to arrest Amin, but like Daoud Khan before him, he refused to surrender. And like Daoud (or Salvador Allende in Chile), he either was shot or committed suicide.

Babrak Karmal, who had been living in exile for 18 months under Soviet control, was brought back to head the government, like other Communists brought in the baggage of the Red Army in Eastern Europe in 1945. The Soviets set about building a new government, with new policies, and also tried to restore some semblance of security to the country. They failed completely at all these tasks.

THE SOVIET OCCUPATION, 1979–89

In 1988, as the Soviets prepared to abandon Afghanistan, the Gorbachev regime put it about that the decision to invade Afghanistan in 1979 had been taken by half a dozen officials, on the spur of the moment, perhaps when they were all drunk. By a nice coincidence, all those officials (including former President Andrei Gromyko) are now dead.

This is the sort of damage control that all governments try. It is quite incredible. The invasion had involved prolonged forward planning and followed an 18-month period during which the Soviet Union had plunged into Afghanistan, its eyes wide open. This had not been the act of a small cabal, but the considered act of a government.

Why did they do it? One explanation – the one favoured by American hawks and those who cannot read a map – can be firmly ruled out. It had nothing to do with Soviet designs upon the Persian Gulf. If they ever wish to close the Straits of Hormuz, they must first defeat and occupy Iran – and they would do that directly, not via a detour through the Hindu Kush. Occupying Afghanistan as the first step to attacking Tehran would be like the United States invading Canada via Alaska. The Soviet invasion of Afghanistan was stupid, but not that stupid.

Nor is it likely that they had any direct designs on Pakistan, if only because success in Pakistan would immediately entail implacable conflict with India while bringing no tangible advantage whatever. They already have a naval base in the Indian Ocean, in Aden, and much good it has done them.

Another suggestion is that the Soviets were afraid of the spread of Islamic fundamentalism from Iran into Soviet Central Asia by way of Afghanistan. But they were already deeply involved in Afghanistan before the fall of the shah. Fear of the fundamentalists may have played a part in keeping them in Afghanistan – but in the event, Soviet intervention has enormously strengthened Afghan fundamentalism and, furthermore, has ruined any hope the Soviets may have entertained of supplanting the Americans in the affections of the Iranians.

The simplest explanation is probably the best. They got sucked into Afghanistan much as the United States got sucked into Vietnam, without clearly thinking through the consequences of their actions, and wildly underestimating the hostility they would arouse. In 1979, it appeared to them that their position within Afghanistan was collapsing, together with the regime. Unless they intervened, Amin would be swept away and Afghanistan would either lapse into anarchy or become fervently anti-Soviet.

Either event would represent the defeat of a policy going back to Lenin, or the tsars.

Lastly, Leonid Brezhnev and his geriatric crew were probably terrified of being the first Soviet leaders to 'lose' a country that had chosen the road to socialism. Never mind that the Communist coup was the work of a few officers and intellectuals and represented only a tiny minority of the population. Afghanistan had a Communist government, and Brezhnev was determined that it would not be overthrown. He may have thought that there was a parallel with events in Hungary in 1956 or in Czechoslovakia in 1968: on both occasions, the government had lost control, but the situation had been saved by the Red Army. After a few months of turmoil, the two countries had settled down and the world community had accepted the event.

They probably expected the same thing to happen in Afghanistan. An overwhelming display of Soviet might would cow the opposition, and then economic assistance, a more subtle policy and the passage of time would reconcile the Afghans to their new form of government. It was a gross miscalculation. It is also worth observing that 30 years after the Hungarian intervention and 20 years after the crushing of the Prague Spring, the USSR and Communism remain utterly detested in both countries.

THE SOVIETS AND THE MUJAHEDDIN

Babrak Karmal broadcast an appeal for Soviet help on 27 December 1979 – from a radio station inside the Soviet Union. His hosts have insisted ever since that they were 'invited' to intervene, by the government of Afghanistan. It is one of the more brazen falsehoods of modern times. Babrak was the complete puppet, who never uttered a word or issued an order that his Soviet masters had not prepared for him. He was so compliant, and therefore so unpopular, that the Soviets finally deposed him on 4 May 1986 and replaced him with Mohammed Najib, a former head of the police, whom they hoped would be a more presentable and competent figurehead. They proved mistaken. Najib was no more able than Babrak to win popular support. For example, although head of a country of profound religious faith, Najib chose to change his name – Najibullah, meaning 'Noble Man of God' – because it was too religious. (He changed it back when he became president.)

The Soviets soon discovered that they had to rule Afghanistan directly. There were simply not enough Afghan Communists left to do the job after the murders, executions and massacres of the previous few years, and Khalq and Parcham continued to fight each other with all the ferocity of a tribal vendetta.

In the wake of the invasion, the whole country rose against the government. The Soviet army held Kabul, but the rebels, known as *mujaheddin* ('holy warriors'), held Kandahar and Herat, the country's second and third largest cities. The Soviets had to retake them with bombers and tanks, and according to one observer, 'in Kandahar, they staged a brutal, block-by-block World War II-style assault.'

The Afghan army collapsed as an effective fighting force, its numbers dropping from about 90,000–100,000 in 1979 to 30,000 by early 1981. Whole units deserted together, taking their weapons with them, and those remaining soldiers who could be cowed or blackmailed into obedience were worthless in a fight.

Soviet troops could take any town or village or valley, but they could not hold them without increasing enormously their forces in Afghanistan. They never had more than 120,000 troops there (compared with over 550,000 Americans in Vietnam at the height of that war), and this was not nearly enough. Possibly they feared having too many casualties. Possibly the Soviet army, suffering severely from the consequences of the falling Soviet birthrate and the enormous needs of guarding the frontiers and occupying Eastern Europe, simply could not find enough troops.

Since they could not spare a million men, they settled for the essential minimum – just enough to hold the main cities and keep the lines of communication open. For the rest of their new fiefdom, they relied on the air force. Rebel areas were bombed mercilessly. Mines were scattered across the countryside, some of them allegedly disguised as toys that children might collect. (There are certainly many legless and armless children in refugee camps.) The Soviets also sent armoured columns into the valleys and destroyed the villages, irrigation works, roads and bridges. It was a policy of scorched earth. Their ambition was to make a solitude and call it peace.

They failed. They drove over 3 million refugees into Pakistan and 2 million into Iran, but once the men had ensured their families' safety, they returned to the fight. They learned to handle modern weapons and, more remarkably, they learned modern tactics – especially the need to obey and to collaborate with other Afghans. They ambushed Soviet convoys, in country uniquely suited to ambushes; they attacked isolated bases and air strips. They infiltrated Kabul and attacked the Soviet embassy, the PDPA headquarters, the Soviet military high command. The Afghan governor of Kandahar lived and worked in a Soviet base. The Mujaheddin even mounted expeditions across the Oxus into the Soviet Union.

The Soviets were never able to conquer the high mountains in the centre of the country – the Hazarajat, comprising a quarter of the total area. Instead, Soviet troops cut off food supplies to starve the people living there. There are hundreds of passes across the mountains into Pakistan. The Soviets tried to block the more important by garrisoning forts in the valleys leading to them. The Mujaheddin laid siege to the forts.

At Christmas 1987, in their last offensive, the Soviets mounted an elaborate rescue of one of the besieged forts, at Khost, 100 miles (160 km) south of Kabul. A heavily armed convoy fought its way into the town to deliver supplies. The Soviet troops then fought their way out again, leaving Khost once more under siege.

A certain caution is necessary when examining atrocity reports and estimates of casualties. At one stage, the United States government insisted that the Soviets used poison gas on the Afghans, but there was never any evidence to support the allegation, and in fact, the same one was made concerning the Vietnamese in Laos, with the same lack of evidence. Reports of booby-trapped toys allegedly scattered across the countryside are also rather dubious.

Seven political parties have since emerged among the Afghan resistance. They are:

- *Hizb-i-Islami* (Islamic Party), led by Yunis Khalis; strong among the Pushtun of Jalalabad. Not to be confused with Hekmatyar's party of the same name (*see below*).
- *Hizb-i-Islami* (Islamic Party), led by Gulbuddin Hekmatyar, which Louis Dupree of the American University describes as pragmatic, opportunistic, revolutionary; mainly Pushtun.

- *Jamiat Islami* (Islamic Society), led by Burnahuddin Rabani, revolutionary Islamic; dominated by non-Pushtuns but including Pushtuns, spread throughout the country.
- *Itehad-i-Islam-Baray Azadi Afghanistan* (Islamic Alliance to Liberate Afghanistan), led by Abdul Rasul Sayyaf, traditionalist.
- *Islami Melli Mahaz* (National Islamic Front), led by Pir Sayyid Ahmad Gailani, modernist, moderate, pro-monarchy; mainly Pushtun in the south and east.
- *Jabahai-yi-Nijat Melli* (National Liberation Front), led by Sigbratullah Mojadidi, traditionalist, pro-monarchy; strong in the south and east around Kandahar.
- *Harakat-i-Inqelab-i-Islami* (Islamic Revolutionary Movement), led by Maulawi Mohammad Mohammadi, mildly revolutionary; strongest in the south-west and west.

In May 1985, the seven came together in Peshawar in a united front, calling themselves the *Islami-Itehad-Afghanistan Mujaheddin* (Islamic Unity of Afghan Warriors, or I U A W), known as the Unity. The parties did not merge. The presidency of the Unity rotated between the seven leaders, with three-month terms. They met to work out a common line, following traditional Afghan tribal practice.

The seven are predominantly Sunni Muslim. Another alliance of four resistance movements was based in Iran, and commanded the allegiance of Afghanistan's Shiites. They controlled much of the centre of the country, and had little contact with the Peshawar Seven.

Between them, the rebel armies of the Unity claimed to have about 150,000 troops in the field, with a comparable number in reserve. Inside Afghanistan, commanders emerged from the ranks. One of these was Ahmad Shah Massoud, who commanded rebels in the Panjsher valley in north-east Afghanistan. He was a brilliantly successful commander, and because his sphere of operations was relatively accessible, he became better known to the outside world than the other leaders. Every year the Soviets mounted offensives against him, with up to 20,000 troops. They occupied the valley, but could not pursue Massoud and his men into the mountains, whence they returned when the Soviets withdrew. It was a pattern repeated throughout the war – only each time it required more Soviet troops, because Massoud's forces improved steadily in number, equipment and training.

One list of resistance leaders included (besides Massoud): Abdul Haq in Kabul, Ismail Khan in Herat, Mullah Maleng in Kandahar, and Jallaluddin Haqqani in Paktia. They are members of either the Islamic Party led by Khalis or the Islamic Society led by Rabani. According to Professor Dupree, these are the two most important and powerful resistance groups because of their strong support inside the country, as opposed to Hekmatyar's group and the monarchists who are prominent in Peshawar but count for much less in the interior.

There is a running dispute between experts on Afghanistan concerning the relative strengths of the various resistance movements. Professor Dupree maintained that the interior resistance groups would work out their differences and set up a coalition government once the Soviets withdrew and the Afghan government 125 was defeated. A less optimistic view was that the conspicuous lack of unity among the seven groups in Peshawar and the continuing, bitter divisions inside Afghanistan along tribal, language and ideological lines would inevitably result in savage civil war. This was no Vietnam, with a single, dedicated revolutionary party. It was a civil war in embryo, with the rebels united only by detestation of the foreigner and his puppets.

Furthermore, according to the pessimists, the party most likely to win was that led by Hekmatyar, which was as hostile to the United States as it was to the Soviet Union, and would turn Afghanistan into an Islamic republic and slaughter all opposition.

The remaining armed forces in Afghanistan were, of course, those of the Communist Party (PDPA). Its forces, heavily armed and trained by the Soviets, numbered about 100,000. There were reports that the Soviets had issued passports to the PDPA cadres, permitting them to escape to the USSR if the regime collapsed.

From the beginning, the United States played a large part in helping the resistance. Arms were first sent to the Mujaheddin by the Carter administration; the quantity was increased steadily during the Reagan administration; and by the mid-1980s, all pretence that this was a secret operation had been dropped. The US spent a total of $3 billion (in the end, $600 million a year) helping the Afghan rebels, and Saudi Arabia, China and other countries together spent another billion. In 1986, the US started delivering Stinger (American) and Blowpipe (British) anti-aircraft missiles in large numbers, and by the summer of 1987, by some accounts, the Soviets were losing one plane or helicopter a day to these missiles. As a result, they could no longer fly low over Afghan villages and strafe them, but instead had to bomb from a great height, which meant they could not give close support to their convoys on the ground. The Stinger in particular proved a lethally effective weapon. Some of the Mujaheddin sold their Stingers to Iran for use against Iraq or even against the United States.

One consequence of the war has been the collapse of the effort to eradicate opium cultivation in Afghanistan and Pakistan. According to the US State Department's 1988 report on narcotics, Afghanistan now produces between 400 and 800 tons of opium a year, second only to Burma. It is quite possible that this is an underestimate: for obvious reasons, exact measurements are difficult. There is now an extensive opium trade across the Khyber Pass, and the Afghans, whatever side they support, participate in the world's largest entrepôt of smuggled goods. The effects on Pakistan have been, in the short term, to increase national income hugely and, in the long term, to corrupt the regime and the people and to promote addiction and crime.

DIPLOMACY

The invasion of Afghanistan proved a disaster for the USSR. For years, the United Nations had supported every Soviet resolution denouncing the West, but after the invasion, the UN voted every year, by increasing majorities (119 to 19, 130 to 19), to denounce the occupation, naming the Soviet Union and demanding that it pull out its troops. Fidel Castro supported the Soviets in public but, in private, lamented that his own influence in the world collapsed. He had hoped to be elected chairman of the Non-Aligned Movement at a meeting in New Delhi in 1982, but instead, he met vigorous criticism for his support of the Soviet Union. The only truly non-aligned country to refrain from criticizing the USSR was India, whose animosity towards Pakistan overrode all other considerations.

The invasion also destroyed the Soviet Union's *détente* with the United States. The SALT II treaty, laboriously negotiated over seven years and signed on Waterloo Day, 18 June 1979, was never offered to the US Senate for ratification because of it. The USSR had been installing medium-range nuclear missiles – SS-20s – in Eastern Europe, and Nato decided to reciprocate by installing American missiles in Western Europe. There can be little doubt that the European determination to stick with this decision, despite an immense Soviet diplomatic campaign against it, was strengthened by the events in Afghanistan.

Jimmy Carter foolishly took the invasion as a personal affront, and cancelled American participation in the 1980 Olympic Games in Moscow. On 23 January 1980, he proclaimed the 'Carter Doctrine', which stated that 'An attempt by any outside force to gain control of the Persian Gulf will be regarded as an assault on the vital interests of the United States, and such an assault will be repelled by any means necessary, including military force.' Then he set about forming the Rapid Deployment Force. The RDF had nothing to do with Afghanistan, and the Soviet occupation of Afghanistan had nothing to do with the Gulf. Mr Carter had become over-excited because the Soviet invasion had followed on the heels of the seizure of the American embassy in Tehran. He wanted to be seen to be doing something forceful and decisive, even if it did nothing to help the Afghans or impress the Iranians.

For the next nine years, American policy oscillated between 'making the Soviets bleed' and trying to find a solution to the Afghan problem. The 'Bleeders' won, and at an expenditure of $600 million a year, the US effectively caused the Soviet Union to haemorrhage until it decided to get out of Afghanistan. That result astonished the hard-liners in Washington, who had been so convinced that the Soviets were, by definition, expansionist that they had found accepting Gorbachev and *glasnost* almost impossible. The consequence of American policy and the Soviets' abrupt decision to abandon Afghanistan was that Afghanistan might be left in total anarchy after the Soviet withdrawal, a Lebanon of central Asia, tempting all its neighbours (Iran, Pakistan and the USSR, again) to intervene.

Under both Carter and Reagan, however, the United States took care to keep its own involvement in Afghanistan as discreet as possible. This was not easy when it involved moving $600 million-worth of arms a year, but by and large, it was successful. The purpose was to prevent the Soviets from turning the war into an East–West or anti-colonialist struggle, with the Americans as the villains. The Soviets did their best to present a counter-image, but American discretion ensured that the world, and the Afghans, continued to see the fight as exclusively a North–South struggle, or an anti-imperialist war with the Soviets as the imperialists.

In June 1982, the UN convened talks between the Afghan and Pakistani governments in Geneva, under the direction of a UN under-secretary, Diego Cordovez, an Ecuadorian lawyer. These were called 'proximity talks' because the Pakistanis would not recognize or negotiate with the Kabul government. The two delegations never met: for six ineffectual years, Cordovez travelled backwards and forwards between their offices, mediating. No agreement could ever be reached: the real principals were the Soviets and the Afghan resistance, and no change in direction could be attained without a change of policy in Moscow.

This at last occurred in February 1988 – or, at least, was finally revealed then. There had been many signs that the Soviets were sickening of the war. One effect of Gorbachev's *glasnost* was that Soviet newspapers at last started reporting the war seriously, and carrying news of death, dismemberment and the miseries returning soldiers brought with them. It soon became apparent to foreigners in Moscow that the war was deeply unpopular. After a final dispute with Washington over when or whether the two sides would cut off arms supplies to their respective clients, Gorbachev finally announced the Soviet withdrawal on 7 April 1988. He chose a most unlikely pretext, visiting a collective farm near Tashkent. He had just met President Najibullah in that city, to inform him of the decision and demand his acquiescence, much as Henry Kissinger had extorted South Vietnam's assent to the Paris agreement of 1973. The television cameras caught Gorbachev chatting casually with the farmers in a field, and calmly informing them that the withdrawal would begin the following month.

The agreement was finally signed in Geneva on 14 April by Pakistan and the Kabul government. The Soviet foreign minister, Edward Shevarnadze and the US secretary of state, George Shultz, signed as guarantors. It was not at all clear what that meant, and there were plentiful ambiguities in the text. The Soviets said that they would begin their withdrawal on 15 May, and complete it in nine months, but it was probable that they would maintain a considerable presence after that, and it was also quite clear that the war would continue. The US and the USSR each agreed not to arm their respective clients so long as the other refrained from doing so. On 10 April 1988, a major Mujaheddin arms and munitions dump in Rawalpindi exploded, killing several hundred people. The size of the explosion demonstrated graphically the quantity of arms that the Americans and their allies had supplied to the Afghan resistance. Whether or not the US and the USSR felt bound by the promise to suspend arms deliveries, it was clear that each side in Afghanistan had adequate supplies to continue the fight at full pitch.

The Soviet withdrawal began, on schedule. The Western press was invited to watch the troops as they left Kabul and as they arrived at the Oxus to be welcomed with flowers, speeches and the joy of their relatives. Soviet television broadcast these touching scenes, a further demonstration both of *glasnost* and of the vast improvement in Soviet public relations technique under Gorbachev.

The Geneva agreement provided that the Soviets would pull out half their 120,000 troops by 15 August, and complete their withdrawal by 15 February 1989. The prospect that Najibullah would not long survive their departure evidently did not disturb them. The withdrawal was conducted efficiently and successfully. The last Soviet soldier, Lieutenant General Boris Gromov, crossed the Friendship Bridge just before noon on 15 February 1989, to be met by his 14-year-old son, carrying a bouquet of flowers. Gromov, the last Soviet commander in Afghanistan, never looked back. He denied that his troops had been defeated and insisted that they had achieved their 'international duty'. Soviet losses were 15,000 killed.

Even before the last Soviet troops had withdrawn, the Mujaheddin mounted a full-scale attack on Jalalabad, the principal city on the road from Kabul eastwards to the Khyber Pass. The siege continued for several months, unsuccessfully. The government drew comfort from its success, and the Mujaheddin began fighting among themselves. Gulbuddin Hekmatyar's Islamic Party attempted to assert its control over other groups, including resistance movements inside the country. The Americans continued to support the Peshawar government in exile, but with increasing reservations.

One of the provisions of the Geneva agreement was that the former UN high commissioner for refugees, Saddrudin Aga Khan, would supervise the return home of the approximate 7 million refugees. It promises to be a long and expensive task. According to one guerrilla leader, 60 per cent of the houses in Afghanistan have been destroyed, and 60 per cent of arable land has been taken out of cultivation because canals and irrigation systems have been damaged or destroyed. If the refuges return *en masse*, there will be mass starvation.

FURTHER READING

American University, *Afghanistan: A Country Study*, Washington D.C., 1986.
Amnesty International, *Afghanistan: Torture of Political Prisoners*, London, 1986.
Chaliand, Gerard (trans. Tamar Jacoby), *Report from Afghanistan*, New York, Viking, 1982.
Dupree, Louis, *Afghanistan*, Princeton, N.J., Princeton University Press, 1973.
— *Red Flag over the Hindu Kush*, Field Staff Reports, American Universities, New York, 1968 etc.
Fraser, George MacDonald, *Flashman*, London, Herbert Jenkins, 1969.
Girardet, Edward, *Afghanistan: The Soviet War*, New York, St Martin's Press, 1985.
Hopkirk, Peter, *Setting the East Ablaze*.
Klass, Rosanne (ed.), *Afghanistan: The Great Game Revisited*, New York, Freedom House, 1988.
Leber, Jerri and Rubin, Barnett E., *A Nation Is Dying*: *Afghanistan under the Soviets*, Evanston, Ill., Northwest University Press, 1988..

BANGLADESH

Geography	55,126 sq. miles (142,776 sq. km). Rather smaller than England and Wales.
Population	103 million (1986). It is growing at 2.5% p.a. The population density is 2000 per sq. mile.
GNP per capita	$160
Refugees	50,000 in India.

HISTORY

Bangladesh became independent as a result of the break-up of Pakistan in the civil war of 1971 (*see* Pakistan, pp. 207–13). The country was in turmoil, with the defeated Pakistani army, the remaining adherents of a united Pakistan, the Indian army and the Bangladeshi guerrilla army (the Mukti Bahini) all fighting in the most crowded country on Earth. Bangladesh was born in violence, and the violence has continued to this day.

The group most loyal to Pakistan in what was to become Bangladesh were the Biharis. These were Urdu-speaking Muslim refugees from the Indian province of Bihar who had fled to East Pakistan in 1947 to escape from the massacres of partition: in 1946, 30,000 Muslim Biharis were massacred by Hindus and more were slaughtered in 1947. In the general horrors of partition, 1.3 million Muslims from India fled to East Pakistan, a million of them from Bihar. In turn, about 3.3 million Hindus fled East Bengal for India.

The Biharis never assimilated with the Bengalis, and when Mohammed Ali Jinnah, the founder of Pakistan, proclaimed Urdu the national language of both east and west divisions, over strong opposition from the Bengalis, the Biharis found themselves in a favoured position in East Pakistan, taking the government jobs that required Urdu. When tension between the two wings of the country reached a peak in 1970–1, the Biharis in the east were the natural victims of Bengali persecution, and hundreds were murdered in Dacca and other cities. When President Yahya proclaimed martial law in the East in March 1971, arrested the Awami League leader Mujib Ur-Rahman and suppressed the League, the Biharis rallied to the Pakistani cause, and took their revenge on their Bengali persecutors by joining the Pakistani armed forces in the effort to suppress Bengali nationalism. Bangladesh now claims that 3 million people were murdered during the period March–December 1971. The real number is probably between 300,000 and half a million.

The massacres continued until the very end of 1971, and many Biharis were murdered after the Pakistanis surrendered. On one infamous occasion, on 18 December, a Bengali terrorist leader killed a number of mostly Bihari prisoners in Dacca soccer stadium, before a vast and cheering crowd. A British television crew was present and televised the event.

Many Biharis died during the following months, but not the vast numbers usual in communal disturbances in the subcontinent. Several hundred thousand remain, 18 years later, living miserable and unwanted in the slums of Dacca. Neither Bangladesh, Pakistan nor India will rescue them.

INDEPENDENT BANGLADESH

The unquestioned leader of the new state was Sheikh Mujib, leader of the Awami League, who became prime minister. However, whatever his skills as an opposition leader, he had none as head of government. He alienated many of those who had contributed most to the fight for independence, and ran the government in an authoritarian, paternalistic style despite natural disasters, famine and rapidly spreading disorder.

In December 1974, Mujib declared a state of emergency. In January 1975, he amended the constitution, making himself executive president and banning all opposition. On 15 August 1975, Mujib and several members of his family were murdered by a group of army majors.

They installed one of Mujib's ministers, Khondakar Mushtaque Ahmad, as president and arrested Mujib's closest associates. Senior army officers disapproved of these developments, and on 3 November, Brigadier Khalid Musharaf staged a coup. The majors escaped to Libya, but Musharaf arrested the chief of staff, General Zia Rahman. He did not make himself president, putting a judge, A. S. M. Sayem, into that position. The jailed Mujibist ministers were murdered.

On 6 November, there was a further coup, instigated by survivors of Mujib's private security force, the JSD, and Musharaf was killed. Sayem remained President, but real power was taken by General Zia.

Zia had played an important role in the war of independence, and now quickly brought the country's security problems under control and set about reforming the administration and military. He was the most popular and successful of Bengali leaders since independence, and in April 1977, he became president. Political life resumed, and elections were held in February 1979; Zia's newly formed Bangladesh Nationalist party won them.

The country was united behind Zia, but elements in the military opposed him. There were several attempted coups and mutinies, and on 30 May 1981, Zia was murdered at the instigation of the army commander at Chittagong. The rebellion was put down by the chief of staff, General Hossain Muhammed Ershad, and the rebel general, his family and many others were killed.

Ershad in due course made himself president. He lacks the charisma of Zia, and his government has made no perceptible progress in solving the country's economic problems. In elections on 3 March 1988, Ershad's party won a large majority, but since the vote was boycotted by the opposition parties (including the 131

Awami League, now led by Mujib's daughter, and Zia's Nationalist party, led by his widow, the Begum Khaleda Zia), the elections offered no solutions. There was much violence before the voting, with several hundred people killed.

THE PROBLEMS OF POLITICS AND DEMOGRAPHY

The fundamental political problem in Bangladesh is the lack of political legitimacy of the regime. Since independence in 1971, there have been four coups, and three heads of government have been assassinated. General Ershad's greatest achievement has been his own survival, and that is not enough to offer any hope to one of the poorest nations on Earth.

However, Bangladesh's real problem is demographic. It is the most densely populated of the world's nations, except for the city states of Singapore and Hong Kong. Its *per capita* income, about $160 a year, is half that of Haiti, and as the population continues to increase relentlessly, the average income continues to drop. Bangladesh is very fertile, watered by two of the great rivers of the world, the Ganges and the Brahmaputra, and built of silt washed down from the north Indian plain and Tibet. But the Malthusian dilemma remains: Bangladesh can barely feed itself in the good years; if the monsoons fail, there will be a famine on a scale the world has not known.

Bangladesh is also extremely low-lying – much of it at or just above sea level. With the deforestation of the Himalayas has come a great increase in the height of the spring floods, with consequent inundation of the Bangladeshi countryside. In 1988, there were severe floods resulting in untold damage. If the 'greenhouse effect' causes the levels of the oceans to rise, Bangladesh may become uninhabitable.

THE CHITTAGONG HILL TRACTS

Eastern Bangladesh includes the first ranges of the Burmese hills. The 600,000 tribal people of the region, who are Buddhists of Tibetan origin, began a guerrilla campaign in 1976, which has so far resulted in the deaths of at least 1500. They accuse the government of encouraging settlement by Muslim Bengalis: there are now at least 300,000 Bengalis in their hills. The same cause has provoked similar uprising in Indian districts farther north and east.

Under the British, the Chittagong Hill Tracts were administered entirely separately from the rest of India, and there were strict laws to prevent outsiders settling there. Under the Government of India Act, 1935, the Tracts were defined as 'totally excluded areas', outside the rule of Bengal and Assam. The same rules applied to hill districts that are now in India and in Burma. There are 13 major tribes in the Tracts, about half their number being Chakmas (who are also the main tribe in Tripura state, over the border in India).

The legal protections offered the tribes were severely reduced by the government of Pakistan, and were abolished altogether by the government of Bangladesh after it became independent in 1971. The theory was that any citizen of Bangladesh had the right to live anywhere in the country. As a result, the tribesmen are rapidly going the way of the American Indians.

In 1951, 9 per cent of the Tracts' population was non-tribal. By 1974, that had increased to 11 per cent, and in 1980, non-tribal people comprised a third of the population. There is no doubt that the percentage has increased still more since then. The government actively encourages Muslim Bengalis to settle in the hills. Since the population of Bangladesh is rising at a rate of 2–3 million a year, settling a few hundred thousand Bengalis in the high hills above Chittagong is not going to make much difference, but in their desperation, the flood of Bengalis into the area will continue.

In 1972, responding to the pressure from the plains, a group of tribal leaders formed the Chittagong Hill Tracts People's Solidarity Association (known by its initials as the JSS). The JSS then formed a military wing, the Shanti Bahini, which in the mid-1970s began attacking army outposts and harassing Bengali villages. Hundreds of people were killed during this campaign. General Ershad offered the Shanti Bahini an amnesty in 1983, and claims that 3000 men surrendered. However, the government's settlement policy was not changed, and there was a sharp increase in Shanti Bahini attacks in 1985, and the troubles have continued ever since: in the last week of April 1988, 36 Bengali settlers were murdered in two hill villages; on 30 April, 13 Bengalis were killed; and on 21 May, another three died.

The government has sent large numbers of troops to suppress the uprising, and according to an Amnesty International report, they have acted with great brutality. A group of local politicians, at a press conference in Dacca in April 1980, described a massacre of some 200 villagers by Bengali troops. Amnesty has found evidence of several other massacres, some provoked by tribal attacks on settlers.

On 31 May 1984, Shanti Bahini terrorists murdered over 100 Bengalis in their villages. In revenge, troops killed hundreds of tribal villagers in the neighbouring hills. Amnesty International reports include details of incidents given by survivors, including horrific accounts of torture and of the rapes of many women before they were murdered. According to the US Committee for Refugees, there are 49,000 refugees from the Tracts in squalid camps in the Indian state of Tripura, of whom 20,115 crossed the border in 1987. Amnesty has stated:

The information available to Amnesty International leads the organization to believe that tribal villagers detained for questioning by military and paramilitary personnel are regularly tortured. Such prisoners are generally kept in pits or trenches seven or eight feet deep ... prisoners are reported to have been held in groups of up to 15 or 20 at one time in these conditions ... The techniques of torture which former prisoners reported to be most frequently used during interrogation are: extensive beating, with rifle butts and sticks, on all parts of the body; pouring very hot water into the nostrils and mouth; hanging the prisoner upside down, often from a tree ... hanging the prisoner by the shoulders for long periods and then beating the soles of his feet ...

FURTHER READING

American University, *Bangladesh, a Country Study*, Washington D.C., 1985.
Amnesty International, *Bangladesh: Unlawful Torture and Killing in the Chittagong Hill Tracts*, London, 1986.
Baxter, Craig, *Bangladesh: A New Nation in an Old Setting*, Boulder, Colo., Westview Press, 1984.
Minority Rights Group, *The Biharis in Bangladesh*, London 1982.
O'Donnell, Charles Peter, *Bangladesh: Biography of a Muslim Nation*, Boulder, Colo., Westview Press, 1984.

BURMA

Geography	261,217 sq. miles (676,552 sq. km): the size of Texas, or of France, Belgium, Holland and Denmark combined. It is divided by a series of mountain ranges running north to south from the Himalayas (19,000 ft/6000 m) to the Bay of Bengal and to the border with Thailand. The central plain is traversed by the Irrawaddy River, the delta of which was the richest rice-producing area in the world before World War II.
Population	37.6 million. All the inhabitants of Burma are referred to as Burmese; the majority language group are the Burmans. There are over 100 languages spoken. Although there has been no ethnic census since 1931, approximate tribal or ethnic divisions among the major tribes (there are dozens of minor ones) are:

> Burman: 25,400,000
> Shan: 4,180,000
> Karen: 3,500,000
> Arakan: 2,280,000
> Indian: 750,000
> Mon: 700,000
> Wa: 500,000
> Kachin: 500,000
> Chin: 500,000
> Naga: 100,000

Religion	85% Buddhist. Many Karen, Kachin and Chin are Christians, converted by American Baptist missionaries.
Resources	Burma is well endowed and is underpopulated, compared with other South Asian nations. It has three-quarters of the world's teak, besides oil, minerals (including tungsten), rubies and jade. Burma is the world's largest producer of opium.
GNP per capita	$200
Refugees	In Burma: 1000 from Bangladesh; 800 from China. From Burma: 20,000 in Thailand.
Insurgents	The American University country study for Burma (1983) lists 28 insurgent groups operating in Burma, whose forces range in size from the Burmese Communist Party (8000–15,000) and the Karen National Union (5000–8000) down to the Kayah New Land Revolution Council (50) and the Karenni People's United Liberation Front (70). Their total manpower was between 27,000 and 44,000. Apart from the Communists, who have a clear political programme, the insurgents are concerned with preserving their own autonomy and, some of them, with controlling the opium trade.

In the summer of 1988, the military government of Burma collapsed under the weight of civilian protest. Burma had been ruled as a socialist, military dictatorship by General Ne Win since 1962, and the country had been reduced to abject poverty. It was one of the most introverted countries in the world, on a par with Albania or North Korea. It was also one of the poorest, largely because of the 'Burmese Way to Socialism'. In 1987, the UN defined Burma as one of the world's 'least-developed countries', one of a select group of the ten poorest.

Eventually, the incompetence of the regime provoked an uprising which began among students and spread to the rest of the population. Ne Win resigned in July and the country rapidly slipped into anarchy. Mass demonstrations in the streets of Rangoon and other cities overthrew all authority, and for a while, it seemed that Burma would follow the example of the Philippines and South Korea in instituting a democratic government after a popular uprising. However, in Burma there was no charismatic leader like Corazon Aquino to unite the opposition, nor could the United States exert its influence to achieve a democratic result. The Burmese army recovered its nerve and authority, and staged a coup on 18 September, restoring the authority that it had held since 1962. The new regime, or the old regime with a few new leaders, suppressed the opposition, broke the general strike and drove student revolutionaries underground. Burma's economic crisis continued and worsened, and the government braced itself for the next upheaval.

These events took place in Rangoon, Mandalay and other cities of the Burman heartland. On the periphery, there have been continuous insurrections against the central authorities since 1947: the Karen rebellion is probably the longest-lasting war of the century. In 1984, the government mounted a brutal offensive against the Karen and other insurgents but did not succeed in defeating them. Conversely, the tribal insurgencies could never overthrow the government. That requires the Burmans themselves to rise in revolt.

HISTORY

In the 19th century Burma, like so much of the world, was annexed to the British empire. First, the East India Company seized the coastal provinces in the First Burma War (1824–6); then south Burma was annexed in 1852 and the rest of the country in 1885. The last king, Thibaw, was exiled to India, and Burma was ruled as a province of British India until the 1930s.

It was a prosperous colony, thanks to its rice, oil, teak and other riches. The Irrawaddy delta with its capital at Rangoon was rapidly developed into a major rice-growing area. Prosperity and, eventually, the development of the institutions of a nation state were concentrated in the river valley and the delta. The hill country was always treated separately, partly to protect the tribesmen, partly on the divide-and-rule principle. While, in India, the British developed educational and political institutions that eventually produced a unified, independent state, for most of their time in Burma they contented themselves with administration and police functions. (George Orwell – Eric Blair – was a Burma policeman.) Finally, in 1937, the British separated Burma from India and began to develop its political institutions. This was partly a reaction to nationalist agitation that had begun among Burmese students and reached a climax in 1938 when oil workers marched on Rangoon in support of the students.

During the Japanese war with China, supplies to China were sent over the mountains into Yenan via the 'Burma Road'. In 1942, in order to cut that road and to threaten India, Japan occupied Burma. Thirty Burmese nationalists, led by the most prominent of the former student leaders, Thakin Aung San, then 27, had gone to Japan for military training in 1940. These 'Thirty Comrades' included several of the men who were to become the leaders of independent Burma, among them Thakin Shu Maung, who later took the *nom de guerre* Ne Win ('Brilliant like the Sun'). ('Thakin' is an honorific, meaning 'master', a title that had been reserved for the British, like *sahib* in India; the Thirty Comrades adopted it to assert their Burmese independence.) Aung San formed a Burmese army allied to the Japanese, based on the Thirty Comrades, and during the Japanese invasion Ne Win led a sabotage mission into Rangoon.

Japan hoped to use Burma as a base from which to invade India, and therefore built the Burma–Siam railway over the Three Pagodas pass from Siam. They proclaimed Burmese independence in August 1943, with Aung San as minister of defence, and Thakin Nu as foreign minister, and they established a Burmese army in which Ne Win was a brigadier. However, the Japanese soon alienated the Burmese by their arrogance and brutality, and after their invasion of India failed in 1944, Aung San formed the Anti-Fascist People's Freedom League, and joined the British when they invaded Burma. On 27 March 1945, on a signal from Mountbatten, the British commander, Aung San's troops attacked the Japanese in the rear, greatly helping the British advance. The British had conducted a long and difficult campaign in Burma, notable for the exploits of Orde Wingate's Chindits (British) and Merrill's Marauders (American).

The war destroyed Burma's industrial base, including the oil industry, the railways, rolling stock and river fleet. The British, after a period of hesitation, decided that Burma should become independent at the same time as India. A conference of a majority of the many nationalities in Burma was held in February 1947, and the Burmese Union was voted into existence: an achievement that was chiefly due to Aung San, the most capable and charismatic of Burmese leaders. He and seven of his ministers were assassinated in July by a disgruntled rival, and the leadership then fell to Nu, who assumed the honorific U (meaning 'uncle'). He signed the treaty establishing Burmese independence, in London on 17 October 1947. Independence day, an auspicious date chosen by the Buddhist astrologers, was 4 January 1948.

INDEPENDENT BURMA

U Nu was not the man to cope with the tribal insurrections that immediately broke out, and which have plagued Burma ever since. The economy was in ruins: the standard of living did not recover to 1940 levels until 1975, and has declined since then. From the start, the country's problems were compounded by the imposition of socialism, and were seriously aggravated after the 1962 coup.

The British had governed Burma proper as they had done the states of India. The hill tribes, comprising at least half the country, were defined as 'scheduled' areas and were administered separately, as were the coastal provinces that had been conquered first; Kayah state, on the Thai border, was never conquered at all. Like the Sikhs or Pathans in India, the hill tribes were considered 'martial races' by the British, as opposed to the supposedly peaceable Burmans, and so the Karen of the south-east and the Kachin of the north-east were recruited into the British army. These divisions were exacerbated by the Karens' adoption of Christianity and their loyalty to the British during the war, when the Burmans, at first, sided with the Japanese. After independence, bringing these diverse peoples into a proper union proved quite beyond the capacity of the Burmans.

On Independence Day, Red Flag Communists were already in revolt, and there was a rebellion among Muslim separatists (the Mujahids) in the coastal province of Arakan. The White Flag Communists revolted on 27 March 1948. (The differences between the two factions were the result of the conflicting ambitions of their leaders.) Then part of the national army that Aung San had founded launched a revolt, and two of the five battalions of the regular army mutinied. Finally, in January 1949, a revolt began among the Karen in the south-east, and the Karen regiments in the army mutinied. U Nu dismissed the commander-in-chief, a Karen, and replaced him with Ne Win, who was to remain in control of the Burmese army until 1988.

Burma almost disintegrated. Mandalay was captured by Kachin rebels on 13 March 1948, and Rangoon was saved by the loyalty of regiments composed of another tribe, the Chin, and by the disunity of the various rebels. By degrees, the government was able to reassert its control of the Irrawaddy valley, recapturing Mandalay on 24 April.

In 1948, as the Communists won the Chinese civil war, a defeated Kuomintang (KMT) army, 12,000 strong, escaped into Burma and occupied part of the Shan state on the eastern frontier. The KMT army, known as the Chinese Irregular Forces (CIF), defeated Burmese armies sent after them, and rapidly expanded the area under their control. They were supplied by Taiwan and the United States, which had fantasies of using them against China.

The CIF and tribal rebels in south-east Burma formed part of a 'warlord' system that controlled the 'Golden Triangle' in Burma, northern Laos, Cambodia and Thailand. This soon developed into the world's major opium-growing area, and by 1953, over 80 per cent of the Burmese army was fighting the CIF there. The CIF are still in Shan state, although much diminished.

After recovering from the dangers of the immediate post-independence period, the country drifted steadily downhill, its economy deteriorating despite many fanciful socialist plans, and its political problems getting steadily worse. The first military coup took place in November 1958, with U Nu's connivance, and the army under Ne Win applied itself to solving the country's problems. It achieved some superficial success.

An election was held in February 1960, which U Nu won, and the army retired to its barracks. U Nu made Buddhism the state religion, which infuriated the animist and Christian Karen and Kachin. The Shan were also moving into opposition: under the 1947 agreement setting up the Union, they had the right to secede, and were considering the possibility. Then U Nu announced that he would nationalize the import trade, part of which was in the hands of a corporation controlled by the army. On 2 March 1962, Ne Win seized power.

THE MILITARY DICTATORSHIP

U Nu and his ministers, and Shan leaders who had gathered in Rangoon to consider their future, were all arrested. Ne Win and his colleagues then set about   137 imposing their peculiar vision on the country. Its guiding principles included: xenophobia, which took the form of an equal dislike for Britain, China, the United States, the Soviet Union and Burma's immediate neighbours; Buddhist theology, with its abhorrence of gambling and ostentation and its supposed advocacy of holy poverty; and old-fashioned authoritarianism.

Ne Win himself was a notorious womanizer, gambler and golfer: wise foreign ministers chose their ambassadors to Rangoon from among diplomatic golfers, who did their business with the party leader on the links. He also had a house in Wimbledon in London, where he spent several months a year, and when he discovered that his children were growing up barely literate, because of the inadequacies of the Burmese educational system, he sent them to school in England. A few years after the coup, the British returned King Thibaw's regalia to Ne Win, hoping to placate him. The gesture had no good effect.

The regime published three documents laying down the principles of the 'Burmese Way to Socialism', as one of them was called. The key document was entitled 'The System of the Correlation of Man and His Environment (the philosophy of the Burma Socialist Programme party)', which mixed Buddhism and socialism into an eclectic Burmese mush. The results have been protracted economic stagnation: foreign firms, starting with the British Imperial Chemical Industries (I C I) and the Burmah Oil Company, were expelled; banks and, in 1963, all major industries were nationalized; and about 200,000 Indians and Pakistanis were expelled. The regime denied citizenship to anyone of foreign extraction and, in 1978, started registering the inhabitants of the western border areas, where there is a Muslim minority, the descendants of immigrants from Bengal. About 200,000 Muslims fled to Bangladesh. Most of them eventually returned, but their position remained precarious until the end of the regime. In 1969, U Nu, who had been released from prison in Rangoon, tried to launch an invasion and insurrection from Thailand; he failed.

Although it was less brutal than Cambodia under the Khmers Rouges and less corrupt than Indonesia, the Ne Win regime was entirely capable of extreme violence to protect itself. It demonstrated the point four months after the 1962 coup, when a student demonstration in Rangoon was put down with great brutality, with scores or perhaps hundreds of people killed. Foreign news organizations were forbidden, the press was nationalized and Burma shut itself away from the world. By strange coincidence, a Burmese, U Thant, became acting secretary-general of the UN when Dag Hammarksjold was killed in 1961, and secretary-general in 1962, the year of the coup.

THE REBELLIONS

The various insurrections continued. They fall into three categories: first, the Burmese Communist party, a class by itself, because it wants to overthrow the government and take its place; second, ethnic groups, whose object is to preserve their tribal autonomy; third, warlord groups, who are chiefly interested in the opium trade. At its widest extent, up to 40 per cent of the country was controlled by insurgents, but this comprised a much smaller fraction of the population.

The Burmese Communist party (BCP), aided by the Chinese, is based in

138 Shan, a territory stretching several hundred miles along the Chinese frontier,

north of that held by the Chinese Irregular Forces (CIF). Apart from the dedicated Communists – the residuum of the Red Flag and White Flag Communists who took to the hills in 1948 – the bulk of BCP support comes from a loose coalition of minority groups, representing the Shan and other ethnic insurgents. The BCP proposed to establish a People's Republic of Burma, to represent the working classes of the country, and, rather improbably, accused Ne Win of subservience to foreign imperialists. In 1968, the BCP's leader, Thakin Than Tun, instigated a 'cultural revolution' on the Maoist model among his followers, but it proved unpopular and Tun himself was murdered. The BCP's problem is that while most of its members are from ethnic minorities and thus the party has little appeal to Burmans, the party's leaders, mostly living in Peking, are Burmans who are therefore distrusted by the tribes. A further problem is that the BCP controls the most productive poppy fields in the Golden Triangle. For a while, it tried to reduce production, but soon the temptation of the huge profits to be made proved too much, and production resumed full blast.

The Karen rebels control the 600 miles of jungle and mountain along the Thai border in south-east Burma. Other rebel groups control the borders to the north, while Chin and Naga rebels control the mountains that separate Burma from India. These last two cooperate with their relatives across the border, who are in revolt against the Indian government. In 1976, nine ethnic groups (soon to be joined by a tenth) formed an alliance – the National Democratic Front (NDF) – to demand autonomy from Rangoon.

Among the original nine was the Karen National Union, which had, in various forms, been in rebellion since 1949; its army is the Karen National Liberation Army, about 5000 strong. Military operations and the local administration are financed by smuggling jewels and teak into Thailand. The Karens claim that they do not take part in the drug trade: that would be against their Baptist faith. Their allies farther north are less fussy.

The other members of the NDF are the Kachin, Shan, Wa, Mon and Arakan, as well as various minor tribes including Karenni, Paluang, Lahu and Pa-O, and together they claim to have 35,000 insurgents. That may have been true in the early 1980s but is probably a considerable exaggeration now.

In 1984, the Burmese army mounted a new offensive against the KNLA and overran two Karen strongholds. In successive attacks, it succeeded in driving about 20,000 people from their homes to live in camps along the Thai border. The KNLA fights in the traditional guerrilla manner, ambushing army patrols and attacking isolated outposts. It has also planted bombs in towns and villages: the government claims that the KNLA put a bomb on a train near Rangoon on 9 January 1988, which killed nine and wounded 38 people. Since 1986, the offensives have been extended to Communist and Kachin insurgents in the north-east, and Mon rebels in south Burma.

The strongest of the NDF armies is probably the Kachin Independence Army (KIA), the military arm of the Kachin Independence Organization (KIO). The Kachin live on the Chinese frontier, in the most inaccessible parts of the country. In an offensive in 1987, the army overran the headquarters of both the KIO and the KIA, but the two organizations still claim 4000–8000 troops and control of half of Kachin state.

According to an Amnesty International report issued in May 1988, based on interviews with 70 Karen refugees in camps on the Thai border, the civilian population in rebel areas has suffered heavily from counter-insurgency drives. They have been rounded up into 'strategic hamlets', often separated from their fields, and many have been summarily shot. Amnesty claims to have documented 200 cases of extra-legal executions of Karens and believes that there are many more. It has also found numerous cases of torture. The report says:

Countless villagers have been seized to work as porters or guides for the army. Many have died as a result. Captured villagers are force-marched until they fall dead from sickness or exhaustion, or are killed for not working hard enough, or blown up in minefields through which they are forced to lead troops. A Karen farmer, now a refugee, was travelling with a friend to buy land for growing rice, when they ran into an army patrol. They were accused of links with the rebels and were forced to become porters. His friend died after being severely beaten by the soldiers. 'The last time I saw him, he was lying alongside the path and was shivering. He could not walk or stand up. The soldiers took his load from his shoulders and left him behind. We could not help him. We could just look at him, take a look at him as we passed by.'

The report includes 60 such stories. In conclusion, Amnesty International states: 'So numerous and similar are the accounts of human rights violations given by the refugees that, in Amnesty International's opinion, they show a consistent pattern of gross violations of human rights.'

The peoples of the remote mountains and jungles of eastern and south-eastern Burma and of the contiguous areas of Laos and Thailand have lived outside the world community for nearly 50 years. The Burmese and Thai armies frequently mount military operations to attack war lords, smugglers, Communists or ethnic insurgents, but have never established their control. The area is of great interest to the outside world because of the opium poppy. More than half the heroin in the world comes from the Golden Triangle and that proportion increases as eradication programmes succeed in Turkey. The Burmese government, even with American assistance, is not capable of controlling the tribal territories.

Ne Win obtained the support of the United States government by promising a vigorous fight against narcotics. The Americans supplied helicopters, planes and chemicals to spray the opium-producing areas, and the government stated that it planned to eradicate 20,234 hectares of poppy fields in 1988. However, the rebels claim that the supplies are used to fight them, and that units of the regular Burmese army are in fact engaged in the opium trade. According to the US State Department, Burma is the world's largest producer of opium: in 1987, between 925 and 1230 metric tons of opium were produced, compared to 700–1100 tons in 1986. In 1988, Burma produced over 1200 tons of raw opium, Laos produced 100–200 tons and Thailand 27 tons. The total crop yields about 140 tons of heroin.

The story of one of the opium war lords – the half-Chinese, half-Shan known as Khun Sa (or Chang Chi-fu) – can stand as an illustration of the mores of the Golden Triangle. He was leader of the Shan United Army (SUA), ostensibly nationalist insurgents but, in fact, a territorial, armed opium cartel. Khun Sa was allied with the CIF but, in the early 1960s, quarrelled with them and was appointed by the Burmese government as militia leader in his native district, Loi-maw. He developed the drug business, with his own opium-refining centre across the border in Thailand, and, by 1964, had set himself up as a drug smuggler and independent warlord. In 1967, the CIF put an embargo on the SUA opium trade, and Khun Sa fought an opium war with his former allies that year. A SUA caravan of opium was pursued across the hills into Laos, where it was seized by the Laotian army (then allied with the US Special Forces and the CIA in the war against the Vietnamese Communists). Khun Sa was captured by the Burmese.

Loss of their leader made the SUA decline until 1973, when Khun Sa's brother kidnapped two Soviet doctors working in a Soviet-built hospital. They were released in exchange for Khun Sa, who was sent home under house arrest. Two years later, he bribed his guards, escaped, and resumed command of the SUA.

That same year, 1975, the Burmese army defeated the CIF and broke its control of the opium trade in the Shan hills. Khun Sa and his SUA filled the vacuum and were soon the dominant force in the trade throughout the Golden Triangle. The SUA, with 1400–8000 men, not only produced its own opium but also bought opium from other insurgent groups, including the Burmese Communist party. The SUA shipped the opium to the Chinese syndicates in Thailand, and also smuggled gold, jewels and jade out of the country.

This profitable business was disrupted in 1981. The Thai army sent a patrol into SUA territory, and it was promptly defeated. It had to be rescued by a much larger force, and the Thais then mounted regular offensives in 1982 and 1983 and destroyed the SUA bases in Thailand. However, the defeat of Khun Sa was not permanent, nor did it mean defeat for the opium trade: Khun Sa's eclipse allowed other warlords to rise to prominence.

THE UPRISING

Like other dictators before him, Ne Win endeavoured to conceal his authority. He resigned from the army in 1972 and, in 1981, resigned as president, citing ill health. But like Mao Tse-tung and Stalin, he retained his essential position as leader of the party. A succession of other generals or former generals held the positions of president, prime minister or minister of defence, but Ne Win was always in command.

The regime started to unravel in September 1987. A currency reform was abruptly announced, robbing everyone in the country of their savings: all banknotes in denominations of 25 kyats (pronounced *chats*) or greater were abruptly declared worthless. The official rate of exchange was then 6 kyats to the US dollar, the black market rate 40. Ne Win said that the reform was aimed at black marketeers – who were, in fact, the only people keeping the economy afloat – and admitted that some reforms were necessary. In March 1988, the first student demonstrations occurred in Rangoon, set off by a brawl in a tea-house, during which a student was killed. Other students then organized a protest march into Rangoon, and the army and police broke up the demonstration with great violence, killing a number of them (estimates of the dead range up to 200) and arresting 3000.

Further demonstrations broke out three months later. On 21 June, after several days of continuous rioting, the government closed the universities and imposed a dusk-to-dawn curfew on the capital and other cities. Burma Radio reported: 'Five police personnel were killed and 26 others seriously wounded as a result of an attack   **141** by an unruly mob armed with swords, sticks and catapults. A member of the mob also was killed and several others wounded.' The true death doll was very much higher, as the government later admitted: some reports from diplomats suggested that about 1000 demonstrators were killed by troops under the command of General Sein Lwin, and in one instance, over 40 people were asphyxiated in a bus.

These events brought the regime's opposition into the open all over the country. A former general, Aung Gyi, who had taken part in the 1962 coup but turned his back on his former colleagues soon afterwards, distributed a series of open letters to Ne Win, remarking, 'The country has plunged to the bottom politically, economically and socially. The moral decay is the most deplorable.'

Ne Win, who was then 77, announced his resignation at a party conference on 23 July. 'Since I am indirectly responsible for the March and June affairs and because of my advanced age, I am resigning from both party chairmanship and also as a member,' he said. He went on: 'Bloodshed in March and June showed the lack of trust and confidence in the government. To find out whether the majority or the minority are behind the demonstrations, a referendum must be held so the people can choose between the existing one-party system or a multiparty system.' He also warned the country against further disorders, saying, 'I have to inform the people throughout the country that when the army shoots, it shoots to hit.'

A number of Ne Win's senior colleagues retired with him, but the party was not yet ready to give up power. His suggestion of a referendum on the one-party system was rejected by the conference, and Sein Lwin, who had commanded the Burmese riot police since the 1962 coup, and put down the student demonstrations in March, was appointed party chairman and president. He immediately arrested Aung Gyi and other prominent dissidents, but the demonstrations continued, and on 3 August he proclaimed martial law in Rangoon.

Mass demonstrations followed – in Rangoon, Mandalay, Pegu and other cities. Troops fired into the crowds, and large numbers of people were killed every day. Monks, students, workers, middle-class people and office workers all poured into the streets and confronted the troops. It was a replay of the events in Manila in 1986. On 10 August, troops burst into a hospital in Rangoon, looking for wounded protesters, and shot down a number of doctors and nurses who tried to protect them. The following day, the army sent tanks against demonstrators at the city's main pagodas, and protestors built barricades throughout the city. By then, there were running, daily battles between the army and 100,000 or more demonstrators in Rangoon.

On 12 August, Sein Lwin resigned. The government admitted that 100 demonstrators had been killed since he had been appointed president, but the real total was probably at least 1000 (the students said it was 3000). With the government in retreat, the crowds took to attacking party offices and other government buildings and burning them to the ground, and also attacked and burned the houses of political leaders.

On 19 August, the party named U Maung Maung president. He had been attorney-general and one of the authors of the 'Socialist Party Programme' and the 'Burmese Way to Socialism', and was a close associate of Ne Win. On 23 August, there were further enormous demonstrations in Rangoon, denouncing the new government and demanding democracy. The next day, Maung Maung lifted martial law in Rangoon, released 1700 political prisoners (including Aung Gyi) and announced that there would be an extraordinary party conference in September to consider ending one-party rule. By then, the ministers and the generals controlled no more than a few government buildings in Rangoon, their party headquarters, and the main army camps. The crowds controlled the rest, and there was considerable fear of anarchy.

The 82-year-old U Nu – who in 1980 had been invited home from Thailand by Ne Win and had entered a monastery – then emerged from retirement and tried to form a committee of opposition figures. Aung Gyi attempted to assert his claims, but many people distrusted him because he had been associated with Ne Win in 1962. Aung San Suu Kyi, the 43-year-old daughter of Aung San, the independence leader who had been assassinated in 1947, returned from her home in Oxford where her husband was teaching, and appealed for unity. So did a grandson of the late UN secretary-general U Thant.

THE COUP

On 18 September, the army seized power in a coup that had been meticulously prepared in advance. The chief of staff, General Saw Maung, filled Rangoon with troops and broke up the demonstrations. In a statement broadcast to the nation, Saw Maung said: 'In order to halt in a timely way the deteriorating conditions on all sides across the country, and for the sake of the interests of the people, the defence forces have assumed all power in the state.' Many Burmese suspected that Ne Win, who had remained in seclusion since resigning in July, still exercised real power.

Hundreds of demonstrators were killed in the first few days of the new regime. The government admitted 60 dead in the first two days, and later raised the figure to 425. Foreign diplomats suspected that up to 1000 people were killed before the last resistance was crushed in October. The general strike collapsed on 3 October. Student rebels left the cities and universities by the thousands and sought out the ethnic rebels in the mountains to offer their services, and to acquire some serious training in revolutionary warfare. There were various estimates of the numbers involved: there were perhaps 5000 in the first few weeks, with more following them in succeeding months.

The opposition at last united and, on 27 September, chose Aung Gyi as chairman of their new alliance, named the National League for Democracy. Another former military man, U Tin Oo, became vice chairman, and Aung San Suu Kyi became secretary general. The government announced that it would open negotiations with them, but they hesitated to accept the invitation for fear of losing popular support. However, they registered their party, just in case genuine elections were planned.

The coup did nothing to help the economy. The United States, Japan, West Germany and others suspended all aid to Burma, which had relied on foreign contributions to finance 35 per cent of the capital budget. Now all its foreign exchange reserves were being consumed to buy rice to feed the population.

In an attempt to appease the demonstrators, the government dissolved the Burma Socialist Programme party and confiscated its property. Leading members then formed the National Union party, which was evidently the same clique that 143 had misgoverned the country for 26 years. However, the opposition was permitted to function, some press freedoms were permitted, and the regime promised that there would be elections in the new year.

FURTHER READING

American University, *Burma: A Country Study*, Washington D.C., 1983.
Amnesty International, *Burma: extrajudicial execution and torture of members of ethnic minorities*, London, 1988.
Cady, John, *A History of Modern Burma*, Ithaca, New York, Cornell University Press, 1958.
Steinberg, David, *Burma: A Socialist Nation of Southeast Asia*, Boulder, Colo., Westview Press, 1982.
Tinker, Hugh, *The Union of Burma*, Oxford University Press, 1959.

CAMBODIA

Geography	69,898 sq. miles (181,305 sq. km). Size of West Germany. 'Cambodia' is the English version of the common Western transliteration of the country's name. The French call it 'Cambodge'. An alternative transliteration is 'Kampuchea', and the two names are used interchangeably. Under the alternative spelling, the Cambodians are known as 'Khmers'.
Population	Unknown. It was officially 8.6 million in 1975.
GNP per capita	$80.00
Refugees	314,450 in other countries.
Casualties	From 1970 to 1975, between 700,000 and 1,100,000 people were killed during the civil war and the American war against the Vietnamese Communists. From 1975 to 1979, the Khmers Rouges killed between 1 million and 2 million people. Up to 100,000 people were killed in the Vietnamese invasion that began in December 1978, and in the Khmers Rouges' retreat. The Vietnamese admit to losing 25,000 men killed during the occupation (1978–88). A conservative assumption would be that at least twice as many Cambodians were killed during the same period, not counting those who died of starvation. Perhaps 50,000–100,000 people died as a result of the guerrilla war since 1979.

Between 1975 and 1978, Cambodia suffered the single most comprehensive disaster that has befallen any country in the world since 1945. The Communist government (the 'Khmers Rouges', or 'Red Cambodians'), who had won a protracted civil war, set about exterminating the intellectual, entrepreneurial, administrative and landowning classes, and emptying the cities of their inhabitants. It has been calculated that as many as 25 per cent of the population, up to 2 million people, were murdered or died of starvation in those three-and-a-half years. In this century, only the Jews of Europe and the Armenians in Turkey have suffered a comparable devastation, and only in the Soviet Union of Stalin did another government impose genocide upon its own people.

HISTORY
A thousand years ago, Cambodia was a rich and powerful kingdom, extending far   145

into Siam (Thailand) and into what is now southern Vietnam. Its kings built an enormous temple-city at Angkor Wat, one of the marvels of the world, and their power was based upon a vast and sophisticated irrigation system, maintained by slave labour. The empire declined in the 14th century, and in 1431 the Siamese captured Angkor Wat. Cambodia then subsided into a small and impoverished kingdom, ground down between Siam and the Empire of Annam (Vietnam), both of which, over the centuries, progressively annexed most of Cambodia. It is one of the great divides of the world: Vietnam is a product of Chinese Confucian civilization; Siam, Cambodia and Laos derived their cultures from Buddhist India.

The country was saved from complete dismemberment by the French, who conquered Vietnam in the mid-19th century and established a protectorate over Cambodia in 1864. They forced Siam to restore provinces it had annexed, and built up Phnom Penh as a pleasant French tropical town. They left the king of Cambodia on his throne, as they did the king of Laos and the Emperor of Annam, while depriving him of all power (and changing dynasties twice in a century). They excavated and restored the temples and palaces at Angkor Wat, and educated a small, élite class in Paris, but otherwise left the Cambodians to live as they always had.

It was a peaceful, charming and indolent country, apparently undisturbed by the tensions and conflicts of the 20th century. In the centre of Cambodia is an inland sea, the Tonle Sap, whose waters flow down a river of the same name into the Mekong River at Phnom Penh. Every year, as the flood waters of the monsoon come down the Mekong from the far Himalayas, the waters of the Tonle Sap river turn and flow up into the lake, and flood the countryside. Every year, the king and his court were rowed out into the lake to honour the phenomenon. They would cast flowers into the water and watch them float downstream, pause, and then float back upstream marking the onset of the floods that would ensure the next rice harvest.

Cambodia escaped virtually unscathed from World War II and the French war in Indochina, which ended at the Geneva conference in 1954 with the partition of Vietnam. Cambodia was declared independent in 1953 and King Norodom Sihanouk, who had been put on the throne in 1941 as a callow, 19-year-old puppet, began his reign in earnest. Sihanouk, born in 1922, remains one of the key players in Cambodia. He was described by William Shawcross thus:

Norodom Sihanouk presided feudally over Cambodia from 1941 to 1970 as king, chief of state, prince, prime minister, head of the main political movement, jazz-band leader, magazine editor, film director and gambling concessionaire, attempting to unite in his rule the unfamiliar concepts of Buddhism, socialism and democracy.

In 1955, to prepare for elections mandated by the Geneva treaties, Sihanouk abdicated in favour of his father, proclaimed himself a commoner and established a political party that won the elections. He was undoubtedly one of the most colourful of hereditary rulers, and although he ceased to be king in 1955, he ruled as an absolute monarch until his overthrow in 1970. A skilled diplomat, intelligent, charming, with a clear view of the dangers facing the country, he was also corrupt, autocratic and short-sighted in his domestic policies. He alienated the educated classes, many of whom joined the opposition or fled to the jungles to join the Khmers Rouges, and patronized and bullied his ministers and the army. He kept the loyalty of the peasantry, however, and perhaps he still does.

146

Cambodia might have developed in the same way as Thailand or Malaysia, gradually evolving into a modern state, had it not been for the Vietnam war. That ferocious conflict inevitably spilled over into Laos and Cambodia. The Cambodian frontier is 40 miles (65 km) from Saigon, and the mountains and thick jungles on the Cambodian side provided ideal sanctuary for the Vietcong and for infiltrators from North Vietnam. Prince Sihanouk's government was powerless to prevent this violation of Cambodian neutrality.

In 1954, Vietnam was far more advanced economically and socially than Cambodia. It had a population of 30 million, of whom 18 million lived in the north, 12 million in the south. Cambodia's population was 6 million. To this demographic disparity was added the limitless military support provided to the North Vietnamese by the Chinese and Soviets, and to the South Vietnamese by the Americans. Cambodia could have protected itself against one of those powers only by committing itself irrevocably to the other. Sihanouk, naturally, wished to back the winner, and in the circumstances of the early 1960s, this meant at first bending with the wind from Hanoi, and later trying to accommodate to the increasing demands of the United States and South Vietnam.

In 1963, while Sihanouk was still secure in his government, a small group of Communists led by Pol Pot (then known as Saloth Sar), Ieng Sary and others left Phnom Penh and started an insurrection in the northern jungles, but for many years, they posed no serious threat to the government. A further group of leftists – some of whom, including Khieu Samphan, had been members of Sihanouk's government – joined them in 1967.

Pol Pot was born in Kompong Thom in 1928, son of a peasant family. He attended a technical college in Phnom Penh and, in 1949, went to Paris on a scholarship to study radio electronics. Like other young Cambodians who studied in France, he fell under the influence of the French Communist party, an organization of ultra-Stalinist orthodoxy. On his return to Phnom Penh, he earned a living teaching history and geography at a private school, and as a journalist. He made his name in left-wing politics, joined the illegal Communist Party, rising to the position of deputy general secretary.

Khieu Samphan was born in 1931, son of a minor civil servant. He became the Khmers Rouges' commander-in-chief during the war and head of state afterwards. He, too, went to France on a scholarship, in 1954. His thesis, offered at the University of Paris in 1959, and entitled 'Cambodia's Economy and Industrial Development', later provided the rationale for the Khmers Rouges' economic policies. It maintained that Cambodia could only develop on the basis of prosperous agriculture; that the existing landowning classes made that impossible; that the cities were parasites; and that Cambodia's existing international economic relationships were inimical to real economic progress. He maintained that the solution was to move the urban population into the countryside and set them to work there, and to collectivize agriculture.

Khieu Samphan worked as a journalist when he returned to Phnom Penh and, unlike Pol Pot, remained within the system until 1967, when he fled Phnom Penh to escape arrest, and joined Pol Pot. He was not admitted to the inner circle of those who had taken to the hills in 1963, but unlike others who joined at that stage, he escaped with his life.

Cambodia's first involvement in the Vietnam war developed in the eastern mountains and in the obscurity of the jungles. As the Communist insurgency developed in South Vietnam, supplies and men came down the Ho-Chi Minh trail from North Vietnam. The trail was a vast network of paths through mountains and jungle, much of it in Cambodia.

It was a long and difficult route over which to move modern weapons, and soon the Vietcong started looking for alternatives. In the 1950s, the Chinese had built a port for Cambodia on the Gulf of Siam, which was named Sihanoukville (subsequently Kompong Som), and the Americans built a 'Friendship Highway' to connect it to Phnom Penh. In 1965, Sihanouk broke diplomatic relations with the United States after President Johnson sent the Marines ashore at Danang. In 1966, Chou En-lai, the Chinese prime minister, demanded that Sihanouk permit supplies for the Vietcong to be landed in Sihanoukville and transported along the Friendship Highway to the Vietcong bases on the frontier.

Sihanouk agreed. If he had refused, the Vietnamese Communists would have extended their direct control over eastern Cambodia, and swung their support behind Pol Pot's Communist insurgents, whom Sihanouk had named the Khmers Rouges. In 1969, there were no more than 4000 active Khmers Rouges guerrillas in Cambodia.

Sihanouk, after rejecting American military aid in 1963, had nothing with which to oppose the heavily armed Vietcong. His army was 30,000 strong, of whom only 11,000 might be considered combat-ready, and their equipment was obsolete and inadequate. Sihanouk thought he had no choice. He allowed the Vietcong to use Sihanoukville, and it quickly became their main supply route. His decision led inevitably to American intervention in Cambodia. That in turn ensured the overthrow of Sihanouk in 1970 and, in 1975, Pol Pot's victory and the horrors that followed.

In an attempt to balance his policy of helping the Vietcong, Sihanouk began to veer back towards the American side. On 18 March 1969, in 'Operation Breakfast', the US Air Force conducted a massive bombing attack on what it believed were the Communist general headquarters inside Cambodia. The attack did not produce the desired results, and the USAF began a continuous and secret air offensive ('Operation Menu') against the 'sanctuaries' – the Communist bases in Cambodia. Sihanouk knew of these bombings but did not protest. In June 8 that year, he allowed the American embassy in Phnom Penh to reopen.

However, Sihanouk was distrusted by the Americans, particularly by President Nixon and his secretary of state, Henry Kissinger, who never tried to win his support or use his popularity and skills as a barrier against the Vietnamese. Until it was far too late, Washington failed to understand the depths of Cambodian–Vietnamese hostility. They were obsessed by the 'domino theory', which assumed a unified Communist conspiracy. Besides, Cambodia was only a sideshow. The main event was in Vietnam.

On 18 March 1970, the prime minister, General Lon Nol, seized power during Sihanouk's absence in Moscow. It was a confused and improvised coup, essentially arising out of a dispute between Sihanouk and his government over Cambodia's part in the Vietnam war. The United States welcomed the change in government.

On 30 April 1970, American and South Vietnamese forces invaded Cambodia to 'clear out the sanctuaries'. Five days later, on 4 May, four students at Kent State University in Ohio were killed by National Guardsmen during a protest. The American–Vietnamese forces withdrew from Cambodia at the end of June, having achieved very little.

After the invasion, Sihanouk set up a government in exile in Peking together with the Khmers Rouges, and Lon Nol proclaimed the republic. The Vietcong and Chinese now offered the Khmers Rouges every support, and their offensive against the Lon Nol government was rapidly extended across the whole country, the name and mystique of Prince Sihanouk being used among the peasantry to reinforce the Khmers Rouges' position.

By 1972, Cambodia was almost as completely engulfed in war as Vietnam itself. There were over 3 million peasant refugees in the cities, and North Vietnamese troops occupied much of eastern Cambodia, while the Khmers Rouges controlled the north. The Americans bombed both continuously.

On 27 January 1973, the United States and the three parties in Vietnam signed a peace agreement in Paris. One of its clauses provided for an ending of foreign interference in Cambodia. The Americans soon withdrew all their remaining troops from Vietnam, but continued bombing Khmers Rouges positions in Cambodia until August, when President Nixon finally acceded to congressional pressure to stop. From beginning to end, the United States Air Force dropped 539,129 tons of bombs on Cambodia, 257,465 tons in the last six months, at a total cost of $7 billion. By comparison, during the whole of World War II, 160,000 tons of bombs, not counting the atomic bombs, were dropped on Japan. This frightful onslaught destroyed the country, driving half the population into the cities as refugees, but it did not deter the Khmers Rouges – though it may have prevented them seizing Phnom Penh in 1973. On the contrary, it encouraged their fanaticism and hatred of the Americans and their 'puppets'.

The war continued in Vietnam, though its nature changed while the Communists prepared for their final offensive, and it intensified in Cambodia. The Khmers Rouges had 50,000 soldiers by then and were not affected by the Paris treaty, although it greatly increased their suspicions of the Vietnamese. It seemed to the Khmers Rouges that Hanoi, like Washington, was treating Cambodia merely as a sideshow.

Lon Nol's army was too corrupt and inefficient to stop the Khmers Rouges without continuous American support. The final attack began on New Year's Day, 1975, and continued as the last Communist offensive in Vietnam got under way. Lon Nol fled the country on 1 April, the American ambassador and his staff were evacuated by helicopter from Phnom Penh on 12 April, and the Khmers Rouges entered the city on 17 April. On 30 April, Saigon fell to the Communists.

DEMOCRATIC KAMPUCHEA

The Khmers Rouges began their rule by driving the entire population of Phnom Penh – 2.5 million people – into the countryside. Most were refugees from the war and the American bombing, whose villages had been destroyed and who had nowhere to go. Patients from hospitals were wheeled on stretchers out of the city, with distraught nurses holding their I V bottles over them, in futile attempts to keep   149 them alive. Westerners sheltering in the French embassy, waiting to be evacuated, listened in horror to the constant rattle of machine-guns as the victors massacred their opponents. All the officials of the defeated government who did not escape, and all captured officers, were summarily executed. The Chans, a mountain tribe that had adopted Islam in the Middle Ages, were slaughtered for their religion: about 60,000, the large majority of the Chans, were murdered.

For three years and eight months, Cambodia was a country without cities, without a currency. Religion, the family unit and all property were abolished. The Khmers Rouges blew up the central bank and dumped the currency reserves in the street, as so much garbage. Applying an economic theory that had been set out in Khieu Samphan's student thesis, the government set about eliminating all traces of industry and urban society, which it considered corrupted by the West. Its intention was to establish a peasant, Communist society, and then to build a new order upon that basis. The result was to return Cambodia to the Dark Ages, with an élite governing class directing a nation of slaves.

In Cambodia in 1975, 'intellectuals' were defined as anyone wearing glasses, speaking a foreign language, graduates of universities or high schools, or possessed of a professional qualification. 'Entrepreneurs' were shopkeepers and self-employed artisans, as well as anyone involved in the management of any business. 'Governing and administrative classes' included anyone who had ever held a government position or who had served in the armed forces or police of the defeated regime. All those who had lived in cities, including the refugees, were defined as 'new people', a class the Khmers Rouges were determined to obliterate. 'Landowners' were those who owned anything beyond the smallest possible family farm as well as those who resisted the forced collectivization of every farm in the country. All the families of these people were deemed equally guilty, and they were all killed, or worked to death, as slave labour. Old people and 'new' people together were to be bent to the needs of 'advanced socialism'.

A further horror was the very large number of very young boys in the Khmers Rouges armies and execution squads. Teenagers and children as young as 10 or 12 were instructed to beat their prisoners to death or to disembowel them (to save ammunition), slaughtering men and women, old and young. The Khmers Rouges did not gas their victims, hundreds at a time, or machine-gun them in large groups, as the Germans had. Each murdered Cambodian was murdered individually. The film *The Killing Fields*, based on first-hand recollections, shows one method of execution: a man whose hands were suspiciously soft, therefore possibly an intellectual, was pulled out of a chain gang by the guards; a woman then put a plastic bag over his head and tied it around his neck so that he suffocated. There were 4000 Khmers Rouges in 1969; the tens of thousands who participated in the mass killings were all recruited between 1970 and 1978.

When the Vietnamese occupied Phnom Penh in January 1979, they found a converted school, called Tuol Sleng, that had been used as the security office of the party's Central Committee. It was a torture centre and place of execution for senior cadres, and 20,000 people had been murdered there. It had been directed by a man called Kong Kech Eav, who used the name Duch. Meticulous accounts of the atrocities had been preserved, including the numbers killed every day, together with photographs of the prisoners as they arrived and at the moment they were killed.

150 Less important Cambodians were taken to the killing fields, and butchered. The skulls were set out in rows and their bones piled in heaps together.

Amnesty International's report on Cambodia quotes from a progress meeting of Tuol Sleng's staff, at which it was noted:

The enemy will not confess to us easily. When we use political pressure, prisoners confess only very little. Thus, they cannot escape from torture. The only difference is whether there will be a lot of it or a little. Torture is a necessary measure . . . It is necessary to avoid any question of hesitancy or half-heartedness, of not daring to torture, which makes it impossible to get answers to our questions from our enemies. This will slow down and delay our work.

The Amnesty report continues: 'Methods of torture included beatings, whippings, administration of electric shocks, forced feeding with excrement, and near-suffocation and near-drowning.'

Tuol Sleng (also known as S21) was an Asian Dachau – with two differences: far fewer of its inmates survived (only seven survivors are known), and when the SS had tortured their prisoners, it had been for medical experiments or to frighten other inmates; torture had not been an integral part of the German camp system. In 'Democratic Kampuchea', it was essential that the more important prisoners, and all party members, confess and admit their errors, under torture, before they were killed. Tuol Sleng was the realization of George Orwell's 'Ministry of Love'.

The ruling group in Cambodia between 1975 and 1978 consisted of a 'Gang of Six'. Pol Pot became prime minister and secretary of the Communist party. The others were Ieng Sary, who was foreign minister; Son Sen, minister of defence; two sisters, Khieu Ponnary, who directed the Association of Democratic Women of Kampuchea, and Khieu Thirith, minister of social action (Ponnary was married to Pol Pot, Thirith to Ieng Sary). The sixth member was Son Sen's wife, Yun Yat, minister of education.

After the Khmers Rouges victory, Prince Sihanouk returned to Phnom Penh as nominal head of state. He was kept in house arrest most of the time, though he was occasionally allowed abroad to sing the praises of the Khmers Rouges government. Sihanouk thus bears some of the blame for the horrors that overwhelmed his country.

Like other revolutions, the Cambodian revolution soon began to devour its children. After they had exterminated their enemies from the old regime, Pol Pot and the Angka – the Organization of the Khmers Rouges, which was the country's government – set about systematically killing everyone who had any connection with the Vietnamese. That included up to half the Cambodian Communists and four of the ten people who had led the Khmers Rouges to victory in 1975. The documents found in the Tuol Sleng included detailed transcripts of their interrogations.

In the summer of 1978, the purges culminated in a series of massacres in eastern Cambodia, the area of the country that had been most closely involved with the Vietnamese. Leading cadres were summoned back to Phnom Penh a few at a time, and were never heard of again. Then Pol Pot sent his army to surround party headquarters in the east. So Phim, the commander in eastern Cambodia and a member of the five-man Politburo of the Cambodian Communist party, shot himself. Some 3000 Khmers Rouges and perhaps 30,000 civilians retreated into the jungles, and put up a desultory resistance, while the peasants took advantage of 151 the fighting among their rulers to attack the communal kitchens and other symbols of the regime. Pol Pot soon defeated the opposition and slaughtered everyone he could find: about 100,000 people were killed in three months, and one-third of the surviving population was marched into western Cambodia. Pol Pot denounced his enemies as 'Khmer bodies with Vietnamese minds'. His rage extended across the border and he sent his troops in a series of raids into Vietnam, where they massacred thousands of peasants.

These were not the first border raids: in September 1977, Cambodians had attacked Vietnamese villages, massacring hundreds. In October and December 1977, Vietnam had retaliated by mounting full-scale military incursions into Cambodia.

None of this deterred Pol Pot. He simply broke diplomatic relations with Hanoi in December 1977. However, after the renewed attacks in the late summer of 1978, Hanoi decided that it was no longer possible to tolerate the Khmers Rouges, and a guerrilla army of dissident Cambodians was formed, including the surviving leaders of the eastern district who had taken refuge in the jungles. Many of them had taken part in earlier massacres of Vietnamese on both sides of the border, but Hanoi turned a blind eye to their past. Among them was Heng Samrin, who was rescued when the Vietnamese sent an armoured column into Cambodia in September 1978.

If the Cambodians had possessed any political skills, or if Pol Pot had been less crazed with ideology, the country could doubtless have preserved its independence and territorial integrity by playing China off against Vietnam. But Pol Pot proclaimed that each Cambodian could and would kill 30 Vietnamese; Cambodia could thus lose 2 million of its people while wiping out the 50 million Vietnamese, and recover the lost territories to the east, including Saigon. On 24 December 1978, Vietnam invaded Cambodia, taking Phnom Penh on 7 January; by the end of the month the Vietnamese had occupied most of the country (*see* Vietnam, pp. 235–41).

The Pol Pot regime was able to put up even less resistance than Lon Nol's government had in 1975. This was due partly to a lack of military supplies, but it was chiefly due to the country's detestation of the regime. The retreating Democratic Kampucheans took several hundred thousand peasants with them, and attempted to set up enclaves under their control in the mountains. While this phantom government lasted, it continued to impose by terror its fantasies of 'advanced socialism'. Scores of thousands – perhaps 100,000 – died, and the remainder were only saved from starvation by an international relief operation in 1979. The Vietnamese overran these last pockets of resistance by the end of that year, and the Khmers Rouges retreated to a series of camps along the border with Thailand.

THE VIETNAMESE OCCUPATION

Vietnam immediately set up a quisling government in Phnom Penh, headed by Heng Samrin. Only the Soviets and their client states and India recognize it, and Vietnam has failed to destroy the guerrilla resistance. The Khmers Rouges are the most important element in the resistance movement; other armies are led by or owe allegiance to Prince Norodom Sihanouk, the former head of state, and to non-Communist groups. China supports the Khmers Rouges, while the West and

Thailand give a little, ineffective, support to the non-Communist resistance whose bases are along the Thai border. For nine years, until the Vietnamese announced their intention to withdraw, in May 1988, the stalemate was absolute. All that could be said for it was that it was preferable to government by Pol Pot.

In 1984-5, the Vietnamese undertook a massive offensive along the border to capture all the refugee camps and military bases of the Khmers Rouges and Son Sann's KPNLF (*see below*). The offensive achieved its aims, but did not destroy the Khmers Rouges. The refugees simply moved over the border into Thailand, and the Khmers Rouges' army split up into guerrilla bands, which continued to harass the Vietnamese and the Phnom Penh regime's army. They were supported and armed by China via a 'Deng Xiaoping Trail' running from China through the jungles of northern Thailand. Their strategy was to wait out the Vietnamese, and then return to power. When Vietnam announced that it intended to withdraw by 1990, it appeared that they would attain that objective.

After the resistance bases along the Thai border had been destroyed, the Vietnamese set about building a fence and laying minefields the length of the frontier. They found themselves in the position of the Americans in Vietnam, trying to hold together a weak and dispirited local government while also attempting to keep the guerrillas out of the country.

Some accounts of the horrors inflicted on Cambodia by Pol Pot had come out during his three years in power. They were not always believed, particularly by those who had most vocally opposed American involvement in Vietnam. After the Vietnamese occupation of the country, however, it became impossible to doubt. Foreign governments and journalists, and the United Nations, were invited to inspect the evidence. It was irrefutable.

International revulsion against the Khmers Rouges did not solve the problem of who was to govern Cambodia. Western states, which had been allied to the Soviet Union during World War II, had acquiesced in the imposition and maintenance of alien governments in Eastern Europe. They were not going to make the same mistake in Cambodia, however horrible the regime that had been replaced.

The Cambodian government set up by the Vietnamese has no more legitimacy than the government set up by the Soviet Union in Afghanistan in 1979 (or than the governments of Eastern Europe). China and the United States and its allies recognized the coalition headed by Prince Sihanouk as the legitimate government of Cambodia and ensured that it retained Cambodia's place in the United Nations. These governments are at constant pains to insist that they do not recognize the Khmers Rouges and are continually embarrassed by the fact that Khieu Samphan, a prominent Khmer Rouge, represents the coalition in international gatherings, and travels frequently to the west.

THE TWO COALITIONS

There are now two alliances directly involved in Cambodia. On one side are the Vietnamese and the government they have set up in Phnom Penh, the People's Republic of Kampuchea. Opposing them is the loose grouping known as the Coalition Government of Democratic Kampuchea, which consists of the Khmers Rouges, Prince Sihanouk's party and the non-Communist Khmer People's National Liberation Front (KPNLF), led by Son Sann. In the background, but playing essential roles, are China, the Soviet Union, the United States and Thailand.

THE PEOPLE'S REPUBLIC OF KAMPUCHEA

The Phnom Penh government is led by Heng Samrin, who heads the (pro-Vietnamese) Cambodian Communist party (the Kampuchean People's revolutionary Party), and Hun Sen, who is prime minister. They are both former Khmers Rouges who fled Phnom Penh during the purge of Cambodians who had connections with Vietnam.

A 1985 report by American civil rights advocates, the Lawyers' Committee for Human Rights, found 'a pervasive pattern of officially sanctioned torture, inhumane treatment and disrespect for individual liberty' in Cambodia. Amnesty International, in 1987, was able to document a consistent pattern of political oppression, illegal executions and torture by the regime. The People's Republic thus fits the pattern of most other Communist states, but is infinitely preferable to the Khmers Rouges.

The regime claims to control virtually the whole national territory, but guerrillas mount frequent attacks on government convoys, and in fact, the government's writ probably does not run in the remoter parts of the country, particularly in the west and north. The regime's army of 30,000 is not nearly large enough to defeat the opposition armies if the Vietnamese were not there to back it up.

Cambodia, like Vietnam, is desperately poor. A catastrophic famine after the Vietnamese victory in 1979 was somewhat mitigated by an international relief effort. The country's agriculture is naturally rich and the country relatively under-populated, so Cambodia can feed itself, at least in rice, now that there is adequate security in the rice-growing areas. But it is a subsistence economy, and the few foreigners permitted to visit Phnom Penh have found the population, particularly the children, severely undernourished. They report that the city is now partly repopulated, but that life appears to be drab and miserable. Life expectancy is 45 years and infant mortality is 21.6 per cent (compared to 60 years and 9.8 per cent in Vietnam). The standard wage is about $2.00 a month.

THE COALITION GOVERNMENT OF DEMOCRATIC KAMPUCHEA

The Khmers Rouges   After their defeat in 1979, the Khmers Rouges, seeing that they needed international support, reorganized their movement. Pol Pot relinquished the title of prime minister, handing over to Khieu Samphan. Initially, they set up a fictitious united front: the Patriotic and Democratic National United Front of Great National Union of Kampuchea. In June 1982, this organization was dissolved when the Khmers Rouges entered into a coalition with Prince Sihanouk and Son Sann.

Whatever the organization, Pol Pot remained secretary of the Central Committee of the (anti-Vietnamese) Communist party, and commander-in-chief of the Khmer Rouge army – the National Army of Democratic Kampuchea. He and his closest associates are either still in Cambodia, directing the resistance, or else in China. The Khmer Rouge army is about 40,000 strong, the largest in Cambodia, and controls refugee camps housing about 70,000 people along the

border.

The Khmer People's National Liberation Front   This anti-Communist organization was set up by Son Sann, who was prime minister of Cambodia under Prince Sihanouk on various occasions. It attempts to bring together all Cambodians who are not wholly committed to the Vietnamese puppet regime or to the Khmers Rouges, and it enjoys the support of the Thai government and the West, although that support is more moral than military. It controls most of the refugee camps in Thailand and has at least some guerrilla forces operating inside Cambodia, but it is no real threat to the Phnom Penh regime nor, probably, could it survive a direct clash with the Khmers Rouges.

In the Lawyers' Committee for Human Rights report, it was stated that, although the KPNLF was committed to human rights, and

despite periodic efforts by the KPNLF's top leadership to enforce discipline among its troops and to establish the rule of law in KPNLF border settlements, a situation of lawlessness often prevailed there. During the worst of these episodes, both non-combatants and troops were beaten, detained under harsh conditions, and sometimes killed by military or administrative personnel.

The National United Front for an Independent, Neutral, Peaceful and Cooperative Cambodia   This grandiosely named organization (known by its French acronym of FUNCINPEC) consists of Prince Sihanouk and his entourage. They directly control some small camps along the Thai border, and claim to have a guerrilla army inside Cambodia, but in fact, the Front's entire strength is Sihanouk himself. He retains a considerable diplomatic reputation abroad, and it is assumed that he would wield great influence in Cambodia if the Vietnamese withdrew and he were permitted to return to Phnom Penh. He is titular head of the three-party coalition. In December 1987 and January 1988, he conducted negotiations with the People's Republic government, in Paris; the negotiations failed.

In May 1987, and again in January 1988, Sihanouk announced that he was resigning as head of the coalition, citing, on the first occasion, attacks on his supporters by the Khmers Rouges and, on the second, differences with the KPNLF. His announcements were not taken seriously.

THE OUTSIDE POWERS

Cambodia remains a sideshow. Vietnam's chief concern is its own wretched condition and relations with China. The Communist Vietnamese occupied Cambodia for the same reason that their predecessors in Saigon invaded it, to clear the approaches to Saigon and to avoid facing a war on two fronts. After their border war in 1979, relations between China and Vietnam remain as tense as any in the world. The Vietnamese fear their giant neighbour to the north, and the Chinese fear encirclement. China's main concern is the danger from the Soviet Union, and it considers Vietnam a client state of the USSR. It therefore supported Pol Pot when he was in power in Phnom Penh, and supports him now.

The Soviets, in turn, use their position in Vietnam (and are welcomed there) as a threat to China. Vietnam could not maintain its armies in Cambodia without Soviet support – and when there was a change of policy in Moscow, Vietnam changed, too. It does not seem to be a coincidence that, within a six-month period, the USSR should have decided to withdraw from Afghanistan, Vietnam from Cambodia and Cuba from Angola.

Thailand supports the guerrillas, of all sorts, through fear of the Vietnamese. It has no wish to have so powerful and belligerent a state as Vietnam on its borders. Thailand is host to 75,580 refugees from Laos, 293,210 from Cambodia and 15,710 from Vietnam. (For the Thai–Laos border war, 1987–8, *see below*).

As for the United States, it has discovered that the fall of the dominoes in Indochina did not affect its security in the slightest. It would like the Soviets to leave Cam Ranh Bay, if that could be arranged, but that is not a high American priority. The trauma of the Vietnam war has not been forgotten, and the American people have no wish to involve themselves in Indochina again. When the Philippines demanded a great increase in the rent the US pays for its bases there, threatening to close them if the claim were not accepted, the Reagan administration took the demand calmly. If the Soviets pull out of Vietnam, there will no longer be any essential reason for so large an American presence in the Philippines.

It will be noted that none of the players is in the least concerned with ideology or morality.

THE FUTURE

The key to Cambodia's future is in Moscow and Peking. Mikhail Gorbachev wants to improve the Soviet Union's relations with China, and the Chinese insist that the USSR must end its connection with Vietnam, and that Vietnam must end its occupation of Cambodia.

In the spring of 1988, the first signs of a possible settlement appeared. There were by then between 125,000 and 140,000 Vietnamese troops in Cambodia, down from a maximum of 180,000 during the 1984–5 offensive. On 25 May, Vietnam announced that it would withdraw 50,000 troops from Cambodia by the end of the year, and complete its withdrawal by 1990. Later, it moved the date up to September 1989. At the end of June 1988, it withdrew its military command from Cambodia, putting its remaining troops there under Cambodian command. In a press conference in Saigon on 1 July, a Vietnamese general revealed Vietnam's casualties during its war in Cambodia: 30,000 killed in the Khmers Rouges' attacks across the border in 1977–8; and 25,000 during the Vietnamese invasion and nine years of occupation. Many of the dead were victims of malaria and of mines left by the Khmers Rouges. The Vietnamese also claimed that they had already withdrawn 25,000 troops from Laos.

After nine years' effort, Vietnam was at last admitting failure. There can be little doubt that the decision was the result of Vietnam's own economic catastrophe (there was a real danger of famine), and pressure from the Soviet Union. If the Soviets could withdraw from Afghanistan, they could also oblige Vietnam to withdraw from Cambodia, an occupation that causes them almost equal political embarrassment to no perceptible advantage. The USSR subsidizes Vietnam to the tune of $2 billion a year, half of which goes to the occupation of Cambodia and most of the rest to maintaining Vietnam's defences against China. For Gorbachev, there were large savings to be made by diplomacy.

The Vietnamese decision to pull out of Cambodia instantly provoked a flurry of diplomatic activity. There seemed to be several possible results: a coalition government headed by Sihanouk, including some or all of the various factions; a resumption of the civil war; or a return of the Khmers Rouges. It was also possible that these three outcomes would all occur, seriatim.

Foreign observers speculated that Cambodia might become a Far Eastern Lebanon, divided into hostile zones, all fighting each other; or a Burma, with a weak central government and various guerrilla groups controlling the border districts; or a Philippines, with a central government battling a strong and aggressive guerrilla enemy. In the Lebanese parallel, Vietnam would represent Syria, and eastern Cambodia, the country's richest province where 60 per cent of the population lives, would represent the Bekaa valley. However, it does not seem likely that the Cambodians can reach a peaceful settlement among themselves, and it is perfectly certain that Cambodia will never be at peace until the danger of a Khmer Rouge restoration is eliminated.

During the Vietnamese occupation, the non-Communist South-east Asian states, grouped together as the Association of South-East Asian Nations (ASEAN), insisted that the first step was a Vietnamese withdrawal. Now they are faced with the prospect that their opening negotiating position may become a reality.

Their first reaction was to revive an idea that had been floating around for years, that there should be a 'cocktail party' to which the Cambodians would be invited. Not formal negotiations, just a party. Sihanouk chose that moment to resign yet again as head of the coalition government. He denounced the Khmers Rouges, and observed that anyone who believed that they had changed their nature 'has to be naïve or an idiot'.

He sent his son, Prince Norodom Ranariddh, to represent him at the 'cocktail party', which was renamed the 'Jakarta informal meeting' and took place in Bogor, Indonesia, on 25 July 1988. Sihanouk chose to visit Jakarta at the same time, as a 'personal guest' of President Suharto. The other delegates to the meeting were: Vietnamese foreign minister, Nguyen Co Thach; the Phnom Penh government, represented by its prime minister, Hun Sen; Khieu Samphan for the Khmers Rouges; and Son Sann for the KPNLF. They were joined by delegates from Laos and ASEAN nations. The meeting was not a success. Nothing was agreed after four days of talks. None of the Cambodian factions shifted its position (though Sihanouk summoned them to meet him on the third day and lectured them on the need for national unity).

China has a plan: it has proposed a coalition government, headed by Sihanouk, and consisting of each of the four main parties (Sihanouk's FUNCINPEC, Son Sann's KPNLF, the Phnom Penh government and the Khmers Rouges). Each party would be able to veto whoever the other three chose to represent them in the coalition, and there would be a freeze on present troop levels as well as internationally supervised elections. This plan was, of course, rejected: it would leave Pol Pot, whatever his title, in control of the largest army in Cambodia.

The Chinese also floated the suggestion that they might 'invite' Pol Pot and his closest associates to Peking, where they would live in comfortable exile. After a report of this appeared in Western newspapers, Peking denied it – but of all the proposals for saving Cambodia from a return of the Khmers Rouges, that was the

157

only one that might work. China and the Soviet Union also agreed to hold direct talks on the future of Cambodia – in February 1989, the Chinese invited Mikhail Gorbachev to visit Peking for the first Sino–Soviet summit since 1959. If the two sides can reach an agreement, they can doubtless impose it upon their clients.

The other Cambodian factions continued to struggle with their dilemma. In November 1988, Hun Sen, the Cambodian prime minister, visited Sihanouk in Paris in an attempt to form a united front against the Khmers Rouges. He insisted that the Vietnamese would keep their promise and withdraw from Cambodia by March 1990, and promised free elections and a coalition government – from which the Khmers Rouges would be excluded. Sihanouk was much less sanguine. He felt that only China had the force to prevent a Khmer Rouge restoration, and therefore refused to cut himself off from the Chinese by forming an alliance with the Vietnamese puppet government in Phnom Penh.

The Khmers Rouges, in their camps along the Thai border, prepared to invade Cambodia as soon as the Vietnamese withdrew. They mobilized the refugees, drafting every able-bodied young man or woman to carry munitions and material to dumps inside Cambodia, and moved the camps across the border. The Vietnamese retaliated by shelling the camps, driving the refugees back. This could be only a temporary measure. In the years since they were driven out of their last strongholds inside Cambodia, the Khmers Rouges have rebuilt their armies, with Chinese supplies and the complicity of the Thai government. They are now reported to have two years' worth of weapons ready for the next war.

In December 1988, the Vietnamese announced that they would advance their troop withdrawal to September 1989 if a diplomatic agreement could be reached by then. It looked a difficult task. A series of conferences were planned to attempt to resolve the problems, but the main antagonists – the Phnom Penh government and the Khmers Rouges – showed no willingness to compromise. The outcome once again depended on Peking and Moscow.

On 5 April, 1989, Vietnam abandoned its demand that foreign aid for the opposition cease before it would withdraw, and announced that its last 50,000 troops would leave Cambodia by 26 September. A conference was convened in Paris to attempt to avert a resumption of the civil war. It was attended by the four Cambodian parties, the Vietnamese, Chinese and ASEAN governments, with the French and Indonesian foreign ministers as co-chairmen. It broke down on 30 August. The disagreement was over the role of the UN in supervising a ceasefire and elections and, above all, over the composition of the proposed interim government. The Phnom Penh government, led by Hun Sen, refused to admit a role for the Khmers Rouges, and the Khmers Rouges, with their Chinese patrons, and with Prince Sihanouk tagging along behind, refused to accept any solution that excluded them. It seemed only too certain that a new civil war would break out in the New Year. Perhaps the best Cambodia could hope for was a replay of the events in Afghanistan, where the government installed by the invading Soviets has survived their departure, but war rages furiously in the countryside. Anything would be preferable to a return of the Khmers Rouges.

THE THAI-LAOS BORDER WAR, 1987–8

In November 1987, a border dispute between Thailand and Laos erupted into a brief war. The trouble was ostensibly over a 27-sq. mile (43 sq. km) stretch of mountainous territory in the north; a border agreement between France and Siam in 1907 had left the exact line unclear. However, it seems likely that the dispute concerned more than an undemarcated border. These remote hills are the centre of the opium trade, in the Golden Triangle, and are also the route by which China supplies its allies in the Cambodian civil war, as well as that by which anti-Communist Vietnamese guerrillas infiltrate into Vietnam. Finally, there has been an ongoing dispute between the two countries on the refugee question. Hmong tribesmen in Laos have tried to escape into Thailand, and the Thai army has tried to stop them, with mixed success. As noted above, there are 75,000 Laotian refugees in Thailand.

By the time agreement on a ceasefire was reached on 17 February 1988, Laos had lost about 200 men and Thailand between 70 and 100. Laos and Thailand had both moved troops into the disputed district, and Laotian artillery had shelled Thai villages and Thailand had bombed Laotian positions. In June, Vietnam announced that it would withdraw 20,000 men, half its garrison, from Laos. This decision, especially if it is followed by a similar withdrawal from Cambodia, will probably solve the difference between Thailand and Laos.

FURTHER READING

American University, *Cambodia: A Country Study*, Washington D.C., 1979.
Amnesty International, *Kampuchea: Political Imprisonment and Torture*, London 1987.
Becker, Elizabeth, *When the War Was Over*, New York, Simon and Schuster, 1986.
Chanda, Nayan, *Brother Enemy: The War After the War*, New York, Harcourt, Brace, Jovanovitch, 1986.
Lawyers' Committee for Human Rights, *Kampuchea: After the Worst*, New York, 1985.
Ngor, Haing, *A Cambodian Odyssey*, New York, Macmillan 1987.
Shawcross, William, *Sideshow*, New York, Simon and Schuster, 1979.
——, *The Quality of Mercy*, New York, Simon and Schuster, 1984.

CHINA

Geography	3,691,500 sq. miles (9,560,948 sq. km). The third largest country on Earth, under half the size of the USSR, and slightly smaller than Canada.
Population	1096 million. The population is 80 per cent rural – but that leaves almost 220 million, twice the population of Japan, in the cities.
GNP per capita	$300
Refugees	100,000 Tibetans in India. Internal: 350,000, mostly ethnic Chinese, from Vietnam.

China has fought one major war since its revolution in 1949, and that was in Korea. There have also been conflicts with the Soviet Union, India and Vietnam, and with the Nationalist regime in Taiwan, and it has conquered Tibet and suppressed uprisings there. None of the issues that provoked the various conflicts has been resolved, and they may all flare up again. Indeed, there was rioting in Lhasa in 1987 and 1988, and skirmishing with Vietnam on the Spratly islands in 1988.

Obviously, a frontier dispute between such large, powerful and belligerent states as China and the Soviet Union could be a real danger to the peace of the world. For the moment at least, both countries' internal problems are so severe that a serious conflict between them is unlikely. The greatest dangers facing China are internal: when Deng Xiaoping sent the tanks into Tiananmen Square on 4 June 1989, he did not resolve the crisis: he merely postponed it and exacerbated it. All Deng's reforms have failed utterly to resolve the question of the legitimacy of the regime, which has been the central question in China since 1911. How can such a vast and diverse country adapt itself to the modern world? Is the choice still between Communist orthodoxy accompanied by economic stagnation, and political pluralism accompanied by economic progress?

These are matters of great concern to the rest of the world. If China's economy continues to expand smoothly at the rate it achieved in the 1980s (9.4 per cent in 1987), it will overtake the Soviet Union early in the next century, and Japan
and Western Europe soon afterwards. China has ten times Japan's population and

far greater natural resources. If the Chinese now follow the example that Japan has set since 1945, and stick to developing their economy, they will dominate the world in the middle of the next century. Indeed, if it had not been for the Communist revolution, they might have done so by the end of this century.

Conversely, if the Tiananmen massacre permanently blights China's economic growth, and it relapses into violent disputes over the thoughts of Chairman Deng, it may become more prone to foreign adventure, against the USSR, Taiwan or Vietnam.

HISTORY

There is nowhere like it. Only Egypt, as a nation, is older, and only Japan has anything approaching the same continuity. China's size and populousness and the uninterrupted stretch of distinctively Chinese civilization over the millennia are unique. Periodically, the Chinese state disintegrated; it was always reconstituted.

The modern tragedy of China was that, unlike Japan, its 19th-century rulers refused to adapt to the times, resisting barbarian influence to the end. China's last dynasty (Chin) was originally Manchu, nomads who conquered the country in the 17th century. In their decadence, ruled by the malevolent Empress Dowager Tzu Hsi, they allowed China to dissolve in corruption and feudal factionalism. The Chin were finally swept away in the revolution of 1911, which was inspired by Western-educated but wholly Chinese intellectuals led by Sun Yat-sen.

It seemed for a while that China would follow Japan's example and modernize while retaining its essential national characteristics. Western powers, particularly the Americans, were heavily involved in the effort. The Portuguese, Russians, Germans, British and Americans had won extra-territorial bases in China, and the privileged status of foreigners in Shanghai was a constant irritant to Chinese susceptibilities. But these concessions helped China modernize, and until 1937, none of the powers ever tried to conquer China. It was too big.

The Nationalist government itself was never able to establish uncontested control across the whole country; there were coups and short civil wars, and warlords established themselves in various parts of the huge territory. By 1928, Chiang Kai-shek, the leader of the Kuomintang (KMT) party, controlled the country, or most of it. He might have led China into the modern world, but the great depression hit China hard, and in 1931, Japan seized Manchuria, site of much of China's most modern industry, and, in 1937, set out to conquer all China.

The war was as brutal as Hitler's invasion of the Soviet Union. When Japan captured Nanking, the capital, its troops looted the city, destroyed its public buildings and massacred between 40,000 and 200,000 people, according to different estimates. It was the first of the great atrocities of World War II.

China's losses in the war against Japan were enormous, perhaps as high as 20 million. Japan occupied the eastern third of the country, but never defeated it, for the same reasons that Hitler never conquered the Soviet Union: the country was too big, the resistance far stronger than Tokyo had expected, and Western assistance played a crucial role. There is a tendency in the US to minimize the Soviet Union's role in defeating Hitler, and to minimize China's role in defeating Japan. They were both essential.

Another problem Chiang faced from the start, and which ultimately defeated him, was the Chinese Communist party. It was an indigenous creation, at first led   **161** by students who had studied in Europe and imbibed Marxism in the heady days after the Bolshevik Revolution, and like other Communist parties, it took its lead from Moscow. However, the Bolsheviks, except for Trotsky and his followers, were more concerned with preserving the USSR than with world revolution, so they remained allied to Chiang Kai-shek and his Kuomintang, even after Chiang had suppressed the Communists in Shanghai in April 1927, slaughtering at least 10,000 of them. There followed the first of many leadership disputes in the Communist party. Mao Tse-tung and his followers, who wanted to build the revolution among the peasantry, prevailed. Stalin preached moderation to the Chinese Communists until the end, sowing the seeds of the bitter split between the two countries that came into the open in the 1960s.

The party moved into the countryside to regroup. There it was constantly harried by Nationalist troops, and it retreated into South China, where it was in danger of being crushed permanently. In 1934, Mao led his troops in what became known as the Long March, across 6200 miles (10,000 km) of desolate territory to the far north-west. He set out with over 190,000 people, including 100,000 troops, but there were only 20,000 when they arrived in Shensi. Chiang, believing them defeated, left them alone, and turned to face the Japanese.

The Chinese Communists joined the fight against them but, immediately after the war, resumed the revolution. Despite huge quantities of American aid, the Nationalist armies collapsed, and on 1 October 1949, Mao proclaimed the People's Republic in Tiananmen Square in Peking. Chiang took refuge on Taiwan (Formosa), an island that had been occupied by the Japanese from 1895 until 1945.

MAO'S CHINA

By the time Mao died in 1976, his government had a number of achievements to its credit. It had united the entire country, and suppressed banditry and warlords. It had restored national prestige for the first time in centuries: a year after the revolution, China had entered the Korean war and fought the Americans to a standstill, at a time when the United States was at the apogee of its power. Mao had rejected Soviet attempts to turn China into another satellite, and had established China as a leading spokesman of the Third World. In a long duel with Washington, Peking had eventually persuaded the Americans to recognize the People's Republic as the sole legitimate government of China.

Foreign policy – except for the Korean war (see Korea, pp. 197–203) – was a success. Domestic policy was a disaster. Mao inflicted an extreme Communist ideology upon the country, abolishing not only private property and farms, but even the villages that were the heart of Chinese society, and the institution of the traditional family. Perhaps a million landlords were executed, and China's peasants were driven into communes, like the Israeli kibbutzim, only with two essential differences. The kibbutz is a wholly democratic and voluntary society; in the communes, everything from the planting schedule to people's reading matter was directed by the party. The kibbutzim are small and manageable; the communes were huge.

The evident failures of his policies led Mao to try ever more extreme measures. In 1957, he launched a 'self-criticism campaign', proclaiming 'Let a hundred flowers bloom, let a hundred schools of thought contend,' in the hope of radicalizing the party. The Chinese took him literally, and demanded democracy, private property and an end to Communist mismanagement. The campaign was hastily abandoned, and those who had believed Chairman Mao and had raised their voices in complaint were shot or imprisoned. In 1958, he proclaimed the Great Leap Forward, a programme of forced economic development, believing that China could manage in five years what had taken 40 in the Soviet Union. It was a disaster, and set the Chinese economy back by a generation.

THE CULTURAL REVOLUTION

Mao's colleagues succeeded in curbing his powers and, in the early 1960s, set about reforming the economy. Mao struck back in 1966 with the Great Proletarian Cultural Revolution, one of the most extraordinary episodes in modern history. It was suddenly initiated in July 1966, when Mao, then 73, emerged from seclusion and swam the Yangtze River, an event that was given huge publicity and was supposed to show that Mao's revolutionary zeal and strength were unimpaired. There was a great purge of the government, like Stalin's purges in the 1930s, with Mao's oldest comrades in arms accused of treachery.

He incited students to rise against the government at every level – from schools to the central authorities in Peking – attacking 'monsters and demons'. His slogan was 'Bombard the headquarters'. In August 1966, he ordered the formation of 'Red Guards' of students, who would storm the heights of society and attack the 'leading capitalist-roaders', meaning senior party members who opposed him.

On 18 August, Mao addressed a crowd of a million Red Guards in Tiananmen Square. Other rallies followed, culminating in November with one that allegedly was attended by 2.5 million enthusiastic revolutionaries. The Red Guards rushed around the country, singing 'The Great Helmsman' or 'The East Is Red' and waving little red books containing Mao's thoughts. Their favourite 'thought' was:

A revolution is not a dinner party, or writing an essay, or painting a picture, or doing embroidery; it cannot be so refined, so leisurely and gentle, so temperate, kind, courteous, restrained and magnanimous. A revolution is an insurrection, an act of violence by which one class overthrows another.

They attacked 'The Four Olds' – old thought, old culture, old customs, old habits. That meant destroying a great deal of Chinese history and the accumulation of art treasures. Red Guards went to Tibet and destroyed 3000 monasteries and temples, built over 500 years.

Universities were closed for years, party leaders were killed or exiled and anarchy became the watchword. In January 1967, Red Guards seized control of Shanghai, the country's largest city, and Mao urged those in every other city to follow their example. The model was the Paris Commune of 1871. Party leaders were paraded before 'struggle meetings' of Red Guards, to abjure their past mistakes, with dunces' caps on their heads and placards setting out their failings hung around their necks. Sometimes they were driven thus attired through Peking on the backs of trucks.

Mao himself began to worry at the violence that he had unleashed, and began to favour the establishment of joint committees of Red Guards, party cadres and army personnel. These committees sprang up everywhere, replacing the party committees. They were dominated by the army.

163

In early 1967, the tide of revolution ebbed for a while, but soon it returned stronger than ever. Liu Shao-qui, president of China and Mao's principal rival, was denounced as an American spy. His wife was dragged to a struggle meeting, and dressed in silks and high heels and a necklace of pingpong balls. Liu died of privation in jail in 1969.

The Great Proletarian Cultural Revolution reached its peak in the summer of 1967, with the country slipping rapidly into anarchy, factions fighting each other and the Red Guards being constantly egged on by Mao and his supporters. Finally, as fighting broke out between units of the army, even Mao saw that the troubles had gone far enough, and started to rein in the Red Guards. It took several years to bring the country back to reason; the Cultural Revolution officially ran from the spring of 1966 to the spring of 1969, but for years afterwards, there was constant political turmoil and sporadic upheavals.

In the course of the Cultural Revolution, by Western estimates, 400,000 people were killed (the Chinese admit to 35,000 deaths), and the government remained paralysed and ineffectual from 1966 until Mao died ten years later.

In late September 1971, there occurred one of the most mysterious episodes of recent history – the alleged plot and flight of Lin Biao. Lin was minister of defence, and had been officially designated as Mao's 'Close Comrade in Arms and Successor'. He had been the prime mover of the Cultural Revolution, after Mao, and continued to be one of the leading figures in the state. Then suddenly it was announced that he had tried to stage a *coup d'état*, and murder Mao. The plot allegedly involved bazookas, exploding oil storage tanks and bombing Mao's residence. When it was discovered, according to the official story, Lin fled to the airport with his wife, his son and various other people, including five members of the Politburo. They fled in Lin's personal Trident and headed for the Soviet Union, but the plane ran out of fuel over Mongolia and crashed, killing everyone on board. The confusion was so great that the annual celebration of the Revolution on 1 October had to be cancelled.

The only part of this improbable story that can be confirmed is that a plane did indeed crash in Mongolia. Even now, 12 years after the death of Mao, no convincing account has ever been given of what was involved in the dispute between Mao and Lin, and the details of the plot remain unconfirmed. The fall of Lin Biao was followed by a full-scale purge throughout the army and the party.

MAO'S LAST DAYS AND THE GANG OF FOUR

During the early 1970s, Chou En-lai, Mao's long-term deputy and the chief moderating influence in the state, managed to have some of the exiled 'rightists' returned to power. The most important of these was Deng Xiaoping. In the 1950s and 1960s, he had been among the handful of people who governed China, as secretary-general of the Chinese Communist party. As the Cultural Revolution got under way, he had remarked: 'It doesn't matter whether a cat is black or white, so long as it catches mice.' This was taken (correctly) to be an aspersion cast upon Mao's theoretical intransigence, and Deng's slogan became a major charge against him and a rallying cry for his supporters. Having been disgraced in 1966, he had been lucky to escape with his life, and had spent the intervening years working in a

cafeteria in an army barracks.

The rightists' restoration was difficult and gradual – Deng was reappointed to the Central Committee in August 1973 – and was vigorously opposed by the radicals, including sometimes Mao himself. Simultaneously, Chou organized the reversal of alliances, institutionalizing China's hostility to the Soviet Union and, in February 1972, welcoming President Nixon to Peking. Nixon was photographed taking tea with Chairman Mao.

The radicals were not yet defeated. In 1974, they began a 'Criticize Confucius' campaign in which the merits of the long-dead sage were endlessly and passionately discussed: by Confucius, the radicals meant Chou En-lai. Then they started a campaign praising Shih Huang Ti, the first Chin Emperor, who had united China, built the Great Wall – and burned the works of Confucius. He is generally regarded as a ferocious tyrant, but the radicals praised him and his work as a way of praising Mao, and attacking Chou and his protégé, Deng Xiaoping. They also denounced Western music, notably Beethoven, as imperialist and decadent and another manifestation of 'monsters and demons'. However, by 1975, Deng had been restored to all his posts and was once again effectively running the country.

Both Mao and Chou were dying, and the fight was over the succession. Chou died in January 1976, and the leftists then engaged in a last, desperate battle for power. Mao, in his dotage, was manipulated by his wife and her closest associates, later collectively known as 'the Gang of Four'. On 5 April occurred the 'Tiananmen Incident'. The authorities had removed a vast accumulation of wreaths honouring Chou that had been laid on a memorial there, and a huge protest demonstration turned into a riot in which party buildings were burned. Deng was blamed for the riot, and was again deposed, but military friends got him safely out of Peking. All over China, there were immense public demonstrations of popular support for him: Deng was clearly seen to be the heir of Chou En-lai, and the last hope of saving China from a renewal of the Cultural Revolution.

In July 1976, an earthquake killed 800,000 people in Tientsin and the government's incompetence was strikingly revealed (there were no relief operations for weeks). The heavens themselves blaze forth the death of kings: the disaster, like other similar catastrophes in China's long history, was taken as an omen – Mao had lost the Mandate of Heaven, by whose grace the emperors once reigned, and there was about to be a change of dynasty.

Mao died on 9 September 1976. A month later, the 'Gang of Four' were arrested in a *coup d'état* organized by the army, security police and members of the government determined to prevent a return to the anarchy of the Cultural Revolution. No other country of comparable importance has passed through such drama and difficulty since 1945.

Within a year, Deng had established his power over the government, and then started the economic reforms that have already dramatically changed the face of China. The people's communes were abolished, and Communism has been abandoned in agriculture (though complete price freedom has not been entirely restored); self-management of businesses and even the private ownership of firms and a stock market have been introduced in the cities.

The economic changes introduced by Deng after 1976 were revolutionary, but were not accompanied by any loosening of the controls exercised by the Communist Party. Where Gorbachev opened the Soviet political scene to all tendencies while proceeding most cautiously in economic reform, Deng chose the opposite course. Each has now discovered that the two must go together.

The explosion came quite suddenly. Hu Yaobang, the government's leading reformist, had been purged after an earlier spate of pro-democracy demonstrations in Peking in 1987. He died on 15 April 1989, and the next day there was a small demonstration of mourning in Tiananmen Square. It was like the mourning for Chou En-lai in 1976. The students marched on the square, and soon there were demonstrations of hundreds of thousands of people demanding reform, democracy and an end to official corruption. The students occupied the square for six weeks, and quickly won the overwhelming support of the general population. Students in other cities followed their example. They were supported by Zhao Ziyang, the party's secretary general, and soon there was a ferocious battle between Zhao and his supporters, and the hardliners led by Deng, who was 84, and the prime minister, Li Peng. Deng told the Politburo: 'We shouldn't be afraid of bloodshed or pressure from international public opinion . . . We have three million troops.'

The students started a hunger strike, and petitioned the government. Zhao emerged to plead with them to give up the strike, and Li Peng grudgingly agreed to hold a televised debate with their leaders. Martial law was proclaimed but the citizens of Peking protected the students. At the beginning of June, they erected a 'Statue of Democracy' in the square, modelled on the Statue of Liberty. Early in the morning of 4 June, Deng sent the troops and tanks into the square. There was heavy fighting and thousands of people were killed (between 2,000 and 5,000 according to different estimates). Many soldiers were killed by the crowds and their trucks were burnt.

It was a disaster for Deng as well as for the students. He had called in the Old Guard to support his hard line, and now the Old Guard demanded an end to all his reforms. Paradoxically, therefore, reformers hoped for Deng's survival. Foreign trade and tourism came to a standstill. Hong Kong, due to be returned to China in 1997, panicked. It seemed only too probable that a new period of turmoil had begun.

TIBET

Tibet occupies 745,000 sq. miles (1.9 million sq. km) on the roof of the world. It has few natural resources, and until the Chinese conquest in 1950, its 2–3 million people led peaceful lives as shepherds, peasants, small traders and monks. Lhasa, the capital, had a population of about 30,000, but other Tibetan towns contained far fewer people (they would be considered villages in Europe) and most of them served the monasteries. Perhaps 10 per cent of the people lived in these, following 'The Way', under the direction of the Dalai Lama. Tibet was the only complete theocracy in the world.

The Dalai Lama is the reincarnation of one of the aspects of the Buddha. His authority is therefore absolute in Tibet, like the Imam Khomeini's in Iran, the difference being that Buddhism is a pacifist creed. When the Dalai Lama dies, search parties scour the countryside to find the baby who is the new Incarnation. The current Dalai Lama is the 14th in this line, and although he fled Tibet in 1959 and now lives in India, there is no doubt that virtually all Tibetans remain wholly devoted to him.

China had asserted sovereignty over Tibet from time to time over the centuries, and had occasionally enforced it for brief periods. However, the country was so remote, and so poor, that the Celestial Empire usually left it alone.

In the twentieth century there was constant squabbling between Lhasa and successive governments in Peking, and border wars between Tibetans and various Chinese warlords. Peking never renounced its claim to Tibet and, from time to time, contemplated sending an army to enforce it. It was always dissuaded by internal dissensions and by strong British support for Tibet. The 13th Dalai Lama died in 1933, and four years later, Japan invaded China.

Tibet remained undisturbed during the war, though the Americans flew supplies to Chiang Kai-shek 'over the hump' of the Tibetan Himalayas, an exceedingly dangerous route. In 1949, Mao Tse-tung entered Peking. China was at last reunited under a strong and assertive government, and one of its first tasks was to 'reunite' the national territory: on 7 October 1950, a Chinese army occupied Lhasa.

China, at first, did little to change Tibet. The 14th Dalai Lama, by then 16 years old, was left in his palace, the monasteries were undisturbed and the Tibetan government continued to function. However, the Chinese built roads into the country, placed their garrisons at strategic points, and moved the first of several hundred thousand Chinese settlers into Tibet.

The Tibetan peasantry began to resist, and in 1955, a guerrilla movement started in the remoter parts of the country, led by the Kampas in the east. By 1959, there was a full-fledged guerrilla war in the countryside, engaging 200,000 Chinese troops. In one battle in 1958, Kampas wiped out a Chinese garrison of 3000 men.

The Chinese would not tolerate such a situation for long. The key to controlling the country was the Dalai Lama. The Chinese invited him to Peking. He declined. On 9 March 1959, the commanding Chinese general in Lhasa invited him to attend a display at the Chinese barracks there, without his usual entourage of ministers and guards. Tibetans took this as an attempt to take the Dalai Lama hostage, like the Inca Atahualpa in Peru, and a crowd of 30,000 Tibetans gathered around the summer palace to protect him. The Chinese fired shells into the palace grounds in warning and moved troops into Lhasa, and the Dalai Lama then decided to escape. He fled on horseback to India, arriving there with 80 followers on 30 March.

When news of the successful escape reached the Chinese in Lhasa, they dispersed the crowds with great violence, killing about 3000 people. There was a great upsurge of fighting throughout Tibet: the Dalai Lama claims that about 65,000 Tibetans were killed. Over 60,000 refugees fled to Nepal and India.

China now dissolved the remaining institutions of Tibetan independence, and installed a Communist regime. The monks were evicted from their monasteries, which were closed; the Chinese language and Chinese law and customs were imposed upon Tibet. Tibetan guerrillas continued the fight, but without any external support, and facing overwhelming odds, it was a hopeless contest.

Then in 1966, the Cultural Revolution came to Tibet. Red Guards seized control of the country and set about extirpating all traces of feudalism and superstition. It was one of the most comprehensive acts of vandalism in the 20th century, comparable to the conduct of the retreating German army in Eastern Europe. As the Germans had blown up the tsars' palaces near Leningrad, and had demolished Warsaw, so the Red Guards destroyed over 3000 temples and monasteries in Tibet. Sacred books, idols and devotional objects were also destroyed, stolen or shipped back to China. Chinese officers who tried to stop the destruction, including the commanding general, Chang Kuo-hua, were arrested by the Red Guards. The Chinese army then intervened, rescued Chang, and tried to impose order, but state terrorism against the Tibetans, many of whom were murdered, and fighting among the Chinese, continued until 1970.

Chris Mullen, writing for the Minority Rights Group, observed that the destruction of Tibetan culture, shrines, monasteries and artefacts was not spontaneous: it was carefully planned:

First, experts came and marked the precious stones, and they were then removed; then came metal experts who marked the precious metals for removal; the buildings were then dynamited and timber was taken away for use by the local commune, and the stones were left for anyone to use.

A more depressing observation was that

Most of the destruction was carried out by young Tibetans. The Chinese took care to stay in the background. No doubt the Tibetan youth were egged on by the Chinese; no doubt many now regret what they did, but the fact remains that the actual destruction of Tibet's cultural heritage was carried out by Tibetans.

In a rather similar phenomenon, ten years later, young Cambodians were taught to kill their compatriots by the Khmers Rouges.

In 1974, after the storm had abated, the Chinese granted an amnesty to the Tibetans who were in prison and began to repair the damage. In 1980, the general secretary of the Chinese Communist party, Hu Yao-bang, went to Lhasa and publicly deplored the excesses of the period 1959–74, which he blamed on the Gang of Four. (Hu himself was subsequently purged.) Some of the monasteries were restored and a few were reopened. Foreign visitors were allowed into Lhasa for the first time in a generation. They found Tibetans living in squalid conditions under harsh Chinese control, and complete alienation between the two societies.

The results of the new policy were predictable. Tibetans were not persuaded of the merits of their subjection to China simply by a little kindness, not after so much oppression. They began to demand their independence again. There were riots in Lhasa in September and October 1987, led by monks who marched through the city denouncing China; about a dozen people were killed. There were more serious disturbances in March 1988. On 5 March, at least one and perhaps three Chinese policemen were killed in a riot during a religious festival. According to the *Observer*, 30 monks were killed in the Jokhang monastery immediately afterwards, and perhaps 20 other people over the next few days. Foreigners were again expelled from Tibet.

In April, Lord Ennals, a former British Labour party minister, visited Tibet and reported that 2000 Tibetans had been arrested during the demonstrations, and that many had been tortured. In Peking, the Panchen Lama, a leading Tibetan monk who has supported the Chinese since they invaded Tibet, said that five people were killed, including one policeman, and 200 detained during the March riots. He also said that the Dalai Lama would be allowed to return to Lhasa if he gave up his demands for Tibetan independence. Previously, China had insisted that the Dalai Lama must live in Peking. (The Panchen Lama died in January 1989.)

The human rights group Asia Watch reported in July 1988 that several hundred Tibetans were still detained and that 'there is little doubt now that torture is often part of the routine in political arrests and incarceration in Tibet, and that the use of cattle prods is common in such instances.'

The riots were a great embarrassment to the Chinese government, but there is little likelihood that it will abandon Tibet. China is not a multilational state, like the Soviet Union, India, Ethiopia or Nigeria, which might disintegrate under particularist pressure. There are many small nationalities on the fringes of China, but the overwhelming majority of the population are Chinese and will always be able to impose themselves upon the minorities.

So the Dalai Lama and a community of about 80,000 Tibetan refugees live in India and Nepal, and try to preserve Tibetan culture from Chinese oppression. They take consolation from their study of The Way, and hope that a new revolution of the Wheel of Life, that once drove them from their homes, will some day take them back again.

TAIWAN

The People's Republic of China (with its capital at Peking) and the Republic of China (based in Taiwan) both insist that China is one and indivisible. They both claim to represent the country, but since 1978 the United States has recognized the People's Republic. Perhaps one day the two will be reunited, but there is no sign of it now.

On the contrary, Taiwan is growing away from the mainland. It has enjoyed sustained economic prosperity, and is now one of the 'four little dragons' of Asia, along with South Korea, Hong Kong and Singapore, treading in Japan's footsteps. Its indigenous population, though of Chinese origin, feels no particular loyalty to Peking, any more than the Chinese of Singapore do. As the older generation – who crossed from the mainland in 1949 – die or retire, Taiwan becomes steadily more Taiwanese and less Chinese. Martial law was lifted, after 38 years, in July 1987; and after President Chiang Ching-kuo, Chiang Kai-shek's son and successor, died on 13 January 1988, a Taiwanese, Lee Teng-hui, succeeded him. Taiwan is thus quite different from Germany, which is kept divided solely by the Soviet army of occupation, or Korea, which remains one nation divided in two by ideology.

The Chinese have made no real effort to reconquer Taiwan, although in the 1950s they mounted a sustained campaign against two islands controlled by the Nationalists: Quemoy and Matsu, which lie off the Chinese coast. These unfortunate outposts were subjected to a sustained artillery bombardment in 1958–60. That episode is chiefly memorable for the role it played in the 1960 American presidential election, in which Vice-President Nixon and Senator Kennedy solemnly debated whether the United States should go to war to defend Quemoy and Matsu. If Mao ever seriously contemplated attacking them, he was dissuaded by his colleagues, and perhaps by Soviet pressure. The Chinese soon turned to symbolic attacks, firing shells that would scatter propaganda pamphlets rather than high explosives over the islands. They mounted loudspeakers to harangue the Nationalist garrisons, and the Nationalists did the same thing in retaliation. It was a pointless exercise, and it lasted for years.

169

Nowadays, China professes to have nothing but benign intentions towards Taiwan, but explicitly refuses to give up the right to use force to reconquer the lost province. It hopes that Taiwan will voluntarily return to the motherland. It is a vain hope – unless China gives up Communism altogether.

THE SINO–SOVIET DISPUTE AND THE BORDER WAR OF 1969

The border incidents between the USSR and China in 1969 were not themselves serious. A few dozen soldiers were killed fighting over an island in the Ussuri river which divides the two countries in the Far East, due north of the town of Vladivostok.

The territory was not important, but the symbolism was: China maintains that large areas of the Soviet Union, notably the Pacific province, including Vladivostok, were stolen from China in a moment of weakness in the late 19th century. The thefts were ratified in the 'unequal treaties' forced upon the Manchu (Chin) dynasty by imperial Russia.

Those were only a few of the unequal treaties; others were imposed by Germany, the United States, Britain and Portugal. Germany lost its position in China after 1918, the Americans withdrew after World War II, and the Communist occupation of Shanghai put an end to the foreign zones there. The last treaty ports, Hong Kong and Macao, will be ceded to China in 1997 and 1999, respectively.

But Russia, now known as the Soviet Union, will not cede Vladivostok, southern Siberia or the areas China claims in Central Asia. The dispute over the island in the Ussuri was therefore fraught with significance. Beyond territory, the dispute goes back to what Mao considered to be Stalin's treachery and to continuing Soviet bullying. There were also doctrinal disputes: Mao called the United States a 'paper tiger', and professed not to fear nuclear weapons.

The two countries' growing dispute was kept secret during the 1950s, and even after it burst into the open, in 1960, hardliners in Washington continued to believe it a fraud, saying that the two countries remained united under Moscow's leadership in a campaign to conquer the world. Many Americans had invested so much rhetoric in denouncing a world-wide conspiracy directed from the Kremlin that they found it impossible to adapt to reality. The same people today refuse to believe in Gorbachev's reforms.

In 1958, the Soviets abruptly suspended aid to the Chinese nuclear programme. In 1959, Nikita Khrushchev visited the United States, to Mao's deep displeasure; when the Soviet leader went to Peking for the 10th anniversary of the Communist revolution, on 1 October 1959, he was greeted with bitter attacks in party newspapers. In the Chinese manner, they were ostensibly directed against one of Mao's Chinese rivals.

In 1960, Mao launched a violent newspaper campaign against Yugoslavia; once again, the real target was Khrushchev. In July, Khrushchev retaliated by recalling all Soviet aid workers from China. They brought back their blue-prints, leaving incomplete projects everywhere, and for several years China was seriously isolated.

Throughout the 1960s, the Chinese continued to be bitterly opposed to both the Soviet Union and to the United States. By the end of the decade, however, they had concluded that, despite the latter's involvement in Vietnam, the danger from the north was more to be feared. The doctrinal disputes carried on, with Mao accusing Khrushchev and his successors of 'revisionism', meaning abandonment of true Marxist principles. The Chinese began actively seeking friends and allies in the Third World, offering themselves as a proper revolutionary alternative to the Soviets.

On 2 March 1969, 300 Chinese troops occupied the island of Damansky, which the Chinese call Chenpao, in the Ussuri river, which is the boundary between China and the USSR in the north-east. The island has no strategic or economic value: it is small and uninhabited, and at that point, the river runs through a barren and marshy territory, itself almost completely unpopulated. The invading Chinese ambushed a small Soviet patrol, killing 23 and wounding 14. The Soviets sent reinforcements, who were in turn ambushed. Then both sides withdrew from the island.

The Soviets protested bitterly and publicly. The Chinese accused them of frequent violations of their border (by the summer, they had a list of 429 such incidents). There were huge anti-Soviet demonstrations outside the Soviet embassy in Peking, and even larger ones outside the Chinese embassy in Moscow.

There was further fighting on Damansky/Chenpao on 15 March, with tanks and artillery and more casualties. There were other clashes along the Amur river frontier, north of the Ussuri, in April and May, and also far to the west on the Sino–Soviet frontier in Central Asia. (Henry Kissinger concluded that the Soviets were probably the aggressors, because the Central Asian incidents occurred only a few miles from a Soviet railhead and hundreds of miles from the nearest Chinese railhead.) The Soviets also began to speculate in public about the necessity for a pre-emptive strike against Chinese nuclear installations, and they even sounded out the Nixon administration for its reaction to such an attack.

Kissinger and Nixon decided that the time had come for a rapprochement with China, and Chou En-lai had evidently come to the same conclusion. By 1970, it was clear that the United States wanted to leave Vietnam, which would eliminate the chief source of direct difficulty between the two countries. The reversal of alliances was consummated, after a secret trip to Peking by Henry Kissinger in 1971, by Nixon's visit to China in February 1972. A document signed by Nixon and Chou – the 'Shanghai Communiqué' – set the course of the two countries' future relations. The Americans then abandoned Taiwan to its fate, although full diplomatic relations with Peking were not established until 1978. By then, the new alliance was a fundamental part of both nations' foreign policy. It was not challenged during the last upheavals of Mao's lifetime, and was embraced by Deng Xiaoping, who visited the US in January 1979, and informed President Carter that China intended to attack Vietnam the following month.

Richard Nixon considers the 'China policy' to be the greatest achievement of his presidency. It was also the most conspicuous failure of Soviet policy. China remained implacably opposed to the Soviet Union until Mikhail Gorbachev initiated a *rapprochement* in 1988, and has built up a nuclear arsenal with missiles capable of hitting Moscow. Conversely, the Soviets have been obliged to move nearly half their army to defend their 4000-mile (6400-km) border with China, thus weakening their positions elsewhere in the world. It is a heavy price for an uninhabited island.

171

Mikhail Gorbachev, as part of his attempt to correct the errors of his predecessors, has proposed negotiations with China on the border dispute and on other matters outstanding. China insists that the Soviet Union must first force Vietnam to evacuate Cambodia and must itself withdraw from its bases in Vietnam and pull its troops back from the border. Gorbachev has begun to meet all these conditions, for domestic reasons as much as from a desire to lessen tensions with Peking, and on 16 May 1989, Gorbachev visited Peking for the first Sino–Soviet summit since 1959. The meeting may have reduced tensions between the two countries, but it was overshadowed by the pro–democracy demonstrators, who were then occupying Tiananmen Square. Gorbachev had to be smuggled through back streets and side doors to meet the Chinese leaders, and found them so distracted by their domestic difficulties that they could scarcely consider the implications of his visit. Its meaning was clear enough for all that: both sides wanted a reconciliation, the USSR for economic, China for political reasons. It was ironic that the two powers should have decided to bury the hatchet just as their internal problems overwhelmed the ideological causes that had provoked the long estrangement.

(For the border war with India in 1962, *see* India, pp. 175–78. For conflicts with Vietnam, and the question of the relationships between China, the USSR, Vietnam and Cambodia, *see* Vietnam, pp. 236–40 and Cambodia, pp. 145–59.)

FURTHER READING

American University, *China: A Country Study*, Washington D.C., 1981.
Bonavia, David, *The Chinese*, New York, Lippincott and Crowell, 1980.
Dietrich, Craig, *People's China: A Brief History*, Oxford University Press, 1986.
Garside, Roger, *Coming Alive: China after Mao*, New York, McGraw Hill, 1981.
Gascoigne, Bamber, *The Treasures and Dynasties of China*, London, Jonathan Cape, 1973.
Harding, Harry, *Second Revolution: China after Mao*.
Hinton, Harold C., *The People's Republic of China – a handbook*, Boulder, Colo., Westview Press, and Folkstone, Dawson, 1979.
Kissinger, Henry, *White House Years*, Boston, Little, Brown, 1979.
Richardson, Hugh M., *Tibet and Its History*, Boulder, Colo., Shambhala, 1984.
Salisbury, Harrison E., *Tiananmen Diary*, Boston, Little, Brown, 1989.

INDIA

Geography	1,269,346 sq. miles (3,287,593 sq. km). As large as Western and Central Europe, or roughly half the size of the continental United States. There are 22 states and ten union territories. Half the states have larger populations than Britain, France or West Germany.
Population	Reached 800 million in the course of 1988, growing at a rate of about 16 million a year. The great majority are Hindu; there are also 90 million Muslims, substantial Sikh and Christian communities and small Jewish and Buddhist communities. There are 50 major regional tongues in India, of which the Constitution recognizes 16 as official languages. Hindi (spoken by a quarter of the population) and English apply to the whole country. There are hundreds of other languages and dialects.
GNP per capita	$270
Refugees	Internal: 6000 Indians, 100,000 Tibetans, 125,000 Tamils from Sri Lanka, 50,000 Bangladeshis, 5600 Afghans and 1100 Iranians.

Since independence in 1947, India has fought three wars with Pakistan (the last in 1971), and a border war with China. There has been a long series of civil disputes in many parts of the country, notably in Assam along the north-east frontier. The latest and most serious is an uprising among the Sikhs, which led to the assault on the Golden Temple in Amritsar in 1984, an event that was followed by the assassination of the prime minister, Indira Gandhi, by members of her Sikh bodyguard. The Temple had to be besieged and taken by the army a second time in May 1988.

In 1974, India became the sixth country to explode a nuclear device, and ever since, Pakistan has been determined to do likewise. There is such hostility between the two that there is always the possibility of another war between them, which does not mean that a nuclear war is at all probable. India is now the dominant power in a region with a population of over 1 billion. Although it is politically allied to the Soviet Union, it is, like China, one of the great independent power centres in the world. It is too big to be dominated by any other nation. On the contrary, it is much more likely to exert intolerable pressure upon its 173 neighbours: there are now 60,000 Indian troops in Sri Lanka, and its government was forced to accept an Indian plan for settling its internal problems (*see*, pp. 229-34).

The only real threats to India come from within. Can a country so populous, so diverse and so poor maintain its national unity? The weight of its increasing population continually drags back its economic progress, thus provoking insoluble social unrest. India has survived so far because it is a democracy, allowing conflicting voices to be heard (the states are frequently in fierce opposition to New Delhi). However, the government has become the fief of the Nehru dynasty, and powerful leaders or ambitious officers may not always resist the temptation to try to solve the country's immense problems with a gun.

HISTORY

India should not be considered a nation state, like Britain, Mexico or China. It is better compared to Europe: a geographically separate entity, with many nations and languages, which all share a common history and civilization.

Indian history goes back 5000 years. A long series of immigrants and conquerors have come over the mountains from the west and from Central Asia, building empires and leaving cities and monuments behind them. The British came by sea, with other Europeans, and established trading posts in the 17th century. In the 18th, they set out to conquer India, and by the mid-19th century, they controlled the entire sub-continent from the Himalayas to Ceylon. It had never been completely united before, and its unity did not survive the passing of the British Raj.

The British gave India its independence at midnight, 14 August 1947. The greatest failure in British imperial history was the partition of India into two nations: one Muslim (Pakistan); the other ostensibly secular, but in fact Hindu (India). In the early days of the independence movement, Muslims and Hindus were united fighting the British, under the spiritual leadership of Mahatma Gandhi. It is possible that, if India had been given independence in the 1930s, it would have remained united. A vigorous imperialist movement in the Tory party in London, which was then overwhelmingly dominant in Parliament, ensured that the timid governments of those days would not attempt so bold a step. The principal leader of this Tory rearguard was Winston Churchill. His subsequent achievements should not obscure his contribution to a disaster in which at least half a million people were killed.

Because of the vagaries of Muslim proselytization in the Middle Ages, the areas of Muslim majority in India were in two separated parts: the Punjab, the Land of the Five Rivers, in the west; and East Bengal in the east. Pakistan therefore came into existence divided into two, and separated by the breadth of Hindu India. The other appendages of British India – Burma and Ceylon – became independent separately.

The partition was one of the most savage events of the century: 12 million people fled their homes, and hundreds of thousands of people were killed in inter-communal massacres. The lowest estimate was 500,000, a more probable total is between 800,000 and 1 million. Trainloads of refugees passing from one side to the other were stopped and everyone on board killed, except the train driver.

Mahatma Gandhi, by prayer and fasting and using all his immense influence, succeeded in restoring order in Delhi. A Hindu fanatic shot him there on 30 January 1948.

The British had ruled half of India directly; in the rest of the country, they had left native princes on their thrones, and ran their states through 'residents' (advisers to the princes). In 1948, the princes were invited to join India or Pakistan. Most of them, for the last time, followed their residents' advice and submitted. The grandest of all, the Nizam of Hyderabad, a Muslim prince in Hindu south India, refused. The new government sent in the army, and no more was heard of independent Hyderabad.

THE FIRST INDO-PAKISTANI WAR

The largest of the princely states was Kashmir in the far north. It is predominantly Muslim, although with a substantial Hindu minority in Jammu. The Nehru family were Kashmiri Brahmins, and the maharajah of Kashmir was a Hindu descendant of a British ally in one of their 19th-century wars, who had been put on his throne as a reward for his loyalty.

The maharajah, too, hoped for independence in 1947, but the government of Pakistan sent Muslim tribesmen into Kashmir to seize the country, and the maharajah therefore signed a treaty of accession to India on 27 October 1947. There followed the first war between India and Pakistan.

It was not a serious conflict in military terms. The Indians and Pakistanis both sent troops, who fought a series of skirmishes before agreeing to a ceasefire in January 1949. By then, India controlled most of Kashmir, but the two countries have never recognized the status quo: each still claims the whole territory.

THE WAR WITH CHINA

The border war between India and China in 1962 was a fiasco that abruptly ended India's role as the moralizing, peace-loving leader of the Third World. Despite this, India managed to save some shreds of its diplomatic reputation after the humiliating defeat of its army, largely because of the country's undeserved reputation as the apostle of peace, and because of China's deserved reputation for ruthless egoism. In fact, India was the aggressor, China the victim, and when it had beaten the Indians, China behaved with striking diplomatic restraint.

The complete military mastery of the region by the British allowed them to set India's northern borders where it best suited them. The frontier was mapped and the line drawn by Captain Henry McMahon of the Indian Army, starting in 1893. As a result, the border has since been known as the McMahon line, much as the border between Maryland and Pennsylvania is named after two earlier British surveyors, Charles Mason and Jeremiah Dixon.

There were problems with the demarcation, the chief of which was that China never accepted the McMahon line. This was an academic difficulty at the time, because China did not then control Tibet, and Britain was far more powerful. However, this situation changed after the British left India and the Chinese Communists seized power in Peking in 1949 and occupied Tibet in 1950 (*see* China, pp. 162–72). If the British had still controlled India, they would doubtless have settled the frontier question expeditiously, just as they had settled the argument over the frontier between Canada and the United States. The disputed territories were not worth fighting for, but India, like many other newly independent nations, considered its frontiers sacred, however remote and inaccessible.

A further problem was discovered at the western end of the line, where it runs through some of the wildest and highest territory on Earth, with passes that rise to 16,000 feet (5200 m) in the towering Pamirs: the line had not been properly demarcated. There were also questions about the exact location of the line further east.

The essentials of the subsequent dispute were that, before the British came, there had been no precise frontiers: each state's power extended only as far as it could march an army. The British then pushed their armies as far as civilization went in the mountains, which meant along the foothills. Finally McMahon, being a tidy-minded European cartographer, drew his line along the crest of the mountains. China rejected this extension of British territory, which the British never policed, and insisted that the frontier should remain in the foothills.

Independent India claimed everything. It even asserted its control over a clearly Tibetan enclave on the south side of the line, in the east: the 'Tawong tract'. China did not protest, and the matter might have remained undecided except that China required a corner of the western end of the border for a road into Tibet. This province is called the Aksai Chin, and is part of the Tibetan plateau and virtually uninhabited. China needed it because it was the only practical route from Sinkiang, its westernmost province, into Tibet. Beyond lies the impassable Gobi desert.

So, in 1956, China built its road. It is 750 miles (1200 km) long, 112 miles (180 km) of it in territory claimed by India.

The Indians found out about the road the next year, by reading Peking newspapers that boasted of this remarkable piece of engineering. India demanded that China evacuate the Aksai Chin. China proposed, in exchange, that the whole frontier be surveyed, and intimated that it would recognize the McMahon line in the east if India accepted its claim to the Aksai Chin and the strategic road, in the west.

India refused categorically, and even refused to negotiate the question with China. Prime Minister Jawaharlal Nehru – who had endlessly lectured and scolded the Americans, British and others on the folly of using force in international affairs, and had constantly recommended negotiations as an infallible solution to all disputes – proved as unyielding and demagogic as the most corrupt Western politician. There is some debate whether he was hypocritical or merely weak, but what is beyond dispute is that his government whipped up a storm of chauvinism. Public and Parliament demanded that the Chinese be driven out of India, and Nehru promised to do so.

To prove his determination, he ordered a campaign against Portuguese Goa, and then allowed the Indian army to occupy the colony (and two other minute Portuguese enclaves) in December 1961. The Indian army then moved what troops it could find up to the Chinese frontier and began to implement the government's new 'forward policy'.

Unfortunately, Nehru had allowed the army to deteriorate sadly since independence. It retained many of its traditions, but its equipment was outdated and insufficient, and it was quite incapable of fighting a mountain war. The syncophantic officers whom Nehru had put in command concealed this fact from him, or at least failed to persuade him of their predicament.

The army was ordered to send patrols into the disputed areas and establish permanent posts there. They had immense difficulty doing so: there were no roads, and everything had to be portered through the Himalayas. The Chinese, on the high plateau, had built themselves all-weather roads and faced no such problems. There were frequent but minor encounters between Indian and Chinese patrols. The Chinese protested repeatedly, and repeatedly demanded formal negotiations on the frontier. Chou En-lai, the Chinese prime minister, went to Delhi in April 1962, to try to persuade the Indians to settle the matter peacefully. The summit was a complete failure.

In June 1962, in the west, the Indian army was ordered to push forward to the border that India claimed in the Aksai Chin; that would have meant occupying China's road. Indian patrols were sent forward, but the terrain was so difficult that there was no chance of reaching their objective. However, for the first time, there were violent clashes between Indian and Chinese patrols, in the Chip Chap valley. By then, there were about 30 Indian positions scattered throughout the Aksai Chin.

Simultaneously, the army was ordered to establish positions along the eastern section of the McMahon line. At one point, just east of the frontier with Bhutan, an Indian protectorate high in the Himalayas, Indian patrols went beyond the McMahon line to occupy a mountain ridge that McMahon had missed on his map. China again protested, to no effect.

In July, there were further serious clashes between Indian and Chinese patrols in Chip Chap. In September, in the east, the Chinese sent patrols into the vicinity of the most forward of the Indian positions. India took this as an invasion, and the government ordered that the Chinese be expelled from 'Indian' territory. On 9 October, the Indians moved forward of their most advanced positions, knowing their situation was hopeless: they were outnumbered five to one; the Chinese were much better equipped, and held the high ground, while the Indians were pinned in the valleys. The Chinese drove them back, killing seven Indian troops. On 20 October, they attacked again, over-running Indian advance positions in the east – and simultaneously wiping out the Indians in the Aksai Chin.

Although the dispute had originally concerned the western frontier, and China's road, the fighting in the east had become much more serious: the Chinese might clear a way through to Assam.

There was another lull in the fighting, and Indian troops guarding a strategic pass, 15,000 feet (5000 m) high, could hear the Chinese below them building a road to bring up trucks and artillery. Nehru's government, in a last act of folly, ordered the army to attack again. It did so on 15 November, once more failing completely. The next day, the Chinese resumed their advance, and routed the Indians; their defensive positions collapsed and the army broke and fled. Two days later, there was nothing between the Chinese army and the plains. Nehru prepared for the loss of Assam.

At that point, on 21 November 1962, China announced a unilateral ceasefire and withdrawal. It pulled its troops back 12 miles (20 km) behind the McMahon line in the east, and behind the previous frontier in the west. All the weapons and equipment that it had captured were carefully cleaned, polished and delivered to the Indians, against receipt. India reoccupied its lost territories, but abandoned its forward policy. Its casualties were 1383 dead, 1696 missing and 3105 prisoners of war, of whom 26 died in captivity. Chinese casualties were probably about half that.   177

Despite China's largesse, India (like Argentina after the Falklands war) refused to accept defeat and, to this day, continues to claim those mountain wastes as its own. It has not negotiated with China, although the offer of recognition of the McMahon line, in exchange for recognition of China's claim to the Aksai Chin, still stands.

The fiasco led to a change of Indian priorities. India became a close ally of the Soviet Union (even though the USSR had supported China during the war, while America had supported India), and devoted much larger sums to defence. It was therefore better able to face Pakistan in the wars of 1965 and 1971. India also gave up lecturing the rest of the world on what it saw as the merits of non-alignment and pacifism.

Nehru never recovered from the shock. He had a stroke in January 1964 and died on 27 May.

THE SECOND WAR WITH PAKISTAN

In 1965, a trivial dispute between India and Pakistan over the waters of a large tidal area on the west coast, the Rann of Kutch, developed into a border war that spread to Kashmir.

After a serious military engagement in the Rann in April, a ceasefire was arranged by the British in June. However, Pakistan infiltrated guerrillas into Kashmir, in the hope of provoking an uprising against India, and occupied a number of positions. India regained them in August and fought off an attack in the Chamb sector of south-west Kashmir. On 6 September, India counterattacked across the frontier in the Punjab, invading Pakistan between Lahore and Sialkot. The Indians advanced a few miles, defeating the Pakistani forces sent to oppose them, and then, on 23 September, accepted a ceasefire proposed by the United Nations. In all, 20,000 people, most of them civilians, had been killed in the fighting. After strenuous efforts at mediation by the Soviet Union, President Ayub Khan of Pakistan and the new prime minister of India, Lal Bahadur Shastri, met in Tashkent in January 1966, to sign a permanent ceasefire. Blessed are the peacemakers: the Soviets have not often played that role. Immediately after signing, Shastri had a heart attack and died. He was succeeded by Nehru's daughter, Indira Gandhi.

(For the third Indo-Pakistan war, *see* Pakistan, pp. 208–13.)

INTERNAL DISPUTES

There has been constant guerrilla activity by separatist groups along the north-eastern frontiers of India, which, with the founding of East Pakistan in 1947 (later Bangladesh), were virtually cut off from the rest of India. A string of mountainous tribal states there have been invaded by Bengali refugees, both Hindu and Muslim, trying to escape the poverty and over-crowding, as well as the unsettled conditions of their native provinces. Meanwhile, New Delhi has tried to assert its control over tribesmen in the mountains who bitterly opposed their inclusion in India in 1947.

The disparity in force between India and the tribes is so great that India cannot be defeated. However, maintaining thousands of troops on constant alert in the mountains is a continuing drain on Indian military resources. After Rajiv Gandhi came to office in 1984, he set about settling these disputes. So far, he has reached agreements with the Mizo, Tripura and Gurkha rebels. The rebellions in Nagaland and Manipur continue.

NAGALAND

The oldest of these revolts is in Nagaland, a remote, inaccessible country in the mountains between Assam and Burma. In 1944, the Japanese made their assault on India through Nagaland and Manipur, immediately to the south, and were stopped at Kohima and Imphal.

The Naga were conquered by the British with considerable difficulty in the 19th century. They were then allowed great autonomy and strict protection against incursions by people from the plains. In the middle of the century, Baptist missionaries arrived from the United States and converted many Naga to Christianity. The Naga fought bravely on Britain's side in World War II and afterwards, as India prepared for partition and independence, demanded a separate state. On 14 August 1947, the Naga National Council (NNC), led by Z. A. Phizo, proclaimed Nagaland independent. India refused to recognize the gesture.

For the next decade, there were bad-tempered exchanges between the Naga and New Delhi, with the Nagas constantly demanding independence, and the Indians refusing to countenance the idea. By 1955, violence was becoming the norm in the Naga hills. The Indian government declared part of Nagaland a 'disturbed area', and began the long attempt to suppress Naga separatism. In January 1956, the whole region was declared a disturbed area, and in March, the NNC proclaimed a federal government, with a constitution and army, and started fighting for its independence. The rebel Naga were now known as 'the Federals'.

In the following two years, the Indians deployed thousands of troops to control Nagaland. According to the government, 1400 Naga and 162 Indian soldiers were killed. There were frequent and credible reports of massacres and torture by the troops.

By degrees, the Indians won the upper hand. In 1963, in belated recognition that the Naga are a special case, Nagaland was made a separate state in the Indian union. It was by far the smallest, with a population then of 350,000 (it is now about 700,000). Later, other states, equally small, were carved out of the hill country (*see below*). The Naga then were split between those who accepted Indian control in a separate state as the best they could get, and those who continued to fight for full independence. There was a ceasefire from 1964 until 1966, and in 1973, a faction of the Federal forces surrendered. The Indian army kept up the pressure, and on 11 November 1975, a key group of the Naga underground leadership accepted defeat and signed a ceasefire at Shillong, in the neighbouring state of Meghalaya. After 20 years of conflict, a measure of peace returned to Nagaland, but Phizo, in exile in London, and a group of Communist Naga, led by J. H. Muivah, refused to surrender. Muivah had sought help from China in 1966, and now he established his command across the border in Burma (where related tribes are also fighting for their independence).

Muivah and his followers have set up a National Socialist Council of Nagaland, and claim an army 2000 strong. They may still enjoy some support from China. They are more a constant irritant than a danger to the Indian government, but the army still has to patrol and carry out surveillance of the border area, and suffers occasional casualties.

MANIPUR AND MIZORAM

These two states, formerly administratively part of Assam, were the scene of secessionist insurgencies for over 25 years. In 1961, the Mizo National Front was formed, partly in response to what its leaders considered Indian callousness during a famine. In February 1966, the MNF launched an insurrection that, for a while, dominated the whole district. The Indian army soon recovered control, and imposed its rule by moving villagers in 'village regrouping programmes', or strategic hamlets.

The government's reaction to the Mizo revolt followed the pattern in Nagaland: heavy military repression, followed by the creation, first of a 'union territory' called Mizoram, then of a full-fledged state of Mizoram. At the same time, the other hill districts were separated from Assam, and the states of Tripura, Meghalaya and Manipur were set up.

The Mizo revolt continued until 25 June 1986, when Rajiv Gandhi signed an agreement with the rebels that met many of their demands, in exchange for their acceptance of the permanency of the Indian union. Mizoram was declared a separate state and the MNF leader, Laldenga, became prime minister. In February 1987, there were elections in Mizoram, and the MNF won a majority in the state assembly, defeating Gandhi's Congress party. In the course of the insurgency, according to Indian estimates, about 1500 people had been killed.

In Manipur, there are still two guerrilla movements: the People's Liberation Army and the Revolutionary Army of Kuneipak. They both have ideological links to China, but they draw their strength from local opposition to the steady encroachment of immigrants from Bengal. Like the other tribesmen of the north-east frontier, they fear that they will eventually be swamped by the desperate millions from Bangladesh.

TRIPURA

Tripura, covering about 4000 sq. miles (10,000 sq. km), is an Indian enclave surrounded on three sides by Bangladesh. Its southern edge borders on the Chittagong Hill Tracts, where members of the same tribes as the Tripurans are in revolt against the Bangladeshi regime (see Bangladesh, pp. 130–33), and its mountains are covered with dense jungle. In 1980, a group calling itself the Tripura Volunteer Force (TVF), led by Bijoy Kumar Hrangkhawl, started fighting for the state's independence. It was particularly opposed to a Marxist party that had won local elections in Tripura, on the strength of immigrants from Bengal. By then, the tribal people were in a minority in their own homeland: the first wave of Hindu immigrants had fled to the hills during the partition of India and in the early years of East Pakistan; a further 100,000 have followed since the independence of Bangladesh in 1971. The TVF started the war by massacring over 1000 Bengali settlers. In the fighting since then, another 1000 people were killed. The TVF had an army of only about 400 men but also thousands of supporters who could be called on if necessary.

In February 1988, the Marxist party in Tripura was defeated in an election, and Hrangkhawl decided that it was time to settle with the federal government. After three months' secret negotiations, the rebels agreed on 12 August to surrender their arms and end the fight. In exchange, the government pledged to stop further immigration from Bangladesh, increase tribal privileges and expand the authority of the local councils in the tribes' autonomous region.

The dispute is not finished, however. Hrangkhawl also demands that the 100,000 Bengalis who have settled in Tripura since 1971 should be expelled. That is not possible, and the deep animosity between the two peoples will continue.

THE GURKHAS

The state of West Bengal is sandwiched between the Himalayas and Bangladesh, and is much more populous than the other north-eastern districts. About 19 million people live there, concentrated along the Brahmaputra river valley, including Gurkhas in the west, around Darjeeling, and a great variety of other peoples further east. Opposition to the central government has been strongest among the Gurkhas (who are related to the Nepalese who still serve in the British army). Small-scale guerrilla war has persisted for years.

There has been a steady infiltration of people from Bengal, both Hindu and Muslim. The first anti-foreign riots occurred in 1979, and since then, there has been constant trouble and occasional massacres. In 1983, during an election campaign that Indira Gandhi forced on the state, 3000 people were killed, including 600 women and children in the Muslim village of Nellie. Their menfolk were off on a raid.

The troubles continued until July 1988, despite the efforts of the Indians to police the country. In February of that year, the Gurkha National Liberation Front attacked a police patrol and lost six men, and in April, a schoolteacher and a journalist were murdered in separate incidents: they were decapitated, and their heads put in nylon bags and left in public places. In all, at least 300 people were killed in the disturbances.

The Gurkhas never rose in full-scale revolt, as had Nagaland or Mizoram, although about 5000 people were killed. If they ever did, controlling them would be far more difficult. The Indian government has devoted considerable development funds to the region in the hope of persuading the people of the benefits of membership of the Indian union. However, the fundamental problem – the conflict between hillsmen and immigrants from the plains – will continue.

The government's policy of conciliation was finally successful when the Gurkha leader, Subhas Ghising, concluded a peace agreement on 25 July 1988. The chief clause in the settlement was the provision of an autonomous Gurkha district around Darjeeling, the Gurkha's main town, which will have a population of about 1.4 million. Its assembly will have control over such matters as education, health, finance and transport, but it will remain part of West Bengal.

THE NAXALITES

A group of revolutionary Communists broke away from the Communist Party of India in 1969, to form the Communist Party of India (Marxist-Leninist), and tried to start a revolutionary war among the peasantry. They concentrated on the district around Naxalbari, in West Bengal, and became known as the Naxalites. 181

They murdered officials and attacked police posts. The government proclaimed a state of emergency, and succeeded in killing or arresting most of the terrorists. Several hundred people had been killed in the disorders. The Naxalites appeared to be thoroughly defeated by the early 1970s, partly because a Communist government had been elected in West Bengal and had met many of the peasants' demands. However, Naxalite activity has now revived: their particular brand of terrorism has been reported in many parts of the country, from Kerala and Tamil Nadu in the south to Assam in the north-east and Bihar and Andhra Pradesh in north-central India.

In Andhra Pradesh, Naxalites have killed over 200 people since 1984, including 35 policemen, and the rate of killing has risen sharply: ten police were murdered in an ambush in August 1987. It is believed that there are about 5000 Naxalites there, including 500 or so terrorists, calling themselves 'Peoples' Wars'. In December 1987, the Peoples' Wars kidnapped a group of senior officials and held them hostage until Naxalites were released from jail. In Bihar, Naxalite bands skirmish with the private armies of local landlords, and in Punjab they have allied themselves with Sikh secessionists.

THE SIKHS

The Sikh insurgency is by far the most serious that India has confronted since independence. It continues today as the most severe challenge to the central government.

There are about 15 million Sikhs in India, most of them in Punjab state where they are in the majority. They follow a religion founded in the 15th century in the Punjab and developed by a succession of ten gurus, or sages. It is an amalgam of Islam and Hinduism: it is monotheistic, like Islam, and utterly rejects the Hindu caste system, but it also accepts reincarnation and Hindu fatalism. The Sikhs' holy city is Amritsar, where they built their Golden Temple. (The word *amritsar* means 'pool of nectar' and refers to the sacred pool that surrounds the temple.) The last of the ten gurus ordered his male followers never to shave or cut their hair, always to carry a dagger, and to take the name *Singh* ('lion'). Women, who were given far more independence than Hindu women, took the name *Kaur* ('princess').

In the early 19th century, the Sikhs conquered the Punjab under the Maharajah Ranjit Singh. His capital was Lahore, and in his turban he wore the Koh-i-Noor diamond which had been a principal possession of the Moghul emperors. Ranjit Singh died in 1839, his successors squabbled among themselves, and within a decade, the British had conquered the Punjab. An escaping prince was captured by the British, and the Koh-i-Noor was found hidden in his turban; it was sent to London and put in Queen Victoria's imperial state crown.

The British appreciated the Sikhs' martial qualities and recruited them in large numbers into their armies. During the Mutiny, ten years after the last Sikh war, Sikh regiments remained loyal and joined in the reconquest of north India, and 100,000 Sikh soldiers fought alongside the British in World War I.

On 13 April 1919, a British general ordered his troops to fire into a crowd in the Jallianwala Bagh, a market place in Amritsar. They were demonstrating illegally against the British and the temple authorities who supported them. The
soldiers killed 379 people and wounded 1200. The Sikh temple authorities

applauded the massacre, an attitude which led to sustained agitation for reform which, in turn, brought a majority of Sikhs to support the independence movement. The reformers founded the Akali Dal, which later developed into the political party that is now at the heart of the dispute between New Delhi and the Sikhs.

At the time of partition, the Sikhs, who were scattered across the Punjab, demanded their independence, but were ignored. When the Punjab was divided, 40 per cent of Sikhs were left in Pakistan, and suffered the worst of the massacres that followed. In their turn, the Sikhs in the east massacred Muslims and drove them into Pakistan. When the red tide subsided, most of the Sikhs were concentrated in the Indian area of the Punjab, around Amritsar. They particularly regretted the loss of Lahore, Ranjit Singh's capital, just across the border.

For the next 35 years, the Sikhs prospered. Their farms became the most productive in India, thanks to their own industry and skill and the government's irrigation projects; the city dwellers adapted to modern industry and commerce. Punjab became one of the richest provinces in India. However, prosperity brought danger: Sikh fundamentalists feared that their religion would be absorbed back into Hinduism. At first, they preached strict adherence to the rules prescribed in the Holy Books, but in the early 1980s, some of them began seriously to advocate a separate Sikh nation, which they would call Khalistan, 'land of the pure'. At the head of this breakaway movement was Sant Jarnail Singh Bhindranwale (*Sant* means 'holy man'). Bhindranwale believed it was the Sikhs' right to kill their enemies, and he led a militant faction that openly resorted to terrorism.

The disturbances began in 1981, when the Akali Dal presented a list of 45 demands to the central government, which, though stopping short of full independence, would have given the Sikhs complete control of Punjab state. Indira Gandhi's government rejected them. The first political assassination followed in September 1981, when a Hindu newspaper editor was murdered.

In September 1982, a conference of Sikhs declared holy war against the Indian government, and a series of increasingly serious incidents began. Sikh terrorists, taking their lead from Bhindranwale, attacked and killed government officials or Hindus whom they wished to drive out of Sikh areas. In April 1983, a senior police officer, a Sikh, was murdered as he left the Golden Temple after performing his devotions. The government did nothing. Police officers who arrested Sikh militants were also murdered, together with their entire families.

The government vacillated between conciliation and firmness, and thereby lost the advantages of either. Indira Gandhi allowed Bhindranwale to turn central Amritsar into a fortress, a 'no-go area' policed by his militant followers, who stockpiled a vast arsenal of weapons in the Golden Temple complex. A retired Sikh general, Sahbeg Singh, devised fortifications and defensive positions for the temple area. It became a base for terrorists, not all of them religious fanatics: some Naxalites emerged to join Bhindranwale.

In October 1983, after a busload of Hindus had been massacred, a state of emergency was declared in Punjab. Parts were declared a 'disturbed area', and the army was brought in to maintain order. Two weeks later, a train passing through Punjab was derailed, killing 219 people. There were riots in Chandigarh, the state capital, which is also capital of the neighbouring state of Haryana – one of the

Sikhs' demands was for full control of Chandigarh. There were anti-Sikh riots in Haryana in which Sikhs were murdered. Terrorism continued to increase and the police were incapable of dealing with it.

Bhindranwale ordered the murder of a succession of politicians, police and journalists. The government seemed unable to defend them, and by early 1984, it was in danger of losing control of the state completely. In March and April there were over 80 political murders in Punjab.

There were last-ditch negotiations between the government and leaders of the Akali Dal. Mrs Gandhi offered to meet most of the Sikhs' demands, including giving them control of Chandigarh, but Bhindranwale refused to compromise. The murders continued, and the Sikhs announced that they would prevent movement of grain out of Punjab. There was no doubt that the threat was real, and that it would have brought about catastrophe: Punjab is the granary of north India.

By this point, by the government's count, Bhindranwale's terrorists had murdered 169 Hindus and 39 Sikhs. Others had been killed in riots and accidents provoked by the terrorists, bringing the total to 410, not counting those killed in the train derailment. The murder rate was increasing rapidly: 23 people were killed in the 24 hours before Mrs Gandhi took her decision. On 2 June 1984, she authorized the army to occupy the Golden Temple.

Beforehand, in a last example of government incompetence, and the complicity of police with the extremists, 200 young Sikhs, including criminals and Naxalites, were allowed to escape. Operation Blue Star was launched on 3 June, one of the sacred days of the Sikhs' calendar, and the temple was crowded with the faithful, as well as Bhindranwale's fighters.

All Punjab was shut down. All road, rail and traffic was stopped, the frontier with Pakistan was closed, and the press were kept out. The authorities were afraid of a general uprising by Sikh villagers, appalled at the attack on the Golden Temple.

For two days, the army laid siege to the temple and attempted to force Bhindranwale to surrender; he preferred martyrdom. On the evening of 5 June, tanks were brought in to assault the temple.

Immediately to the west of the Golden Temple, itself surrounded by the sacred pool, is another sacred edifice, the Akal Takht, where Bhindranwale had set up his headquarters. The army first attacked and occupied a number of outlying buildings, and then turned its attention to the Akal Takht. They tried sending in commandos, but they were easily repulsed by heavy fire from General Sahbeg Singh's gun emplacements. So the army blasted its way into the Akal Takht with its tanks.

The building was severely damaged. Bhindranwale, Sahbeg Singh and their senior supporters were all killed, martyrs to the cause. In all, by the official count, 493 Sikh militants and civilians and 83 troops were killed. However, about 1600 civilians, known to have been inside the temple complex when the attack began, remained unaccounted for, and it is possible therefore that the real casualty figure was much higher.

The Golden Temple was damaged, but not severely. The Akal Takht was ruined, and the temple's library was destroyed. The army had also attacked 37 other Sikh temples, searching for terrorists.

The attack on the Golden Temple provoked mutinies by Sikh troops and disturbances throughout Punjab. Mrs Gandhi tried to blame Pakistan for the troubles, denouncing 'outside interference' – in fact, there is no evidence at all that Pakistan was in any way involved. Mrs Gandhi and her supporters, carried away by their own eloquence, also tried to blame the CIA and even the British for the consequences of their own incompetence.

On 31 October 1984, Mrs Gandhi was shot and killed by two Sikhs guarding the prime minister's bungalow in New Delhi. She had been on her way to give a television interview to the British wit and playwright Peter Ustinov. The two Sikhs surrendered immediately, and were taken away by the police. One of them was then murdered in the police station, the other severely beaten. Riots broke out immediately, incited by members of the ruling Congress party. Hindus were brought by bus from the suburbs of Delhi and turned loose in Sikh neighbourhoods. According to government figures, 2717 people were killed (almost all of them Sikhs), 2150 in Delhi. The police and army stood by throughout the day of massacres; 100,000 Sikhs fled Delhi, half back to Punjab, half to refugee camps set up for them in the country near the capital.

The situation was only brought under control when Mrs Gandhi's son, Rajiv, who had been sworn in as prime minister to succeed her, visited a devastated Sikh neighbourhood and told the army to restore order. (The Sikh who admitted killing Mrs Gandi was executed in January 1989, along with another Sikh who had been convicted of conspiracy with the assassins.)

Killing Bhindranwale did not end terrorism in Punjab. Although the murder rate declined in the second half of 1984 and in early 1985, it then rose sharply. On 23 June 1985, 329 people were killed when an Air India plane crashed in the sea south of Ireland, on a flight from Toronto to London, and investigators believed that it had been destroyed by a bomb. A few hours later, a bomb concealed in a suitcase exploded at Tokyo Airport, killing two baggage handlers. The suitcase had arrived on another flight from Canada, which was late. If it had been on time, the suitcase and the bomb would have been transferred to another Air India flight from Tokyo to India, and would have exploded in midair. There can be little doubt that the two bombs were the work of Sikh terrorists.

In 1985, 65 people were killed in Punjab; in 1986, 609; in 1987, 1566; and in 1988, 2000. Of those killed between 1985 and 1987, 1819 were the victims of terrorism, and 421, by official count, were terrorists killed by security forces. The death rate in the early months of 1988 was even higher than the year before, with over 900 killed in the first four months. In March alone, 225 people were murdered, including ten people attending a Sikh wedding; a group calling itself the Khalistan Commando Force, one of four Sikh terrorist organizations, claimed responsibility for that atrocity. On 3 March, terrorists attacked a Hindu festival and machine-gunned the audience, killing 34. On 31 March, 33 people were killed, including 18 members of a Hindu work brigade who were dragged out of their huts, lined up in a courtyard and slaughtered.

The terrorists once again took refuge in the Golden Temple, and once again the government and moderate Sikh leaders seemed incapable of controlling them. There have been reports that Naxalites have resumed operations: a number of those murdered have been members of the legal Communist party, who have opposed Naxalite terrorism.

On 9 May, a Sikh gang crossed the border into Haryana state and attacked a Hindu wedding, killing 13 people. On the same day, the government at last sent troops into Amritsar again, and once again laid siege to the Golden Temple. Five people were killed on the first day of the siege. However, this time, instead of storming the temple, troops cut off its water and electricity and waited for the terrorists to surrender. There was constant sniping from minarets inside the temple complex, and army sharpshooters, taking up positions in buildings overlooking the complex, shot a number of terrorists. Terrorists outside Amritsar continued the campaign of killings: more than 190 people were killed during the first week of the siege, and the government rushed reinforcements to Punjab. About 800 people, mostly civilian worshippers, left the temple the day after the siege began, and 146 Sikhs surrendered on 15 May. Three days later, the last of the Sikhs in the temple gave themselves up. The army immediately found 16 bodies inside the temple, people who had been killed by the extremists; later, after excavating in the cellars, more bodies were found, bringing the total to 41 men, women and children. Many of them had been tortured.

Over the next five days, Sikh terrorists killed a further 245 people in Punjab, most of them Hindu migrant workers brought in to work in the paddy fields. There was a mass exodus of these workers, with disastrous effects on the incomes of the Sikh farmers who employed them. By the end of 1988, 2000 people had been killed, and the murders continued in 1989 at a rate of 200 a month.

In an attempt to come to terms with the Sikhs, the government released a number of their leaders who had been jailed on 4 March. They included Jasbir Singh Rode, who was immediately installed as head priest in the Golden Temple. He has continued to voice most of the extremists' demands, but not the most divisive: the call for Khalistan. At the end of May, all five priests at the temple, including Rode, were dismissed by the Sikh governing committee, which alleged that they were pandering to terrorism.

So far, most of the Sikhs have not supported the extremists, and therefore a large part of the terrorists' campaign is directed against other Sikhs, to frighten them into support for Khalistan. The government in New Delhi, first under Indira Gandhi and now under her son Rajiv, has proved incapable of resolving either the political problem or the security problem. The dilemma is clear: unless terrorism can be brought under control, the extremists will defeat the government and will establish Khalistan. But suppressing the terrorists may require such a degree of force that all the undecided Sikhs will rally to the cause.

The Sikh terrorists have been beneficiaries of the Afghan war: there have been so many weapons flowing into Pakistan that the Sikhs have no difficulty obtaining all they need. The Indian government blames Pakistan. It is probable that, at most, Pakistan is guilty of benign neglect in policing the border, but the crisis has become so serious that it could well have serious effects upon Indian–Pakistani relations.

An additional problem now confronts India: its involvement in the civil war in Sri Lanka (*see* Sri Lanka, pp. 227–34). In July 1987, Rajiv Gandhi agreed to send Indian troops to north Sri Lanka in order to police a ceasefire and peace settlement that he had brokered between the Sri Lankan government and the rebel Tamils. It was intended to be a brief and uneventful intervention, but the fighting resumed between Sinhalese and Tamils, and in October, the Indian army laid siege to Jaffna. It lost 500 men in the operation and has suffered a steady attrition ever since. There is no end in sight.

There are now 60,000 Indian troops in Sri Lanka, and large numbers in Punjab and the north-east. It is apparent that maintaining Indian hegemony in the region is going to be a costly business.

THE MALDIVES

On 3 November 1988, a band of Tamil mercenaries from Sri Lanka invaded the Maldive islands and attempted to overthrow the government. They had been hired by a former president who had been deposed in 1980 and now hoped for a restoration. The Indians promptly sent troops to Male, the capital, and restored the government. The mercenaries fled on the boat that had brought them, and were later captured by the Indian navy. In all, 12 people were killed during the attempted coup.

The Maldives are a chain of islands in the Indian Ocean, south-west of India. They were a British protectorate in the days of the Raj (like the Seychelles further west) and India remains the dominant influence, even though the Maldive republic is an independent country. This was the second Indian intervention in the internal affairs of a neighbour in two years (the first was Sri Lanka). Some other neighbours worried that Rajiv Gandhi might develop imperial delusions and start policing the whole region, where India is by far the most powerful nation.

FURTHER READING

Akbar, M. J., *India, the Siege Within*, London, Penguin, 1985, and *Riot after Riot*, New Delhi, Penguin, 1988.
American University, *India: A Country Study*, Washington D.C., 1985.
Choudkury, G. W., *India, Pakistan, Bangladesh and the Major Powers*, New York, Macmillan, 1985.
Fishlock, Trevor, *India File: Inside the Subcontinent*, London, Murray, 1983.
Galbraith, John Kenneth, *Ambassador's Journal*, Boston, Houghton, Mifflin, 1969.
Hardgrave, Robert L., *India Under Pressure: The Prospects for Stability*, Boulder, Colo., Westview Press, 1984.
Hart, Henry C., *Indira Gandhi's India: A Political System Reappraised*, Boulder, Colo., Westview Press, 1976.
Maxwell, Neville, *India's China War*, New York, Pantheon Books, 1970.
Mehta, Ved, *A Family Affair: India Under Three Prime Ministers*, Oxford University Press, 1982.
Minority Rights Group, *India, the Nagas and the North-East*, London, 1980.
Tully, Mark and Satish, Jacob, *Amritsar: Mrs Gandhi's Last Battle*, London, Jonathan Cape, 1985.

INDONESIA

Geography	741,031 sq. miles (1,919,263 sq. km). More than 13,000 islands, stretching across 3500 miles (5600 km) of ocean; it is therefore wider than the North Atlantic.
Population	165 million. The most heavily populated island is Java (the size of England), with over 100 million people – double England's population density. There are 10 major ethnic groups and over 300 smaller ones, speaking more than 200 distinct languages; there is also a rich and resented Chinese minority (about 4 million people). The official language is Bahasa Indonesia, a modernized version of Malay. 90% of Indonesians are Muslims but, for most of them, their adherence to Islam is nominal. Among the small minority of devout Muslims, there is a further minority of fanatics who want to establish an Islamic republic. The island of Bali is Hindu, and Ambon in the South Moluccas is Calvinist. The national motto is 'Unity in Diversity'.
Resources	Oil; gas; minerals; hardwoods and other tropical products; fish.
GNP per capita	$500
Refugees	Internal: 2490 Vietnamese. External: 9500 from (Indonesian) West Irian in Papua New Guinea.
Casualties	Between 400,000 and 1 million people were killed in the massacres of 1965, and at least 100,000 people have been killed in East Timor since 1975.

Indonesia is the fifth most populous nation on Earth. It has large natural resources, and although it is not developing as rapidly as South Korea or Taiwan, it is clearly moving in the same direction. In another generation, unless it is engulfed by political or economic disaster, it should reach the position that Japan attained 20 years ago. The world will then have to take notice.

HISTORY

The first Europeans to reach Indonesia were the Portuguese and Spanish, in the early 16th century, and they found an eclectic civilization. Indonesia was originally Hindu; then it accepted Buddhism, and for centuries the two religions coexisted peacefully. One of the greatest of all Buddhist temples was built at

188

Borobudur, and a few miles away was Prambanam, an immense Hindu religious centre. In the Middle Ages, Islam reached the islands, brought by Arab traders, and overlaid and absorbed the Hindu–Buddhist traditions. However, those traditions were never lost, partly because of the arrival of the Europeans.

Trade between the Spice Islands, as they were called, and Europe was enormously lucrative, and for over a century the European powers fought among themselves for its control. By the middle of the 17th century, the Dutch had driven out all rivals except for the Portuguese, who retained a small colony on Timor, east of Java, and the Spanish in the Philippines.

The Dutch empire was centred on Java, where they built Batavia (now Jakarta, capital of Indonesia) as a Far Eastern Amsterdam. They did not seek to convert their subjects to Christianity: the people of Ambon, the principal clove-producing island in the South Moluccas, were first converted by the Portuguese and were only later persuaded by the Dutch to give up Catholicism and adopt Calvinism. The Dutch were almost exclusively concerned with trade, and only took on the administration of the hinterland and farther islands to protect their trading posts and to keep their rivals out.

By the mid-19th century, the islands had been divided upon wholly artificial lines between the British in Malaya and North Borneo, the Dutch in what is now Indonesia, and the Spanish in the Philippines; the Dutch, British and Germans divided up New Guinea between them. The 20th century brought the inevitable stirrings of nationalism. The first Communist party in Asia – the PKI – was founded in Batavia in 1920, and in 1927 Achmad Sukarno founded the Nationalist party.

This latter organization became the dominant force opposing the Dutch. The Japanese occupied Indonesia in 1942, and Sukarno and his chief lieutenant, Mohammed Hatta, cooperated with the new order, they said, to further the cause of independence. Sukarno continued to collaborate after Japan annexed Indonesia in 1943, even though the Philippines and Burma had been proclaimed independent, and he acquiesced in the recruitment by the Japanese of slave labour in Java. The occupation caused several hundred thousand deaths.

In 1944, as the Americans were closing in on them, the Japanese reversed themselves and, hoping to make Indonesia an ally, accepted the principle of independence for that country. The new state was to include Portuguese Timor, Malaya, Singapore and British Borneo (though Sukarno had laid claim only to the Dutch East Indies). An independent Indonesia was finally proclaimed, with Sukarno as president, on 17 August 1945 – two days after Japan had surrendered to the Americans.

Sukarno was able to establish himself firmly before the Dutch returned, forming an army equipped with weapons taken from the Japanese. The first of the Allies to reach Indonesia were the British, and in October 1945, there was a full-scale battle between British and Indonesian troops at Surabya in eastern Java.

The Dutch recognized Sukarno's republic, but only in Java: they resumed control of the rest of the Dutch East Indies, set up a 'Netherlands Union' and progressively reduced the territory controlled by the republic, so that, by January 1948, it was confined to central Java. Then leftist members of the Indonesian army

189

staged a coup against Sukarno in Madiun, in Java. The Communist party supported them and was brutally suppressed by General Abdul Haris Nasution, one of Sukarno's top commanders.

In December 1948, another Dutch offensive captured the republic's last bases at Jogjakarta, and Sukarno and Hatta were captured and exiled to Sumatra. That was the last spasm of Dutch imperialism. They had no allies: the British had abandoned India, and the Americans threatened to cut off Marshall Aid if the Dutch did not give Indonesia its independence. Meanwhile, on the ground, they were finding it impossible to control such a vast, populous and disaffected country. Sovereignty was transferred on 17 December 1949, although the Dutch retained West New Guinea, much to their subsequent sorrow.

The new government set about establishing its control of the islands, putting down a series of revolts. Calvinist Ambon, in the Moluccas, which had supported the Dutch, proclaimed its independence and had to be conquered. In April 1950, 12,000 Ambonese soldiers and their families were evacuated to the Netherlands (*see* Terrorism, pp. 553–54).

In the mid-1950s, the central government was weak and divided: there were attempted coups; an extremist Islamic movement, Darul Islam, was fighting the government in central Java; and a group of dissident army officers started a rebellion in Sumatra. The rebels in Sumatra and the Celebes were able to persuade the CIA that Sukarno was anti-Western, and the agency began secretly shipping arms to them. Despite this, President Eisenhower stated, 'Our policy is one of careful neutrality, a proper deportment all the way through, so as not to be taking sides where it is none of our business,' and the secretary of state, John Foster Dulles, told a congressional committee in March 1958, 'We are not intervening in the internal affairs of this country.' They were both lying.

The CIA was not only sending arms to the rebels, it was also bombing government positions. One of the raids hit a hospital by mistake, and on 18 May 1958, a B-26 crashlanded in government territory in Ambon. Its pilot, an American named Allan Pope, was captured. The plane was empty, but shortly before it had crashed, parachutes had been seen floating to earth. They were found to be bearing cases of Springfield rifles, and the cases were marked 'Interarms', the name of a major American arms company that had close links to the CIA. Its owner, Sam Cummings, denied that he had had anything to do with that particular shipment, but the provenance of the guns was unimportant. What counted was that the CIA had been caught red-handed. Sukarno never trusted the Americans after that.

Sukarno proclaimed a new political philosophy – 'Guided Democracy', as opposed to the parliamentary sort – and his two allies were the army chief-of-staff, General Nasution, and the PKI. He proclaimed a state of emergency in March 1957 and, in 1959, launched a campaign against Dutch control of West New Guinea, which he called Irian Jaya (West Irian). The Dutch were preparing West New Guinea for eventual independence, and refused Sukarno's demands. In retaliation, he nationalized all the immense Dutch holdings in Indonesia, a step that brought the country to the verge of bankruptcy. The army had to step in to run the nationalized companies, and thus became a major force in the country's economy. Sukarno sent 'volunteers' into West New Guinea in 1960.

Once again, the Dutch found themselves without allies, and in 1963, 'West Irian' was added to Indonesia.

By then, the economy was in serious trouble. Sukarno invented yet another new political philosophy – Nasakom (Nationalism, Religion and Communism) – and expelled 119,000 Chinese. Neither measure helped.

In 1960, the British ceded their two colonies in Borneo – Sarawak and North Borneo (Sabah) – to Malaya, to form part of the new federation of Malaysia. Sukarno called out the mobs to protest. British property was nationalized, and Sukarno announced that Indonesia 'must gobble Malaysia raw'. The Indonesian army began armed incursions into Malaysian Borneo and across the straits into Malaya itself. The British sent an army to protect Malaysia, and the defeat of the Indonesian 'confrontation' contributed to a severe loss of prestige for Sukarno. To compensate for the defeat, Sukarno had the British embassy burned in September 1963, along with the houses of many British and Australian citizens. (*See* Malaysia, pp. 204–6.)

THE 1965 COUP

Sukarno announced that 1965 would be 'a year of living dangerously'. The PKI was by now the dominant political force in Java. In the early morning of 1 October, a group of middle-rank officers led by Lieutenant Colonel Untung, a commander of the presidential guard, attempted a coup against the army command. It is possible that Sukarno and the PKI knew about the coup in advance.

Six senior generals were murdered and their bodies thrown down a well at a place called the Crocodile Hole on Halim air base, near Jakarta. Among those killed was General Achmad Yani, the chief of staff. General Nasution, the minister of defence, escaped through a back passage from his bedroom, but his five-year-old daughter was killed. The rebels seized the radio station and announced the coup, saying that the generals had been plotting against Sukarno. They proclaimed a new government, led by the 'September 30 Movement'. Sukarno moved to Halim, a decision he was never able to explain.

The commander of the reserve army, General Suharto, had not been on the list of generals to be killed, an oversight that the plotters did not live long enough to regret. He found that most of the army was not involved and would still obey orders, and he quickly gathered an overwhelming force of loyal troops, led by a tank division, which rolled over the rebels. Within 24 hours, the coup was over.

Violent anti-Communist demonstrations broke out in Jakarta and the rest of Java, and the mobs and the army set about slaughtering Communists wherever they could find them. By the time the massacres subsided, several hundred thousand people had been killed. The dead included most of the leaders of the PKI. The party had 3 million members, and the army now systematically hunted down all its cadres and shot them. Most of those who died, however, were villagers and many had nothing to do with the PKI; they were victims of local hatreds. So many bodies were thrown into the rivers that they became a serious health problem. In one district in West Java, suspects were decapitated by guillotine, and their heads piled up in the villages, to set an example. Many Chinese (according to one estimate, 20,000) were among the victims, and mobs attacked the Chinese embassy.

The total number of those killed remains in dispute. The official government figure is 80,000. Muslim leaders, whose people did most of the killings, admit to 500,000 and other estimates go up to 1 million. The usual compromise estimate is that 400,000 people were killed. A number of former PKI officials are still in jail, and from time to time some of them are still brought out and executed: nine died in this way in 1986, and a former member of the politburo, who was arrested in 1968, was executed in November 1987.

Suharto took control of the government and progressively eliminated Sukarno's influence. It was an elaborate and subtle process, typically Javanese: Sukarno had been the country's dominant political figure for decades, and had clearly been favoured by beneficent spirits; he had to be eased out gradually, as it became clear that the spirits no longer supported him. When the process was completed, he was legally deposed in March 1968, and died in 1970.

SUHARTO'S RULE

Suharto reversed Indonesia's alliances. He broke diplomatic relations with China (they were finally resumed in 1989) and became a close associate of the United States. Sukarno's half-baked socialism was abandoned, and a group of American-trained economists (the 'Berkeley Mafia') was put in charge of the country's economy and rescued it from disaster.

Suharto has now ruled Indonesia for over 20 years, and was elected to another five-year term in 1988. He has wrapped his dictatorship in a philosophy called the 'New Order', which exacts deference and obedience to authority. Some opposition is permitted, rather more than in China or Singapore, but not much. Opposition parties were permitted to win 30 per cent or more of the vote – to an assembly that has no authority. Indonesia has enjoyed economic growth and stability, standards of living have risen dramatically and Indonesia now feeds itself. *Per capita* GNP rose at an annual rate of 4.2 per cent between 1965 and 1985. But there is a steady undercurrent of dissatisfaction at the continuing vast gap between the small, rich governing class, and the huge mass of the urban poor.

The national oil company, Pertamina, collapsed in 1975 in a major scandal: a high court case in Singapore had to resolve a dispute between the heirs of a Pertamina official, who had officially earned $600 a month yet left an estate worth $32 million. The rapacity of Suharto's own children is a source of much criticism: they are known collectively as TOSHIBA, an acronym of their first names, or as 'the family business'. The allegations of corruption do not, however, extend to Suharto himself, who is accused of only being too lenient with his wife and children. The parallel with the Philippines is obvious.

There is also a parallel with Iran, not only because the shah's family was notoriously corrupt, but also because his regime was overthrown by an Islamic revival. The dangers from Islamic fundamentalism remain of acute concern to Indonesia. Islamic fanatics hijacked an Indonesian airliner in 1981; and there were serious Islamic disturbances in Jakarta in September 1984, during which troops opened fire on demonstrators. The government reported that nine people were killed; Muslim organizations say the true number was 400–600; and Amnesty International concluded that at least 30, and possibly many more, died.

The difference between Indonesia and Iran or the Philippines is that there is no ayatollah or Corazon Aquino to rally the opposition. The middle classes remain quiescent and so far there have been only minor student disturbances and nothing of the scale of those in South Korea or the Philippines. However, in November 1987, at least ten students were killed in Ujung Padang in the Celebes, in a riot that started as a student protest against a new rule obliging riders of motorcycles to wear helmets.

For many years now, Indonesia has been on the short list of countries whose regimes are likely to be overthrown. Others on that list – Iran, South Korea, the Philippines, Burma – have duly passed through the fires. So far, Indonesia has remained untouched. However, the most adroit dictatorship cannot last for ever. Suharto, who was born in June 1921, has governed Indonesia since 1965. Indonesia must now be near the top of the list.

EAST TIMOR

The Portuguese retained their colony in East Timor (and a small enclave on the north coast of West Timor) until after the Portuguese revolution of April 1974. It was a small, neglected and impoverished colony, covering about 7400 sq. miles (19,000 sq. km). About one-third of the population was Catholic. Joseph Conrad described the capital, Dili, as 'that highly pestilential place'. The colony was occupied by Japan during World War II, and about 40,000 people were killed or died of starvation.

After the Portuguese revolution, the new leftist government in Lisbon abandoned all the colonies that Portugal had kept around the world, except Macao on the Chinese mainland. Three political parties were established in East Timor: Fretilin (*Frente Revolucionaria de Timor Leste Independente*), which advocated immediate independence; UDT (*União Democratica Timorense*), which wanted a continuing association with Portugal, leading to independence; and Apodeti (*Associacão Popular Democratica Timorense*), which wanted integration with Indonesia. Apodeti probably had 5 per cent of popular support, the other two sharing the remainder in equal proportions. Portugal remained in nominal control, but in fact, Lisbon was far too preoccupied with its own political problems and the crises in Angola and Mozambique to concern itself with the fate of East Timor. As in Angola at the same time, the Portuguese government favoured the most left-leaning of the colonial political parties – in this case, Fretilin, which quickly became the dominant force in East Timor.

On 10 August 1975, the UDT attempted a coup. There was a brief civil war between it and Apodeti, on the one side, and Fretilin on the other. Fretilin won, at a cost of about 1500 lives. Portugal then washed its hands of the place: its civil administrators withdrew to an island off the coast of Dili, and Fretilin was left in control.

On 28 November, Fretilin proclaimed the Democratic Republic of East Timor. Indonesia sent 'volunteers' to occupy Dili on 7 December, and the Indonesian army then set out to conquer the country. By the following spring, there were 30,000 Indonesian troops there. The Indonesians set up a puppet regime, which in May 1977 called for integration with Indonesia. On 17 July, East Timor became Indonesia's 27th province.

The Indonesian troops started to massacre the Timorese as soon as they   193 arrived – perhaps 2000 civilians were killed in Dili in the first few days. Fretilin had formed an army of 20,000 during the 18 months that it had controlled East Timor, and it had been armed by the departing Portuguese. There was soon a full-scale war between it and the Indonesian army. The Indonesian air force bombed villages indiscriminately, and the army used heavy artillery against Fretilin and its civilian supporters. Thousands of people suspected of Fretilin sympathies were arrested, tortured and murdered. Timorese peasants were moved into resettlement centres where they could be properly policed, and the traditional village life of the Timorese people was thus utterly destroyed. Estimates of the number of people killed or dead of starvation or illness caused by the war range between 10 and 30 per cent of the population. A conservative estimate would be 100,000 dead out of a population of perhaps 650,000 in 1975.

The Fretilin army put up a stout resistance, but by the end of 1978, it had been largely destroyed. Its leader, Nicolau Lobato, was killed on 31 December 1978, and the remnants of the Fretilin resistance took to the hills.

In 1981, in 'Operation Security', the Indonesian army rounded up as many Timorese men between the ages of 15 and 55 as they could find, and marched them against Fretilin positions, as a 'fence' to protect the army. There was a brief ceasefire in 1983, and when that broke down, another massive 'Operation Clean-Sweep' was mounted.

Amnesty International reports numerous instances of torture, extralegal executions, massacres and mistreatment of civilians. International relief agencies, allowed into East Timor in 1979, found widespread famine, and for a while East Timor was reported as a new Biafra. The country was ruined, much of the population had been regrouped in 'resettlement areas' and the surviving coffee plantations had been taken over by the Indonesian army. For the most part, East Timor has been completely closed off from the world: its inhabitants are not allowed to leave, and visitors from the rest of Indonesia, or from the outside, apart from a few journalists, are forbidden to enter. There are, of course, no political freedoms at all, no civil liberties, no press.

Fretilin survives, conducting a persistent, low-level guerrilla campaign against the government. In 1988, the Indonesian commanding general said that fewer than 100 Indonesian soldiers are killed every year by guerrillas. (He did not say how many Timorese were killed annually.) He also stated that guerrilla activity was now limited to the hills in the east and south-east, and consisted of ambushes of government convoys and attacks on settlements. The government puts the number of guerrillas at 500–1000. Fretilin claims it has 3000, and says that it killed 165 Indonesian soldiers in 1987. There are said to be about 20,000 Indonesian troops in East Timor.

Through all this, the world did nothing. In September 1974, Australia, in the person of Labour prime minister Gough Whitlam, acknowledged to Suharto that it would be best for East Timor to join Indonesia. In 1975, Australia was distracted by a constitutional crisis, an event that may even have encouraged the Indonesians to invade East Timor. US President Ford, with his secretary of state Henry Kissinger, visited Jakarta on 5–6 December 1975, the day before the invasion, and did nothing to dissuade Suharto; nor did they condemn him afterwards. Even as news of the massacres came out, the major powers, East and West, ignored it. Indonesia is too populous, rich and influential in the Third World for the United States, China or the Soviet Union to risk its displeasure. India, equating East Timor with Goa (another Portuguese colonial relic that India had annexed, without serious opposition from the Goans), supported Indonesia. Thus the four most populous nations on Earth supported the fifth, Indonesia, in a small act of genocide.

The United Nations condemned the annexation in 1976 and has since repeated that condemnation on a number of occasions, although each time with fewer votes against the Indonesian government. The Soviet Union had always voted against Indonesia, but that is the extent of its disapproval.

In recent years, Indonesia has tried to win the loyalty of the Timorese by investing heavily in East Timor, now spending more there *per capita* than in any province except Jakarta. The standards of living, health, education, sanitation and so on have all improved dramatically, although the political control is as tight as ever. Perhaps, eventually, the carrot may prove more persuasive than the stick.

In November 1988, the Washington human rights group Asia Watch issued a report on Indonesia and East Timor, stating that the situation had improved. More than 100 political prisoners had been released in East Timor in that year and there had been 'comparatively few' cases of illegal disappearances in recent years. The report stated that 'some of the worst excesses of the occupation have abated, but the Timorese people continue to suffer daily violations of fundamental rights'.

IRIAN JAYA

Formerly Dutch New Guinea, it is one of the most backward areas in the world. Its tribes, many still in the Stone Age, speak 800 distinct languages. Cannibalism and headhunting persist there: in 1975, a group of 13 Christian converts were killed and eaten by their heathen brethren while the European missionary was away.

Indonesia annexed Irian Jaya in 1963, with only the most perfunctory consideration for the wishes of its inhabitants. In the past few years, following attempts to resettle people from Java in the virgin forests of the outer islands, including those of Irian Jaya, a low-level guerrilla insurgency has started up there. The Free Papua Movement (OPM) was founded in 1963, based on the more educated classes, and motivated by tribal resentments. It relies to some extent on other tribes across the border, in Papua New Guinea, an independent nation that occupies the eastern half of the immense island. The OPM claims that several thousand Indonesian troops have been killed and larger numbers of civilians, but there are no means of verifying its claims. The OPM leader, Jacob Prai, was arrested in Papua New Guinea in 1979 and sent to Sweden.

There is no chance that the Irian Jaya guerrillas will win, any more than Fretilin will: the indigenous populations are too small, relative to that of Indonesia. However, New Guinea is so large and so wild and the terrain so difficult that it may also be impossible for Indonesia to win.

FURTHER READING

American University, *Indonesia: A Country Study*, Washington D.C., 1983.
Amnesty International, *Indonesia/East Timor: Violations of Human Rights*,
  London, 1985.
Dunn, James, *Timor – A People's Betrayal*.
Emmerson, Donald K., 'Invisible Indonesia', *Foreign Affairs*, Vol. 66, no. 2, 1987.
Picken, Margot, 'The East Timor Agony', *New York Review*, 4 December 1986.

KOREA

Geography	*North Korea*: 46,814 sq. miles (121,248 sq. km). *South Korea*: 38,452 sq. miles (99,590 sq. km). Between them, they are about the size of Great Britain.
Population	*North Korea*: 20.8 million. *South Korea*: 41.6 million.
GNP per capita	*North Korea*: $1170*. *South Korea*: $2370.

The Korean war lasted from 1950 to 1953. Since then, the two Koreas have grown steadily further apart and at an accelerating rate, as South Korea's economy continues to expand at a phenomenal pace while the north stagnates. In December 1987, South Korea held a presidential election, which returned a democratically elected president – Roh Tae Woo – for the first time in decades. The following April, South Korea passed a further test of democracy: President Roh's party was defeated in legislative elections, and the president now has to cope with a parliament dominated by the opposition.

Meanwhile, North Korea has been ruled by Kim Il Sung for over 40 years. He has developed an extravagant cult of his own personality, and has prepared his son for the succession, hoping to establish the only Communist dynasty.

The border between the two Koreas is one of the most dangerous in the world. North Korea itself remains erratic and belligerent: North Korean assassins murdered 17 members of an official South Korean delegation visiting Rangoon in October 1983; and in November 1987, two North Korean terrorists planted a bomb in a K A L airliner in Abu Dhabi, which exploded over the Indian Ocean, killing all 115 people on board.

HISTORY

Korea developed its national identity over the centuries in the course of constant wars with China and Japan, both of which invaded it frequently. In 1907, Japan, fresh from its victory over Russia in Manchuria, established a protectorate over Korea and, in 1910, annexed it.

On 8 August 1945, the Soviet Union declared war on Japan and invaded Manchuria and Korea – two days after the atomic bomb was dropped on 197

Hiroshima, and one week before the Japanese surrender. The United States had ardently solicited Stalin to join in the war against Japan, and had now to cope with the consequences. Truman had no wish to see the Soviets established in Korea, just across the strait from Japan, and proposed that the isthmus should be provisionally divided along the 38th parallel, roughly halfway down. Stalin, who did not intend to begin a conflict with the US in the Far East, immediately agreed, and Korea, which had just escaped from Japanese colonialism, was suddenly partitioned by the two superpowers.

The Soviets immediately started building up a Communist state in the north. It must be said that, although it was imposed by the Red Army, the People's Republic of Korea has since survived on its own, the last Soviet troops having been withdrawn in 1949. The Americans were more preoccupied with Japan, and neglected their zone of Korea. Diplomatic efforts to arrange for the country's reunification were fruitless: the two sides refused to agree. Stalin would tolerate only a Communist Korea, Truman a democratic one.

The North Koreans built up an army 200,000 strong and resolved to reunify the country by force. Whether Stalin ordered the attack or merely acquiesced is now a subject of only academic debate. At the time, it was seen as a further step in the Soviet dream of conquering the world.

In a speech to the National Press Club in Washington on 12 January 1950, the secretary of state, Dean Acheson, remarked that the American 'defensive perimeter runs along the Aleutians to Japan and then goes to the Ryukyus [a string of islands south of Japan, including Okinawa].' He did not mention Korea. His enemies later alleged that this was to invite North Korea's attack. The allegation was part of the McCarthyite onslaught on the Truman administration (what Acheson called 'the attack of the primitives'), which does not necessarily mean that the primitives were wrong. Soviet diplomacy, not to mention North Korean diplomacy, was always inept, and it is at least possible that Acheson's omission, combined with their ignorance of the United States, led them into catastrophic error.

The invasion began on 6 June 1950. By early August, North Korea had occupied the whole of South Korea except for a pocket in the south-east. American troops in Korea were routed, and reinforcements sent from Japan did hardly better. In their defence, it must be said that the US army in the Far East had been allowed to run to seed, the big rearmament programme launched by the Truman administration having been directed towards building up American forces in Europe. Even at the height of the Korean war, the best new troops raised in the United States were shipped to Europe. Korea was a sideshow.

The day after the attack, President Truman ordered General Douglas MacArthur to defend South Korea. The general, abandoning his role of proconsul in Japan, sent sufficient troops across into Korea to protect the last redoubt, ordered the air force to bomb North Korean supply lines, and prepared a counterattack.

The United Nations, which the USSR was then boycotting, branded North Korea as aggressor and authorized the United States to form a UN command to defend the South. Its allies rallied to the call, sending contingents to fight alongside the Americans. The bulk of the UN force, however, was always the American army.

On 15 September, MacArthur landed his troops on the west coast of Korea at Inchon, near Seoul. Although the North Koreans were already seriously over-extended, and their defeat, once the United States had entered the war, was inevitable, the Inchon landings were one of the century's most remarkable feats of war. They were improvised in three months and carried out brilliantly, and in a matter of weeks MacArthur liberated the whole of South Korea and drove his armies into the North.

Perhaps if he had proceeded more cautiously, perhaps if he had kept his mouth shut, perhaps if Washington had proposed to recognize the Chinese Communist government (which it had refused to do since 1949) and invited it to a settlement of the Korean question, the Chinese would have permitted the defeat of North Korea and the reunification of the country. As it was, MacArthur drove his armies up to the Chinese frontier, proclaimed his intention of reuniting Korea unilaterally and threatened to carry the attack across the Yalu river into China. The Chinese sent numerous warnings to Washington that they would not tolerate such a result. The warnings were ignored, and in October, the People's Liberation Army crossed the Yalu.

The UN forces – principally American but including British, Canadian, Turkish and various other contingents – were taken wholly by surprise, and were driven back in rout. Seoul fell to the Chinese and North Koreans. It was only with the greatest difficulty, and in the midst of winter, that MacArthur managed to establish a defence line across the peninsula. In the following year, with skilful use of the terrain, and thanks to its overwhelming technical superiority, the UN command was able to drive the Chinese back approximately to the line of the former frontier. The general in command of operations was now Matthew Ridgeway, who had succeeded MacArthur when President Truman relieved the latter of his command on 11 April 1951, for insubordination. The Americans dug in and resisted 'human wave' attacks by the Chinese for over two years. A ceasefire was finally signed on 27 July 1953.

According to figures issued by the UN command, the Korean war resulted in the following casualties:

● United States: 37,904 dead, including 12,939 missing in action, presumed dead; 101,368 wounded.
● Other United Nations contingents: 4521 dead, among them 537 British and 312 Canadians.
● South Korea: 103,248 killed; 159,727 wounded.
● The US high command calculated that North Korea lost 316,579 killed and China 422,612. It also calculated that 2 million civilians, north and south, were killed or injured.

While the casualty figures for UN forces are precise, the ones attributed to the North Koreans and Chinese must be treated with extreme caution. For one thing, their precision is clearly spurious: for China, for instance, the breakdown was 401,401 killed and 21,211 missing, presumed dead – figures that are too pretty to be accurate and, obviously, too accurate to be accurate. Evidently they were reached by some statistical method. Furthermore, as experience in Vietnam showed 15 years later, American generals are entirely capable of inflating the body count. I. F. Stone   199 remarked that the high command was claiming Chinese losses equivalent to a full division a day during their mass offensives, a rate of attrition three times greater than the German army suffered at Verdun.

However, even heavily discounting the number of battlefield dead from the official 884,964, and taking a conservative number for civilian dead, the total deaths caused by the Korean war in three years were probably between 1 and 1.5 million.

POST-WAR KOREA

The country, both north and south, was utterly devastated. It was reduced to the level of Germany in 1945, its cities rubble, its industries destroyed. Both parts of the country set about the long painful business of restoration, complicated by the implacable hatred each side had for the other. The Chinese armies withdrew in 1958 but the Americans remain: South Korea is, despite Acheson's remarks, well within the American defensive perimeter.

With Hong Kong, Taiwan and Singapore, South Korea has now become one of the 'four little dragons' – East Asian countries that are following Japan's example in the pursuit of industrial growth. Its population is more than double the North's, its GNP nearly four times as great and rising far more rapidly. The comparison with Germany is striking. However, the East German regime survives because of the Soviet occupation, and East Germany has not the faintest intention of invading the West. In addition, North Korea spends 22.2 per cent of its GNP on defence, South Korea 5.5 per cent. As a proportion of the population, the North Korean armed forces are almost three times as great as those of the South (the actual numbers are North Korea: 784,000 men; South Korea: 600,000). Partly as a result, South Korea continues to pull ahead economically.

North Korea under Kim Il Sung is an oddity: a smaller country dedicated to invading and defeating a larger and far stronger one – whose defence is guaranteed by the United States. A sensible regime would cut its defence expenditure to the bone and concentrate on economic development. The fact that a government can follow a completely senseless policy for decades, can provoke South Korea by acts of flagrant terrorism and can seriously contemplate a second Korean war is another reminder of the power of irrationality in human affairs.

On 18 January 1968, 31 North Korean commandos, disguised as South Korean soldiers and civilians, crossed the demilitarized zone (DMZ) between the two countries and headed for Seoul with the intention of assassinating President Park Chung Hee. They reached the capital on 21 January but were intercepted by police, and a gun battle broke out, during which five of the commandos, one South Korean policeman and five civilians were killed. Some of the commandos were later killed in a fire-fight with American troops as they tried to escape back across the DMZ, and the commander of the operation was captured and admitted that his object had been the president. Park survived another attack, in August 1974, that killed his wife, but was finally assassinated by his chief of police, during a private dinner party in October 1979.

In October 1983, President Chun Doo Hwan of South Korea paid a state visit to Burma. On 9 October, he went to lay a wreath at the martyrs' memorial in

Rangoon, which commemorates Thakin Aung San, founder of independent

Burma, who was assassinated in 1947. Chun's car was delayed by traffic, and just before he arrived, a bomb demolished the memorial, killing 21 and wounding 46. The dead included the Korean foreign minister, Lee Bum Suk, the economic planning minister and deputy prime minister, Suh Suk Joon, and the minister for commerce and industry, Kim Dong Whie. The others were advisers to the president, journalists and security personnel.

Just before the explosion, the South Korean ambassador had arrived in a large car and a bugler had begun to practise 'The Last Post'. Presumably the terrorists, watching from a distance, had assumed that the president had arrived and the ceremony was beginning, and so detonated the bomb by radio. Three bombs had been concealed in the roof of the memorial; only one exploded.

Two days later, police arrested their first suspect, who tried to blow himself up with a hand grenade. The same day, villagers reported two suspicious foreigners to police, and when the latter approached them, they, too, tried to commit suicide with grenades (one succeeded) and three policemen were killed. The two wounded men were found to be North Koreans, and confessed that they had been sent to assassinate President Chun.

Six days before the opening of the Asian Games in Seoul in 1986, a bomb exploded in Seoul airport, killing five people. South Korea blamed the North.

On 29 November 1987, Korean Airlines flight 858, en route from Europe to Korea via the Middle East, exploded over the Indian Ocean, killing all 115 people on board. Two passengers had left the flight at its last stop, Abu Dhabi on the Persian Gulf. They were stopped by security guards, and both immediately swallowed cyanide. The man, Kim Sung Il, aged 70, died; the woman, Kim Hyon Hui, aged 26, survived.

She was extradited to South Korea, and there confessed. The two were North Korean intelligence agents, and had been given orders 'personally written' by Kim Chong Il, President Kim Il Sung's son. The woman had been trained to behave and look Japanese, and the two had left a bottle of liquid explosive (disguised as liquor) and a detonator in a radio in the overhead rack on the aircraft. She said that the attack had been designed to destabilize South Korea during its presidential election campaign, and to increase international nervousness about the forthcoming Olympic Games there. She told a press conference in January 1988 that she had since changed her allegiance, after watching South Korean television, and being driven around Seoul by her interrogators.

South Korea sometimes overreacts to the threat from the North. In 1986, as Seoul was in the throes of preparations for the 1988 Olympics, the North Koreans began construction of a large hydroelectric dam on the Pukhan river, which crosses the DMZ and flows through Seoul on its way to the sea. South Korea claimed that the North planned to finish the dam before the Olympics, allow a huge reservoir to accumulate behind it and then suddenly to blow up the dam, releasing the water. The flood would sweep through Seoul, drowning 2 million people, including the visitors and athletes at the Games. It was all rather improbable, but the South Koreans, much agitated, built a 'peace dam' on the river, on their side of the DMZ, to divert the flood. They finished it in record time, at a cost of $250 million; then they observed that the North's dam was hardly started, and was clearly years from completion.

201

In May 1988, South Korean students began a series of anti-American demonstrations. They blamed the United States for the division of the country, which is preposterous, and for supporting a long series of authoritarian Korean governments, which is not preposterous at all. They claim, in particular, that the United States was responsible for the Kwangju massacre in May 1980, in which South Korean troops, who were theoretically under American command, killed hundreds of demonstrators. The students now demanded the expulsion of the 40,000 American troops, and immediate reunification.

They proposed to march to the North to make their point. President Roo ordered the police to stop them, but admitted the possibility that the South was too rigid in its approach to the North. He therefore proposed a resumption of direct talks, and three sessions were held at the truce village, Panmunjom. The meetings were not a success. The South wanted the North to participate in the Olympics, and the North refused – unless it could be co-host. South Korea rejected that demand. The other, permanent subject of disagreement concerns America's presence in South Korea. Despite the student demonstrations, the Seoul government has no intention of asking them to leave. So the talks broke off, acrimoniously.

There is undoubtedly a great deal of Korean xenophobia. The United States is pressing South Korea to open its domestic market to American exports, to reduce the huge trade deficit. This is considered offensive by many Koreans who have built their astonishing economic development on hard work and the American market, and they are easily persuaded that the Americans really want to return them to their previous penury. Resentment at past American policies is also profound: the United States did indeed support a series of unsavoury military presidents, and accepted the argument that, because of the danger from the North, democracy could wait. Furthermore, the presence of the US is exceedingly visible (there is a huge American base in suburban Seoul), and it is perfectly acceptable for conservative Koreans to join the radicals in deploring American influence.

Evidently the far left – that is, Maoist Communism – has many adherents. The majority of Koreans, of course, have no wish to be taken over by Kim Il Sung, and perhaps the Korean radicals will go the way of the Japanese radicals of the 1950s and 1960s, who blamed the US for all their ills, real or imaginary. There was so much anti-Americanism in Japan that, in 1960, President Eisenhower had to cancel a state visit at the last moment. Those former Japanese radicals are now senior management in Japan Inc., and perhaps today's Korean radicals will follow the same route.

It is also possible that they will maintain the Maoist faith, like the Filipino radicals who demonstrated against the United States in 1970–2, and then formed the New People's Army (*see* The Philippines, pp. 214–26). The difference is that the Philippines then slipped into the Marcos autocracy, while Korea has just escaped from a prolonged military dictatorship. The demonstrations and the bizarre desire for a united, Communist Korea are tests for Korean democracy. If the government can cope with the challenge, including Molotov cocktails thrown at police and assaults with clubs and iron bars, without resorting to excessive force itself, South Korea will survive. In the long series of demonstrations during 1986–7, which led to free elections for the presidency in December 1987 and for the legislature in April 1988, there were countless violent clashes between riot police and demonstrators. But the police at all times kept their discipline, and it appears that they were guided by the principle that the rioters were Koreans, their children, who were the country's future, and therefore they never used live ammunition. (The contrast between this and Israel's methods of riot control during the simultaneous *intifada* was striking.)

The improvements in relations between China, the US and the USSR have left North Korea isolated, like Vietnam. It is unlikely that there will be any significant diplomatic progress until after Kim Il Sung dies, and in the meantime, there will always be a danger of further conflict between North and South.

The 1988 Olympics in Seoul were a great success. Stringent security precautions were taken, for fear of terrorism from the North, but there were no incidents. (China and the USSR, which both sent teams, had promised to use their influence with North Korea to ensure the peace.) The games allowed many South Koreans to demonstrate their irritation with the United States. The cheerful chauvinism of American television, which ceaselessly patronized Korea and everything Korean throughout the games, and a few incidents of boorish behaviour by American athletes were given great play in Seoul. Conversely, Americans were angered by the constant manifestations of anti-Americanism they encountered.

Koreans had more pressing concerns. The transition to democracy continued and proved continually painful. A parliamentary inquiry into the misdeeds of the former military regime revealed a pattern of corruption that implicated former President Chun, and suggested that the Kwangju massacre was a result of deliberate government policy. Members of Chun's family were arrested and charged with corruption, and a series of violent demonstrations by students and other radicals forced President Roh Tae Woo to abandon his friend and patron, and insist that he appear on television and apologize for his errors. Chun was then sent into internal exile in the country. The demonstrations continued.

FURTHER READING

Alexander, Bevin, *Korea – The First War We Lost*, New York, Hippocrene Books, 1986.
American University, *North Korea: A Country Study*, Washington, D.C., 1982.
——, *South Korea: A Country Study*, Washington, D.C., 1981.
Amnesty International, *South Korea: Violations of Human Rights*, London, 1986.
Hastings, Max, *The Korean War*, New York, Simon and Schuster, 1987.
MacDonald, Callum, *Korea: The War before Vietnam*, New York, Free Press, 1987.
Stone, I. F., *The Hidden History of the Korean War*, New York, Monthly Review Press, 1952.

MALAYSIA

Geography	127,672 sq. miles (330,669 sq. km). Malaysia comprises the Malay peninsula (50,670 sq. miles; 131,235 sq. km) and Sabah and Sarawak on the north coast of Borneo.
Population	15.9 million, of whom 2.5 million live in the Borneo territories, the rest in Malaya. About 7 million are Malays, 4 million Chinese, 1.3 million Indian (mostly Tamils). The others are the indigenous tribes of Borneo.
Resources	Tin, rubber, tropical produce; rapidly developing light industry.
GNP per capita	$1850
Refugees	90,000 from the Philippines, 8220 from Vietnam.

The last traces of a Communist insurgency sputter along in the jungles on the Thai frontier. The 'confrontation' with Indonesia (*see* Indonesia, pp. 188–96) has subsided, and the two countries are now allied in the ASEAN (Association of South-East Asian Nations). There were serious anti-Chinese riots in Kuala Lumpur in 1969, in which hundreds of people were killed, but since then, the predominantly Malay government and the Chinese and Indian communities have worked to reduce social inequities and racial tensions. They have been notably more successful than, for example, the government of Sri Lanka. At the moment, Malaysia is a bastion of stability and ethnic harmony in a dangerous world.

Malaysia has a special role in an account of contemporary conflicts. The Communist insurgency, 1948–60, was soundly defeated, and the American intervention in Vietnam was a fruitless attempt to repeat that success. The Malayan experience unfortunately proved to be unique.

HISTORY

The Malay peninsula came under British control in the 19th century as an appendage of the Indian empire and because of the activities of a British adventurer, Stamford Raffles. He set up a trading emporium on Singapore island in 1819, which developed rapidly into the Straits Settlements, the greatest trading centre in South-east Asia. In order to protect Singapore, the British extended their influence to the peninsula. Another adventurer, Sir James Brooke, cleared the pirates out of

Sarawak on the north-western coast of Borneo, and set himself up as the 'White Raja of Sarawak'.

On 10 December 1941, the British navy in the Far East suffered a humiliation even greater than Pearl Harbor, when the Japanese attacked and sank the battleship *Prince of Wales* and the cruiser *Repulse* at Singapore. Singapore itself was captured on 15 February 1942; most of the numerous British and Australian PoWs died in the camps. The Japanese incited the Malays against the Chinese, and thousands of the latter were executed. Resistance started first among the Chinese, led by the Communist Party, in both Malaya and Singapore, and was ruthlessly suppressed.

After the war, and as a result of the humiliating defeat that the British had suffered at the hands of the Japanese, the citizens of the British empire in Asia concluded that the days of empire were over. The British were constrained to agree with them. The last Brooke Raja of Sarawak was summarily dispossessed by the government in London; Malaya became independent in 1957; and in 1963, Singapore and the territories in Borneo (which were still British colonies or protectorates) were federated with Malaya to become the country now known as Malaysia. Singapore withdrew from the federation in 1965, and the British protectorate of Brunei, possessed of large oil revenues, declined to join and went it alone.

THE EMERGENCY

The Malaya Emergency began in June 1948. Communist terrorists attacked government posts, police and military patrols in the rubber plantations and tin-mining areas; the first victims were three European plantation managers. The insurgents intended to follow classic guerrilla strategy and wreck the economy by killing planters and their managers, by slashing rubber trees and by blowing up or burning essential buildings at the plantations or mines. They also made a speciality of attacking Malayan officials.

Almost all the Communist terrorists – known to the British army as 'CTs' and to themselves as the Min Yuen – were Chinese, and the fighting was at least partly a continuation of the animosities stirred up by the Japanese. The CTs' greatest successes occurred in 1949–51, culminating in the assassination of the British high commissioner, Sir Henry Gurney, in an ambush on 6 October 1951. During the course of the Emergency, one in ten of the rubber planters were murdered.

The British responded by gathering together the Chinese workers of the plantations and mines into 'new villages'. About 300,000 squatters lived on the fringes of the plantations and provided the 'sea' in which the CT 'fish' could swim, under Mao's prescription for guerrilla war. By 1952, the British had moved the squatters into 400 new villages, securely under government control. They offered many advantages in health, sanitation and other facilities, but also imposed considerable hardship on the people involved. After the Emergency ended, the new villages survived and throve: for the first time, Chinese immigrants and their descendants had leases on their houses and were a recognized part of Malayan society. Part of the campaign against the CTs involved providing everyone with an identity card; these gave the Chinese proof of residence and citizenship, and a stake in the success of independent Malaya.

The policy succeeded in cutting the CTs off from popular support and, more important, from their only source of supply. It was the model for the 'strategic hamlets' policy that the Americans tried in Vietnam.

The other British method for fighting the terrorists was to train their conscript army in the techniques of guerrilla warfare. Small foot patrols scoured the jungles, ambushing the CTs; this was known as 'jungle bashing'. It was calculated that 1000 hours of jungle bashing might be needed for one contact with a CT.

The British proved better guerrilla fighters than the Malayan Communists. They had another advantage: they brought in Dayak trackers from Borneo. They divided the country, whose topography lends itself to such practices, into districts, each of which was in turn subjected to a most thorough search. As each district was declared 'white,' the British moved their troops, police and planes on to the next. They started this intensive clearance operation in the south and worked north. By the time of independence, the remaining 500 or so CTs had been driven across the border into Thailand.

Ten years later, when Sukarno sent Indonesian guerrillas into Sarawak, the British demonstrated that they had not lost their skills. The Indonesians were roundly defeated by the same methods that had beaten the Malayan Communists.

The essential difference between the British experience in Malaya and the Americans' in Vietnam (and the Philippine government's today) is that the Malayan insurrection was limited to a minority among a distinct ethnic group. The majority of the Chinese did not support the CTs and were separated from them in their new villages, while the majority of the population, the Malays, actively opposed the Communists. In Vietnam, no such distinction was possible, nor is it possible in the Philippines. The other element in the British strategy, sending British soldiers into the jungles on foot patrol, to play cat and mouse with the guerrillas, was not tried extensively in Vietnam.

At the height of the Emergency, there were 40,000 regular troops in Malaya (including the Malay Regiment), 70,000 police who were almost entirely Malays, and up to 250,000 'Home Guards' who defended their own villages and communities.

At the start of the Emergency, the CTs had 4000 to 5000 guerrilla fighters, and in the early 1950s, they had perhaps 8000 men. In the course of the Emergency, about 13,000 suspected terrorists were killed. The British lost 525 men killed, including Malay soldiers and police.

FURTHER READING

American University, *Malaysia, a Country Study*, Washington, 1985.

Gullick, J. M., *Malaysia*, New York, Praegar, 1969.

James, Harold and Shiel-Small, Denis, *The Undeclared War: The Story of the Indonesian Confrontation, 1962–66*, London, Leo Cooper, 1971.

McKie, Ronald, *The Emergence of Malaysia*, New York, Harcourt, Brace and World, 1963.

PAKISTAN

Geography	310,403 sq. miles (803,941 sq. km). Somewhat larger than the UK and France combined.
Population	About 100 million. The major ethnic groups are: Punjabis, about 60%; Sindhi, 12%; Baluchi, 4%; Pushtun (Pathan), 11%. The population is 70% Sunni Muslim, 30% Shiite, many of them Ismaili. Urdu is the official language, but English is widely spoken.
GNP per capita	$350
Refugees	3,541,000 Afghans.

On 17 August 1988, the military ruler of Pakistan, General Mohammed Zia el-Haq, was killed in a plane crash. Three months later, on 16 November, general elections were held. They were conducted fairly and openly, and the Pakistan People's party, led by Benazir Bhutto, won 92 of the 215 seats in the National Assembly. She became prime minister on 2 December – the first woman to head the government of an Islamic country and, at the age of 35, the youngest head of government in the world. She now has to grapple with the social and economic problems that have defeated every Pakistani government since independence.

Pakistan was in the midst of a profound political crisis when Zia was killed. His death abruptly removed one of the principal causes of that crisis: the blood feud between him and the opposition that had subsisted since he overthrew Zulfikar Ali Bhutto in 1977 and hanged him. The underlying antagonisms between Pakistan's regions and between the army and civilians remain.

Pakistan has lurched from crisis to crisis since it was born in the disaster of the Indian partition in 1947. It has fought three wars with India, and lost all of them. (For the first two, *see* India, pp. 173–87.) The third, in 1971, was East Pakistan's war of independence, and ended with the formation of Bangladesh. There have been two military coups, the second of which, in 1977, brought Zia to power. There have been dissident movements in Baluchistan and Sind, and frequent disturbances in all parts of the country. The latest have been in Karachi, provoked by the influx of refugees from Afghanistan.

Because the chief concern of Pakistan's foreign policy has been its enmity towards India, it developed a close alliance with China, which fought a border war with India in 1962. There is now an all-weather road over the Himalayas from Sinkiang in western China into northern Pakistan, as a symbol of that alliance. Pakistan inherited from the British a profound distrust of the USSR. It considered Afghanistan as a buffer state, and when the Soviets occupied it in 1979, the Pakistanis naturally supported the resistance. Equally naturally, India has developed close relations with the Soviet Union, on the principle that 'the enemy of my enemy is my friend.' India was the only independent country of any consequence that refrained from criticizing the Soviet occupation of Afghanistan.

The United States has supported Pakistan from its inception, on the same principle – its staunch opposition to the Soviets – and American relations with India have therefore always been cool, despite the fact that India is a democracy while Pakistan has usually been a military dictatorship. The only time that the balance of American favour tilted towards India was during the Kennedy administration, when John Kenneth Galbraith was American ambassador to New Delhi. However, after the 1965 war, the United States suspended arms sales to both countries, a policy that in effect penalized Pakistan as India continued to be supplied by the USSR.

During the 1971 war, President Nixon ordered his administration to 'tilt' in favour of Pakistan, and his national security adviser, Henry Kissinger, strove strenuously to obey the order. (News of it was leaked to Jack Anderson, a Washington columnist, who published it.) The 'tilt' did Pakistan no good. Nixon's successors have followed the same preference, even after a Pakistani mob sacked the American embassy in Islamabad in November 1979, killing two American servicemen, while the authorities did nothing to protect it. Arms sales to Pakistan were resumed during the Carter administration, and during the Afghan war, Pakistan became a major recipient of American aid. There is, however, strong pressure from Congress to cut that aid, because of Pakistan's nuclear programme and because of the nearly one-third of the world's heroin that is manufactured in the frontier districts.

HISTORY

In the long run-up to India's independence, there were two main political parties: the Congress party, led by Nehru, Patel and Gandhi; and the Muslim League, led by Mohammed Ali Jinnah (known as the Quaid-i-Azam) and Liaquat Ali Khan. The Congress party wanted a united India; the League advocated a separate state for Muslims, consisting of north-east India and East Bengal. The disadvantages of this scheme, apart from the permanent hostility between the two nations that has ensued, were that a huge number of Muslims, now 90 million, would be left as a minority in India, and that the country's two wings would be separated by 1000 miles of Indian territory. When independence came in 1947, it was accompanied by immense movements of population and immense bloodshed: 12 million people were driven from their homes, in India and in Pakistan, and about 800,000 people were murdered.

For a variety of reasons that are still hotly debated, Pakistan, unlike India, proved incapable of establishing a stable democratic form of government. Jinnah died in 1948 and Liaquat Ali was assassinated in 1951, and the series of weak and ineffectual governments that followed were faced with Baluchi and Pushtun unrest and with increasing differences between the two wings of the country. The fundamental conflict was between the Bengalis, who were by far the most numerous of Pakistan's ethnic groups and, in due course, became an absolute majority in the nation, and the Punjabis, who numbered 60 per cent of West Pakistan's population and dominated that region. Each group thought that it should lead the nation. Civilian government collapsed under the strain, and on 7 October 1958, the president, General Iskander Mirza, abrogated the constitution and proclaimed martial law, appointing General Ayub Khan as martial law administrator. On 28 October, Ayub packed Mirza off into exile in London and took full power.

Ayub pursued economic development on lines recommended by the United States, and achieved some success. However, he failed to resolve the country's underlying political problems, and started and lost a war with India in 1965. In 1968, he celebrated his decade in power with considerable pomp and so provoked the Pakistanis that riots broke out all over the country. Ayub was forced to resign in March 1969, and was succeeded by another general, Yahya Khan. Political parties were revived and elections were called for November 1970.

THE WAR OF 1971 AND THE INDEPENDENCE OF BANGLADESH

The main parties in the country were now the Awami League in East Pakistan, led by Sheikh Mujib Ur-Rahman, and the Pakistan People's party (PPP), led by Zulfikar Ali Bhutto, who had been foreign minister under Ayub. The PPP was based in the Punjab and Sind; it had no support in the North-west Frontier Province (Pushtunistan), or in Baluchistan. The elections were postponed when a cyclone devastated East Pakistan, killing 250,000 people in November 1970.

When voting finally took place in December, the Awami League won 160 of the 162 National Assembly seats allocated to East Pakistan, and the PPP won 81 of the 138 seats allocated to the West. Sheikh Mujib had an absolute majority and insisted that he would form the government as soon as parliament convened. He would then carry out his party's electoral platform, which amounted to stripping the federal government of all power except over foreign affairs and defence.

Yahya and Bhutto both refused to accept the prospect. The stalemate was absolute, and on 25 March 1971, Yahya proclaimed a state of emergency in East Pakistan, dissolved the Awami League and arrested its leaders, including Mujib, and denounced them as traitors.

Yahya's army in the East was 40,000 strong, and was progressively increased to 75,000. It set about ferociously repressing the 75 million Bengalis, and before the end of the year, it had killed at least 300,000 people. (The Bangladeshis now claim that the total killed was 3 million, which is clearly a great exaggeration.) On 14 April 1971, in a village near the Indian border, Mujib's surviving associates proclaimed an independent Bangladesh, but on the approach of the Pakistani army, they prudently moved to Calcutta. India offered Bangladesh every support. It began to train Bengali guerrillas – the Mukti Bahini – one of whose first 'achievements' was the murder of the governor of East Pakistan, Abdel Monen Khan. Soon there were 100,000 Mukti Bahini, led by Bengali officers who had deserted from the old Pakistan army. Refugees from Bangladesh began to pour over the border into India: in the end, there were over 10 million of them.

209

The Nixon administration offered some succour to Pakistan (the famous 'tilt'), although it was obvious that it would not succeed in restoring Pakistani unity. Kissinger had arranged to use Yahya's government as his super-secret channel to China, and in July, as his staff informed the press that he was ill, he flew from Islamabad to Peking. The United States' pro-Pakistan policy was much resented in India, which in August signed a 20-year treaty of peace, friendship and cooperation with the Soviet Union. Indira Gandhi toured Western countries and Moscow to explain that India would have to intervene unless Pakistan renounced its war in the East. The Indians forbade Pakistani planes to overfly Indian territory. They therefore had to make the long trip around, via Sri Lanka.

The massacres increased in frequency and the guerrilla fighting became rapidly more serious. The guerrillas announced a generalized offensive in November, and on 22 November, the Indian army crossed the border at numerous points into East Pakistan and began an advance on Dacca. The Indians later denied that they had invaded, saying that they had waited until Pakistan attacked them.

Yahya declared a state of national emergency and, in desperation, began preparations for a general war against India on all fronts. On 3 December, the Pakistani air force attempted to repeat the Israeli achievement of the Six Day War of 1967, and destroy the Indian air force on the ground. It failed. In 1967, the Israelis had taken the Egyptians completely by surprise and won the war in a 30-minute air raid; in 1971, the Pakistanis attacked the wrong airports, missed the planes on the ground when they found the right ones, and their planes were in turn attacked and destroyed by the Indians.

On 4 December, India openly poured troops into East Pakistan and, in a five-pronged attack, soon defeated the Pakistani army there. It surrendered on 16 December. Simultaneously, the Indians had crossed the border into West Pakistan.

Kissinger, whose distaste for India is quite remarkable, claims that there was a real danger that India, supported by the Soviet Union, would dismember West Pakistan as well, annexing Kashmir. He claims that American diplomacy prevented this eventuality by using its leverage in Moscow to induce the Soviets to dissuade India. In any event, on 17 December, Indira Gandhi announced a unilateral ceasefire.

Yahya Khan's military government collapsed. He resigned on 20 December, and Bhutto took power. It was a sequence of events to be repeated by the Greek colonels in Cyprus and the Argentinian junta in the Falklands war.

During his four-and-a-half years as head of the government, Bhutto succeeded in restoring Pakistani self-confidence and a semblance of unity, but he provoked much opposition in the army and in large sectors of the population. The PPP won elections in March 1977, an event that provoked widespread rioting and protest in districts dominated by the opposition. The army took power in a coup on 5 July 1977, and the chief of staff, General Zia el-Haq, made himself president. On 4 April 1979, despite vehement protests from governments around the world, Zia had Bhutto hanged on a charge of plotting the assassination of a political rival.

When Zia died, Pakistan was faced with a serious challenge from the Afghan and Iranian refugees. There are about 3.5 million Afghans in Pakistan, most of them in camps in the North-west Frontier Province (NWFP), but also thousands elsewhere in the country. In addition, about 20,000 refugees from Iran live mostly in Karachi.

There is constant tension between various Afghan factions, between Shiites and Sunnis, between followers of the ayatollah and his enemies, a situation that, particularly in Karachi, is compounded by conflicts between Biharis (refugees from eastern India) and other Pakistanis. Hundreds of people have been killed or wounded in riots or bombings and by assassination. More than 200 were killed by bombings in 1987: on 14 July 1987, 72 people were killed by car bombs in Karachi and hundreds were injured.

The Pakistani government hopes that the Afghan refugees will all return home in the next year or two, but it is not likely that Pakistan's communal tensions will disappear so quickly. A further problem is that India accuses it of fomenting trouble in the Punjab by arming Sikh dissidents.

Pakistan is on the verge of making its first atomic weapons. (India has already demonstrated its capacity to do so.) In 1987, Pakistani businessmen in several countries, including the United States and Canada, were discovered to be buying the various components needed for a plant to separate weapons-grade plutonium from used fuel in nuclear power plants. The conspiracy was evidently directed by the Pakistani government. In May 1988, the *New York Times*, in a report attributed to official US sources, stated that Pakistan had successfully tested a surface-to-surface missile capable of delivering a nuclear warhead to Delhi or Bombay. India had tested a similar missile in February.

In December 1985, Zia at last lifted martial law, which he had imposed in 1977. Politics revived, after a fashion, and Benazir Bhutto, daughter of the late president, emerged as leader of the PPP. There was a national assembly, a prime minister, a government and a constitution, but it was all a sham. Zia remained the absolute ruler, the dictator. On 29 May 1988, because the civilian government he had installed was showing signs of independence, he dissolved parliament (without consulting the government), dismissed the prime minister, Mohammed Khan Junejo, leader of the Muslim League, and announced that there would be elections in November. The news was greeted with the greatest scepticism: Benazir Bhutto was not alone in believing that the elections would be a fraud.

On 17 August 1988, President Zia was killed when his military C-130 suddenly crashed shortly after taking off. The president had been on an inspection at a military base, along with several senior officers and the American ambassador, Arnold Raphel. One of those killed was the chairman of the joint chiefs of staff, General Akhtar Abdul Rehman, who had directed the vast logistics operation involved in moving arms to the Afghan resistance. Zia had been a staunch supporter of the resistance, and his supporters suspected that the Afghan secret service was responsible for his death. Subsequent investigations failed to find any proof of sabotage, however, and they ruled out the possibility that the plane had been hit by a missile or had exploded in the air.

The new government promised to hold the elections as scheduled in November, and the acting president, Ishaq Ghulam Khan, and the new chief of staff, General Mirza Aslam Beg, kept this promise. The elections were the first expression of democracy that Pakistan had enjoyed since 1972, and were hotly debated between several political parties. Benazir Bhutto succeeded in extending the PPP's reach beyond her father's strongholds in Sind, but still needed the support of other parties to win a majority in the assembly. She also needed the army's support; as a

211

result, she promised to maintain the army in all its power and privileges and to continue supporting the rebels in Afghanistan.

Unlike Corazon Aquino in the Philippines, Bhutto was not swept to power in a popular uprising against a detested regime. On the contrary, Zia was clearly hugely popular: half a million people attended his funeral. Furthermore, Aquino controlled the military; Bhutto does not. She may be prime minister, but real power in the country is still exercised by the army and its commander, General Beg. Bhutto's party is divided into bitterly contesting factions, and opposition parties, particularly in the Punjab, have the power to bring her down if the going gets rough.

When Zia died, the country was as split as it had been 11 years earlier, when he had taken power. Relations with India were scarcely improved and the country's economy was sustained by American aid and by remittances from expatriate workers in the Persian Gulf. Bhutto has also to grapple with the consequences of the Afghan war, notably the 3.5 million Afghan refugees now in Pakistan, and the enormous increase in the number of guns loose in the community. It is a depressing prospect.

BALUCHISTAN

Baluchistan is the largest of Pakistan's provinces, but the least populous, being largely mountain and desert. There are about 6 million Baluchis: the 4 million in Pakistan occupy the territory west of the lower Indus valley; the remainder occupy a considerable part of southern Afghanistan and south-east Iran. They have long agitated for a separate state: their division between three nations, all of whom mistrust and oppress them, is a historical accident, another consequence of thoughtless imperial expansionism by the British in the 19th century.

In 1973, the endemic tribal fighting and resistance to government control developed into a full-scale insurrection. At the height of the fighting, there were 55,000 tribesmen in the guerrilla armies. Bhutto sent 70,000 troops to suppress them. The shah of Iran, concerned that the fighting might spread among Iranian Baluchis, sent 25 Huey-Cobra gunships and their crews; they devastated Baluchi villages as they had the villages of Vietnam, and as the Soviets, later, were to devastate Afghanistan. The Pakistani air force bombed villages and suspected guerrilla positions, while Afghanistan threatened full-scale war in defence of the tribesmen. It was an empty threat: Afghanistan was preoccupied with its own increasing internal problems.

By the end of 1974, the rebels had been driven back into their mountain fastnesses, where they remain. In 1976, two army divisions were sent against them, and there have been frequent punitive expeditions into the mountains since then. One estimate of casualties puts both Baluchi and Pakistani dead at 3000.

PUSHTUNISTAN

Resistance in the North-west Frontier Province has not been as serious as in Baluchistan, but the potential dangers are far greater. The Pushtuns, or Pathans, are far more numerous – 11 million compared to 4 million Pakistani Baluchis. They are more adept at modern warfare, and the war in Afghanistan has demonstrated the effectiveness of guerrilla fighting in those remote and difficult mountains; it has also put enormous quantities of arms at their disposal. The Pushtuns are divided between Pakistan and Afghanistan, and for many years the governments in Kabul regularly demanded that Pakistan cede Pushtunistan to them. Now the civil war in Afghanistan (*see* pp. 117–29) has driven 3.5 million Afghan refugees into Pakistan, most of them Pushtuns.

In the mid-1980s, the government in Islamabad tried to assert its control over the frontier districts, because the large increase in the opium trade there was causing serious problems with the United States. In March 1986, the government sent a small army, reportedly eight battalions strong, to control a tribal leader near the Khyber Pass. It was to no avail. The opium trade continued to flourish, and smuggling across the Khyber Pass reached astonishing levels: goods from Eastern Europe and the Soviet Union – from refrigerators to caviar – were freely available in frontier villages, as were all sorts of guns. The whole operation was financed by American money brought in by the mujaheddin, by international relief agencies working with the refugees, and by the immense profits of the opium trade. Zia, who wished to establish a purified Islamic republic of Pakistan, instead presided over an irresistible flood of corruption.

FURTHER READING

American University, *Pakistan: A Country Study*, Washington D.C., 1984
Baxter, Craig, *Zia's Pakistan: Politics and Stability in a Frontline State*, Boulder, Colo., Westview Press, 1987.
Choudhury, Golam Wahed, *The Last Days of United Pakistan*, Bloomington, Indiana University Press, 1974.
Hayes, Louis D., *Politics in Pakistan: The Struggle for Legitimacy*, Boulder, Colo., Westview Press, 1984.
Minority Rights Group, *The Baluchis and Pathans*, London 1987.

PHILIPPINES

Geography	An archipelago stretching 1000 miles (1600 km) from north to south, including over 7000 islands which, between them, occupy about 115,000 sq. miles (300,000 sq. km), about the size of Italy.
Population	56 million. There are eight major languages; English, Tagalog (renamed Pilipino to make it more 'national') and Spanish are the official ones. Tagalog is the mother-tongue of 30% and is spoken by 55%. The population is 85% Roman Catholic, 5% Protestant, 5% Muslim; the rest are animists.
GNP per capita	$570
Refugees	External: 90,000, (mostly Muslims) in Malaysia. Internal: 8800 from Vietnam; 2920 from Laos; 230 from Cambodia.

President Ferdinand Marcos was driven from power on 26 February 1986, after 20 years in office. He was succeeded by Corazon Aquino, widow of Benigno Aquino, who was murdered in 1983. President Aquino has to grapple with intractible economic problems. There is also a long-running Muslim insurgency in Mindanao, the main southern island in the Philippines; a Communist revolt centred on the northern island, Luzon; and the continuing danger of an army *coup d'état*. There have been several unsuccessful coups since she took office, and the Communist New People's Army has greatly increased its strength. Aquino and her supporters, who defied tanks and machine-guns in the name of freedom, have made the depressing discovery that Marcos was not the problem, he was a symptom.

HISTORY
The Philippines had no national history before the coming of the Spaniards in 1521. This was not Java or Vietnam, where organized states flourished a millennium before European colonization, and whose people today can look back on the colonial period as an episode, an interruption, in a long history. The Philippines have nothing to look back to before Ferdinand Magellan landed in Cebu, an island in the centre of the archipelago, and a strong element in the modern history of the country is of a nation in search of its own identity.

For 380 years, the Philippines were the remotest part of the Spanish empire. Manila was a trading station where silver from Potosi in South America was exchanged for silk from China. Twice a year, the Acapulco galleon crossed the Pacific bearing treasure in each direction. The Philippines were governed from Mexico until 1821, and during those uneventful centuries, the only episode out of the ordinary was a brief British occupation of Manila in 1762–6, during the Seven Years' War. The Spanish government in Manila had little effect on the rest of the islands: only 5 per cent of the population now speak Spanish. Spain's most lasting contribution was religious: 90 per cent were converted to Catholicism.

By the end of the 19th century, Spain was losing its grip on the remnants of its empire. Cuba was in revolt, and a nationalist uprising started in the Philippines. The Spanish authorities tried to crush it by executing the country's leading intellectual, José Rizal, and buying off the rebels' military leader, Emilio Aguinaldo, but it was clear that Spanish rule was coming to an end.

On 15 February 1898, an American battleship the USS *Maine*, blew up in Havana harbour. The United States used the episode (probably an accident) as a *causus belli* and declared war on Spain. In May, Admiral Dewey destroyed a Spanish squadron in the Philippines; on 1 July, Teddy Roosevelt stormed up San Juan Hill in Cuba; Santiago in Cuba surrendered on 17 July; and on 4 August, American troops were landed at Manila. A peace treaty was signed in Paris on 10 December. Cuba became independent under American protection, and Spain ceded Puerto Rico, the Philippines and Guam to the US. Thus the great enterprise begun by Ferdinand and Isabella in 1492 came to an end, and the United States acquired its first overseas colonies.

It was a flagrant case of imperialist aggression, just the sort of thing the Europeans had been doing for hundreds of years. It was not, however, America's first colonial war: 50 years earlier the United States had summarily annexed a large part of Mexico.

The military governor of Manila was General Arthur MacArthur, a hero of the Civil War and father of Douglas MacArthur. The son's career offers a striking illustration of the acceleration of modern history. He was born on the western frontier, where his father was protecting settlers against Indians, and, as a child, lived in forts that were periodically attacked by Indians with bows and arrows. He lived to command American forces in the Pacific when the first atomic bombs were dropped on Japan.

The Filipinos fought the new occupation. It took Arthur MacArthur two years and 150,000 troops to suppress the insurrection. Aguinaldo vanished from history (though he lived to see the Japanese occupation and Philippine independence), and his deputy Manuel Quezon became the dominant political figure in the country.

President McKinley had proclaimed: 'We will educate the Philippines and uplift and Christianize them, and by God's grace do the very best we can for them.' The Americans devoted themselves to teaching the Filipinos English and developing a modern state on American lines, with executive and legislature, stock market and baseball, universal education and freedom of religion. There was a running debate between Wilsonian Democrats and Taftian Republicans over the date when the Philippines should become independent. Taft, who was President of the US Philippine Commission (the civilian adminstration) in the early years, referred to the Filipinos as 'our little brown brothers', 215 and believed that they should be guided by American wisdom for an indefinite period.

The Philippine élite – the *ilustrados* – assimilated easily to the American system. Their privileges and land-holdings were preserved and they prospered under American direction. The debate on independence was resolved by the administration of President Franklin Roosevelt, which created a Philippine Commonwealth (in effect, self-government under American supervision) to be followed by independence in ten years. The Commonwealth of the Philippines was set up in 1935 and Quezon was elected President. He hired retired US General Douglas MacArthur to form and command a Philippine army.

The Japanese attacked the Philippines on 7 December 1941, ten hours after Pearl Harbor. MacArthur, by now commander of all American forces in the Far East as well as the Philippine army, declared Manila an open city and withdrew to the fortifications of the Bataan peninsula and Corregidor island in the bay. The Japanese occupied Manila on 2 January 1942, and the siege of the fortresses continued for five months before they finally surrendered. By then President Quezon had left the country, and MacArthur had been ordered to Australia. He promised to return.

The élite, who had got on so well with the Americans, found they could live equally well with the Japanese, and collaborated openly. The Japanese set up a quisling government, with José Laurel as president. He was a member of a prominent *ilustrado* family, and his son is now Aquino's vice president.

The mass of the Filipinos detested the Japanese and fought them. The split between the élite and the peasantry, which remains the country's most serious social problem, was greatly exacerbated by this division: it seemed to most Filipinos that the governing classes were traitors to the nation. There was a full-scale guerrilla war against the Japanese, the only one in south-east Asia. In the Philippines, the Japanese could not present themselves as liberators, as they did in Indonesia, Malaya, Indochina and Burma. They were invaders.

The Philippines lost 1 million people killed during the war, most of them civilians. The fighting continued to the very end. A total of 260,000 men fought in guerrilla units, among them Ferdinand Marcos. The most effective guerrilla group was the People's Anti-Japanese Army, or Hukbalahap (known as the Huks), in central Luzon. They were led by Luis Taruc, a Communist, and, by the end of the war, controlled most of the island. They imposed land reform and set up soviets in the countryside, while fighting off the Japanese.

MacArthur landed at Leyte, an island in the centre of the archipelago, on 20 October 1944, and fought his way back to Manila by late January 1945. The Japanese navy put up a last-ditch defence in Manila and destroyed most of the city; it was as badly damaged as Berlin, Warsaw or Budapest. The Japanese murdered 100,000 Filipino civilians, deliberately slaughtering and mutilating children as well as adults. The entire business district and 80 per cent of the southern residential district, together with 75 per cent of the factories, were destroyed. In 1945, per capita production was probably lower than it had been in 1899, and the GNP was 39 per cent of the 1937 level – when the Philippines were still suffering from the Depression.

THE INDEPENDENT PHILIPPINES

216   The Philippines became independent on 4 July 1946. It was a new sort of

independence, one that later bacame known as 'neo-colonialism'. The United States continued to control the Philippines' economy as completely as it controlled the banana republics of Central America. A Parity Act, passed by the US Congress before it approved the Philippines' independence, provided that US companies would enjoy equal rights with local firms to develop the country. The American bases were leased for 99 years, and the United States controlled the exchange rate of the peso. Congress offered compensation for war damage, but only on condition that the Philippines accept the base agreement and the Parity Act.

The Filipinos, of course, resented these limitations on their sovereignty, which have been progressively eliminated since. They also resented that Japan and Germany, former enemies, received far more generous reconstruction aid than the Philippines, which had fought loyally on the United States' side. Furthermore, the question of the collaborators deeply divided Filipino society. MacArthur arbitrarily declared that Manuel Roxas, an old friend who had been vice president under the Japanese quisling government, was innocent of all wrongdoing. In the 1946 election, Roxas defeated President Sergio Osmena, who had succeeded Quezon when he died in 1944, and who had spent the war in Washington. In 1948, Roxas pardoned all collaborators (only one had ever been indicted).

In 1947, the Huks rose in revolt. It was partly a typical peasant uprising, partly a Communist rebellion. It was suppressed by the minister of defence, Ramon Magsaysay, who captured the Huk leaders in 1950 and dispersed their troops. A small remnant, reduced to banditry, survived in the hills of Luzon. Many former Huks were resettled in Mindanao, which solved their problems while enraging the Muslims who lived there and who feared being overwhelmed by Christians from the north.

The pre-war oligarchy reasserted its complete control of the country. Government operated under the patronage system, a sort of institutionalized corruption. The oligarchs prospered, but the rapidly increasing population, millions of whom moved into Manila, sank into abject poverty. Social tensions were much increased by the huge numbers of weapons left over from the war, and Manila became one of the most crime-ridden cities in the world.

Marcos was elected president in 1965. He presented himself as a war hero, who would clear out the corruption of the previous administration. However, his own administration was undistinguished until 1969, election year, when he contrived to be the first Filipino president to win re-election. He managed this by pouring money into the provinces and bribing officials. Political violence increased steadily during Marcos's two official terms. In January 1970, there were student riots in Manila, suppressed with considerable violence. The conflict between police and students proved to be one of the catalysts that helped start the Communist rebellion (see NPA below). In October 1970, grenades were thrown at an opposition, Liberal party rally, killing ten people, and in November 1971, over 200 people were killed in an election campaign.

On 22 September 1972, a bomb was thrown (or, according to other accounts, shots were fired) at the limousine of the defence secretary, Juan Ponce Enrile, and Marcos used this as a pretext to proclaim martial law. The minister was not in the car at the time, and years later, he confirmed what many had immediately suspected – that the attempt was a fake, designed by Marcos to eliminate democratic government. (It is also widely suspected that some of the other bombings were also his work.) The decree proclaiming martial law – known as Proclamation 1081 – had already been signed, on 17 September.

Marcos suspended Congress, *habeus corpus* and the freedom of the press. He arrested opposition leaders (including Senator Benigno Aquino), suspended all opposition newspapers and private broadcasting stations and, in a few days, had imposed a full-scale dictatorship, describing his new regime as 'constitutional authoritarianism'. He also suspended the constitution, one of whose provisions limited a president to two four-year terms.

Many Filipinos welcomed the coup. They were tired of political violence, and Marcos persuaded them that he could deliver prosperity and a quiet life. He deceived them. Marcos's 14-year dictatorship was a disaster for the Philippines. The democracy bequeathed by the United States had not proved strong enough to prevent the coup, and because the US supported Marcos, almost to the end, its own popularity in the Philippines was severely affected. In June 1981, Marcos staged an election and rigged the results to his advantage. The US vice president, George Bush, representing the United States at Marcos's inauguration, said: 'We love your adherence to democratic principle – and to the democratic processes.' It was an unfortunate remark.

Corruption reached astonishing levels. Following the example of Marcos and his profligate wife, Imelda, everyone stole. Imelda was governor of Greater Manila, and her signature was needed on all major government contracts; she took a regular percentage. Government corporations ran up vast debts with American banks so that their officers might award themselves lavish kickbacks. When Marcos finally escaped after the revolution, he left the country with an enormous burden of debt that it has little hope of repaying. The government also alleges he stole several billion dollars, and stashed them away in New York (where he owned a number of expensive buildings), and in banks in Switzerland and in the Caribbean.

The leading opponent to Marcos before the coup was Senator Benigno Aquino, who evidently intended to run for president when Marcos's term expired. He was arrested during the coup, tortured, put on trial and sentenced to death. The sentence was commuted, and in 1980, under pressure from the Carter administration, Marcos allowed him to go into exile. In the summer of 1983, he decided to return home and challenge Marcos directly. His family and friends tried to dissuade him, but he persisted. On 27 August, he flew into Manila airport, on a China Airlines flight from Tokyo. He was accompanied by several friends and reporters, one of whom filmed the events inside the aircraft and tantalizing glimpses through a window afterwards.

The moment the aircraft reached the terminal, security men entered it and arrested Aquino. He was hustled out of the door and down a flight of steps leading directly on to the tarmac. There were shots, and Aquino was killed. The police claimed that the assailant had been a Communist gunman, Rolando Galman, who was himself immediately shot by the police. Nobody believed this preposterous story, and in due course, witnesses, including some of the security guards, recounted that Aquino had been shot in the back of the head as he had gone down the stairs on to the tarmac. Galman had then been thrown out of a police van, whether dead or alive hardly matters: his body had been immediately shot up by the police, to provide the cover story. The murder had been ordered by General Fabian Ver, the chief of staff, Marcos's most loyal henchman. The only question worth asking was whether Marcos had ordered the murder or simply acquiesced.

The event galvanized the Filipinos. Hundreds of thousands of people, who had perhaps grumbled at the regime but had never moved into opposition, now took to the streets. Aquino's funeral was the occasion for the largest demonstrations in Philippine history: millions of people – from every level of Philippine society, bankers to peasants – marched in protest.

The American government was appalled and the Catholic Church, which had so far refrained from overt, institutionalized opposition, now demanded that Marcos must go. Jaime, Cardinal Sin, primate of the Church, gave the lead.

Marcos was sick, suffering a kidney disease, but despite this, he put up a prolonged rearguard action. The writer William Chapman thinks that he might have survived if he had not suddenly decided to call a presidential election for 7 February 1986 to reaffirm his position. It was a disastrous mistake. To general astonishment, the opposition formed a united front at the last moment, presenting Corazon Aquino as candidate for president and Salvador Laurel for vice president, a ticket that had been put together by Cardinal Sin. American Senator Richard Lugar, then chairman of the Senate Foreign Relations Committee, who led a team to act as observers during the election, commented, 'A very disturbing pattern of incidents is emerging. The vote count is being shaped to what President Marcos needs.' Marcos claimed to win the election, by 13 million to 11 million votes, but the fraud was blatant. In one province, an over-zealous supporter obtained a vote of 100 per cent for Marcos, nothing for Aquino.

After the election, Mrs Aquino announced that she had won, and had herself inaugurated. Seeing the way the wind was blowing (it was a gale by then), the defence secretary, Enrile, and the acting chief of staff, General Fidel Ramos, defected to Aquino, and their supporters seized control of military headquarters. When Marcos ordered the nearest military units to suppress the mutiny and armoured cars and tanks rolled into the city, hundreds of thousands of unarmed civilians blocked their route.

President Reagan sent a special emissary, Philip Habib, to persuade Marcos to leave. The desperate Filipino president called Senator Paul Laxalt, an old friend who was also close to President Reagan. However, Laxalt, who was at the White House when Marcos rang, told him – 'on a purely personal basis' – that he should leave. Clearly, the Americans had abandoned him.

The regime collapsed like a house of cards. Marcos tried broadcasting to the nation and had himself inaugurated inside his palace, but the army and the police deserted him. On 25 February, the US military command at Clark air base sent a small fleet of helicopters to take him, his wife Imelda, General Ver and their closest friends to safety. They spent the night at Clark, and were then flown to Hawaii, where US customs officials confiscated the several million dollars worth of gold, currency and jewellery that they had brought with them. Imelda had left her shoes behind, and the first thing she did on the military base where they were first lodged in Hawaii, was to go shopping.

The Marcoses were not left in peace. Federal and state prosecutors, not to mention the Philippine government and authorities in Switzerland and other   **219** countries where Marcos had hidden his fortune, all set to work investigating his crimes. The research was particularly active in New York, where he had bought a series of buildings, worth hundreds of millions of dollars, and allegedly concealed his continuing ownership by transferring them to the Saudi financier Adnan Kashoggi. Ferdinand and Imelda Marcos were both indicted in New York on these alleged offences, and in November 1988, Imelda Marcos went there to be formally charged (Marcos himself was judged too sick to travel). Mrs Marcos was released on bail.

THE MOROS

The Muslims in the Philippines were known to the Spanish as the Moros, a tribute to the centuries of battles between Spaniards and Moors. They are racially and linguistically indistinguishable from Filipino Christians, but their culture and history are different. The Moros are concentrated in the southern islands, Mindanao and the Sulu archipelago. They never accepted Spanish rule, and the Spaniards were never powerful enough to impose it. Indeed, until the British established protectorates in north Borneo in the mid-19th century (see Malaysia, pp. 204–6), there were no clear frontiers in the islands between the territories claimed by the Dutch, British and Spaniards. As late as the 1960s, the Philippines laid claim to British North Borneo, now Sabah, and joined Indonesia in opposing that territory's incorporation into Malaysia.

During the American period, Mindanao and Sulu were brought firmly under Manila's control. The Americans encouraged landless peasants from Luzon to settle in the sparsely populated southern islands, a policy that the independent Philippines has followed, and there are now more Christians than Muslims on Mindanao. This is the Moros' chief grievance: they fear being swamped in a Christian flood. In 1968, a group of Moros formed the Moro National Liberation Front (MNLF). They were inspired by Muslim nationalism in Indonesia and Malaysia and, starting in the 1970s, looked to Arab states from Libya to Saudi Arabia for moral and financial support.

After declaring martial law, Marcos tried to suppress Muslim agitation by disarming the Moros. The MNLF thereupon rose in revolt. By 1974, it had put between 50,000 and 60,000 guerrillas into the field (according to government estimates), and arms from Libya were pouring in to them through Malaysia. Furthermore, the Arabs constantly threatened the Philippines with an oil embargo.

At its height, in 1977, the guerrilla war in Mindanao occupied two-thirds of the army's combat units. Marcos was able to restore a semblance of central control to Moro areas, but was quite unable to suppress the rebellion. He granted a degree of autonomy to the Moros in 1977, after the 'Tripoli Agreement' was signed between MNLF and government representatives, and many of the original leaders of the MNLF emerged from the jungle and took up positions of authority. However, a hardline faction, led from exile by Nur Misauri, continued to demand full independence for Mindanao, Sulu, Basilan and Palawan, perhaps one-third of the national territory. Misuari claims that 100,000 Moros have been killed since 1972; other estimates put the number of deaths at 50,000–60,000.

After the 1986 revolution, President Aquino arranged a truce with the MNLF and persuaded Nur Misuari to return. The new constitution promulgated in 1987 provides an autonomous region for the Moro in Mindanao, but its details remain unsettled.

The Moro resistance has now split into three groups: the original MNLF, based in the Sulu islands, and the Moro Islamic Liberation Front (MILF) on Mindanao, each of which claim about 20,000 members; and the Moro National Liberation Front Reformed. The government has mounted a major economic development project in Mindanao and, by offering jobs and political power to MNLF leaders, has engineered or exacerbated the splits in the movement. In January 1988, a dispute between the MNLF and the MILF led to a shoot-out that left at least 20 people dead and drove 7000 civilians from their homes.

THE NEW PEOPLE'S ARMY (NPA)

The Communist Party of the Philippines Marxist–Leninist (Mao Tse-tung Thought) was founded on 26 December 1968, by a group of 11 student radicals who despaired of the official, pro-Soviet Communist party. They were inspired by radical student movements in Europe and the United States and by the Cultural Revolution in China, and intended to form a guerrilla army in the countryside which would eventually 'surround' the towns, following the Maoist guerrilla formula, and seize power. In March 1969, they formed the New People's Army, with an arsenal of 20 rifles and a few handguns.

This derisory group has since become a formidable military and political force. Its strength is based on an alliance of agrarian discontent and nationalism, defined and led by Marxist theory. It is now moving into the towns, and building a new base in the slums. This is the combination that produced the Chinese and Vietnamese revolutions.

The party is the guiding force behind the National Democratic Front, set up in 1973, which seeks to unite all leftist opponents of the regime. Its original leader and theoretician was José Ma Sison, who wrote under the *nom de plume* Amando Guerrero. He was arrested in 1977, but the revolution continued without him; President Aquino released him in 1986, in an attempt to persuade the NPA to lay down its arms and join the democratic process. Sison and his friends developed their political theories during the 1960s. The Marcos regime was becoming steadily more oppressive, and radical students were influenced by the Vietnam war and the overwhelming American presence in the Philippines. They began demonstrating against the American bases in 1965, and were sufficiently troublesome to serve as one of the pretexts for Marcos to proclaim martial law in 1972.

Sison and his comrades studied Mao's Little Red Book and sallied forth into the countryside to convert the peasantry. In the beginning, they had no success. Sison recruited a last survivor of the Huk revolt, Commander Dante, whom he made military commander of the NPA. Its first operations were a fiasco. Small NPA bands were harried constantly by the police and failed to establish bases as they had hoped; the police captured their entire archives, and published them. The NPA finally retreated into distant corners of Luzon, where they were left alone. Dante was captured at the same time as Sison, but by then, the NPA had produced its own leaders to carry on the fight.

One of the NPA's first successes was its protection of Kalinga tribesmen in the Cordillera mountains of northern Luzon. In 1974, the government proposed to build four dams and a huge hydroelectric plant on the Chico river, flooding a major valley and driving thousands of peasants from their homes. The NPA followed a

221

policy of selected assassination of officials and engineers, and the plan was soon abandoned.

Sison wrote a pamphlet analysing the mistakes of the Huks: *Rectify Errors and Rebuild the Party*. He contended that the first mistake of the guerrillas in the 1940s had been to follow a 'putschist' policy: they had tried to raise an army and march on Manila – and were defeated. The second mistake had been their failure to recognize the political nature of guerrilla warfare: the guerrillas had to win the support of the peasantry before any military action could begin. Third, Sison condemned the Huks for concentrating all their efforts on Luzon, instead of spreading them throughout the country.

This document provided a handbook for the NPA, and the guerrillas prepared for a long war. They devoted themselves to winning the confidence of workers on sugar plantations, landless peasants and small farmers, before attempting any military action. They sent cadres to every corner of the country, so that the Philippine army would have to be spread thinly, everywhere, to pursue them.

Throughout the 1970s, Marcos proclaimed frequent and dramatic victories against the NPA. Filipinos and Americans came to discount these claims, which were clearly completely imaginary, and to assume, therefore, that the NPA was no real threat. The NPA, meanwhile, followed Sison's instructions and steadily spread its influence: by the mid-1980s, it had 20,000 guerrillas, 12,000 modern weapons, the party had 30,000 members and a 'mass base' of 1 million people. This base was the 'water' in which the Communist 'fish' could 'swim' undetected. The NPA was operating in 60 of the Philippines' 73 provinces, and claimed some influence in 25 per cent of the 'barangays', the kinship groups of 100 or so families that make up the foundations of Philippine society. Furthermore, the NPA had established itself as a major force in the slums (barrios) of several cities, including Davao in southeast Mindanao and Bacolod on the island of Negros in the centre of the archipelago.

The NPA has developed rather like the Mafia in classical Sicily, as an alternative police force and government. The Philippine army and police are corrupt, inefficient, and oppressive. The police never patrol the barrios or the remote villages, and the NPA offers its services to discipline unjust landlords, petty crooks and unfaithful husbands. A policy of selective assassination has proved highly popular, and the party claims that peasants willingly pay a small levy – part political contribution, part protection money.

In fighting the NPA, the Marcos regime, according to a 1988 report by Amnesty International, resorted to 'widespread and systematic torture by the security forces'. It states: 'By the time he departed, a pattern of gross and systematic violations of human rights had been well established.' Under martial law (1972–81), the main violations were arbitrary arrest, illegal detention and torture, but after it was lifted by Marcos, the number of 'disappearances' – murders by security forces – increased dramatically. Amnesty reports: 'Victims included politicians, lawyers, priests, church workers, journalists and students, all suspected of engaging in or supporting subversive activities.

The killings were often carried out by vigilante groups operating with government approval. Many of them were set up by local landlords or religious cults, and had names such as 'Lord of the Sacred Heart', (known also as 'Chop-chop' from its practice of mutilating victims with machetes), 'Rock Christ', 'The Red Ones' and 'The Four Ks' (from the Pilipino words for 'Sin, Salvation, Life and Property').

The overthrow of the Marcos regime in 1986 was a mixed blessing for the NPA. It might have corresponded to the overthrow of the Nhu government in South Vietnam in 1963, which was followed by a protracted series of *coups d'état* and a great increase in Communist influence. However, the new president, Corazon Aquino, is hugely popular, and although many of her supporters have been disappointed at her performance and the fact that she has not succeeded in solving the country's problems, she remains a legitimate and popular leader, not at all like the ephemeral and corrupt generals who governed Vietnam after Nhu.

Furthermore, the Communists made a major tactical error during the revolution. They turned down pressing offers by moderates and leftists for a common front, and were left on the sidelines and therefore cannot claim any part of the glory of defeating Marcos. On the contrary, the Aquino government has been able to argue that it genuinely represents the people, unlike Marcos, and that the Communists are fighting against democracy.

On 27 February 1986, immediately after taking power, President Aquino ordered the release of all political prisoners, including Sison and other NPA leaders. The government ratified the UN convention against torture, repealed Marcos's decrees permitting the detention of political prisoners and restored *habeus corpus*. It then entered into negotiations with the NPA, and a 60-day ceasefire was declared on 10 December 1986.

The Communists revelled in their freedom to give interviews on television and invite journalists to their 'liberated areas'. However, after troops opened fire on a peasant demonstration in Manila on 22 January 1987, killing 12 people, the NPA broke off the talks. The ceasefire lapsed and heavy fighting resumed. In the next two months, over 400 people were killed.

The war has not been going so well for the NPA since then. There is now something of a public backlash against Communist terrorism. An attempt to start urban warfare in Manila was defeated: the NPA sent 1200 armed men into the city and over 100 police and officials were murdered. The public was outraged. The Manila NPA brigade announced in December 1987, that no more police would be killed and that targets would be chosen more 'selectively'.

Left-wing parties, notably the Partido ng Bayan founded by Sison, did badly in congressional elections in May 1987 and in local elections the following January. Over 100 people were killed in politically inspired violence during the latter elections. A further difficulty for the NPA was the discovery in Mindanao of mass graves containing hundreds of bodies – people executed by the NPA for suspected 'treason'.

A local militia – the Alsa Masa ('Masses Arise') – attacked NPA positions in their stronghold in Agdao, a slum district of Davao, and drove them out. The government now arms local vigilante groups to defend their villages against the NPA, and many of the crimes attributed to the Marcos vigilante groups are now being committed by the Aquino vigilantes.

Amnesty International found that human rights abuses had increased markedly in 1987 and 1988, and the Aquino government was beginning to resemble the Marcos regime in this respect. In 1986, Amnesty found:

223

strong evidence that the Aquino government's commitment to the protection of human rights and the establishment of legal safeguards had led to major improvements . . . But by the time of Amnesty International's third mission in July 1987, there had been a sharp escalation in political violence, and the government appeared increasingly unwilling or unable to persuade its security forces to respect the safeguards it had promoted so vigorously a year earlier, particularly when members of the military and police were targets of the NPA assassination squads.

The army is reverting to its Marcos-era custom of revenge killings. Amnesty reports a number of specific cases:

● In February 1987, 17 villagers, including six children, were massacred by troops after an NPA attack on a military patrol killed a lieutenant.
● In April, after an NPA attack on a military barracks in which 17 soldiers were killed, military patrols killed at least 13 villagers nearby.
● In the same month, a 25-year old farmer picked up by the army was found strangled with his own shirt: 'His hands were tied, an eye had been gouged out, his fingernails pulled out and there were stab wounds in his chest and one armpit.'

The army contends that the Aquino government is 'soft on Communism', and that its own hands are tied behind its back by the government's attempts to protect human rights. In fact, however, not a single military man has been convicted of a human rights abuse since Aquino took power. Rather, the number of 'disappearances' increased sharply in 1988 as military intelligence arrested suspects without warrants and without ever admitting what it was doing. A group called Find, set up under the Marcos dictatorship and devoted to attempting to trace missing people, remains busy. In the 21 months after Aquino became president, Find listed hundreds of 'disappearances', of which 212 remained unexplained at the end of the period. One leader commented: 'Many of them, we assume, they were "salvaged" already' – 'salvaged' being current Filipino euphemism for 'killed'.

In March 1988, police arrested five Communist leaders in Manila, including Romulo Kintanar, commander of the NPA, and Rafael Baylosis, the party's general secretary. A great many incriminating documents, including minutes of politburo meetings, were found – stored on computer disks, for this is a modern revolution. They showed that the party is seriously divided on which tactics to follow. The arrests were described by police as a body blow to the NPA: Kintanar was believed to be the organizer of the 'Sparrow squads', responsible for the wave of assassinations in Manila. However, on 12 November, Kintanar escaped. He and the other terrorist leaders had been held in a military camp – and had all been invited to a party. Kintanar and his wife were picked up by accomplices and simply driven out of the base to freedom.

The NPA is prepared for the long haul and will not be defeated by the loss of some of its leaders. A secret report of the Philippine military, prepared in May 1988 and subsequently leaked to Marcos's former secretary for national defence, the corrupt and vicious Juan Ponce Enrile (who published it), showed that the NPA had won 66 of 67 major battles with troops in the first three months of the year. If it is to be defeated, the Philippine army must be reformed and must improve its tactics – first of all, by remembering that its duty is to protect the Philippine people, not to terrorize them. A start was made with the dismissal, on 23 November

1986, of Enrile, who had deserted his master at the last moment and joined Aquino. However, General Fidel Ramos, who had been commander of the Philippines Constabulary before the revolution, when torture and the extralegal execution of suspects became routine, has now taken Enrile's place.

THE AQUINO GOVERNMENT

The government finally enacted its long-promised land reform in June 1988, but it was immediately criticized as insufficient by leftists and moderates. There are many loopholes in its proposals to break up the big estates, including a provision that the law need not apply to some corporations. This clause apparently would exclude President Aquino's own family sugar estate, the Hacienda Luisita. The fundamental problem, in the Philippines as in Central America, is that the growing population has long since outrun the land available. Even if all the land were redistributed, there would still be hundreds of thousands of landless families, and the distributed plots would be too small to support those who obtained them.

In the short term, the greatest danger to the Aquino government comes from the army. There have been many attempted coups, the most violent on 28 August 1987, in which more than 50 people were killed. Led by Colonel Gregorio 'Gringo' Honassan, the insurgents attacked the presidential palace and the government's Channel 4 television station, and were repulsed; they then seized several private television stations and Camp Aguinaldo. The police chief in Cebu City, the country's second largest city, joined the rebellion and arrested the local military leaders. General Ramos brought in loyal troops who attacked Camp Aguinaldo with tanks, artillery and World War II bombers. It was notable that there was more noise than real military action: neither side wanted to cause too many casualties. President Aquino's son was nearly killed: arriving at the palace, he was stopped by rebel troops who murdered his three bodyguards; the young Aquino managed to save himself by pleading for his life.

The coup collapsed. Honassan escaped, only to be arrested on 9 December. He was imprisoned on a naval gunboat in Manila harbour, awaiting trial, but on 2 April 1988, he bribed his guards and escaped with 14 of them in two rubber boats, and joined the opposition.

The most dangerous, however, was the series of sham coups threatened by Enrile's supporters, which were apparently designed to force Aquino to hand over real power to the secretary of defence. In the end, Aquino forced Enrile to resign. He is now a senator and leader of the opposition – in fact if not in name, the political heir to Marcos.

Aquino is now faced with the long and laborious business of persuading the peasantry to stop supporting the NPA. Before this can happen, a number of things need to be done: the military have to be prevented from committing excesses while patrolling the countryside; large sums need to be devoted to social and development projects; the endemic corruption in the administration has to be ended; the economy must be revived, to raise the deplorably low living standards of the urban poor; thorough-going civilian control has to be imposed on the armed forces; and the Philippines has to be restored to the orderly habits of settled democracies. It will take her and her successors decades, if the NPA does not get there first.

225

FURTHER READING

American University, *Area Handbook for the Philippines*, Washington, 1984.
Amnesty International. *Philippines: Unlawful Killings by Military and Paramilitary Forces*, London 1988.
Chapman, William, *Inside the Philippine Revolution*, New York, W. W. Norton, 1987.
Kouisar, Lucy, *Corazon Aquino: The Story of a Revolution*, New York, George Braziller, 1987.
Manchester, William, *American Caesar: Douglas MacArthur*.
Steinberg, David Joel, *The Philippines: A Singular and a Plural Place*, Boulder, Colo., Westview Press, 1982.

SRI LANKA

Geography	25,322 sq. miles (65,610 sq. km). The size of Ireland. In 1972, when the country became a republic, ending its connection with the British crown, its name was changed from Ceylon to Sri Lanka, a more precise transliteration of the Sinhalese.
Population	16 million, of whom 74% are Sinhalese (Buddhists), 18% are Tamils (Hindus), the rest Christians and Muslims. The latter are descendants of Arab traders and mostly speak Tamil.
GNP per capita	$400
Refugees	Internal: 100,000. External: 125,000 in India.
Casualties	According to human rights groups, 12,000 to 16,000 people have been killed since 1983. The official figure in early 1988 was 7000.

Sri Lanka was paradise. No country on Earth is more beautiful, and its citizens and all visitors alike agreed that nowhere was life more pleasant. Back in the misty Middle Ages, there had been invasions from India and wars between Sinhalese and Tamil principalities. But that had been long ago.

The Portuguese set up trading posts in the 16th century, and were replaced by the Dutch and then the British. It seemed a beneficent colonialism. The Pax Britannica ensured peace and prosperity throughout the 19th century and came peacefully to an end in 1948, shortly after the independence of India. The British established a modern system of government and the English language – but the governing classes were Sinhalese and the junior clerks and teachers were Tamil.

Nearly three-quarters of the population are Sinhalese (who are Buddhist), 18 per cent Tamil (who are Hindu). The rest are Muslims and Christians, and all lived peacefully together for 20 years after independence.

The country was resolutely democratic: governments frequently lost elections, and handed over to the parliamentary opposition. The economy was soundly based on the export of tea, timber and other tropical produce, and tourism. There seemed to be no reason why it should not develop modern industry.

It was not to be. Ceylon, which changed its name to Sri Lanka in 1972, instead became a case study in the dynamics of national dissolution. Sinhalese chauvinism and the demagoguery of Sinhalese politicians, the half-baked Marxism of successive 227 governments, and nationalist and racist fantasies among unemployed and highly educated Tamil youths, led to racial tensions, riots, killings and finally full-fledged terrorism and civil war.

Sri Lanka was typical of the Third World states that the European empires created: its population consisted of ethnic groups whose only loyalty was to the group, not to the nation. It did have two advantages over most other states: its frontiers were uncontested (it is an island), and one of those ethnic groups comprised the large majority of the population.

But 20 miles (32 km) from the northern tip of Sri Lanka is India, and the southernmost state of the Indian union is Tamil Nadu whose 56 million people are Tamils like their cousins in Sri Lanka. There is a similar situation in Cyprus, where the Turkish minority, like Sri Lanka's Tamils, comprise 18 per cent of the population. Tamils in Sri Lanka could always count on the support of the state government in Madras, as the Turks in Cyprus can count on Ankara; and the Sinhalese, like the Greeks in Cyprus or the Irish, although in a majority on their island, saw themselves as the victims of a neighbour much more powerful than themselves. They considered the Tamils not as a minority to be conciliated and protected but as a threat to national survival. It was a self-inflicted injury. Treated as a danger, Tamil nationalism burst into flames and now threatens the very existence of the state.

HISTORY

During the colonial period, the British administration discouraged missionary activity among the Sinhalese but permitted it among the Tamils, and mission schools were set up in what was then northern Ceylon where there is a Tamil majority. A century and a half of European education produced a well-educated class of Tamils who filled most of the junior places in the government and supplied most of the professional classes – lawyers, doctors and the like. The Sinhalese owners of the great tea plantations went to universities in Britain.

After independence, the Sinhalese came to resent this Tamil predominance in the professions (the same thing happened in many other former colonies), and as Sinhalese education improved and Tamils lost their positions, Tamils came to resent their lost opportunities.

In 1956, Solomon West Ridgeway Bandaranaike was elected prime minister. He was heir to one of the grandest Sinhalese families, English educated and an unscrupulous demagogue who built his power by whipping up his compatriots' hatred of the Tamils. He made Sinhalese the national language and, when Tamils demonstrated in protest, suppressed the demonstrations brutally. He imposed quotas for Tamils in the government, professions and universities, and nationalized much of the economy. In 1956, Tamils held roughly half of government jobs; by 1980, their share had dropped to 11 per cent. Bandaranaike offered a golden, Marxist future to the country, socialized the economy, and set it on the road to bankruptcy.

He was assassinated in September 1959, and was later succeeded by his widow Sirimavo Bandaranaike, the first woman to head a democratic government anywhere in the world. She pursued her husband's policies, driving the economy into chronic depression, and encouraged discrimination against the Tamils.

Unemployment became endemic among young Sinhalese and Tamils alike, and in each community, extremists began to preach violence, blaming their social and economic problems upon the other community. Episodic inter-communal riots became increasingly frequent during the 1960s and 1970s. In 1971, a Sinhalese revolutionary organization – the Janatha Vimukthi Peramuna (People's Liberation Front) – staged an uprising, which was then bloodily repressed. By the government's count, 2000 people died; others claim that 10,000 were killed by security forces suppressing the J V P.

The J V P had been founded in the late 1960s by Rohana Wijeweera (born in 1945), a medical student who had attended the Patrice Lumumba University in Moscow. The party remained underground after the 1971 coup attempt, but was legalized in 1977. Wijeweera ran for president in 1982, but after the 1983 riots in Colombo, the party was suppressed again, and Wijeweera went underground. He has seized the opportunity of the conflict with the Tamils to develop an ultra-Sinhalese programme, promising death and destruction to the Tamils and also to Sinhalese who oppose him – starting with President Jayewardene himself.

THE TIME OF TROUBLES

The government's incompetence finally provoked a crisis. Mrs Bandaranaike was defeated in an election in 1977, and replaced by another Sinhalese grandee, Junius Richard Jayewardene, then aged 70. He changed the constitution to make himself president (there is an executive prime minister, on the French model), and when he was re-elected in 1982, postponed legislative elections indefinitely. He tried to reverse his predecessor's economic policies and reduce tensions between Sinhalese and Tamils. He failed. Perhaps it was too late. Mary Anne Weaver (*see* p.234) thinks that the essential problem was that he considered the crisis a matter of terrorism, to be dealt with by the police, not a matter of communal relations, to be settled by political means.

By then, the Tamils had called in help from Tamil Nadu. The complexities of Indian national politics led Prime Minister Indira Gandhi to permit the Madras government to help the Tamils in Sri Lanka. Tamil terrorists were trained in Tamil Nadu, arms and munitions of all sorts were smuggled across the narrow strait, and the Sri Lankan navy was quite unable to stop it.

Extremist Tamils, brought up on tales of Sinhalese oppression, began to talk of Tamil Eelam, an independent Tamil state in northern and eastern Sri Lanka. The principal town of the north is Jaffna, on a peninsula running towards India, the largest of a string of fishing villages and small towns that are the heart of the Tamil insurgency. Velupillai Prabakaran, son of a fisherman, was born in one of those villages in 1954. When he was four, he saw an uncle burned alive during the riots that followed the imposition of Sinhalese as sole national language. He is now the supreme commander of the most violent of the terrorist organizations, the Liberation Tigers of Tamil Eelam, commonly known as the Tamil Tigers.

Prabakaran sees himself as the perfect terrorist: he prides himself as a marksman and carries out many killings himself. Although his role model is clearly Fidel Castro, he is not an educated man nor is he a Marxist. His favourite recreation is said to be watching Clint Eastwood movies.

The Tigers began with robberies and murders. In 1975, Prabakaran and two comrades shot the mayor of Jaffna, a Tamil they considered a quisling. The Tigers then began a campaign of assassination of Tamils employed by the central government.

In July 1983, Prabakaran led a commando attack on an army post in Jaffna, killing 13 Sinhalese soldiers. Sinhalese rioted in Colombo and other cities, and according to the government, 140 people, most of them Tamils, were killed. Mary Anne Weaver thinks the total was 1000, and that $300 million worth of property damage was done in Colombo alone, and 100,000 Tamils were driven from their homes. The riots were largely inspired and led by the JVP, which now re-emerged from obscurity to become almost as serious a threat to the government as the Tigers. It probably has at least 2000 full-time fighters.

The 1983 riots gave an immense boost to the Tigers: thousands of young Tamils fled to the jungles and started guerrilla training. In addition, Tamil members of parliament were expelled.

Violent incidents multiplied. On 14 May 1985, the Tigers attacked a sacred Buddhist shrine at Anuradhapura. More than 150 Sinhalese were killed, and a great deal of damage done to the temple and to the sacred Bo tree, grown from a cutting taken from the tree under which the Lord Buddha found enlightenment. The Tigers then took control of Jaffna and most of the northern province, driving the Sinhalese out and isolating army and police in their barracks.

The security situation in the rest of the country deteriorated rapidly. The Sri Lankan army, which had served only ceremonial functions for nearly 40 years, was quite unable to contain the Tigers, who had been well trained by Indian officers in Tamil Nadu. The soldiers were undisciplined and incompetent, and slaughtered hundreds of Tamil civilians. Instances of torture, massacre and extralegal executions multiplied: Amnesty International has compiled a long list of Tamils who have been arrested by the security forces and have never been heard of again.

It was not until a veteran of World War II, General Cyril Ranatunge, was brought out of retirement and set to work training new recruits, that effective discipline was introduced and the army began to do its job, and there were no more reports of army massacres. The army more than doubled in size, to 25,000, as did the other security forces, to 50,000. Defence spending increased by 1700 per cent, to $500 million a year.

The crisis was reached in 1987. On 17 April, Good Friday, the Tigers ambushed a convoy of buses in the centre of the country. The 128 Sinhalese passengers, all unarmed, and including many women and children, were separated from the Tamils and Muslims and then murdered. On 21 April, a bomb at the central bus terminal in Colombo killed 113. The central government resolved to recapture control of the Jaffna peninsula.

The army mounted a general offensive – Operation Liberation – on 26 May. In two weeks, the army had occupied the outlying districts in the northern province, doing immense damage and killing 132 guerrillas and 300 civilians, at a cost of 62 military deaths. Before attacking, the air force bombed the province, destroying scores of villages.

Then India intervened. On 3 June 1987, Prime Minister Rajiv Gandhi authorized a fleet of fishing boats to deliver 'humanitarian' supplies to the besieged Tamils in Jaffna. The boats were turned back by the Sri Lankan navy, and the next day Gandhi ordered the Indian air force to drop the supplies by parachute. The drops amounted, officially, to only 25 tons of 'humanitarian' supplies, but their symbolic importance was enormous. If India was going to intervene, the Colombo government had no chance of victory.

Gandhi had several objects in mind. They did not include encouraging Tamil separatism: that would set the worst possible precedent for restive parts of the Indian union, such as Punjab or the north-east. He did, however, want to retain the political support of the Tamil Nadu government. (He failed: after a general mêlée in the state legislature in January 1988, Gandhi suspended the government, and in elections in January 1989, his Congress party was soundly defeated.) Gandhi also wanted to enforce Indian hegemony over its neighbour: he objected to Sri Lanka's pro-Western policies, and still more to the fact that Jayewardene had sought help from China, Pakistan, South Africa and Israel and from British mercenaries to train the armed forces. Lastly, he coveted Trincomalee harbour on Sri Lanka's east coast, one of the finest natural harbours in the world, comparable to New York, San Francisco or Sydney.

The Sri Lankan army suspended its offensive. Negotiations began between the government and the Indians, who consulted the Tamil parties, including the Tigers and their terrorist rivals (there are, in all, five terrorist groups). Jayewardene, who had offered autonomy to the Tamil northern province the previous December, now extended the offer to include the eastern province, which is disputed between Sinhalese and Tamils; Trincomalee is its principal city and prize. The two provinces would be merged and run by a Tamil-led government which would have wide powers. A referendum would be held in the eastern province by the end of 1988 to ratify this arrangement. Tamil and English would be made co-equal national languages with Sinhalese. In exchange, the Tamil terrorists would surrender their arms. India would police the ceasefire.

All the Tamils accepted the proposal except Prabakaran, who was put under house arrest in New Delhi. However, militant Sinhalese, incited by the JVP, demonstrated against the agreement in Colombo on 28 July, and started a riot in which 70 people were killed. The next day, Gandhi flew to Colombo to sign the agreement. One of the Sinhalese soldiers in the guard of honour tried to attack him.

For a tense week, the Tigers refused to surrender their arms. Finally, on 4 August, Prabakaran returned from New Delhi and ordered his troops to turn in their arms. At a mass meeting in Jaffna, he announced: 'We have no choice but to toe the line of the Indian government. If we don't, there will be an armed confrontation with the Indian army. We don't want that. India is a powerful country and we are unable to do anything to stop it.' Tons of arms were then surrendered, perhaps one-fifth of the Tigers' arsenal. (Eight months later, it emerged that the Indian government had paid the Tigers a large sum of money for their cooperation.)

There was a brief moment of hope. Despite all the killings and 'disappearances', despite the hatred between Tamils and Sinhalese and the bitterness of Tamils whose villages have been destroyed, the agreement clearly provided the basis for a permanent settlement.

Gandhi sent the first units of what became a 60,000-man army of occupation to police the northern province. But there was barely a pause in terrorism. The Tigers set about assassinating members of rival terrorist groups: within six weeks, they had killed at least 150. The Indians did nothing to intervene. Prabakaran took control of the interim council, for the north and east provinces.

The JVP remained bitterly opposed to the settlement. On 18 August, two grenades were thrown into a meeting room in Parliament House and the room was sprayed with machine-gun bullets. The attack almost killed President Jayewardene; two other politicians were killed. In April 1988, police claimed that they had arrested the culprit, a cleaner who was a member of the JVP.

The ceasefire lasted less than two months. On 3 October 1987, the Sri Lankan navy intercepted a trawler off Jaffna carrying 17 Tigers, including three of Prabakaran's closest aides, one of whom was suspected of planting the bomb in the Colombo bus depot. They were smuggling a large consignment of arms from India. The authorities insisted on bringing them to Colombo. At the airbase, as they were about to enter the plane to fly south, they all simultaneously swallowed cyanide. (The Tigers carry cyanide capsules at all times, and are sworn to kill themselves rather than be captured.) Thirteen of the 17 died.

The Tigers at once repudiated the peace settlement. There was an immediate series of terrorist attacks in eastern Sri Lanka, including the murder of eight Sinhalese soldiers held by the Tigers. At least 188 people were killed, and Jaffna was once again under the control of the Tigers.

The event was a serious blow to Gandhi, who was committed to keeping the peace. He ordered his army to occupy Jaffna; they laid siege to the town and eventually took it. It was not a glorious episode. The Tigers in Jaffna held out for 17 days against the full might of the Indian army, which used its arsenal of Soviet-made rockets, helicopter gunships and artillery against them. The Indians lost at least 460 men (the official figure), but failed either to defeat or capture the Tigers – most of whom escaped with their weapons. Between 300 and 400 Tigers and as many as 1000 civilians were killed.

There were various estimates of the number of Indians killed by Tamil terrorists, and of Tamils killed by Indian soldiers. A year after their arrival, the Indian army said that they had lost 530 men, and had themselves killed about 2000. Sri Lankan officials (not necessarily any more reliable) claimed that, by the end of the year, up to 1000 Indian soldiers had been killed by Tamil fighters, and over 1000 wounded. There were 50,000–65,000 Indian troops policing the Tamil territories, but terrorism continued unabated: 25 people were killed in one incident on 27 December 1987; another ten on New Year's Eve (the Tigers entered a Sinhalese village 26 miles (42 km) south of Trincomalee, lined up the villagers against a wall, and shot them). The previous May, the Tigers had killed 23 people in the same village.

This had become part of the Tigers' strategy. They intended to clear Sinhalese villagers out of the eastern province which they claimed for their own, along with the north, and they did it by murdering the villagers. By the spring of 1988, the entire Sinhalese population of Trincomalee had fled.

The new year proved just as bloody as 1987. On 23 February, after Tigers shot four Indian soldiers in an ambush, Indian troops killed 20 Tamils. The next day, in a speech to Parliament, President Jayewardene offered a new amnesty to the Tigers and to the JVP, who had by then murdered over 200 government officials, police and supporters of the 1987 agreements. On 2 March, Tigers disguised in army uniforms shot six adults and nine children in Colombo. Three days later, a mine exploded under a truck near Trincomalee, killing 19 people, including six women and two children, most of them Sinhalese. There were further bomb attacks on buses throughout northern and eastern Sri Lanka in March and April: in April, a bus filled with shoppers south of Trincomalee was bombed, killing 26; another bus was attacked killing six. Forty Muslims were killed in raids on their villages in the eastern province.

While the Indians fight the Tigers in the north, the Sri Lankan army fights the JVP in the south. There are more than 10,000 Sri Lankan troops pursuing the 2000 JVP terrorists.

In the previous five years, between 7000 and 16,000 people had been killed and over half a million driven from their homes – and the rate of killings was increasing rapidly. The cost to the economy was catastrophic. The tourist industry was dead. The northern and eastern provinces were battlefields, and many tea plantations in the north-central highlands had been abandoned for fear of terrorists.

On 10 May 1988, the government and the JVP signed a ceasefire. The JVP agreed to abandon terrorism and the government agreed to legalize the organization and release imprisoned members, except those accused of murder. However, the agreement collapsed immediately, and the JVP pursued a violent campaign to disrupt provincial elections on 2 June, bombing government buildings and attacking polling stations.

India has been sucked into the fight, and the Indian army, which came to keep the peace, is now under fire from both sides, like the British in Northern Ireland. By the summer of 1988, the Indians had imposed a semblance of order in northern and eastern Sri Lanka, by means of heavy patrols in the towns and on the main roads, but the Tigers remained active in the countryside and were evidently entirely capable of mounting further attacks whenever they wished.

In June 1988, India announced that it would withdraw between 3000 and 5000 of its troops from Sri Lanka. It was a symbolic gesture. Gandhi said that the bulk of the army would remain until after provincial elections in the north and east, and until an effective ceasefire had come into effect. There was no sign whatever that any such peace was likely.

Jayewardene offered the Tamils all the concessions that might have averted the troubles 20 years before, but the Tigers were not pacified. They had tasted blood, and there was little hope that they would abandon the fight. The 60,000 Indian troops in Sri Lanka trying to control the Tamils were faced with a hopeless task and no obvious means of escaping.

As for the JVP, its campaign continued to increase in violence throughout 1988. On 10 September, the Indian High Command announced, in Jayewardene's name, the formal decision to merge the northern and eastern provinces. It was a further demonstration of Sri Lanka's subordination to India, and provoked a further excess of JVP terrorism. Colombo was closed down for a day when the JVP put up posters denouncing the proposed merger and demanding a general strike.

On 15 September, Jayewardene decreed that there would be a presidential election in December, and that he would not be a candidate. He was by then 82 years old, and it was time to retire. There were also to be provincial elections in the   233 new northeastern province in November, and in preparation for the event, the Tigers and the JVP stepped up their terrorist campaigns (it seemed entirely likely that they were now cooperating). For example, the Tigers massacred 47 people in a Sinhalese village on 10 October.

Jayewardene tried once again to persuade the JVP to suspend terrorism and participate in the presidential election. He was unsuccessful, and the JVP exerted itself, by the usual methods of murder and and intimidation, to disrupt the voting. In mass JVP demonstrations in Colombo and other southern towns on 10 November, at least ten people were killed by troops. There was a series of strikes in Sinhalese districts, including hotels and other service industries, and the government ordered all remaining tourists to leave the country. By then, JVP terrorists were killing people at the rate of 25 to 50 a day. Sinhalese areas were administered by the army; schools and universities were closed; and public services such as rubbish collection and public utilities such as electricity were failing.

The provincial elections took place in November, despite the Tigers' efforts. As a sideline, some of the Tigers offered their services to an exiled politician from the Maldive islands, west of Sri Lanka, and attempted a coup there. They were frustrated by the Indians (*see* India, p. 188).

The presidential election took place on 19 December. The turn-out was about 55 per cent, far lower than was usual in Sri Lankan elections, but a creditable total considering the extreme level of violence and intimidation from both Tamil and Sinhalese terrorists. Jayewardene's United National Party candidate, the prime minister Ranasinghe Premadasa, won a narrow victory over Sirimavo Bandaranaike, trying to make a comeback. She promptly charged fraud. In his last act as president, Jayewardene dissolved parliament and set new elections for February. Premadasa was sworn in on 2 January 1989.

The new President was no more successful in resolving the country's conflicts than the old one. He lifted the state of emergency, but it was an empty gesture. The JVP terror campaign continued, mixing xenophobia and Marxism in a deadly combination. The Tigers continued to fight the Indians, the government and other Tamil parties and there was increasing tension between the Sri Lanka government and the Indians. President Premadasa demanded that all Indian troops be withdrawn by 29 July 1989, the second anniversary of their arrival. They refused to leave. The Indian army was accused of massacring Tamil villagers: Sri Lanka was looking more and more like Lebanon.

FURTHER READING

De Silva, K. M., *A History of Sri Lanka*, London, C. Hurst, 1981.
Manor, James (ed.), *Sri Lanka in Change and Crisis,* London, Croom Helm, 1984.
Shwartz, Walter, *The Tamils of Sri Lanka*, London, Minority Rights Group, 1986.
—— *Sri Lanka: Disappearances*, Amnesty International, London, September 1986.
Weaver, Mary Anne, 'The Gods and the Stars', *New Yorker*, 21 March 1988.

VIETNAM

Geography 129,086 sq. miles (334,331 sq. km). The size of Norway.
Population 63 million.
Refugees External: about 1 million since 1975; 46,000 still classified
as refugees in various countries. Internal: 21,000 from
Cambodia.

On 30 April 1975, Communist Vietnam won the greatest of all wars of national liberation, and the most difficult of all Communist revolutions. Late on the evening of the 29th, the American ambassador and his staff were rescued from their embassy by helicopter. The last Marines left early in the morning, a few hours before North Vietnamese tanks rolled into Saigon.

At a cost of 2.5 million lives, Ho Chi Minh and his successors won independence and national unity. They could have obtained it all freely from the French 25 years earlier if they had renounced their revolution. Fourteen years since that day in 1975, triumph has turned to dust and the revolution is on the point of collapse. Vietnam is in perpetual conflict with China and in hopeless occupation of Cambodia, and the economy is in ruins. Vietnam's only ally, the Soviet Union, is showing clear signs of fatigue and Vietnam's only hope of survival is to evacuate Cambodia, and come to terms with the West. In the spring of 1988, it announced sweeping economic reforms, which amounted to abandoning the policies it had followed since 1954, and at the end of the year, it said that all Vietnamese troops could be out of Cambodia by September 1989.

Vietnam can barely feed its population and, in 1988, made several direct appeals to the United States for food aid. Annual inflation is running at 1000 per cent, and the standard of living is dropping steadily. Average income is now estimated to be about $100 a year. By comparison, Haiti, the poorest country in the Western Hemisphere, has a *per capita* income of $330 p.a.

Thousands of Vietnamese are fleeing by boat and overland – to Hong Kong, Malaysia and Thailand. They are frequently attacked by Thai pirates, who murder the men and rape the women. Since the glorious revolution in 1975, over 1 million refugees have fled the country.

HISTORY

For nearly 30 years, American policy in East and South-east Asia was based upon the 'domino theory'. Washington assumed that there was a worldwide Communist conspiracy, directed from Moscow, which would attack one country after another: if China went, Vietnam would go; if Vietnam went, Cambodia would go; and then Thailand, Malaysia and so on. Each country 'lost' to the West would be added to a united Communist world empire ruled from the Kremlin, what Ronald Reagan described as the 'evil empire'.

However, the events of the 1970s showed that nationalism and ethnic hostility were far more potent forces than ideology. Once American pressure was withdrawn, the dominoes immediately started fighting among themselves. Soviets and Chinese went to war, as did the Chinese and Vietnamese, and the Vietnamese and the Cambodians. Cambodia looked to China as an ally against Vietnam, just as Vietnam looked to the Soviet Union as an ally against China. China allied itself with the United States against the USSR, and the US found itself a silent partner in an anti-Vietnamese, and therefore anti-Soviet, alliance that included the Khmers Rouges. It is one of the most elegant examples of power politics in modern times.

It is easy to be wise after the event. The domino theory looked perfectly plausible at the time, and there is plenty of evidence that the Chinese and Vietnamese believed in it, too. China steadfastly supported the Vietnamese Communists through all their wars, starting when Mao's armies occupied South China in 1949 and provided Ho Chi Minh with secure bases from which to overrun Tonkin. The Sino–Soviet dispute in the 1960s and 1970s, however, caused the North Vietnamese serious and increasing problems. China simultaneously demanded that Vietnam take its side against the USSR, and itself set about establishing a *de facto* alliance with the United States, Hanoi's greatest enemy. In February 1972, Mao received President Nixon in Peking at the height of the US bombing offensive against North Vietnam. North Vietnam needed both China and the USSR. The Chinese claim that they spent $20 billion in aid to Vietnam over the years, an enormous sum for a poor country, and the Vietnamese Communists were always armed by the Soviet Union.

From the start, the Vietnamese resented Chinese bullying. There was 1000 years of animosity between the Celestial Empire and its sometime vassal, the Empire of Annam, and all the years of French colonialism, revolution and the wars of Indochina could not change that basic antipathy.

Relations between the two countries began to deteriorate seriously immediately after the Communist victory in 1975. China continued obsessively to fear the Soviet Union, which it accused of attempting to encircle it by extending its hegemony to Vietnam. It was a self-fulfilling prophecy: the Vietnamese did not allow the Soviets to establish a permanent base in Cam Ranh Bay until China attacked Vietnam in 1979; after that episode, Soviet military aid to Vietnam escalated dramatically.

China's hostility to the Soviet Union was not entirely paranoid – and even paranoiacs can have enemies. There had been serious border clashes between the two countries in 1969 (*see* China, pp. 170–72), and much more serious threats from Moscow. But fearing encirclement was pure foolishness. China is too big for any alliance to encircle or dominate or conquer it – but, foolish or not, that was what the Chinese feared.

The Communist victory in Vietnam permitted a revival of the millennial hostility between it and Cambodia (*see* pp. 145–59). Pol Pot was the most extreme ideological fanatic in the world, but he was also a Cambodian nationalist who detested the Vietnamese who had devoured one-third of the national territory over the centuries: Saigon had originally been a Cambodian village, and all of the Mekong delta had once been part of Cambodia.

The Khmers Rouges provoked their first conflict with Vietnam on 4 May 1975, barely two weeks after they took Phnom Penh. They seized two islands in the Gulf of Siam that the French had allocated to Vietnam, and massacred the several hundred Vietnamese inhabitants. A survivor who returned to one of the islands three months later found it littered with skulls.

An American cargo ship, the *Mayaguez*, blundered into this confrontation on 12 May, and was captured by the Cambodians. President Ford ordered a massive air strike against Cambodian coastal bases in retaliation. It was the last American raid of the Vietnam war, killed thousands of Cambodians, caused great damage, cost the lives of 41 US Marines and other military personnel and did nothing to save the 40-man crew of the *Mayaguez*. They had already been released.

The Vietnamese reoccupied the islands, evicting the Cambodian garrisons. Pol Pot, who had no choice, apologized, claiming that the Cambodian incursion had been due to an excess of zeal by the local commander. In fact, it had been a quite deliberate attempt to seize territory before the new Vietnamese government could assert its claim. It was a failure, but an omen of things to come.

The Khmers Rouges were naturally the ideological pupils of Mao Tse-tung, and constantly praised the extravagances of the Cultural Revolution. But when the Gang of Four were arrested in October 1976 and a new pragmatic regime took power in Peking, the Khmers Rouges instantly applauded. Although Deng Xiaoping had staked his life and career on fighting extremism in China, he continued to defend Pol Pot and the Khmers Rouges, despite his profound detestation for their principles, because of his even more profound detestation for Vietnam and the Soviet Union.

THE WAR OVER CAMBODIA

The Khmers Rouges were constantly the aggressors in the troubles with Vietnam, first massacring Vietnamese living in Cambodia, then attacking across the border and slaughtering Vietnamese villagers. In December 1978, the Vietnamese invaded Cambodia and soon occupied the whole country (*see* Cambodia).

As relations between Vietnam and Cambodia deteriorated, the Chinese responded by suspending all technical and economic aid to Vietnam in the summer of 1978. In retaliation, Vietnam persecuted and expelled the large numbers of Chinese living in Vietnam; as a result, in that year, about 150,000 of them fled overland to China, and 250,000 more fled by boat (of these, 30,000–40,000 perished at sea). The unhappy saga of the 'boat people' was one of the many horrors of the decade.

The Vietnamese occupation of Cambodia was a severe diplomatic setback to China, the worst since General MacArthur invaded North Korea in 1950. This time, however, China's own territory was not endangered, and Peking informed Pol Pot that he would have to win his own salvation, by resuming guerrilla warfare.

THE CHINA–VIETNAM WAR

The blow to Chinese pride could not be endured, and the Chinese decided to teach Vietnam a lesson. On 17 February 1979, Deng Xiaoping launched a full-scale invasion, sending 75,000 troops across the border at 20 different points. The whole operation soon involved a quarter of a million men. Deng presumably thought he could repeat the achievements of the 1962 war against India, when China had indeed delivered a sharp lesson in military reality. This time, things happened differently.

The People's Liberation Army of China was the largest in the world, but it had not fought seriously since Korea and had been debilitated by the political battles of the intervening years. In addition, its armament was woefully inadequate and antiquated. The Vietnamese, by contrast, had fought continuously since 1946, and were well equipped with modern Soviet weapons, not to mention the billions of dollars' worth of American equipment captured in 1975.

The war lasted 16 days. By sheer weight of numbers, the Chinese cleared the border posts and captured five provincial capitals. By an historical irony, the chief of them was Lang Son, the site of the first major defeat that the Viet Minh had inflicted on the French, in October 1950, after the Chinese Communist victory had given them a secure base beyond the border.

This time, it was the Chinese who captured Lang Son, and they razed it to the ground, together with the four other provincial capitals. Those five towns were the last in North Vietnam that had survived intact since French colonial days, because the Americans had not bombed so near the frontier for fear of provoking Chinese intervention.

The Chinese failed to defeat the Vietnamese, and after suffering heavy casualties, Deng proclaimed victory and withdrew his troops. About 20,000 people had been killed, by Chinese count, an equal number on each side. For once, the large majority were soldiers.

The episode was a serious defeat for China, and it failed totally to achieve its main objective: to induce the Vietnamese to leave Cambodia. The Vietnamese found it unnecessary to move a single division out of Cambodia to send north. However, in the long term, the war was to prove exceedingly costly to Vietnam: not only were several provinces devastated (ten years later, they have still not recovered), but it became necessary to build fortifications and to maintain large forces on permanent alert along the northern border.

For the next ten years, there were repeated skirmishes between Vietnamese and Chinese troops, sometimes involving thousands of men. The two sides shelled each other's positions constantly: for months on end, China would fire 10,000 shells a day at Vietnamese positions. It was considered a sign of improved relations when the daily total dropped to 700 in 1988.

The war graphically illustrated the disastrous consequences of Mao Tse-tung's and Lin Biao's belief in the invincibility of guerrilla armies. Deng was able to blame Mao and the Gang of Four for the defeat and set about purging the army of Maoists. Foreign defeat thus strengthened Deng's domestic position.

THE SPRATLYS DISPUTE

The first conflict between modern Vietnam and China occurred even before the
238 Communist victory in Saigon. It concerned two chains of islands in the South

China Sea, claimed by both Vietnam and China. These are the Paracels, off the coast of Vietnam, and the Spratlys, far to the south. The Chinese claim is exiguous (the Spratlys are closer to Borneo than to China), and the islands, tiny coral atolls, are of no strategic or economic value unless oil is found in the ocean surrounding them. Taiwan, the Philippines and Malaysia also claim the Spratlys, but have never seriously asserted their claims.

In 1972, the Thieu regime of South Vietnam started hawking oil concessions in the islands. China promptly occupied the Amphitrite chain in the Paracels. South Vietnam thereupon sent a small naval contingent to another part, the Crescent Islands, and to the Spratlys. In 1974, the North Vietnamese, in turn, announced that they would sell oil leases in the South China Sea, and the Chinese reacted by occupying the Crescent Islands, evicting the South Vietnamese.

North Vietnam did not contest China's claims as long as the war continued, but on 11 April 1975, as its armies were closing in on Saigon, it sent a small naval force to occupy the Spratlys. China instantly protested. The dispute has simmered ever since, with occasional naval demonstrations. In January 1988, the Chinese sent a military force ashore in the Spratlys, and on 14 March, Chinese naval vessels sank a Vietnamese gunboat there, Vietnam reporting three men killed and 74 missing. Vietnam then sent naval reinforcements to the islands, and issued dire warnings against a proposed Chinese oceanographic expedition. China, in turn, denounced Vietnamese naval preparations. In the event, Vietnam withdrew, and left China master of the field.

No one knows if there is oil under the South China Sea, or if it could be exploited. No oil company is going to take the risk of exploring in a zone disputed between such belligerent neighbours.

Their dispute, of course, is not really about oil, or remote coral islands. There is a deep-seated national rivalry, exacerbated by the Chinese fear of the Soviet Union, and the immediate cause for their hostility is Cambodia. That Vietnam, in effect, allowed China to annex the Spratlys in 1988 was one of the first signs of its fundamental change of policy towards its neighbours.

MODERN VIETNAM

Vietnam, in 1988, was facing famine. There had been a series of poor harvests in previous years, a problem compounded by the relentless increase in the population and the catastrophic effects of Communism on agricultural productivity. In 1981, the government abandoned strict Communist principles and allowed farmers to sell whatever they produced beyond a quota that they were obliged to sell to the government. Production increased in five years from 13 million to 18 million tons, but it is not enough to match an annual population growth of 2.6 per cent.

In April 1988, for the first time, the Vietnamese government appealed to the United States. The State Department replied that the US 'had no interest' in helping Vietnam as long as it continued to occupy Cambodia. The US sanctions imposed in 1979, after the Vietnamese invasion of Cambodia, remain in force. In May, admitting that 3 million people were already on the brink of starvation, Vietnamese officials appealed to the world community: the Europeans sent 10,000 tons of rice; the USSR sent 60,000 tons. The 1987 shortfall had been 1.5 million tons, and the 1988 harvest was no better. The National Assembly was told in June

239

1988 that rice production *per capita* had dropped from 581 lb in 1982 to 506 lb in 1987. Vietnam was facing disaster.

Finance, too, was a grave problem. In the first few months of 1988, inflation reached 60 per cent a month. In March, the central bank introduced new banknotes, denominated in 1000, 2000 and 3000 dong (the national currency), and the rate of inflation rose still further. In 1987, the government, abandoning its principles, enacted a law on foreign investment which it claims is the most liberal in the Communist world, but so far there has been no foreign investment. Indochina is too unsettled to tempt prudent capitalists.

Ho Chi Minh City (formerly Saigon) suffers from inadequate water and electricity supplies. A major hydroelectric project built with Soviet aid north-west of the city was opened in March 1988, and immediately had to close: it was so badly constructed that the turbines broke when they were started up, and the dam itself was unsafe. In May, the local press reported unconvincingly that repairs had been completed.

Vietnam had no friends other than the Soviet Union and its own puppet states, Laos and Cambodia. When Rajiv Gandhi visited Hanoi in April 1988, he refused to offer Vietnam any support in its dispute with China over the Spratlys, even though India is usually resolutely hostile to China and supports the USSR's allies.

In May 1988, Vietnam announced that it would withdraw half its troops in Cambodia – 50,000 men – by the end of the year, and complete the withdrawal by 1990. It later specified that all its troops would be withdrawn by September 1989, if a political settlement could be reached by then, or March 1990 at the latest. At the same time, it announced that it had already cut its military presence in Laos from 45,000 to 20,000. It seemed that Vietnam was at last bowing to necessity and, probably, to Soviet pressure. It has discovered the limits of independence.

Vietnam then tried to improve its relations with China and the United States, but discovered that both countries preferred to wait until the withdrawal from Cambodia was complete. Vietnam eased its persecution of its Chinese minority, and admitted that it has much to learn from Deng's economic reforms. It also tried to satisfy American demands for the return of the remains of US servicemen killed during the Vietnam war.

Vietnam remains a paradox: it is one of the poorest nations in the world, with one of the world's largest and most powerful armies which, in 1975, was surpassed only by those of the United States, the Soviet Union and China. It had the power to over-run Cambodia in a month and to hold it indefinitely – but not to defeat the Khmers Rouges, because they were supported by China. Cambodia has been described as 'Vietnam's Vietnam', and the comparison is exact – with one difference. The US, in economic terms, could afford the Vietnam war; Vietnam could not afford its war in Cambodia, even though the Soviet Union footed the bill.

Vietnam and Cambodia are the extreme modern examples of the price of revolution. It may be debated whether Ho Chi Minh and his comrades would have launched the struggle in 1946 if they had known in advance that the cost would be 5 million dead. What cannot be doubted is that they, and their successors, failed in their ultimate purpose. They have communized Indochina, but they have also ruined it. It was never part of their dream that, 40 years after they began, and decades after their victory, they would have to go begging to the United States and China for food to save their people from starvation.

FURTHER READING

Chanda, Nayan, *Brother Enemy, the War after the War*, New York, Harcourt, Brace, Jovanovitch, 1986.

MIDDLE EAST

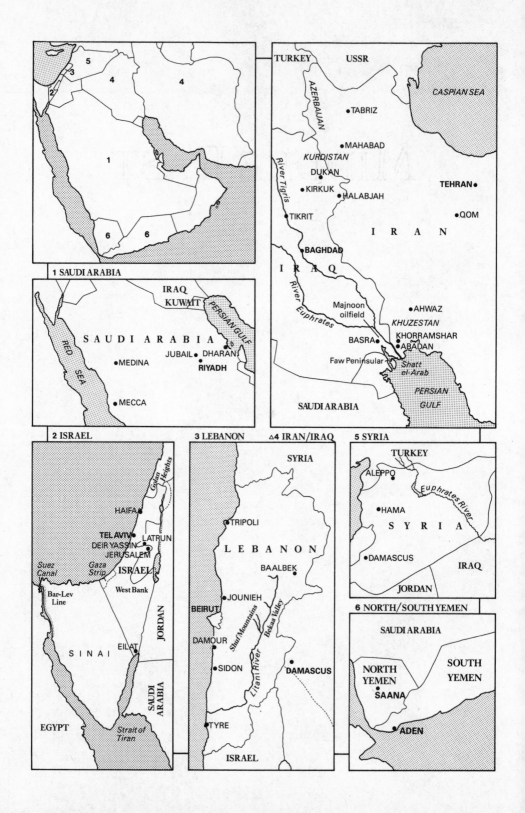

1 SAUDI ARABIA

5
3
2
4
4
1
6
6

2 ISRAEL

IRAQ
KUWAIT
PERSIAN GULF
S A U D I   A R A B I A
RED SEA
•MEDINA
JUBAIL• •DHARAN
RIYADH
•MECCA

△4 IRAN/IRAQ

TURKEY   USSR
CASPIAN SEA
AZERBAIJAN
•TABRIZ
•MAHABAD
KURDISTAN
River Tigris
DUKAN•
•KIRKUK
•HALABJAH
TEHRAN•
•QOM
TIKRIT•
I R A N
BAGHDAD
I R A Q
River Euphrates
Majnoon oilfield
•AHWAZ
KHUZESTAN
KHORRAMSHAR
BASRA• •ABADAN
Faw Peninsular
Shatt el-Arab
SAUDI ARABIA
PERSIAN GULF

3 LEBANON

SYRIA
•TRIPOLI
L E B A N O N
•BAALBEK
•JOUNIEH
BEIRUT•
Shuf Mountains
Bekaa Valley
•DAMOUR
Litani River
•SIDON
DAMASCUS•
•TYRE
ISRAEL

5 SYRIA

TURKEY
ALEPPO•
Euphrates River
•HAMA
S Y R I A
•DAMASCUS
IRAQ
JORDAN

2 ISRAEL

Golan Heights
HAIFA•
TEL AVIV•
DEIR YASSIN• •LATRUN
JERUSALEM•
Suez Canal   Gaza Strip
ISRAEL
Bar-Lev Line   West Bank
JORDAN
S I N A I
EILAT•
SAUDI ARABIA
EGYPT
Strait of Tiran

6 NORTH/SOUTH YEMEN

SAUDI ARABIA
NORTH YEMEN   **SOUTH YEMEN**
SAANA•
•**ADEN**

IRAN

Geography	636,367 sq. miles (1,648,184 sq. km). Four times as big as California; three times as big as France.
Population	45 million. 45% speak Persian, 23% speak related languages (Kurdish, Luri, Baluchi), 26% Turkic languages (the Azer-baijanis in the north-west and the Turkomen in the north-east).
Resources	Oil reserves of 48.5 billion barrels; considerable other mineral wealth; exports wide variety of goods, ranging from pistachio nuts to carpets and caviar.
Refugees	Internal: 1 million Iranians; 2.6 million Afghans; 400,000 Iraqis. External: abroad; 800,000 (under a different classification) live in Turkey.
Casualties	No reliable figures for Iran–Iraq war. Best estimates are that Iran lost between 400,000 and 600,000 killed, and Iraq between 100,000 and 150,000.

On 20 July 1988, the Ayatollah Khomeini reluctantly accepted the UN proposal for a ceasefire in the Gulf war, saying, 'The acceptance of this issue is more lethal to me than poison; but I surrender to God's satisfaction. I have drunk this for the sake of God's satisfaction.' Whatever the military situation or the long-term prospects for Iran, the ayatollah clearly considered that he had suffered a devastating defeat:

Today Khomeini has bared his chest to all the arrows of misfortune and calamitous events and, in front of all the artillery and missiles of the enemy and just like all lovers of martyrdom, is counting the days until achieving martyrdom.

When the ceasefire took effect on 20 August, the problem for the UN and the states involved was to liquidate the war and to try to deal with its underlying causes. The key to both was the future of the Islamic revolution in Iran.

HISTORY
Persia is one of the oldest states on Earth, with a continuous history stretching back to Cyrus the Great, whose career of conquest began in 549 BC. Shah Mohammed celebrated what he claimed as the 2500th anniversary of the founding   245

of the empire in 1971, in a ceremony at Persepolis which cost Iran $100 million. His arithmetic and his political judgment were both faulty.

In the centuries after Cyrus, the Persian empire was frequently conquered but it just as frequently recovered. It was always an empire: one of its peoples ruled over the others. The Persians themselves have been in a minority at all times, and have therefore had to adapt their government to the needs of their subjects. Modern nationalism has now infected the Kurds, Azerbaijanis, Arabs, Baluchis and Turkomen who make up the majority of the population of Iran and will continue to trouble the Persians' control.

The country was called Persia from the time of Cyrus until the 1930s, when Shah Reza, in a moment of Fascist enthusiasm, changed it to Iran. He wished to assert that the Persians were the original Aryans and therefore an even purer *volk* than his much admired Nazis.

The roots of the Iranian revolution go back to the origins of the modern monarchy and the policies of Reza Khan Pahlevi, the general who made himself shah in 1925. He was a tough, no-nonsense reformer, who modelled himself on Kemal Ataturk of Turkey. But where Ataturk's reforms took hold, Reza Shah's did not. Turkey, after the collapse of the Ottoman empire, was ready for reform; Persia was not. More important, Ataturk pursued his reformist policies consistently for 20 years, and left competent reformers and the structure of a reformed state behind him; Reza Shah established a dynasty. When he was deposed by the British in 1941, for pro-Axis policies, all his achievements depended upon the capacity of his heir:

> And all to leave what with his toil he won,
> To that unfeather'd two-legged thing, a son.

The son was Mohammed Reza, second and last shah of the Pahlevi dynasty, who wholly lacked his father's forcefulness and ability. Reza's reforms had been opposed by the clergy, the Ulama, but unlike Henry VIII or Ataturk, he had failed to bring them under control. He had attacked them and dominated them but had never crushed them. His son failed even to dominate them, merely earning their undying enmity.

The secular National Front, led by Mohammed Mossadegh, succeeded briefly in driving Mohammed Shah from his throne. He was restored by the army, aided by the CIA, an episode that gave both institutions an exaggerated idea of their influence. The events of 1953 came back to haunt the Americans a quarter of a century later.

Ruhollah Khomeini, born in 1902, developed his political ideas in opposition to Reza Shah. By the 1930s, he was already a prominent theological scholar, Koranic exegete and leader of the clerical establishment in Qom, the theological centre of Persia. The defeat of the National Front in August 1953 left the clerical Ulama as the centre of opposition.

Khomeini's role in the Ulama grew steadily. In 1962, he led a fight against a law giving the vote to women and non-Muslims in local council elections, denouncing it as an 'attack on the Koran and Islam'. The shah backed down (unlike his father, who would never have tolerated such opposition), and in June 1963, Khomeini launched a violent attack on the regime. There were riots, ruthlessly put down by the regime, and paratroopers attacked Khomeini's seminary at Qom and arrested him. There were further riots, in Tehran and in Qom, all vigorously suppressed. Some students were thrown off the roof of the seminary, others were drowned in a lake; a total of at least 200 people were killed. After the revolution, the general who directed the operation was one of the first to be shot.

Khomeini was released in August 1964, and the shah tried to calm the unrest by holding elections. Khomeini called for a boycott, and was arrested again. He was released the following spring, but then the government introduced another unpopular measure: the Status of Forces Law, which extended diplomatic privileges to all American military personnel in Iran. The measure was so unpopular that the shah had trouble getting the bill through the rubber-stamp parliament, the Majlis. Khomeini depicted it as an insult to Iranian nationalism, 'a document for the enslavement of Iran', 'an acknowledgement that Iran is an American colony'. This time he was deported to Turkey. A year later, in 1965, he moved to the Shiite holy city of Najaf in Iraq.

From that sanctuary, he continued to attack the shah and his government. His role in the events of 1962–4 assured him a large following among students at Qom, many of whom later emerged as clerical leaders of the revolution.

THE OLD REGIME

The collapse of the monarchy in January 1979 was both surprising and inevitable. Surprising, because the shah had ruled without sustained opposition for 25 years, had a 400,000-man army, a large and effective police force, and a sinisterly effective secret police, Savak. Furthermore, the enormous revenues of Iran's oil industry should have permitted a steadily expanding economy, which, in turn, should have ensured the loyalty of the population.

The revolution was, however, inevitable because of the tyranny, corruption and economic and political ineptitude of the regime. The shah had little native ability and pursued policies that alienated, successively, all the important elements of the population: the peasants, the clerics, the urban middle class, the big industrialists, the students. When opposition started to develop in 1977, the pent-up hostility and rage of the country burst uncontrollably forth. The shah had no idea how to cope with this sudden turn of events. He alternately promised reforms and ordered his army and police to crush the opposition.

In January 1978, seminary students in Qom took to the streets in a pro-Khomeini demonstration. The police opened fire, killing a number of them. The period of mourning in Iran lasts 40 days: 40 days after the Qom killings, there were further demonstrations and further killings. The pattern was repeated. The protests swept the country. In September, during the festivities marking the end of Ramadan, there were a series of huge demonstrations in Tehran. The shah proclaimed martial law, and on 8 September, the police opened fire on the crowd in Jaleh Square, killing hundreds. The massacre became known as 'Black Friday', and the square and its martyrs' monument remain the preferred site of revolutionary demonstrations, an Iranian Place de la Bastille.

The shah's response was uncertain and erratic. In turn, he granted concessions, sacked his prime minister, arrested the commander of Savak, and ordered the army to maintain order. He hoped that Washington would tell him what to do, and was confused by the conflicting signs from the Carter administration: on the one   247 hand, the secretary of state, Cyrus Vance, advised him to negotiate with the opposition; on the other, the national security adviser, Zbigniew Brzezinski, wanted him to crush the opposition with whatever force was necessary.

In October 1978, on the shah's urging, Khomeini was expelled from Iraq; he moved to a suburb of Paris, Neuphle-le-Château. It was a decisive event. There were excellent telephone and telex links between France and Iran, and Khomeini's messages were sent to Tehran every day and spread around the country. It was revolutionary propaganda conducted by telex and Xerox. Khomeini was by now the spokesman for the revolution, and all opposition in Iran gathered around him. Moderates thought they could use him. They were mistaken.

The shah continued to vacillate between firmness and conciliation, but it was too late for either policy to save him. He consulted the opposition, who either refused to deal with him, or demanded that he leave the country. He appointed an opposition politician, Shahpour Bakhtiar, as prime minister, who took the job on condition that the shah go abroad at once.

The shah fled the country on 16 January 1979. The generals and guardsmen who saw him off were in tears; Bakhtiar and other politicians were barely civil to him. The prime minister announced a series of important measures: he abolished Savak, decreed freedom of the press, proposed a number of essential democratic reforms. It was all useless. On 31 January, Khomeini flew in to Tehran – like Lenin to the Finland station – and on 11 February, he proclaimed the Islamic republic.

THE REVOLUTION

There have been plenty of violent changes of regime in the world in this century: in the past 40 years, the monarchies of Egypt, Iraq and Libya were all swept away in army coups; Greece, Turkey, Spain and Portugal have all swung between military and civilian governments; there have been three changes of regime in France since 1940. However, in all those cases, the essential instruments of the state survived, as they did in all the coups of Latin America except Cuba.

What happened in Iran was not an ordinary coup; it was a revolution. The police, the courts, the whole structure of state authority collapsed and the vacuum was filled by militant clerics and students. The constitution, the laws, the education system, the entire economy were overthrown. It was a change as catastrophic as the Russian or Chinese revolution, the collapse of the Ethiopian monarchy or the overthrow of the Portuguese colonial regimes in Africa. What is more, Iran was a relatively modern, developed state, not a primitive backwater like Ethiopia, nor had it suffered devastating wars like Russia and China. Nevertheless, it went from a 20th-century dictatorship to a medieval theocracy in 18 months.

There was an immediate reversal of Iran's foreign policies. The Israeli embassy in Tehran was abandoned precipitously. American technicians manning listening posts in north-east Iran, spying on the Soviet missile testing sites across the border, were hastily brought out, leaving most of their equipment behind them. The US embassy was attacked on 14 February, and the US consulate at Tabriz in the west – a major outpost and site of important encounters – was sacked by a mob.

Five days after Khomeini took power, the first executions occurred, of senior officers in the shah's army. Soon a revolutionary terror was under way: at least 582 were executed between February 1979 and January 1980, and in the following 18 months, a further 906 executions took place. After the assassinations of the summer of 1981 (*see below*), when the revolution was clearly in danger, there were mass killings throughout the country: the clandestine opposition compiled a list of 7746 people executed between June 1981 and September 1983. Historian Shaul Bakhash calculates that, in all, 10,000 were executed between 1979 and 1983. The killings continued throughout the war with Iraq, and in 1988, after the ceasefire, at least 3000 prisoners were taken out of the jails and shot. The regime thus eliminated surviving monarchists and leftists together.

Like other revolutions, there was constant competition between relatively moderate leaders and the extremists, and the extremists always won. The difference in Iran was that the victorious extremists were Islamic fundamentalists, not leftists.

Mehdi Bazargan, the first prime minister appointed by Khomeini (Bakhtiar had wisely got out), lasted nine months. He tried to keep the machinery of the state functioning and to establish relations with the United States. However, the latter goal was soon unachievable: the former shah – who had led a peripatetic existence since his exile, moving from Morocco to Panama to the Bahamas, looking for a country to take him in – was admitted into the US on 22 October 1979 for medical treatment (it was later revealed that he was suffering from inoperable cancer). The event provoked an uproar in Iran, which claimed that the United States was the instrument of counter-revolution. On 1 November, Bazargan met Brzezinski in Algiers. On the 4th, the American embassy in Tehran was seized and 53 hostages taken, and on the 6th, Bazargan resigned.

Abol-Hasan Bani-Sadr became president in January 1980, under a new constitution. He had been closely associated with Khomeini in Paris, but was less extreme than his thorough-going Islamic colleagues, whom he referred to as 'a fistful of Fascist clerics'. He hoped to bring the revolution under control, but he failed completely and, in the end, had to flee for his life. His authority as president was undermined by the leaders of the Majlis, by the Revolutionary Guards, by revolutionary committees (the 'Komitehs'), by the students who had seized the American hostages, and, above all, by Khomeini himself who had as little time for moderation as Mao Tse-tung.

A full-fledged revolutionary struggle was under way, and the hostages were an important weapon for the extremists. In addition, in an instance of criminal negligence, the embassy allowed its files to fall into their hands. The last ambassador to the shah, William Sullivan, had shipped the files back to Washington at the end of 1978, as the regime disintegrated, keeping only skeleton files; when the embassy was first attacked on 14 February 1979, these few documents were promptly shredded. However, after Sullivan left the files were all brought back from Washington, and when the embassy was occupied, most of them were found intact. Many Iranian politicians were arrested – and some were executed – because the files revealed that they had had dealings with the Americans before the revolution.

Leftist groups in Iran, as well as the clerical extremists, used the hostage crisis as a means of discrediting moderates and the United States. Khomeini made various impossible conditions for their release, and Bani-Sadr tried to manoeuvre between the intransigence of the extremists (including Khomeini) and US demands for the hostages.

On 24 April, the Americans attempted a hare-brained rescue of the hostages, which failed lamentably with a loss of eight lives. The extremists used the event to prove American perfidy, and to demonstrate that there remained many traitors active inside Iran. There was a purge of the armed forces commanders, and two alleged coup plots were discovered; over 100 officers were executed.

Bani-Sadr was increasingly pushed on to the sidelines, and hostilities opened between leftists and Islamic extremists. In modern Iran, this meant that hundreds of people were killed in riots and arbitrary executions, as the clerics, encouraged by Khomeini, increased their attacks on the leftists.

Simultaneously, the tribal minorities in Iran rose in revolt. The most important were the Kurds in the west (*see* pp. 296–304) and the Azerbaijanis in the north-west, but there was also serious trouble among Baluchis in the east and other tribes along the Soviet border. The country seemed to be disintegrating.

When, on 22 September 1980, Iraq attacked on the ground and in the air (*see* Iraq, pp. 261–68), the revolution was saved by the shah: he had bought such enormous quantities of military equipment, he had trained such large numbers of military men, that the army managed to hold off the initial Iraqi attack. As in the Soviet Union in 1941, the regime had hurriedly to release hundreds of army and air force officers from jail to save the fatherland.

The crisis restored the army as a force in national affairs, but also led to a consolidation of the Revolutionary Guards: they suffered frightful casualties at the front, but as the war continued, they were developed into a cohesive and formidable fighting force, a sort of SS which, sooner or later, is bound to come into conflict with the army.

The war with Iraq diverted the Iranians from the hostages affair. President Carter had seized all Iranian assets in the United States and in American banks abroad. Iran needed the money for the war and, besides, Saddam Hussein of Iraq was now the enemy. As 1980 drew to a close, negotiations for the release of the hostages in exchange for the frozen assets were concluded, with considerable help from the Algerian government, acting as mediator. The hostages were finally released on 20 January 1981, just as President Reagan was being inaugurated in Washington.

Bani-Sadr tried to use the war emergency as a means of restoring his authority but failed, and the political battles grew steadily more intense. His supporters were attacked and sometimes killed by members of the clerical parties. Then the prime minister, Mohammed Ali Rajai, stripped Bani-Sadr of all power, and in late March 1981, Khomeini abandoned him to the wolves. He was dismissed as commander-in-chief of the army by the Ayatollah in June and went into hiding.

The leftists made one last effort to seize power. The Mujaheddin – by far the largest organization, a nationalist, socialist group that believed in 'revolutionary terror' – formed a loose alliance with Communists and Kurdish socialists, and sent their followers into the city streets to do battle with the Revolutionary Guards. The battles lasted several days and hundreds of people were killed. On 21 June, Bani-Sadr was impeached by the Majlis – a crushing defeat for the moderates and the left. On 29 July, Bani-Sadr and the Mujaheddin leader, Massoud Rajavi, fled the

country.

By then, the Mujaheddin had begun a terror campaign in Tehran. On 28 June, a car bomb demolished the headquarters of the government party, the Islamic Republican party, killing four cabinet ministers and over 30 other officials, and the party's secretary-general, Mohammed Beheshti, probably the most important figure in the government after Khomeini himself. On 30 August, a bomb killed the new president, Mohammed Ali Rajai, who, as prime minister, had been Bani-Sadr's nemesis; others killed included the new prime minister and the head of the police. Another bomb, a week later, killed the prosecutor-general.

The assassinations spread in waves across the country, resulting in the deaths of hundreds of officials. In September, the Mujaheddin took to the streets again, in an attempt to bring down the regime, just as the shah had been brought down three years before. There were street battles, culminating on 27 September with a day-long engagement between Mujaheddin and Revolutionary Guards. The Guards prevailed.

The government reacted violently, executing thousands of supposed enemies. Most of those shot were leftists, but the jails were emptied of imprisoned royalists and other opposition figures. Bani-Sadr's foreign minister, Sadegh Ghotbzadeh, who had worked for Khomeini for years, was accused of plotting, and executed. The Ayatollah Shariatmadari, the spiritual leader of the Azerbaijanis in Tabriz, was stripped of his office.

It was the revolution's most dangerous moment. The regime made no distinction as to age or sex. Boys as young as 12 were shot for taking part in demonstrations; over half those executed were students. Most of the opposition groups were wiped out, leaving only the Kurds in their mountains and the Mujaheddin, who were numerous enough and practised enough to survive, though they had been seriously affected. For the time being at least, the Islamic republic had defeated its enemies.

In 1986, the French government, under pressure from Iran, expelled Massoud Rajavi from Paris. He moved to Baghdad, and claimed that he was continuing to organize a guerrilla campaign against the regime. It does not appear that he has enjoyed any notable success, although in the last days of the war, he invaded Iran and briefly occupied a border town.

THE TWILIGHT OF THE AYATOLLAH

The Ayatollah Khomeini remained the uncontested leader of Iran, but in his old age (he was born in 1902), the inevitable struggle for the succession got under way. Events in China have shown how difficult it is to predict the course of events in such circumstances. A leading cleric might inherit Khomeini's office but not his authority. The final outcome depends on the balance of force between the army, the Revolutionary Guards and the Islamic Republican party.

Politics in Tehran were dominated by the war with Iraq. To begin with, the enthusiasm of the Revolutionary Guards brought success. The initial Iraqi offensive was stopped outside Abadan and Ahwaz, and the first Iranian counter-offensive in 1981 drove the Iraqis back on their own frontiers. Iran won two major victories: in February 1984, its armies captured Majnoon island, one of Iraq's major oilfields, on the central front; and in February 1986, they crossed the Shatt el-Arab and seized the Faw peninsula. Then the great attack on Basra in December 1986 failed: after the guns had pounded the city for weeks on end, the guards charged across the open ground towards the Iraqi positions, like the British at the Somme or the French at Verdun, and met the same fate. In modern warfare, the defensive, when properly organized, is once again stronger than the offensive, whatever the revolutionary enthusiasm of the attackers.

There were constant demonstrations in Tehran and other cities, in which hundreds of thousands of young men vowed themselves to martyrdom, but there were also constant funerals as Iranians buried their sons. The limits of the nation's zeal for martyrdom were reached: seven years was enough. To begin with, the Revolutionary Guards, like Mao's Red Guards 20 years before, had believed that their enthusiasm and faith could overcome every obstacle. Did not the Ayatollah promise paradise to every martyr? However, events have shown that martyrdom is not sufficient, that religious enthusiasm no longer wins wars. What is more, the Muslims of the world did not rally to the ayatollah's preaching. Even the Shiites of Iraq preferred the vicious tyranny of Saddam Hussein, Sunni though he was, to the Ayatollah's Shiite paradise: Hussein was an Arab, Khomeini a Persian, and 13 centuries of hostility are not to be dispersed by a Friday sermon. The only people who allowed themselves to be seduced by the Ayatollah were the desperate Shiites in Lebanon, and not even all of them heeded the call.

The economy was collapsing. War and revolution had taken their toll. Only war industries survived, and the standard of living was dropping precipitously. There were no longer enough recruits for the Revolutionary Guards; the Iranian war machine was no longer capable of supplying the huge armies that had marched singing to war in the early days. The vast stock of weapons accumulated by the shah was exhausted. Iran's great advantage over Iraq – the fact that its population was four times as great – was lost if there were no rifles for the soldiers.

The country was sliding steadily into bankruptcy. Strict Islamic law forbids usury, and Khomeini interpreted that to mean that Iran could not borrow against future oil revenues to meet the expenses of war. Iran paid cash, and when the reserves were exhausted, Iran had to rely on income from its oil exports. Oil revenue dropped from $20 billion in 1982 to $5 billion in 1988. At an OPEC meeting in June 1988, Saudi Arabia, who had broken diplomatic relations with Iran two months earlier, vetoed a last, desperate Iranian initiative to cut production and thus raise prices again.

By 1988, Iran's imports for civilian purposes, including such essential items as equipment for the oilfields, had been cut to a trickle, in order to keep up the purchase of armaments, but still there was not enough money to pay for the weapons the army needed. The war had by then come home to civilians. The steady bombardment of Tehran and other cities by Iraqi missiles is said to have driven a large part of the capital's population into the country. The attacks were nowhere near as severe as the V-1 and V-2 attacks on London during World War II, let alone the bomber offensives, but they certainly further depressed Iranian morale.

Internal opposition reappeared in public for the first time in years. Khomeini's first prime minister, Mehdi Bazargan, wrote an open letter to the Ayatollah in May 1988, stating that the war policy was a failure: 'Since 1986, you have not stopped proclaiming victory, and now you are calling on the population to resist until victory. Is that not an admission of failure on your part?' The letter went on to point out that Iraq's economy was surviving, while Iran was on the brink of bankruptcy.

In 1988, instead of mounting another general assault, Iranian troops pushed through the Iraqi defences in the Zagros mountains and captured nearly two of their divisions and their general. The frontline was now in sight of the dam that provides most of Baghdad's water, but there were another 100 miles (160 km) of mountain before the Iranians could break into the plains. It was their last success, and it was more than counterbalanced by the loss of the Faw peninsula on 17 April, and the loss of further territory on the approaches to Basra on 25 May. In those two battles, Iraq recaptured almost all the territory in the south that it had lost during the war; on 26 June, it also recaptured Majnoon island and, on 11 July, drove the Iranians out of Kurdistan. These Iraqi victories were won rapidly and easily. The Iranians put up very little resistance. They seemed exhausted.

At the end of May, Khomeini issued a decree renouncing his position as commander-in-chief of the armed forces and naming Ali Rafsanjani to the post. He was instructed to 'coordinate the armed forces, the Revolutionary Guards, the security forces and volunteer mobilization forces'. Whatever significance the appointment had in the succession struggle, it evidently pointed to another serious problem facing Iran: the conflict between the armed forces and the Revolutionary Guards. In the short term, it put the pragmatists in control of the war machine.

Hojatolislam Ali Akbar Hashemi Rafsanjani, speaker of the Majlis, was the Iranian official who had been approached by the Reagan administration in 1985–6 in an attempt to win the release of American hostages in Lebanon – an affair that came to be known as 'Irangate'. The American rationale was that Rafsanjani might very well emerge as Khomeini's successor, and establishing contact with him in advance would suit American long-term interests. His favour would be won by selling arms to Iran, and in return, he would arrange the release of the hostages.

The secret discussions continued for several months, and included a visit to Washington by Rafsanjani's son, who was given a tour of the White House by Oliver North, a member of the National Security Council staff, who was to become the central figure, on the American side, in the Iran–Contra scandal. Several arms deliveries were made, including anti-tank and anti-aircraft missiles, and two American hostages in Lebanon were released. It has never been clear whether Rafsanjani accepted the American premiss – that improved relations were ultimately desirable.

A man of great subtlety and flexibility, unlike some of his rivals who are unbending fanatics, Rafsanjani's personal concern was to win the succession struggle, which would not necessarily be concluded immediately upon Khomeini's death. Command of the armed forces would either give him the weapons he needed to succeed, or make him the inevitable scapegoat for losing the war. The fact that the Ayatollah accepted responsibility for the ceasefire offered Rafsanjani some protection. Only time will show whether it is enough.

DIPLOMACY

Throughout the war, Arab states and the United Nations tried continually to mediate between the two sides. One early effort was made by Algeria, but it ended abruptly when, on 3 May 1982, Iraq shot down the plane carrying the Algerian foreign minister, Mohammed Ben Yahia, and 12 of his colleagues. They had been flying to Tehran, and the Algerians suspect that the shooting was deliberate. That episode followed Saddam Hussein's first effort to escape from the trap he had dug for himself: in March 1982, he had offered to withdraw Iraqi forces to the international frontier. Iran had rejected this plan; it would recapture its own territory with its own forces, and it demanded that Hussein be deposed, Iraq be formally declared the aggressor, and that Iraq pay reparations for the costs of the war. The two sides held these positions for the next six years.

The UN Security Council finally agreed to Resolution 598 on 20 July 1987. This called for an immediate ceasefire, provided for an international commission to consider the question of war guilt, and laid down mandatory sanctions that might be enforced against either state if it persisted in the war. After some hesitation, Iraq accepted the resolution, but Iran rejected it outright. For the next year, the United States tried to persuade the other members of the Security Council to approve sanctions, but never got very far. It was only the series of defeats inflicted on Iran in the spring of 1988 that finally tipped the balance.

Just before Iran accepted the ceasefire, on 3 July, a US warship, the USS *Vincennes*, shot down an Iranian civilian airliner, Iranair flight 655, killing all 290 people on board. It was a striking illustration of the inadequacies of modern technology. The *Vincennes* was equipped with the most modern and sophisticated anti-aircraft system in the world – the Aegis system – but it depended upon every sailor working as precisely and as calmly as every computer. One of the weapons' officers misread the signals and mistook the airliner for an F-15.

On 18 July 1988, Rafsanjani announced that Iran would accept Resolution 598. Two days later, Khomeini's statement was read over the radio. It was full of the old, fiery denunciations of his enemies:

We have repeatedly shown in our foreign and international Islamic policy that we have been and are intent on expanding the influence of Islam in the world and lessening the domination of the world devourers. Now if the servants of the United States cite this policy as being expansionist and motivated to establish a great empire, we will not fear it but welcome it . . . We must smash the hands and the teeth of the superpowers, particularly the United States. And we must choose one of two alternatives – either martyrdom or victory, and we regard both as victory.

He continued to threaten Saudi Arabia and Kuwait: 'All of you will be partners in the adventurism and crimes created by the United States. We have not yet engaged in any action that would engulf the entire region in blood and fire, making it totally unstable.' He admitted freely that the war was lost:

The acceptance of the resolution was truly a very bitter and tragic issue for everyone, particularly for me. Up to a few days ago, I believed in the methods of defence and the stances announced in the war . . . However, due to some incidents and factors which for the moment I will refrain from elaborating on and which, God willing, will be made clear in the future, and in view of the opinion of all the high-ranking political and military experts of the country, whose commitment, sympathy and sincerity I trust, I agreed with the acceptance of the resolution and the ceasefire.

The Iranians then moved their operations to the negotiating table, in what promised to be long and bitter disputes with Iraq over a peace settlement. Both sides claimed sovereignty of the Shatt el-Arab. Iran had abandoned its effort to

254

overthrow Saddam Hussein, but refused to renounce any of its other demands.

Iran faced immense economic and social problems after the war, and it was evident that it could not hope to restore its oil industry, let alone the rest of the economy, without outside help. The government moved cautiously to improve relations with the West, but in the spring of 1989 Khomeini issued a ruling that the Pakistan-born British author, Salman Rushdie, should be executed for blasphemy and apostasy. That sudden demonstration of fundamentalist intransigence brought all diplomatic progress to a halt. Khomeini died on 3 June 1989, but his spirit continued to dominate Iran. His successors did not lift the death sentence on Rushdie. Rafsanjani was elected president and purged the most militant fundamentalists from the government, but gave no public sign of wanting a reconciliation with the West. In particular, he made no effort to secure the release of hostages held in Beirut. Iran remained an outlaw state, brooding on its revolution.

FURTHER READING

Amnesty International, *Iran: Violations of Human Rights*, London, 1987.
Avery, Peter, *Modern Iran*, New York, Praegar, 1965.
Bakhash, Shaul, *The Reign of the Ayatollahs: Iran and the Islamic Revolution*, New York, Basic Books, 1984.
Bernard, Cheryl, *The Government of God: Iran's Islamic Republic*, New York, Cornell University Press, 1984.
Hiro, Dalip, *Iran under the Ayatollahs*, London, Routledge and Kegan Paul, 1985.
Mortimer, Edward, *Faith and Power: The Politics of Islam*, London, Faber and Faber, 1982.
Shawcross, William, *The Shah's Last Ride: The Fate of an Ally*, New York, Simon & Schuster, 1988; London, Chatto & Windus, 1989.
Sick, Gary, *All Fall Down – America's Tragic Encounter with Iran*, New York, Random House, 1985.

IRAQ

Geography	167,568 sq. miles (433,999 sq. km). About the size of Sweden.
Population	16.5 million. About 50% are Shiite Muslim Arabs 25% Sunni Arabs, 20% Kurds (Sunni) and 5% Christians. 75% speak Arabic, the remainder speak Kurdish, Turkish or Persian.
Resources	Oil reserves set officially at 44.5 billion barrels, but which are certainly far larger; world's largest exporter of dates.
GNP per capita	$3020 (1980). The war reduced this total substantially.
Refugees	Internal: 20,000–50,000 Iraqis; 75,000 Iranians. External: 404,000.

The war between Iraq and Iran, which lasted from September 1980 until the ceasefire of August 1988, was the most violent since the Vietnam war. It was by far the most costly conventional war since Korea, with regular armies fighting set-piece battles. It was a national war, from first to last, unlike those other conflicts. Indeed, it soon developed into an ethnic war, with Arabs fighting Persians as they have done since at least the 7th century AD, the first century of the Hegeira. The Ayatollah Khomeini proclaimed a *jihad* (holy war) calling on the Shiites to fight the heretical Sunnis. He soon discovered that the Iraqi Shiites, who are in the majority in Iraq, are Arabs first: they supported their Sunni government, to defeat the Persian invaders.

The war ended when Iran sued for peace (*see* Iran, pp. 245–55). The regime could no longer muster the troops and armaments needed to defend the fatherland, let alone break through the Iraqi line to Baghdad. Iraq accepted the ceasefire along the international frontier. There were to be no territorial changes as a result of the war, although the dispute over the line of the border in the Shatt el-Arab river remained unresolved. Iraq claimed victory, but had failed to obtain its principal objectives: to occupy Khuzestan, Iran's Arabic-speaking province on the plains of Mesopotamia, and to overthrow the revolutionary regime in Tehran.

There are no reliable figures for the number of people killed in the war. Iran probably lost between 400,000 and 600,000 men killed, and Iraq between 100,000 and 150,000.

256

HISTORY

Iraq, like so many states of the modern world, is an entirely artificial creation, arbitrarily drawn on a map by the British and the French when they partitioned the Middle East after 1918. It is a land of most ancient quarrels. In 539 BC, Cyrus the Great, king of Persia, conquered Babylon and slew Belshazzar the king. The shah of Iran celebrated the 2500th anniversary of the foundation of the Persian monarchy in 1971 – at least ten years late. The Arabs celebrate a different anniversary: the Persians ruled Mesopotamia for 1100 years, a reign interrupted only by Alexander the Great and his successors, but in AD 637, the Arabs defeated the Persians in the battle of al-Qadissiya, one of the decisive events of history. For most of the following 1300 years, Mesopotamia was united with Syria (which then included Lebanon and what are now Israel and Jordan). The state was ruled from Damascus and then from Baghdad until the 16th century, and part of that time it extended over most of modern Iran and central Asia. Under the Abbasid caliphate (750–1258), Baghdad was one of the greatest centres of learning in the Western world. It was destroyed by Hulagu Khan, Genghiz Khan's grandson, in 1258. He made a pyramid of the skulls of all Baghdad's scholars, theologians, poets and administrators, and threw all the libraries into the Tigris. The river ran black with the ink. It was one of the great disasters of history.

The Dark Ages in the Middle East continued for three centuries, punctuated by the conquests of Tamburlaine, who sacked Baghdad in 1401. In the 16th century, Mesopotamia was a battleground between the Safavids in Persia and the Ottomans in Constantinople: the Ottoman empire controlled Baghdad from 1534 to 1918, with occasional, bloody, interruptions by the Safavids, as the latter tried repeatedly to conquer Mesopotamia and liberate the Shiite holy places there. The ancient battles between Arabs and Persians, from the 7th to the 12th century, are all vividly remembered in both countries, and played a large part in their war propaganda.

So did the disputes between Sunni and Shiite Muslims, which also began in the 7th century in Mesopotamia. They started as a fight for the succession to the empire founded by Mohammed and the first caliphs – between the Umayyads (Sunni) and Mohammed's son-in-law Ali and grandson Hussein. Hussein was defeated and killed in battle at Karbala in 680, and is buried at Najaf, and these two cities in Iraq are now the holiest shrines of the Shiites. Najaf has the largest cemeteries in the world: hundreds of thousands, perhaps millions, of Shiites have been brought for burial there. Iran is 80 per cent Shiite and Iraq, although it has always been ruled by Sunnis, has a Shiite majority.

The history of Iraq since 1918, like the history of Syria and Lebanon, has been a continuing struggle by the state to form a nation out of the diverse peoples, languages, religions and traditions that exist within its frontiers.

The British drew up the modern frontiers of Iraq and Jordan, and installed kings of the Hashemite dynasty in Baghdad and Amman. The family, imported from Arabia, has survived in Jordan, a desert kingdom, but never won acceptance in Mesopotamia, the oldest urban civilization in the world, where the royal family was thought subservient to the British and Americans.

An army coup overthrew the monarchy on 14 July 1958, at the height of President Nasser's influence in the Arab world. Nasserites were fighting for power in Syria, Lebanon and Jordan, as well as Iraq. The royal government

257

distrusted the army, and took care that its units had no ammunition for their guns. However, two battalions ordered to the Jordanian frontier, to be ready to help King Hussein if there were a revolt, were issued ammunition. They were under the orders of Brigadier Abd al-Karim Kassem and Colonel Abd al-Salam Arif: unknown to the government, Kassem was chairman and Arif a senior member of the secret Free Officers Committee, which had been planning a coup for years.

Instead of heading west, they drove into Baghdad in the early hours and seized the Ministry of Defence, and other key posts in the capital. Arif set up his headquarters at Broadcasting House, and coordinated the attack on the royal palace. A desultory siege lasted into the morning and then the crown prince, Abdul Illah, surrendered. The royal party was ordered into the courtyard: King Feisal II, his uncle the crown prince, several women (including the king's sister and Abdul Illah's mother) and a number of servants, about 25 people in all. They were lined up against a wall and shot.

The prime minister, Nuri es-Said, had escaped from his house and taken refuge in Baghdad. He was caught the next day, trying to escape disguised as a woman, and was lynched by the mob. His body, and the crown prince's, were tied behind Land Rovers and dragged through the streets of Baghdad. Scores of officials of the old regime suffered the same fate: it was the revolution's favourite means of execution. Some of the victims, wounded in earlier shootings, were taken from their hospital beds to be dragged. The British embassy was sacked. For a while there was a ban on Western tourists visiting Baghdad, and personal sanctions were sometimes enforced against those who ignored it.

THE RISE OF THE BA'ATH

After the 1958 coup, Abd al-Karim Kassem became president. Within two months, he had removed Arif, who was sympathetic to the Ba'ath party and to the Nasserites; Arif was sentenced to death, but was pardoned in 1962. Kassem relied on the support of the Communist party against the Ba'ath, and he proved an incompetent, eccentric and xenophobic leader. The dangers of the situation were demonstrated in October 1959, when he barely escaped assassination: the leader of the assassination squad, who escaped, wounded, was Saddam Hussein.

The Kurds in the north rose in revolt (see The Kurds, pp. 297–300), and in 1961, Kassem tried to annex Kuwait. Britain, then still allied to Kuwait and governing the Gulf sheikhdoms, sent troops to protect Kuwait against attack. Kassem backed down. The only casualties were a few British soldiers who suffered heatstroke: they had arrived in one of the hottest places on Earth dressed for an English summer.

A new army plot was put together by Arif and Colonel Ahmad Hasan al-Bakr, a leader of the Ba'athists, and this coup occurred on 8 February 1963. It was a more elaborate and difficult operation than the 1958 coup, but it ended in the same way. The plotters seized the key points of the city, and laid siege to the Ministry of Defence. Kassem's Communist supporters took to the streets in his support, but they were mown down by the troops: hundreds were killed.

Kassem held out in the ministry all day and, in the evening, escaped with a few aides. Early the following morning, he was arrested and taken to Broadcasting House, which was again serving as coup headquarters. After a violent shouting match with Arif, Kassem was shot, with his three surviving aides, in a television studio. Pictures of the event were then broadcast.

Al-Bakr became prime minister and Arif was given the nominal post of president. The new Ba'ath government then devoted itself to massacring members of the Iraqi Communist party, who were mostly Shiites. The government itself, however, was deeply divided between the Nasserites, led by Arif, and the pro-Syrians, led by al-Bakr. Arif briskly resolved the difficulty by staging a coup against the government on 18 November 1963. He declared the Ba'ath party illegal and set about purging the government of all its members. He then prepared the way for a union with Egypt and Syria, but at the last moment called it off (the Syrians were equally unenthusiastic) and started purging his Nasserite former colleagues instead.

There were more attempted coups by Nasserites and Ba'athists. In April 1966, Arif was killed in a helicopter crash, apparently accidentally, and was succeeded by his brother, General Abd el-Rahman Arif. He tried to resolve the economic crisis brought on by his predecessors' economic policies and to solve the continuing Kurdish problem, but the concessions he proposed to the Kurds were unpopular with Iraqi nationalists, including the Ba'ath party. After the Six Day War in 1967, Arif moved his government sharply to the left, encouraging Iraqi Communists and others.

On 17 July 1968, the Ba'ath and an alliance of conservatives and moderates staged a *coup d'état*. For once, no one was killed. Arif was packed off into exile, al-Bakr became president and a new government of national unity was formed. Ba'athist officers quickly took control of the army and, on 30 July, staged another coup, dismissing all non-Ba'ath ministers. Most of the leading members of the new government were from the town of Tikrit, north of Baghdad, and several of them were closely related to each other, including al-Bakr and Hussein; in due course, they all dropped the cognomen 'al-Tikriti' to conceal the fact. Not all Tikritis remained members of the inner circle, however: in 1971, Saddam Hussein exiled General Hardan al-Tikriti, and later had him assassinated in Kuwait.

The Ba'ath has maintained itself in power since 1968 by a policy of ruthless terrorism, killing off its opponents, whether Communists, Nasserites, pro-Syrians, Islamic fundamentalists or dissident Ba'athists. On 27 January 1969, nine Jews and five others were hanged in public in Baghdad, allegedly as Israeli spies. The small surviving Jewish community in Iraq has since made every effort to escape.

The first attempted coup against the regime occurred two months after it took power, and there have been many since then, all unsuccessful. In July 1973, one of them led to the death of the defence minister, General Hammad Shihab (al-Tikriti).

Despite its brutality, and its reliance on the secret police, the Ba'ath regime did have a number of achievements to its credit. For example, its survival during the long war with Iran showed that it had considerable popular support, but its main success was economic. Iraq played a leading part in the first OPEC price rise in 1973–4; the large oil revenues that ensued were used sensibly, and the country made rapid progress until the war in 1980. The Ba'ath foreign policy was intransigent and selfish. It professed undying hostility to Israel, gave some encouragement to Palestinian terrorism, bought arms from the Soviet Union and concluded a treaty of friendship with it in April 1972, and denounced the United States on every occasion. However, Iraq was never a subservient 259 satellite to the Soviet Union, and when it became necessary to seek support in the West, Saddam Hussein changed his tune without the slightest shame.

The history of Iraq has continued to be a bitter and bloody contest between the competing forces in Iraqi society: the Ba'ath party (see Syria, pp. 330–32), which is secular and socialist and led by Sunni Arabs from the town of Tikrit; the Shiite majority of the population; the Communist party, whose members are mostly Shiite; various other leftist and Nasserite factions; the Kurds; and the army. Saddam Hussein al-Tikriti, the current Ba'athist president, has tried to use the war with Iran as a means of uniting the country against the Persians and thus overcoming its divisions. However, since he established his power by executing potential rivals in the party and army, massacring Communists and religious Shiites, murdering the principal Iraqi Shiite religious leader, and has used poison gas against Kurdish villages, he may not succeed.

For decades, there had been a running border dispute between Iraq and Iran over the Shatt el-Arab river, which is the confluence of the Tigris and Euphrates and marks the southern border between the two countries. Iran claimed that the frontier lay along the middle of the river – the *thalweg* – Iraq claimed that it was on the east bank, and since 1937, the Iraqi view had prevailed. In addition, from 1961 to 1975, Iran had given every assistance to Kurdish rebels in northern Iraq. The war was a steady drain on Iraqi resources, and finally, in 1975, Iraq accepted Iran's claims on the Shatt in exchange for Iran abandoning support for the Kurds. The agreement was announced at an OPEC meeting in Algiers in March, and a treaty signed in Baghdad in June. The Iraqis, despite the great advantage they drew from the treaty, considered it a national humiliation and awaited an opportunity to reassert their claims to the waterway.

The tensions between Sunni and Shiite, and between the secular Ba'ath party and militant Islam, were greatly exacerbated by the Iranian revolution. The Ayatollah Khomeini had been living in exile in Iraq since 1965, in Najaf. There he was closely associated with an Iraqi ayatollah, Baqir al-Sadr, who advocated the establishment of an Islamic republic in Iraq. The agreement with Iran on the Shatt el-Arab waterway and the Kurds also contained a clause forbidding each side to allow opposition movements against the other. In September 1978, belatedly, the Iranian government demanded that Iraq expel Khomeini, and he was sent to Paris. This proved a mistake: he found Paris much more congenial as a base of operations against the shah, and the expulsion confirmed his animosity towards Iraq.

Immediately after the Iranian revolution in February 1979, the new regime in Tehran began inciting Iraqi Shiites to revolt. The Shiites make up the majority in Iraq and thus presented a serious challenge to the government. A Shiite Islamic party, the Dawa, under Iranian influence, was plotting against the regime and had started a terrorist campaign. Saddam Hussein, who was then vice-president and the strong man of the government, put the Ayatollah al-Sadr under house arrest in Najaf. There followed serious riots in Shiite neighbourhoods in Baghdad, which were put down with great brutality.

On 16 July 1979, Hussein persuaded the president, Hasan al-Bakr, to resign and took his place; he then vigorously set about consolidating his position. On 28 July, Baghdad Radio announced that 'a treacherous and lowly plot, perpetrated by a gang disloyal to the party and revolution has been discovered'. Five leading members of the Ba'ath Regional Council and 16 other senior figures were executed in the presence of Saddam Hussein and 'leading party cadres'. The radio announcement stated that the five 'were in contact with a foreign side' (i.e. Syria); one report suggested that four of them were Shiites. Then, after the attempted assassination of one of his closest assistants in April 1980, Hussein had the Ayatollah al-Sadr and his sister summarily hanged. He thus showed the brutal instincts of the true tyrant. The repression of the Shiites was intensified, and 15,000–20,000 of them were expelled to Iran and hundreds were executed.

By 1980, Saddam Hussein was firmly in control in Iraq. Oil revenues had risen from $1.8 billion in 1973 to $26.1 billion in 1980, and early in 1981, the price of oil reached $35 a barrel, five times its level in 1973. Iraq was not the only country to imagine that the golden years would last for ever.

In the 18 months following the flight of the shah, in January 1979, Iran had slid to the brink of disintegration. The army had lost virtually all its senior officers, and seemed incapable even of controlling the Kurds and Azerbaijanis. The Institute of Strategic Studies in London calculated that 60 per cent of the Iranian army deserted in the wake of the revolution. A ferocious battle for power was under way in Tehran between leftists and moderates and Islamic fundamentalists. Iran's behaviour, particularly its occupation of the American embassy and its seizure of the hostages, had isolated it among the community of nations, and by breaking with the United States, Iran had lost its chief military supplier: the shah had bought fleets of modern aircraft, but most were grounded through lack of spares and poor maintenance. The Iraqis claimed that 'There is a government on every street corner in Iran.'

Iran's policy of generalized militancy extended to its relations with Iraq. Instead of conciliating its neighbours while it sorted out its domestic problems, it stirred up Shiite fundamentalism in Iraq. Saddam Hussein, newly installed as president in Baghdad, protested bitterly. At the same time, Iran's troubles seemed to him to provide a good moment to revive Iraq's claim to the whole of the Shatt el-Arab. Neither of these matters can, however, seriously be considered a *causus belli*. The real reason for Iraq's aggression was undoubtedly a desire to take advantage of Iran's difficulties, to inflict a humiliating defeat on it and to defeat and perhaps overthrow Khomeini. Possibly Hussein hoped to annex Khuzestan, the Iranian province on the plains where most of its oil is found. Khuzestan's population is largely Arab, and perhaps Hussein thought they would welcome being freed from the Persians' yoke.

THE WAR WITH IRAN

On 17 September 1980, Hussein announced that he was abrogating the 1975 treaty, and five days later, his armies mounted a general offensive. The Iraqis drove into Iran; Khorramshar, Iran's largest port, fell at the end of October; and Ahwaz, the provincial capital of Khuzestan, and Abadan, the country's oil capital, were threatened.

Although it seemed at first that Iraq would win easily, it quickly became apparent that the Iraqi armies were badly led and lacking in offensive spirit, and that Iraq had grossly underestimated Iran's military capability. The Iraqi offensive

261

stalled at the end of 1980, with the Iranians clinging to a toehold in Khorramshar and holding Abadan against heavy Iraqi shelling. Iraqi troops were stopped well short of Ahwaz. In the spring and summer of 1981, Iran counter-attacked, and drove the Iraqis back from the approaches to Abadan.

The excuses that Hussein offered to explain the early defeats were remarkable. According to the writer Christine Moss Helms, he said that Iraq's lines of communication had originally been too long, Iraqi forces had been too widely dispersed and the reservists had been inexperienced, and the Iranians had fought better, had been defending their homeland and had had better intelligence and better knowledge of the terrain. Furthermore, Iraq had been at a disadvantage because it had relied on tanks, and the Iranians had unsportingly attacked at night, when the tanks could not manoeuvre. In most nations, a general responsible for such miscalculations would be relieved of his post; in many, he would be shot. However, Iraq is a one-party dictatorship, and Saddam Hussein has so far survived. It should be noted that the Ba'ath is a civilian party: only Saddam Hussein himself had a military background, although he was only a lieutenant in 1959 when he left the army and devoted himself to revolutionary politics. Iraq is like the Soviet Union in 1941, and military considerations are always subordinated to political ones, including the need for the ruling party to keep absolute control of the army.

While all this was going on, one of the most dramatic incidents in recent Iraqi history occurred on 7 June 1981, when the Israeli air force bombed the Osirak nuclear reactor that the French had been building on the outskirts of Baghdad. The Israelis sent eight F-16s, each carrying two 2000-lb bombs, escorted by six F-15s. They flew high over Jordan, and then at rooftop level to Baghdad, to pass under Iraqi radar. No planes were lost. Neither Iraqi nor Saudi radar, nor the American AWAC planes patrolling the Saudi skies, saw them come or go. (The Americans claimed rather lamely that they were looking the other way.) One French technician and a number of Iraqis were killed. The Israeli government, led then by Menachem Begin, claimed that Iraq was preparing to develop nuclear weapons. The French technicians (and the Iraqis) denied it.

The war went on. Iran retained the initiative until the spring of 1988. A generalized offensive in 1982 cleared the Iraqis from Khorramshar on 24 May, and drove them back to their frontier. In another series of offensives, the Iranians pushed across the border in Kurdistan and across the desert towards the Tigris, and in February 1984, they seized Majnoon island in southern Iraq. It is an area that used to be marsh, and which was inhabited by the Marsh Arabs, a wholly separate and distinct tribe whose territory and way of life had been sacrificed to the oil industry. The marshes had been drained and the oil rigs set up: there were over 6 billion barrels of oil reserves to be found there. Capturing the area was a major victory for Iran. Both sides tried to infiltrate troops through the marshes, with heavy losses.

One of the weapons the Iraqis used to repel the Iranians was poison gas, both the mustard gas that had been used in World War I, and nerve gas. The only other occasion that gas had been used since 1918 was when Mussolini employed it in Abyssinia in 1935 (see Ethiopia, p. 28). Iranian soldiers who had been gassed were
taken to Europe to be treated.

In 1986, Iranian troops crossed the marshes at the mouth of the Shatt al-Arab and occupied the Faw peninsula. The following year, they mounted a massive onslaught on Basra, Iraq's second largest city, and almost broke through its defences. Most of the population fled: for many months, the city was in range of Iranian guns, which shelled it mercilessly. By then, the Iraqis had developed considerable defensive skills and were able to hold the Iranians off Basra, but in doing so, they left the northern front undermanned.

Every year, Iran mounted offensives against Iraq, and every year Iraq held the line. The Iranians suffered immense casualties, sending fanatical Revolutionary Guards against Iraqi emplacements, like European soldiers going 'over the top' on the Western Front in World War I. Shiism proclaims the importance of martyrdom, and hundreds of thousands of Iranians volunteered to give their lives for the cause. The Guards would attack in human waves, driving back the Iraqis whatever the cost, preparing the way for the regular Iranian army. It was not until the Iraqis had dug substantial defensive lines, like the trenches on the Western Front, that they were able to stop the Guards. Even then, there was always the danger of a sudden breakthrough, like the capture of the Faw peninsula in 1986.

Although the fighting was exceedingly costly, Iran, which in 1980 had a population comparable to that of Britain or France in 1914, did not suffer the same scale of casualties as those two countries had by 1918 (nearly a million for Britain, 1.3 million for France). Although estimates vary greatly, Iran probably lost between 400,000 and 600,000 dead between 1980 and 1988, Iraq about 150,000 killed, 500,000 wounded and 70,000 captured. In the attacks on Basra in January 1987, Iran lost 25,000 to 30,000 dead, and Iraq 5000 to 10,000. Iran could afford the disparity: its population is 45 million, compared with 15 million in Iraq.

THE TANKER WAR

From the time the southern front stabilized at the end of 1980, Iran was able to prevent all Iraqi oil exports through the Shatt. In April 1982, as the tide of war turned against Iraq, Syria closed Iraq's pipeline to the Mediterranean, and it appeared for a while that Iraq would be strangled economically before it was defeated militarily.

The other Arab states came to the rescue. Iraq has one of the most unpleasant governments in the region and had shown constant hostility to the monarchies in Jordan, the Gulf and Saudi Arabia. However, the threat of Persian fundamentalism was far more to be feared, and thus the conservative Arab states could not afford to let Iraq be defeated. King Hussein of Jordan opened Aqaba to Iraqi imports (chiefly arms), pipelines were hurriedly constructed across the desert to the Red Sea, and through Turkey to the Mediterranean, and for a while, Iraqi exports also went through Kuwait. Above all, the conservative Arabs subsidized Iraq directly, to a tune of billions of dollars a year. In the eight years of the war, the subsidy reputedly came to $60 billion.

The tanker war started in 1984. Iraq attacked Iranian tankers and the main Iranian oil terminal at Kharg island, which was easily within reach of Iraqi air bases. Iran retaliated by attacking Kuwaiti and other Gulf tankers, on the grounds that, since those countries were supporting Iraq, their commerce was a legitimate Iranian target. However, neither side succeeded in seriously damaging   263 the other's exports. The price of oil, which started to drop sharply in 1982, was never seriously affected by the tanker war. Iran simply moved its main oil depot to Larak island in the Straits of Hormuz: small tankers from Kharg and other oilfields would carry oil to Larak and there transfer it to supertankers.

In 1987, Kuwait persuaded the United States to offer protection to the Kuwaiti oil fleet. Eleven Kuwaiti tankers were transferred to American registration, and the United States began patrolling the Gulf to protect them. On 17 May, an Iraqi Super-Etendard fired two Exocet missiles at an American frigate, the USS *Stark*, apparently mistaking her for an Iranian warship. The *Stark*'s defences were not functioning, she was severely damaged and 37 American sailors were killed. Iraq apologized profusely and the Reagan administration accepted the excuses offered. Thereafter American ships were put on permanent maximum alert, and close collaboration between the US forces, Saudi and American AWACs (radar planes) and Iraq was instituted to ensure that there was no repeat of the incident. Iran then accused the Americans of helping Iraq, and there was clearly some substance to the charge. When an American warship shot down an Iranian airliner on 3 July 1988 (*see* Iran, p. 254), the mistake was partly due to the ship's fear of a repetition of the *Stark* incident.

Iran retaliated by sowing mines in the Gulf, and several ships were hit. An American frigate, the USS *Samuel B. Roberts*, was hit by an Iranian mine on 14 April 1988 and severely damaged. In further retaliation, the US navy sank six Iranian warships and patrol boats, and destroyed two Iranian oil platforms.

THE AIR WAR

Another feature of the Iran–Iraq war was the use of bombers and missiles to attack cities. Iraq launched the first bombing raids on Iranian cities in 1984, starting with an attack on Dizful in February, and later it extended them to Tehran and other urban areas. These attacks never attained the intensity of those in earlier 20th-century wars – neither side had enough bombers – but as the conflict dragged on, the number of civilian casualties caused by the air war increased steadily.

In 1987, Iraq began using missiles against Iranian cities. These were Soviet-made Scud missiles, modified to carry as far as Tehran, which became the chief target; one report alleged that 4 million Tehranis, half the population, had fled the city. Other cities were hit, too, though not so severely, among them Shiraz, Kermanshah and Isfahan. The last is one of the most beautiful cities on Earth, comparable to Venice, and the possibility that its monuments might be damaged was the most serious threat to the world's cultural heritage since 1945. Iran retaliated by sending its own missiles against Baghdad.

THE IRAQI VICTORY

In a military sense, however, the tanker war and the air war were sideshows. What counted was the war on the ground. In the spring of 1988, in its last offensive, Iran attacked in Kurdistan, driving its armies to within sight of the great Darbandi Khan reservoir and hydroelectric plant at Dukan, which supply Baghdad. Iran captured over 4000 Iraqi troops, including a divisional commander, and took 400 square miles (640 sq. km) of territory. Losing the dam would have been a major defeat for Iraq. The Iranians had been advancing steadily through the mountains

264

towards Kirkuk, and if they had broken through to the plains, they might have won the war. To stop them, Iraq used poison gas. In March 1988, an Iraqi Kurdish village, Halabjah, then under Iranian occupation, was hit by gas. The bodies of at least 100 civilians – women, children and elderly men – were shown to Western reporters brought down from Tehran for the occasion. Iran claimed that 2000 people had been killed, and a subsequent UN report confirmed the use of poison gas.

Despite the dangers of the Iranian attack in Kurdistan, the Iraqis sent no reinforcements, confident that they could hold the line. Besides, they needed their troops in the south: on 17 April, they launched a surprise offensive on the Faw peninsula and, in three days' heavy fighting, drove the Iranians back across the Shatt el-Arab. Liberating Faw after two years was Iraq's biggest victory and the decisive battle of the war. The following month, in another offensive, the Iraqis cleared the approaches to Basra, recovering virtually all the land lost earlier in the war. Reports from the front, both at Faw and outside Basra, indicated that the Iranian resistance was surprisingly weak. The army that had shown such courage and *élan* early in the war now broke in a rout, and fled before the Arabs.

In June, Iraq attacked on the central front and recaptured the Majnoon oilfield that had been seized by Iran in 1984, and in a series of limited offensives to the east of the river, they recovered the last few miles of Iraqi territory occupied by the Iranians. In the same month, exiled Iranians – Massoud Rajavi's National Liberation Army – attacked across the border in Kurdistan. The NLA, formed of anti-Khomeini Mujaheddin (*see* Iran), reportedly has 15,000 troops, armed by the Iraqis – not enough to tip the balance in the war, but sufficient to play a role in Iran if the revolutionary regime collapses. Their summer offensive took an Iranian town, Mehran, which they held for a few days before pulling back behind the frontier. The incident was part of a series of small offensives in Kurdestan designed to push the Iranians back from the Dukan dam.

There were a number of reasons for Iraq's victories in 1988. The first was Iran's war-weariness, and perhaps also the loss of its revolutionary enthusiasm. A second reason was that Iraq, despite American efforts to prevent arms sales to both sides, had always been able to obtain the weapons and ammunition it needed. After the failure of its first offensive in 1980, the Baghdad regime mended its relations with Saudi Arabia, Kuwait and Jordan, and consolidated its good relations with Turkey. It kept its distance from the Soviet Union and went to great lengths to present itself as a reasonable, modern state fighting a fanatical aggressor in Tehran. This policy won it sympathy, if not arms, from Washington (and diplomatic relations, which had been broken in 1967, were at last resumed). In turn, better relations with the Americans permitted the development of fruitful relations with European arms dealers, notably the French.

The conservative Arabs supplied the money, the Europeans sold the arms, but the war was won by the steadfastness of Iraqi soldiers. Meanwhile Iran, isolated by its own fanaticism, found it impossible to supply its armies. A further Iraqi advantage was geographic: the battlefields were all within easy reach of Iraqi bases, supplied by the main roads running the length of the country, and as a result, Iraq could move troops easily and rapidly. Iran, by contrast, had to move troops and supplies down from the Iranian plateau, over high mountains and along winding and difficult roads.

On the ground, the Iraqi generals fought a defensive war from 1981 until 1988, allowing the Iranians to exhaust themselves in a series of offensives – in much the same way that the Germans had conserved their energy from 1914 until 1918, allowing the Allies to beat fruitlessly upon the Western Front, and then had launched one last assault towards Paris. The Iraqi armies held the line, most notably during the Iranian attacks on Basra in 1986–7, and the Ba'ath regime had the strength and sufficient popularity to hold the home front. That is, in many ways, the most remarkable of its achievements: in 1980, very few people would have predicted that Saddam Hussein could survive seven years of stalemate.

THE CEASEFIRE

These Iraqi victories were the last straw for Iran. On 18 July 1988, the government in Tehran announced that it would accept the ceasefire that the UN had proposed. The Ayatollah himself confirmed that he had approved the decision, and on 8 August the foreign ministers of the two countries, meeting UN secretary-general Pérez de Cuellar in New York, announced that the ceasefire would take effect on 20 August.

A UN peacekeeping force was hurriedly assembled and sent to the Gulf. There was some small-scale fighting, during which the Iraqis pushed the Iranians out of Kurdistan and demonstrated that they could penetrate Iranian territory at will, at least on the central front. After the ceasefire, Saddam Hussein turned his attention to the Kurdish rebels in the north and rapidly restored central authority throughout all Iraqi Kurdistan. The war was over.

(*For a more detailed account of the diplomatic manoeuvring that led to the ceasefire, see* Iran, *pp. 253–55, and for the reconquest of Kurdistan, see* The Kurds, *pp. 299–300.*)

AFTER THE WAR

Iraq had started the war, in 1980, to recover complete control of the Shatt el-Arab, to stop Iran inciting Iraqi Shiites to revolt and to humiliate and possibly overthrow the Ayatollah Khomeini. Hussein may also have coveted Khuzestan. It was a clear case of aggression. Eight years later, a few of these objectives had been obtained, and Iraq celebrated a great victory. The cost, however, had been enormous. Iraq may have lost 150,000 soldiers killed, incurred debts of $60 billion to other Arab states, suffered immense damage to Basra and other cities and, of course, earned the undying enmity of Iran, a much larger and richer neighbour. The war also led to the militarization of Iraqi society, and it was not at all certain that the Ba'ath party would always retain the loyalty of the army. In the euphoria of its victory parades and celebrations, in August 1988, the regime exulted in triumph. Later, the bills would come due.

The war was over, but the quarrel was not. Iranian and Iraqi delegations met in Geneva under the auspices of the UN, to convert the ceasefire agreement into a peace treaty. All the signs were that these would be long and arduous negotiations. To begin with, both sides continued to claim full sovereignty over the Shatt el-Arab waterway, and Iran continued to insist that Iraq be branded an aggressor.

The regime faced much unfinished business in other fields, too. First, there were
the Kurds, who tried incessantly to take advantage of Iraq's difficulties, and

whose leaders allied themselves with the Persians against the Arabs. They were not forgiven. In the last week of August, during the opening meetings of the Geneva conference, Iraq launched a new offensive in Kurdistan to wipe out one of the major resistance movements. Once again, Iraq used poison gas. (*See* The Kurds.)

Then there was the quarrel with Syria. Iraq's battle-tested armies were now free to reopen the question of the Euphrates dam (*see* Syria, p. 355) and reconsider the matter of Syria's alliance with Iran. Then there was Israel: since 1948, Iraq has been its noisy but ineffective enemy; it is much more formidable now and, among other matters, has yet to avenge the destruction of its nuclear reactor.

Lastly, there is the question of Iraq's future relations with the conservative Arab states to the south, with the West and with the USSR. Before the war, Iraq was on the worst of terms with Saudi Arabia and Kuwait, bitterly hostile to the United States, and allied to the Soviet Union. During the war, it became dependent on oil money from the conservative Arabs and to some extent upon arms sales from the West. The USSR faded out of the picture diplomatically, while continuing to provide the bulk of Iran's arms. The question now is whether Iraq will pursue its currently much improved relations with Washington, or revert to its previous hostility.

CHRONOLOGY OF THE IRAN–IRAQ WAR

1980

17 September	Saddam Hussein abrogates treaty with Iran on the Shatt el-Arab frontier, and claims whole river for Iraq. Iran rejects the claim.
22 September	Iraq bombs Tehran and invades Iran. It occupies Khorramshar and reaches the outskirts of Abadan before it is stopped. By the end of year, Iraq's offensive has failed.

1981

May	Iran's first counter-offensive pushes Iraq back from Abadan, and crosses border on central and northern fronts.

1982

29 March	Saddam Hussein proposes mutual withdrawal to frontier, and ceasefire. Iran rejects proposal.
24 May	Iran recaptures Khorramshar.

1984

22 February	Iran attacks on central front; captures Majnoon island.
27 March	Iraq starts tanker war in Persian Gulf with missile attacks on Iranian oil tankers. Iran retaliates by attacking Saudi and Kuwaiti tankers.
November	Iraq resumes diplomatic relations with US.

1985

11 March	Iran crosses the Tigris and attacks Basra; repulsed. The 'war of the cities' begins with missile attacks on Tehran and Baghdad.

1986

9 February	Iran crosses the Shatt el-Arab in night attack, and occupies the Faw peninsula.
25 February	Iran captures Chwarta in Iraqi Kurdistan.
12 August	Iraq bombs Iranian oil base on Sirri island in Persian Gulf.
24 December	Iran launches major offensive against Basra, and is repulsed after several weeks' fighting.

1987

23 April	Kuwait appeals for help in tanker war. U S agrees to 'reflag' Kuwaiti vessels, making them American, and to protect them.
17 May	Iraqi jet attacks USS *Stark*, killing 37 sailors.
20 July	UN Security Council resolution calls for ceasefire.
22 July	First US-flag tanker convoy escorted through Gulf by US Navy.

1988

16 March	Iranian offensive in Kurdistan takes Halabjah. Iraqi counter-attack, using gas, kills over 2000 civilians.
18 April	U S navy destroys two Iranian oil platforms, sinks six Iranian boats, in retaliation for mining of USS *Samuel B. Roberts*. Iraq recaptures Faw peninsula.
26 June	Iraq retakes Majnoon island.
3 July	USS *Vincennes* shoots down Iranian civilian airliner, killing 290 passengers and crew.
11 July	Iraq retakes Halabjah and other Kurdish areas occupied by Iran.
18 July	Iran announces it will accept immediate ceasefire.
30 August	Iraq launches a new offensive against the Kurds.

FURTHER READING

Bulloch, John, *The Persian Gulf Unveiled*, New York, St Martin's Press, 1985.

The Cambridge History of Islam, Cambridge University Press.

Dann, Uriel, *Iraq under Qassem*, New York, Praeger, 1969.

Helms, Christine Moss, *Iraq, Eastern Flank of the Arab World*, Washington, Brookings Institution, 1985.

Khaddouri, Majid, *The Gulf War: The Orgins and Implications of the Iraq–Iran Conflict*, Oxford University Press, 1988.

——, *Republican Iraq*, Oxford University Press, 1969.

——, *Socialist Iraq*, Washington D.C., Middle East Institute, 1978.

Marr, Phoebe, *The Modern History of Iraq*, Boulder, Colo., Westview Press, 1985.

Mortimer, Edward, *Faith and Power – The Politics of Islam*, London, Faber and Faber, 1982.

Penrose, Edith Tilton, Iraq: *International Relations and National Development*, London, E. Benn Boulder, Colo., Westview Press, 1978.

ISRAEL

Geography	7993 sq. miles (20,702 sq. km); about one-quarter the size of Scotland. Occupied territories: 2847 sq. miles (7115 sq. km).
Population	4.2 million Israeli citizens:

- 3.5 million (82.9%) Jews
- 550,000 (13.5%) Muslims
- 86,000 (2.3%) Christians
- 53,000 (1.3%) Druse

There has been no census of the Arab population of the occupied territories since 1967. In 1988, it was estimated to be:

- West Bank: 790,000
- Gaza strip 540,000
- East Jerusalem: 130,000

There are 12,000 Druse living on the Golan Heights. In 1987, there were about 51,000 Israelis living on the West Bank, 2000 in the Gaza strip, 6700 on the Golan Heights.

Refugees	385,630 people on the West Bank and 459,070 in the Gaza strip are classified as refugees by UNRWA (1988).
Casualties	As of 20 April 1988, the 40th anniversary of Israel's independence, the number of Israelis killed in the various wars and in lesser conflicts was computed to total 16,450.

During its pre-history as a Jewish colony in Palestine and for the first 20 years of its independence, Israel saw itself as David confronting an implacable Arab Goliath who was intent on its destruction. It was a reasonable enough myth. The turning-point came in 1967, when David defeated the combined armies of Egypt, Jordan, and Syria, and captured the Old City of Jerusalem and the heights of Samaria and Judea. Since then, Israel has been the dominant military power in the Levant, and all the international sympathy once felt for embattled David slowly leached away and was progressively transferred to the oppressed Palestinians. By 1982, when Israel invaded Lebanon and bombed Beirut, only the United States remained an unquestioning friend, partly because of the size of the Jewish community there, partly because the Soviet Union supported the Arabs, who became associated in the American public's mind with the forces of evil. Arab terrorists turned their weapons against Americans and, of course, cemented the American–Israeli alliance further.

When President Anwar Sadat of Egypt decided to make peace with Israel, the United States served the essential role of mediator. For ten years after that, successive American governments sought to persuade other Arab governments to follow Egypt's example, without success. The Arabs contended that it was impossible without the consent of the Palestinians, and that the true representative of the Palestinians was the PLO. Finally, in 1988, Yassir Arafat, the PLO's chairman, who had for decades refused to recognize Israel's existence and had promised to drive the Jews into the sea, bowed to reality and agreed that there should be two states between the Jordan river and the Mediterranean – Israel and Palestine – and that he must open negotiations with Israel to achieve this objective. The United States reluctantly but decisively accepted this transformation. Israel had lost its last diplomatic support, and was now alone against the world.

HISTORY

Not many nations have a birth certificate. Israel's took the form of a letter from Sir Arthur Balfour, British foreign secretary, to Lord Rothschild, dated 2 November 1917:

Dear Lord Rothschild,

I have much pleasure in conveying to you, on behalf of His Majesty's Government, the following declaration of sympathy with Jewish Zionist aspirations which has been submitted to, and approved by, the Cabinet:

'His Majesty's Government view with favour the establishment in Palestine of a national home for the Jewish people, and will use their best endeavours to facilitate the achievement of this object, it being clearly understood that nothing shall be done which may prejudice the civil and religious rights of the existing non-Jewish communities in Palestine, or the rights and political status enjoyed by Jews in any other country.'

I should be grateful if you would bring this declaration to the knowledge of the Zionist federation.

Yours sincerely,

Arthur Balfour

It will be noted that this 'Balfour Declaration' – with which the French government also associated itself – did not promise Palestine as the national home for the Jews – it promised a national home *in* Palestine. Nor did it define the territorial boundaries of Palestine.

Seventy years later, it is both impossible and profitless to establish whether Balfour and his colleagues were being disingenuous. It is at any rate clear that, within a very few years, the British government had discovered that the two promises in the Declaration could not both be kept: the Jews and the Palestinians could not both be satisfied.

One month after the Declaration was written, the British army commanded by Lord Allenby occupied Palestine: an Australian unit reached Bethlehem on Christmas Day, allegedly prompting a British trooper to remark, 'I'll bet the shepherds watched their flocks that night.' After the war, the British and French divided the Levant between them, the British taking Iraq and Palestine and the French taking Syria, as mandates under the League of Nations. Although the United States did not join the League, a resolution of Congress approved these arrangements.

In the absence of the United States, Britain and France controlled the League, and were therefore able to set the terms of the mandates to their satisfaction. These terms provided that the mandatory powers were to rule the territories in the interests of their inhabitants. The Balfour Declaration was incorporated into the British mandate for Palestine, making a 'national home for the Jews' an international obligation. The British and French defined the northern boundary of Palestine, now the frontier between Israel and Lebanon, and the British ceded eastern Palestine, known as Transjordan, to the Emir Abdullah ibn Hussein (*see* Syria, p. 329). The wishes of the Arab inhabitants of these territories were not considered, although President Wilson sent an investigative commission to the Levant, which concluded that the Arabs had no desire whatever to be subjected to a foreign government, but that if such subjection were unavoidable, they would prefer an American mandate to a British one, and a British mandate to a French one.

On 1 July 1920, Sir Herbert Samuel, a prominent British Jewish politician, assumed office as high commissioner in Palestine. On the Sabbath following the Feast of Ab, which commemorates the destruction of the Temple, Samuel attended services in the Great Synagogue in Jerusalem and read from the Book of Isaiah: 'Comfort ye, comfort ye my people, saith your God. Speak ye comfortably to Jerusalem, and cry unto her that her warfare is accomplished.' He was the first uncontested Jewish governor of Jerusalem since Titus had destroyed the Temple in AD 70.

This auspicious beginning soon deteriorated into ill-tempered conflict between the British mandatory power and the Jews in Palestine, and by the end of the mandate, Britain was actively trying to strangle Israel in its cradle. From the start, British relations with the Arabs were bad. That problem was compounded in 1921 by a mistake of Samuel's that would have disastrous consequences over the years. Samuel arranged for the election of Haj Amin al-Husseini as Grand Mufti of Jerusalem, hoping thus to appease the more radical Arabs. However, Husseini turned out to be a fanatical opponent of the British and the Zionists, and he went on to thwart all attempts at compromise and incited the Palestinians to repeated acts of terrorism. During World War II, he went to Berlin, and formed an alliance with Hitler.

PALESTINE

In the last years of Ottoman rule, Palestine was an obscure and decaying province of a declining empire. Jerusalem itself probably had a Jewish majority in the later 19th century, but in the rest of Palestine, the Jews were heavily outnumbered. Zionist claims that Palestine was unpopulated, or that its Arab inhabitants drifted in and out of the territory without establishing themselves, are entirely fanciful. The first Zionist immigrants settled along the coastal plain, and the first Jewish agricultural settlement, Petach Tikva, was founded in 1878, east of modern Tel Aviv. A number of other settlements were established before 1914, but the Jewish community was never very large. Serious immigration only began with the mandate.

At the time of the Balfour Declaration in 1917, the population of Palestine – that is, the area between the Jordan river and the Mediterranean – was stated to consist of about 610,000 Arabs (Muslim and Christian) and 50,000 Jews. The number of Jews had declined by one-third during World War I, because of Turkish persecution, but many of those who had fled the country returned after the British conquered Palestine, and were followed by a wave of Jewish immigrants. Among those who came back was David Ben Gurion, an immigrant from Russia, who had been expelled by the Turks for socialist agitation. By 1922, there were 84,000 Jews and 668,000 Arabs.

Jews bought land from the Arabs, often from absentee landowners, much of it completely valueless. In 1922, the Jewish Agency owned 148,263 acres (60,120 hectares), and by 1939, this had increased to 383,354 acres (155,140 hectares). The Jews drained the swamps and irrigated the desert; they established kibbutzim to cultivate and occupy the land. In a generation, the Jewish area, roughly half of habitable Palestine, was changed beyond recognition. The desert bloomed, forests were planted on the hills and the Jews built a city for themselves on the coast: Tel Aviv. It was founded in 1909, and within 30 years, people from Poland and Russia had created for themselves the life of a Mediterranean port, like Alexandria or Tunis, Piraeus, Marseille or Genoa.

Furthermore, the Jews in those first, all-important creative years laid out the institutions of a modern state. In 1919, a centralized Hebrew school system was set up, and the following year, Samuel decreed that Hebrew, along with Arabic and English, should be one of the state's official languages. In the same year, an elected Jewish assembly and the Histadrut (General Federation of Labour) were instituted. In 1921, a chief rabbinate was set up. In 1924, the Technicon (Israel Institute of Technology) was opened in Haifa and, in 1925, the Hebrew University in Jerusalem, on Mount Scopus. Also, in 1920, the Haganah, the military arm of the Jewish Agency was established, to protect Jewish settlements against banditry. From these beginnings, in a direct line, a quarter of a century later, came the social organizations, the political parties, the Knesset (parliament), the educational system and the army of independent Israel.

There was large-scale Jewish immigration into Palestine in the early 1920s, but in the latter part of the decade, it dropped to a trickle, and indeed, there was considerable Jewish emigration. Palestine was still a 'national home', not yet a refuge. The Soviet Union had clamped the gates shut on emigration, and Russian Jews were forced, therefore, to share with other Soviet citizens the delights of Bolshevism. However, even though the United States had ended free immigration, there was no great movement of Jewish emigration towards the alternative, Palestine. Poland alternated between bouts of anti-Semitism and liberalization, but France had recovered from the wave of anti-Semitism evinced in the Dreyfus affair, and the Weimar Republic in Germany had swept away the last restrictions on the Jews. It was a last flowering of European Jewry. In addition, it should be remembered that among the Jews, the Zionists were just one sect and by no means the most important. The 'national home' was considered by many to be an interesting experiment, but no more.

This reduction in Jewish immigration could also be put down to the fact that immigrants' lives in Palestine were hard, subject to constant difficulties from the British authorities and to the vagaries of Zionist funding from abroad. Furthermore, in the later 1920s, Palestine suffered a severe economic recession, and there was rapidly increasing Arab resentment at what Jewish immigration there was. Small-scale rioting became a normal feature of life, and there were frequent attacks on Jewish settlements. After a serious outbreak of Arab rioting in 1929, including the massacre of some 60 Jews in Hebron, the first of a series of British commissions went to Palestine; on their return, they (like the ones that followed) made the observation that free Jewish immigration and the rights of the Palestinian Arabs were mutually exclusive.

This was an academic point at the time, because Jewish immigration then was very low. However, from a total of 4075 immigrants in 1931, the number rose to 9553 in 1932, and this was followed by a great flood: in 1933, 30,327 Jews came to Palestine; in 1934, 42,359; and in 1935, 61,854. The British were therefore finally faced with the consequences of their promises. There was an Arab uprising in 1936 in which 80 Jews, 28 British and 197 Arabs were killed. The British attempted to solve their dilemma by restricting Jewish immigration, just as the greatest disaster in the modern history of the Jews was beginning.

THE HOLOCAUST

Hitler came to power on 30 January 1933. One of the fundamental tenets of the Nazi party was virulent anti-Semitism and, from the beginning of the Third Reich, the hand of the state was heavy upon the Jews. They were excluded from public life, from teaching and from the professions, and severe restrictions were put on their economic activities. The Nuremberg Laws of 15 September 1935, which deprived Jews of citizenship, further depressed the conditions of Jewish existence. For several years, however, persecution went no further. From 1933, many German Jews panicked and fled, some abandoning all their possessions because they were not allowed to take more than a derisory sum abroad. In the event, their panic and flight was shown to be the course of wisdom, and all those who counselled patience were deceived.

The persecution of the Jews increased sharply as Hitler consolidated his power in Germany, and built up the Reich's economic and military power. After the *Anschluss*, the annexation of Austria on 12 March 1938, Austrian Jews were subjected to brutalities and humiliations that were a harbinger of things to come. Adolf Eichmann, a Gestapo official of Austrian origin, was sent to Vienna to supervise the expulsion of as many Jews as possible, the confiscation of their property and their total exclusion from Austrian society. Hitler then decreed the expulsion from the Reich of all Jews of foreign nationality. On 7 November 1938, a junior German official in the embassy in Paris was assassinated by a 17-year-old Jewish student, whose family, of Polish origin, had lived in Germany since 1914, and had just been expelled. In revenge, the German government, under the direction of Goebbels, organized a nationwide pogrom against the Jews, on the night of 9/10 November – the *Kristallnacht* ('glass night'), so named because of the number of windows that were broken. Synagogues, homes and businesses were burned to the ground, over 100 Jews were murdered, and thousands were taken into 'protective custody' in concentration camps. They had to buy their way out.

From that moment, the Jews in Germany and Austria were desperate to escape, as were those in neighbouring countries, such as Czechoslovakia and Poland, which were evidently next on the list.

After the Arab uprising in 1936, the British sent another commission to Palestine, headed by Lord Peel. Dr Chaim Weizmann made an eloquent plea for the Jews trapped in Europe: 'There are in this part of the world six million people doomed to be pent up in places where they are not wanted, and for whom the world is divided into places where they cannot live, and places where they cannot enter.'

Peel concluded once again that Zionist and Arab aspirations were incompatible, and, for the first time, drew the inevitable conclusion: Palestine should be partitioned between a Jewish state and an Arab state, the latter to be federated with Transjordan. The Jews, at Dr Weizmann's urging, accepted the proposal, even though the area to be allocated to them was very small. The Arabs rejected it, a decision they have since had reason to regret: they have frequently been offered a separate state, but each time, as Israel expanded, the Arabs were offered less territory. The latest version was offered by the US secretary of state, George Shultz, in 1988; the Palestinians and Jordan still rejected it, and the Israeli government found procedural grounds for rejecting it, too.

The Arab insurrection continued from 1936 to 1939, when the British finally put it down, and during that period the Haganah expanded to defend Jewish settlements. Curiously, at a time when the British were bent on appeasing Germans and Arabs alike, the authorities in Palestine helped the Haganah. Orde Wingate, a Scottish officer and a passionate Zionist, organized night patrols to defend the Haifa pipeline, and many of the Israeli army's future leaders began their careers fighting at his side. For the first time in centuries, Jews fought to defend themselves. It turned out to be a lesson of crucial importance.

In the summer of 1938, President Roosevelt called an international conference at Evian in the French Alps to discuss the Jewish refugees. Delegates from 31 nations gathered to listen to the pleas of all the Jews of Central and Eastern Europe and then, in turn, to explain why nothing, unfortunately, could be done for them. The British were particularly insistent that a limit had been reached for emigration to Palestine.

After Evian, the United States agreed to take 30,000 German Jewish refugees a year, and Britain took an equal number. Of the 685,000 Jews in Germany and Austria, about 426,000 emigrated between 1933 and 1940. The 100,000 who reached the US, the 65,000 who reached Britain and the 140,000 who reached Palestine were saved. However, many went to France, Poland or, like the family of Anne Frank, the Netherlands, where the Gestapo eventually found them. The Jews of Eastern Europe had no escape.

The British called an Arab–Jewish conference in March 1939. It met in St James's Palace in London, and was a total failure. The Arabs – and, in particular, the Palestinians – made demands so extreme that they could never be accepted. They also refused to meet the Zionist delegation, and the Zionists therefore were spared the embarrassment of having to refuse the terms that the British wanted to propose. The day the conference broke up, Hitler occupied Prague.

The fall of Czechoslovakia was the direct result of the British government's policy of appeasement. After the final destruction of Czechoslovakia, Britain gave a guarantee to Poland and prepared for war. Appeasement was abandoned – as far as the Germans were concerned. However, calculating that the Jews would support Britain against Hitler no matter what, because they had no choice, and that in any event the Arabs were far more important to the war effort, the British government decided to appease the Arabs by selling out the Jews.

The 'infamous White Paper' was issued on 17 May 1939. It stated that Palestine would not be partitioned, that it would obtain its independence in 1949 and that Arabs and Jews should spend the next decade preparing for that event. Jewish immigration was to be strictly limited. In the year that Hitler laid his hand upon the 3 million Jews of Poland, Britain would permit only 35,000 Jews to enter Palestine. In each of the following four years, 10,000 more refugees would be granted entry, and for the remaining five years of the mandate, there would be no Jewish immigration without the consent of the Arabs.

This is considered by Jews today as part of their general betrayal by the democracies. However, it is important to remember that the Germans did not start systematically killing the Jews before Operation Barbarossa, the invasion of the Soviet Union, in June 1941; the Wannsee conference, at which the German government decided formally to murder all the Jews in Europe, took place in January 1942. The British and American officials who refused to admit Jews escaping from Germany considered them to be refugees from political and economic persecution, not people fleeing for their lives. Between 1933 and 1941, as the German armies occupied most of Europe, the Jews were seemingly in a not much worse position than the rest of the populations of Poland, Yugoslavia, Greece, France, Holland and the Soviet Union. In the course of World War II, a total of 25 million civilians, of all nationalities, races, ethnic groups and religions, were killed.

To the charge 'What did the Allies do to save the Jews?' the answer is that in September 1939, two years before the Holocaust began, Britain, France and the British dominions declared war on Germany, the only countries to do so before being attacked. In June 1941, the Soviet Union and, in the following December, the United States both involuntarily joined the war. The Allies fought Hitler to the death, and destroyed him. It was the Red Army that liberated Auschwitz, the British who liberated Belsen, the Americans who liberated Dachau.

The charge of which the Allies can be accused is not that they did nothing for the Jews: after all, they did defeat Hitler. It is that, before the war, they did not foresee the Holocaust, and provide for the Jews who wished to escape, and that after the murders began, they made no effort to save those few thousand who might have been smuggled out of Hitler's Europe.

The British maintained the policy of the White Paper, and restricted Jewish emigration to Palestine to a trickle. When refugee ships reached the eastern Mediterranean, they were forceably taken into Haifa and most of the refugees were then sent to Mauritius or Cyprus. The incident that the Israelis remember most vividly concerned a group of refugees from Roumania who managed to charter an ancient cattle boat, the *Struma*, and escape to Turkey at the end of 1941. They hoped to be sent overland to Palestine (the Germans controlled the Aegean), but the British refused to admit them. The Turks, therefore, would not let them land. The *Struma* sank off Istanbul on 24 February 1942, killing 767 people.

In 1942, the outside world learned about the Holocaust. It was a crime without precedent. Unlike many of the casualty figures given in this book, the number of those murdered has been computed accurately. The numbers of Jews in all the countries occupied by Hitler from 1939 is known. The number of those who escaped and those who survived is also known, and the usual demographic rules can be applied to determine the number of natural deaths and births during those six years. The total of Jews murdered comes to 5,820,000.

The Germans calculated that there were 10 million Jews in Europe, and they intended to kill all of them. In the end, they murdered more than one-third of all the Jews in the world. If they had defeated the Soviet Union, they would have completed their work in Europe, and if Rommel had defeated the British at El Alamein, the Germans would have conquered the Middle East, including Palestine, and the Holocaust would have been extended to the Jews there and to the Sephardic Jews of North Africa.

The Germans were crazily systematic. Elderly, bedridden Jews were carried on stretchers to trains in Holland, and shipped across all Europe to the death camps in eastern Poland, there to be murdered. As the Red Army drove back the Germans from the east, and even after the Western Allies had breached the Siegfried Line in the west, the Gestapo was still requisitioning trains to carry Jews to Auschwitz. Skilled Jewish workers, making munitions for the Wehrmacht, were sent to their deaths.

The Holocaust is the central event in the history of Israel. The Arabs argue, with much justification, that the world has made the Palestinians pay for crimes committed by Germans. They would have done better to make the moral effort to understand the effect of the memory of Auschwitz and Majdanek. The phrase 'Never again' is not a slogan, it is a programme. In particular, Nasser in 1967 would have profited from more understanding of this vital point.

THE END OF THE MANDATE

David Ben Gurion stated the Jewish position on the White Paper: 'We shall fight the war against Hitler as though there were no White Paper, and we shall fight the White Paper as though there were no war.' Virtually the whole Yishuv (the Jewish people in Palestine) followed his lead, the only exceptions being a tiny group of fanatics led by Avraham Stern, whose hatred of Britain led them to propose an anti-British alliance with Hitler. Although the Holocaust had not yet begun, it was still a bizarre proposal. It is only worth mentioning today because the 'Stern Gang', as the British called it, or 'Lehi' (Israel Freedom Fighters) as it was known in Hebrew, mounted attacks on British troops and assassinated a number of British officials during the war, and, in 1948, assassinated the UN commissioner, Count Bernadotte. One of its members was Itzak Shamir, later leader of the Likud party and prime minister of Israel.

Large numbers of Palestinian Jews served in the British armed forces, and late in the war, the British formed a Jewish Brigade that served in Italy. In Palestine itself, the Haganah was armed and trained by the British and its élite corps of commandos, the Palmach, was used in operations throughout the Middle East. The Stern Gang continued to attack the British, even as Rommel's armies were at the gates of Cairo. Stern himself was killed in a shootout in Tel Aviv in June 1942. In October 1944, the survivors of the gang assassinated Lord Moyne, the British minister resident in the Middle East, in Cairo. Ben Gurion and the

Haganah then cooperated with the British in rounding up the terrorists in Palestine, and Ben Gurion used the opportunity to settle accounts with the Revisionists. These comprised the right-wing opposition party, the Herut (Liberals), led by Menachem Begin; their military arm was the Irgun Zvai Leumi (Etzel). The political battle between the two factions continues to this day.

After the war, the British continued the policy of the 1939 White Paper. Jewish immigration was, in theory, sharply limited: the hundreds of thousands of survivors then in resettlement camps in Europe would stay there. The Arabs in Palestine would be supported and a 'bi-national state', dominated by the Arabs, would be set up. In fact, however, about 200,000 immigrants were able to reach Palestine between 1944 and 1948. The British thus enraged the Jews by announcing a policy of refusing immigration, while in fact permitting it and so enraging the Arabs.

It was an extraordinary period. The same government that gave India its independence in 1947 continued to play the imperial game in the Middle East as though nothing had changed. The British nowadays insist that they nobly gave away their empire, unlike the French, who fought to keep theirs. This is not true. The British had to be forced out of India, and they clung to portions of the Middle East for more than 20 years after the war. A mixture of force and political pressure had to be used to prize them loose from Iraq, Egypt, Palestine and Aden.

Ben Gurion turned to the Americans for support. He demanded that 100,000 refugees should be permitted to emigrate to Palestine, and President Truman supported the demand. There was a war of independence in Palestine, with the Haganah and Irgun fighting the British, but compared with other such wars, it was not very violent. Ben Gurion's calculation was that British public opinion, exhausted from World War II, and horrified by the discovery of the camps in Europe (particularly Belsen), would not tolerate the situation for long.

The most dramatic incident in the conflict occurred on 22 July 1946, when the King David Hotel in Jerusalem, which was being used as British military head-quarters, was blown up. The explosion killed 25 British, 40 Arabs and 17 Jews. It was a reprisal for a major British security operation in June, and had been ordered by Begin after a misunderstanding between the Haganah and Irgun. Ben Gurion and the Haganah commanders bitterly denounced the attack – though their own involvement was far greater than they admitted.

On 29 July, the British hanged three Irgun terrorists, and the next day, Begin ordered the hanging of two British hostages, sergeants captured earlier. Their bodies were booby-trapped and hung upside down in a grove where the British would find them. This action, like the murders of Moyne and Bernadotte and, later, the Deir Yassin massacre, were a disgrace to the Israeli cause, and have been particularly remembered when Begin, Shamir or their apologists have denounced Arab terrorism. At the time, most Israelis were horrified and never tried to justify Jewish terrorism. That remains a fundamental difference between most Israelis and most Palestinians.

Ben Gurion's calculation was correct. The British had no stomach for the fight, and on 18 February 1947, the foreign secretary, Ernest Bevin, announced that they would abandon the mandate. In May, the United Nations set up a Special Committee on Palestine (UNSCOP) which recommended the country's 277 partition into two states. Count Bernadotte, a Swedish diplomat who had played a considerable role in saving the surviving Jews in Europe during the last months of the war, was made UN commissioner to Palestine. After he was murdered, he was succeeded by the black American diplomat, Ralph Bunche. The UN partition plan was approved by the General Assembly on 27 November.

Once again, the Jews accepted it, although the proposed frontiers were indefensible, and the Arabs rejected it *in toto*. The British announced that they would evacuate Palestine on 15 May 1948, whether the UN was ready to administer the territory or not.

THE FIRST ARAB–ISRAELI WAR

The Palestinians prepared for war, aided by the armies of neighbouring Arab states. The most formidable of these turned out to be the Arab Legion, the army of Emir Abdullah of Transjordan (later Jordan). Its commander, Lieutenant General Sir John Glubb, and many of its officers were British, and the Arab officers had been trained by them. The wars between the Arabs and Israelis have demonstrated with great force the truth of the old adage that there are no bad soldiers, only bad officers. The Arab armies in 1948–9 (except the Arab Legion) performed badly because they were badly led, and the Israeli army performed brilliantly because it was brilliantly led. In 1973, the Israelis were much disconcerted to discover that, with good officers, both Egyptian and Syrian troops could be formidable soldiers.

In 1948, not only were the Arab armies badly led, but the Arab states were corrupt, incompetent and constantly squabbling among themselves. There was no coordination between the attacking forces, and Israel's scanty forces and still more scanty armaments could be moved between fronts without disaster.

The fighting started before the British left, and the British showed a clear partiality towards the Palestinian guerrillas over the Jews. The most shameful episode occurred on 13 April 1948, when a Jewish convoy tried to relieve Mount Scopus, just east of Jerusalem, where the Hebrew University and Hadassah hospital were under siege. They were ambushed by the Arabs. Most of the 80 or so people in the convoy were medical staff, doctors and nurses, but there were troops and munitions as well. The British had outposts in the area but did not intervene, despite repeated pleas from Jewish officials. The entire convoy was wiped out.

A much more dramatic and important incident had occurred a few days earlier, on 9 April, when a troop of Irgun guerrillas fought a skirmish at the Arab village of Deir Yassin, west of Jerusalem, and then massacred over 250 Arabs, almost all of them civilians. Begin was theoretically responsible, because he commanded the Irgun. In some mitigation, it has been suggested that he was merely a political figurehead, offering a figleaf of respectability to the Irgun terrorists. Certainly he was never a military man, nor himself involved in terrorism (unlike Shamir).

News of the massacre spread rapidly and played a decisive part in inducing Arabs to flee. There has been a continuous debate ever since over the responsibility for the refugee problem, with Israelis arguing that the Arabs ordered civilians to leave the battle zone for their own safety, and Arabs claiming that the Israelis followed a policy of mass terror. In the BBC recordings of all the broadcasts emanating from Arab capitals at the time, there are no instances of official Arab incitements to civilians to flee. Quite the contrary: people were urged to stay in their villages. However, in some cases local Arab commanders did undoubtedly urge civilians to get out of the way. Conversely, there was no deliberate Israeli policy of driving out the Arabs, though there were undoubtedly times where local commanders did just that. A more typical case was Haifa, where the Jewish authorities begged the Arabs to stay, but they left anyway.

One Deir Yassin was enough. The Arabs fled. But civilians always try to escape: the modern history of Europe is filled with desperate columns of refugees escaping from one invading army or another. In 1967, tens of thousands of Arabs on the West Bank fled from the Israelis instinctively, as they had in 1948, though there were no massacres. When they discovered that there was no danger, they went home again. By the end of the fighting in 1949, about 800,000 Arabs were refugees. They, and their descendants, form the heart of the Arab–Israeli problem today.

As the British pulled back to the ports, Jews and Arabs fought for control of the areas they had evacuated. The Jews tried to defend all their settlements but, after a bloody defeat at Etzion, south of Jerusalem, accepted that some places would have to be abandoned. (It is notable how few were permanently lost.) The last British commander left Haifa on 15 May. The day before, in Tel Aviv, David Ben Gurion had proclaimed the independence of Israel.

The armies of Lebanon, Syria, Jordan and Egypt immediately invaded Israel, to join the Palestinian 'Arab Liberation Army'. The war lasted until 7 January 1949, punctuated by two truces. Israel's victory over the Palestinians, Lebanese and Syrians was complete. The whole of northern Palestine was conquered, and at the end of the war, Israeli troops were in contol of much of southern Lebanon. On the central front, the Israelis and the Arab Legion fought to a standstill. The Legion seized Latrun, a dominant position on the Tel Aviv–Jerusalem road, and held it against repeated Israeli attacks. They occupied the Old City of Jerusalem, including all the major shrines, drove the Jews out of the Jewish Quarter, and besieged Jewish West Jerusalem. The siege was broken when the Israelis constructed a 'Burma road' through the hills to bypass Latrun, and after the war, they left the wrecks of the tanks and armoured cars that had been destroyed along the 'Jerusalem corridor', as memorials to the fighting. The Jordanians retained the high ground of Palestine – Samaria and Judea – as well as the Old City of Jerusalem. These territories came to be known as the 'West Bank'.

In the south, the Israelis defeated the Egyptians decisively and drove them out of the whole country except for the Gaza strip. They were prevented from occupying that last pocket by threats from the British: when an Israeli force invaded Sinai and advanced on El Arish on the north coast, threatening to cut off the Egyptians in Gaza, the British informed Israel that they would intervene, under the terms of their treaty with Egypt, unless Israel withdrew immediately. Faced with *force majeure*, Israel complied. The RAF patrolled the Sinai to make sure Israel had withdrawn: the Israeli air force shot down five British Spitfires. Seven years later, Egypt abrogated the treaty with Britain, and the following year, 1956, Britain and Israel invaded Egypt together.

During the Israeli offensive against the Egyptians in October 1948, an Egyptian brigade of about 4000 men was cut off at Faluja, a small town north-east of Gaza. The brigade remained under siege until the final armistice with Egypt 279 was signed in Rhodes, on 24 February 1949. They put up a highly creditable defence, and the Israelis gave them full military honours when they marched out. Among them was Major Gamal Abdel Nasser who later recounted that the idea of forming a group of 'free officers' to overthrow the regime which he blamed for the disaster first occurred to him during that four months' siege.

The armistice negotiations were conducted under UN auspices. The agreement with Lebanon, under which Israel withdrew its forces from that country, was signed on 23 March; the armistice with Jordan was signed on 3 April, and with Syria on 20 July. In the meanwhile, between 6 and 10 March, the Israelis had sent a small force down the length of the Negev desert to occupy the hamlet of Um-Rashrash on the Gulf of Aqaba. They renamed it Eilat.

The first war against the Arabs was the most costly of Israel's wars: just over 6000 Israelis were killed, including over 4000 soldiers. It was also the most dangerous and difficult. The victories in 1956 and 1967 were more dramatic, but the war of independence was the war of survival, in which Israel's very existence was in doubt.

ISRAEL AND THE ARABS

The Arabs who had signed armistice agreements with Israel in 1949 continued to refuse to recognize its existence. They referred to 'occupied Palestine', promised the refugees that they would soon return home in glory, and prepared for the next war. The Arabs' policy towards Israel consisted of bombast interspersed with bombing. The chief sufferers were the refugees, in the Gaza strip, on the West Bank and in Lebanon. They led a life of unrelieved squalor, like American Indians on reservations, supported only by the United Nations Relief Works Agency (UNRWA). The inhabitants of Gaza were not even allowed to leave that territory, which became a huge concentration camp. Refugees elsewhere were hardly better off.

The Arabs' defeat in 1948 was followed by a string of upheavals. The Egyptian prime minister was assassinated on 12 December 1948. The first of a long series of coups occurred in Syria on 30 March 1949, and King Farouk of Egypt was deposed by the Free Officers on 26 July 1952.

Abdullah had annexed the West Bank to his emirate, Transjordan, made himself king and gave the kingdom the new name of Jordan. Only Britain and Pakistan recognized the annexation. He was secretly negotiating frontier adjustments with Israel, and had initialled an agreement designed to lead to a peace treaty when, on 20 July 1951, he was shot outside the El-Aqsa Mosque in Jerusalem. His 16-year-old grandson, Hussein, who was with him at the time, became king a year later, when his father was declared insane.

The Arab leaders were by now prisoners of their own rhetoric. They had promised to destroy Israel, and if they tried another road, they might be killed.

Nasser was the driving force behind the new Egyptian government and, in due course, made himself president. He discovered a talent for demagogic rhetoric and was soon behaving like a latter-day Mussolini, rousing the crowds with exhortations and dreams of national grandeur. He promised to unite all Arabs, like the caliphs of old, but it turned out that, in his vision, the caliphate would be a

Nasserite empire ruled from Cairo.

His first success was to drive out the British, who had first occupied Egypt 80 years earlier and had remained camped along the Suez canal. They had no business there, ten years after the war, and went sulkily, in the summer of 1956. Nasser then initiated the first terror campaign against Israel, arming and training Palestinian *'fedayeen'* to cross the border and attack Israeli targets from the Gaza strip and from Jordan. Israel began to retaliate.

Nasser's socialistic pronouncements and anti-imperialist speeches annoyed the British and Americans. Late in 1955, he made a deal to buy huge quantities of arms from Czechoslovakia. This was the Soviet bloc's first introduction to the Middle East and displeased London and Washington still further. Nasser gave every support to the FLN in Algeria who were in revolt against the French, and so added France to his list of opponents. His great domestic ambition was to dam the Nile at Aswan. The United States had offered to finance the project, but, in July 1956, after the Czech arms deal, it pulled out. Nasser retaliated by nationalizing the Suez canal.

THE SUEZ CAMPAIGN

Israel had by then established itself as a functioning, modern state. It had taken in over 800,000 immigrants, half of them from Arab countries. The Haganah had been developed into a modern and highly efficient citizens' army – the Israeli Defence Force (*Zahal* in Hebrew).

The terrorist attacks across the border were by now becoming intolerable. The Arab states, who had agreed at Rhodes to pursue negotiations towards a permanent peace treaty, had done nothing of the sort, and now Nasser was evidently planning to reverse the verdict of 1948, and reconquer Palestine.

In the summer of 1956, Israel and France began secret negotiations to mount a joint attack on Egypt. Later, they were joined by the British. Their plan was to overthrow Nasser. Israel wanted to clear out the *fedayeen* bases in the Gaza strip, and hoped that a further defeat would impel Egypt to negotiate for a peace treaty. France aimed to end Egyptian support for the FLN. British participation in the conspiracy is much more difficult to explain. The prime minister, Sir Anthony Eden, and the foreign secretary, Selwyn Lloyd, claimed that allowing Nasser to get away with nationalizing the Suez canal would be an act of appeasement comparable to the Munich agreement of 1938, which set the stage for World War II. What were never clearly examined were Britain's long-term interests in the Middle East, which were to ensure tranquillity, keep out the Soviets and assure oil supplies. The Suez campaign was to have the exact opposite results.

The Israelis crossed the border on 29 October 1956. Paratroopers seized the Mitla pass in western Sinai, and by 1 November, the Israelis had taken the whole of eastern and central Sinai. Another attack at Rafah, the southern end of the Gaza strip, cut off the Egyptian forces there, and by 2 November, the Israelis had reached the Suez canal. In a last detail, a commando raid occupied Sharm El-Sheikh at the southern tip of the peninsula on 4 November. The victory was complete. Nasser lost most of his army's tanks and other heavy equipment.

The British and French were astonished at the speed of Israel's victory – they had planned a leisurely invasion. On 31 October, the two governments had issued an ultimatum, ordering both sides to withdraw from the canal. Israel had promptly accepted; Egypt had understandably rejected it. The British then had bombed Egyptian air bases, wiping out the Egyptian air force. An invasion fleet had set sail from Malta on 1 November, after the war was all but finished. British paratroops landed in the canal zone on 5 November, and on the 6th, British and French troops landed at Port Said. The operation has become known as the 'Suez affair', but in fact, the British never reached the town of Suez, which is at the southern end of the canal.

British and French dilatoriness allowed international opposition to reach hurricane proportions. President Eisenhower threatened economic reprisals, and the Soviet Union offered to send troops to Syria and Egypt. That was bluff: at the time, the USSR was fully engaged in suppressing the Hungarian uprising. There was a run on the British pound, and British troops were scarcely ashore before the order came to cease fire. The whole operation ended in a humiliating fiasco. The ceasefire took effect at midnight on 6 November, and the British and French soon withdrew from Egypt, leaving the Israelis to fend for themselves. Under strong American pressure, they finally left the Gaza strip in March 1957. Their occupation of the strip had been marred by two incidents: on 3 November, immediately after the fighting, Israeli troops panicked and killed 275 civilians at Khan Younis; and on 12 November, they killed 111 Palestinians in a refugee camp at Rafah.

A UN peacekeeping force was set up in Sinai to separate Egyptians and Israelis. One of its posts was at Sharm El-Sheikh, and Israel was at last able to develop Eilat and to send ships through the Strait of Tiran into the Red Sea. President Eisenhower guaranteed that the strait would be kept open by whatever means were necessary.

THE SIX DAY WAR

The next Arab–Israeli war blew up abruptly and unexpectedly in the spring of 1967. It was provoked by Syria, where the Ba'ath party had just taken power and needed to demonstrate its revolutionary and anti-Zionist zeal.

From the Golan Heights, Syrian artillery positions could shell Israeli villages in Galilee, and did so. In addition, the Palestine Liberation Army – the military wing of the Palestine Liberation Organization (PLO) founded in 1965 and led by Ahmed Shukeiri – had begun raiding across the border from Jordan and Syria. At the same time, Syria, Jordan and Lebanon planned to divert the headwaters of the Jordan river, to deprive Israel of two-thirds of its water. The Israelis announced that diverting the water would be tantamount to a declaration of war, and so would closing the Strait of Tiran or stationing non-Jordanian Arab troops on the West Bank.

On 7 April 1967, after the Syrians shelled Israeli villages again, the Israeli air force was sent to attack the gun positions. The Syrian air force was sent to defend them, and lost six MiGs to Israel's French-built Mystères. Syria feared that Israel intended to mount a pre-emptive strike against it, and appealed to Egypt for help. The Soviet Union informed Egypt that Israel had massed 11 brigades along the northern frontier – a report that was completely untrue.

Nasser was at a low point. His armies were involved in a hopeless war in North Yemen (*see* The Yemens, pp. 338–41); his influence in Jordan, Syria and

Iraq was non-existent; and his relations with Saudi Arabia were violently hostile. His dreams of pan-Arabism had gone aglimmering. So he seized the opportunity to mount a political offensive against Israel.

There has been much debate since whether he had ever intended to go to war. Certainly, he was not ready for it when it came – which is another count against him. His apologists claim that all his rhetoric was bluff, that he had had no intention of fighting – but heads of government of major countries cannot complain when their pronouncements are taken seriously. He closed the Strait of Tiran, formed a joint military command with Syria and Jordan, mobilized his armies and moved them into Sinai, and announced that the final war for the liquidation of Israel was imminent. There have not been many occasions since 1945 when military action has been wholly justified. The Six Day War was one of them.

Tensions escalated rapidly in May. On 17 May, Nasser demanded that the UN pull its peacekeeping force out of Sinai, and the secretary-general, U Thant, did so immediately, to the amazement and scandal of Israel and many other members of the UN. On 20 May, Nasser sent seven divisions into the Sinai. Tourists fled Israel, except for a few hardy souls who stayed for the battle and were then drafted to dig tank traps. The place of the missing tourists was taken by hordes of foreign journalists expecting war, who came for a ringside seat.

On 2 May, Nasser declared the Strait closed. Israel called on the United States to honour Eisenhower's promise made in 1956. The State Department had never heard of it. Hasty research produced a copy of the letter in the presidential library at Abilene, Kansas, but the Israelis were informed that the promise had expired when Ike had left office. They learned, to their dismay, of the discontinuities between administrations: only a treaty ratified by the US Senate is binding.

President Johnson and the British government tried to mediate, to find a way of guaranteeing freedom of navigation through the Strait without actually enforcing it. Negotiations might take some weeks – and since Israel used the passage relatively seldom, there was no hurry. Then, on 26 May, Nasser, in a speech in Cairo, announced that the time had come to destroy Israel. All Araby was mobilized: Israel was surrounded by 250,000 enemy troops. Furthermore, Israel could not wait. It had mobilized its armies – that is, the entire able-bodied manhood of the country – and it could not maintain that status for very long.

Then France, which had been Israel's staunchest ally, suddenly abandoned it. General de Gaulle informed Israel that it should reach a compromise with Egypt. The Israeli prime minister, Levi Eshkol, formed a government of national unity, invited Menachem Begin into the Cabinet for the first time and made Moshe Dayan (who had been chief of staff in 1956) minister of defence.

On the Arab side, King Hussein submitted to overwhelming pressure. To save his throne and perhaps his life, he gave in to the general hysteria and made his peace with Nasser. The Jordanian army was put under the command of an Egyptian general.

Nasser had decided that he would strangle Israel. If it accepted the closing of the Strait, it would be a great victory for him. If it tried to break out, the overwhelming Arab superiority would defeat the attempt – and then Israel would be crushed. What he failed to take into account was that the government in Tel Aviv could make the same calculations.

The Israelis undertook a campaign of strategic deception. On the weekend beginning Friday, 2 June, they demobilized part of their armed forces and lowered the state of alert of the remainder. The beaches were crowded. Dayan gave a press conference and remarked that he expected nothing to happen for several weeks, or months. It seemed that the crisis was diminishing. The British ambassador informed his government there would be no war, and the first wave of returning journalists (from the *Sunday Times*) left for home on Monday morning. As their plane flew peacefully over the blue Mediterranean, the pilot informed them on the intercom that the war had begun.

The formal decision to fight was taken at the weekly cabinet meeting on Sunday, 4 June. Soldiers and airmen were recalled from the beaches, and the army moved into position. At 7.45 the following morning, Monday, 5 June, the Israeli air force attacked the Egyptians. They flew low across the Mediterranean, under the sightline of the Egyptian radar (but watched by the British on radar from Cyprus; they gave first news of the war to London). Then they turned inland, and attacked Egypt from the west – the wrong way. Egyptian pilots had expected a traditional dawn attack, out of the rising sun, and had waited in their aircraft every morning. When the attack did not come, they went to breakfast. Thus, the Israelis caught the Egyptian air force on the ground, defenceless, and they destroyed it.

In 500 sorties, the Israelis destroyed 309 out of Egypt's 340 combat-ready planes, including all 30 long-range bombers. The Egyptians promptly announced that they had destroyed 400 Israeli planes. Believing the boast, the Syrian and Jordanian air forces attacked Israel. By the evening, the Jordanian air force had been wiped out, Syria had lost two-thirds of its aircraft and an Iraqi squadron was destroyed on the ground at a base in Jordan. In all, the Israelis destroyed 393 Arab aircraft on the ground and 58 in the air, with an Israeli loss of 26.

Then the Israeli army attacked the Egyptians. An official Israeli announcement later stated that the Egyptians had attacked first, and the Israelis 'went out to meet them'. This was untrue. The Israelis again drove through the Egyptian army at Rafah, cutting off the Gaza strip, attacked the Egyptians in central Sinai, and then advanced north to the coast and due west across the peninsula.

They had complete control of the air, and used it with devastating effect. The lasting memory of the war is the image of 20-mile (32-km) convoys of Egyptian vehicles, heading west towards safety, strung out along the roads in the Sinai, each vehicle destroyed. The Israelis first hit the tanks at the head of the convoys, then the ones at the rear, and then destroyed everything in between at their leisure.

In four days, they reached the Suez canal. The Egyptians had lost 15,000 men by Israeli count, 10,000 by their own. Since the Israelis buried the bodies, their figure is reliable. Israel had taken 5000 prisoners, and an enormous booty in vehicles and weapons. Nasser admitted his army had lost 80 per cent of its heavy equipment.

The war incited passionate interest all over the world. Jews everywhere rallied to Israel's support, and the world's press flooded into the Middle East. The *Sunday Times* reporters turned around and flew back to Cyprus, with a number of others. (One of them was Norman Fowler, home affairs correspondent for *The Times*. From Cyprus, he hired a boat that landed him in Beirut and promptly departed. The local authorities gave him a one-hour visa, which fortunately sufficed to get him to the British embassy, which then organized a longer-term visa. He is now a senior member of the British cabinet.)

At the outset of the war, King Hussein was informed through the UN that Israel would not attack Jordan unless provoked. The Israelis expected the Jordanian air attack, and perhaps a small token ground offensive, and were prepared to ignore them. However, the Egyptian general commanding the Jordanian army, General Riadh, ordered a general offensive. King Hussein, perhaps misled by the lies put out by Nasser and Egyptian headquarters, and believing a great Arab victory was under way, allowed the attack to take place. The Jordanians shelled Tel Aviv and West Jerusalem, and moved their troops forward to threaten the Tel Aviv–Jerusalem road.

On the first day, the Israelis held the Jordanians off. On the second, they encircled East Jerusalem and drove in the Jordanian defences on the northern and southern flanks of the West Bank. On the third day, Wednesday, 7 June, they completed the occupation of the whole of the West Bank, capturing Hebron, Nablus and Ramallah, and seized the Old City of Jerusalem. For the first time since 1948, Jews said their prayers at the Wailing Wall and the chief rabbi blew the *shofar* in triumph.

Thursday was devoted to mopping up in the Sinai. The Israelis returned to Sharm El-Sheikh. The government debated whether to complete the agenda by dealing with Syria, which had shelled Galilee but had otherwise played no part in the war. The UN Security Council was in session, and the Soviet Union was trying to arrange a ceasefire before its friends were completely destroyed. The Israelis felt that the Syrians had started the fight, and should pay the price, and they also wanted to protect northern Israel against future attack.

Therefore, on Friday, 9 June, the Israeli army stormed straight up the cliffs overlooking Lake Tiberias. In two days' fighting, they cleared the Golan Heights, capturing Kuneitra and huge quantities of Syrian armaments. The road to Damascus was open when Syria finally accepted a ceasefire.

Israel lost 705 men in the Six Day War, the Arabs 20,000–25,000.

THE WAR OF ATTRITION

The period between the 1967 and 1973 wars was a violent one. President Nasser launched a war of attrition against Israeli positions on the eastern shore of the Suez canal, on the assumption that Israel's reluctance to take casualties and Egypt's superiority in heavy artillery would give him the advantage. The Israelis protected themselves by building an immense line of fortifications along the canal to house their garrisons: the 'Bar Lev line', named after their chief of staff. It was the largest work of engineering undertaken in Israeli history.

Israel retaliated against the incessant Egyptian attacks by using their air superiority to hit targets all over Egypt. In addition, Israeli commandos blew up power lines near the Aswan dam and captured an entire radar station on the Gulf of Suez and carried it back in triumph; another raid set fire to the refineries at Suez, creating a spectacular blaze that lasted for days. The Israelis attacked military installations near Cairo, and this eventually induced Nasser to call on the Soviets for help. The Soviets constructed greatly improved anti-aircraft defences west of the canal. They also sent their latest surface-to-air SAM-3 missiles to Egypt, with 285

Soviet crews, and Soviet pilots began flying missions in Egypt: suddenly, the war between Egypt and Israel had reached dangerous levels.

A ceasefire was arranged on 8 August 1970, and the Egyptians and their Soviet allies immediately began to move their defences forward, so that an Egyptian attack across the canal would be protected against the Israeli air force. For their part, the Israelis used the ceasefire to strengthen the Bar Lev line, despite suggestions that it was a new Maginot line. As the ceasefire continued, Israel reduced its defensive positions along the canal.

Nasser died suddenly on 28 September 1970, and his successor, Anwar el-Sadat, postponed the plans for an immediate attack across the canal. Sadat proved a more patient and subtle leader than Nasser, and an altogether more formidable opponent of Israel.

THE YOM KIPPUR WAR

President Sadat sent his armies across the Suez canal on Yom Kippur, the Day of Atonement, 6 October 1973. He achieved complete tactical surprise. He had repeatedly announced an imminent offensive – and nothing had happened. The Israelis therefore assumed that he was all bluff and no substance. The Egyptian and Syrian armies had frequently conducted exercises near the front lines without attacking. When they did so again, in September 1973, it was not taken seriously.

Syrian manoeuvres were put down to nervousness following an aerial dogfight in which the Israeli air force shot down 13 Syrian planes on 13 September. Even the abrupt departure from Alexandria of visiting Soviet ships and the evacuation from Egypt and Syria of the families of Soviet military personnel on 5 October did not alert the Israelis or the Americans. Most serious of all, the Israelis underestimated their enemy. The high command did not share the general contempt felt by many Israelis for the Arabs, but they were guilty of overconfidence. Henry Kissinger observed that 'the October surprise was the culmination of a failure of *political* analysis on the part of its victims'. The Israelis were certain that they would win any war, knew that Egypt and Syria must understand that Israel's victory was virtually assured, and therefore assumed that the Arabs would not attack. But Sadat was after a political, not a military victory.

He had concluded that Egypt could only recover the Sinai and reopen the Suez canal, which had remained closed since 1967, through negotiations with Israel. But he must approach those negotiations as an equal, not as a defeated suppliant. Ever since the Six Day War, Israel, in the standard phrase, had been waiting for the phone call in which the Arabs would propose peace. But no Arab could make such a call after a defeat: King Abdullah had done so, and had been killed for it. (After his huge political victory in the Yom Kippur War, Sadat did make that call – and he, too, was shot. It was a depressing lesson for other Arab leaders.)

Sadat's war was a close-run thing. Israel won the fighting on the ground and, but for American pressure, would have destroyed the Egyptian army – and Sadat himself. Sadat had a Soviet promise of support against defeat, but at the last moment, the Soviets backed down in the face of American support for Israel. The Americans then insisted that Israel hold its hand. It could have won a total victory – but what would have been the point of that?

The most conspicuous difference between 1973 and previous wars was that the Egyptians and Syrians fought well, bravely and tenaciously; they never broke and ran, as they had in 1956 and 1967. It was the first truly modern war – with a full panoply of missiles and electronic defences – and only the Battle of Kursk in 1943 had involved more tanks.

The chief features of the Bar-Lev line, along the eastern bank of the canal, were its high banks of sand. When they attacked, the Egyptians blasted through the artificial dunes with water cannon. The crossing was relatively easy, and soon Egypt had two large armies on the eastern bank; the initial Israeli counterattacks were beaten off with heavy losses.

At the same time, Syria attacked across the Golan Heights. This was more dangerous to Israel. Syrian tanks almost reached the escarpment overlooking Galilee before they were stopped by the heroic efforts of the vastly outnumbered Israelis. Syria had attacked with 1400 tanks and, in the course of the war, was to lose 1150 of them.

When the Israelis counterattacked, they managed to drive the Syrians back towards Damascus, but they were then stopped by a flank attack mounted by two Iraqi armoured divisions and a Jordanian armoured brigade. The Iraqis did not fight particularly well – not nearly as well as the Egyptians and Syrians – but their presence diverted the Israelis from their intention of moving to within artillery range of Damascus.

On the southern front, after the Egyptians had established themselves across the canal, they mounted a large-scale assault on Israeli positions, on 14 October. The battle involved 2000 tanks, and the Israelis beat back the attack. By then, the war had lasted far longer than Israel, or anyone else, had expected. The Soviets had begun an airlift of supplies to the Egyptians and Syrians, and on 9 October, the Israelis appealed to the US for help: they were running out of ammunition and had lost 49 planes and 500 tanks (though many of these had been lost through poor maintenance). On 13 October, President Nixon ordered a full-scale resupply airlift, taking tanks and planes out of American depots to replace Israeli losses. The American airlift consisted of 20 flights a day, carrying 2000 tons of material, far outdistancing the Soviet effort.

The Israelis counterattacked through a gap in the Egyptian front and across the canal on 16 October, and for a crucial 24 hours, local Egyptian commanders did not realize what was happening. It was a perilous operation: for one thing, it was several days before the supply route was assured. After that, things moved rapidly, as the Israelis drove south to encircle the Egyptian 3rd Army. The Arabs asked for a ceasefire, and Henry Kissinger, the US secretary of state, flew to Moscow on 20 October to settle the terms.

UN Security Council Resolution 338, passed just after midnight on 22 October, provided for a ceasefire with the armies in place, to be followed by negotiations for a lasting peace. The Israelis, however, had not completed the encirclement of the 3rd Army. They violated the ceasefire and reached Suez, on the western bank of the canal at its southern extremity, on 24 October.

The 3rd Army's 45,000 men and 250 tanks were now cut off on the eastern bank and in Suez. Israel wanted to destroy them and only refrained from doing so under extreme pressure from the Americans. Sadat demanded a joint US–Soviet force to   287 patrol the ceasefire line and, when Nixon rejected the idea out of hand, invited the Soviets to send an army on its own. The Soviet Union had put seven divisions on alert and, on the 23rd, informed Washington that it would accede to the Egyptian request. That would have meant war between the USSR and Israel. Kissinger informed Sadat, regretfully, that if the Soviets went to Egypt, the US would fight them, on his territory. At midnight, American forces worldwide were put on 'DefCon III'. (American forces have five degrees of 'defence condition', ranging from 'DefCon V,' peacetime, to 'DefCon I', all-out war.) The Soviets backed down.

So did Israel. The Egyptians were allowed to send medical supplies, food and water to their isolated 3rd Army, and negotiations for a disengagement began at Kilometre 101 on the Suez–Cairo road. There followed a period of intense diplomacy, conducted by Henry Kissinger, as a result of which the Israelis and Egyptians signed a disengagement agreement on 17 January 1974, and the Israelis and Syrians on 31 May. The Israelis pulled back from the Suez canal to the line of the hills to the east, and Egypt was at last able to reopen the canal and free the ships that had been trapped since 5 June 1967. On the Golan Heights, Israel agreed to withdraw slightly behind the 1967 line, and the Syrians recovered Kuneitra. Demilitarized zones were established along both fronts.

ISRAEL AND THE ARABS

The Yom Kippur War demonstrated that Israel was not invincible, and it restored Arab pride. It did not, however, lead immediately to peace anywhere. There was a four-year hiatus during which the best efforts of Kissinger and other mediators failed to make any progress. Then, on 11 November 1978, Sadat cut through the fog of difficulties by inviting himself to Jerusalem. Menachem Begin welcomed the proposal, and the formal announcements were made in interviews with Walter Cronkite broadcast on American television three days later.

Sadat arrived in Jerusalem on 19 November. It was one of the most extraordinary moments in recent history, the whole world watching on live television as Sadat was met off the aircraft by Begin. A few minutes later, Sadat was presented to Golda Meir and bowed over her hand in greeting. That day, he visited the el-Aqsa Mosque, the Church of the Holy Sepulchre, and the Yad Vashem memorial to the Holocaust. On the 20th, he laid a wreath at an Israeli war memorial, and addressed the Knesset. 'If you want to live with us, in this part of the world,' he said, 'in sincerity I tell you that we welcome you among us with all security and safety.' However, he added, 'There can be no peace without the Palestinians,' and the settlement 'must be based on justice, and not on the occupation of the land of others . . . You have to give up once and for all the dreams of conquest and the belief that force is the best means of dealing with the Arabs.'

Israel had been waiting for that phone call, for face-to-face negotiations with the Arabs, for recognition. Sadat's gesture answered their every prayer, or appeared to. The negotiations that followed were difficult and protracted, and required the personal intervention of President Jimmy Carter. Begin and Sadat met Carter at Camp David on 6 September 1978, and signed a framework agreement at the White House on the 17th. Further negotiations were needed, and involved Carter himself in shuttle diplomacy, before a peace treaty was finally signed, on the lawn in front

of the White House, on 27 March 1979.

Under the terms of the agreement, Israel withdrew progressively from the entire Sinai peninsula. Begin tried to keep an Israeli settlement just over the border in the north, but failed. A dispute over the exact line of the frontier west of Eilat, where the Israelis had built a resort called Taba, dragged on for over a decade. (The arbitors eventually decided in Egypt's favour in November 1988.) The peace agreement was put under severe strain by the war in Lebanon, but peace with Israel was generally popular in Egypt, even if the Israelis themselves were not. Sadat paid for the treaty with his life: he was assassinated in 1981 by soldiers in his own army who believed that he had betrayed Islam and Egypt. His successor, Hosni Mubarak, was able to escape personal blame for the treaty while at the same time pursuing Sadat's policies of peace with Israel and a close alliance with the United States. It seems likely that, as long as he and like-thinking politicians retain power in Cairo, peace will be preserved.

THE *INTIFADA*

The Camp David agreement provided that there would be negotiations leading to 'autonomy' for the Palestinians living in occupied territory. These negotiations never took place. For almost ten years, that did not appear to matter. Israel had a peace treaty with Egypt, *de facto* peace with Jordan, and a secure border with Syria. It tried to secure the remaining border, with Lebanon, by military means and succeeded, up to a point (*see* Lebanon, pp. 305–22). The PLO can still occasionally mount raids against Israel, and there are still terrorist actions against Israelis abroad, but they are pinpricks. In a military sense, Israel is more secure now than it has ever been.

On 9 December 1987, the first of a series of demonstrations by Palestinians – in the Gaza strip and on the West Bank – showed how illusory that security was. Boys and young men took to stoning Israeli patrols; the Israelis fired back, with live ammunition, killing some of their tormentors. There was a general strike in Gaza and the West Bank, and shops closed in sympathy.

The Palestinians call the uprising the 'intifada', from the Arabic verb 'to shake loose'. An underground committee was formed to direct it. By the first anniversary of the *intifada*, in December 1988, the Israeli army had killed 366 Palestinians and wounded over 20,000 in attempting to repress the disturbances. Eleven Israelis were killed in the same period, including a woman and her three children who were killed when a bus was fire-bombed near Jerusalem on 30 October, two days before the Israeli general election. By then, over 5000 young men had been arrested, and were held in detention centres, including tented camps in the Negev; a few were expelled (36 in 1988).

The Israeli authorities vowed to suppress the riots with whatever means were necessary. The minister of defence, Yitzak Rabin, ordered his troops to beat every rioter they caught, to break their arms and fingers. When the rioters took to throwing Molotov cocktails, in the summer of 1988, and there were cases of arson in Israel proper as well as in the occupied territories, Rabin authorized his men to shoot anyone seen with a firebomb. Palestinian houses were also blown up and trees cut down, but other means for controlling the disturbances were less draconian. Remittances from abroad were intercepted, farmers' markets in the Jordan valley were closed down, concrete barricades were erected at street intersections.

The rioters insisted that Palestinian police, mayors and other local officials resign. Those who hesitated were threatened with death, and a few notorious collaborators were murdered. To the Israelis' horror, the troubles spread to Israeli Arabs. Jewish settlers on the West Bank sometimes took matters into their own hands. In one particularly horrifying incident, a party of Israeli children on a nature hike passed through the fields of an Arab village. A man in a field shouted at them, and one of the two guards with the children shot and killed him. Other people then took the party into the village. The same guard panicked, fired and killed another Arab and one of the Israeli children. All Israel cried for vengeance and several houses in the village were blown up before discovering that the girl had actually been killed, accidently, by the guard – a psychopathic Israeli settler.

By degrees, the rioting died down, periodically flaring up again, but the problem at its core remained as acute as ever: after 20 years' quiescence, the Palestinians in the occupied territories had started to protest against their condition.

On 9 December 1988, the first anniversary of the uprising, Israel mounted a massive raid on the headquarters of Ahmed Jibril's Popular Front for the Liberation of Palestine-General Command (*see* Arab terrorism, pp. 526–47) outside Beirut. Jibril's barracks were destroyed and 20 members of his command killed. Israel intended the gesture as a demonstration that it was not to be intimidated by the *intifada*.

THE DILEMMA

There are now about 540,000 Palestinians in the Gaza strip, 790,000 on the West Bank, 130,000 in East Jerusalem, 650,000 in Israel proper. Of the total population of Israel and the occupied territories – about 5.6 million – over one-third are Palestinian. Meron Benvenisti of the West Bank Data Project believed in 1983 that this ratio was likely to be maintained, as the lower Jewish birthrate would be compensated by continuing immigration. Jewish net immigration has dropped since then.

It is the absolute number of Palestinians, not the proportion, that is the problem. The Gaza strip is now one of the most densely populated places on Earth. Its population was 385,000 in 1967, and this has been increased by approximately 155,000, all young, alienated and hostile.

Zionist irridentists, led by Itzak Shamir, refuse to surrender any territory: Shamir voted against the peace treaty with Egypt because it represented a retreat. A minority of Israelis advocate abandoning Gaza and the West Bank, but even if Israel retreated to the 1967 frontier, with or without Jerusalem, the problem would remain. It has been the same problem since the Balfour Declaration in 1917: how is the Jewish national home to survive in a country with a large, and hostile, Arab population?

A separate and genuinely independent Palestinian state as a solution is an illusion, not because the conservative Likud party opposes it, or because the PLO would dominate it, but because Jews and Arabs are now so hopelessly intermingled throughout the whole of Palestine/Israel, the economic life of the two communities so completely fused together, that they cannot be separated. They are like Siamese twins sharing one liver and stomach. They are destined to live together, whatever form of political organization they set up. Even if the 51,000 Jewish settlers on the West Bank could be repatriated, which they cannot be, economic integration has passed a point of no return. There are a mere 2000 Jews in the Gaza strip, and they could certainly be removed, but the Palestinians there cannot survive without Israel. That is where they work, where their economic future lies. A Palestinian state would remain economically a part of Israel. Its independence would be entirely spurious.

So what are the Israelis to do? The Jewish hawks say that Israel must control the entire territory because it is the Promised Land, and for reasons of national security. A few extremists say that the Palestinians should be expelled, but that would only work if foreign states would take them in, and there is little likelihood of that. Jewish doves say that Palestine should be partitioned again, as do the American government and the Europeans. Arab doves ask to be allowed to form a Palestinian state, and then they will make peace.

Many of the refugees (perhaps most of them) in Gaza and the West Bank, and also in the camps in Lebanon, demand their land back, the return of their houses in Jaffa and Haifa, and the restoration of their villages in Galilee. What is more, all the Palestinians of the diaspora must be allowed to return, if they wish, all 2 million of them. And the Jews? They must go back whence they came. They demand this despite the fact that they lost their lands 40 years ago and the great majority of the refugees have been born in exile; that most of today's Israelis were born in Israel; that tens of millions of refugees in other countries have made new lives and given up their hopes of returning.

Now it may be that if a Palestinian state were set up, the diaspora would not wish to return. It may be that, with a state of their own, Palestinian resentments would face away, and they would come to accept Israel as freely as Anwar Sadat did. Well-meaning foreigners say that Israel has no choice, must accept the risk, just as it accepted the risk of giving up the Sinai. It appears that Israel is not ready to do so.

In the course of persuading Israel to accept the 1974 disengagement agreements, Kissinger promised that the United States would never negotiate with the PLO unless it met certain stringent conditions (*see below*). For 14 years, that promise was a millstone around the necks of successive secretaries of state and presidents. The way to make peace is to negotiate with your enemy, and Americans have negotiated with Mao Tse-tung and the Ayatollah Khomeini, and Ronald Reagan himself went to Moscow to make peace with the 'evil empire'. But they could not negotiate with Arafat because of Kissinger's rash promise – and Jewish voters insisted that that promise must be repeated at every election.

The Israelis, who once demanded that their enemies negotiate with them, now themselves refuse to negotiate. For some of them, of course, this is simply a tactical ploy. They have no wish to make peace with the Palestinians because there are no concessions they are willing to offer. They will concede nothing, neither land nor political authority. On the contrary, they insist on the Jews' continued right to seize more land from the Arabs to build new settlements.

Other Israelis, probably the majority, simply detest Yassir Arafat, who to them symbolizes the terrorist, haranguing the UN General Assembly with a pistol stuck in his belt. Arafat's men have murdered scores of Israelis. PLO soldiers under Arafat's command have also attacked and killed Israeli soldiers, and although that is not strictly terrorism (*see* Terrorism, pp. 493–500), Israelis consider it a distinction without a difference.

291

The first condition that Kissinger set for opening a dialogue with the PLO was that it must formally recognize Israel's right to exist, in the terms of UN Resolutions 242 and 338. Later, a further precondition was added, that the PLO should renounce terrorism. For 14 years, Arafat and his comrades refused to accept these conditions publicly, although privately they repeatedly assured visitors that they did indeed recognize that Israel was there to stay. At last, in December 1988, after an elaborate diplomatic minuet set off by King Hussein, Arafat pronounced the irrevocable words and the United States agreed to talk to him. It was one of the worst shocks to the Israelis in their history.

Israel increasingly resembles South Africa. The main difference is that the blacks in South Africa are a large majority, while the Palestinians in Israel and the territories comprise only one-third of the population. The other difference is that the South Africans set up 'Bantustans', quasi-independent tribal states that are, in fact, totally controlled by white South Africa. Israel refuses to set up a Palestinian Bantustan on the West Bank and in the Gaza strip. The similarities are that the settlers – Jews or white South Africans – enjoy all the usual democratic rights while the indigenous population has none. Arabs and blacks can be expelled from their land and their homes under emergency regulations, and their property handed over to the dominant race. From 1948 to 1968, in Israel proper, almost 250,000 acres (over 100,000 hectares) of Arab land were confiscated by the Israeli government to make room for Jewish settlers. The Palestinians are subjected to constant harassment and police surveillance, and their economic condition is substantially inferior to the settlers' – just like black South Africans.

The *intifada* has demonstrated that the young Palestinians do not accept their situation. It has also demonstrated that Israel does not accept that Palestinians have the same rights as Jews: they are the enemy. No civilized country shoots its own citizens when they throw rocks at the police. The Israelis have made no serious effort to learn riot control: they send fully armed troops to fight stone-throwing teenagers, ignoring the experience of the South Koreans, the Japanese, the British in Northern Ireland and the French, who all have specialized riot police. Japanese rioters are far more dangerous than Palestinians – they are more numerous and disciplined – but the Japanese police do not shoot them. The British are still paying the price for sending the paras into Londonderry in 1972, and the Koreans have yet to forgive the state for the killings in Kwangju (*see* Korea, p. 202). The Israelis will pay for years for the error of shooting so many rioters.

ISRAEL AND HER NEIGHBOURS

The year 1973 was a high point for the Arabs. For one short period, they were united against Israel, their armies behaved creditably, they unleashed the 'oil weapon' (*see* Saudi Arabia, pp. 323–27), and the PLO came into its own as the recognized representative of 'occupied Palestine'. Since then, things have never been the same. Syria and Iraq have been on the brink of war, as have Egypt and Libya, and, indeed, Libya and all her other neighbours. Sadat make a separate peace with Israel, pulling the most powerful Arab state out of the perpetual confrontation, and the extremists have been fighting a losing political battle against Egypt ever since. The oil weapon, after bringing spectacular wealth to the oil states in the 1970s and early 1980s, failed as a result of increased production and conservation in the West. The Palestinians were defeated by Israel in Lebanon and took to fighting among themselves.

The United States largely ignored the Middle East after the Marines were withdrawn from Beirut early in 1984. The Reagan administration concentrated on Central America and relations with the Soviet Union, although George Shultz made a last, fruitless effort to promote a settlement in the summer of 1988. He suggested an international conference, to be promoted by the United States and the Soviet Union, as a means of getting Israel, Jordan and the Palestinians together. The eventual solution would, once again, be a federation between the occupied territories and Jordan. After several visits to the Middle East, Shultz retired baffled. None of the principals would accept his proposals.

The perpetual stalemate was finally broken by King Hussein. On 31 July 1988, he formally renounced his claim to the West Bank. His grandfather, King Abdullah, had annexed the area in 1949, and Hussein had lost it during the Six Day War in 1967. Ever since, Jordan had claimed it as part of the kingdom, had continued to pay the salaries of public officials (most notably the teachers) and had issued passports to the Palestinian inhabitants. The decision meant that there was now no one to challenge the Israelis except the Palestinians themselves.

Moderate Arabs, Egypt, Jordan, Saudi Arabia and, surprisingly, Iraq used their influence with the PLO to persuade it to moderate its position. They were joined discretely by the USSR where the new government of Mikhail Gorbachev was showing signs of wanting to return to Middle East diplomacy in a less hamfisted way than in the past.

Ever since 1967, the chief sticking point had been the PLO's adamant refusal to recognize Israel. On 15 November 1988, the Palestine National Council (PNC), meeting in Algiers, proclaimed an independent Palestinian state. Over 40 years after UN Resolution 181 partitioned Palestine and proposed a Jewish and an Arab state there, the Palestinians at last accepted the decision. The PNC specifically accepted the crucial UN Security Council Resolutions 242 and 338, which proclaim the right of every state in the region to live within secure and recognized boundaries. This meant that it was recognizing Israel, but on that occasion, neither Arafat nor any of the other delegates could quite bring themselves to say so. The significance of this decision was also diminished by their equivocation over terrorism. The council insisted on the Palestinians' right to 'resist Israeli occupation' and, while rejecting 'all forms of terrorism', did so 'in accordance with UN resolutions'. Those resolutions have often approved 'liberation struggles'. The council agreed formally to negotiate with Israel in the context of an international peace conference, on condition that Israel accepted that the Palestinians had political rights, and proposed that independent Palestine should enter a confederation with Jordan.

The most extreme Palestinians were not represented at the Algiers meeting, and others, led by George Habash, could only be persuaded with difficulty to accept the resolutions. Habash further muddied the waters by insisting that the PLO still demanded the whole of Palestine.

Two weeks earlier, on 1 November, Israel had endured a general election that had left the Knesset hopelessly divided. A majority of the electorate had rejected the Labour party's call for negotiations with the Arabs (but not the PLO), but had also rejected the extremism of Likud and its allies. The balance was held by religious parties, which had quite different agendas: they wanted to amend the Law of Return by limiting conversions to Judaism to those following strictly Orthodox rites. It seemed a minor point because it would affect only a handful of people annually, but it had great symbolic importance. The majority of American Jews, who are members of Reform or Conservative congregations, took the proposal to mean that their own Jewishness was being denied by the government of Israel. The alliance between Israel and American Jewry, which was the very foundation of the state's security, was shaken.

The Algiers conference fell in the midst of the first round of haggling over the composition of a new Israeli government, and when they were not arguing over religious dogma, both sides in Israel continued to denounce the PLO. Shamir said that the only thing the PLO could do to win his approval would be to disband.

Arafat made another speech before the UN General Assembly meeting in Geneva on 13 December (the venue had been changed from New York when the Americans refused Arafat a visa). Once again, the Americans found its content inadequate. A US State Department spokesman insisted that afternoon that nothing had changed, that Arafat still refused to issue an unequivocal denunciation of terrorism, and to recognize Israel explicitly. It appeared as though Shultz was going to leave the stage as secretary of state having contributed nothing towards progress in the Middle East.

However, in the background, intensive negotiations were taking place. The Swedes were the key mediators, urging Arafat to make the last step and urging the Americans to accept his statement as sufficient. The same arguments were made by the Arab moderates, by the Europeans, and by the Turkish prime minister, Turgut Ozal, who happened to be in Washington.

On the following day, Arafat gave a press conference in Geneva, his fourth or fifth 'clarification' of the Algiers resolution. He stated that he accepted UN Resolutions 181, 242 and 338. He also said: 'I repeat for the record that we totally and absolutely renounce all forms of terrorism, including individual, group and state terrorism.' It was enough. That evening, Shultz announced that the United States was ready to open a dialogue with the PLO.

It was a *coup de théâtre*, beyond question the most important diplomatic development in the Middle East for years, and a dramatic conclusion to a year that had been full of remarkable events.

It left Israel totally isolated. The Americans insisted that they would continue to support Israel's security, but they had pulled the rug out from under its diplomatic position. Shultz himself would play no part in the ensuing negotiations: he was due to hand the State Department over to James Baker on 20 January. The series of events that had begun with the *intifada*, and had continued with Hussein's abandonment of the Palestinians to their own devices, had led ineluctably to the PLO at last accepting the need to negotiate directly with Israel, and the United States accepting the need to negotiate with the PLO. It remained to be seen how much pressure President Bush would exert on the Israelis to bring them to the table.

FURTHER READING

American University, *Israel: A Country Study*, Washington 1979.

Benvenisti, Meron, *The West Bank Data Project*, Washington, American Enterprise Institute, Studies in Foreign Policy, 1984.

Frankel, William, *Israel Observed*, London, Thames and Hudson, 1985.

Grossman, David, *The Yellow Rain*, New York, Farrar, Straus and Giroux, 1988.

Hertzog, Chaim, *The Arab–Israeli Wars*, New York, Random House, 1981.

Kissinger, Henry, *White House Years*, Boston, Little, Brown, 1979.

——, *Years of Upheaval*, Boston, Little, Brown, 1982.

Laqueur, Walter, *The Road to War, 1967*, London, Weidenfeld and Nicolson, London, 1968.

Lucas, Noah, *The Modern History of Israel*, New York, Praeger, 1975.

MacLeish, Roderick, *The Sun Stood Still*, New York, Atheneum, 1968.

O'Brien, Conor Cruise, *The Siege*, New York, Simon and Schuster, 1986.

Perlmutter, Amos, *Israel: The Partitioned State*, New York, Charles Scribner's Sons, 1985.

Rabinovich Itamir, and Reinharz, Jehuda (eds), *Israel in the Middle East: Documents and Readings on Society, Politics and Foreign Relations, 1948 to the Present*, Oxford University Press, 1984.

Sadat, Anwar el, *In Search of Identity*, New York, Harper and Row, 1978.

Shazli, Lt. Gen. Saad el, *The Crossing of the Suez*, San Francisco, American Mideast Research, 1980.

Shipler, David, *Arab and Jew*, New York Times Books, 1986.

Sykes, Christopher, *Crossroads to Israel*, Cleveland, World Publishing Co., 1965.

The Kurds

The Kurds are an ancient people partitioned among Iraq, Iran, Syria, Turkey, Lebanon and the Soviet Union. They have never been a nation nor have they ever, in modern times, been united under one government. The frontier between Persia and the Ottoman empire ran through the middle of Kurdish territory, a line that still divides them. They have now learned nationalism, at the same time and in the same school as the Turks, the Persians and the Arabs, and have fought a series of unsuccessful campaigns against the governments of Ankara, Tehran and Baghdad.

Only the roughest estimate can be made of the total number of Kurds. The highest figure offered is 20 million – certainly an exaggeration. David McDowall, author of the Minority Rights Group report, suggests the following estimate of the Kurdish population in 1980:

Country	Total population	Kurds	%
Turkey	44,500,000	8,455,000	19
Iraq	13,500,000	3,105,000	23
Iran	37,700,000	3,701,000	10
Syria	9,200,000	734,000	8
Lebanon	—	60,000	—
USSR	—	265,000	—
Total:		16,320,000	

There are also believed to be about 350,000 Kurdish 'guest workers' in Western Europe.

The Kurds live in a territory covering about 250,000 square miles (640,000 sq. km). They are all Muslim, at least 80 per cent of them Sunni, the rest Shiite. They claim to be the descendants of the ancient Medes, one of the founding kingdoms of the Persian empire, who certainly lived in what is now Kurdistan, and their language is related to Persian. The numerous dialects are often as mutually incomprehensible as were many Italian dialects in the 19th century or French patois before the Revolution.

296   The most famous of all Kurds was Saladin, who was actually born outside

Kurdistan, in Tikrit in Iraq (later the birthplace of Saddam Hussein). Saladin made himself ruler of Egypt and Syria and liberated Jerusalem from the Crusaders. He had no interest in Kurdistan.

The situation of the Kurds is an example of the difficulty of reconciling the idea of a nation state with the real world. A homogenous nation within settled frontiers is the exception to the rule, even in Europe. The Kurds are not united, but neither are the Arabs nor the Turks. The Kurds' misfortune is not that they are separated, but that they are oppressed by the dominant races in the countries where they live.

The Kurds living in the Ottoman empire were generally loyal subjects, serving with distinction in Ottoman armies. During World War I, the Russians opened a front against Turkey in the Caucasus. During three years of warfare, the Armenian community in eastern Turkey was destroyed in a series of pogroms in which the Kurds participated enthusiastically (*see* Terrorism: Forlorn hopes, pp. 548–54). Another small community, the Christian Assyrians, was also driven out of its homelands; the remnants settled in Iraqi Kurdistan after the war, and were later slaughtered in the first Kurdish revolt. In 1920, the League of Nations – meaning, in this case, the British – contemplated establishing independent states for the Armenians and the Kurds. The rump Ottoman government in Constantinople signed the Treaty of Sèvres, which provided, among other concessions, for the creation of Kurdistan.

Kemal Pasha then raised the banner of Turkish nationalism in revolt, and he and his followers restored Turkish independence and settled its frontiers. Many Kurds joined him, preferring the Turks to the Armenians or the Greeks. The Treaty of Sèvres was quietly abandoned, and its replacement, the Treaty of Lausanne, signed in 1923, made no mention of the Kurds. The latter, having remained loyal to the caliph, suddenly found themselves subject to a secular government that insisted they were Turks, not Kurds at all, and to British and Arab rule from Baghdad. The first Kurdish revolts ensued, and they have continued, in one form or another, ever since. They have been notable as much for the ferocity with which the different Kurdish tribes and families have fought against each other as for the consistency with which they have fought Turkish, Iraqi and Iranian governments.

THE KURDS IN IRAQ

In 1943, when Iraq was occupied by the British and bitterly divided between pro-Axis and pro-Allies factions, the Mullah Mustafa Barzani, who was hereditary religious and secular leader of his tribe, set up an autonomous region around his home town of Barzan, which he held for two years. In 1945, the Baghdad government reasserted its authority in Kurdistan, and Barzani led the fight against it. He was defeated and, in 1946, moved to Mahabad, in north-west Iran, where Kurds under the patronage of the Soviet Union had set up a Kurdish republic (*see below*). When the Iranian government reoccupied Mahabad, Barzani fled to the USSR, where he lived until the Iraqi revolution in 1958.

The regime of the Iraqi general Abd al-Karim Kassem at first promised the Kurds autonomy, but when Barzani started asserting his authority in Kurdistan in the north of the country, the government went to war. The first phase of the war lasted from 1961 to 1970, and took the form of many such insurrections: after 297 recovering from its initial reverses, the government controlled the main towns and periodically occupied the larger valleys, but never reached the Kurds' positions in the mountains. The Iraqi air force therefore bombed Kurdish villages indiscriminately, but without affecting the Kurds' will to resist. Barzani's army – the Pesh Merga (the phrase means 'those who walk before death') – numbered 50,000–60,000 men, and at the height of their success, the Kurdish rebels controlled all the mountains in north-east Iraq, and their guerrilla bands reached the outskirts of Mosul, Arbil and Kirkuk, the principal cities in Iraqi Kurdistan. At various times, the Kurds were supported by Iran, the USSR, Israel and the US.

Thousands of people were killed, mainly civilians. One estimate puts the civilian death toll between 1961 and 1970 at 100,000 and military deaths at 9000. A total of half that, or 50,000, seems more probable.

In March 1970, the Iraqi government offered autonomy to the Kurds and a ceasefire came into force. However, the two sides could never reach agreement on the details of the proposed relationship. The main sticking points were Barzani's demands that he retain the Pesh Merga under his own command, and that Kurdistan include Kirkuk, the province that produces 70 per cent of Iraq's oil. The Baghdad government made its final offer – autonomy without Kirkuk – on the fourth anniversary of the March Manifesto and, when Barzani rejected it, ordered a renewed offensive.

The Iraqi army drove into Kurdistan, and Barzini made the mistake of renouncing traditional guerrilla tactics and, instead, fought a conventional war against the Iraqis. He had 40,000 troops (the Pesh Merga) and 60,000 militiamen, and he overestimated his strength. The Kurds were defeated and, by the end of the year, had been driven into the furthest recesses of their mountains, up against the Turkish and Iranian frontiers.

The Pesh Merga survived for a while, holding off an Iraqi army 100,000 strong, thanks to support from the Iranians in the form of heavy artillery, and, secretly, from the CIA. The Ba'ath government in Baghdad was in its most militantly leftist phase, closely allied to the Soviet Union and bitterly hostile to the West. Iran and Iraq were, as usual, enemies, and there were serious border disputes between the two.

In 1975, in an abrupt reversal of policy, the shah of Iran and Dr Henry Kissinger, the US secretary of state, decided to abandon the Kurds and reach an agreement with the Iraqi government. The Iranian and the Iraqi governments signed an agreement settling their disputes during an OPEC meeting in Algiers on 6 March 1975. American clandestine military aid to the Kurds was abruptly ended and, more important, so was Iranian aid. The frontier was closed and the Kurds were left to their fate. Mustafa Barzani and tens of thousands of his followers fled to Iran (Barzani died in the United States in 1979), and the Iraqis celebrated their victory in the usual manner, by executing as many of the rebels as they could lay their hands on. The short war had cost the lives of 7000 Iraqi troops, by official count, and 2000 Kurdish troops, according to Barzani. The real totals were probably much higher, perhaps 20,000 all told, and there were 600,000 refugees.

Barzani's Kurdish Democratic Party (KDP) went into eclipse, and rival Kurdish leaders took up the fight. The most notable of them was Jalal Talabani, of the Patriotic Union of Kurdistan (PUK). Talabani had opposed Barzani since the 1950s. His tribal base is in Suleimaniya, in southern Kurdistan, a much more urbanized region than Barzan in the north. After the débâcle of 1975, Talabani took refuge in Syria with about 4000 armed followers. He was given a Syrian passport by President Assad, and his small army was posted along the Iraqi border to guard it against the Ba'athists of Baghdad. At that time, relations between Syria and Iraq were particularly tense: they nearly went to war in 1975. Turning Talabani loose in Iraqi Kurdistan during the Iran–Iraq war was another instance of the fratricidal tendencies of Syrian and Iraqi Ba'athists. Then the PUK merged with two other, Marxist Kurdish groups and, in 1978, was reported to have fought several pitched battles with the KDP and the residuum of the Pesh Merga.

In 1984, the Iraqis offered Talabani a further measure of autonomy in exchange for continued opposition to the Barzanis and the KDP. However, two years later, Talabani and Mustafa Barzani's son, Massoud, reached an agreement, brokered by the Iranians, and set up an alliance between the PUK and the KDP. Kurdish guerrillas then started attacking Iraqi positions in south Kurdistan as well as the north.

When Iran sued for peace, on 18 July 1988, the Iraqis immediately turned their attention to the Kurds. Saddam Hussein's army swept through Iraqi Kurdistan and, within a month, had driven the Kurdish forces in a rout over the border into Turkey and Iran. There was some evidence that Iraq had once again used poison gas, but the reports were not confirmed. The Turkish government had to take care of about 60,000 refugees, and hastily put up tent camps to receive them. It was a temporary measure: tents are no adequate protection for civilians in a Turkish winter.

Six weeks later, Turkey managed to send a number of the refugees into Iran (Massoud Barzani's party claimed that 30,000 had been expelled). They could not return to their homes in Iraq, because their homes no longer existed: the Iraqi army had systematically obliterated their villages. The government alleged that the destruction was for the villagers' own good, that they would be better off in modern towns – described as 'complexes that have all the necessary infrastructure' – being built for them at the foot of the mountains. Elsewhere, they might have been called 'strategic hamlets'. The Iraqi authorities claimed that 20,000 Kurds returned from Iran after Saddam Hussein offered them an amnesty on 6 September.

THE KURDS AND THE WAR

One of the principal fronts in the war between Iran and Iraq was in Iraqi Kurdistan. The topography favoured the Iraqis: a succession of high mountain ranges, the Zagros, run parallel to the border; successfully crossing one range offered the Iranian attackers the opportunity to contemplate the next. Nevertheless, year by year, the Iranians pushed through the highest mountains and, in March 1988, were within sight of the Darbandi Khan lake and dam at Dukan, whence a series of passes lead down into the plains. It was their furthest advance.

Throughout the eight years of war, there was a constantly shifting series of alliances on both sides of the border. The Iranians recruited many Kurds to help fight Iraq, despite the betrayal of 1975 and the ruthless suppression of the Iranian Kurds in 1979–83. By early in 1984, the Iranian army had reasserted its control over virtually all Iranian Kurdistan – killing an estimated 27,500 Kurds in the 299 process. At the same time, many Kurds in Iraq fought against Iran – and always Kurds fought each other on both sides of the border, and across the border. As ever, the tribes followed their leaders, nursing ancestral grievances and vendettas. The traditionalist Kurdish Democratic Party (KDP), now led by sons of the Mullah Mustafa, supported the government in Tehran against the KDPI, while Baghdad supported leftist Kurds against Tehran.

The Iraqi Kurds had more success than the Iranian Kurds in preserving some control over parts of their territory, but only for as long as the war with Iran lasted – for example, in September 1987, Kurdish guerrillas briefly occupied Kanimasi, an Iraqi Kurdish town near the Turkish border. Kurdish bands operating throughout Iraqi Kurdistan assassinated government officials and ambushed military convoys. In retaliation, the Iraqis destroyed Kurdish villages, moved the population into easily controlled valleys and cleared them out of the old, labyrinthine cities of Kirkuk and Arbil, and filled the province with troops. Rebel leaders claim that Iraq destroyed over 1000 villages between 1987 and 1988.

The 1986 agreement between Talabani and the Barzani faction proved to be another case of the Kurds backing the wrong horse. They assumed that Iran would win the war and hoped to establish an autonomous Kurdistan on at least the Iraqi side of the frontier. The Kurds remained divided, however: in the waning days of the war, the Iraqis were able to send large bands of leftist Kurds across the border to occupy, temporarily, a number of Iranian Kurdish towns.

In March 1988, during the last Iranian spring offensive, the Iraqi air force used poison gas – both cyanide and mustard gas – against the Kurdish town of Halabjah, which the Iranians had captured. The Iranians alleged that 2000 people were killed in the incident, and when Western reporters were taken to the town, they counted at least 100 bodies, all civilians. In April, Iran reported a further series of Iraqi gas attacks on Kurdish villages.

THE KURDS IN IRAN

Like their cousins in Iraq and Turkey, Iranian Kurds tried to set up an independent state after World War I, but they were suppressed by General Reza Khan, who made himself shah in 1925 (see Iran, p. 246). In World War II, the British occupied most of Iran. The Soviet Union controlled a small area in the north, and the Azerbaijanis, with Soviet support, set up a republic of their own in Tabriz in January 1946. Simultaneously, a tribe of Kurds seized the opportunity to set up the Republic of Mahabad, but Kurds in other areas conspicuously failed to rally to the flag. Mustafa Barzani, driven out of his stronghold in Iraq, for a while provided an army to defend Mahabad, but when the Soviets withdrew from Iran, the Iranians reoccupied both Tabriz and Mahabad in December 1946. Barzani then fled to the USSR.

Iranian Kurds were largely quiescent during the rest of the reign of Shah Mohammed, who had succeeded his father in 1941. When Barzani returned to Iraq in 1958, and later started the Kurds' revolt, he was supported by the shah out of enmity for Baghdad, and used his influence to keep the Iranian Kurds loyal to the throne. This included arresting and executing any Iranian rebels who came his way. The Ba'ath regime in Baghdad tried to stir up anti-shah feeling among the Kurdish Democratic Party of Iran (KDPI), a leftist organization established during the Mahabad republic, which was ideologically much closer to the Ba'ath than to Barzani. However, Barzani's influence in the border lands was so strong that the KDPI would not challenge him, or fight against the Iranians.

After the collapse of the Iranian monarchy in 1979, the Kurds there took the opportunity to establish their autonomy. They seized control of their provinces and helped themselves to the huge stores of weapons that the shah had accumulated in barracks and arsenals near the Iraqi frontier. The conflict between the KDPI and traditional tribal leaders continued. Most Kurds are Sunni, but there was a large Shiite community in southern Kurdistan that supported Khomeini.

The KDPI joined the opposition to Khomeini and took part in the fighting in Tehran and elsewhere. For a while, the revolutionary government lost control of the Kurdish provinces, and there were wholesale massacres of Persians and Kurds in disputed areas. However, the Iranian Kurds were not supported from outside, and Khomeini was able to send his army into Kurdistan, to be followed by revolutionary courts that set about executing all opposition Kurds they could find. The Kurds took to the mountains and started a full-scale guerrilla war. There were attempts to negotiate but without success. The government controlled the towns, while the KDPI controlled the mountains. Then, in September 1980, Saddam Hussein invaded Iran.

THE KURDS IN SYRIA

The Kurds in Syria are less numerous and less militant than their relatives in Iraq. Most of them live in the north-east, along the Turkish and Iraqi frontiers, but there are Kurdish centres elsewhere, some of them relics of Kurdish military colonies established in the Middle Ages. The Kurds were given the Crusader castle, Krak des Chevaliers, to guard in the 14th century. When the French returned in 1920, they cleaned up the castle and evicted the Kurds. The French left again, in 1945. The Kurds are still there.

After the merger of Syria and Egypt in 1958, a policy of settling Arabs in Kurdistan was introduced and continued until 1976. Under the guise of land reform, tribal land was confiscated and given to Bedu from the desert. The Kurdish language is no longer taught in schools, and all signs of Kurdish culture are rigorously suppressed.

One reason for the Kurds' mistreatment in Syria was that the French had encouraged separatism among Syria's many minorities, and had promoted Kurds in the army. The first three coups in independent Syria, all in 1949, were carried out by Kurdish generals. Furthermore, Kurds dominated the Syrian Communist party, which was a rival to the Ba'ath (now dominated by another minority, the Alawites). Kurdish Communists now play an enthusiastic part in the terrorism in Lebanon, to which about 50,000 Kurds have fled to escape from persecution and economic distress in Syria.

However, a high proportion of Syrian Kurds have accepted the regime and serve in the army. The Syrians have also encouraged a Marxist party – the Kurdish Workers' Party – which carries on guerrilla warfare and terrorism in Turkey. Its leader, Abdullah Ocalan, lives in Damascus.

THE KURDS IN TURKEY

The largest number of Kurds live in eastern Turkey – perhaps 8–10 million people. Whereas the Kurds in Iraq, Iran and Syria are confronted by unstable governments (which, in the case of Iraq and Syria, are minority military dictatorships), the Kurds in Turkey are a minority, comprising about 19 per cent, in an otherwise homogeneous nation, which has a population of about 50 million, a secure government and a fierce determination to maintain national integrity. In addition, Turkish Kurds have, in common with their relatives in Iraq and Iran, an ineradicable delight in fighting among themselves.

The Kurds were, for the most part, loyal subjects of the Ottoman caliph, but they have been much less loyal to the secular state set up by Ataturk. In 1925, the Dervishes incited the Kurds to revolt, demanding the restoration of the caliphate. Ataturk ruthlessly suppressed the uprising. Hundreds of villages were burned and between 40,000 and 250,000 people were killed. The leaders of the revolt were executed, and Ataturk used the occasion to launch some of his major reforms: the suppression of the order of Dervishes, and the outlawing of the fez, the headgear that was the outward and visible sign of the Turk's adherence to Islam.

The Turks then set about suppressing the Kurds as a separate people, in the most sweeping way possible, by flatly denying their existence. They claim that the Kurds are 'Mountain Turks', and insist that they must be educated in Turkish and adopt the Western manners of modern Turkey. (In 1979, a former minister of public works was sentenced to two years' hard labour for saying in public: 'In Turkey, there are Kurds. I, too, am a Kurd.') In fact, the Kurds are no more Turkish than the Welsh are 'Mountain English'. The languages are totally distinct, and the separate history of the Kurds goes back at least 1000 years before the first Turkish tribes arrived from Central Asia.

There has been constant unrest in the Kurdish provinces of Turkey for many years for a number of reasons: the central government's anti-Kurdish policies; the political unrest that swept Turkey in the 1970s and led to the army coup in 1980; and the wars in Iranian and Iraqi Kurdistan. For decades, the eastern provinces have been under martial law, ostensibly to guard the frontier against Soviet incursions but, in fact, to control the Kurds.

The year 1965 saw the establishment of the Kurdistan Democratic Party of Turkey (KDPT), a traditionalist, separatist organization with links to the Mullah Mustafa Barzani in Iraq. The Turkish Workers Party (TWP), a doctrinaire socialist party, supported the Kurds and had many Kurdish members, and was therefore suppressed by the government. In 1967, there were mass demonstrations in the Kurdish provinces against the suppression of Kurdish cultural and political activity, and in 1969, the Organization of Revolutionary Youth (DDKO) was set up by militants from the TWP to start a guerrilla war against the government.

The latter periodically deported tens of thousands of Kurds from eastern Turkey, and resettled them in central Anatolia or allowed them to move to the cities. In another instance of the law of unforeseen consequences, many of these transplanted Kurds then took up radical politics and joined the far-left Turkish parties that started a campaign of terrorism against the government in the 1970s. Then some of them returned to their villages and introduced notions of nationalism, socialism and armed resistance to their tribal relatives who would not normally have considered such things.

The troubles in the east were one reason for the army 'coup by communiqué' in March 1971, when the army induced the politicians to hand over power to a government of technocrats, and instructed the new regime to solve the country's problems. The army then set about suppressing all signs of Kurdish nationalism in the east, but with little success.

By the late 1970s, Turkey was disintegrating into civil war between right and left, with open revolt in the Kurdish provinces, and urban terrorism that killed 5000 people between 1978 and 1980. A number of Kurdish parties and terrorist groups were active, the most radical being the Workers' Party of Kurdistan (PKK; also known as the Apocus), which fought both the Turkish state and also traditional Kurdish leaders. In September 1980, the army staged another coup. It then repressed the Kurds with a heavy hand.

The disturbances increased with the Iran–Iraq war. In May 1983, the Turkish army mounted a major operation over the border in Iraq to clear out Kurdish guerrilla positions. By official count, in the four years 1984–8, 185 Turkish soldiers, 480 Kurdish civilians and about 200 guerrillas were killed. On 1 April 1988, government forces killed 20 guerrillas with the loss of three military men, including the pilot of a helicopter that was shot down, in a battle near the Syrian frontier. The troops discovered and attacked a guerrilla band in a cave, after a guerrilla attack on a village had resulted in the deaths of nine people. In early May, terrorists massacred 25 Turkish villagers in two separate incidents near the Syrian border. A few days before, terrorists had hanged a village teacher whom they had accused of being an informer.

The government reported that the killers were members of the Workers' Party of Kurdistan, which has its headquarters in Damascus and can only operate across the frontier with the assistance of the Assad regime. So far, Turkey has taken no drastic exception to this provocation, but if the guerrillas seriously extend their activities, it might consider retaliation. Since Turkey is a member of Nato, and the USSR is Syria's patron and ally, the dangers are obvious.

The Turkish government is taking a firm military line against the rebels, but it has also launched a major economic development scheme for south-east Turkey, in Turkish Kurdistan, based upon a series of dams for irrigation and hydroelectricity. The Kabban dam, the largest in Turkey, has been completed, and the much larger Ataturk dam is under construction. When it is finished, by the year 2000, its associated irrigation and industrial projects should provide work for 3 million people, many of them Kurds.

FURTHER READING

American University, *Turkey: A Country Study*, Washington D.C., 1980.
American University, *Iraq: A Country Study*, Washington, 1979.
Edmonds, Cecil, *Kurds, Turks and Arabs*, Oxford University Press, 1957.
Ghareeb, Edmund, *The Kurdish Question in Iraq*, Syracuse University Press, New York, 1981.
Ghassemlon, A. R. *et al.* (ed. Gérard Chaliand; trans. Michael Pallis), *People without a Country: The Kurds and Kurdistan*, London, Zed Press, 1980.

Kinnane, Dirk, *The Kurds and Kurdistan*, Oxford University Press, 1964.

Lewis, Bernard, *The Arabs in History*, London/New York, Hutchinson's University Library, 1950.

——, *The Emergence of Modern Turkey*, Royal Institute of International Affairs, Oxford University Press, 1968.

McDowall, David, *The Kurds*, London, Minority Rights Group, 1985.

O'Ballance, Edgar, *The Kurdish Revolt, 1961–1970*, Hamden, Conn., Arclion Books, 1973.

Pelletiere, Stephen C., *The Kurds: An Unstable Element in the Gulf*, Boulder, Colo., Westview Press, 1984.

LEBANON

Geography   3950 sq. miles (10,400 sq. km). About half the size of Wales.
Defined by its topography: a narrow coastal strip along the
Mediterranean, 120 miles (200 km) long, and two mountain ranges
parallel to the coast – the Lebanon and Anti-Lebanon mountains –
with the narrow Bekaa valley between them. At its widest,
Lebanon is 60 miles (100 km) across.

Population   About 4 million (there has been no countrywide census since
1932). The capital Beirut had a population of over 1 million in
1975; the second city, Tripoli, has a population of about 600,000.
Estimated confessional breakdown of Lebanon

Maronite Christian	900,000
Orthodox Christian	250,000
Greek Catholics	150,000
Armenians	175,000
Palestinian Christians	30,000
Other Christians	50,000
Shiite Muslims	1,100,000
Sunni Muslims	750,000
Druse	200,000
Palestinians (Sunni)	300,000
Others (inc. Kurds)	100,000

Note: Islam is divided into two main sects: the Sunni, the majority
sect (90% worldwide); and the Shiites, who are dominant in Iran
and are in a majority in Iraq (they are in a minority elsewhere).
Sunnis and Shiites consider each other to be heretical. Both
consider the Druse to be a heretical Islamic sect.

The Maronite Christians are the result of a heresy of the 4th–7th
centuries, in which they broke from the orthodox Church because
of their belief in the solely divine nature of Christ. Since the 16th
century, however, they have been an Eastern Church in union with
the Roman Catholic Church but retaining their own rite and canon
law.

Principal domestic military forces
- Lebanese Army (Maronite): 15,000
- Lebanese Force (formerly Phalangist militia; Maronite): 10,000–
15,000
- Progressive Socialist Party (Druse, some Kurds): 5000
- Amal Militia (Shiite): 10,000
- Palestine Liberation Organization (PLO): at least 6000 and
growing

- Hizbollah ('Party of God'; pro-Khomeini Shiite): unknown
- South Lebanon Army (pro-Israeli): 1500

There are also militias controlled by dissident Maronites, Syrian Christians, pro-Syrian and anti-Syrian Sunnis, anti-PLO Palestinians, anti-Amal Shiites and various local groups.

Foreign military
- Syrian army: 20,000–30,000
- Israel: classified
- United Nations Interim Force in Lebanon (UNIFIL) (polices southern border): 7500

Refugees   Internal: 400,000–800,000, including 288,180 Palestinian refugees.

Casualties   The Lebanese government estimated in 1988 that 176,000 people had been killed since the civil war began in 1975.

Myself against my brother. Myself and my brother against my cousin. Myself, my brother and my cousin against the foreigner.

Arab proverb

A scorpion asked a rat to carry him across the Jordan. 'How do I know you won't sting me?' asked the rat. 'If I stung you, I would drown,' replied the scorpion. So the rat took the scorpion on his back and started to swim the river. Halfway across, the scorpion stung him. As he died, the rat cried out, 'Why did you do that?' The drowning scorpion replied, 'Because this is the Middle East.'

Israeli story

Before 1975, Lebanon had few of the attributes of a real nation, but at least its innumerable factions contrived a degree of mutual toleration. That comity has completely disintegrated. There is no Lebanon. When President Amin Gemayel's term ended in September 1988, there was no one to succeed him: the contending factions could not agree on a candidate, so the Christians and Muslims each set up an administration – which administered nothing. When a new president is finally chosen, he, too, will administer nothing. Lebanon is not even a geographical entity any more, with the Syrians permanently installed in the north and east, and the Israelis in the south. Beirut, once the most cosmopolitan and lively city in the Middle East, is a ghost town, its centre destroyed, its commerce, banking and social life ruined. Lebanon's main industry now is the export of hashish, and the country survives on remittances from hundreds of thousands of emigrants. It is the extreme case, in the modern world, of a nation tearing itself to pieces.

HISTORY

Through all its history, except during the Crusades, Lebanon was part of Syria. However, the Maronite Christians and the Druse living on and near the wild and inaccessible Mount Lebanon maintained a degree of independence from the Ottoman empire and, by the 19th century, had established a right to self-government. They celebrated it by fighting a civil war in 1860, and provoking foreign, notably French, intervention.

After World War I, France was awarded Syria as a mandate by the League of Nations and, in 1920, created Lebanon. The Maronites' and Druses' Mount

Lebanon fastnesses were enlarged by the addition of the coastal strip, including the port cities of Tripoli, Beirut and Sidon, and the Bekaa valley and the crest of the Anti-Lebanon to the east. The new state had a small Christian majority.

The Syrians have never recognized Lebanon's separate identity, claiming that it should be part of Greater Syria (which they sometimes also say should include Jordan and Palestine). Many Lebanese Muslims and non-Maronite Christians shared this view, objecting to their forcible inclusion into a Maronite-dominated state.

France was compelled, by Britain, to give Lebanon and Syria their independence in 1943. To begin with, Muslim and Christian leaders in Lebanon agreed to work together. In an unofficial deal, later known as the National Pact, they laid down that the power of the state should be kept at a minimum, leaving the various confessional groups to run their own affairs as they wished. The enfeebled government would be controlled by a Maronite president and a Sunni prime minister, with a Shiite as president of the Chamber of Deputies; in Parliament, there would be a permanent ratio of six Christians to every five Muslims.

There was one essential weakness in this system. It precluded the emergence of any national sentiment. People considered themselves Maronites or Druse, Sunni or Shiite, never as Lebanese. Other Middle Eastern states formed of the fragments of the Ottoman empire tried to turn themselves into nations. Lebanon never did.

The religion-based appointments and the parliamentary ratio reflected the diversity of Lebanese society at the time. However, in subsequent decades, the numerical balance of the population changed radically. In particular, the Shiite Muslims, the poorest and most oppressed section, overtook the Sunnis and the Maronites. By 1975, Muslims were in a clear majority and would not indefinitely accept a Maronite stranglehold on the presidency.

The country was actually run by a shifting alliance of notables: landowners from the mountains or rich merchants from the cities. Some of the leading families go back to Ottoman times, including the Jumblatts (Druse), Franjiehs (Maronite) and Karamis (Sunni). Others rose to prominence during the Mandate, including the Chamouns and Gemayels (both Maronites). Pierre Gemayel visited Berlin in 1936 and, impressed by the Nazis' efficiency, founded a quasi-Fascist party, the Phalange, which in due course recruited its own militia.

Lebanon throve as the West's gateway to the Arab world. It was the Middle East's banking and commercial centre and was also the base for Western news organizations – and intelligence operations. Generations of journalists, diplomats, scholars and spies learned Arabic at the American University in Beirut or at the British Foreign Office school overlooking the city. The Lebanese, and most particularly the Maronites, maintained close links with France, as well as with Britian and the United States. Arabs from Saudi Arabia and the Gulf came to Beirut to escape the shackles of Arabian austerity.

The prosperity of the 1950s and 1960s never touched the underclass of Shiites and Palestinians, who were excluded from the political process. Lebanon was also corrupt, which offended those who did not benefit from that corruption. It had little industry to occupy the lower classes; the ports and roads were antiquated and neglected; and, above all, there was a growing schism between the élite and the   307 working class. While the élite looked West, the Muslim majority increasingly looked to radical Arab regimes: Egypt in the 1950s and 1960s, the PLO or Iraq in the 1970s, and the 1980s, some of them looked to the Ayatollah's Iran.

THE FIRST CIVIL WAR AND AFTERWARDS

In 1958, these pressures exploded in a brief civil war. In February, Egypt and Syria proclaimed their union, and President Nasser preached pan-Arab radicalism and encouraged revolution throughout the Arab world. In July, the Hashemite monarchy was overthrown in Iraq, King Hussein was threatened in Jordan and serious troubles broke out in Lebanon when President Camille Chamoun decided that he would run for a second term. He appealed for help: President Eisenhower sent the Marines into Beirut, and the British, briefly, sent troops to bolster Hussein.

Twenty years later, people looked back nostalgically to that episode. The shooting always stopped for lunch, and local ceasefires were arranged by telephone to enable people to go shopping. Legend has it that, as the Marines came up the beach, watched by admiring bathing beauties, they were greeted with enthusiasm by ice-cream vendors. The dispute was settled, or at least papered over, by removing Chamoun and asking the Marines to go home.

Afterwards, however, Lebanon increasingly developed into a battleground between foreigners, most notably the Palestinians and the Israelis. Israel had first invaded Lebanon during its war of independence in 1948, and for a year it occupied the country as far as the Litani river. In the aftermath of that war, about 100,000 Palestinian refugees had come to Lebanon. Most of them, and their descendants, still live in camps immediately south of Beirut, and around Tyre and Sidon in south Lebanon, Tripoli in the north, and at Baalbek in the Bekaa valley.

Lebanon stayed clear of the 1956, 1967 and 1973 wars between Israel and its Arab neighbours, and profited from the instability of the rest of the Middle East. The joke in Israel was that no one knew which Arab country would make peace first, but everyone knew which would come second: Lebanon. Things did not work out like that. Neither the Arab militants nor Israel would respect Lebanon's neutrality. On 26 December 1968, Arab terrorists attacked an El Al plane at Athens airport, killing two people. Israel retaliated two days later by raiding Beirut airport and blowing up 13 aircraft belonging to Middle East Airlines, which were parked there. More Palestinians had come to Lebanon after the Six Day War in 1967, and two years later, Nasser obliged the Lebanese government to give the PLO free rein in southern Lebanon. The PLO then mounted its first raids across the border into Israel – and Israel mounted its first retaliatory attacks. When King Hussein drove the PLO out of Jordan in 'Black September' 1970, its commandos and headquarters moved to Beirut, and armed Palestinian units took over the camps.

By then, the Shiites of southern Lebanon and the Beirut slums had become radicalized under the leadership of the Imam Musa Sadr. They rejected Maronite and Sunni leadership and allied themselves with the Palestinians against the government. They were also militantly anti-Israeli, partly because of the increasingly frequent and bloody Israeli raids upon southern Lebanon. Musa Sadr founded his own army – the Amal Militia – and played a large part in the civil war of 1975. He disappeared in Libya in 1978, presumably murdered by Khadafy.

308

The Maronites were divided into three clans. Chamoun's power base was in the urban centres of Beirut and Damour, on the coast south of Beirut. The Gemayels controlled Jounieh, on the coast north of Beirut and in the mountains behind, and Suleiman Franjieh, who was president from 1970 to 1976, controlled the Maronite heartland in the northern recesses of Mount Lebanon. A shoot-out in a church between members of the Franjieh clan and supporters of President Chamoun in 1957 had left over 20 people dead. By 1975, the Gemayels were the most powerful clan because they controlled the largest militia (known as the Kataib) through their party, the Phalange.

THE SECOND CIVIL WAR

The civil war was sparked on 13 April 1975 by the massacre by the Kataib of about 25 Palestinians who had been travelling in a bus through the Christian village of Zgharta, near Tripoli in northern Lebanon. The Phalange had been consecrating a new church at the time, and thought the sudden appearance of a bus-load of Palestinians an intolerable provocation – so they shot them.

The PLO retaliated against unoffending Christians, and the vendetta began, with over 100 people killed in the north during the first ten days of September. The fighting slowly expanded and grew steadily more violent, progressively sucking in all the many opposing factions of Lebanese society. By the end of the year, the civil war had become a conflict between Maronites and Muslims, and the Maronites were winning.

The government collapsed on 7 May. President Suleiman Franjieh appointed a military government, which disintegrated a few days later, and, on 28 May, appointed Rashid Karami as prime minister. The first American hostage, Colonel Ernest Morgan, was kidnapped on 29 June, but he was released unharmed on 12 July. By the autumn, there was a full-scale civil war under way in Beirut, and for the first time, Syria tried to mediate. In December, the frontline between Muslims and Maronites was in the heart of Beirut, with the big hotels along the seafront the main strategic objectives of the two sides. Meanwhile, the Christians had laid siege to Palestinian camps, notably Tal al-Zaatar in East Beirut, and Muslim and Druse armies, joined by the PLO, were besieging two Christian towns: Zahle, in the Bekaa valley; and Damour, south of Beirut, which was Camille Chamoun's fiefdom.

The PLO intervention turned the tide against the Maronites. Damour was overrun on 21 January 1976, and its inhabitants massacred or driven out. Christian villages in the north around Tripoli, in the southern mountains and in the Bekaa were attacked and destroyed.

In February, Muslims started deserting the Lebanese Army, and in March, the army split into Christian and Muslim units. The Muslims called themselves the Lebanese Arab Army and joined the PLO, Druse and various Muslim militias in the drive towards the Christian heartland. On 21 March, Muslims captured the Holiday Inn, the key to downtown Beirut. After that, the Christians were confined to the eastern part of the city.

In desperation, the Maronite leaders called on the Syrians for help. Syria, fearing anarchy, leftist revolution and Israeli intervention on its borders, acceded, and President Assad turned on his former allies, the PLO, Druse and left-wing Sunni militia. The Syrian army crossed the border in strength in April and, on 1 June, mounted a full-scale intervention. They provided cover for a Christian counter-attack on Palestinian positions, notably Tal al-Zaatar on the Christian side of Beirut. Michael Aoun, now nominal leader of the Maronites, first made his name by directing that operation. The camp fell on 13 August.

The Syrian army moved towards the southern border, but stopped at the 'Red Line' drawn by Israel, 5 miles (8 km) from the frontier. A ceasefire was promulgated in November. The Lebanese government calculated that 35,000 people had been killed in the fighting since April 1975.

In May 1976, under extreme Syrian pressure, Lebanese politicians had agreed to elect a new president, Elias Sarkis, and he took office on 23 September. The brutal repression of the PLO continued. On 27 September, four Palestinian terrorists seized a hotel in Damascus in protest, and took 90 hostages. Four hostages and one terrorist were killed when the Syrian army stormed the place: the three surviving terrorists were hanged publicly the next day. On 11 October, another group of Palestinians attacked the Syrian embassy in Rome. They called themselves 'Black June', after the date of the Syrian intervention in Lebanon.

On 2 February 1977, the Druse leader, Kemal Jumblatt, one of the principal opponents of the Maronites, was assassinated, possibly by the Syrians. His son, Walid, immediately took his place. The Christians and Syrians soon fell out, chiefly on the issue of the Christians' relations with Israel: the Israelis were now arming and training Christian militias and independent army units in southern Lebanon, and these forces were attacking PLO positions there. The Syrians started shelling Christian East Beirut. Assad patched up his quarrel with Arafat, and faced with this new alliance against them, the Christians turned for help to the Israelis.

THE FIRST ISRAELI INVASION

In March 1978, Israel invaded Lebanon, officially in retaliation for a PLO raid on Israel which had killed 32 people. A large group of Palestinian troops had landed on the coast north of Tel Aviv, and had commandeered a bus filled with civilians, most of whom were killed at an army roadblock. In fact, Israel was already preparing to invade, and simply used the bus incident as a pretext. The army occupied the country as far as the Litani river, with the object of crushing the PLO: over 2000 people were killed and 250,000 driven from their homes. After some months, President Carter insisted that Israel pull back to its own borders, and a UN force (UNIFIL) was sent to police the border. However, Israel had by then established its own private Christian Lebanese army, led by Major Saad Haddad, along the frontier, which pushed UNIFIL further north. In Israeli terms, the invasion had not been a success – partly because it was widely anticipated, and the PLO had been able to escape to the north, and partly because the Israelis did not hit the main PLO bases in Beirut. The minister of defence, Ariel Sharon, determined to avoid those errors next time.

At this point, the Maronites started fighting among themselves. Pierre Gemayel's son, Bashir, attempted to overrun the Franjieh fief in the north, starting by ordering the assassination of the former president's son Tony on 13 June; his wife and daughter and 30 other people were also killed. Ever since, the

Franjeih and Gemayel clans have remained bitter enemies (Franjieh may have played a role in the murder of Bashir Gemayel in 1982). The Franjiehs have allied themselves with Syria while the Gemayels called in the Israelis. The latter also suppressed the Chamoun militia in 1979, and incorporated it into the Kataib, now renamed the Lebanese Forces.

Israel began a policy of 'pre-emptive strikes' against supposed Palestinian targets in Lebanon, bombing that country much as the United States had once bombed Cambodia. However, the PLO had mobile rocket launchers, mounted on trucks, with a range of up to 15 miles (24 km), and in July 1981, they launched a rocket attack on northern Israel. In retaliation, the Israelis bombed Beirut, killing 120 people. Three days later, the PLO launched a massive rocket attack that hit a score of targets throughout northern Israel. After that, a ceasefire was arranged by the US mediator, Philip Habib, and rocket attacks ceased.

In the spring of 1981, the Syrians had moved a large number of Soviet anti-aircraft missile batteries into eastern Lebanon to protect their armies against Israeli air attacks. The Israelis rather perversely denounced the move as provocative, insisting on their right to patrol the skies of Lebanon uncontested, bombing what they willed. But for a strenuous American diplomatic effort, there might have been another war between Israel and Syria on the issue.

Sharon was convinced that the only way to ensure Israel's security was to eliminate the PLO from Lebanon and install a friendly government there. Israel had long since entered into an alliance with the Lebanese Forces of Bashir Gemayel, providing most of their weapons. Now Sharon started planning a summer campaign. He informed the US secretary of state, Alexander Haig, who offered no objection.

'OPERATION PEACE IN GALILEE'

The next Israeli invasion – dubbed 'Operation Peace in Galilee' – began on 6 June 1982, Israel offering as a pretext the attempted assassination of its ambassador in London (see Arab terrorism, pp. 526–47). The Israeli government announced that it wished to establish a demilitarized zone to extend 15 miles (24 km) north of the frontier to protect northern Israel from rocket attacks (of which, in fact, there had been none since the ceasefire).

Sharon had other ideas, and pushed his armies up to Beirut, placing the city under siege. At least 10,000 people, most of them civilians, were killed in this first phase of the war. In violent fighting with the Syrian army, the Israelis seized the southern Bekaa valley and inflicted a humiliating defeat on the Syrian air force: between 8 and 10 June, Israel shot down 61 Syrian MiGs at a loss of one Israeli plane; they also destroyed 17 of Syria's 19 SAM sites. On 11 June, Israel announced a ceasefire with Syria, which the latter immediately accepted: meanwhile, Israeli troops completed their advance to Beirut. On 22 June, the Israelis seized the Beirut–Damascus highway, cutting off 10,000 Syrian troops in Beirut (including a unit of special forces commanded by Rifaat Assad, President Assad's brother).

The PLO was routed in fighting in the countryside, but put up a stout defence in Beirut. The Israelis had no experience of urban warfare, and their initial attacks were repulsed. (They hoped that the Christian militias would do the work for them, but Bashir Gemayel declined the honour.) The Israeli air force inflicted immense damage on West Beirut: the attacks, televised around the world from the safety of Christian East Beirut, provoked comparisons with the Luftwaffe's attacks on Rotterdam and London, or the USAF attacks on Hanoi. Eventually, on 19 August, the United States brokered an agreement with Israel, the Arab nations and the PLO, and the latter evacuated Beirut – about 6000 fighters by road to Damascus, and another 8000, including the high command, by sea – under the protection of American, French and other Western troops.

The Americans had suggested that they would remain in Beirut, and Israel had promised not to move into West Beirut. In the event, the American and other Western troops left immediately, and Israel marched into West Beirut and set up positions around the refugee camps.

On 23 August, Bashir Gemayel was elected president of Lebanon by the Chamber of Deputies. He promised to unite the country and make peace with Syria and his Maronite and Shiite enemies – and conspicuously refused to sign a peace treaty with Israel. Three weeks later, on 14 September, he was assassinated by a bomb at Phalange party headquarters, together with 26 party supporters. The assassin was a member of a left-wing Syrian Christian party, allied at various times to the PLO and the Druse. The murder was possibly committed at Syrian instigation and perhaps with the complicity of Suleiman Franjieh.

On the following day, Israel completed its occupation of West Beirut. Then, at Israel's request, the Lebanese Forces entered the Palestinian refugee camps of Sabra and Shatila to hunt for PLO terrorists. They massacred between 700 and 2000 people. In the international outcry that followed, Israel was blamed, although no Israelis had been directly involved.

THE AMERICAN INTERVENTION

The US government and its allies promptly sent troops to protect the refugee camps: a 5800-strong Multi-National Force (MNF), consisting of US Marines, and French, British and Italian contingents. To begin with, the MNF, like previous armies of occupation, was welcomed because it brought stability to West and South Beirut. The Shiites and Palestinians soon turned against it, however, as it became apparent that the MNF was intended to assist the largely Christian Lebanese Army.

The Israelis remained in Beirut, still hoping that a permanent peace treaty could be concluded – but in vain. The PLO infiltrated back into the camps and Shiite militias soon began to attack Israeli positions. The Israeli HQ at Tyre was destroyed by a car bomb on 11 November 1982, killing 90; it was blown up a second time, by another suicide driver, on 5 November 1983, this time killing 28 Israelis. A suicide car bomb was launched against the US embassy on 23 April 1983, destroying the building and killing 16 Americans (including the chief CIA expert on the Middle East) and 33 other people.

On 17 May 1983, Secretary of State George Shultz arranged a 'withdrawal agreement', signed by Amin Gemayel (Bashir's brother, who had taken over the presidency on 23 September 1982) and the Israelis, providing for the total withdrawal of foreign forces from Lebanon, a general settlement there and a peace treaty between Lebanon and Israel. However, Syria and most of the other Lebanese factions refused to sign.

Meanwhile, Israel had turned West Beirut over to the Lebanese Army, which began to round up Palestinian and Shiite suspects. At the same time, the Maronites, under Israeli protection, seized control of the predominantly Druse Shuf mountains overlooking Beirut to the south-east. In July 1983, the Druse and Shiites struck back and drove the Army out of West Beirut. A ceasefire was declared, and the Army returned.

Then the Israeli government, shaken by domestic and international opposition, and guerrilla attacks on its positions, pulled back from Beirut. On 17 August it took up positions on the Awali river just north of Sidon, 20 miles (32 km) south of Beirut, and, at the end of the month, abruptly abandoned the Shuf, leaving the Lebanese Forces to their fate. Immediately, a mixed force of Druse and Shiite militia attacked them and won a decisive victory. The Lebanese Forces were driven out of the Shuf – and 75,000 Christian civilians fled their homes. The United States tried to help by shelling Druse villages with the big guns of the battleship *New Jersey* anchored off the coast, convincing proof the US was no longer neutral in the domestic disputes of the Lebanese.

The American Marines and other Western troops remained in their positions in Beirut, although there was no longer any clear reason for their presence. On 23 October a suicide driver broke through to the US Marine barracks near the airport, and the bomb he carried killed 241 Marines. Simultaneously, another truck was driven into the French barracks, killing 58.

The Druse stepped up their shelling of American and French positions around the airport. In retaliation on 17 November, French Mystères attacked what were believed to be terrorist bases in the Bekaa valley. Not to be outdone, and on the pretext that the Syrians had fired on unarmed American reconaissance planes, 28 American aircraft from carriers out in the Mediterranean attacked Syrian anti-aircraft missile sites in Lebanon on 4 December. Two planes were lost: an A-7 Corsair, whose pilot baled out safely over Christian territory; and an A-6E, whose pilot, Lieutenant Robert Goodman, was captured by the Syrians, and the other member of the crew was killed. On the same day, eight Marines were killed by a shell falling on their bunker. The American politician, the Reverend Jesse Jackson, went to Damascus early in the New Year, and persuaded President Assad to release Lieutenant Goodman on 3 January 1984.

The dominant local military force was now the Amal Militia, headed by Nabih Berri. His troops occupied West Beirut in February 1984 and, as the Israelis retreated south, Amal followed and took their place. The Lebanese Army was left with only the Maronite heartland, East Beirut and a tiny enclave around the presidential palace.

The Multi-National Force was now isolated and in constant danger, and served no purpose whatever. After insisting, repeatedly, that the Marines would remain, President Reagan suddenly announced, on 2 February, that they would be 'redeployed to the fleet'. The other Western garrisons promptly followed the American example. The French left a small observer force, which was subject to repeated attack until it, too, was finally evacuated in April 1986.

On 20 September 1984, the American embassy in Beirut was blown up by a car bomb for the second time. After the original building, near the seafront in West Beirut, had been demolished in April of the previous year, the embassy had been moved to a rented office building in the supposed security of East Beirut; this security was provided by Christian militiamen under American supervision. The second attack was carried out like the first, and like the attack on the Marine barracks: a car packed with several hundred pounds of explosives was driven at great speed through the checkpoints and up to the building. Its driver was heading for the underground carpark, and if he had made it, the whole building would have been demolished and everyone in it killed. By happy coincidence, the British ambassador to Lebanon, Donald Miers, was visiting his American colleague, Reginald Bartholemew. Miers' British bodyguard was standing outside the embassy, saw what was happening and managed to shoot the driver before he could reach the carpark entrance. The car hit a wall and exploded. About 20 people were killed. The two ambassadors were slightly injured.

THE NEW STALEMATE
The chief beneficiary of Israel's progressive withdrawal was Syria, which advanced its troops into central Lebanon. The destruction of the military power of the PLO had long been a Syrian objective, and had now been partly achieved by the Israelis. Syria set about completing the process.

Dissidents within the PLO accused Yassir Arafat of incompetence and weakness, because he had lost Beirut and had then opened negotiations with King Hussein of Jordan, and President Mubarak of Egypt, both of whom supported an American peace plan that would have involved recognizing Israel. The dissidents attacked Arafat's supporters in PLO camps in Baalbek in the Bekaa valley, but the loyalists regrouped in two camps near Tripoli in north Lebanon. In October 1983, the Syrians and their Palestinian clients, together with Franjieh's Christians, besieged the Palestinian camps, and the city of Tripoli itself, which was controlled by a fundamentalist Sunni sect, the al Tawhid.

After heavy fighting and many civilian casualties, Syria occupied the camps, but refrained from storming Tripoli, for political-religious reasons. Arafat, who had gone to the city, was allowed to evacuate it with his troops, once again claiming victory in defeat. He moved his HQ to Tunis.

PEACE EFFORTS
In the autumn of 1983, Syria sponsored a meeting of Lebanese notables in Geneva, in the hopes of settling the many disputes of Lebanon. President Gemayel made many concessions, including a new division of parliament giving Muslims equal representation with Christians. He was, however, repudiated by the Lebanese Forces once ruled by his brother, which seized East Beirut from the Army. A further meeting in Lausanne in March 1984 broke up on the question of the presidency: Suleiman Franjieh refused to abandon the Maronite claim to that office.

There was fighting between the Sunni militia in West Beirut – the Murabitun, which was allied to the PLO – and the Druse. Meanwhile, the Shiite community was badly split; fundamentalists under Syrian protection challenged Berri's Amal Militia, and there was a great increase in the fundamentalists' influence in south Lebanon. The same groups that sent their young martyrs on suicide attacks against Western and Israeli positions were now challenging the main-line Muslim leaders.

In February 1985, Israel withdrew from the Sunni city of Sidon, and there was an immediate settling of accounts with suspected collaborators. On 12 March, the Lebanese Forces, under Samir Geagea, repudiated President Gemayel's leadership and attacked Sidon. In April, a coalition of Syrian-supported Druse, Sunni, Palestinian and Shiite forces – all the Muslims in Lebanon – attacked the Lebanese Forces and defeated them. The Christian population in the hills behind Sidon, 75,000 people, were driven north.

Then in May, Amal tried to capture the Palestinian camps in Beirut and was beaten off, with heavy civilian casualties on both sides. Amal kept the camps under siege and shelled them regularly until early 1988.

LEBANON TODAY

On 8 March 1985, a car bomb exploded outside a building in West Beirut controlled by the Hizbollah, an extremist, pro-Iranian Shiite sect. The bombing was directed at the Hizbollah leader, Sheikh Mohammed Hussein Fadlallah, who is believed to be the director of the Islamic Jihad terrorist group responsible for most of the kidnappings of Westerners (*see below*). In the explosion, 80 people were killed and 256 wounded. Fadlallah escaped: he had been delayed by the importunings of a woman suppliant. It was later reported in Washington that the director of the CIA, William Casey, had asked Saudi Arabia to finance a Maronite terrorist group in an attempt to assassinate Fadlallah. By this time, car bombs had become the weapon of choice of all parties among Lebanon's factions, and were causing more casualties than the shelling.

Attacks on Israel's remaining troops increased rapidly, soon reaching four a day, and there was a steady flow of casualties. Eventually the occupation proved too costly, and the Israelis completed their withdrawal in June 1985, taking many thousands of Palestinian and Lebanese prisoners with them. However, they left a 1500-strong 'South Lebanon Army' (SLA), commanded first by Saad Haddad and, when he died in 1984, by former General Antoine Lahad. It controls a strip along the border and a narrow finger of territory running north to Jezzine, in the mountains above Sidon. The Israelis periodically undertake operations beyond the SLA zone, including a sweep through 25 villages in February 1986, after two Israeli soldiers were captured; 15 people were killed in that operation.

In the summer of 1985, after the disaster in the south, Geagea was removed as commander of the Lebanese Forces. His replacement Elie Hobeiqa – who had commanded the troops that had perpetrated the Shatila and Sabra massacres in 1982 – went to Damascus on 9 September and made his peace with the Syrians, and on 28 December, he, Berri and Jumblatt signed an agreement on a new constitution. This brief moment of hope lasted all of two weeks. On 15 January 1986, Geagea, now allied with Gemayel, mounted a coup in the Lebanese Forces and ousted Hobeiqa. The Sunni were also dissatisfied with the Damascus agreement, which therefore collapsed.

There was renewed fighting between Christian and Muslim militias in Beirut, provoked by an attempt by Hobeiqa, supported by Syria, to seize the Voice of Lebanon radio station. Fighting also broke out between Geagea's Lebanese Forces and the Lebanese Army, which had been painfully reconstituted by the Americans; it disintegrated once again.

315

Amal had been besieging the Palestinians in their South Beirut camps since the spring of 1985. By December 1986, 60 per cent of the Shatila camp had been destroyed in the shelling, but the Palestinians continued to resist. The PLO commandos, banished to Tunis in 1982, were now returning to Lebanon, supported by the Hizbollah faction of Lebanese Shiites and the Druse; Palestinian artillery in the Druse-controlled mountains shelled Amal positions in West Beirut. In December, Amal, supported by Shiite units of the Lebanese Army, mounted a full-scale assault on the camps, with tanks and 'Stalin Organs' (multiple rocket launchers). They failed to capture them.

On 5 July 1986, the Syrians returned to Beirut for the first time since 1982, and restored order in West Beirut. Syrian troops began to demolish the barricades that made up the 'Green Line' dividing Christian and Muslim Beirut.

In February 1987, they once again tried to stop the fighting, and this time, they attacked the Hizbollah militias in South Beirut. In four days, they cleared the streets of armed gangs, and assaulted a Hizbollah strongpoint, slaughtering 23 militiamen. They did not, however, clear out the camps or rescue any of the Westerners held hostage. In April, they advanced to the two Palestinian camps, Shatila and Burj el Brajneh, which the Amal Militia had been besieging since 1985, but they did not interfere.

On 20 January 1988, the Amal Militia abandoned its siege of the two camps, as an act, said Nabih Berri, Amal's leader, of solidarity with the Palestinian rioters in Gaza and the West Bank. The siege had cost at least 2500 lives. Amal was now free to resume its battle with the Hizbollah. The fighting started in Nabatiye in south Lebanon in April. To begin with, Amal had the upper hand and occupied a number of Shiite villages that had been controlled by Hizbollah; they also attacked Iranian Revolutionary Guards who were operating in the district. Israel contributed in early May by invading south Lebanon and clearing out a series of Hizbollah strongholds, the most important of which was the village of Maydun: 40 Hizbollah militiamen and three Israeli soldiers were killed in the operation. The fighting then spread to Beirut.

The two sides used heavy artillery and mortars in the slums, and hundreds of people were killed. In four days of fighting, Hizbollah defeated Amal, and took control of the coastal highway past the airport. On 14 May, the Syrians intervened to protect Amal from further defeat, and cautiously moved troops into the slums. The caution was necessary: on 26 May a car carrying four Syrian generals, the most senior officers in Lebanon, was attacked in a Hizbollah district by a dozen gunmen; the generals escaped. On 28 May, after protracted negotiations, Hizbollah pulled back from the positions it had captured, and allowed the Syrians to occupy them with 7000 troops and 50 tanks. The Lebanese police calculated that 660 people had been killed that May in fighting between the Shiite factions, between PLO factions in the camps, and in car bombings, which continued to be the favourite terrorist weapon in Lebanon.

TERRORISM

Naked terrorism has been a constant in all the fighting since 1975. The Shatila and Sabra massacres were nothing new. Muslims had massacred hundreds of Christians in the prosperous Christian town of Damour, south of Beirut. Their objective had

316

been to clear the area of Christians, and they succeeded. In the same month, Christian militiamen massacred Palestinians in a refugee camp in Karantina in North Beirut, in a Christian area they wanted cleared. The Druse, the PLO, the Sunni militias, the Syrians, the Israelis – they have all sought to achieve their ends by slaughtering their enemies.

Assassination is a favoured political statement in the Middle East, particularly in Lebanon. The Druse leader, Kemal Jumblatt, was assassinated in February 1977. In June 1978, Bashir Gemayel had Tony Franjieh assassinated, and was himself assassinated in September 1982. Prime Minister Rashid Karami was killed by a bomb planted in his helicopter on 1 June 1987, and in February 1988, a bomb was found in President Amin Gemayel's plane. Foreign murderers play their part: President Assad was suspected of complicity in several assassinations, and Colonel Khadafy of Libya probably ordered the murder of the Shiite leader Musa Sadr, who disappeared in Libya in August 1978.

In such a context, killing and kidnapping Westerners was no exceptional tactic. The Islamic Jihad clearly aimed at ending all Western influence in Lebanon. Sometimes – as in the hijacking of a TWA flight in 1985, in which the plane was brought to Beirut and its passengers carried off to Shiite strongholds there – the terrorists made political demands (*see* Arab terrorism, pp. 526–47). On that occasion, they wanted PLO prisoners in Israel to be released. When the United States bombed Libya in April 1986, Lebanese terrorists retaliated by murdering two British and one American hostage, because some of the US planes were based in England.

The principle of political dealings with terrorists was often denounced by Israeli, American and European politicians, but each country was ready to deal on occasion. In 1985–6, the US government secretly negotiated with the Iranians to win the release of American hostages in Lebanon. Two were released, apparently as a result of the delivery of American arms to Tehran. The Israelis exchanged prisoners with the PLO, and the West Germans and French paid ransom for their citizens.

Western governments repeatedly warned their citizens to leave Lebanon. Some refused, and paid with their liberty: a new wave of kidnappings early in 1988 merely confirmed the danger. Among those kidnapped was a US Marine, Lieutenant Colonel William Higgins, serving with UNIFIL, who was abducted on 17 February. A few days earlier, the Frenchman Jacques Merin, reportedly the No. 2 man on the Lebanon desk of the French secret service, was shot in East Beirut just after leaving a meeting with Lebanese security officials. He had presumably been engaged in negotiations for the release of French hostages in Lebanon – they were eventually released in May.

The tensions between Maronites and Muslims, and within the Maronite community itself, that were at the origin of the civil war continued. President Gemayel's term expired in September, and although the office has no power, fighting for the succession (it cannot be called an election) was intense. The Syrians first supported Suleiman Franjieh. However, he was unacceptable to the Gemayel clan, and when the Chamber of Deputies gathered in August to elect a new president, the Christian militias ensured that there would be no election by the simple method of preventing enough deputies to attend to form a quorum.

317

Subsequently, Syria supported another candidate, Mikhail Daher, but he, too, proved to be unacceptable to the Maronite extremists. Thus, when Gemayel's term ended on 22 September, the office became vacant. Gemayel, as his last act, appointed General Michel Aoun as prime minister. He was the Maronite commander of the largely Maronite Lebanese Army, an organization that had played a small and inglorious part in the civil war but which had also been built up into some semblance of efficiency with American help.

Aoun formed an alliance with Geagea, who continued to command the principal Christian militia. Their avowed intention was to expel the Syrians from Lebanon and then settle accounts with the rival militias. Their alliance broke down in February 1989, when serious fighting between their armies began.

The Muslims of all shades, and the Druse and the Maronite followers of Suleiman Franjieh, all denounced Aoun's new government as illegal, and continued to give their allegiance to the government of Selim Hoss, a Sunni who had been appointed acting prime minister on the assassination of Rashid Karami, but had never been voted formally into office because the Chamber of Deputies could not meet. Aoun offered seats in his cabinet to Muslim military men. They refused. Hoss, in turn, formed a government excluding the Maronites.

The split was of great symbolic importance, pushing Lebanon to the brink of permanent partition, but it had little practical consequence. There had been no effective national government for years, and local administration was entirely in the hands of local warlords. All that the new dispensation changed were the circumstances of Lebanon's diplomats abroad, who now had not one but two powerless foreign ministers to report to. They resolved the dilemma by ignoring both. They assumed that, sooner or later, a president would be chosen, through some face-saving formula, though he would be as completely powerless as Gemayel had been. In the meantime, since Lebanon had no foreign policy, their diplomatic confusion did not matter very much.

In March 1989, Aoun attacked the Syrians in their positions in and around west Beirut. He demanded that Syria withdraw completely from Lebanon and apparently hoped that he could provoke the international community to force the withdrawal. Beirut then suffered the worst devastation of its long martyrdom. The world community, as usual, did nothing. Aoun's only support came from Israel and Iraq, a curious alliance based on their joint detestation of Syria. It proved sufficient to prevent the Christian heartland from being overrun by Moslem armies in their first offensive, but not nearly enough to defeat the Syrians. Aoun's artillery shelled west Beirut and the Syrians, Druse and Lebanese Moslems shelled east Beirut. Most of the city's inhabitants fled, those that remained taking refuge in cellars and air-raid shelters. The guns systematically destroyed the city: now it resembles Berlin in 1945. In September, Aoun threatened to unleash 'Christian terrorism' against the Americans, because of their failure to come to his aid. The United States thereupon evacuated their embassy from Beirut.

There is no Lebanese state, no government, no common citizenship or sense of national solidarity between the factions. There is no Lebanon, only ruins.

Chronology of the Civil War in Lebanon

1975

13 April	25 Palestinians massacred by Christian militia (Kataib) in Zgharta, north Lebanon. Muslims retaliate by killing Christians, and by end of year, full-scale civil war is under way. PLO supports Muslims. Christians attack PLO camps and Muslims.
7 May	Government collapses. Rashid Karami appointed prime minister 28 May.
21 September	Syria sends high-level mediation team. It fails.
8 December	General Muslim offensive in downtown Beirut. Heavy fighting around seafront hotels. Maronites lay siege to Tal al-Zaatar, a Palestinian camp in East Beirut.

1976

21 January	Druse army captures Damour, Christian town south of Beirut, driving out inhabitants.
March	Lebanese army splits between Christian and Muslim units. Muslims, aided by Druse and PLO, win upper hand, occupying Christian positions throughout country.
1 June	Syria intervenes, to support Maronites. Syrians occupy much of south Lebanon and the Bekaa valley, dividing the combatants in Beirut. Death toll computed at 35,000 so far.
23 September	Elias Sarkis installed as president.

1977

2 February	Kemal Jumblatt, Druse leader, assassinated. Syrians turn on Maronites, begin shelling East Beirut. Maronites turn to Israel for help.
September	Israel raids deep into south Lebanon, supporting Christian forces.

1978

12 March	PLO raid on Israel kills 32.
15 March	Israel occupies south Lebanon, as far as Litani river. 2000 people killed, 250,000 driven from their homes.
11 April	Israel begins withdrawal.
13 June	Tony Franjieh assassinated on orders of Bashir Gemayel.

1980

March	Syria withdraws its troops from Beirut. Frequent Israeli air raids and incursions into south Lebanon.

1981

April	Further fighting between Christians and Syrians. Syrians move SAM-7 batteries into Bekaa valley and central Lebanon.
July	PLO launches rocket attack on Israel. Israel retaliates by bombing Beirut. Three days later, PLO rockets hit score of targets in northern Israel. President Reagan's special envoy, Philip Habib, arranges ceasefire.

1982

3 June	Abu Nidal gang attempts to assassinate Israeli ambassador to London.
6 June	Israel launches 'Operation Peace in Galilee'. Israeli armies advance to Beirut and lay siege. Israel defeats the Syrian army in the Bekaa valley and the Israeli air force shoots down 61 Syrian MiGs and destroys 17 of Syria's 19 SAM sites.
11 June	Israel announces a ceasefire with Syria.
22 June	Israel takes the Beirut–Damascus highway, completing encirclement of (Muslim) West Beirut.
19 August	US mediates an agreement between Israel, Syria and the PLO, allowing the latter to evacuate Beirut, protected by American, French and other European troops.
23 August	Bashir Gemayel elected president of Lebanon.
14 September	Gemayel assassinated.
15 September	Israel completes occupation of West Beirut. Lebanese Forces enter Palestinian Shatila and Sabra camps, and massacre between 700 and 2000 people. US and other Western troops return to protect camps.
23 September	Amin Gemayel inaugurated president.
11 November	Israeli military headquarters at Tyre destroyed by suicide car bomb, killing 90.

1983

23 April	Suicide car bomb attack on US embassy in West Beirut kills 49 people.
17 May	US Secretary of State George Shultz arranges for Amin Gemayel and the Israelis to sign a 'withdrawal agreement' which includes *de facto* recognition of Israel. The agreement is repudiated by other Lebanese factions and Syria.
June	Israel pulls out of Shuf mountains overlooking Beirut, and Beirut itself.
July	Druse and Shiites expel Maronites from West Beirut.
17 August	Israel pull back to Awali river, 20 miles (32 km) south of Beirut. Druse and Shiites occupy Shuf, expelling 75,000 Maronite villagers. USS *New Jersey* shells Druse villages in a vain attempt to help the Maronites.
October	PLO dissidents, supported by Syria, attack Arafat's remaining bases in Lebanon, in the Bekaa valley and near Tripoli, in north Lebanon. Arafat once again flees by sea.
23 October	Truck bomb attacks kill 241 US Marines and 58 French soldiers in their barracks.
1 November	Syria sponsors meeting of Lebanese factions in Geneva, to find a peace settlement. It fails.
5 November	Second suicide car bomb attack on Israeli HQ in Tyre kills 25.
17 November	French air force bombs suspected terrorist bases in Bekaa valley.
4 December	28 American planes sent to attack Syrian anti-aircraft bases. Two planes lost, one pilot captured. Eight Marines killed by a shell hitting their bunker near Beirut airport.

1984

February	Amal Militia occupies West Beirut.
2 February	President Reagan announces that US Marines will be 'redeployed to the fleet'.
12 March	Further peace meeting between the factions, in Lausanne, fails.
20 September	Another suicide car bomb attack on new US embassy in East Beirut kills 20.

1985

February	Israel withdraws from Sidon.
8 March	Car bomb explodes outside Hizbollah (pro-Iranian Shiites) HQ in West Beirut, killing 80.
12 March	Maronites under Samir Geagea attack Sunni positions around Sidon. In April, Geagea's forces defeated: 75,000 Christians driven from their homes in and around Sidon.
May	Amal lays siege to Palestinian camps in Beirut. The siege continues for nearly three years.
June	Israel withdraws from southern Lebanon, except for a small area along the frontier.
9 September	Geagea's successor as leader of Maronite forces, Elie Hobeiqa, goes to Damascus and signs peace agreement with President Assad. On 28 December, he signs an agreement with Walid Jumblatt (for the Druse) and Nabih Berri (for the Shiites).

1986

15 January	Geagea and Gemayel depose Hobeiqa as commander of Maronite forces and repudiate his peace agreement. There is heavy fighting in Beirut between the two Maronite factions.
5 July	Syrians return to Beirut; attempt to restore order.
December	Amal mounts a full-scale assault on Palestinian camps. They are seriously damaged, but hold out.

1987

20 January	Archbishop of Canterbury's personal envoy Terry Waite kidnapped and taken hostage.
February	Syrians move into South Beirut and attack Hizbollah positions.
1 June	Prime Minister Rashid Karami assassinated.

1988

January	Amal gives up siege of camps, ostensibly as sign of support for the Palestinian uprising against the Israelis.
April	Amal and Hizbollah start fighting again. Israel intervenes in May by attacking villages controlled by Hizbollah. Between them, they drive Hizbollah out of south Lebanon. Hizbollah, supported by the PLO, defeats Amal in South Beirut. Syria intervenes again, and sends troops to separate two sides.
18 August	Chamber of Deputies fails to elect a new president.
22 September	Amin Gemayel's term as president expires. Gemayel names as successor General Michel Aoun, a Maronite who commanded the (Christian) Lebanese Army. Aoun offers positions in the government to Shiite, Sunni and Druse leaders. Acting prime minister, Selim Hoss, a Sunni, asserts that he continues in office. Lebanon thus is formally partitioned.
18 October	A meeting of the Chamber of Deputies fails to elect a new speaker.
December	Heavy fighting between Amal and Hizbollah resumes.

1989

February	Fighting breaks out between Aoun's Lebanese Army and Geagea's Lebanese forces.
March	Aoun declares war on Syrians and new civil war progressively destroys Beirut.

FURTHER READING

Becker, Jillian, *The PLO: The Rise and Fall of the Palestine Liberation Organization*, New York, St Martin's Press, 1984.

Bulloch, John, *Final Conflict, the War in Lebanon*.

Cobban, Helena, *The Making of Modern Lebanon*, Boulder, Colo., Westview Press, 1985 and *The P.L.O.*, Cambridge University Press, 1984.

Eveland, Wilbur Crane, *Ropes of Sand: America's Failure in the Middle East,* New York, W. W. Norton, 1980.

Gabriel, Richard A., *Operation Peace for Galilee*, New York, Hill and Wang, 1984.

Gilmour, David, *Lebanon, the Fractured Country*, New York, St Martin's Press, 1984.

McDowall, David, *Lebanon: A Conflict of Minorities*, London, Minority Rights Group, 1986.

Rabinovitch, Itamar, *The War for Lebanon, 1970–1983*, New York, Cornell University Press, 1984.

Randall, Jonathan: *Going All the Way: Christian Warlords, Israeli Adventurers and the War in Lebanon*, New York, Viking, 1983.

Schiff, Ze'ev and Ya'ari Ehud, *Israel's Lebanon War*, New York, Simon and Schuster, 1984.

SAUDI ARABIA

Geography	837,972 sq. miles (2,263,579 sq. km). The size of Western Europe. All desert except the mountains behind Mecca and in the south-west.
Population	12 million
Resources	Oil: the largest reserves in the world. Officially 169 billion barrels, but they are certainly far larger than that. In 1982, oil revenue was $99 billion; in 1988, it was estimated at $22 billion.
GNP per capita	$6930

Saudi Arabia is the personal creation of Abdul Aziz ibn Abdul Rahman (1886–1953). In a series of campaigns between 1901 and 1924, he led his followers to the conquest of the peninsula, on camels and on foot, and following the green flag of Islam. It is an empire, like that of Alexander, Genghiz Khan or Tamburlaine, conquered by a leader of genius. It is the last of its kind.

Abdul Aziz was also known as Ibn Saud, an honorific title meaning 'head of the Saud family'. The al Saud are a family, not a tribe, and Saudi Arabia is the only country in the world to be named after a family.

So far, Saudi Arabia has survived its founder's death because the al Saud have formed themselves into a corporation whose ruling principle is that its members must offer a united front to the world and must put the family's interests ahead of their own. Also, the country's enormous wealth enables the government to buy off most opposition.

There is greater strength in a vast and cohesive family than in other, monogamous dynasties, such as the Pahlevis in Iran. There are about 4000 members of the House of Saud: King Abdul Aziz had 42 sons and 20 daughters, and his brothers, cousins and his own sons have been nearly as prolific. When the king of Saudi Arabia proves incompetent, he can be removed. Four of the sons of Abdul' Aziz have succeeded each other on his throne, and plenty of able-bodied sons remain: the youngest was born in 1947. The next generation may prove less orderly: one of them assassinated King Feisal in 1975. However, danger is more likely to come from outside: from those who are excluded from the government 323 because they are not members of the House of Saud; from revivalist sects who believe that the kingdom is insufficiently puritanical; from the armed forces, built up under American supervision to defend the kingdom from the Iranians; from greedy Arabs; or from some combination of these possible threats.

Fundamentalist fanatics seized the Great Mosque in Mecca in 1979 and were finally defeated when the government brought in the army. The protracted war between Iran and Iraq was a continuing threat to Saudi Arabia and the Gulf emirates, and its settlement puts enormous power into the hands of Saddam Hussein, president of Iraq. Another problem for the Saudis comes from constant American pressure on them to take an active part in resolving the dispute between Israel and its neighbours. The kingdom's enormous wealth is a danger as well as a protection: there are many populous and powerful states near by that might be tempted to impose a redistribution of the riches of Araby.

HISTORY

The al Saud family had, at various times in earlier centuries, ruled a large but poverty-stricken kingdom in the desert. Arabia had occasionally been united, but never for long. No tribe had ever been powerful enough to establish permanent rule over the others, and no outsider had coveted the barren wastes. The Turks controlled Mecca and Medina, but left the desert alone.

In 1891, when Abdul Aziz was 17, the al Saud were driven out of their ancestral lands and their capital, Riyadh. The family subsisted on the charity of neighbouring tribes until, in January 1902, Abdul Aziz led the attack that recaptured Riyadh, and from that base, in a series of desert wars, he conquered most of the Arabian peninsula. Kuwait and the other Gulf emirates only escaped his control because they were protected by the British. After World War I, he prepared to attack Transjordan, Syria and Iraq, to follow in the footsteps of the first caliphs, but was again stopped by the British. Had it not been for them the whole peninsula and the 'fertile crescent' might have been united in one enormously rich and powerful kingdom, ruled by a caliph of the House of Saud. How long it would have lasted is a different question.

Abdul Aziz completed his conquests in 1924, when he seized the holy cities of Mecca and Medina from the Shareef Hussein, whose family then moved to Iraq and Jordan. In 1934, in one last attempt at expansion, Abdul Aziz sent an army to conquer the Yemen, but it was defeated.

Saudi Arabia was allied with Britain and the United States during World War II, and on 12 February 1945, King Abdul Aziz visited President Franklin Roosevelt aboard the USS *Quincy* in the Great Bitter Lake, part of the Suez canal. He brought a large suite with him, and enough sheep to feed them, and they all camped on deck, to the wonderment of the American navy. These two remarkable statesmen, despite many misunderstandings and disagreements, then sealed an alliance that has persisted ever since.

Shortly after World War I, an American oil man had visited T. E. Lawrence (Lawrence of Arabia) in Oxford and asked whether it was worth prospecting for oil in Arabia. Lawrence had replied categorically that there was no oil to be found there, and the American had returned happily home.

Well No. 7, the first great Arabian gusher, came in on 20 March 1938. It had been drilled by the Standard Oil Company of California (Socal). World War II interrupted further exploration, and it was not until the 1950s that Saudi Arabia became a major oil producer, but two decades later it became the world's second greatest, after the USSR, and by far the largest exporter. It has the biggest oil reserves in the world, officially 169 billion barrels (but certainly far larger), compared with 66 billion in Kuwait, 67 billion in the USSR and 26 billion in the United States.

MODERN ARABIA

Saudi Arabia's reputation for inscrutable stability was shattered on 20 November 1979 when a group of about 200 fanatical tribesmen from the desert seized the Great Mosque in Mecca. They were followers of an eloquent preacher, Juhayman ibn Muhammed ibn Saif, who believed that his brother-in-law was the Mahdi, a spiritual leader who appears once a century. (The previous Mahdi had been responsible for the death of General Gordon in Khartoum.)

The rebels denounced the alleged decadence of the House of Saud and called on all Arabs to overthrow it. They held off the Saudi army until 4 December. The mosque was slightly damaged in the fighting (the Saudis showed more concern and skill than the Indians did when they attacked the Golden Temple in Amritsar five years later). The rebels were driven out of the buildings that surround the vast courtyard in which stands the Kaaba, the stone structure that is the holiest site in Islam. They took refuge in the cellars, along with their families and hostages, and had to be ferreted out one by one, fighting to the last.

The Mahdi and 116 other rebels were killed, as were 127 soldiers and a dozen civilians. Juhayman was captured and he was executed, along with 62 other survivors, on 9 January 1980.

When the mosque was seized, the government panicked. All communications were cut: it feared that this was part of a *coup d'état*, or a foreign invasion. The confusion spread rumours around the Islamic world: Iran and Libya blamed the United States, and a mob in Islamabad, Pakistan, burned the American embassy, killing a Marine guard and another soldier, while government troops watched.

There were also riots in the kingdom's eastern provinces, the oil territories. Saudi Arabia is overwhelmingly Sunni Muslim, but there is a Shiite minority of about 200,000 people in the east, and they were incited to revolt by the success of the Ayatollah Khomeini's revolution across the Gulf in Iran. The Shiites thought themselves neglected and treated as second-class citizens. These disturbances were briskly suppressed.

THE HAJ RIOTS

One of the duties laid upon the faithful is to go in pilgrimage to Mecca to pray at the Kaaba within the Great Mosque. The pilgrimage, the Haj, follows set rituals and is performed in the month that ends in the Feast of the Sacrifice. In 1987, the Haj took place in July and August.

Organizing the pilgrimage is an immense task, and the Saudis devote a good part of the national budget to it. Two million people come every year, and in 1987, these included 155,000 Iranians. This posed a particular problem, because the Ayatollah Khomeini had called repeatedly for the faithful to rise and overthrow the House of Saud, whom he considered to be heretics. His anger was more political than theological, however: Saudi Arabia had given lavish support to Iraq in its war with Iran.

On 31 July, a riot occurred in Mecca that resulted in the deaths of 402 people, by the Saudi count: 275 Iranians, 85 police and 42 pilgrims of various other nationalities. A further 649, including 303 Iranians, were hospitalized.

The Saudis claimed that the Iranians had deliberately started the riot by marching on the Great Mosque, waving placards with Khomeini's picture on them and chanting anti-Saudi slogans. This had outraged the Saudis: a demonstration on such a holy occasion was, they said, unheard of. They claimed that police had showed great restraint when they had confronted the demonstrators and tried to stop them from approaching the mosque. The rioters had beaten and stabbed them, and when the police had charged, they had panicked and fled. Most of the dead were killed in the stampede.

Other accounts are more complicated. For a start, in the long history of the Haj, there have been plenty of demonstrations. More to the point, the Iranians had negotiated with the Saudi authorities in advance over the question of whether they could parade with pictures of the Ayatollah. They claimed that all they had wanted to do was to hold a prayer meeting before dispersing, that they had been victims of an unprovoked attack, and that the police had used their guns – a charge the Saudis indignantly denied.

Whatever its immediate cause, the riot was clearly a direct consequence of the hostility between the two governments, and whatever the exact sequence of events, the riot was equally clearly chiefly the fault of the Iranians.

There was a riot in Tehran, the Saudi and Kuwaiti embassies there were sacked and four Saudi diplomats were arrested and manhandled. Afterwards, the Ayatollah proclaimed a *jihad*, a holy war, against the Saudis. It had no immediately discernible effect, but the Saudis awaited the next Haj with some trepidation.

Relations between the two countries deteriorated steadily. In the year following the Haj riot, Iranian gunboats periodically attacked shipping, including Saudi shipping, in the Gulf. In March 1988, King Fahd revealed that Saudi Arabia had acquired long-distance surface-to-surface missiles from China, and would use them against Iran if the attacks continued. In the same month, Saudi Arabia for the first time announced limitations on the numbers of pilgrims who would be allowed to attend the Haj – 1000 pilgrims for every million Muslims in the world, and the Iranian quota was 45,000. Iran immediately refused to accept any limitation, and in April, the Ayatollah announced that Iran would send 150,000 pilgrims. 'They shall perform their obligation, which is to declare deliverance from the infidels, the US and Israel,' he said. 'It would be impossible for them to go on the Haj and not stage demonstrations against global oppression, for declaring deliverance from infidels is among the political obligations of the Haj. Without it, the Haj is no Haj.'

Later that month, after Iranian saboteurs set fire to a petrochemical plant in Jubail in Saudi Arabia's oil province, and after an Iranian attack on a Saudi tanker, Saudi Arabia broke diplomatic relations with Iran. In April, Saudi Arabia rejected a new plan, put forward at an OPEC meeting and supported by Iran, that would limit oil production and raise prices.

On 15 June, Iran announced that no Iranians would go on pilgrimage that year: 'Either 150,000 Iranians will go, or no Iranian will go,' an official said. It appeared to be a victory for the Saudis. In fact, Iran was by then losing the war with Iraq, and its government was moving painfully towards its decision to accept a ceasefire. It had evidently concluded that this was no time for further troubles with Saudi Arabia.

At the same time that the Saudis were facing down the Iranians, they were demonstrating their independence of the United States by requiring that the American ambassador, Hume Horan, be recalled. He was not declared *persona non grata*: that would be an affront. Instead, the US State Department was informed that he would no longer enjoy 'access' to the higher reaches of the Saudi government. The ostensible reason for Saudi displeasure was that Horam had delivered an official American protest at the purchase of the Chinese missiles. A deeper reason appeared to be that Horam, unlike most American diplomats, spoke fluent Arabic and interested himself closely in Saudi internal politics. Most important was the fact that the Saudis resent that the United States, and particularly Congress, insists that relations with the Arabs be governed by their concern for Israel. Every time the Saudis try to buy American weapons, the sale is either refused or weighed down with conditions by Congress, for fear that the arms might be used against Israel.

Later that summer, Saudi Arabia placed a large order for weapons (including aircraft and missiles) with British firms, making the British their largest arms supplier. This decision cost the American armaments industry $30 billion in lost business. One Saudi diplomat observed that his countrymen were tired of being insulted. Shortly afterwards, a large order for arms for Kuwait went through Congress without any trouble. The Saudis had made their point.

FURTHER READING

American University, *Saudi Arabia: A Country Study*, Washington D.C., 1984.
Holden, David and Johns, Richard, *The House of Saud*, New York, Holt Rinehart & Winston, 1981.
Lacey, Robert, *The Kingdom: Arabia and the House of Sa'ud*, New York, Harcourt, Brace, Jovanovich, 1981.
Mortimer, Edward, *Faith and Power: The Politics of Islam*, London, Faber and Faber, 1982.

SYRIA

Geography	71,498 sq. miles (185,179 sq. km). Twice the size of Portugal.		
Population	10.9 million, divided as follows:		

Religion	Percentage of population	Language
Muslim		
Sunni	57.4	Arabic
Sunni	8.5	Kurdish
Sunni	3.0	Turkish
Sunni sub-total	68.9	
Schismatic Muslim		
Shiite	1.0	Arabic
Alawite	11.7	Arabic
Ismaili	1.0	Arabic
Druse	3.0	Arabic
Total Muslim	85.6	
Christian		
Eastern Orthodox	4.7	Arabic
Armenian	4.0	Armenian
Other Christian	5.4	Arabic
Total Christian	14.1	
Other (Yazidis, Jews)	0.8	Arabic

GNP per capita	$1560
Refugees	259,850 Palestinians and 4000 Iranians.

HISTORY

Like most of the other states of the Middle East, Syria was conjured into existence after World War I from the wreckage of the Ottoman empire. It had always been a province of a larger state, except for a brief moment of Umayyad glory in the 7th–8th centuries.

Syria was ruled by the Turks from the 16th century until 1918 with occasional interruptions, including conquests by Napoleon and the 19th-century Egyptian ruler, Mohammed Ali. What are now Iraq, Syria, Lebanon, Jordan and Israel were then divided into various administrative districts, but they were all an integral, undivided part of the Ottoman empire. This did not mean that the people of the area had any unified national sentiment. When the League of Nations gave France a mandate to rule Syria, all that united its inhabitants were arbitrary lines on the map, drawn by the French. However, 85 per cent of the population were Muslims of one sort or another, and 90 per cent of the population spoke Arabic. On this basis, successive regimes have tried to construct a nation.

In 1919, the British, then the dominant power in the Middle East, had separated Iraq from Syria and southern Syria from the rest of the province, partly to create a buffer zone to the north of the Suez canal, partly to meet the promise made in 1917 to create a 'national home for the Jews'. The new entity was called Palestine, a biblical name revived for the occasion.

The British had intended that the Emir Feisal, son of the Hashemite King Hussein of the Hejaz, Shereef of Mecca, should become king of Syria, and Feisal's brother Abdullah was to become king of Iraq. Feisal, who had led the Arab revolt against the Turks with the assistance of T. E. Lawrence, installed himself in Damascus in 1918. However, the French had not assented to these arrangements, and when Syria became a French mandate and the new rulers arrived in Damascus in July 1920, they evicted Feisal. He appealed to the British who, as a consolation prize, made him king of Iraq in 1921. (The Hashemite Kingdom of Iraq lasted until 1958, when Feisal's grandson, King Feisal II, was killed in a military coup.)

The Emir Abdullah was left homeless, so he set out from Mecca to reconquer Syria and drive out the French. He got as far as Amman, then very loosely under British control, in March 1921. There, advised of the strength of the French position, he decided that, for the moment, discretion was the better part of valour. He would stay in Amman, in a territory he named Transjordan. The British acquiesced in this *coup de main*, and their new Palestine protectorate was divided into two. When the British gave up the mandate in 1948, Abdullah went to war with Israel, and emerged in control of Jerusalem and the West Bank. He annexed these territories and proclaimed the kingdom of Jordan. He was assassinated in 1951 at the el-Aqsa Mosque in Jerusalem.

Meanwhile, the French, in turn, further subdivided Syria, to create Lebanon. In 1939, Turkey demanded, and obtained, Iskanderun (Alexandretta) and Antioch in the north-west.

France was persuaded to give Syria and Lebanon their independence after World War II. The persuasion was not gentle: their British sent an army to Damascus in 1941 to dispossess the Vichy regime. (One of their Palestinian soldiers, Moshe Dayan, lost an eye in the fight against the French, in a skirmish in southern Lebanon.) In May 1945, the French put down rioting in Damascus by shelling the city. The British government threatened to occupy Syria unless the French departed, which, finally, they did. The present borders of Syria were set when, in 1967, it lost the Golan Heights to Israel as a result of the Six Day War (*see* Israel).

As for the Syrians, this history of a land chopped about by foreigners, all without the least regard for the wishes of its inhabitants (except for the Christians in Lebanon), has left them xenophobic and suspicious. They have never recognized Lebanon as an independent country *de jure*, though they have accepted the reality of its separate existence, and from time to time, they have revived their claims to 'southern Syria', meaning Israel and Jordan, and to Alexandretta.

329

THE BA'ATH

The Ba'ath (Arab Renaissance) party was founded in 1940 in Damascus by Michel Aflaq and Salah al-Din al-Bitar. Aflaq was a Christian, and from the start, the party attracted Arab minorities because it based its pan-Arabism on language, history and ethnicity, not Islam.

Alflaq's objective was 'Unity, Freedom and Socialism'. The Ba'ath was strongly opposed to the colonial powers, France and Britain, an attitude which naturally developed in later years into anti-Americanism and hostility to Israel. The party denounced all the Arab states set up after 1918 as illegitimate. It wanted to revive Arab national consciousness and unite all the Arabs in one state, from the Atlantic to the Gulf, from Marrakesh to Mecca.

The Ba'ath is divided into 'regional commands', one for each of the Arab states. The regional Ba'ath parties in Syria and Iraq eventually seized power, but failed to unite. The pull of nationalism, even in such artificial states, proved stronger than ideology.

After the French departed, Syria was ruled by a succession of ephemeral, authoritarian governments, punctuated by *coups d'état*: there were 15 coups and attempted coups between 1949 and 1970. The Ba'ath party in Syria went underground in 1950, and played an important part in the opposition to the government. Ba'athists were soon influential among army officers, particularly among the Alawites, a heretical Muslim sect concentrated in Latakia province, along the Mediterranean.

In 1958, with the government on the verge of collapse, the Ba'ath took the lead in uniting Syria with Egypt, as the United Arab Republic (UAR). The Ba'ath considered this the first step towards uniting all Arabs, but President Nasser of Egypt saw things differently. He set about suppressing the party in Syria, sowing the seeds for the enmity between the two countries that has persisted ever since. Nasser also sent his vice-president, General Abdul Hakim Amir, as his viceroy to Damascus. Amir made himself, and the Egyptians, deeply unpopular as he ruthlessly repressed all Syrian independence. The general, Nasser's most loyal follower, was later made scapegoat for the Egyptian débâcle in 1967 and committed suicide.

On 28 September 1961, an army coup in Syria abruptly ended the union with Egypt. Egyptian officials were shipped home and a deep frost settled on relations between Cairo and Damascus. They were only reconciled in 1967, just in time for the Six Day War.

After the breakup of the UAR, Syria went through a period of great instability. To begin with, there was a conservative reaction, and Nasser's socialist measures were repealed. Then there were elections followed by a coup on 28 March 1962.

That coup was reversed in April, only to be followed during the next four years by a bewildering series of coups, counter-coups and changes of government. The Ba'ath had formally reconstituted itself in May 1962, and Salah al-Din al-Bitar, a leader of the civilian wing of the party, became prime minister for the first time in March 1963. He had constantly to fight against Nasserites who staged frequent coup attempts, riots and assassinations, and there was a prolonged struggle for power between various factions of the Ba'ath itself. In July 1963, a major Nasserite coup attempt was suppressed and its leaders were executed. As a result, General Amin el-Hafiz became military dictator.

The two main factions of the party were: the 'civilians', though their titular leader, Hafiz, was a general who advocated unity with Iraq and Egypt; and the 'military' wing, which was described as 'regionalist', meaning nationalist. On 23 February 1966, in the bloodiest coup to date, the military purged the civilians, arresting Hafiz and the two founders of the party, Michel Aflaq and Bitar. Aflaq died in Baghdad in 1989. Bitar and his wife were murdered in London in 1980.

In the new regime, power was shared between two generals, Salah al-Jadid and Hafez el-Assad. Jadid was the senior of the two, but Assad was minister of defence. The government, under Jadid's urging, allied itself with the Syrian Communist party and instituted a general purge of all other parties and tendencies in the Ba'ath. The government demonstrated its pan-Arab enthusiasm by various highly provocative gestures against Israel, which contributed largely to the tensions that provoked the 1967 war. Syria's humiliating defeat seriously undermined the positions of such radical leaders as Nasser and Jadid, and permitted Assad to extend his influence in Syria. However, Jadid remained in control of the party, and he continued to advocate extreme measures in foreign policy.

In September 1970, when King Hussein suppressed the PLO in Jordan, Jadid sent a tank brigade to the rescue. The United States moved the Sixth Fleet to the eastern Mediterranean, and the Israelis ostentatiously mobilized their armies on the Golan Heights. The Jordanian army and air force attacked the Syrian tanks, and drove them back across the frontier; Assad, commanding the Syrian air force, refused to provide air cover.

Despite this fiasco, Jadid retained control, and on 12 November, a party congress censored Assad. The next day, he struck back, arresting Jadid and his supporters. Following tradition, he then carried out an extensive purge of the party, and suppressed the Communist party. Assad has exercised complete power in Syria ever since.

ASSAD'S SYRIA

The Ba'ath achieved its first, precarious taste of power in Iraq and Syria at the same time, in *coups d'état* early in 1963. However, it lost power in Baghdad in November, and by the time it recovered, the leaders of the two parties were at daggers drawn. They have been bitterly opposed ever since, to the extent that Syria was allied with Iran in its war with Iraq. One of the differences between the two parties is that the Syrian Ba'ath has been run by the army since 1966, while the Iraqi Ba'ath maintain a civilian leadership. The chief difference is personal: if the two countries merged, one set of leaders would dominate the other. Since Iraq is more populous and far richer, the Syrians would probably be the losers – and they have resisted the idea.

The original group of revolutionary officers was dominated by Alawites. By the time he had made himself all powerful, Assad had established other members of the sect in key positions throughout the party, government and, above all, the military. Furthermore, he set up separate armed forces – the 'Special Forces' – under the command of two of his brothers-in-law, and the 'Defence Companies' under the command of his brother Rifaat el-Assad. These units are mainly composed of Alawites, and they have steadily expanded in size – the American University 331 country study on Syria put their number at 20,000–34,000 in 1978 – and are provided with every military luxury. They resemble Hitler's SS: they are loyal to the party and its leader, and to their own leaders, but not to the state. They have the added refinement of tribal loyalty. They are also utterly ruthless, as the suppression of the revolt in Hama in 1982 demonstrated (*see below*). Their weakness, which emerged in 1984, is the rivalry between their various leaders.

By the time Assad had eliminated all his opponents, the Ba'ath government, in Syria as in Iraq, was no more than a military dictatorship, its ideology a burned-out shell covering a ruthless tyranny. Assad retains power, like Saddam Hussein, by murdering his opponents, putting down rebellion with overwhelming force, and sending his assassins abroad to pursue those who escape. The Ba'ath is now like the Party in *1984*; as Orwell wrote:

We know that no one ever seizes power with the intention of relinquishing it. Power is not a means, it is an end. One does not establish a dictatorship in order to safeguard a revolution; one makes the revolution in order to establish the dictatorship. The object of persecution is persecution. The object of torture is torture. The object of power is power.

A report issued in 1987 by Amnesty International asserted that 'torture is a regular experience for thousands of political prisoners in Syria.' The report continued:

Brutal methods of torture have been described to Amnesty International by former inmates of Syrian prisons. Similar methods have been described by former detainees tortured by Syrian forces in Syria. One, known as the Black Slave, involves strapping the victim onto a device which, when switched on, inserts a heated metal skewer into the anus. The Washing Machine is a hollow spinning drum, similar to that of a domestic washing machine, into which the victim's arms are pushed and spun until they are crushed. There is the Syrian Chair, a metal chair to which the victim is bound by the hands and feet. The chair's backrest is then bent backwards, causing acute stress to the spine. Meanwhile, metal blades fixed into the chair's front legs cut into the victim's ankles ... A variation of this form of torture, known as the Confessional Chair, is practised in Lebanon.

Syria has used assassination to pursue its ends for many years. On 29 August 1960, long before Assad came to power, the Jordanian prime minister, Hazza al-Majali, was murdered by a bomb placed in his office, at a time when King Hussein should have been there; Hussein mobilized his army and nearly went to war as a result. There have since been other frequent, Syrian-inspired attempts on Hussein's life. In 1980, Assad had Salah al-Din al-Bitar, one of the founders of modern Syria, murdered in exile, much as Stalin had Trotsky murdered in Mexico. In October 1986, Britain broke diplomatic relations with Syria when it was established that Syria had been deeply implicated in an attempt to blow up an El Al plane on a flight from London. A Jordanian terrorist, holding a Syrian passport and acting on orders from Syrian intelligence, had seduced an Irish girl, got her pregnant and put her on a flight to Israel with a bomb in her suitcase. It was found by Israeli security men. The terrorist had gone straight from the airport to the Syrian embassy.

There are few dictatorships in the world as odious as Syria. However, both the Alawite clique in Syria and the Tikriti clique in Iraq have, as their base, a minority community, and both face extreme political and military difficulties. They are unlikely to survive for ever.

THE MUSLIM BROTHERHOOD

Islamic fundamentalist fanaticism is not restricted to the Iranians. It has been a constant threat in Syria and Iraq, and, to a lesser extent in Egypt, where the Muslim Brotherhood had its origins. Its aim was resistance to foreign (particularly British) domination of Arab lands, and opposition to the secularizing, Western tendencies of Arab governments.

The Brotherhood was founded in 1929 by Hasan al-Banna, an Egyptian, and developed into a mass movement during the 1930s and 1940s. It took the lead in opposing King Farouk's regime after the war, and at the end of 1948, following Egypt's defeat in the first war with Israel (in which the Brotherhood had played an inglorious part), the Brotherhood was suppressed. On 28 December, a young Brother shot the prime minister, Nokrashy Pasha, and on 12 February 1949, Banna was murdered by the Egyptian police.

In the aftermath of the 1952 revolution in Egypt, the Brotherhood was driven underground by Nasser. Its surviving leaders went abroad, and developed the movement in Jordan and Syria and in the Palestinian diaspora. Among its Palestinian recruits were Yassir Arafat, who later founded Al-Fatah, the main party in the Palestine Liberation Organization, and his deputy and military commander, Khalid Wazir, who was murdered by Israeli commandos in 1988.

The Brotherhood, which made many converts in Syria in the 1950s, was suppressed there after the union with Egypt in 1958, and not restored to legality after the union was ended in 1961. The Ba'ath party, and particularly the Alawites, had no intention of allowing a fundamentalist, Sunni party to extend its influence in Syria. The first demonstrations of Sunni displeasure took place in Hama in April 1964. The regime responded by sending the army to shell the Sultan Mosque there, killing dozens of people. There were more serious demonstrations in 1967 and 1973 against the regime's secular policies. In 1967, the riots were provoked by an article published in an army magazine, which implied criticism of Islam, and in 1973, they were sparked off when a new constitution failed to make Islam the state religion and conspicuously admitted the possibility that a non-Muslim might become head of state. Although this was fundamental Ba'ath doctrine, Assad hastily backed down; the constitution was amended to insist that the president must be a Muslim – but most Sunnis do not consider Alawites to be proper Muslims.

Between 1973 and 1979, a number of Alawite officials and Soviet advisers were assassinated, but the regime had been chiefly concentrating on suppressing left-wing Ba'athists and missed the significance of the attacks. Then, on 16 June 1979, Captain Ibrahim al-Yussuf, a Ba'ath party political officer and a Sunni Muslim, assembled the cadets of the Aleppo Artillery School. He ordered the Sunni among them to leave the room, and then ordered his accomplices to open fire. They machine-gunned the remaining cadets, all Alawites, killing 60 of them (some sources put the number at 32).

Extremist Sunni all over the country rejoiced that the heretics had been killed, and the massacre ignited all the hatred that Assad had suppressed. For the next three years, Syria was engulfed in a virtual civil war. The rebels, who claimed to be heirs to the Muslim Brotherhood, assassinated Alawite officials, officers and Soviet military and civilian personnel. There were frequent car bombings in

Damascus and other cities, killing hundreds of people. By early 1980, there had been 300–400 political killings, and the two major northern cities, Aleppo and Hama, were in the hands of the Brotherhood.

In March 1980, there was a general strike throughout the country in support of the Brotherhood and its demands for an Islamic republic. It seemed as though Syria was about to go the way of Iran.

President Assad resorted to extreme force to put down the revolt. On Easter Sunday, 6 April, the army surrounded Hama and Aleppo. The Special Forces conducted a series of sweeps through the two cities, arresting thousands of people and shooting anyone suspected of belonging to the Brotherhood. By the end of the year, at least 1000 people had been executed.

The terrorism continued. In April 1981, after an attempt on the life of President Assad, another 200–300 men were publicly executed in Hama. Even that proved insufficient: another 150 officials were murdered that year. In February 1982, the Brotherhood took control of Hama. Assad sent in his brother Rifaat with artillery and tanks on a full-scale assault. Between 2000 (the official figure) and 20,000 people were killed, and a third of the city was levelled.

These extreme measures restored at least the semblance of calm to Syria, but the assassinations and bombings continued, though at a lower rate. In 1986, more people were killed by terrorists in Syria than in all the heavily publicized terrorist attacks in Paris and Istanbul and in the Karachi airport incident – in March alone, terrorist bombs killed 150 people in Syria. The underlying tensions there remain as acute and dangerous as ever. The most dangerous for the regime is the alienation of the Sunni majority from the Alawites. Even with Alawite officers in key positions throughout the army, and with Alawite 'special units' to serve as the regime's praetorian guard, a minority comprising 12–15 per cent of the population cannot hope to dominate the country for ever. The disaffected Sunni officer who carried out the Aleppo massacre had been passed over for promotion, in favour of an Alawite, and was taking his revenge.

The Muslim Brotherhood has gone underground again. It has had no pre-eminent leader since Banna was murdered in 1949, but his doctrines are undoubtedly embraced by large numbers of Syrians. Those doctrines also remain influential in Egypt, where periodic uprisings by fundamentalists have disturbed the government. The fundamentalists' most dramatic achievement was the assassination of President Sadat in October 1981.

MODERN SYRIA

In November 1983, Assad had a heart attack, and vanished from public view for several months. There was a brief and very public dispute between Rifaat Assad, the president's brother, General Ali Haider, who commanded the Special Forces, and General Shafiq Fayyad, commander of the 3rd Armoured Division. It was a battle for the succession, and it was all in the family: Haider and Fayyad are both Assad's brothers-in-law (and are both Alawites). In March 1984, Rifaat sent his tanks into Damascus, where they confronted Haider's and Fayyad's troops. Assad from his sickbed resolved the crisis by sending Rifaat into exile. The president recovered and resumed control of the government, but the problems of the succession had been starkly demonstrated.

In Rifaat's absence, the Defence Companies were reportedly dissolved. On 11 September 1984, the minister of defence, Mustapha Tlas, was quoted in foreign newspapers as saying that Rifaat had been exiled 'for ever'. Rifaat riposted the next day with a statement from Geneva asserting that the Tlas quotation was a fabrication. He proved the point by returning to Damascus on 26 November.

According to the Amnesty report, Haider's Special Forces have been stationed in Lebanon since 1985, where they are responsible for the torture, ill-treatment and deliberate killing of innocent civilians.

Besides its internal differences, Syria faces a number of external problems. By far the most serious is Lebanon (*see* pp. 309–22). Syria has intervened in that unhappy country in an attempt to restore the peace, but without success. Its difficulties were demonstrated in the spring of 1988 when a full-scale civil war broke out between the two factions of Shiites – Amal, supported by Syria, and Hizbollah, supported by Iran. The Hizbollah was winning the fight on the ground when Syria intervened in a series of diplomatic efforts to obtain a ceasefire. Syria had risked ostracism in the Arab world by allying itself with the Iranians against a fellow-Arab state, Iraq, and now the same Iranians were stirring up their followers in Syria's own backyard.

The great danger in Lebanon was that Syria would be sucked into an impossible conflict, like Israel and the United States before it. Assad's evident reluctance to use force against the Hizbollah showed that he knew how unpopular such a course would be.

Syria's continuing enmity with Iraq may also develop into a serious problem now that the Iran–Iraq war has ended. Iraq did its best to ignore Syria throughout the war: it could not cope with a war on two fronts. But now that Saddam Hussein's regime has survived the conflict, it can turn its attention seriously to its fellow Ba'athist regime in Damascus, which stabbed it in the back during its darkest hours.

Even before the war, in 1975, relations had been so tense that the two governments had mobilized their armies along the frontier. The proximate cause of the dispute had been water: Syria was building a large dam on the Euphrates, with Soviet help, and Iraq had charged that Syria was stealing its water resources. The dispute had subsided, partly thanks to Saudi mediation.

The real dispute, however, had been the personal and political conflict between Assad and Hussein for leadership of the Ba'ath party. Assad has shown great political skill in chosing his allies and discomforting his enemies, but he has now accumulated an impressive array of the latter.

Among them, of course, is Israel, but ever since the 1973 war, Syria has taken care not to provoke its most powerful enemy. The level of intransigent, anti-Zionist rhetoric from Damascus has never slackened, but it was notable that, when Israel invaded Lebanon in 1982, Syria did not intervene. The Israelis allowed the Syrians in Beirut (they included Rifaat el-Assad) to depart unmolested, and the Syrians, most of the time, kept out of harm's way. At the beginning of the conflict, the Israelis had seized a pretext to attack Syrian anti-aircraft batteries in the Bekaa valley and, in the process, had shot down a large part of Syria's air force. The memory of that episode proved a sufficient reminder to the Syrians of the need for caution.

The Syrian economy is in great difficulty. Defence takes a huge part of the national budget (by some reports as much as 50 per cent), and other resources are committed to those scourges of the Third World: grandiose projects such as the Euphrates dam. The Soviets can supply weapons for the armed forces, but they are notoriously incapable of providing the assistance and advice needed to help developing countries escape from poverty. Furthermore, the Gorbachev government has started to apply rigid criteria to its aid programmes, and is not nearly as generous as it used to be.

Syria has virtually nothing to export and no reserves to pay for its imports. It has been a client of the Soviet Union for over 20 years, and has very little to show for it. Although Syria is not in as parlous a state as Ethiopia or Vietnam, its dependence is almost as great. Assad has so completely alienated every other potential ally that he has nowhere else to turn. Gorbachev will not abandon Syria: it provides his entrée to the Middle East. In the long term, however, he may discover the dangers of being too closely allied to an unpopular regime. If Assad goes the way of the shah, Soviet influence in Syria may collapse as abruptly as did American influence in Iran.

One of the few cards Assad can play against the West is the fate of the score of Western hostages held in Beirut. It was generally assumed that, although he might not be able to guarantee their release, they could not be released without his assistance. However, as the influence of the Hizbollah and its Iranian patrons has expanded in Lebanon, this argument has lost much of its force. In May 1988, the French government arranged for the release of the last three French hostages in Lebanon through negotiations with Iran, not Syria.

The United States has been reluctant to confront Assad too firmly, fearing for the lives of the American hostages in Lebanon, and hoping that, sooner or later, Syria can be persuaded to follow Egypt's example and expel the Soviets and trade land for peace with Israel. In prolonged negotiations with Assad after the 1973 war, Henry Kissinger managed to induce Syria to accept a permanent ceasefire in exchange for a strip of territory on the Golan Heights, including the regional capital, Kuneitra. That was the last time that Syria showed any flexibility.

(*See also* The Kurds pp. 296–304.)

FURTHER READING

American University, *Syria: A Country Study*, Washington D.C., 1987.
Amnesty International, *Syria: Torture by the Security Forces*, London, 1987.
Antonius, George, *The Arab Awakening*, New York, Capricorn, 1963.
Devlin, John, *The Ba'ath Party from Its Origins to 1966*, New York, Praeger, 1966.
Glubb, John Bagot, *Syria, Lebanon, Jordan*, New York, Walker, 1967.
Hureau, Jean, *La Syrie aujourd'hui*, Paris, Editions, J.A., 1977.
International Journal of Middle East Studies.
Middle East International, London.
Mortimer, Edward, *Faith and Power: The Politics of Islam*, London, Faber and Faber, 1982.
Petran, Tabitha, *Syria*, New York, Praegar, 1972.

Runciman, Steven, *A History of the Crusades* (3 vols.), Cambridge University Press, 1951–54.

Seal, Patrick, *The Struggle for Syria*, Oxford University Press, 1965.

Sinai, Anne and Pollack, Allan, *The Syrian Arab Republic: A Handbook*, New York, American Academic Association for Peace in the Middle East, 1976.

THE YEMENS

NORTH YEMEN (THE YEMEN ARAB REPUBLIC)

Geography	75,000 sq. miles (195,000 sq. km). Rather larger than Benelux.
Population	8 million
GNP per capita	$550
Refugees	61,200 from South Yemen have lived here since 1986.

SOUTH YEMEN (PEOPLE'S DEMOCRATIC REPUBLIC OF YEMEN)

Geography	112,000 sq. miles (290,000 sq. km). The size of Italy.
Population	2 million
GNP per capita	$480

Note: the frontiers of both states are ill-defined and their sizes are therefore approximate.

HISTORY

The Yemen was the home of the Queen of Sheba. It was known to the Romans as *Arabia Felix* – Happy, or Prosperous Arabia – an early case of distance lending enchantment. South Yemen is barren desert. So is much of North Yemen, but that country is chiefly mountainous and enjoys a relatively temperate climate. It produced myrhh and frankincense, both highly esteemed in antiquity.

Various monarchies succeeded each other in the area, each ruling different proportions of the mountains and deserts, which were inhabited by a multitude of independent tribes. The various Arab caliphs and dynasties sometimes controlled the Yemen, sometimes not. The Turks ruled for a while, and King Abdul Aziz (Ibn Saud) sent his warriors to conquer North Yemen in 1934, and was defeated.

The whole country, north and south, remained quite ignorant of the outside world until the 1960s – except for Aden. That port, on the extreme southern extremity of the Arabian peninsula, was annexed by Britain in 1839, as part of the string of naval bases it established around the Indian Ocean to protect the Indian empire. After the opening of the Suez canal, Aden became an important coaling station on the route to the subcontinent.

Yemen was ruled from Saana by imams who were both religious and secular leaders. They were rigidly authoritarian and conservative, opposed to all modernization, and like the tsars in Russia, the imams ruled by absolutism tempered by assassination. Their absolutism was, however, moderated by the need to retain the loyalty of the tribes. The tradition of assassination has survived the fall of the imamate.

The British had imposed a wholly artificial division between North and South Yemen, in order to exert some control over Aden's hinterland. They called the south the Aden Protectorate and signed treaties with the various sheikhs who governed it.

Out of imperial habit, Britain retained Aden after losing India in 1947, and even expanded the dockyards and built an oil refinery. The Imam Yahya of the Yemen was assassinated in 1948 in an attempted coup, which was put down by his son Ahmad. The new imam permitted some modernization, and he joined the rest of the Arab world in hostility to Britian during the Suez war of 1956. In one of the many transitory unions of which the Arabs are so fond, he united the Yemen with Nasser's United Arab Republic (Egypt and Syria) in 1958. The union was called the Union of Arab States, and had no purpose except to vex the British and the Saudis. It was dissolved in December 1961. The imam remained as authoritarian and reactionary as his predecessors.

The loss of the Suez canal in 1956 did not alter British policy, although rising Arab radicalism, the inevitable consequence of the need for a modern workforce in the port, made holding Aden increasingly difficult. The rationale for keeping Aden was that it was needed as a base for operations in the Gulf, which was still a British protectorate. Meanwhile, some military men in North Yemen had learned revolutionary tactics in Egypt and plotted against the imam.

On 19 September 1962, at the height of the influence and megalomania of President Nasser of Egypt, the old Imam Ahmad died. On 26 September, the Egyptians organized a coup in Saana and immediately flew in troops to protect the new government. This was exactly the technique that was to be employed by the Soviet Union in Afghanistan 17 years later, and the results were very similar.

The tribes refused to recognize the regime. Ahmad's heir, who had ruled Saana for a week, rallied them and attacked the Egyptians. The royalists were supported by the Saudis and the British, and the Egyptians were quite unable to defeat them. Nasser's air force tried bombing guerrilla bases in Saudi Arabia, and the two countries were on the verge of war until President Kennedy made it clear that the United States would support the Saudis.

Meanwhile, Britain's position in Aden was becoming untenable. The Colonial Office set up a Federation of South Arabia, to be dominated by conservative sheikhs from the back country, in the hope of leaving a pro-British government behind them, but the radicals easily defeated it. In 1967, after Egypt's humiliating defeat in the Six Day War, Nasser abandoned his attempt to conquer North Yemen and Britain abandoned South Yemen. The Egyptians pulled out in October and the British in November.

INDEPENDENCE
The two Yemens entered the new era with a series of coups and assassinations that have continued ever since. The regime that the Egyptians left behind in North Yemen was overthrown within a month. The civil war continued until 1970 when

an agreement between the various factions was brokered by the Saudis. The new government looked to Saudi Arabia as its natural ally.

In the South, the country was renamed the People's Democratic Republic of Yemen, and allied itself with the Soviet Union. Aden was bankrupted by Britain's departure and the closing of the Suez canal. The USSR stepped into the breach. In exchange for naval facilities, it has armed the South Yemenis and provided some minimal economic assistance. South Yemen has since become a most obdurately Communist state, an Arabian Cuba. Its Communist practice, however, has been seriously modified by the intransigent conservatism of the tribes (which are always in a state of revolt or incipient revolt against Aden). For example, it is the only Communist state in the world with a state religion, Islam. Furthermore, South Yemen depends upon remittances from 100,000 of its citizens working abroad, mostly in Saudi Arabia and the Gulf States, who are there subject to the conservative doctrines of those staunchly anti-Communist regimes. The expatriates insist that their money go to their families, and the government is forced therefore to tolerate a degree of quite unCommunist free enterprise.

Both Yemens have been notable for the frequency and bloodiness of their changes of government. Despite the fact that they have proclaimed their ambition to unite, they have fought numerous border skirmishes and one all-out war, in 1979. In 1977, a North Yemen president was assassinated, possibly because he had planned to visit Aden. On 24 June 1978, a messenger from President Salim Rubai Ali of South Yemen was shown into the office of President Ahmad al-Ghashmi of North Yemen, in Saana. In the messenger's briefcase was a bomb, which exploded, killing both men. Two days later, President Rubai Ali was himself killed in a coup in Aden. There have been other coups and other assassinations in both countries since then.

During the 1970s, South Yemen was governed by a triumvirate of Ali Nasser el-Hassani, Abdel Fatah Ismail and Salim Rubai Ali, all veterans of the fight against the British, who had attained this position after coups in 1969 and 1971. Rubai was president until the unfortunate events of June 1978; then there wer two.

Ismail became president, but was overthrown by his fellow-*duumvir*, Hassani, in 1980; he escaped to Moscow, where he spent five years acquiring the reputation of a dogmatic Communist. Hassani, by now president, was considered marginally more moderate and, by the mid-1980s, was cautiously developing slightly less chilly relations with the West and with conservative Arab regimes.

Ismail, temporarily reconciled with Hassani, returned in the autumn of 1985 and resumed his place in the politburo. A new triumvirate was formed comprising Hassani, Ismail and the vice-president, Ali Ahmed Antar. These new arrangements were not to Hassani's liking. He summoned a meeting of the politburo on 13 January 1986, at 10 a.m., but he himself did not attend, having departed secretly for his tribal base in the mountains, leaving his Mercedes behind to deceive his colleagues. When they were all seated, waiting for Hassani, his bodyguards opened fire on them with machine-guns. Antar was killed immediately, as was the minister of defence, Saleh Muslih Quassem. Ismail died of his wounds later. Their own bodyguards rushed into the room, and the ensuing gun fight resulted in the deaths of about 20 people. A few members of the politburo who had managed to escape through a window immediately rallied their supporters. A savage battle broke out in the centre of Aden; it lasted ten days.

The Soviet Union was taken totally by surprise. Its diplomats and military advisers fled, taking refuge in a Soviet freighter in the harbour. Westerners were evacuated more comfortably, aboard the Royal Yacht *Britannia*, which had been sailing down the Red Sea on its way to New Zealand to meet the Queen. The *Britannia* ferried the refugees from Aden to Djibouti on the African coast opposite.

Witnesses reported seeing heavily armed tribesmen pouring into the city. During the fighting, the army was divided along tribal rather than ideological lines. The navy supported Hassani, and its ships shelled opposition tanks. President Hassani lost, and fled to Ethiopia. As his troops retreated from Aden, they demolished the Soviet embassy. The prime minister, fortunately for him, was out of the country during these events. He waited until the fight was over, and then returned to assume the presidency.

The government later reported that 4230 members of the ruling party had been killed in the fighting, and it seems likely that the total number killed was about 13,000. Over 60,000 refugees fled to North Yemen.

Aden is important to the Soviet Union. It provides a base in the Indian Ocean, enabling the Soviets to play a role in the Middle East controversies. The Soviets' position there is evidently precarious, and it is entirely possible that they will be evicted in the next tribal upheaval. The British used troops to hold Aden in the 1960s, and were eventually driven out by a mass uprising in the city. In 1986, the Soviets simply fled when the civil war broke out. They did not have the troops to impose a decision, and it seems likely, after their Afghan experiences, that they will not embark on any new adventures. Their position depends upon the balance of forces between the tribes and within the politburo, and that can change from one day to the next.

FURTHER READING

American University, *The Yemens: A Country Study*, Washington, D.C., 1986.
Bidwell, Robin, *The Two Yemens*, Boulder, Colo., Westview Press, 1983.
Pindhan, B. R., *Economics, Society and Culture in Contemporary Yemen*, London, University of Essex Press.

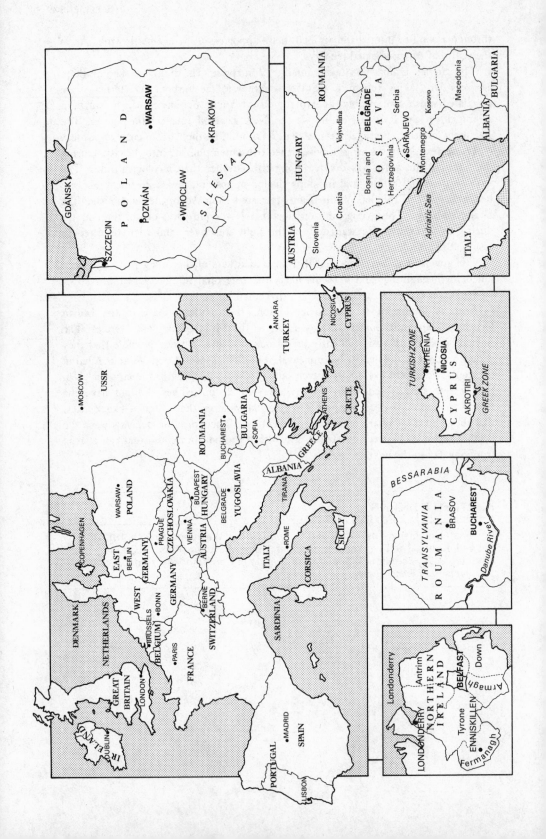

EUROPE

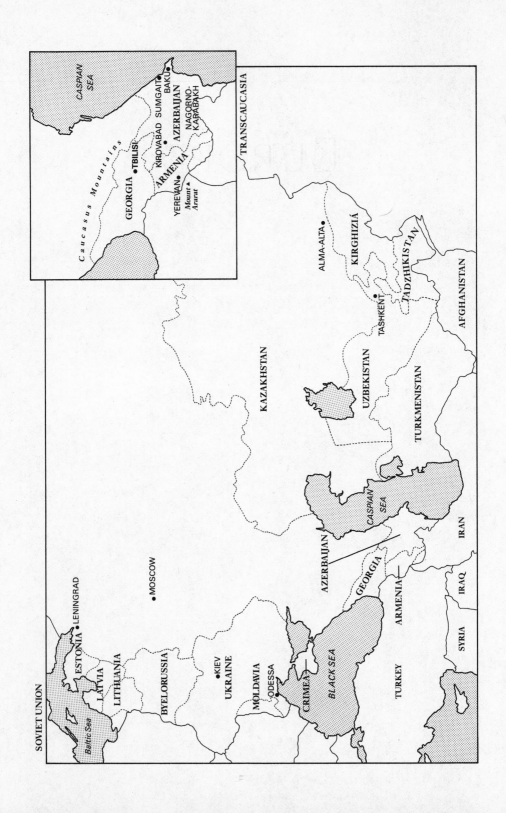

CYPRUS

Geography	3572 sq. miles (9255 sq. km). Divided into Greek (60%) and Turkish (40%) zones, as well as two small British 'sovereign bases' – at Akrotiri and Dhekelia on the south coast – which, between them, cover 99 sq. miles (256 sq. km).
Population	672,000: 80% Greek, 18% Turkish. There are 180,000 Greek and 20,000 Turkish refugees, and Turkey has sent 50,000 settlers to North Cyprus. There are also 30,000 Turkish soldiers in North Cyprus, and the 'green line' separating the two parts of the island is policed by 2000 UN troops.
GNP per capita	$4360. There is a great disparity between the (Turkish) north and the (Greek) south.

Cyprus is one of the world's latent trouble spots. It was forcibly partitioned by Turkey in 1974, and the Turks keep a 30,000-man army there to maintain this. Cyprus is the source of permanent and extreme tension between Greece and Turkey – ostensible allies in Nato – and therefore a cause of serious weakness to the alliance in the eastern Mediterranean.

Cyprus is notionally an independent nation, and it is a member of the United Nations. The majority of its population (about 500,000 people) consider themselves Greeks by nationality, unjustly separated from their homeland. The Turkish minority consider themselves Turks living in Cyprus: their loyalty is to Ankara. There is a Turkish government in Cyprus, established in 1983, calling itself the Republic of North Kibris. It is recognized by no other power than Turkey.

Cyprus's miseries are the legacy of nine centuries of warfare between Greeks and Turks, but more immediately they are the direct result of British colonialism and the policies of the British Conservative government of the 1950s. In addition, President Richard Nixon and, particularly, his secretary of state Henry Kissinger bear a direct responsibility for permitting the crisis of 1974, the partition of the island and the continuing stalemate.

HISTORY

Cyprus, the birthplace of Aphrodite, was Greek throughout history – although   345 foreigners occupied it from time to time, including Richard I of England and the Venetians – until the coming of the Turks. They conquered the island in 1570, and over the centuries, a number settled there until, in the 1950s, they comprised some 18 per cent of the population. They lived amicably among the Greek majority both as rulers and, after Turkey ceded Cyprus to Britain in 1878, as fellow-subjects.

The British prime minister of the time, Lord Beaconsfield (Benjamin Disraeli), demanded Cyprus as the price for mediating a peace between Turkey and Russia. On returning to London, he announced: 'I bring peace with honour – and Cyprus.' By looking at an inadequate map, he had presumably been misled into beliving that Cyprus would be another useful naval base on the sea route to India, like Gibraltar, Malta and the Suez canal. In fact it has no usable harbours and served no real imperial purpose whatever.

Cyprus should have been ceded to Greece after World War I, but Britain did not then believe in giving up her colonies voluntarily. After World War II, a case could be made that Greece was too unstable, and might fall to Soviet Communism, and that Cyprus should be protected from that danger. However, by the 1950s, the Greek civil war was over and the Greek Cypriots demanded the right to self-determination. In their case, that would have meant *enosis*, union with Greece. In a completely unforgivable act of British stupidity, the Conservative government announced that it would 'never' give up Cyprus – a colony whose retention met no conceivable British national interest.

The Greek Cypriots resorted to terrorism. The terrorist organization, EOKA, was led by Colonel George Grivas, an extreme right-wing retired officer of the Greek army who used the *nom de guerre* Dighenis. The political leadership of the Greek Cypriots was assumed by Michael Christodoros Mouskos, who took the title Archbishop Makarios III when he became Orthodox primate of the island. The British army failed to supress EOKA and failed to catch Grivas. They succeeded, however, in banishing Makarios to the Seychelles.

The Cyprus emergency was a constant irritant in British domestic politics. It was the last hurrah of British imperialism, and when the Labour MP Barbara Castle said that British troops had tortured their prisoners, she was so mercilessly abused by irate Conservatives that she had to grovel in apology. She was right, for all that.

Grivas fought a cautious, skilful campaign of sabotage and assassination. It was not a guerrilla campaign: the terrain was not suitable. The British had 40,000 troops and police on the island in 1956, all of them hunting for Grivas. Of these, 105 soldiers and 51 police were killed, the vast majority by accident – 21 soldiers were killed in a forest fire, exactly 20 per cent of British military deaths. The unit that suffered the worst losses was the Royal Norfolk Regiment, which lost 18 men, most of them teenagers doing their National Service; five of these were killed in the fire, and only two were killed by EOKA.

A total of 238 civilians were also killed, of whom 203 were Greek Cypriots, most of them EOKA fighters. In the first serious fighting between Greeks and Turks, in 1958, 115 people were killed.

Britain finally admitted defeat in 1959, but still refused the Cypriots the right of self-determination. The Turks were by then playing an active part in Cyprus's future, and they insisted that *enosis* must never be permitted because, they said, a Greek base 50 miles (80 km) off their southern coast would be a mortal danger. The argument was, and is, preposterous. Turkey is overwhelmingly more powerful than Greece. Cyprus could be no more dangerous to Turkey than Cuba is to the United States. The Turks, however, believe in the danger from the south. Like Disraeli, they are misled by maps and dreams of encirclement.

To prove their point, in 1955, the Turkish government of Adnan Menderes fomented an anti-Greek pogrom in Istanbul, in which over 2000 people were killed and the remaining Greeks in the city were driven out. That ended a connection going back to Byzantium, and a community dating from the founding of the city by Constantine the Great in the 4th century. Menderes was hanged for his crimes in September 1961.

There was no need for Britain to accede to Turkey's wishes in 1959, but the British naturally disliked Makarios and the Greeks because they had wronged them. Greece had been an ally in World War II while Turkey had been neutral, but by the 1950s, Turkey was a much more important member of Nato and therefore won British and American support in its disputes with Greece.

The British did not call Turkey's bluff. Instead, in conferences in London and Zurich in 1959 and 1960, it arranged for an independent Cyprus, with a Greek president, Makarios, and a Turkish vice-president, Rauf Denktash; Turkey was also allowed to base a small number of troops there. Cyprus was forbidden to unite with Greece. The only other country in the world whose sovereignty is similarly circumscribed is Austria. The British kept two air bases on the southern coast, and Britain and Turkey were named guarantors of the settlement.

INDEPENDENT CYPRUS

The constitution was unworkable, and collapsed in 1963. Former EOKA terrorists attacked Turkish villages, and took hostages. The Turkish contingent on the island cut the road from Nicosia to Kyrenia on the north coast, and the Turks threatened to invade. On Christmas Day, the British sent troops to the island, at Makarios's invitation, to keep the peace. They were notably unsuccessful, and the Greeks continued to harass the Turks, driving them out of their homes.

Diplomacy was tried. The British got the UN to send a permanent force to Cyprus – UNFICYP – to police the 'green line' between the two communities in Nicosia. President Lyndon Johnson sent former secretary of state Dean Acheson to mediate between Greeks and Turks. He offered the sort of plan which would have been welcomed by everyone ten years earlier: Cyprus would be united with Greece; Turkey would have sovereign bases on the island; the Turkish community would have two autonomous cantons; there would be compensation for any Turk who wanted to leave; Greece would cede to Turkey the small island of Kastellorizon, off the coast of Anatolia. The Acheson plan was rejected by all sides.

Grivas returned to the island, inciting violence against Turks, and founded a new paramilitary force, EOKA-B. In April 1967, there was a military coup in Greece. In September, Grivas organized an attack on a Turkish village in which 27 Turks (and two Greeks) were killed. Turkey informed its allies that it intended   347 to invade, and was only dissuaded by the vigorous intervention of President Johnson, who now sent another mediator: Cyrus Vance, a former secretary of the air force and a future secretary of state. Johnson threatened, in effect, to expel Turkey from Nato if it invaded Cyprus, and insisted that Greek troops should be removed from the island. About 10,000 went home.

An uneasy peace was maintained until 1974. The Turkish Cypriots looked after their own affairs, and Archbishop Makarios remained titular president of the whole. The next crisis was precipitated by the EOKA terrorists, whose Fascist sympathies were by now quite clear. They acted under instructions from Athens.

Nixon and Kissinger disliked Makarios, whom they accused of leftist sympathies, and they approved of the Athens military junta, considering it more reliable than the Greek political parties. The junta authorized EOKA, now led by a gangster called Nikos Sampson (Grivas having died on 27 January), to assassinate Makarios. When several attempts failed, Sampson organized a coup and seized power on 15 July 1974. Makarios was rescued by the British.

Kissinger refused to condemn the coup, and openly expressed relief at the overthrow of Makarios. In his defence, it should be noted that he was distracted: at that moment, the Watergate crisis in the United States had reached its final paroxysm. Turkey told all the world that it would not tolerate *enosis*, and when the United States failed to use its influence to reverse the coup or to deter Turkey, the Turkish prime minister, Bulent Ecevit, ordered an invasion. Turkish forces, including parachutists, landed on 20 July and quickly established beach-heads along the northern coast, and in a landing zone near Nicosia.

The leader of the Athens junta, General Dmitrios Ioannides, ordered a full-scale attack on Turkey. The armed forces refused, arrested Ioannides, proclaimed an end to the junta and, on 23 July, handed power back to the civilians. It was a sequence of events the Argentinian junta might have considered before invading the Falklands in 1982.

The British convened a conference in Geneva to resolve the Cyprus crisis. It was a complete failure. Kissinger declined to exert any pressure on Turkey, and the Turks therefore refused to evacuate the island. When the Greeks refused to meet Turkey's demand that the island be partitioned, the Turks conducted a second invasion, on 13 August, and partitioned the island themselves, driving the Greeks out of roughly 40 per cent of it. Turks from the Greek zone fled north, Greeks in the north fled south. About 200,000 people lost their homes, 180,000 of them Greeks. This division has remained unchanged ever since.

CURRENT STATUS

The Greek zone in Cyprus, contrary to all expectations, has flourished since 1974. Makarios died in 1977, but his immediate successors followed the same policies. The Greeks' success has been helped by the collapse of Lebanon: Cyprus has become the bolt-hole and listening base for the Middle East. The Turkish zone, on the other hand, has stagnated: Turkey's own continuing political and economic problems preclude the sort of assistance that 'North Kibris' would need to develop into a viable economy.

Relations between the two communities remain as bad as ever. There are

periodic negotiations, under UN sponsorship, but they have never made any progress. The Turks remain adamantly opposed to reunification of the island, let alone *enosis*. The only power that might make them change their minds, the United States, has remained aloof, for the same reason that it permitted the Turks to invade Cyprus in the first place. For many years, it disliked the Greek government because it was headed by the leftist Andreas Papandreou, and it always attached far more importance to good relations with Turkey. Although the US imposed an arms embargo on Turkey in 1974, on the grounds that American-supplied weapons had been used illegally, the embargo was lifted in 1978.

As for the British, their role as guarantors of the independence of Cyprus is clearly at an end. However, they have at last found a use for Cyprus – as a listening post. On 5 June 1967, British radar stations on the hills above Akrotiri and Larnaca watched the Israeli air force fly far out over the Mediterranean and then sweep in upon the unsuspecting Egyptians from the west. The same bases provide American intelligence with excellent facilities for observing events throughout the Middle East, both electronically and with the SR-71A 'Blackbird' spy plane.

Cyprus's position is not an unfailing advantage. The PLO and Israel's secret service, the Mossad, fight their dark and desperate battles there, and there have been many murders, on both sides. In March 1978, in Nicosia, two PLO terrorists killed Youssef el-Sebai, the editor of *El-Ahram* and a close friend of Anwar Sadat of Egypt. They then seized 30 hostages and barricaded themselves in a hotel. After negotiations with the Cypriot authorities, they were allowed to take 15 hostages to Larnaca airport and board a Cyprus Airways aircraft that would take them to freedom. However, no Middle Eastern country would allow the plane to land and it eventually returned to Larnaca. Meanwhile, 54 Egyptian commandos had been flown to the airport, without informing the Cyprus government, and on 19 March, they stormed the plane. They were mown down by the Cypriot National Guard, who thought they were PLO terrorists; 15 Egyptians were killed. The chief hijacker, known as Samir Kadar, was deported to Syria in 1982; he was believed to be a senior operative in the Abu Nidal terrorist organization and, in July 1988, was apparently killed in a car carrying a load of explosives in Greece.

There have also been terrorist attacks on civilians: in September 1985, three terrorists – two Arab, one British – seized an Israeli cruise boat and murdered the four people on board. In February 1988, the PLO chartered a ferry, planning to fill it with 130 Palestinians whom the Israelis had expelled, and sail it to Haifa in a publicity stunt. It was crippled by a limpet mine off Limassol, presumably by Israeli agents. In the same month, a powerful bomb exploded in a car near the Israeli embassy, killing three people including the car's driver; the bomb had gone off early. Exasperated, Cyprus expelled 66 foreigners, mostly Arabs, whom it suspected of terrorist sympathies.

Also in February 1988, a new president took office in Greek Cyprus, George Vassiliou, who promised a 'peace offensive' to resolve the dispute. In the first round of the election, Makarios's successor, President Spyros Kyprianou, had only come third: the electorate was evidently tired of the perpetual stalemate. However, the key to changing the situation was in Ankara.

Turkey has applied to join the European Community, but the Cyprus imbroglio is an insuperable barrier. The question is whether the Turks can be persuaded that joining the EC is more important than retaining the 'Republic of North Kibris'. 349

The Turkish prime minister, Turgut Ozal, visited Greece in June 1988, for official talks with Papandreou. The encounter achieved nothing, but was considered a success because it was the first meeting for many years. On his return to Turkey, Ozal survived an assassination attempt by an ultra-nationalist.

Meanwhile, the UN secretary-general, Javier Pérez de Cuellar, once again took on the Sisyphean task of bringing the Greek and Turkish Cypriots together. On 24 August, he gave a lunch in Geneva for President Vassiliou and Rauf Denktash, and won their agreement to begin negotiations designed to resolve the question by the summer of 1989.

He quickly met the limits of compromise: Vassiliou and Denktash met in Nicosia in September, and again at the UN in New York in November 1988, and the talks all but collapsed. The Greeks proposed the reunification of Cyprus on the basis of 'three freedoms': all Cypriots would have the right to live anywhere in the island, might acquire property anywhere and could move about freely. Denktash said that those freedoms should be postponed for 18 years and then be subject to severe restrictions. Vassiliou rejected the conditions out of hand, and though the two agreed to meet again, it was quite clear that Denktash would not abandon his 'Republic of North Kibris' until the government in Ankara obliged him to. That day has not yet dawned.

FURTHER READING

American University, *Cyprus: A Country Study*, Washington D.C., 1979.
Crashaw, Nancy, *The Cyprus Revolt*, Boston, Allen and Unwin, 1978.
Durrell, Lawrence, *Bitter Lemons*, London, Faber and Faber, 1957.
Hitchens, Christopher, *Cyprus*, New York, Quartet Books, 1984.
Minority Rights Group, *Cyprus*, London, 1984.
Stern, Laurence, *The Wrong Horse*, New York, Times Books, 1977.

EASTERN EUROPE

Bulgaria
Geography: 42,823 sq. miles (110,911 sq. km)
Population: 8,982,000

Czechoslovakia
Geography: 49,371 sq. miles (127,870 sq. km)
Population: 15,357,000

East Germany/German Democratic Republic (DDR)
Geography: 41,645 sq. miles (107,860 sq. km)
Population: 16,646,000

Hungary
Geography: 35,919 sq. miles (93,030 sq. km)
Population: 10,647,000

Poland
Geography: 120,348 sq. miles (311,700 sq. km)
Population: 37,495,000

Roumania
Geography: 91,699 sq. miles (237,500 sq. km)
Population: 22,862,000

Yugoslavia
Geography: 98,766 sq. miles (255,803 sq. km). Yugoslavia is a federation of six republics: Slovenia, Croatia, Bosnia and Hertzegovinia, Serbia, Montenegro and Macedonia
Population: 23,273,000
GNP per capita: $2300

(The World Bank does not offer GNP figures for Warsaw Pact countries.)

There is much debate in Europe, east and west, over which of the Communist countries will collapse first. Will the explosion come in Budapest as in 1956, in   351

Prague as in 1968, or in Poland as in 1980? There have even been signs of unrest in East Germany and Roumania, so the possibility of trouble there cannot be discounted. Perhaps, as in 1956, more than one government will fall together.

In Poland, in September 1989, the Communist Party handed over much of its power to a government headed by Solidarity. Hungary has promised to hold free elections by the summer of 1990. The Czech government continued to oppose all reforms, despite increasing signs of dissent, and in the autumn of 1989, the East German regime entered its worst crisis since 1961, as 100,000 of its citizens fled West.

The Soviet Union is now living with the consequences of one of Stalin's fundamental misjudgments. He determined in 1945 that the USSR should never again be left vulnerable to attack from the Germans, who, in 1918, had occupied the Ukraine and, in 1942, had reached Stalingrad. Stalin decided that the best way to ensure safety was to install a buffer of client states from the Baltic to the Adriatic. There has been a hot debate over the extent to which Stalin, at the time, was concerned with the spread of Communism. By 1948, with the Cold War well under way, Stalin concluded that there should be not merely client states but Communist client states to protect his western borders, and that became Soviet policy. A decade later, Khrushchev was still fantasizing about a world Communist state. But in 1945, Soviet national security came first and Communism a long way second.

Stalin's misjudgment was ironic: he failed to appreciate the real shift in the balance of power in the world of which he was the chief beneficiary. The Soviet Union after 1945 was so overwhelmingly powerful that no imaginable combination of European states could confront it. Its only superior was the United States across distant oceans, which might oppose the Soviet Union but would never consider attacking it by land. The USSR no longer needed buffer states. On the contrary, as over 40 years of history have demonstrated, the satellites that Stalin installed in East Germany, Poland, Czechoslovakia and the rest have always been a burden to the Soviet Union. For one thing, suppressing their independence turned the United States from an ally into an enemy, and Nato was formed because of the Communist coup in Czechoslovakia. For another, the clear evidence of Soviet tyranny was enough to ensure that Western Europe would not voluntarily adopt Communism.

The USSR was therefore obliged to take on the burden of 100 million resentful subjects in poverty-stricken countries, whose defence (and oppression) would be a permanent lien on the Soviet economy. The satellites have cost the USSR far more than they are worth – for, in strategic terms, they are worth nothing. Stalin continued to be guided by the imperatives of Russian history, going back centuries, at the moment the atom bomb and the collapse of Europe made his concerns redundant.

East Europeans, with the limited exception of the Bulgars, detest the Russians. The tsars suppressed the Polish state in the 18th century, and ruled Poland until 1917; the new Soviet Union tried to conquer it in 1920. In 1939, Stalin, Hitler's ally, annexed eastern Poland, and 15,000 officers of the Polish army were murdered by the KGB at Katyn. Although the Red Army liberated Poland from the Nazis, they did so as conquerors – and they waited at the gates of Warsaw in August 1944, while the Nazis destroyed the city. The Soviets also arrived in Hungary as conquerors in 1944 – where they had put down a nationalist uprising in 1848. They repeated the feat in 1956. The Soviets still occupy a large part of Roumanian national territory: Bessarabia.

With this historical background, it is not at all surprising that the imposition of Soviet Communism on Eastern Europe has always been deeply unpopular. The regimes in East Germany, Poland, Czechoslovakia and Hungary survive because they are supported by the Red Army. Stalin built a vast prison for the East Europeans, as an unnecessary barrier against Western aggression. His successors, desperate to reduce tensions with the West so that they can salvage their collapsing economy, can already see the limits of *détente*: normal relations with the West will not be possible until the Red Army pulls out of Eastern Europe – and if it does that, the governments there will collapse, like dominoes. The Soviets' situation is probably not yet desperate enough to accept that humiliation, though events may force it upon them, as in Afghanistan. Like Eastern Europe, the USSR is still Stalin's prisoner.

EAST GERMANY

The first crack in the solid Stalinist façade of Eastern European Communism occurred in June 1953, in East Berlin. It was a spontaneous uprising of the German working class against Communist oppression, and it was immediately and ruthlessly suppressed by Soviet troops.

Stalin had died on 5 March 1953, and the struggle for succession had begun at once. The East European regimes were pawns in the battle. Some powerful men in Moscow, including Beria and Malenkov, considered settling their differences with the West in one sweeping gesture: the abandonment of East Germany (the German Democratic Republic, DDR). The possibility that a general settlement might have been achieved in 1953 has tantalized historians ever since. Churchill, then in his last term as British prime minister, went to see Eisenhower, who had taken office as president of the United States in January, and proposed a joint approach to Moscow in the belief that the occasion of Soviet disarray should be seized. Eisenhower, however, spurned the idea. In any event, the man who eventually came out on top in Moscow, Nikita Khrushchev, showed himself a firm believer in maintaining Soviet hegemony in Eastern Europe. Later, the proposal for 'abandoning' the DDR became one of the charges made against Malenkov.

Of all the countries in Eastern Europe, the DDR was the place most likely to welcome Communism in 1945. There was a long tradition of radical socialism in Berlin: Hitler always hated the city for that reason. After the war, a group of German Communists who had survived the purges of the 1930s was installed in East Berlin and, in 1949, set up their 'Democratic Republic'. They pushed industrialization as rapidly as possible, emulating the efforts of the Soviet Union under Stalin, and, in the spring of 1953, announced a 10 per cent increase in the workers' 'norms' – that is, all workers were required to increase their productivity by 10 per cent without any increase in wages.

The measure was hugely unpopular. On 16 June, there was a spontaneous work stoppage at a building site in East Berlin, and it spread to the whole Soviet zone in a matter of hours. That evening, the radio station in the American zone broadcast a call for a general strike, and the next day, the whole country came out on strike. 353

Mass meetings of workers denounced the government, the regime and Communism itself, to the utter dismay of party functionaries who had devoted their lives to the workers' cause and now saw themselves repudiated.

Whatever their internal debates about a general settlement, the Soviet politburo had no intention of allowing the East Germans to reassert their independence. Soviet troops were deployed in large numbers in the major cities, notably Berlin. The citizens of West Berlin watched helplessly as Soviet tanks and troops in armoured cars shot down the last demonstrating workers and students.

The party and state did not collapse, as their counterparts in Hungary were to do in 1956. There was no time for popular fury to overturn the state: the Soviets had acted too quickly. However, there is no doubt that, without Soviet intervention, the DDR would never have survived. By official count, 21 people were killed.

The DDR's next crisis was in August 1961, when it built the Berlin Wall to prevent its citizens from escaping. East Germany remained quiet for a generation after that: it was more prosperous than its Communist neighbours, though its economy suffered from the same underlying weaknesses, and by the late 1980s was falling rapidly behind West Germany's.

Erich Honecker and his politburo in East Berlin resisted the reform movement emanating from Gorbachev's Moscow for as long as possible, but in 1989 were swept away by a tide of popular discontent. It began in the summer as tens of thousands of East Germans escaped to the West through Hungary and Czechoslovakia. Honecker fulminated against the Hungarians but his compatriots, by the hundred thousand, took to the streets to demand freedom to travel. Gorbachev offered no support and in October, Honecker resigned. His successor, Egon Krenz, bowed to the inevitable and on 9 November lifted all travel restrictions. The Berlin Wall was breached. It was the beginning of the end for the DDR, whose government was forced to promise free elections and democracy. The end of Communism in Germany was suddenly near, with reunification looming behind, and a complete reordering of the post-war settlement in Europe.

POLAND

After the great victory in 1945, Stalin hesitated over what course to follow in Eastern Europe. It is not clear that he intended to force Communism upon Poland and the rest immediately – they were not ready for it. What is certain is that, whatever happened, Stalin would never give up control of the countries that the Red Army had conquered. In a famous meeting with Winston Churchill in Moscow in October 1944, the two of them agreed that the region would be in the Soviet Union's sphere of influence. It became a major Soviet grievance when Churchill welshed on the agreement, in the famous Fulton, Missouri speech declaring the Cold War in 1946, and when the United States welshed on the Yalta agreement by reopening the question of the frontiers of Poland in 1947.

The first governments that Stalin authorized in Eastern Europe in 1945 were coalitions: Communists comprised the most important parties but did not completely dominate. After the West broke up the wartime alliance, there was an abrupt shift in Stalin's policies, and all opposition to Communism was suppressed. Moderate Communist leaders, such as Gomulka in Poland and Nagy in Hungary, were dismissed, and Stalinists were put in their place. In 1948, a long night of tryanny descended upon Eastern Europe.

The Stalinist experiment ended in failure in 1956. Workers and peasants had at first welcomed the nationalizations of industry and the distribution of land. For example, Imre Nagy in Hungary made his name and ensured his popularity by distributing the Esterhazy and Church estates to the peasants. However, after 1948, agriculture was collectivized on the Soviet model and the workers were driven in a mad rush towards industrialization. Their standards of living dropped precipitously, there was never enough to eat, and peasants who were moved to the cities found that there was nowhere to live.

In June 1956, workers at an engineering factory in Poznań in western Poland came out on strike against working conditions and food shortages. They demanded higher wages, and soon there were riots, including an attack on a local prison. The government sent in tanks and at least 80 people were killed. All across the country, the authority of the party was shaken and officials, seeing the writing on the wall, hastily revised their policies. It was too late.

Władysław Gomulka had been prime minister between 1945 and 1948, and was remembered as a moderate and sensible leader. He had been dismissed and arrested, but starting a tradition that has been maintained in each succeeding crisis, he was not executed. On the contrary, he was kept in reserve.

As the situation continued to deteriorate after the Poznań riots, Gomulka's followers, fearing a further explosion, started an opposition Communist party in the factories, and challenged the government in Warsaw. In October, after further disturbances, the government collapsed and handed all power to Gomulka.

On 19 October occurred one of those melodramatic events that have marked Polish history. The party's Central Committee gathered to confront the crisis, and Nikita Khrushchev and the Soviet politburo arrived unexpectedly to join their deliberations. The Soviet army was at the gates of Warsaw, its troops were pouring into the country from every direction, and the Polish army and militia moved out to confront them.

Gomulka faced Khrushchev down. The Polish party, unlike the Hungarians a week later, was united behind him. Gomulka insisted that the Poles be permitted to decide their own future, but he gave Khrushchev two guarantees: Poland would remain a loyal ally to the USSR, and would maintain its Communist form of government. On the morning of 20 October, after a night of dispute, Khrushchev accepted the guarantees. The Red Army returned to its barracks, the Soviets promised not to interfere in Polish affairs in future, and Khrushchev returned to Moscow.

It was a spectacular victory for the Poles – what came to be known as 'The October'. The Hungarian uprising on 23 October was a direct response to it, but in the longer term, it solved nothing. The collectivization of agriculture was abandoned, forced industrialization was slowed down but the fundamental contradiction remained. Indeed, it was cemented by Gomulka's promise to Khrushchev. The root of the trouble was that the Poles had rejected Soviet Communism, and Gomulka could not keep both his explicit promise to Khrushchev and his implied promise to his fellow-citizens – prosperity and independence. It is not surprising then that, by 1968, Gomulka was totally discredited, and Poland was steadily   355 slipping backwards, particularly in comparison with its three Communist neighbours: the DDR, Czechoslovakia and Hungary.

One of the components of the 1956 settlement had been the restoration of the liberties of the Catholic Church. Its primate, Cardinal Wyszynski, became spokesman for the opposition. By the 1960s, the party was again attacking the Church.

The party, sensing the crisis to come, split into competing factions. The anti-Gomulka faction beat the nationalist drum, reviving forbidden memories of the non-Communist resistance to the Germans – and also reviving the odious tradition of East European anti-Semitism. It was the most discreditable episode in modern Polish history, a wave of state-supported anti-Semitism. The Germans had murdered 3 million Polish Jews and most of the surviving 250,000 had left for Israel after the war. The remainder were in every way loyal Poles, many of them loyal Communists. Now they were hounded out of the country.

1968 was the year of the 'Prague spring'. Gomulka detested it, and connived with Brezhnev to suppress it. Poles were self-obsessed, and showed little sympathy for the Czechs. After all, they said, what had Czechoslovakia done for Poland in 1956? The journalist Neal Ascherson quotes one Polish comment: 'They greeted Russian tanks with red flags in 1945, and they gave us no help in 1956. Now they can get what's coming to them.'

In December 1970, Gomulka won his greatest diplomatic triumph. The West German chancellor, Willy Brandt, came to Warsaw to sign a treaty recognizing the western frontiers of Poland. Germany at last gave up its claims to Danzig (Gdańsk), Stettin (Szczecin) and Breslau (Wroclaw), and to East Prussia and Silesia. Brandt also knelt in prayer at the memorial to the Warsaw ghetto.

On Saturday, 12 December, the government announced steep price rises in food and other commodities. The following Monday, there was a protest demonstration by workers from the Lenin shipyard in Gdańsk. The next day, shipyard workers in Gdynia came out on strike, and the first real riots took place in Gdańsk, in which a number of people were killed and party headquarters were burned down. Riots spread along the Baltic coast, and Gomulka ordered them suppressed by any and all means. Troops fired on workers, and by the end of the week, the whole area was in open insurrection. In a hasty politburo meeting on 20 December, Gomulka was summarily dismissed, protesting vehemently, and Edward Gierek, party leader from Silesia, took his place. He made conciliatory speeches and broadcasts, calling on the workers to end their strikes, and sent the troops back to barracks.

There were further disturbances after Christmas, and once again, the situation was slipping out of control. Gierek and his senior colleagues went to Szczecin on 24 January 1971, and drove to the shipyard in a taxi. For nine hours, they argued with the striking workers and at last persuaded them to end the strike. They repeated the same remarkable dialogue in Gdańsk the next day. The price rises were rescinded a month later, after a further strike in Łódź.

December 1970 to February 1971 had seen a stunning victory for Polish workers – not for the liberal Communist intellectuals who had supported Gomulka in 1956, but for the Polish working class. When the new regime failed to live up to its promises, just like the Gomulka regime in 1956–70, the workers became completely disillusioned with all forms of Communist government.

In 1976, the government again announced steep increases in food prices. Meat went up by 70 per cent, sugar by 100 per cent, butter and cheese by 30 per cent. Strikes swept the country, and party headquarters at Radom were burned to the ground. The price rises was 'withdrawn for further discussion'. It was not only a political humiliation for the government, it was an economic disaster: by then, food prices in the shops were subsidized by 70 per cent. In the aftermath of the 1976 crisis, workers – including Lech Walesa, an electrician at the Lenin shipyard at Gdańsk – who had played prominent roles in the strikes were sacked. A group of Warsaw intellectuals then formed a Committee for the Defence of Workers' Rights (KOR), its principal leaders being Jaček Kuron and Adam Michnik.

There was a great shift in power in Poland on 16 October 1978, the day that Karol Wojtyla, the Cardinal Archbishop of Kraków, was elected pope. The Church had always been the most powerful institution in Poland, taking second place only recently to the Soviet army. Now it suddenly received an enormous reinforcement: its head was now the Vicar of Christ on Earth. John Paul II instantly became the personification of the nation.

In August 1980, the government again tried to raise food prices by as much as 100 per cent. There were sporadic strikes in various parts of the country – and then the management of the Lenin shipyard in Gdańsk tried to sack Anna Walentynowicz for agitation. Her comrades called for her reinstatement, the shipyard closed – and Lech Walesa, who had been sacked in 1976, returned to take command of the strike committee. Strikes spread to the rest of the Baltic region, and then to the rest of the country, including the mining districts in Silesia, and Warsaw itself. In bitter negotiations with the Gdańsk strikers, the government finally conceded their right to form free trade unions. The entire Gierek team was swept away. Gierek himself had a heart attack on 6 September, and was thus spared the indignity of being fired. Free trade unions were formed throughout the country, and were registered by the government. They took the collective name 'Solidarity', after the name of a workers' newspaper published in Gdańsk.

For 18 months, Poland was in a ferment. Solidarity rapidly evolved from a trade union into a political movement, constantly probing the limits of its power. The government retreated step by step, liberalizing the press and broadcasting, even allowing the formation of a farmers' branch of Solidarity. That was a major concession because it amounted to permitting the revival of the pre-war Peasants' party. The USSR watched these developments with great unease. In November 1980 and again in March 1981, it threatened to intervene directly. Troops were massed on the borders and the other Communist countries were lined up to join them. Poland was again threatened with invasion from east and west, as in 1939.

The new party leader was Stanislaw Kania, a moderate and cautious aparatchik, who tried to hold the party together while conceding Solidarity's most pressing demands. A party conference was held in July 1981, at which most of the old guard was deposed. The party had new and radical members, but it was much too late. General Wojciech Jaruzelski, the minister of defence in 1980, had won some popularity by refusing to allow troops to be used against strikers. He had become prime minister in February 1982, and started to grapple with the economic crisis while Kania battled on with Solidarity. Kania's authority was, however, melting away, and on 18 October, he handed over control of the party to

357

Jaruzelski. Later events showed that planning for the subsequent *coup d'état* was already at that point far advanced. By December, there was a naked struggle for power between the government and Solidarity, and on Sunday, 13 December 1981, Jaruzelski imposed a 'state of war' (the Polish equivalent of a state of emergency) and suppressed Solidarity. Solidarity and KOR leaders were arrested, and all civil liberties were suspended. Gierek was also arrested, together with many other former leaders.

The workers resisted as best they could: they occupied their factories, shipyards and mines; Solidarity leaders refused to negotiate with the government. The Church denounced the imposition of martial law, and a number of workers were killed (seven by official count, many more by Solidarity's estimate). By degrees, the resistance was beaten down, and Poland relapsed into sullen apathy. The cycle of history began again. In 1945, 1948, 1956 and 1970, new regimes had taken over the country, with greater or lesser optimism, and tried to solve its problems. They had all failed. In 1956, 1970 and 1980, the regimes had simply collapsed in the face of public disorder. (There seems to be a roughly ten-year cycle in post-war Polish history.) Jaruzelski understood perfectly that, if he could not solve the problems that had defeated his predecessors, he, too, would be driven from office.

Solidarity survived as a sort of government-in-exile, illegal, proscribed but at any moment liable to arise from its ashes. There are four centres of power in Poland: the Church, whose enormous influence is demonstrated every time the pope visits the country; the workers, whose chosen representatives are the leaders of Solidarity; the Red Army; and the government. The striking difference between Poland in 1980 and Czechoslovakia in 1968, and the USSR in 1988, is that, in Poland, the reform movement arose from among the workers, who then invited the intellectuals to join them. In Czechoslovakia, and in Gorbachev's Soviet Union, the radicals seized the commanding heights of the party and then appealed for the workers to join them. In Poland, the workers have the additional strength of the Church to support them.

Jaruzelski's government remained in power because it was supported by the Soviet Union, and because many of the Poles assumed, as they did in 1956 and 1981, that no matter what happened in Afghanistan, the Balkans or in Africa, the USSR would not permit Poland to escape. It was a theory that a more radical generation will put to the test. It nearly happened in October 1984, when members of the secret police kidnapped and murdered Father Jerzy Popieluszko, a popular parish priest who was an outspoken supporter of Solidarity. There was an explosion of outrage, and for a while, the priest's monument was the scene of enormous daily demonstrations. The regime arrested the men responsible and put them on trial. They were convicted, but there was widespread suspicion that they had been acting on orders from senior ministers.

Poland is an extreme case of a general failure of Communist economies, and is in a situation similar to that which much of Africa finds itself. Food prices are heavily subsidized to keep the urban workers quiet. This means that peasants are not paid enough to enable them to modernize their farms (whether privately owned as in Poland, or collective as in the USSR), and so agriculture declines. City dwellers are faced with the conundrum: what is the point of guaranteed low prices for food if there is nothing to buy?

The only solution to the agricultural crisis, in Poland or in Africa, is to restore a market economy, to free prices. In Poland, as in Sudan, Morocco and a dozen other countries, the attempt was met by riots, and the Polish economy has been declining steadily since the declaration of martial law. In a referendum in the spring of 1988, when the government consulted the electorate on reforms, its proposals were soundly rejected, and therefore abandoned. In May, there was another outbreak of strikes, which were put down with difficulty, and in August, industrial unrest began again, starting in the Silesian mines and spreading to Gdańsk. On both occasions, the demand for the restoration of Solidarity was raised. The government could no longer impose its policies, nor could it win the country's assent. All it could do was overawe the workers, for the moment. The paralysis was total – a sure recipe for disaster.

Jaruzelski was perfectly aware of the danger. During the August strikes, he summoned a plenum of the central committee at which the party's failures were openly debated. Jaruzelski himself admitted his lack of success, and called for 'a courageous turnaround' by the government. It was an extraordinary admission by Jaruzelski who, as head of the government, had been given dictatorial powers six-and-a-half years earlier to resolve Poland's long-standing difficulties. He told the plenum (and the speech was broadcast) that solving Poland's problems 'demands the courage to break with old sterotypes and barriers, the courage to use new and unconventional means, and, first of all, effective ones.' He invited Lech Walesa and other Solidarity leaders to meetings with the government, in a 'round table' to consider possible reforms.

Round-table negotiations between the government and Solidarity opened in December and continued until April, 1989. Solidarity was legalized and the constitution was revised. A new office of president was instituted. Parliament would consist of a lower house (the Sejm) and a Senate. Most power would be reserved for the Sejm, which would elect an executive prime minister.

Elections were held in June 1989. All Senate seats were freely contested, as were 161 of the 460 Sejm seats. The Communist Party was reserved 173 seats, and 126 were set aside for the Peasants and Democratic parties, which were allied to the Communists. Free elections were promised by 1994.

The first round of the election, on 4 June, produced a Solidarity landslide. The party won 99 of the Senate seats (the hundredth was won by a millionaire, running as an independent). Solidarity won all the freely contested Sejm seats, defeating many independents including candidates put up by the Catholic hierarchy. The Communists were humiliated. Many of their candidates in uncontested races failed to win a majority because voters crossed their names off the ballot. They had to face a run-off on 18 June – and many of them were only elected when Solidarity instructed its supporters to vote for them. Lech Walesa was not a candidate. He decided to lead Solaridity from outside parliament, perhaps awaiting the call to assume the presidency.

The new parliament elected Jaruzelski president, with some difficulty: the Peasants and Democratic parties, seeing the way the wind was blowing, deserted the Communists. Jaruzelski won a majority of seven only because some senior Solidarity figures voted for him. He then nominated the minister of the interior, Czeslaw Kiszczak as prime minister.

The economy was collapsing. Walesa floated the idea of Solidarity taking power, and the two minor parties deserted the Communists altogether. Kiszczak failed to form a government and on 24 August, Jaruzelski bowed to the inevitable and nominated Tadeusz Mazowiecki, editor of a Solidarity magazine, as prime minister. He was confirmed by parliament on 12 September. The Communists kept the ministries of defence and the interior, thus retaining ultimate power in the state, and had a few minor ministries. The rest went to Solidarity and its new allies.

So long as the Party controls the police and army, and every government ministry and agency is packed with Communists, it could still, in theory, resume power and arrest Walesa and Mazowiecki again. However, it is more likely that the tide, now running strongly against the Communists, will sweep them finally away – unless there is a counter-revolution in Moscow and the Red Army is sent to restore order in Warsaw once again.

HUNGARY

The key event in the recent history of Eastern Europe was the Hungarian uprising in October 1956, and its suppression by the Red Army. As Soviet tanks pounded government buildings, the last cries for help were broadcast over the radio to the West. The West did nothing, except open its doors to the 200,000 refugees who poured across the Austrian border.

In subsequent years, in the hopes of avoiding a repetition of the crisis, the Soviets permitted the Hungarian government to experiment with a looser form of economic organization than the stringent Stalinist model that had been imposed throughout Eastern Europe. When this was done, the government acquired a certain measure of acceptance and even popularity. That proved to be an illusion. The reforms have not worked: Hungary's economy is in a profound crisis, and there can really be no doubt that the Communist regime would be swept away as rapidly as in 1956 if there were any certainty that the Soviet Union would not intervene again.

In 1956, the Hungarian economy was in difficulty and the party was seriously split. On the one hand were the Stalinists, led by the party secretary, Matyas Rakosi, one of the most detestable figures in East European history, and his closest collaborator, Erno Gero. The rival faction was led by Imre Nagy, who had been the first Communist prime minister of Hungary (1945–8) and had supervised the distribution of the land to the peasants. He had been purged from government and party when Stalinism was imposed upon Eastern Europe in 1948, and was thus not involved in the purges that followed. After Stalin died, he had been restored to power in 1953 on the orders of the Soviet politburo, in an attempt to redirect the economy. It is reported that Molotov, of all people, told Rakosi: 'Will you finally understand that you can't forever govern with Soviet bayonets?'

Nagy instituted various reforms, but was again deposed after 18 months, in March 1955, victim of Rakosi's intrigues in Moscow. The crisis deepened progressively, and in June 1956, after the riots in Poznań and the upheavals in the Polish party, Rakosi was removed as first secretary and sent into exile in the Soviet Union. He was replaced by Gero, who was as detested as his mentor.

The Hungarian uprising happened amazingly rapidly. The spark that set it off was the news of the Polish October. Encouraged by the success of the Polish demonstrators, who had brought Gomulka back to power, students and intellectuals held mass meetings on the evening of 22 October 1956, in the colleges and universities of Budapest. They passed a series of resolutions demanding changes in government personnel and policy. There were mass demonstrations the next day, and by the evening of 24 October, the government had collapsed and what remained of the Communist party controlled only a few buildings in Budapest. The huge statue of Stalin in the centre of the city was pulled down.

It was a national revolt: its symbol, from 23 October onwards, was the Hungarian flag with a hole in its centre, where the hammer and sickle had been cut out. The revolutionaries demanded that 15 March be restored as a national holiday, commemorating the revolution of 1848, and replacing the anniversary of the imposition of Communism by the Red Army in 1944. Most important of all, they demanded that all Soviet troops in Hungary be withdrawn.

With Erno Gero's reluctant agreement, Imre Nagy was brought back as prime minister. However, Gero did everything in his power to thwart Nagy, and thus ensured that the party was paralysed. Gero himself clung to office until 25 October, when he was evacuated from Budapest in a Soviet tank. As the writer Tibor Meray put it, he had devoted 40 years to Communism and now, 'Sitting in his tank, he carried away nothing but the hatred of the people, a stomach eaten by ulcers, and eyes nearly blinded from overstrain.' Gero was replaced by János Kádár, who had been imprisoned and tortured by the Rakosi regime. Earlier, as minister of the interior, he had interrogated Laszlo Rajk, the principal victim of the 1949 purge trial – and himself an implacable scourge of the people's enemies.

Nagy was swept along by the tide of revolution. He lacked Gomulka's flexibility and clarity and failed to seize control of the revolution until the very end. Constantly urged on by worker and student delegations, he had to fight off the remaining Stalinists, and negotiate with the Soviets.

In the first panic on the evening of 23 October, Gero had asked the Soviets to intervene, which resulted in heavy fighting on the 24th. Shooting outside the parliament building, in which about 70 people were killed, was started by the secret police, the AVH, many of whose officers were lynched. In the next two days, there was sporadic fighting throughout Budapest between students and Soviet forces. That was when the students threw their Molotov cocktails at the Soviet tanks.

The government had by then collapsed completely throughout the country. Local committees were set up in the various districts of the capital and in provincial cities. The Soviets were unsure of themselves and did not attempt to restore order. On the 28th, they withdrew from Budapest, and Nagy and the Hungarians claimed a great victory.

Communism had been overthrown on one splendid rush of enthusiasm. The Hungarian army refused to oppose the demonstrators, the police disintegrated and the AVH went into hiding. Nagy formed a coalition government with other political parties and started to put an administration together. The Hungarians were filled with the exaltation of revolution, and they demanded that all Soviet troops leave by 1 January, and that Hungary abrogate the Warsaw Pact and declare itself neutral.

361

The Soviet leadership hesitated for several days over which course to follow. Two senior members of the politburo, Anastas Mikoyan and Mikhail Suslov, were in Budapest and negotiated with Nagy. They promised that Soviet troops would be withdrawn and that Hungary was free to decide her own future. However, by 1 November, Khrushchev and the rest of the politburo had decided to intervene. Their decision was undoubtedly influenced by two coincidences: it was the week before the American presidential election, the worst time for Washington to decide anything; and three days after Israel had invaded Egypt (*see* Israel, pp. 311–38). The West, therefore, was wholly distracted, and the Soviets considered that they would have a free hand in Budapest. Troops were moved across the border in large numbers and stationed at all the air fields and major communications centres in the country. Budapest was surrounded.

Nagy was informed of these developments, and demanded an explanation from the Soviet ambassador, Yuri Andropov. Nagy insisted that he was a loyal Communist and friend of the Soviet Union. He had lived in Moscow for years and knew all the Kremlin leaders well, and he could not believe that they would order the overthrow of the Hungarian government. Had not Mikoyan and Suslov formally assured him only the day before that the Soviet Union accepted the new government, would withdraw Soviet troops and would respect the decision to abrogate the Warsaw Pact?

The news from the countryside was increasingly ominous. There was a further series of meetings with Andropov, in the course of which the ambassador constantly refused to give any explanation of Soviet troop movements. The Hungarian party politburo, including Kádár and Ferenc Munnich (who defected to the Soviets two days later), voted to take Hungary out of the Warsaw Pact. Informing Andropov of the decision, Kádár told him, 'What happens to me is of little importance, but I am ready, as a Hungarian, to fight if necessary. If your tanks enter Budapest, I will go into the streets and fight against you with my bare hands!'

The government ratified the decision, and announced it to the people. Hungary was now neutral, like Austria. Then Nagy played his last card: he demanded that the Western powers guarantee Hungary's neutrality, like Austria's, to provide assurance that it would not join an alliance against the Soviet Union.

Negotiations were to begin immediately with the Soviets on the withdrawal of their troops, and a first meeting with a Soviet military delegation was held at the Ministry of Defence. The Soviets demanded that their war memorials be respected, and the Hungarians agreed at once. It was arranged that a further meeting would be held, at Soviet headquarters outside Budapest, on Saturday evening, 3 November.

For a last brief autumn day, the Hungarians thought they had won. Nagy, who was under no illusion, extended his government by including ministers from other political parties, miraculously revived after a decade's persecution. Radio Free Europe cheered the victory and urged Hungary to purge the last Communists from the government. On Saturday evening, Colonel Pal Maleter, the minister of defence, led a delegation of Hungarian officers to Soviet headquarters. The talks went well for the first hour, then General Ivan Serov, head of the KGB, burst into the room and arrested them.

Early the following morning, Soviet tanks entered Budapest. At 5.20 a.m.,

Nagy broadcast to the nation:

This is Imre Nagy, president of the council of ministers of the People's Republic of Hungary speaking. Today at dawn, Soviet forces launched an attack against the capital with the obvious purpose of overthrowing the legal Hungarian democratic government. Our troops are fighting. The government is at its post. I notify the people of our country and the entire world of these facts.

An hour later, the playwright Gyula Hay made a last broadcast:

This is the Hungarian Writers' Association speaking to all writers, scientists, writers' associations, academics and scientific organizations of the world. We appeal for help to all intellectuals in all countries. Our time is limited. You all know the facts. There is no need to review them. Help Hungary! Help the writers, scientists, workers, peasants, and all Hungarian intellectuals. Help! Help! Help!

By six o'clock, Nagy had learned that Kádár and Munnich had formed a new pro-Soviet government. The Soviets were now in the centre of Budapest, and Nagy took refuge in the Yugoslav embassy. There was no organized resistance by the Hungarian armed forces, but the workers in their factories and districts put up a valiant, futile struggle for several days. They were overwhelmed, as were their friends elsewhere in the country. There was a general strike throughout Hungary which was gradually suppressed. The last strike committee dissolved itself in January 1957.

Nagy was lured out of his refuge on 22 November by promises of security and was arrested. He was executed 18 months later, along with Colonel Maleter and a number of other leaders of the former government.

THE KÁDÁR YEARS

After they had restored order in Budapest, the Soviets handed over power to János Kádár's new government. It took several years before he was able to reconstitute the Communist party and set up a properly functioning administration. When that was achieved, he set about dealing with some of the problems that had caused the revolution.

He could not touch the most basic question – relations with the USSR – but he mitigated the Stalinist economic policies of the Rakosi period and established what Khrushchev called 'Goulash Communism'. The Soviets gave him a free hand: they had no wish to reimpose Stalinism, as long as Hungary remained loyal to Moscow. Hungary prospered, in East European terms, and over the years, the Hungarians were allowed a degree of freedom that other East Europeans were denied. They could travel abroad, dissidents were harassed but not suppressed, and there was little censorship of foreign publications.

Hungary claims to have inspired Mikhail Gorbachev's *glasnost* policy, and it is certainly true that the Hungarians have long enjoyed the freedoms that Gorbachev has now introduced in the USSR. However, there are limits to their liberties, and the relatively liberal economic policies that have been followed since the early 1960s have failed to raise Hungary to Western levels of prosperity. Because they can visit the West freely and read Western books and newspapers, Hungarians can see for themselves how rapidly they are falling behind.

They are constantly testing the limits of their freedoms. The essential point is that Kádár's economic reforms did not go far enough. The economy went into deep depression by the mid-1980s, with a heavy burden of foreign debt and no means of paying it – and without credit, Hungary could not continue modernization. In May 1988, a party conference swept away the old leadership and installed a new government under Karol Grosz, which may be the Communist party's last chance to win the confidence of the people.

In November 1988, a 40-year-old economist, Miklos Nemeth, who had studied at Harvard University, was made prime minister. The appointment was described as a first step towards separating the government and the Communist party, but the opposition remained sceptical: it claimed that the government would continue to obey the party's orders. Nemeth insisted that reform was inevitable, and would include the legalization of opposition parties and trade unions, as well as free elections under a new constitution, to be introduced in 1990. Nemeth is not the most liberal of party leaders: there are several prominent members of the politburo who want to go much further and faster. However, there is no denying that Hungary is once again leading the way for the whole bloc. In December 1988, parliament voted to legalize opposition parties, and a plenum of the Central Commmittee confirmed the decision the following February. The tide of reform was running strongly.

Grosz and Nemeth, unlike Jaruzelski in Poland or the governments of Roumania and Czechoslovakia, retain a measure of popular support. They can hope that, by liberating the political system, they will not immediately provoke an irresistible demand for real democracy that will sweep them away like their predecessors in 1956. Time will tell. Older Hungarians remember vividly the events of 1956. The younger generation may be ready to try again.

CZECHOSLOVAKIA

The joke in 1956 was that all the nations of Eastern Europe were behaving out of character: the Soviets were behaving like Germans, the Hungarians like Poles, the Poles like Czechs and the Czechs like swine.

By this it was meant that Hungarians throwing stones at Soviet tanks were as gallantly foolish as the Polish cavalry who had charged against Hilter's panzers in 1939; the Poles who bluffed the Soviets out of occupying Warsaw were showing the same ability to bend to the wind that had saved Prague, alone in Central Europe, from destruction in the war; while the Czechs under Antonin Novotny's quisling government slavishly obeyed the USSR.

In Czechoslovakia in 1968, things happened differently. As in Hungary 12 years earlier, the regime was rotting from the head, but the Czech party succeeded in finding alternative leaders who took control and introduced a sweeping series of reforms. In January 1968, the party conference deposed the Stalinist general secretary, Antonin Novotny, and elected a reformist Slovak, Alexander Dubček. In the spring, Novotny was also removed as president and replaced with a popular general, Ludvik Svoboda. Then the 'Prague Spring' began. Dubček proclaimed 'socialism with a human face': an end to censorship, a restoration of democratic rights to non-Communists and an abandonment of rigid, Stalinist economic policies. The reformers' problem was that Czech workers had lost all confidence in the party and, despite strenuous efforts by party intellectuals, did not rally behind the reformers until it was too late. Elections for the XIVth party conference were held, and it was clear that the old guard was going to be swept entirely away. Such a thing was intolerable to Leonid Brezhnev, then the Soviet leader. On 20 August 1968, the Soviet Union invaded Czechoslovakia. On that occasion, the Poles, Hungarians and East Germans all behaved like swine: they joined the invasion.

Soviet troops seized the airport and sent three columns of tanks into Prague. One occupied the residence of the president, one the prime minister's office, the third the party headquarters, where a meeting of the politburo was in session when the Soviets entered. They made the committee members, including Dubček, lie on the floor. (One of them commented later, 'For some time, all we could see of our allies was their boots.') The leaders were then taken to the airport and loaded into a Soviet plane. Through the windows, they observed four men apparently carrying a corpse towards the aircraft, and concluded that their turn would be next – until the 'corpse' started struggling. It was Oldrich Cernik, the prime minister, who had been arrested at his office and refused to move. The prisoners were flown to Poland, where they were incarcerated for 60 hours, without being allowed to wash, shave or change. Then they were flown to Moscow.

They assumed that they would be shot, but instead they were driven straight to the Kremlin and taken to a large room, where they waited. Then Brezhnev marched in, followed by the Soviet politburo, and said, 'How nice to see you gentlemen.' President Svoboda, whom the Soviets wished to retain in office, had been brought to Moscow separately, but he refused to talk to them without Dubček and the others, a refusal they now believe saved their lives. The prisoners were browbeaten into signing a 'Moscow protocol' approving the invasion. They were then sent back to Prague, where in due course they all lost their jobs, and were replaced by quislings.

The Soviets' justification for their intervention in Czechoslovakian affairs was the 'Brezhnev doctrine', which stipulates that if a Communist government gets into trouble, other Communist states may come to the rescue. The doctrine was greeted with much indignation in the West, although Western powers had enforced their own version of the doctrine on numerous occasions – in Greece in 1944 and 1946, for instance, and in the Dominican Republic in 1965, three years before the Soviet invasion of Czechoslovakia. Brezhnev formally stated his doctrine a month after the event:

The weakening of any of the links in the world socialist system directly affects all the socialist countries, which cannot look on indifferently when this happens. Thus, with talk about the right of nations to self-determination, the anti-socialist elements in Czechoslovakia actually covered up a demand for so-called neutrality and Czechoslovakia's withdrawal from the socialist community. However, the implementation of 'self-determination' of that kind, or, in other words, the detaching of Czechoslovakia from the socialist community, would have come into conflict with Czechoslovakia's vital interests and would have been detrimental to the other socialist states. Such 'self-determination', as a result of which Nato troops would have been able to come up to the Soviet borders, while the community of European socialist countries would have been rent, would have encroached, in actual fact, upon the vital interests of the peoples of these countries and would be in fundamental conflict with the right of these people to socialist self-determination.

Two days after the invasion, the elected delegates to the party conference met clandestinely in a factory in Prague. By then, Czech workers had called a general strike and were trying to defend the achievements of the Prague Spring. It was all 365 in vain. Dubček and his colleagues were kept on as figureheads until the following summer, but all power was wielded by the old guard, and the workers' councils were ground down and suppressed.

Dubček – who in 1969 was replaced by Gustáv Husák, party leader from Slovakia – was luckier than his Hungarian counterpart Imrie Nagy: he was not shot. For a while, he was ambassador to Turkey, then he was given a menial job as a forestry worker in Slovakia, where he still lives. The government marked the 20th anniversary of the invasion by publishing virulent attacks on him, perhaps because they fear that some new upheaval might bring him back to power. He is now about the same age as Winston Churchill in 1940, Imre Nagy in 1956 and Charles de Gaulle in 1958. In November 1988, he was allowed to travel abroad for the first time in years, to accept an honorary degree at the University of Bologna in Italy. He gave several newspaper interviews and made a speech at the degree ceremony in which he vigorously defended the policies of the Prague Spring and, by implication, attacked everything that had happened since.

The Czechoslovak government has been wholly subservient to the USSR since 1968, obeying the Soviets in all things, suppressing dissidents, chanting the praise of the great Soviet motherland on every occasion. Husák retired at the end of 1987, and was replaced by Miloš Jakes. The regime was more than surprised when Gorbachev was cheered in the streets during a visit to Prague early in 1988. When his spokesman was asked what the difference was between the Prague Spring and Gorbachev's *glasnost*, he replied: 'Twenty years.'

The Czech economy has suffered less than that of Poland or Hungary: after all, Czechoslovakia had been a modern state before the Communist coup in 1948. However, the present government is detested and a sudden explosion is entirely possible. A new generation has grown up, who might take *glasnost* seriously.

The government has no intention of loosening the reins. In October 1988, the prime minister, Lubomir Strougal, was forced to resign. He had been the leading advocate of economic reform, and although he never proposed to go as far as Hungary, his suggestions were rejected by the politburo. Evidently, the Czechoslovak party intended to stick with the model it had adopted in 1968. The police firmly repressed the small demonstrations that were held in Prague in August to commemorate the 20th anniversary of the 1968 invasion. Then on 28 October – the 70th anniversary of Czechoslovakia's independence from Austria – there was a larger demonstration in the capital. It had been called by Charter 77, the principal dissident movement, and was also broken up by police. It was the first sign of serious popular unrest in years.

THE BALKANS

In Poland and Czechoslovakia, the only relevant question is the future of their relations with the USSR. The Balkans are more complicated. The six nations there (seven, counting Turkey) have yet to settle questions far older than Marxism.

The spark that lit the fuse of World War I was the assassination at Sarajevo on 28 June 1914 of the Archduke Franz Ferdinand, heir to the throne of Austria-Hungary, and his wife. They were shot by a Serbian terrorist as they rode through the city in an open carriage. Sarajevo is the capital of Bosnia, a province that had been annexed by Austria in 1908 but had been coveted by Serbia for 50 years. Austria suspected, rightly, that the Serbian government was implicated in the assassination. Serbia was also a threat to Austrian control of the Slavic lands of Crotia and Slovenia, as well as Bosnia, and Vienna used the murders as a pretext to extort a complete surrender by the Serbian government in Belgrade. In the calamity that followed, millions died, four empires were destroyed, Lenin and Trotsky imposed Bolshevism upon Russia and the scene was set for a second and greater war 20 years after the first.

Austria-Hungary is one with Nineveh and Tyre. Its rule over half of the Balkans and Central Europe has been replaced by the Soviet empire, which is now ineluctably moving towards the same condition of decay and disintegration that afflicted the Hapsburgs' domains in 1914. The animosities among the Balkan people are as great as ever, and no one can seriously expect the present tranquillity to last for ever.

The Balkans suffered a long succession of wars between the middle of the last century and 1945. The cause was always the same: the rising nationalism of the various parts of the region and the impossibility of establishing mutually acceptable frontiers between any of them. That useful word 'Balkanization' was coined to meet the case. In 1919, during the negotiations following World War I, the powers made a valiant effort to settle the Balkan frontiers once and for all. Harold Nicolson recounted entering the American president's room in Paris, and finding Woodrow Wilson and David Lloyd George on their hands and knees, pushing the maps of Eastern Europe around the floor, while Clemenceau observed them sardonically from his chair. The borders were established in the Treaty of Trianon, the garden annex to the Peace of Versailles, and they were confirmed in 1945 with two exceptions: parts of Roumania and Czechoslovakia were annexed by the Soviet Union, and the border between Italy and Yugoslavia was adjusted in the latter's favour.

The heavy hand of the Red Army has kept the peace ever since. The status quo was only challenged once, in Budapest in 1956, but the irredentist claims are not forgotten. As the grip of the USSR is loosened, Hungary once more concerns itself with the fate of the Hungarian minority in Roumania. The Yugoslav federation barely holds together and is particularly threatened by a large and restive Albanian minority in the south. Bulgaria has been persecuting its Turkish minority and has certainly not forgotten its claims on southern Yugoslavia and on the Dobrudja in southern Roumania. The Roumanians, while fearing irredentist claims from Bulgaria and Hungary, look covetously over the border at Soviet Moldavia.

None of this means that a renewal of the Balkan wars is likely, although the most dangerous dispute, between Hungary and Roumania, might possibly escalate into an uncontrollable conflict. The Balkan people must wait for the Soviet Union to abandon its hegemony over them before they can start killing each other again.

THE TRANSYLVANIA DISPUTE

In 1867, the Hungarians attained equality with Austria in what became known as the Austro-Hungarian empire. The Austrian emperor was also king of Hungary, and Hungarians ruled over part of what is now Yugoslavia and roughly half of modern Roumania and Czechoslovakia. They lost it all in the   367 collapse of the empire in 1918. The victors confined the Hungarians to their native plains, excluding a third of them, 3 million people in all. These separated brethren lived in Czechoslovakia and in Yugoslavia and, above all, in central Roumania.

This is Transylvania, which both Hungarians and Roumanians claim as the cradle of their nations. For over 1000 years, Magyars, Roumanians and Germans, with smaller Jewish and gypsy communities, lived there, co-mingled but distinct: many villages and towns have three names, one in each of the major languages. The number of Hungarians is hotly disputed: Hungary says there are 2.5 million; Roumania says there are only 1.7 million. There are now about 300,000 Germans there, the only large East European German community that was not expelled in 1945, and there are also several hundred thousand Hungarians in eastern Roumania, far from Transylvania, including 200,000 in Bucharest.

The largest Hungarian communities are in central and eastern Transylvania separated from the motherland by a wide territory that is chiefly Roumanian. Those areas could not be restored to Hungary without making large numbers of Roumanians subjects of Budapest, reversing the present irredentist claims and creating a wholly impractical frontier. The peacemakers in 1919 decided that it would be better to leave the Transylvanian Hungarians in Roumania while at the same time guaranteeing them every possible political and civil right. Besides, Hungary was one of the nations that had started the war, and lost it.

In the 1930s, Hungary joined the Axis and was a loyal ally to Hitler until his defeat was certain and the Red Army was at the Danube. When Germany partitioned Czechoslovakia, in 1938–9, Hungary took a large slice for itself. After the Hitler–Stalin pact, which among other things allowed Stalin to annex part of Roumania (*see below*), Hungary demanded Transylvania. Roumania could not refuse. The Hungarians did not seize all the territory they had lost in 1918, but merely took northern Transylvania. They persecuted Roumanians living there, and the Roumanians persecuted Hungarians living in southern Transylvania. Both nations were allied to Germany, which insisted they keep the peace, and both prepared to fight each other as soon as the war was over. Hungary also annexed part of Yugoslavia in 1941. However horrible the present Roumanian regime, and however relatively moderate the present government of Hungary, the Hungarians' history of ruthless aggression and oppression of their neighbours should not be forgotten. The neighbours remember.

After they liberated the Balkans, the Soviets restored the pre-war frontiers (adjusted to their own convenience) and declared that Leninist internationalism would solve the 'nationalities question'. They meant that, in the future, the Marxist rule of the primacy of class over nation would resolve all difficulties. It is one of the more absurd errors of Communist theory.

The Hungarians in Roumania have suffered steady and increasing persecution since 1945. President Nicolae Ceauşescu of Roumania stated the case succinctly:

Our party and state are faced with the duty to take conscientious action to provide every one of our citizens with the sort of conditions under which the nation and the nationalities can fulfil themselves and, at the same time, make it possible for national differences to diminish and gradually to disappear under Communism.

Hungarians in Roumania have resisted attempts to make them 'disappear'.

Despite this, Hungarian schools, formerly in their hundreds, have almost all been closed or merged with Roumanian schools, until now there are only eight left, and the director of each of these is a Roumanian. The Hungarian university at Cluj has been merged with a Roumanian university. The few remaining Hungarian language magazines and newspapers are heavily censored, very small and worthless; newspapers from Budapest may not be sold in Transylvania. Tourists from abroad must stay in government hotels; this ruling means that Hungarians from Hungary may not stay with their relatives in Transylvania. Tourism, in any case, is severely discouraged.

Ceauşescu is now engaged in imposing a final solution to the Hungarian problem. Early in 1988, he announced that 8000 of the 13,000 villages in Roumania would be wiped out, to be replaced by 'agro-industrial centres'. The ones to go are almost all Hungarian. Hungarians have been obliged to adopt Roumanian Christian names to get jobs, and all Hungarian towns and villages in Transylvania have been given Roumanian names.

On 27 June 1988, tens of thousands of Hungarians marched on the Roumanian embassy in Budapest to protest against Ceauşescu's policies. It was an event without precedent in Eastern Europe. The Hungarian government permitted, even encouraged the demonstration, and is now playing the nationalist card – but, so far, only against Roumania. Hungarian refugees from Roumania are now welcomed in Hungary, and Budapest has protested vigorously and frequently against Roumanian persecution of its Hungarian minority. The Hungarian government insists that it has no irredentist claim on Transylvania – it still pays lip-service to socialist internationalism – but the Hungarian people have quite other intentions. They have no time for socialism or internationalism.

ROUMANIA

Apart from the Greeks, the Roumanians are the oldest nation in the Balkans. They were colonized by the Romans and learned Latin; Roumanian, though heavily corrupted by Slav and Turkish words, is a Romance language. When the Hungarians conquered Dacia, and the Slavs flooded the whole peninsula, the Roumanians survived, and when they finally escaped Turkish domination in the 19th century, they looked to the West for inspiration while the Bulgars and Serbs looked to Mother Russia.

Hungarians and Roumanians are hopelessly intermingled in Transylvania (*see above*), and Roumania has quarrels with its other neighbours. North of the Danube is Bessarabia, now the Moldavian Soviet Socialist Republic, which was an historic principality of Roumania. The tsars wrested it from Turkish control in the 18th century. Southern Bessarabia was ceded to Roumania after the Crimean War, but it had to hand it back to Russia in the Treaty of Berlin in 1878. When the Russian empire collapsed in 1917, Roumania claimed the lost province. In 1939, in his treaty with Hitler, Stalin stated that the Soviet Union would now recover Moldavia, and in June 1940, immediately after the defeat of France and Britain's expulsion from the Continent, the Soviet foreign minister, Molotov, informed the Roumanians. He also told them that the USSR would annex Bukovina, an area of northern Roumania which had been part of the Austro-Hungarian empire. He scrawled a new line on a map, in thick pencil, carelessly including areas of Moldavia that had never been part of Russia. The Soviets insisted on imposing the Molotov line.

Exactly a year later, when Hitler invaded the Soviet Union, the Roumanians joined him. They recovered their lost territories, and Hitler also permitted them to annex Odessa and its hinterland, which they called Transnistria. It was a short-lived empire: when the tide turned, the Soviet Union took back Moldavia and Bukovina, adding eastern Czechoslovakia for good measure.

In the Balkan wars, 1912–13, and in both world wars, Roumania and Bulgaria contested the southern Dobrudja, an area in the Danube delta. It is now Roumanian again. Stalin may have amputated north-east Roumania, but he restored its territories to the south and west.

The current Roumanian government is the most corrupt and inefficient of all Communist regimes. President Nicolae Ceauşescu rules with the aid of his wife, children and other relatives in a grotesque 'cult of the personality' exceeded only by that in North Korea. Roumania resembles Orwell's vision of a Communist dictatorship in *1984*: a miserable tyranny where the people starve in the cold and their every act is monitored by the Thought Police. Roumania continues to be a reminder of the economic conditions in Europe in the late 1940s, when everything was rationed. There is not enough electricity to heat buildings during the winter, or even to light them adequately at night.

Ceauşescu has also decided to leave his mark on Bucharest by demolishing a number of important 19th-century buildings, including the cathedral, to make way for new avenues. In all, a third of the city centre is being razed.

About 50,000 refugees from Roumania have moved to Hungary since 1981, and the numbers increased sharply in 1988. Most of them are ethnic Hungarians, but some are native Roumanians, escaping the economic calamity caused by Ceauşescu's policies. The Roumanian–Hungarian border now resembles the Iron Curtain of 30 years ago, with people to the east desperate to escape the horrors of their native country to reach the comparative freedom and affluence of Hungary. For the first time in the history of European Communism, people are trying to get into a Communist country – and are being welcomed.

It is not only the ethnic Hungarians who protest. In November 1987, there were large demonstrations against the regime in Brasov, one of the country's largest cities. The workers there were protesting against austerity measures imposed by the government. The riots were suppressed, but it is entirely possible that they will be repeated. The governments in the rest of Eastern Europe may assume that, if the worst comes to the worst, the Soviet Union will come to the rescue. Ceauşescu can make no such assumption, and the Roumanians know it. The possibility of an explosion in Roumania is very high.

BULGARIA

The Bulgarians believed in 1914 that the great powers had unjustly deprived them of parts of their national territory after the various 19th-century wars and the Balkan wars of 1912 and 1913. So on the outbreak of World War I, they allied themselves with the Central Powers and annexed the southern Dobrudja from Roumania, western Macedonia from Serbia and eastern Thrace from Greece. Forced to restore all these territories in 1918, they tried again in 1940. Once more the Bulgarians joined the Germans, once more they annexed their neighbours' territories and once more they were defeated.

Despite all the movements of population of the 20th century, there remains a considerable Turkish community in Bulgaria, several hundred thousand strong. It is impossible to be more precise as Bulgaria denies that there are any Turks at all, and in the 1970s, it set out to prove the point by ordering all citizens to adopt Bulgarian names. The measure was aimed at the Turks, and has been accompanied by various punitive measures. All this is flatly contrary to Communist doctrine, not to mention the UN Declaration on Human Rights and the Helsinki Final Act, but it is standard Balkan practice.

The wide territory of Macedonia, now in southern Yugoslavia and northern Greece, is another sensitive area. Greece claims that everyone living within its frontiers is Greek. The Yugoslavs claim that Yugoslav Macedonia, one of the constituent republics of their federation, is populated entirely by Slavs whose language and culture looks north to Belgrade, not east to Sofia. The Bulgars assert that the Macedonians speak Bulgarian, which is true, and that the territory ought to be incorporated into Bulgaria, which does not necessarily follow: all those who speak French, for instance, do not consider themselves French. As for Greece, there can be no doubt that many people in Greek Macedonia and Thrace speak Bulgarian, not Greek. The Greeks, meanwhile, lay claim to southern Albania, which they call Northern Epiros.

Despite these territorial disputes, Bulgaria is the most tranquil of Soviet satellites. It is conspicuously better governed than Roumania to its north, and its traditional alliance with Russia persists. In the wake of Gorbachev's reforms in Moscow, Bulgaria's leader, Todor Zhivkov, who has ruled the country since 1954, contemplated similar reforms, announcing in July 1987 that they would be introduced at the next party conference. He abandoned the idea at the last moment, and the conference, in January 1988, was remarkably unremarkable. Bulgaria will not take the lead in any new reform movement in the Balkans.

YUGOSLAVIA

The Yugoslav and Albanian Communist parties, unlike all the others, won their revolutions without any help from the Red Army. Tito then broke with Stalin, in 1948, and lived to tell the tale. The Soviets did not impose their hegemony upon Belgrade – one reason why the Communist regime survives in Yugoslavia today.

The other is a consequence of the fragmentation of the country. There are six constituent republics in Yugoslavia, all enjoying a great measure of autonomy. Tito and his successors have made a virtue of weakness. Where Stalin imposed an iron tyranny upon the 100 or so nationalities in the USSR, a tyranny solidly based on the numerical predominance of the Russians, Tito preserved his state by a complicated balancing act between the three major nationalities – Serbs, Croats and Slovenes – and the lesser minorities. (He was himself a Croat, which helped keep that republic in the federation.) It is not a democracy, but national rights and individual freedoms are respected in Yugoslavia far more than elsewhere in Eastern Europe.

The rights and privileges of the minority communities, cut off from their compatriots by the frontiers of 1919, are all, in theory at least, protected by the 371 constitution. This theoretically admirable state of affairs is most severely tested in Kosovo (or Kossovo), the region, now part of Serbia, that lies immediately north and east of Albania. About 90 per cent of its population of approximately 1 million people speak Albanian, and most of them are Muslims; they are also known as the Shqiptars. In 1981, there were pogroms in Kosovo directed at the Serb minority, many of whom were murdered. There were the usual Balkan reports of frightful atrocities perpetrated by the Albanians.

No one in his right mind would wish to be united with modern Albania, the most reclusive and one of the most tyrannical states in the world, but the Kosovo Albanians want their independence from Belgrade. The Serbs reject any such proposition, partly because Kosovo is a traditional part of Serbia (the Turks defeated the Serbians in a famous battle there in 1389, a Balkan Flodden), and partly because secession by Kosovo might lead to the disintegration of Yugoslavia.

The Yugoslav government, at least since the 1960s, has been far less oppressive than other Communist governments in Eastern Europe, and as a result, popular discontent has a safety valve denied the Roumanians and Czechs. But now, discontent is steadily increasing, and the collective government set up after Tito's death, with a rotating presidency, quite lacks the authority to deal with the underlying economic and political problems.

National antagonisms persist. Serbs have not forgotten that the Croats and Slovenes joined the Germans in the last war. The Fascist Croatian government set up by Hitler was fanatically Catholic and persecuted Orthodox Serbs and helped the Gestapo ship off the Jews to Auschwitz. Films survive of congregations of Serbs being offered the choice of conversion to Catholicism or death; the films conclude with the machine-guns slaughtering them. In all, about 700,000 people were murdered by the Croation government. One of the men most responsible, the police minister Andriya Artukovitch, afterwards lived peacefully in California for over 30 years, escaping all efforts to have him prosecuted for war crimes, until the mid-1980s when he was finally extradicted to Yugoslavia.

The Croats, conversely, resent domination from Belgrade, as do the Slovenes. Other distinctions go back to the Austro-Hungarian period and beyond: in the north, people use the Latin alphabet, are Catholic, and look West; in the east and south, people are Orthodox, use the Cyrillic alphabet, and their cultural traditions are linked to the East; in Kosovo, of course, the people pray towards Mecca.

Yugoslavia would like to be the Communist Switzerland of the Balkans, with its many nationalities cohabiting peacefully together. It isn't. Its survival so far has been a miracle, and has owed a great deal, from 1948 until recent times, to the deep hostility felt by its different populations towards the USSR. However much Croats and Macedonians may have disliked Belgrade, they much preferred it to Moscow. Now that threat is lifted, and they are free to quarrel among themselves. They are increasingly availing themselves of that dispensation.

In 1988, the signs of dissolution became evident. Serbs began to demand that their numbers and historic role as leaders of Yugoslavia be recognized. The Serb party leader, Slobodan Milosevic, put himself at the head of this nationalist movement – supporting demands that Kosovo should lose its autonomy and be reintegrated into Serbia – and won a degree of popularity that no Yugoslav leader has enjoyed since Tito. As a result, of course, he was widely distrusted in the other regions.

Milosevic organized a mass demonstration of 100,000 Serbs in the Vojvodina, a province in the north-east of the country, which led to the resignation of the local government. Serbs want Vojvodina to be reunited to Serbia, and they also have their eyes on Bosnia-Hertzegovina, another of Yugoslavia's constituent republics with a Serbian majority but large Croatian minorities. Any rearrangement of Yugoslavia along these lines would indeed restore Serbia to its lost domination of the country.

On 20 October 1988, the party politburo ruled against Milosevic and voted to uphold the loose system bequeathed by Tito. The Serbian leader would not accept the verdict and, in November, succeeded in forcing the resignation of party leaders in Kosovo, whom he accused of abetting the 'persecution' of the Serbian minority. The following week, he called out the people of Belgrade in an enormous demonstration of at least 600,000 against the alleged Albanian atrocities in Kosovo. Meanwhile, the Albanians were themselves demonstrating in Pristina, the capital of Kosovo, demanding the reinstatement of the dismissed officials.

Milosevic claimed to be a sound democrat, but there are plenty of Yugoslavs who remember another national leader who rose to power demanding the restoration of the 'rights' of his *volk*, and then annexed a series of neighbouring countries to reunite the dispersed Germans with the Reich. Milosevic, fortunately, lacks Hitler's power base, but the sudden revival of Balkan chauvinism is a nasty reminder of the persistence of nationalism and xenophobia in Europe.

FURTHER READING

Ascherson, Neal, *The Polish August: the Self-Limiting Revolution*, New York, Viking, 1982, and *The Struggles for Poland*, New York, Random House, 1987.
American University, *Yugoslavia: A Country Study*, Washington D.C., 1979.
Gadney, Reg, *Cry Hungary! Uprising, 1956*, New York, Atheneum, 1986.
Minority Rights Group, *The Hungarians of Roumania*, London, 1978.
Gati, Charles, *Hungary and the Soviet Bloc*, Durham, N. C., Duke University Press, 1986.
Khrushchev, Nikita, *Khrushchev Remembers*, edited by Edward Crankshaw, translated by Strobe Talbott, Boston, Little, Brown, 1970.
London, Kurt (ed.), *Eastern Europe in Transition*, Baltimore, Md., Johns Hopkins University Press, 1966.
Meray, Tibor, *Thirteen Days that Shook the Kremlin*, translated by Howard L. Katzander, New York, Praegar, 1959.
Wolff, Robert Lee, *The Balkans in Our Time*, Cambridge, Mass., Harvard University Press, 1956.

NORTHERN IRELAND

Geography	5462 sq. miles (14,147 sq. km), slightly larger than Connecticut. It comprises the six north-eastern counties of Ireland: Antrim, Armagh, Down, Fermanagh, Londonderry and Tyrone. Often called the 'Six Counties' by Catholics. Also known as Ulster, especially by Protestants, although the ancient province of Ulster included three other counties – Cavan, Donegal and Monaghan – which are now part of the Irish Republic.
Population	1,537,000. Of these, 950,000 are Protestant, 600,000 are Catholic. The principal city is Belfast, with a population of 420,000, of whom 100,000 are Catholic, 320,000 Protestant. (The Irish Republic has a population of 3.2 million, of whom about 100,000 are Protestant, the rest Catholic, in an area of 27,136 sq. miles [70, 282 sq. km]).
Constitutional status	Northern Ireland is part of the United Kingdom of Great Britain and Northern Ireland (UK). It has the same status as Scotland and Wales. It elects 17 members to the Parliament in London as its share of the overall population of the UK. It is administered by a secretary of state for Northern Ireland (analogous to the secretaries for Scotland and for Wales), who is responsible to Parliament. Local affairs are administered by locally elected officials, at county and city level.

The exigencies of the war against terrorism have led to restrictions on various civil rights, including trial by jury and freedom of speech. Legal provisions permitting the detention of suspects without charge for up to seven days have been declared illegal by the European Court. |
| **Economy** | Northern Ireland enjoyed great prosperity in the 19th century, thanks to the textile industry (chiefly linen) and the shipbuilding industry in Belfast: Harland & Wolff were at one time the largest shipbuilders in the world (they built the *Titanic*). Shipbuilding has been in decline since World War I, and the remaining yards survive on government subsidies; the linen industry has all but disappeared. Government efforts to stimulate new investment and modern industries have not met with much success, in large part because of IRA terrorism. Agriculture is relatively prosperous, thanks to the pricing policies of the European Community. Unemployment, at 18.6%, is higher than the British average (10.2%) and in some areas reaches 40%; it is twice as high among Catholics as among Protestants. |

Armed forces   At the end of 1988, there were 10,600 regular British troops in Northern Ireland, 6200 members of the Ulster Defence Regiment and 8200 full-time and 4600 part-time members of the Royal Ulster Constabulary, making a total of 29,600 security personnel. The Provisional IRA was thought to consist of about 300 full-time terrorists and up to 1500 'reservists'.

Casualties   About 2700 people were killed from 1969 to the end of 1988. Of these:

     31% were members of the security forces
     14% were members of paramilitary groups
     55% were civilians

Of the civilians, 69% were Catholic, 31% Protestant. Of the total:

     44% were killed by the Provisional IRA
     18% were killed by other Republican groups
     27% were killed by 'Loyalist' terrorism
     10% were killed by the British army
     2% were killed by the RUC
     0.28% were killed by the UDR

In 1988, 93 people were killed in Northern Ireland. Of these, 5 were police officers, 21 were members of the regular army, 11 were members of the Ulster Defence Regiment and 56 were civilians. About 20 of the 'civilians' were members of the IRA. Three RAF men were murdered in the Netherlands, one British soldier was murdered in Belgium and another in London. Three IRA terrorists were killed in Gibraltar.

By comparison, Washington, DC, which has a population of 620,000 (less than half that of Northern Ireland), had about 375 murders in 1988.

Things fall apart; the centre cannot hold;
Mere anarchy is loosed upon the world,
The blood-dimmed tide is loosed, and everywhere   ﹀
The ceremony of innocence is drowned;
The best lack all conviction, while the worst
Are full of passionate intensity.
         W. B. Yeats, 'The Second Coming'

The gunmen aren't dying for the people: the people are dying for the gunmen.
         Sean O'Casey

HISTORY

On Easter Monday, 24 April 1916, Patrick Pearse stood on the steps of the General Post Office in Sackville Street, Dublin, and proclaimed the Irish Republic: 'Irishmen and Irishwomen: In the name of God and of the dead generations from which she received her old tradition of nationhood, Ireland, through us, summons her children to her flag and strikes for her freedom.'

It was the first nationalist uprising of the 20th century, and it was firmly suppressed by the British army. Six years later, after a guerrilla war marked by many atrocities on both sides, most of Ireland won its independence. The Protestant majority of the Six Counties insisted on remaining united with Great   375

Britain. The Provisional Irish Republican Army and other terrorist organizations are still fighting to unite Northern Ireland with the Irish Republic. Their objective is supported by a large majority of the Catholic population (Nationalists) who, however, generally oppose their terrorist tactics. The Protestant majority (Unionists) want to remain part of the UK, and support security measures taken by the British government to defeat terrorism. There are now about 10,000 British troops (down from 25,000 in the mid-1970s) and twice that number of local police fighting the IRA.

The IRA terrorist campaign is the longest lasting and the most violent in Europe. Over 2700 people have been killed since August 1969, and a further 25,000 have suffered serious injury. 'The Troubles' show no sign of ending. Although there is less violence than there was ten years ago, an average of seven or eight people are killed a month. In 1988, 93 people were killed, the same as in 1987.

> The Irish must go to Hell or Connacht.
> Oliver Cromwell

The British first conquered Ireland in the 12th century. They succeeded in imposing their laws and, eventually, their language, but the majority of the Irish never willingly accepted their forced union with England. Resistance acquired a religious cast, which it has retained, when Great Britain, but not Ireland, embraced the Protestant Reformation in the 16th century. Ever since, all Protestants in Ireland have supported the Union, and most Catholics have opposed it.

At the end of the 16th century, after a revolt in Ulster, Elizabeth I confiscated all the land of the province. She and her successor, James I, granted the land to Protestant settlers from England and Scotland, in the Ulster plantation, which is exactly contemporary with the American colonies of Virginia and Massachusetts. Northern Ireland has had a Protestant majority ever since. The Protestant presence is even older: Carrickfergus was a Protestant town in the reign of Henry VIII. Catholics and Protestants have opposed each other, sometimes peacefully, sometimes violently, for nearly 400 years. This is a civil war, not a colonial war.

Catholic Ireland still remembers the revolt of the 1640s, which was eventually suppressed, with memorable brutality, by Cromwell. Much Protestant mythology goes back to the events of those years and to the second Irish civil war of the late 17th century, 300 years ago. After King James II was expelled from England in 1688, Catholic Ireland rose in his defence. Two episodes in that war are still celebrated every year: the Catholic siege of Londonderry (which was defended by Protestant apprentices, the 'Prentice Boys') in August 1689; and the Battle of the Boyne, on 12 July 1690, in which the Protestant King William III defeated his father-in-law, the Catholic King James. Protestants annually mark these two anniversaries with parades during the 'marching season'. One of their songs has the following chorus:

> We're up to our knees in Papish blood,
> We're up to our knees in slaughter:
> King Billy slew the Papish crew,
> At the Battle of Boyne Water.

In the wake of yet another rebellion, the (Protestant) Irish Parliament in Dublin was suppressed in 1801, and the political union of the two kingdoms was enacted. Irish Catholic men finally won the vote in 1829, shortly before the greatest disaster in Irish history, the potato famine of the 1840s. It cost hundreds of thousands of lives and led to a mass emigration to Great Britain, North America and Australia. The population, 8 million before the famine, has never recovered. The emigrants' descendants, and particularly those in the United States, have kept their religion and sense of Irishness over the generations. John F. Kennedy, for instance, was a fourth-generation American – his great-grandparents had emigrated during the famine – but he still proclaimed his Irishness. One of his nephews, visiting Belfast 140 years after his great-great-grandparents had left Ireland, repeated the assertion that he was Irish and had every right to meddle in Irish politics.

THE EASTER RISING AND THE WAR OF INDEPENDENCE

> *Was it for this the wild geese spread*
> *The grey wing upon every tide;*
> *For this that all that blood was shed,*
> *For this Edward Fitzgerald died,*
> *And Robert Emmet and Wolfe Tone,*
> *All that delirium of the brave?*
> *Romantic Ireland's dead and gone,*
> *It's with O'Leary in the grave.*
> W. B. Yeats, 'September 1913'

The Irish, by now well represented in the British Parliament, continued throughout the latter half of the 19th century to demand Home Rule (a measure of autonomy). The debate reached a fever pitch in London just before World War I, with the Liberal government proposing Home Rule and the Conservatives opposing it. Partition as a solution was discussed for the first time, and there was a long debate on whether to include Fermanagh and Tyrone (two counties equally divided between Catholics and Protestants) in the proposed Protestant enclave, but when the war began, this discussion was postponed for the duration.

Irish extremists, who had been plotting a new insurrection for years under the direction of their secret society, the Irish Republican Brotherhood, decided that their time had come. In 1916, they organized the Easter Rising. This was suppressed, at a cost of 1350 dead, and some of its leaders were shot, but the event brought the Republicans wide public support. In the 1918 general election, their political wing, Sinn Fein (pronounced *shin fain*, 'Ourselves Alone'), won most of the Catholic constituencies and a slight majority of the Catholic vote. The elected members seceded from the British Parliament and formed the first Dáil, an Irish Parliament in Dublin, with Eamon de Valéra as President of the Republic.

They formed the original Irish Republican Army, under the command of Michael Collins, which fought a guerrilla war against the British from 1919 to 1921. In 1920, the British partitioned Ireland, setting up legislatures with limited powers in Dublin (for the 26 counties that now make up the Republic) and in Stormont, outside Belfast, for the six Protestant counties of the north-east. The IRA continued to fight for an independent, united Republic, and eventually the British government offered 'dominion status' (the same degree of independence as Canada) on two conditions: that the Irish government renounce the Republic,   377 recognizing George V as King of Ireland, and agreement that the Six Counties had the right to remain in the union with Great Britain. A treaty on those lines was signed in London on 6 December 1921.

THE PARTITION DEBATE

There was intense opposition to the treaty among extremists in the IRA, led by de Valéra, who baulked at giving up the Republic. They lost the vote in the Dáil, but refused to recognize their defeat. When the independent Irish Free State was set up in 1922, they fought, and lost, a brutal civil war on the issue (1922–3), in which far more Irishmen – about 4000 – were killed, or executed, than the British had killed between 1916 and 1921. Today's Catholic mythology has it that the Dáil debate and the civil war were fought on the issue of partition. In fact, the question of partition went by default at the time, because both sides assumed that Northern Ireland would soon see the necessity of remaining in a united Ireland rather than existing as a separated appendage of Great Britain. De Valéra and his fellow extremists argued that giving up the Republic meant giving up Irish independence, and they were prepared to kill their former comrades to reverse the decision.

They were all mistaken. Ireland quickly assumed full independence, was neutral in World War II and was finally proclaimed a republic in 1949, all without any further impediment from Britain. And the Protestant majority in the North held firm to the Union. With their semi-autonomous parliament in Stormont, they ruled the Catholic minority with a heavy hand. That minority was deprived, by gerrymandering and blatant fraud, of many of its economic, social, and political rights. The ironic consequence of Irish independence was a sharp deterioration in the status of the Northern Catholics.

Partition, which was a mere line on the map in 1920, has developed into a real border as the two parts of Ireland have gone their separate ways. The South wished to establish its independence from Britain, but this also meant differentiating itself from Northern Ireland. Today, divorce, contraception and abortion are all legal in the North, illegal in the South. The British welfare state and education subsidies are far more generous than those in Ireland, and apply to Northern Ireland. The standard of living there is consequently much higher than in the Republic, and there is very little trade across the border.

The question of partition subsided into the background of Irish concerns. The Northern Protestants, of course, thought the matter settled once and for all. The Northern Nationalists, brooding on the wrongs being done to them, did not forget. In a speech after World War I, recalling the pre-war debates on the line the border should take, Winston Churchill remarked on the tenacity of Irish quarrels: 'As the deluge subsides and waters recede, we see the dreary steeples of Fermanagh and Tyrone emerging once again. The integrity of their quarrel is one of the few institutions that has been unaltered in the cataclysm that has swept the world.' Seventy-five years later, the dispute continues.

AFTER PARTITION

In the late 1920s, de Valéra and his followers abandoned violent opposition to the state and accepted the monarchical British constitution and democratic politics. In effect, this meant accepting partition. Their political party, Fianna

Fáil ('Warriors of Ireland'), came to be the largest in the Free State, and forms the present government of the Republic. The original pro-treaty party, Fine Gael ('The Irish Race'), is now in opposition. Ironically, it was a Fine Gael government that finally proclaimed the Republic in 1948, during one of de Valéra's brief periods in opposition. A dissident splinter faction of the IRA continued a small-scale terrorist campaign against the government in Dublin and against partition. De Valéra, when he became prime minister, interned them. There were bombings in England and Northern Ireland in 1938 and a further outbreak of violence in 1956, both short-lived.

In 1968, following the example of the civil rights movement in the United States, Catholics in Northern Ireland began agitating for their political and social rights. For instance, the city of Londonderry (known to Catholics as Derry) had a Catholic majority, but the city council was gerrymandered to keep the Protestants permanently in power. The civil rights movement met with a great deal of success, and was supported by all Northern Catholics and by the British government, then led by Harold Wilson (Labour).

THE TROUBLES

Many talk about a solution to Ulster's politial problem but few are prepared to say what the problem is. The reason is simple. The problem is that there is no solution.

British political scientist, Professor Richard Rose

In July 1969, a peaceful civil rights demonstration in Londonderry was broken up with great violence by Protestant paramilitary police (the 'B Specials'). Protestants attacked Catholics throughout the province, and the local militia and police stood by, or actively helped.

The British government intervened, sending the army to keep order in August 1969. This was welcomed by Catholics because it protected them from Protestant violence. After a period of indecision, the government set about correcting the civil rights abuses of Northern Ireland, but they encountered intractible opposition from Stormont. Therefore the government, then led by Edward Heath (Conservative), dissolved the Northern Ireland parliament and government in 1972, and the province has been directly ruled from London ever since, except for a brief interval when the institution of a Northern Ireland Assembly was attempted (unsuccessfully) in 1974.

The rump of the old IRA was stirred into action by the events of 1969. Recruiting new members proved easy: memories of 50 years of discrimination were enough. As the cycle of terrorism and repression got under way, the IRA expanded rapidly. The world-wide economic recession of the 1970s severely affected Northern Ireland, where the major industries – shipbuilding and textiles – collapsed. Unemployment was (and remains) very high throughout the province, and disproportionately severe among Catholics, providing a ready pool of recruits.

In the aftermath of the Londonderry disturbance in August 1969, Catholics set up 'No Go' areas in the Catholic districts of that city (the Bogside) and of Belfast (around the Falls Road), building barricades and preventing the police and army from entering. The IRA developed rapidly behind those barricades.

379

Bloody Sunday

The moment the very name of Ireland is mentioned, the English seem to bid adieu to common feeling, common prudence and to common sense, and to act with the barbarity of tyrants and the fatuity of idiots.

Sydney Smith

Terrorists began shooting British soldiers and Irish policemen, and setting off bombs in Protestant villages and in Belfast. The security situation deteriorated rapidly: 15 people were killed in 1969, 25 in 1970, 173 in 1971.

The British government flooded the province with troops, among whom the paratroopers and Scottish regiments made a particular name for themselves. In August 1971, the army entered the 'No Go' areas and dismantled the barricades. On 9 August, the government introduced a policy of interning IRA suspects without trial. Hundreds of people were arrested in massive military operations in the Falls Road area of Belfast and in the Bogside in Londonderry. The British behaved like an army of occupation in what was supposed to be a British province, and achieved the complete alienation of the Catholic population. The cycle reached its final paroxysm when paratroopers opened fire on rioting Catholics in Londonderry, killing 13, on what came to be known as 'Bloody Sunday', 30 January 1972. Two weeks later, rioters in Dublin burned the British embassy, a splendid 18th-century building, while the police watched. Even in a century filled with meaningless political gestures, the notion that the Irish might intimidate the British, or be revenged upon them, by burning down one of their own architectural monuments was particularly bizarre.

The one attempt at an agreement between the British government and the IRA occurred during this period. In 1972, they arranged a ceasefire and secret talks, which got nowhere.

Britain increased the number of troops in the province, disbanded the 'B Specials' and set about dismantling the gerrymandered political system. Londonderry City Council now has a Catholic majority, and has officially changed the city's name to Derry. In 1973, Prime Minister Edward Heath convened a conference at Sunningdale in England, which proposed a system of power-sharing between Protestants and Catholics in Northern Ireland. An Assembly was elected and a power-sharing executive was set up in 1974: the Protestants staged a general strike in protest, and the assembly and executive collapsed together.

The Terrorist Campaign

The atrocities continued. The worst year was 1972, with 474 deaths in Northern Ireland. Of these, 255 were killed by the IRA, 103 by Protestant terrorists, 74 by the security forces and 42 were unclassified (meaning that, for he most part, they were probably caused by the IRA). In the same year, the terrorist campaign crossed the Irish Sea to England, when bombs in two pubs in Birmingham killed 19 and wounded 180. Protestant terrorists were equally busy: in December 1971, a bomb in a Catholic pub in Londonderry killed 15, and in May 1974, a car bomb killed 22 people in Dublin.

In 1978, a bomb in the Le Mon café in Belfast, killed 12 people and injured 23. In 1979, Lord Louis Mountbatten, aged 78, a distinguished statesman and a relative of the Queen, was murdered in Ireland, with three other people – a woman older than he and two young boys. On the same day, a bomb under a road at Warrenpoint near the border blew up an army truck, killing 18 soldiers. A bomb also severely damaged the 11th-century Westminster Hall, one of the most important public buildings in London.

In 1981, a group of IRA prisoners went on hunger strike to demand 'political status'. Ten of them died, including Bobby Sands who had been elected a Member of Parliament while in prison. There were more bomb attacks in London that year: one bomb was concealed in a bandstand in Regent's Park; another exploded in Chelsea as a bus carrying soldiers went by; a third exploded near a parade of the Queen's Horse Guards in Hyde Park.

At Christmas 1983, a bomb went off in the street near Harrods department store in London, killing five and injuring more than 80; one of the dead and many of the injured were American tourists. In 1984, a bomb in the Grand Hotel, Brighton, just missed killing or injuring Prime Minister Margaret Thatcher, who was attending the Conservative party conference. Another powerful bomb was found shortly afterwards, concealed in a tourist hotel in London. Altogether, about 100 people have been killed by terrorist acts in Great Britain, and about 60 in the Irish Republic, including the British ambassador. The British ambassador to the Netherlands was also murdered, as were three RAF men in 1988, and several other atrocities were prevented by security forces.

The bombings in Birmingham and London, the Mountbatten murder and the Brighton bombing were the most spectacular events and aroused the most anger, but the IRA's campaign has been mostly concentrated in Northern Ireland itself. There have been many assassinations of judges, policemen, soldiers, and public officials. On many occasions, IRA gunmen shot their victims in the presence of their families, once on the steps of St Patrick's Cathedral in Armagh. A soldier on leave was murdered in his parents' house in Derry, and on one occasion the congregation of a Protestant church was machine-gunned during Sunday service. There were also many attacks on police and army barracks, and South Armagh, which was originally mostly Catholic, and from which virtually all Protestants have been driven, became a favourite battleground between the IRA and the police.

These acts of terrorism provoked Protestant reprisals, and a great deal of the British police effort has been devoted to preventing Protestant and Catholic paramilitary forces from slaughtering each other. Protestant terrorist organizations – the Ulster Volunteer Force and the Ulster Defence Association – have murdered a number of prominent Nationalists; and they attempted to assassinate Bernadette Devlin (now McAliskey) and her husband: she had been a leader of the 1969 civil rights movement and later a Member of Parliament. The Protestant terrorists have murdered hundreds of Catholics, mostly at random, and have also assassinated a number of IRA suspects; they have used car bombs and have bombed pubs and public buildings as indiscriminately, though not so frequently, as the IRA. People have been driven from their homes, and as a result, there is now an almost complete residential segregation between Catholics and Protestants in Northern Ireland.

The IRA has grown increasingly sophisticated in its use of weapons. The Brighton bomb, for instance, was concealed in the hotel for a month before the Tory party conference. Some IRA experts learned their trade in the British army;

others were trained in Libya. Protestant terrorists have usually been former soldiers.

THE NEW IRA

The IRA has changed considerably since 1969. Its old guard has been progressively eliminated, and replaced by much younger and tougher men. The first of the new generation was a group of Marxists who were more interested in international Communism than in fighting the British. The movement split, and a dissident group, which proved to be the large majority, broke away and formed the Provisional IRA, known universally as the Provos, devoted to driving the British out of Northern Ireland by violence.

The IRA's political wing, Sinn Fein, also split, into an Official Sinn Fein and a Provisional Sinn Fein. The officials, both political and military, quickly lost most of their supporters, though there were occasional, violent quarrels with the Provos, leading to frequent killings and mutilations on both sides. Apart from killing people, the favourite penalty in Northern Ireland, for all terrorist groups, is 'kneecapping': the victim's kneecap is either shot away or destroyed with an electric drill. Belfast hospitals now lead the world in reconstruction operations on knee-joints. The IRA also favours shaving the heads of and tarring and feathering women who fraternize with the 'enemy'.

Another dissident IRA faction – the Irish National Liberation Army (INLA) – followed a policy of extreme violence and Marxist dogma. It was responsible for some of the most spectacular murders, including the car bomb that killed the British Member of Parliament Airey Neave at the House of Commons in 1979. However, the INLA was severely weakened by police actions and attacks by the Provos in 1986–7.

THE PROVOS' PROGRAMME

The IRA's original objective was to wear down Britain's support for the Protestants in Northern Ireland. They believed that if British troops were withdrawn, the Protestants would accept the situation and agree to the reunification of Ireland. This remains the faith of the IRA's rank and file. However, almost 20 years of terrorism have reinforced Protestant determination to have nothing to do with the Republic, and there can be no doubt at all that a British withdrawal would be followed by a civil war – which the Protestants would win. They are twice as numerous as the Catholics and would control the police and militia (the IRA devotes itself to killing all Catholic members of those organizations). If the IRA won its heart's desire – the abrupt withdrawal of the British – there would follow the setting up of a Protestant Republic of Northern Ireland and, most probably, the expulsion of several hundred thousand people from their homes in Belfast, Derry and the border areas; in the end, there might be no Catholics at all in Northern Ireland. This is the Dublin government's worst nightmare. The IRA, driven south, would, of course, turn its rage upon the Irish Republic.

The Provos' leaders for the past ten years or so have swung around to a Marxist revolutionary policy, like that of the despised Official IRA. They now advocate a united socialist Irish Republic, and look to Lenin and Khadafy as much as to the IRA's old heroes, Patrick Pearse and de Valéra. However, their idea of establishing a Communist Ireland is even further from reality than winning a civil war with the Protestants, or persuading the Protestants peacefully to accept government from Dublin.

IRA men of all persuasions heartily despise the government of the Republic, which they consider an illegitimate, quisling regime because it accepts partition. The Irish in the Republic reciprocate these feelings: they detest IRA terrorism, and although they pay lip service to the ideal of reunification, they will do nothing to bring it about. The Provisional Sinn Fein won less than 3 per cent of the vote in the 1987 Irish elections.

The party does better in the North. It elected one of the 17 Northern Ireland MPs in the 1987 British elections, but it was easily outpolled among Catholics by the Social-Democrat Labour party (SDLP), which managed to win about 25 per cent of the vote in Northern Ireland. Sinn Fein's one MP, who refuses to take his seat in Westminster, is Gerry Adams, believed to be a former Provo chief of staff.

The IRA is thought to have about 200–300 active gunmen (and women) at any given moment. Since its largest operations involve no more than a dozen people, this is quite enough. It could certainly recruit far more if it wished, but the IRA is not a guerrilla army. It is a terrorist organization, and size is irrelevant, and large numbers can be dangerous.

THE TERRORISTS' BANKROLL

The Provos draw their financial support from levies on the Nationalist population of Northern Ireland, from robberies on both sides of the border (post offices are particularly vulnerable), from smuggling and from contributions from abroad. The Provos' total income from these sources is thought to be about £5 million (about $9 million), of which $2–4 million comes from the United States, although American contributions have tended to decline as the conflict has dragged on. IRA members and their families mostly draw unemployment pay from the British government.

Armed robberies in the Republic increased from 11 in 1970 to 306 in 1981, but have diminished with improved security since then. The most profitable of the IRA's sources of income is probably smuggling. The vagueries of Irish and British and European Community agricultural policy, the differences in taxes (the Republic's taxes are far higher than Britain's), differences in the values of the British and Irish currencies – all these factors offer smugglers a golden opportunity. In some places, the Irish border passes through villages (in one notorious case it passes through the house of a well-known Republican), so smuggling is easy. The proposal to eliminate all barriers between members of the European Community by 1992 will end this source of revenue.

The Irish government calculated in 1983 that the total cost of the first 14 years of the Troubles amounted to £11,064,000,000 ($17.6 billion), and continued at a rate of £1,322,000,000 a year; the total up to the end of 1988, therefore would be £18,996,000,000 ($34,922,000,000) at 1982 values. In 1988–9, the direct British subsidy to Northern Ireland – excluding the costs of the army, but including police and prisons – came to about £2000 million ($3.6 billion). The obvious financial cost was chiefly borne by the British and Irish governments, but the losses to the economy, particularly the tourist industry, have fallen on the people of Northern

Ireland, who have also to bear most of the psychological cost of the over 50,000 separate incidents of murder, bombing or arson since 1969.

THE AMERICAN CONNECTION

> More Irish than the Irish, more Catholic than the Pope.
> Old Proverb

The Irish Northern Aid Committee (Noraid) raises funds for the IRA from Irish-Americans by direct solicitations, fund-raising drives in Irish newspapers in the US and collections in bars and at Irish fairs. There is much dispute over how much of the funds reach Northern Ireland, and this source of funding has diminished since the Anglo-Irish treaty was signed in 1985.

American administrations since the Troubles began have steadfastly supported British policy. There was, to begin with, considerable ignorance of the situation there (Senator Edward Kennedy at first called Northern Ireland 'Britain's Vietnam'), but as the IRA campaign developed and large numbers of people were killed, support for the IRA shrank. In particular, four of the most prominent Irish-Americans – Senators Kennedy of Massachusetts and Daniel Patrick Moynihan of New York, Thomas P. ('Tip') O'Neill, speaker of the House of Representatives until 1986 and Hugh Carey, governor of New York until 1982 – took to issuing statements every St Patrick's Day condemning terrorism. The most prominent Irish-American, President Reagan, steadfastly supported the British, and after the 1985 Anglo-Irish treaty, Congress voted an aid package for Northern Ireland.

There are vigorous pro-IRA lobbies in Washington who try to change American policy, by enforcing an American boycott of Northern Ireland, and American supporters of the IRA have always exerted an influence far beyond their numbers (most Irish-Americans detest terrorism as much as the Irish do). The IRA counts on the moral support of its front organizations such as Noraid, and from pro-IRA demonstrations in New York, Boston and other centres of Irish-American influence. As well as a hard core of Irish-Americans, it is also supported by a few non-Irish-American politicians, including Mario Biaggi, who was for many years a congressman from the Bronx until he was jailed for corruption in 1988. Another conspicuously non-Irish supporter is the comptroller of the City of New York, Harrison Goldin.

Irish-Americans are also an important source of weapons. Guns may be bought so easily and cheaply in the United States that the only real difficulty is smuggling them into Ireland. Several boatloads have been intercepted, the most recent in Boston harbour in 1986, and guns have been found in many unlikely places, including the kitchens of the luxury liner, the *Queen Elizabeth II*. Another source of weapons and money has been Libya. A boatload of Libyan weapons was intercepted off the west coast of Ireland in 1974, and a large cache of Libyan weapons was discovered in the Republic in 1986. In 1988, the French navy intercepted a Panamanian ship, the *Eksund*, carrying 150 tons of Libyan arms to the IRA. The cargo included surface-to-air missiles, Kalashnikovs and large quantities of explosives.

ATTEMPTS AT A POLITICAL SOLUTION

The Irish are a fair people; they never speak well of one another.
Samuel Johnson

The British government, led by Margaret Thatcher, and the Irish government, led by Garrett FitzGerald of Fine Gael, signed an Anglo-Irish treaty on 15 November 1985, which institutionalized power-sharing between Catholics and Protestants in Northern Ireland, and gave the Irish Republic a direct role in Northern Ireland affairs. Joint Anglo-Irish committees would meet regularly to discuss policy and reach agreed conclusions, the topics ranging from security matters to anti-discrimination policy in Northern Ireland. The object of the agreement was for the authorities in the province to get to the root of Catholic alienation by dealing with all the specific issues of discrimination in politics, society and the economy. The agreement was welcomed by the Nationalists and by the Republic. Fianna Fáil's leader, Charles Haughey (now Irish prime minister), initially rejected the treaty but changed his tune when it proved exceedingly popular.

British security policy, notably the Stalker affair and the Gibraltar killings (*see below*), have put a great strain on the treaty mechanism. The tepid hope felt when the treaty was signed has now largely dissipated, but the British, the Irish and the Nationalist parties – that is, everyone except the IRA and the Unionists – continue to cling to the treaty because it is the only thing they have. The IRA reject the treaty because it does not meet their basic demand for reunification.

The IRA may lose support among the northern Nationalists, especially if the economy recovers and unemployment drops, but it needs very few members to continue its terrorist campaign.

BRITISH POLICY

The Anglo-Irish treaty was the first attempt by a British government to find a solution to its Irish predicament since 1973. The British would like nothing better than for Irish Protestants and Catholics to live in harmony together in a united Republic, but they recognize that there is no hope of that, because of Protestant intransigence. For 40 years, British law has ensured that no change in the status of Northern Ireland can be made without the consent of a majority of its population, and that commitment holds good, as it must, because it is no more than a recognition of Protestant strength.

Failing a change of heart by the Protestant majority, the British hope that the provisions of the treaty will gradually reconcile the Catholic minority to remaining in the UK by meeting all their legitimate grievances, particularly over discrimination in employment, and police practices. They have abandoned the illusion that they can ever defeat the IRA. The best they can hope for is that the Provos will progressively lose support, and that eventually war-weariness will lead to a *de facto* ceasefire. There are no signs of any such development.

In 1988, the British government strengthened the provisions of anti-discrimination legislation. Previous laws and the Fair Employment Agency were very impressive and democratic on paper, but not very successful in practice, and there continued to be considerable discrimination. This was partly due to the very high level of unemployment: factories with a workforce comprising 90 per cent or more Protestants have not hired any new workers for a decade and therefore remain Protestant strongholds. The new rules strengthen the agency, renamed the Fair Employment Commission, partially in an attempt to comply with the 'McBride principles', enunciated by another of the IRA front organizations in the United States and adopted by a number of American politicians. They lay down stringent rules for non-discrimination in Northern Ireland as preconditions for American investment, and have been made binding on a number of state pension investment funds.

The British legislation introduces for the first time the concept of 'affirmative action': companies that have in the past discriminated against a particular group (in practice, this means Catholics) can now be obliged to hire members of that group in preference to others. The rules will be enforced by a Fair Employment Tribunal and there will be heavy penalties for disobedience.

THE LATEST DISASTERS

As in many anti-terrorist campaigns, the British army and police are faced with a dilemma: in order to combat terrorism effectively and 'restore law and order', they have resorted to measures that frustrate the government's essential long-term strategy – winning the 'hearts and minds' of the Catholics. The British army is not the SS and the police are not the Gestapo, but their tactics have been frequently brutal, particularly in the early days. Amnesty International and the European Court of Justice documented widespread use of torture, and some British policies, notably internment and allowing Bobby Sands and his comrades to starve themselves to death, were amazingly stupid and counterproductive. As a result, though Catholics may detest terrorism and murder, they also detest the police and army and, by extension, the British.

Northern Ireland is one of those places where, however bad the situation, it can always get worse. On 8 May 1987, acting on a tip, police ambushed an IRA squad as it attacked a police station at Loughgall, south-west of Belfast; eight IRA men were killed, including three senior commanders. On Remembrance Sunday, 8 November 1987 in Enniskillen, Co. Fermanagh, in the west of the province, the town had gathered at the local war memorial to mark the anniversary of the Armistice and honour the dead of World Wars I and II. These ceremonies always conclude with a minute's silence at 11 a.m., the hour of the Armistice in 1918; a terrorist bomb that had been concealed in a community centre next to the memorial went off at 10.45, killing 11 people and wounding 55. The IRA later said that the bomb had been aimed at the military honour guard, but there was no honour guard. All the killed and injured were civilians, including many children. It was the largest civilian death toll since a bomb in a pub had killed 17 people in 1982. The IRA apologized for the deaths, grudgingly. The Enniskillen murders were greeted with universal revulsion. They also helped persuade the Irish Dáil to pass an extradition treaty with Britain.

1988 was a bad year. In February, a British soldier shot an IRA man at the border as the latter was walking to a Gaelic football match. The army insisted that the incident was an accident. Then, on 6 March 1988, three unarmed IRA terrorists, two men and a woman, were shot dead by British security men in Gibraltar. It was the most flagrant recent example of extralegal execution in Britain's war with the IRA.

The three terrorists had been plotting a repeat of the Enniskillen massacre: they had loaded a car with explosives and planned to park it next to a parade ground on Gibraltar where the band of the Royal Anglian Regiment was due to perform two days later. When they were shot, they had just reserved a parking space using an entirely innocent car. The car containing the bomb, which had been left over the border in Spain, would have replaced it at a suitable moment an hour or two before the parade.

It turned out that the three had been followed for days by members of the British and Spanish secret services. There had never been any danger that their bomb would explode, although the security forces later insisted that they had believed that the terrorists had already left one on Gibraltar. The three had been leaving Gibraltar, on foot, when a police car drove up. Several men jumped out of the car and shot them dead. The gunmen turned out to be members of the Special Air Services (SAS).

An official version of events was promptly offered. The three terrorists had made 'suspicious hand movements', which led the SAS men to believe that they were about to pull out guns or push a detonator button. Eye witnesses were soon discovered, who disputed this version of events. At least one of the dead men, who had been shot in the back, had been finished off on the ground. A witness said: 'The man on the ground was lying on his back. The man standing over this man had his foot on the man's chest. I then saw the gunman point his gun deliberately at the man that was lying on the floor and fire two or three times into him at point-blank range.' Anyone who cast doubt upon the official version of events was accused of prejudicing the inquest which was to take place in Gibraltar – an inquest that was postponed for months. The British foreign secretary and prime minister, not to mention lesser officials, repeatedly insisted upon the sanctity of the inquest. They tried to prevent British television from broadcasting a report on the killings, including interviews with eyewitnesses. When Amnesty International issued a statement questioning the official version, Mrs Thatcher told the House of Commons, 'I hope Amnesty has some concern for the more than 2000 people murdered by the IRA since 1969.'

The bodies of the three terrorists were shipped back to Belfast. At their funeral on 16 March, a Protestant terrorist shot at and threw hand grenades into the crowd, killing three people and wounding more than 50. He was grabbed by mourners when he ran out of ammunition and grenades, and turned over to the police. Three days later, at the funeral of the victims of the cemetery shootings, two off-duty British soldiers, in civilian clothing, drove by mistake into the funeral procession. They were dragged out of their car, and lynched. Both incidents were televised, and the film of the lynching was later used to identify and arrest some of the lynch mob.

By then, relations between the British and Irish were worse than they had been for years. They had not been helped by the outcome of what came to be known as the 'Stalker affair'. A British policeman from Manchester, John Stalker, had been sent to Northern Ireland in 1984 to investigate three incidents that had occurred in 1982, in which Ulster police had shot six men, killing five of them. Most of the dead had been IRA terrorists, and the allegation was that they had been victims of 'extralegal executions'. Stalker was a good cop and carried out his investigations thoroughly. However, just before they were concluded, he was pulled off the case. On 25 January 1988, the British attorney-general told the House of Commons that, although there was sufficient evidence to prosecute members of the Ulster police for perverting justice, he had decided not to do so. It is not often that public officials admit that they are engaged in a cover-up and intend to continue it. Stalker eventually published his own conclusions. He had found no evidence of a 'shoot to kill' policy, but in the early 1980s, there had been an inclination among the security forces to shoot suspects without warning rather than arrest them.

There had been a long agitation against the convictions of several people for the 1974 Birmingham pub bombings. In March 1988, an appeals court upheld the convictions, which had been obtained largely on the strength of their confessions. It seemed to many Irish people that Britain had lost all respect for the rule of law.

This was not the case. The Gibraltar inquest had been merely postponed, not suppressed: it was held in September 1988. The jury concluded that the killings had been justified because the soldiers 'had reason to believe' that their own lives or the lives of others were endangered. The jury accepted the claim that the SAS men had believed that the three terrorists had been armed and that they had left a bomb in Gibraltar. Furthermore, they had feared that the bomb was equipped with a radio-controlled detonator, and the three terrorists might have been about to set it off. The SAS men, who testified behind screens to protect their identities, said that the terrorists ignored shouted warnings to stop, and seemed to be reaching for guns, or a detonator.

The IRA continued its work. On 29 February 1988, two terrorists blew themselves up while assembling a bomb. On 2 May, three RAF men were killed by car bombs in the Netherlands. On 16 May, Protestant terrorists shot up a Catholic bar, killing three people. On 15 June, six British soldiers were killed by a bomb that had been placed in their car at a school sports day in Lisburn, south of Belfast. On 1 August, the IRA planted a bomb in an army postal depot in London, killing one soldier. On 20 August, eight soldiers riding in a bus from Belfast airport to their barracks were killed by a bomb; it was evident that the IRA had been tipped off about when the bus would leave and what route it would take. Ten days later, three IRA gunmen were shot by the security forces: the IRA conceded that they had been 'on a mission', but the British would reveal none of the details of the incident. On 31 August, two civilians were killed in Derry when they set off a bomb meant for the police; the IRA expressed its regret for an operation 'that had gone tragically wrong'.

With the Gibraltar inquest safely out of the way, the British government moved on to other highly controversial matters. In October, it banned all radio or television appearances by members of the IRA, of Sinn Fein and of certain Protestant terrorist organizations, and ended the ancient right of accused persons in Northern Ireland to remain silent, without prejudice, at their trials. On 29 November, the European Court at Strasburg ruled that the provisions of the Prevention of Terrorism Act which permitted the authorities to hold suspects for up to seven days without charge were violations of the European Convention on Human Rights. A few weeks later, the British government decided that it would not be bound by the ruling. The Act would remain in its present form.

The justification for the ban on broadcasting interviews with members of the IRA and 'Loyalist' terrorist groups and their front organizations was that depriving them of publicity was to deny them oxygen. As for the right to remain silent, the government ruled that, in future, courts would be permitted to 'attach whatever weight they think proper to the fact that a suspect remains silent when questioned'. It announced that the new rule would be extended to Great Britain in due course. To many people, both these measures seemed to be serious restrictions on civil liberties. They are both matters covered by the Bill of Rights in the US Constitution: freedom of speech is absolutely guaranteed under the First Amendment, and the right to remain silent is guaranteed under the Fifth Amendment.

The decision to ignore the ruling of the European Court was an embarrassment to the government: Britain had been one of the original signatories of the European Convention on Human Rights. It had now to argue that the seriousness of the terrorist threat in Northern Ireland made it necessary to repudiate some of that. The decision may have been helped by a dispute that developed in November and December between Britain and Belgium and Ireland. The Belgian police, acting at Britain's request, arrested an Irish former priest, Patrick Ryan, whom the British accused of being an IRA terrorist, alleging that he had delivered explosives to the IRA commandos who murdered a number of British servicemen in Europe. The Belgian courts refused to extradite him to Britain – claiming that the extradition request was improperly drafted – and shipped him off to Dublin before the improprieties could be corrected. The Irish attorney general refused to permit his extradition to Britain on the grounds that the British government and newspapers had made so many prejudicial statements against him that he would never get a fair trial.

At the same time, the British government lengthened sentences for terrorist acts by reducing the periods of remission to which convicts were entitled, from one-half of their sentences to one-third. It also proposed to amend the electoral law to require all candidates in local district council elections to sign declarations that they would not support terrorism or proscribed organizations if elected. It did not seem very probable that any of this would reduce the level of terrorism.

The prospects for a ceasefire, let alone a reconciliation between the two communities, were more remote than ever, and so was any prospect that either side might 'win' the war.

> *To hell with the future, and long live the past,*
> *May God in his mercy look down on Belfast.*
> Modern proverb

NOTABLE INCIDENTS

1969

July	Civil rights march in Londonderry broken up by B Specials.
August	First British troops sent to Northern Ireland.

1970

June	Army imposes 24-hour curfew on Falls Road area, Belfast, conducts house-to-house search for terrorists; 5 people killed.
9 August	Internment without trial introduced.

1971

4 December	Protestant terrorists kill 15 Catholics with a bomb in a Londonderry bar.

1972

30 January	British paratroopers kill 13 Catholic demonstrators in Londonderry, on 'Bloody Sunday'.
22 February	IRA bomb in a bar in Aldershot, England, kills 7 British soldiers.
March	Stormont Parliament dissolved. Britain imposes direct rule on Northern Ireland.

1973

11 November	Power-sharing executive set up by Unionist, SDLP and Alliance parties.
6–9 December	Conference at Sunningdale in England between British and Irish governments and the 3 parties. Agree to a 'Council of Ireland'.

1974

May	Strike by Protestant Ulster Workers' Council forces abandonment of executive and Sunningdale proposals.
17 May	Car bombs in Dublin, planted by Protestant terrorists, kill 22 people.
21 November	IRA bombs in two pubs in Birmingham kill 21.

1976

4 January	5 Catholics murdered in Co. Armagh.
5 January	10 Protestant workers killed on a bus, in reprisal.
21 July	British ambassador to Dublin killed by a bomb.

1978

17 February	IRA bombs at the Le Mon café, Belfast kill 12.

1979

22 March	British ambassador to the Netherlands killed.
30 March	Airey Neave, MP, killed by car bomb at the House of Commons.
27 August	Bomb kills 18 British soldiers at Warrenpoint, Northern Ireland. Lord Louis Mountbatten and 3 others killed by bomb on his boat at Sligo, Ireland.

1980

October	First IRA prisoners' hunger strike. Called off 18 December.

1981

1 March	Bobby Sands begins hunger strike; he dies 5 April. (9 other IRA prisoners eventually starve themselves to death.)

1982

22 July	11 British soldiers killed in two bombings in London, one under a bandstand in Regent's Park.
6 December	Irish National Liberation Army bombs disco in Ballykelly, killing 11 soldiers and 6 civilians.

1983

17 December	Car bomb outside Harrods department store in London kills 5 people, wounds more than 80.

1984

12 October	IRA bomb in the Grand Hotel, Brighton, during the annual Tory party conference, kills 4, narrowly missing Margaret Thatcher.

1985

28 February	IRA mortar attack on police barracks at Newry kills 9 policemen in a cafeteria.
15 November	Margaret Thatcher and Garrett FitzGerald sign Anglo-Irish treaty.

1987

March	Gunfights between rival Republican terrorists kill 12.
25 April	Ulster Chief Justice Maurice Gibson and his wife assassinated by a bomb.
8 May	3 senior IRA men and 5 other terrorists killed in an ambush at Loughgall.
8 November	11 civilians killed during an Armistice day service at Enniskillen.

1988

6 March	3 IRA terrorists shot by British SAS men in Gibraltar.
16 March	3 people killed by a Protestant terrorist during the Gibraltar terrorists' funeral.
19 March	2 British soldiers lynched during the funeral of the victims of the 16 March shooting.
2 May	3 RAF men killed by bombs in Holland.
15 June	6 British soldiers killed by car bomb at sports event.
1 August	1 soldier killed by bomb in army barracks in London.
20 August	8 soldiers travelling from Belfast airport killed by bomb.
30 August	3 IRA gunmen killed by security forces.
31 August	2 IRA suspects arrested crossing West German border from Holland, carrying explosives.
31 August	Elderly Catholic couple killed by IRA booby-trap in Londonderry.
12 September	Bombs demolish home of head of Northern Ireland civil service. Car bomb in Belfast injures 12.
24 November	67-year-old Catholic and his 11-year-old grand-daughter killed by IRA bomb; 8 other civilians wounded. As after 31 August incident, and Enniskillen bombing, the IRA apologises.

FURTHER READING

Amnesty International, *Report of the Amnesty International Mission to Northern Ireland,* London, 1978.

New Ireland Forum, *The Economic Consequences of the Division of Ireland since 1920, The Cost of Violence arising from the Northern Ireland Crisis since 1969* and *Reports of Proceedings, 1983, and conclusions,* Stationery Office, Dublin, 1984.

O'Malley, Padraig, *The Uncivil Wars* (includes a comprehensive bibliography), Houghton Mifflin Co., Boston, 1983.

Rose, Richard, *Northern Ireland: Time of Choice*, American Enterprise Institute, Washington, 1976.

Stalker, John, *The Stalker Affair*, New York, Viking/London, Harrap, 1988.

Watt, David (ed.), *The Constitution of Northern Ireland*, Heinemann, London, 1981.

SOVIET UNION

Geography 8,599,341 sq. miles (22,272,000 sq. km)
Population 281,700,000

The Union of Soviet Socialist Republics (USSR) is a federation of 15 union republics:

Slavs
1   **Russia.** Size: 6,593,850 sq. miles (17,078,005 sq. km). Population: 145.3 million.
2   **Ukraine.** Size: 231,990 sq. miles (600,852 sq. km). Population: 51.2 million.
3   **Byelorussia (White Russia).** Size: 80,150 sq. miles (207,588 sq. km). Population: 10.1 million.

Baltic states
4   **Estonia.** Size: 17,410 sq. miles (45,092 sq. km). Population: 1.55 million.
5   **Latvia.** Size: 25,590 sq. miles (66,278 sq. km). Population: 2.6 million.
6   **Lithuania.** Size: 25,170 sq. miles (65,190 sq. km). Population: 3.6 million.

Moldavia
7   **Moldavia.** Size: 13,050 sq. miles (33,799 sq. km). Population: 4.19 million.

Transcaucasia
8   **Armenia.** Size: 11,490 sq. miles (29,759 sq. km). Population: 3.4 million.
9   **Azerbaijan.** Size: 33,430 sq. miles (86,853 sq. km). Population: 6.8 million.
10 **Georgia.** Size: 26,900 sq. miles (69,671 sq. km). Population: 5.3 million.

Central Asia
11 **Kazakhstan.** Size: 1,048,030 sq. miles (2,714,387 sq. km). Population: 16.2 million.
12 **Kirghizia.** Size: 76,700 sq. miles (198,652 sq. km). Population: 4.14 million.
13 **Tadzhikistan.** Size: 55,240 sq. miles (143,071 sq. km). Population: 4.8 million.
14 **Turkmenistan.** Size: 188,400 sq. miles (487,954 sq. km). Population: 3.4 million.
15 **Uzbekistan.** Size: 173,546 sq. miles (449,482 sq. km). Population: 19 million.

The Russian republic, by far the largest, is itself divided into 16 autonomous republics (the equivalent of American states), 5 autonomous regions (ethnic regions) and 10 autonomous areas (smaller areas inhabited by specific nationalities).

The Soviet Union faces a host of problems. The Communist model has ceased to work: the economy has scarcely expanded for the past decade, and has no possibility of doing so as it is now organized. The first signs of restiveness among the approximately 100 nationalities within the union coincided with the rapid development of *glasnost*, Gorbachev's policy of openness (*see below*). Gorbachev is now in full retreat from the 'forward' policy followed during the Brezhnev era. He has abandoned Afghanistan to its fate, and may do the same to Angola, Nicaragua and Ethiopia. The USSR is also faced with the consequences of its 45 years of oppression in Eastern Europe: it may soon have to confront again the question of sending in tanks to shore up a collapsing regime in Warsaw, Prague or Budapest.

The silent mass of Soviet citizens have begun to stir from their apathy. In 1989, unrest spread from Moscow to every corner of the country, particularly during the elections to parliament in the spring, when scores of party officials were defeated. Economic conditions have deteriorated steadily under Gorbachev, and he is held accountable. The Party has yet to admit defeat, like the Polish comrades, but its authority and self-confidence are rapidly being eroded. How long can it impose a system it no longer believes in, and how long will the Soviet people submit?

THE NATIONALITIES PROBLEM

We should busy ourselves most thoroughly with the nationalities policy at the present stage. This is a most fundamental, vital question of our society.

Mikhail Gorbachev, 18 February 1988

The Soviet Union is not the only federation of many nationalities. India has a larger population and even greater diversity, and many African countries, starting with Nigeria, have to contend with an equal or greater number of rival tribes. The USSR is different from the others, however, because it is the heir to the Russian empire. The minority nations were all conquered in their turn by the tsars of Muskovy. Russians are still in a majority in the population (about 52 per cent), and whatever the doctrines of Leninist internationalism, all non-Russian Soviet citizens to some extent consider themselves victims of 'Great Russian chauvinism'.

In 1989, of the 23 members of the politburo and secretariat of the Communist party, 19 were Russians, two Ukrainians, one White Russian – and one man, the foreign minister Edward Shevarnadze, a Georgian, was a non-Slav. There was no one from Central Asia – and no Armenians or Azerbaijanis.

Some feel discrimination less than others. The White Russians and the Ukrainians are clearly more equal than the Uzbeks and the Khirgiz; and some, perhaps including the Armenians, look to the Russians to protect them from their more powerful neighbours.

The idea of a great federation of different but equal nations is a noble one. The Western Europeans, sick of fighting each other, are slowly building such a federation for themselves, and the Indians are struggling to preserve theirs. The **393** alternative was horribly demonstrated in the partition of India in 1947, when rivers of blood divided the country, and has been revived in the recent revolt by Sikh extremists. Civil wars in Nigeria, Lebanon, Sudan and Ethiopia show where the mirage of national independence can lead, and the wars of the Europeans have devastated the continent for centuries.

The trouble with the USSR is that the Bolsheviks imposed a community of suffering upon the 100 or so ethnic groups they governed. Communism and Russian imperialism have been equal curses in Central Asia and in the Baltic states. When collectivization was imposed upon the Ukraine in the early 1930s, Stalin was motivated as much by a desire to suppress Ukrainian nationalism as to impose Communism upon agriculture. Russian troops surrounded Ukrainian villages and ordered them to deliver all the grain and meat they had stored – and then left them to starve.

Now that the experiment begun in 1917 is coming to an end, Mikhail Gorbachev is looking for a solution to his problems in loosening the grip that the party has exercised on every level of society. He wants *perestroika* ('restructuring') and *glasnost* ('openness'). The Russians may follow him, but the other nationalities may instead use their new freedoms to demand their independence.

There are three main groups of non-Russian peoples in the Soviet Union: on the Baltic, in the Caucusus and in Central Asia. The first signs of dissent came in Armenia in February 1988, but there were also rumblings of dissatisfaction in the Baltic republics and in Moldavia. Central Asia – by far the largest and, potentially, the most dangerous of these areas – remained quiet.

ARMENIA

In February 1988, without any warning, reports reached Moscow of massive demonstrations in Armenia. Hundreds of thousands of people were demanding that Nagorno-Karabakh, an area of the neighbouring republic, Azerbaijan, be transferred to Armenia. There had been nothing like it since the early days of the Soviet Union, and there could be no doubt that this sudden upsurge of nationalistic fervour was the result of Gorbachavian *glasnost*.

The Caucusus, which lie between the Caspian Sea and the Black Sea, were annexed by tsarist Russia in the 19th century. The territory comprises two Christian nations, Georgia and Armenia, and a much larger Muslim republic, Azerbaijan. The Azerbaijanis are, in fact, Turkish, cousins to the 40 million Turks of Turkey, the 6 or 8 million Azerbaijanis of Iran and the millions more in Soviet Central Asia. It is this wider dimension that enabled the Azerbaijanis to win control of Nagorno-Karabakh in the first place, and to retain it ever since.

Parts of tsarist Armenia (Kars) were reconquered by Turkey in World War I. The fate of the Armenians under Turkish rule (*see* Terrorism: Forlorn hopes, pp. 548–54) and the pressures of the Azerbaijanis naturally led the Armenians (and the Georgians) to look to Moscow for protection. During the confusion following the Russian Revolution, Armenia was set up as an independent state, and there was a brief effort by Turks to establish a pan-Turkic commonwealth stretching from the Bosphoros to Samarkand. In the general settlement in 1923, Turkey kept Kars, and the Azerbaijanis were allowed to annex Nagorno-Karabakh as well as another enclave in south-west Armenia, as part of the Bolsheviks' effort to pacify the non-Russian area they had inherited from the tsar.

394   Meanwhile, national movements in Armenia and Georgia were brutally

suppressed, after Stalin was delegated by Lenin to settle the problem. In subsequent years, until the 1950s, the citizens of these two republics could at least take comfort in the thought that, if the Russians governed Armenia and Georgia, Georgians and an Armenian governed Russia: Stalin and the head of the KGB, Beria, were Georgians, and Mikoyan, who for many years was economics minister of the USSR, and was later president, was an Armenian.

The large majority of the people of Nagorno-Karabakh (126,000 individuals) are Armenians, and the remaining 37,000 are Azerbaijanis. It is an autonomous region of the Azerbaijani republic, and its people were apparently driven to protest by the corruption and inefficiency of the region's authorities, and also because of a certain amount of ethnic persecution.

The first demonstrations were in Stepanakert, the region's capital, on 13 February 1988. Two Azerbaijanis were killed, though that fact was not revealed until later. The demonstrations spread to Yerevan, capital of Armenia, a week later. Soon, there were daily gatherings of hundreds of thousands of people. The authorities were quite unable to control the demonstrators and therefore joined them. On 20 February, the Nagorno-Karabakh regional assembly formally demanded that the region be transferred to Armenia. It was a revolutionary demand. The vote was 110 for seccession from Azerbaijan, 17 against and 13 abstentions, and was made along strictly ethnic lines: the abstentions were presumably the senior Communist officials. The party first secretary in the district was dismissed and replaced by a man who had voted for secession.

Moscow was astonished by these developments. 'I must say frankly that the Soviet Communist party central committee has been disturbed by this turn of events,' said Mikhail Gorbachev. 'It is fraught with serious consequences.' The committee turned down the Nagorno-Karabakh demand immediately, but Gorbachev hastily promised to study the matter, in the hope of calming things. The Armenians then agreed to suspend their protests for a month.

Western reporters were not allowed to visit Armenia, but videotapes brought out of Yerevan showed enormous crowds of people peacefully demonstrating in front of the city opera house. The organizers of the demonstration policed the event, and elected a committee to represent them to the authorities. The demonstrators listened to speeches, including those by government and party officials: it was notable that the demonstrations were not anti-Soviet nor anti-Russian.

The situation became much more serious on 28 February, when there were anti-Armenian riots in Sumgait, an Azerbaijani town on the Caspian. They were apparently sparked off by the belated report that two Azerbaijanis had been killed in the 13 February demonstration in Nagorno-Karabakh, and by the arrival of over 5000 Azerbaijani refugees from Kafan in Armenia. There was a minority of 15,000–20,000 Armenians in Sumgait, a town with a population of 223,000, and during the riots, they were hunted through the streets, beaten and, some of them, murdered. The Soviet radio described the events as a pogrom, and confirmed that 32 people (26 Armenians and six Azerbaijanis) had been killed and 197 seriously injured. A survivor reported to the Armenian community in Moscow that the mob had stormed a maternity hospital and that one pregnant woman had been killed, her womb ripped open and the baby mutilated. Unofficial reports in Moscow stated that over 300 people had been killed. Whether the reports were true or not was less significant than the fact that Armenians could believe such horrors of the Azerbaijanis.

Troops were used to restore order: another report stated that eight soldiers were killed. This was the first time in over 60 years that the Soviet government admitted officially that troops had been used in suppressing civil disturbances (in fact, there have been many occasions when troops have been so employed). In Sumgait, the Armenians were taken to army barracks and makeshift refugee centres to protect them from the Azerbaijanis, and a night-time curfew was imposed for two weeks. The mayor of Sumgait and other top officials were fired.

On 23 March, the presidium of the Supreme Soviet (federal parliament) in Moscow flatly refused to reconsider the boundaries question. It issued a statement denouncing attempts to change the boundaries through street demonstrations, called on the army to maintain order in the two republics and banned unofficial demonstrations. One reason for this stern attitude was undoubtedly the Azerbaijani reaction to the Armenian demands. The Armenians were not anti-Soviet, but the Azerbaijanis showed clear signs of opposition to Moscow. They are Shiite Muslims, like their cousins in Iran, and the USSR has no wish to see nationalist agitation develop in Baku, the capital of Azerbaijan, which is also one of the country's main industrial centres. As some consolation, Moscow also announced a $664 million crash programme of economic and cultural development for Nagorno-Karabakh.

The government then flooded Yerevan with troops, and a mass demonstration planned for 25 March was cancelled. A general strike in Nagorno-Karabakh lasted a few days longer, and then was quietly ended.

In May, there were further disturbances in both Yerevan and in Baku. In the latter, the disturbances were provoked by reports of a riot in Ararat, a town in Armenia, while the Yerevan demonstrations were provoked by reports of the sentences given at the first trials of the people responsible for the murders in Sumgait. (The murderers received sentences of 3 to 15 years, which the Armenians found too lenient.) On 19 May, 200,000 Armenians demonstrated in Yerevan, and there were also reports of strikes and demonstrations in Nagorno-Karabakh. The central government responded by abruptly sacking the first secretaries in both republics on 21 May.

That deed was accomplished by special emissaries of the politburo in Moscow. Yigor Ligachev, who is second in seniority to Gorbachev in the Soviet government, went to Baku and promised that the status of Nagorno-Karabakh would not be changed. News of this promise promptly sparked further strikes and demonstrations in Armenia, and in the disputed region.

The new party leader in Armenia addressed the demonstrators, and promised that the republic's legislature would consider a resolution calling for the transfer of Nagorno-Karabakh, and that Moscow would consider setting it up as a special autonomous region, independent of both Armenia and Azerbaijan. Nothing more was heard of this possible compromise, for the moment at least: in mid-June, the Armenian legislature formally demanded the return of the district, and the Azerbaijani legislature refused to consider the transfer. According to the Soviet constitution, the boundaries of a Soviet republic may not be changed without its consent.

Another general strike in Nagorno-Karabakh continued, and in June, large numbers of Soviet troops were deployed there to keep the peace. On 27 June, the strike was finally ended, just in time for the special Communist party conference in Moscow on 28 June. That event turned out to be an important episode in the evolution of *glasnost*: delegates denounced members of the government, described the crimes of Stalin, and demanded democracy. The 'nationalities question' was virtually ignored.

The dispute resumed in July: a demonstration of 10,000 people closed the Yerevan airport on 6 July, and one demonstrator was killed and several wounded as 3000 troops broke it up. Then the regional assembly in Nagorno-Karabakh voted simply to secede from Azerbaijan. The presidium of the Soviet parliament met to consider the issue on 18 July, and the debate was televised: Gorbachev was shown denouncing those who stirred up the dispute as enemies of *perestroika*. Armenia's demand for the transfer was turned down unanimously. There were further huge demonstrations in Yerevan, Soviet police started arresting Armenian dissidents, one of whom was expelled from the country.

A precarious peace returned to the Caucusus. It lasted two months. Leaders of the two republics and the disputed region were brought together in Stepanakert, where they agreed to end the dispute, to accept the Supreme Soviet's 18 July ruling, and to work together to improve relations. Their good intentions proved insufficient. On 12 September, new demonstrations broke out in Nagorno-Karabakh and immediately spread to Armenia, where the Armenians were protesting that there had been an influx of Azerbaijanis into the district. The government insisted that this was untrue, and that the signs of activity were in fact the first fruits of the central government's decision to improve the local economy.

This time, the government tried to prevent the further spread of trouble by pouring troops into Yerevan and into Nagorno-Karabakh. They kept an uneasy peace for a month, during which there were once again mass demonstrations throughout Armenia. The real trouble began on 22 November.

On that day, there were riots in several cities in Azerbaijan, including the two largest, Baku and Kirovabad. Troops were called in to restore order, and three soldiers were killed trying to protect the Armenian quarter of Kirovabad. The Armenians resumed demonstrating, and two people were killed in Yerevan on 25 November. The government imposed a curfew on the city, and then a general pogrom developed in both Azerbaijan and Armenia. Tens of thousands of people were driven from their homes in both republics. Before, there had been 475,000 Armenians living in Azerbaijan and smaller numbers of Azerbaijanis living in Armenia. Soon there was a mass movement of populations between the two, and the refugees had to be put in tent cities. Twenty-eight people were killed (by official count) in the last week of November, and by that time, 40,000 Armenians had fled Azerbaijan and 30,000 Azerbaijanis had fled Armenia. By early December, the total of refugees had risen to over 100,000.

The Soviet army had an iron grip on the main cities, where the refugees gathered, but could not protect outlying communities. The crisis was rapidly turning into a disaster when the Armenian earthquake of 7 December devastated Transcaucasia. In that cataclysm, the Armenians forgot their irredentist claims on their neighbours. It was certain, however, that the dispute would revive.

THE BALTIC STATES

Estonia, Latvia and Lithuania, the three small states along the eastern shores of the Baltic, were absorbed into the Russian empire in the 18th century. Like Finland, they became independent after the Russian Revolution, and the fledgling USSR recognized their independence in February 1920. In 1940, however, Stalin annexed them again, under the terms of a secret protocol to the Hitler–Stalin pact of August 1939. The annexation was marked by the wholesale deportation of possibly hundreds of thousands of people to Siberia. (One estimate puts the number deported from Latvia as high as 320,000 out of a population of less than 2 million.) The Western powers have always refused to recognize the annexation.

Unlike Armenia, nationalist agitation in any of the three has a tendency to turn immediately into an anti-Soviet demonstration. In the spring of 1988, as the USSR got ready for Gorbachev's special party conference, independent organizations sprang up in all three republics and demanded a degree of independence from Moscow that stopped just short of secession. They wanted the right to manage their own economies and have their own representatives at the United Nations (as the Ukraine and White Russia already do), and openly discussed the possibility of running candidates in elections. The party leadership in all three had to scramble to catch up.

Another difference with Armenia is that Latvia, Lithuania and Estonia are afraid of being swallowed up by Russia. There is no danger of that in the Caucusus, but there are large Russian minorities in each of the Baltic states. It is the same worry that has inspired Welsh, Breton and Basque nationalism in Western Europe. In Lithuania, the population is 20 per cent Russian. In Latvia, only 54 per cent are Latvian, 33 per cent being Russian and the remainder more likely to identify with the Russians than with the Latvians. In Estonia, 65 per cent of the people are native.

The three states' flags, suppressed in 1940, reappeared, with official toleration, and the governments made strenuous efforts to patch up relations with the churches, particularly in Lithuania, which is strongly Catholic. To begin with, Estonia took the lead. The government allowed the formation of an Estonian Front, the nearest thing to an opposition party anywhere in the Soviet Union since immediately after the Revolution. The Communist party secretary was dismissed on 16 June and was replaced by Vaino Valas who had shared a room with Mikhail Gorbachev when they both attended a Komsomol (Young Communist) party school 30 years before. He immediately won the hearts of Estonians by addressing his first central committee meetings in Estonian, instead of in Russian.

All these signs of revived nationalism were permitted by the central government, and public demonstrations in all three Baltic states were peaceful and did not at first involve overt demands for full independence. In each case, people demonstrated on the anniversary of their countries' incorporation into the Soviet Union, in June 1940. In addition, on 24 February 1988, 20,000–30,000 people demonstrated in Tallinn, capital of Estonia, to commemorate its independence day – that is, the day Estonia won its independence from Russia in 1920.

In November, Gorbachev presented a series of constitutional amendments to a meeting of the Supreme Soviet in Moscow. The reforms were much discussed in advance, and the Estonian parliament, in a quite unprecedented gesture, voted unanimously to reject them. The Estonians objected to the provisions that increased the Soviet president's powers and reduced the powers of the country's constituent republics. These objections were over-ruled in Moscow, but afterwards, the Estonians once again proclaimed that they could themselves determine which Soviet legislation they would like to adopt. Then they voted to make Estonian their national language.

The Russian minorities staged strikes in protest and Gorbachev and the Politburo fulminated, but the independence movement continued to gain momentum. On 23 August, 1989, a human chain was formed from Tallinn in Estonia to Vilnius in Lithuania, to mark the 50th anniversary of the Hitler-Stalin Pact.

Estonia, in particular, can never be really independent of the Soviet Union: it is only 80 miles (130 kms) from Leningrad and its economic future is clearly linked to that of the metropolis. Gorbachev hoped that the three republics would take the lead in economic reform, that they would succeed and thus demonstrate the advantages of *perestroika*. Unfortunately for him, the citizens of the three countries, though delighted at the opportunity to recover their economic independence, used the occasion to put their political demands first. The hotheads demanded independence, whatever the consequences, while the Russian-speaking minority, and the conservatives in Moscow, demanded that the independence movement be suppressed. The confrontation was pushing ineluctably towards a showdown.

MOLDAVIA

In Moldavia (Bessarabia), which is populated by Roumanians, a political movement sprang up in 1988 to demand that Moldavian be declared the official language, and that the Cyrillic script be abandoned in favour of the Latin script. On 22 January 1989, there was a mass demonstration in support of these demands in the capital, Kishinev. As in the Baltic republics, party leaders scrambled to join the nationalists. Roumanian was declared the republic's official language, and the Latin alphabet was restored. The Russian-speaking minority went on strike in protest.

No one wanted an immediate reunification with Ceauşescu's Roumania, but it is obvious that the demand will be made when that tyranny is overthrown. In the meantime, Moldavians are asserting themselves as boldly as the Balts.

THE UKRAINE

The most dangerous of all nationalisms in the Soviet Union is in the Ukraine. The USSR can survive without Estonia or Moldavia. It cannot survive without the Ukraine. The first stirrings of nationalism, in 1989, a movement called *Rukh* billed as a defence of *perestroika*, were therefore deeply worrying to Moscow. There was some consolation in the fact that the eastern Ukraine is heavily Russified: the dissidents were first heard in the west, in areas annexed from Poland in 1945, where the Ukrainian language has best survived.

Gorbachev may hope that relations between Russians and Ukrainians may evolve as have relations between Castillians and Catalans in Spain, who have a rather similar history. The difference is that whatever Franco's crimes against the Catalans, they were nothing compared to Stalin's famine in the Ukraine, in which five million people died. Why should the Ukrainians ever forgive the Communist Party?

THE CRIMEAN TARTARS AND CENTRAL ASIA

One of Stalin's most monstrous crimes concerned the Crimean Tartars, a large community of Turkic origin, living on the northern shores of the Black Sea and in the Crimea. At the time of the German invasion, some of them collaborated, and as soon as the Germans were driven out, Stalin retaliated by deporting the entire population to Central Asia. It was only in December 1987 that the government at last granted surviving Crim-Tartars the right to return. There have been small demonstrations by Tartars and their supporters in Moscow demanding that Crim-Tartary be restored as a Soviet republic, a demand firmly rejected by the government, which points out that the area is now inhabited by Ukrainians.

The most vociferous anti-government demonstration in Central Asia occurred in December 1986, in Alma-Ata, the capital of Kazakhstan. People were protesting against Gorbachev's decision to dismiss the local party secretary and member of **399** the politburo, Dinmukahmed Kunaev, and replace him with a Russian. Kunaev had been deeply corrupt: reformers in Moscow have uncovered a whole network of corruption in Central Asia, where they refer to a mafia, which had embezzled billions of roubles. However, as far as the Kazakhs were concerned, Kunaev was one of their own, and they protested bitterly at his dismissal.

They were also protesting at the continuing immigration of Russians into Kazakhstan. This had been the site of Khrushchev's unhappy 'virgin lands' project in the 1950s and 1960s, which had been designed to solve the Soviet Union's agricultural problems at a stroke. It had failed, but in the process, hundreds of thousands of Russians had been imported into Central Asia, and now they are in a slight majority in Kazakhstan.

The politics of the Soviet Union continued to evolve at the same hectic pace in 1989 – and the country's multitudinous problems continued to get worse. There were further outbreaks of ethnic and nationalist violence, in Georgia and Uzbekistan. In both cases, the troubles started with a dispute between the majority and an ethnic minority, in Georgia an indigenous tribe and in Uzbekistan one of the Turkic groups expelled to Central Asia by Stalin.

The Georgian troubles soon turned into an anti-Soviet demonstration. On 9 April, the local authorities sent the troops into the centre of Tbilisi to break up a crowd. The soldiers were not armed, so they used spades taken from their tanks as clubs, and gas that some Georgians claimed was poisonous. Several dozen people were killed. In Uzbekistan, the troubles rapidly developed in to a pogrom, in which hundreds of people were killed.

On 29 March 1989, elections were held for the new Soviet parliament. Many prominent Communist officials were defeated, including the entire party leadership in Leningrad, and in Moscow the dissident Communist Boris Yeltsin won almost 90 per cent of the vote against an official candidate. Andrei Sakharov and other opposition figures were elected, and when the Congress assembled, its deliberations were broadcast live on television. For the first time in the history of the Soviet state, there was a free and open debate on every political and economic issue facing the country.

In April 1989, there were riots in Abkhazia, an autonomous region in northern Georgia, inhabited by a Moslem minority, the Abkhazians. As in Nagorno-Karabakh and Central Asia, the dispute was an ethnic quarrel going back centuries which had been controlled but not resolved by the USSR. In June, there were serious riots in Uzbekistan, when Uzbeks attacked Meskhetians, who are a Caucasian group deported from Georgia to Central Asia by Stalin. Scores of people were killed. It is certain that there will be more such disputes.

FURTHER READING

Binyon, Michael, *Life in Russia*, New York, Pantheon Books, 1983.
Kaiser, Robert, *Russia*, New York, Atheneum, 1976.
Lang, David Marshall and Walker, Christopher J., *The Armenians*, London, Minority Rights Group, 1987.
Smith, Hedrick, *The Russians*, New York, Times Books, 1983.
Congressional Quarterly 'The Soviet Union', Washington, 1982.

LATIN AMERICA

UNITED STATES

MEXICO

MEXICO
CITY

BAHAMAS

HAVANA
CUBA

DOMINICAN REPUBLIC
PORT-AU-PRINCE
SANTO DOMINGO

BELMOPAN
BELIZE
HONDURAS
HAITI

GUATEMALA
EL SALVADOR
NICARAGUA

COSTA RICA
PANAMA
CITY

GRENADA

PANAMA
CARACAS

MEDELLIN
VENEZUELA
GEORGETOWN
GUYANA
SURINAM
FRENCH GUIANA

BOGOTÁ

COLUMBIA

ECUADOR
QUITO
Yari River
Rio Negra

Amazon River
Amazon River

PERU

Madeira River
Tapajos River
Xingu River

LIMA
AYACUCHO

BRAZIL

LA PAZ
BRASILIA

BOLIVIA

CHILE
PARAGUAY

SAO PAULO
ASUNCIÓN
RIO DE JANEIRO

ARGENTINA

SANTIAGO
BUENOS AIRES

FALKLAND
ISLANDS
STANLEY

SOUTH
GEORGIA

MEXICO

BELIZE

GUATEMALA

GUATEMALA
CITY
HONDURAS
TEGUCIGALPA

SAN
SALVADOR

EL SALVADOR
NICARAGUA
Miskito Coast

MANAGUA
Lake
Nicaragua

EL BLUFF

SAN JOSÉ
COSTA
RICA

ARGENTINA AND THE FALKLANDS

ARGENTINA

Geography	1,072,067 sq. miles (2,776,643 sq. km)
Population	30,977,000
GNP per capita	$2350

There have been many countries that have been worse governed than Argentina between 1945 and 1982, nations that also faced extremes of poverty, backwardness, external enemies, the bitter divisions of competing tribes. Argentina suffered from none of those disadvantages. It is large, rich in natural resources, with an educated and homogeneous population and no foreign enemies. In 1945, it had the largest gold reserves of any country in the world after the United States, and it should have developed into another Canada. Instead, for nearly 40 years, it endured an alternation of incompetent Fascist and incompetent military governments.

Argentina's travails culminated in the mid-1970s with a Communist terrorist campaign against the state. It was suppressed with great brutality by the military government, which murdered over 10,000 civilians accused of terrorism. When the military were finally evicted in 1982, they left a bitterly divided and impoverished country, with a heavily indebted Third World economy, which had just suffered a humiliating defeat in a pointless war.

HISTORY

Argentina's troubles go back to the Fascist dictator Juan Perón, who won election to the presidency in February 1946 after a demagogic campaign that overawed the military government. He was the Mussolini of South America, but even more incompetent than the Duce had been. Like Mussolini, he nationalized the banks and foreign companies, took over the universities and recognized the USSR. He delivered rabble-rousing speeches from the balcony of the Casa Rosada, the presidential palace in Buenos Aires, inciting his subjects' chauvinism by abusing Britain and the United States, and indulging every demand of the urban proletariat 403

– the *descamisados* ('shirtless ones') – who were the base of his power. He promised them cheap housing, education, medicine, clothing, bread and circuses – and he was able to make his promises good as long as the gold reserves lasted and there was still foreign property to confiscate. When the bread ran out, the circus became more frenetic. The chief performer was his wife, Eva (known as 'Evita'), around whom Perón developed a semi-religious cult, and whom he had proclaimed *jefa espiritual de la nación* ('spiritual leader of the nation'). When she died, in July 1952, the country was subjected to an orgy of official mourning without modern precedent. In 1955, the army finally deposed Perón. He took refuge on a Paraguayan gunboat in the River Plate, and left the country on 20 September.

The country that he left behind was ruined, and has not yet recovered. Perón had institutionalized corruption among the military, and the workers had been led to believe that prosperity was their right, not something to be worked for, and that their increasing poverty must be a foreign plot. For nearly 20 years, Perón himself, from his exile in Spain, was a constant cause of instability because he offered the prospect of an alternative government, a return to the golden days of the *Juan and Evita Show*. Eva's body had been smuggled out of the country after his overthrow, and he kept it in a private shrine, to be brought back in triumph when the people called.

During that interregnum, the military returned power to civilian governments twice: first to Arturo Frondizi in February 1958, and then to Arturo Ilea in July 1963. They both failed to solve the country's problems and were therefore removed by the military, Frondizi having lasted four years, Ilea three. In 1973, in an attempt to break out of this vicious circle, the military allowed Perón to return. In the long run, the gamble worked, for the time being at least: the golden age did not return and Perónism lost its lustre.

Perón's demagogic touch was gone. He failed to co-opt the left and, instead, turned on it, driving it underground. He died in July 1974.

The extremists, disillusioned with Perón and exasperated by 30 years of Fascist or quasi-Fascist misgovernment, turned to terrorism, calling themselves the Monteneros. Leading industrialists and military men, including one of the generals who had deposed Perón, were assassinated. There were bombs and shootings in the cities, the guerrillas tried to start an insurgency in the countryside and the universities were in permanent revolt. It is, however, important to note that the terrorists were far less numerous than the military claimed and were never a serious threat to the republic. They could have been dealt with as the West Germans dealt with the Baader–Meinhof gang (*see* The Euro-terrorists, pp. 501–14).

Perón was succeeded by his widow Isabel, whom he had made vice president. She proved grossly incompetent and was deposed by the armed forces in March 1976. A junta was established, composed of the commanders of the three services. They responded to the terrorists with martial law and the 'dirty war', dispensing altogether with legal process. People suspected of belonging to the revolutionary parties were arrested, tortured and murdered. No account was ever given of what happened to them: they were *los desaparecidos*, the 'disappeared'. Mass graves were dug in remote cemeteries, and some unfortunates were simply dropped out of aircraft over the ocean.

The military's motto was: when in doubt, kill them. It was effective. Revolutionary terrorism was practically eliminated, but it was replaced by state terrorism. The National Commission on the Disappearance of Persons, set up by the Alfonsín government after the military were overthrown, established dossiers and took testimony on the cases of 8960 people who had been arrested and never heard of again. The commission did not examine every case and officially admits that there are many more. The best estimate is that between 10,000 and 15,000 people were murdered during the 'dirty war'.

In this extremity, a number of courageous women started demonstrating on the Plaza de Mayo outside the Casa Rosada. They were the mothers of the disappeared, and their weekly demonstrations quickly became an intolerable challenge to the regime. By late 1981, midsummer in the Southern Hemisphere, there were thousands of these *Madres de Mayo* demonstrating every Thursday, at first silently and peacefully but soon noisily, insistently demanding their children.

The demonstrations were not the only crisis facing the regime. The country's economic situation was sharply deteriorating, partly because of the international oil crisis but chiefly because of Argentina's chronic governmental incompetence. There was also dissension within the junta: one general, Roberto Viola, was removed as president in December 1981 and replaced by another, Leopoldo Galtieri.

In disposing of his fellow general, Galtieri needed the support of the navy commander, Admiral Jorge Anaya. Anaya had long entertained dreams of liberating the Malvinas, as the Falkland Islands are known in Argentina. Galtieri promised to accomplish the task in 1982. A dramatic victory would solve all his problems at a stroke.

THE FALKLANDS

The Falklands are a desolate archipelago in the South Atlantic, 400 miles (640 km) off the southern tip of South America. There are two main islands, covering 6280 square miles (16,265 sq. km), about the size of Wales. In 1982 they were inhabited by 1800 people and 400,000 sheep.

The Falklands were noted by various explorers in the 16th and 17th centuries. The first to land was a British sailor, in 1690, who named them after an admiralty official, Lord Falkland. Visiting Breton sailors later named them the Malouines, after St Malo; this name was later corrupted to Malvinas. In the mid-18th century, both France and Britain laid claim to the Falklands and set up small military colonies there, though both were hard pressed to justify the need for such an outpost.

France sold her interest to Spain in 1766, and a Spanish fleet was sent from Buenos Aires to expel the British. There was a brief chauvinistic outcry in Britain, memorably denounced by Dr Johnson, in which politicians proclaimed Britain's inalienable right to those untempting islands. Britain threatened war, and Spain agreed to restore the British colony and remove its own garrison, though without renouncing its claim to the islands. The incident was closed. The British evacuated the Falklands in 1774, and they remained unoccupied for the next 50 years.

When Argentina won its independence from Spain in 1816, it laid claim to the Falklands, as heir to Spain's possessions, and in 1826 set up a colony there. **405**

Considering past history, it had every right to do so. If the British had wanted the islands, they should have settled them, or at least left a permanent garrison.

After Waterloo, the British embarked upon an imperial century. Instead of abandoning their long-neglected claims, they reasserted them. If someone else wanted the Falklands, then perhaps they were worth having. This attitude was further complicated by the fact that an expedition to Buenos Aires during the Napoleonic wars had been defeated; the British were certainly not now going to cede even worthless territory to Argentina. Lord Palmerston, the most belligerent of all British foreign secretaries, asserted that Britain had never renounced sovereignty to the Falklands and sent a small naval expedition, which in 1833 summarily evicted the Argentinians. It was this act of aggression that Argentina set out to rectify in 1982.

No doubt about it, the original British action was a case of arrogant high-handedness, but that had occurred 149 years before Galtieri turned his thoughts towards the islands. In international law, Argentina had no case. The islands had been continuously occupied by Britain since 1833, when a commercial enterprise, the Falkland Islands Company, started raising sheep and imported settlers, mostly from Scotland. Their descendants are there still.

True, the Falklands had been taken from Argentina by force. However, if territories seized by force must be returned to their previous owners or their descendants, and if continuous occupation over the generations bestows no rights, then the United States must return Texas and California to Mexico, and France must return Alsace-Lorraine to Germany – and that was indeed the latter's assertion in 1870, with calamitous consequences for both countries. If the Falklands are to be returned because Argentina occupied them for six years 150 years ago, then Germany may reclaim the ancient German cities Breslau, Danzig and Königsburg, the Greeks may reclaim Constantinople, and the Queen of England may reclaim her lost duchies of Normandy, Anjou and Aquitaine.

The essence of the British claim, however, was not historical, but was based on the charter of the United Nations and on the established principles of international law, which give countries, however small, the right of self-determination. The Falklanders wanted to remain British, and that was sufficient.

That Britain was in the right does not mean that it was wise. The Falklands provide no strategic or economic benefit to Britain. Only armchair strategists cherish them, those obsessed with maps who think that they might be useful in controlling the waters around Cape Horn. Prime Minister Margaret Thatcher went to war to protect the right to self-determination of 1800 people, roughly the number who live in a typical block of council flats. Mrs Thatcher would never allow 1800 people in Britain to determine the course of national policy. She has made a career of obliging her fellow citizens to face up to unpleasant choices – closing industries, intimidating trade unions and reforming the health service. The Falklanders, it seems, were somehow different: they were allowed to direct British policy towards the whole of Latin America. It was a remarkable instance of the tail wagging the dog. It is also worth remarking that the 70,000–100,000 British citizens who live in Argentina take a very different view of the Falklands dispute than do those 1800 sheep farmers.

Every Argentinian child had for generations been taught that Britain had robbed Argentina of the Malvinas. They were not taught the horrors of war, nor were they encouraged to examine irredentist claims dispassionately. On the contrary, if Galtieri had not gone to war with Britain, he might have gone to war with Chile, over two other worthless and disputed islands in the channel between Patagonia and Tierra del Fuego. Every Argentinian child knew all about that dispute, too.

At the height of the crisis in 1982, the Argentinian foreign minister complained on American television that, of course, the Malvinas were Argentinian: he had sung songs about it as a child. Argentina's claims were childish, but they were passionately believed, and the nation worked itself into a patriotic fever in a bad cause, very much like European militarists earlier in the century. The British government, and particularly the Foreign Office, was much to blame for failing to take Argentina seriously. The junta's greatest error was that it utterly failed to predict the probable British reaction to an invasion – the most gratuitous case of ignorance and self-delusion since Nasser closed the Strait of Tiran in 1967.

The Galtieri junta was not only carried away by its own rhetoric, it was also exceedingly stupid. The point is illustrated by the timing of the invasion: 2 April 1982. It was in the autumn. If they had waited two months longer, it would have been too late in the year for Britain to mount a counter-offensive, and the Falklands would have been in Argentina's hands undisturbed for the next six months. What is more, the British had just sold one of their last two aircraft carriers to Australia and were preparing to scrap the second, together with several of the other warships that were used in the task force that eventually recaptured the islands. If Argentina had waited another year, the British would not have had the resources to retake the Falklands, and would have been forced to acquiesce in the *fait accompli*.

THE ROAD TO WAR

Argentina and Britain had periodically conducted negotiations over the future of the Falklands. The Foreign Office was disinclined to fight too hard to retain such a small and unimportant colony, but a strong Falklands lobby in the Conservative party set up an instant cacophony every time the notion of renouncing sovereignty over the islands was raised.

Unlike Spain, which tried to win Gibraltar by closing the border and bullying the Gibraltarians, the Argentinians for many years offered every inducement to the Falklanders to think favourably of them: there was a heavily subsidized airlink between the islands and the mainland; medical treatment was provided (Argentina has excellent doctors); scholarships were offered. Argentinian tourists took business to the Falklands, and were always on their best behaviour.

However, the military government was too impatient, needed a success too badly, to allow such a sensible policy the time it needed. Like Franco's Spain in the case of Gibraltar, they were also unlikely to admit that their regime was so unappetizing that no one could be expected voluntarily to join it.

In late 1981 and early 1982, a further round of unsuccessful negotiations was held. Britain again refused to bend on sovereignty. General Galtieri had promised Admiral Anaya that the Malvinas would be returned by the end of 1982, before the 150th anniversary of their occupation by Britain, and so plans for the invasion were dusted off and brought up to date.

There was one further Argentinian miscalculation. During the Carter presidency, Argentina had been subjected to much pressure and criticism because of its abominable record on human rights. The moment the Reagan administration took office, however, all that changed. The Argentinians were welcomed back into the fold. They were invited to send specialists to help anti-terrorist campaigns in El Salvador and to train the Nicaraguan Contras. Galtieri was welcomed with open arms in Washington. The egregious Jeane Kirkpatrick, now US permanent representative to the UN and one of the president's favourites, was well known for her admiration for authoritarian South American regimes. Galtieri assumed that the United States would support Argentina in the coming conflict. It was a costly misjudgment.

THE BEGINNING OF WAR

Argentina needed a *causus belli* and found a most unsatisfactory one – one that precipitated the invasion earlier in the year than military prudence suggested. An Argentinian scrap merchant had contracted to remove an abandoned whaling station from South Georgia, another British island well to the east of the Falklands, and which the Argentinians also claimed. He landed his expedition on South Georgia in mid-March, without first checking in with the British authorities, represented by a small scientific station on another part of the island. He was told to remove himself or obtain permits, and two dozen Royal Marines were sent from the Falklands to enforce the decision.

Galtieri sent troops to protect the Argentinian scrap dealer on 25 March, and occupied South Georgia. At the same time, he ordered the invasion of the Falklands. The Argentinian navy put troops ashore at dawn on 2 April, and they soon occupied Stanley, the capital, and other strategic points.

The British were taken completely by surprise. The Foreign Office had ignored a series of warnings by the embassy in Buenos Aires, in disbelief that the Argentinians would be so rash as to invade British territory. In the 1981 Defence White Paper, the minister of defence had announced plans to get rid of the last naval vessel in the South Atlantic, the converted icebreaker HMS *Endurance*. The same document had also proposed a drastic reduction in the rest of the surface fleet, including elimination of the two aircraft carriers. Henceforth, the Royal Navy's budget was to be devoted to building Trident submarines and their missiles. The Argentinians had read the White Paper and concluded that Britain had written off the Falklands.

They were mistaken. Britain was outraged by the invasion. Even those who thought that the Falklands should be abandoned found it an intolerable affront to the national dignity and asked, 'What sort of people do they think we are?' Britain may have come down in the world since 1945, but not to the point where it could be pushed around by a Latin American military government. The phrase 'tin-pot dictator' was a favourite.

THE EMPIRE STRIKES BACK

The invasion was on a Friday. By the following Tuesday, 5 April, a British naval task force had set sail to recapture the islands – 8250 miles (13,275 km) away – and avenge British honour. The British had not previously had a reputation for successful improvisation in an emergency. This time, they did it magnificently.

The navy being much reduced, merchant ships were drafted into service, including two liners, the *Canberra* and the *Queen Elizabeth II*. The *Canberra* had just completed a cruise, and returned to Southampton on 7 April. Her next cruise was abruptly cancelled, a helipad was carved out of her decks, and she sailed two days later with 2400 troops. The *QEII* was brought into service later and was converted to a troop carrier, like her illustrious predecessors, the *Queen Mary* and the *Queen Elizabeth*, in World War II.

It happens that Britain has retained, as relics of empire, a string of islands down the length of the Atlantic. The Task Force therefore progressed from Portsmouth to Gibraltar to Ascension to St Helena to South Georgia, where the *QEII* and other transports sheltered during the campaign. The problem with the more southerly islands was that, beyond Ascension, with 4000 miles to go, there were no airports. The operation had to be entirely naval, until the army could get ashore.

At the same time, the United States made a determined effort to avert war, while the British successfully lobbied at the United Nations and in Europe to line up world opinion against Argentina. President Reagan called Galtieri on the night of the invasion, begging him to desist, but to no avail. The secretary of state, Alexander Haig, tried shuttle diplomacy, flying between London and Buenos Aires. Admiral Anaya, who had never been to war, told him, 'My son is a helicopter pilot. The proudest day of my life will be when he lays down his life for the Malvinas.' General Haig, who had served in Korea and Vietnam, replied, 'You know, when you see the body bags, it's different.'

When the war started, the Americans gave the British every moral and practical help, including intelligence and armaments shipped from American depots. American public opinion was vociferously pro-British. In 1988, John Lehman, who was the US secretary of the navy in 1982, said that the British might have failed without American help, particularly in intelligence. The two navies even discussed the possibility that the British might lease the USS *Guam*, a 12,000-ton assault ship that can be used as a small aircraft carrier. It was not needed.

The Task Force reached the South Atlantic on 1 May. The first engagement was the recapture of South Georgia, which was easily accomplished. Reconquering the Falklands was more difficult.

There are two main islands in the archipelago, with Port Stanley on the east coast of the eastern island. The British chose to land on the other side of that island, at a place called San Carlos, and use the narrow waterway between the two islands as a shelter for the fleet of cargo ships and landing craft as well as the naval vessels sent to protect them. The landing was on 21 May, and was not seriously opposed. In fact, throughout the fighting, the Argentinian army (consisting almost entirely of conscripts) proved woefully inadequate. Very few units showed any fighting spirit at all, and surrendered to much smaller British forces. The navy was equally unimpressive: a British submarine sank the cruiser *Belgrano*, and after that, the Argentinian navy stayed in port. (The *Belgrano* affair was later the cause of a sharp dispute in Britain, where the government was accused of giving the go-ahead to the navy to sink a ship that was no danger to the Task Force, and which was, in fact, heading away from the Falklands at the time.)

Argentina's honour was redeemed by its air force, its pilots showing immense gallantry and skill. They sank a number of British ships, with heavy loss of life, flying from bases 400 miles (640 km) away, at the limit of their range. The British – with only a limited number of Harriers flying off their two aircraft carriers, and with Rapier and Blowpipe surface-to-air missiles (SAMs) to defend the fleet – found themselves in grave danger. A score of ships, including the liner *Canberra*, were packed into the narrow strait off San Carlos, and they came under constant attack from Argentinian aircraft. Four British ships, including two warships, were sunk by bombs, and the destroyer HMS *Sheffield* and the cargo ship *Atlantic Conveyor* were sunk by French Exocet air-launched anti-ship missiles. Many other ships were damaged, some seriously.

The British have an all-volunteer army, and it bore itself well. The Royal Navy lived up to its traditions, and pilots flying off the aircraft carriers – including Prince Andrew, the Queen's second son – performed creditably.

After they had secured their landing, the British had to cross East Falkland to reach Stanley. It took them three weeks. They charged across the island, and laid siege to the capital, which was defended by Argentinian positions on the surrounding ring of hills. At all times, the British had the initiative over the miserable Argentinian conscripts, who had not expected to have to fight for the Malvinas. The Argentinian forces surrendered on 14 June 1982.

The British took 12,978 prisoners and lost 250 men killed. Five Falklands civilians were killed. The Argentines lost 746 killed, of whom 368 had been on the *Belgrano*.

AFTERMATH OF THE WAR

The prisoners were all repatriated. Within days, the junta had resigned, and mass demonstrations in Buenos Aires demanded a return to democracy. It was the same course of events that had brought down the Greek junta in 1974. A retired general, who was innocent of all involvement in the Falklands fiasco, was brought in to supervise the transition.

There was a presidential election, and Raul Alfonsín, leader of the Radical party, won by a huge majority, with a mandate to clean out the military, investigate the 'dirty war' and punish the guilty – and also to investigate the Falklands war. All the generals and admirals who had been members of the various juntas from 1976 to 1982 are now serving long sentences, as are many of the military murderers and torturers.

Argentina is struggling to build a solid democracy, while trying to cope with the economic disasters left behind by previous regimes. The Falklands question remains unsolved. President Alfonsín can do much, but he cannot yet renounce Argentina's claim to the Malvinas. The irredentist tradition, and all those children's songs, are too strong for him. Books and newspaper accounts of the war, published in Argentina afterwards, were astonishingly mendacious, never suggesting that Galtieri's objective had been wrong, only that the execution of the plan had been defective.

Neither can Mrs Thatcher renounce the Falklands, after the 250 dead and a glorious victory. The British government has spent millions building a modern air base at Stanley and buying the aircraft to enable the Falklands to be reinforced quickly. The Falkland islanders, their lives permanently disrupted by a garrison considerably larger than their own population, have to bear the brunt of the continuing tensions.

Six years after the surrender, Argentina still refused to sign an armistice, and restore diplomatic relations with Britain. Argentina wishes to resume negotiations over the future of the Falklands, including the question of sovereignty. The British have agreed to discuss everything except sovereignty. They say the matter is settled, and it is up to Argentina to recognize reality. In March 1988, the British conducted elaborate military and air exercises in and around the Falklands, to prove to themselves that they would be ready if ever an invasion were again threatened. Argentina protested bitterly at this 'provocation'. The stalemate continues.

As ever, the dangers in Argentina itself remain military intervention and a revival of Perónist Fascism. The armed forces were cowed by their defeat in 1982, and although several coups were attempted against the Alfonsín government, none was condoned by the high command. However, Alfonsín did not dare touch the institution: the same men who ordered the murders of thousands of people still run Argentina's army, navy and air force. Their predecessors had governed the country with brief interruptions for over 50 years, and their successors have not renounced their mission. Furthermore, the Alfonsín regime, however laudable its democratic principles, proved scarcely more competent at managing the economy than previous governments. As a result, Perónism revived from its ashes, in the person of Carlos Saúl Menem, governor of La Rioja province, in whom the passions and frustrations of the mass of Argentinians are now personified.

In April 1982, only a short time ago, hundreds of thousands of people crowded the Plaza de Mayo chanting 'Argentina, Argentina!' as General Galtieri announced that 'The flag of Argentina flies on the Malvinas.' The temptations of military and political demagoguery are as strong as ever, and it is by no means clear that the Argentinians have lost their affection for men in uniform ranting from balconies.

FURTHER READING

Amnesty International, *Argentina: The military juntas and human rights. Report of the trial of the former junta members*, London, 1985.
Burns, Jimmy, *The Land that Lost Its Heroes*, London, Bloomsbury, 1987.
Hastings, Max and Jenkins, Simon, *The Battle for the Falklands*, New York, W. W. Norton, 1983.
Laffin, John, *Fight for the Falklands!*, New York, St Martin's Press, 1982.
Middlebrook, Martin, *Operation Corporate*, London, Viking, 1985.
Sunday Times (London) Insight Team, *The Falklands War, the Full Story*, London, Andre Deutsch, 1982.

CENTRAL AMERICA

Porfírio Díaz, a revolutionary 19th-century president of Mexico, made the celebrated comment: 'Poor Mexico: so far from God, so close to the United States.' For nearly a century, the other nations of Central America – Guatemala, El Salvador, Honduras, Nicaragua, Costa Rica, Panama and, to some extent, Belize (formerly British Honduras) – suffered from a double disadvantage: they were too close to the United States for safety, too far for understanding.

For most of their history, the United States has treated them like colonies, without accepting any of the responsibility for the well-being of their inhabitants that the British and French showed for their colonial empires or the Americans themselves showed in the Philippines. The United States ruled El Salvador, Guatemala, Nicaragua and the rest in the old Spanish manner: it left the administration in the hands of the local oligarchy, and protected that oligarchy against popular discontent, but insisted that American commercial and political interests were always paramount. In the most extreme case, Guatemala and Honduras became the colonies of the United Fruit Company. In Nicaragua, the United States repeatedly sent in the Marines to establish governments to its liking.

This attitude only began to change (and the change is by no means complete) in the 1970s and 1980s as Washington at last began to learn about the realities of the situation in Central America. Policies followed by the Carter and Reagan administrations (there was much more continuity between them than either would admit) began to distinguish in each case between the interests of the military and landed oligarchy and of the country at large. Democratically elected presidents took office in El Salvador, Guatemala and Honduras, and the Reagan administration actively encouraged democracy and land reform, reversing the policies of every other president from Teddy Roosevelt to Gerald Ford. However, they discovered that bringing reform to Central America was as difficult as reforming Indochina had proved.

To a great extent, Central America throughout the 19th and most of the 20th century was a victim of American isolationism. Americans knew little about the place and cared less. They knew far more about China than they did about Guatemala. Early in the century, they neither knew nor wished to know that

412

Guatemalan peasants were obliged to work for United Fruit without pay for 150 days a year 'in lieu of taxes', and that the rest of the year they were paid 25 cents a day. In the 1960s, conditions that Americans would have instantly recognized to be intolerable in Asia, let alone Europe or the United States itself, were ignored or accepted in Central America – and anyone who proposed to change those conditions was instantly branded a Communist.

In 1983, Henry Kissinger led a National Bipartisan Commission on Central America. It was an exceedingly eminent commission, and its report is one of the major state papers of the 1980s. The commission pointed out all the social and economic difficulties facing the region, and concluded that the only way to avert a Communist revolution was to encourage root and branch reform. It recommended that at least $8 billion in aid should be spent on Central America by the end of the decade.

The report was prefaced by a few significant observations:

For most people in the United States, Central America has long been what the entire New World was to Europeans of five centuries ago: *terra incognita*. Probably few of even the most educated could name all the countries of Central America and their capitals, much less recite much of the social and political backgrounds. Most members of this Commission began with what we now see as an extremely limited understanding of the region, its needs and its importance.

That was a remarkable admission for a former US secretary of state.

After Woodrow Wilson sent 'Black Jack' Pershing chasing after Pancho Villa in northern Mexico in 1916, the United States left Mexico to its own devices. Its government has pursued agrarian reform, economic nationalism (it confiscated American oil interests) and has frequently indulged in anti-American gestures. The United States has never suffered in the slightest from those policies. Mexico has escaped the curse of its proximity to the United States (though not its remoteness from the Deity), as the United States has come to understand something of its southern neighbour.

The rest of Central America was not so fortunate. Instead of leaving those half-dozen small countries to work out their own destinies, the Americans have constantly interfered. Nicaragua was directly administered by the United States for 20 years and then handed over to the Somoza dynasty. Although Franklin Roosevelt proclaimed a 'good neighbour policy', promising to keep his hands off Latin America, it turned out that this meant a benevolent indifference to the installation of Fascist and military dictators throughout the region.

In the 1950s, the 'good neighbour' policy was abandoned: the Americans now took an active interest in Latin America, meaning that it actively encouraged and sustained right-wing regimes. The CIA engineered a coup in Guatemala in 1954, and Washington then gave strong support to a regime that eventually massacred about 100,000 peasants (during that period, only the Khmer Rouge government in Cambodia and Idi Amin in Uganda managed a higher rate of killing their own people). The Somozas of Nicaragua – and, in the Caribbean, Batista of Cuba and Trujillo of the Dominican Republic – were all supported by successive administrations in Washington.

The tide turned at last in the late 1970s. In the 1980s, during the Reagan   413 administration, Washington tried to build up democratic centrist parties in El Salvador, Guatemala and Honduras, by forcing the military to hand over power to civilians, and then supporting those civilians against attack from left and right. As Mr Reagan's term drew to its close, the three governments were barely surviving. Meanwhile, the administration tried everything short of sending in the Marines to overthrow the Marxist government in Nicaragua, on the improbable pretext that it was a menace to the United States.

However gloomy the prospects in Central America, it is important to note the evolution of political thinking in Washington. Those Democratic paladins Woodrow Wilson and Lyndon Johnson never hesitated to send troops to Central America and the Caribbean to impose their political views. Ultra-conservative President Ronald Reagan used them once, in Grenada: they were undoubtedly popular on the island, and they were removed within a year. They have never been used in Nicaragua.

A turning point in El Salvador occurred in December 1983, when the then US vice president, George Bush, personally delivered the message to the military regime that the United States insisted on free elections and an end to human rights abuse. There were free elections the following spring. In June 1988 during a tour of Central America, Reagan's secretary of state, George Shultz, repeatedly reaffirmed the United States' commitment to human rights and democracy, and told the various army commands directly that the United States would never support any new military governments. Both Bush and Shultz, acting for President Reagan, were following in the footsteps of Jimmy Carter, whom Reagan had endlessly attacked for 'softness' in pushing for human rights reforms in Latin America.

On a wider canvas, and over a longer term, the main hope for the whole of Latin America is the evolution of their societies away from the old divisions between peasantry and oligarchy. For this to happen there, as in Asia, people will have to move to the cities, education will have to improve, society and the economy will have to diversify. It then becomes increasingly difficult for a military or political clique, of left or right, to exercise its dictatorship: governments need the support of the citizenry in order to function. This historic evolution applies as much to Sandinista Nicaragua as it would to Fascist El Salvador. The alternative to democracy is chaos.

EL SALVADOR

Geography	8056 sq. miles (20,865 sq. km). The size of Wales.
Population	4.9 million
GNP per capita	$820
Casualties	Over 60,000 killed since 1979.
Refugees	Internal: 450,000 Salvadorans, 200 foreign. External: 15,100 in Honduras, 120,000* in Mexico, 500 in Guatemala, 7200 in Nicaragua, 600 in Panama, 2900 in Belize, 6200 in Costa Rica.
Political parties	• *The Christian Democratic Party* (PDC): led by José Napoleón Duarte since the 1960s. A traditional, centrist, reformist party, closely allied to the Church. Popular support based on middle classes, traditional trade unions and peasant associations. After forming the government 1984–9, now in a state of collapse.

● *Democratic Revolutionary Front* (FDR): coalition of three
leftist parties, one clearly Marxist, the others not:
National Democratic Union (UDN): Communist party's front
organization. Military counterpart is FAL, one of the components of the FMLN (*see below*).
National Revolutionary Movement (MNR): a socialist party,
member of the Second International (like the British Labour
party and the French Socialist party). Leaders are Guillermo
Ungo and Eduardo Calles.
Popular Social Christian Movement (MPSC): formed by dissident Christian Democrats protesting against Duarte's 1980
decision to join the military-dominated government. Leaders
are Hector Dada and Rubén Zamora.
● *National Conciliation Party*: official party of the oligarchy
before the 1979 coup. From 1961 onwards, chose the president
from the armed forces.
● *Republican National Alliance* (Arena): formed in 1981. One
of most openly Fascist in Latin America. Symbol is a sword
and a cross. Draws much of its strength from charismatic
leadership of Roberto d'Aubuisson. Party is militantly anti-
Communist and opposed to land reform, unions and all negotiation with rebels. Proclaims 'the individual's right to acquire,
maintain and use property as a projection of human personality',
and is thus the mouthpiece of the oligarchy. Won widespread
popular support because it offers a clear-cut alternative to
Communist rebels and to ineffective centrist governments.

The rebels

The first guerrilla movements were formed after Soccer War
in 1969 (*see below*), but did not begin to campaign until after
the Sandinista victory in Nicaragua in 1979. In March 1980,
four separate and competing organizations formed a united front
under sponsorship of Fidel Castro of Cuba; in October, the
alliance adopted the name *Farabundo Martí National Liberation
Front* (FMLN). The original four were later joined by the Salvadoran
Communist party. All five are Marxist and revolutionary.
● *People's Liberation Forces* (FPL): most extreme unit of
FMLN. Founded in 1970 by Salvador Cayento Carpio,
former secretary general of the Communist party; he modelled
FPL and its campaign on the Vietnamese struggle. On 12 April
1983, Carpio committed suicide in Nicaragua after one of
his henchmen killed another prominent member of the party,
Comandante Ana María (Dr Melida Anaya Montes). FPL re-
mains the largest guerrilla organization and is now led by
Leonel Gonzalez.
● *People's Revolutionary Army* (ERP): founded in 1971.
Members chiefly drawn from middle class and Christian Democratic youth. Its leaders are Joaquin Villalobos, who has become
the chief FMLN strategist and spokesman, and Ana Guadalupe
Martínez. Political wing is called People's League of February
28 (LP-28); one of its chief assets is clandestine Radio Ven-
ceremos ('We Shall Overcome'). Both the FPL and the ERP are
openly Communist, and are advised by Shafik Handal, the
Salvadoran Communist party's most noted political strategist.
● *Armed Forces of National Resistance* (FARN): broke away
from the ERP in 1975 in dispute over whether organization
should concentrate on armed resistance or building a political
base. ERP leaders accused the chief spokesman of the latter
tendency, the poet Roque Dalton, of being a CIA agent, and

415

shot him. His followers then seceded. FARN specialize in kidnapping members of the '14 families'. Its leaders are Ferman Cienfuegos and Saul Villalta. In February 1988, the Salvadoran army claimed to have killed Cienfuegos, but apparently they were mistaken.
• *Central American Revolutionary Workers' Party* (PRTC): founded in 1976 by Roberto Roca. Smallest of the guerrilla armies.
• *Armed Forces of Liberation* (FAL): military wing of the Salvadoran Communist party.

In the early 1980s, it seemed as though El Salvador was about to follow Nicaragua down the road of Communist revolution. An odious military regime, overthrown in 1979, had been followed by a succession of ineffective juntas that were all incapable of defeating the guerrillas or of controlling the right-wing death squads that operated freely throughout the country. At the height of the fighting in 1981–2, guerrillas were operating in the suburbs of San Salvador, and the death squads were killing 20 or 30 people a day and dumping their bodies by the roadside.

The United States intervened with advice, money and weapons, but Congress refused to permit the Reagan administration to send troops to El Salvador. In elections in 1984, Salvadorans freely voted for the Christian Democratic candidate for the presidency, José Napoleón Duarte, and for a while it seemed as though the United States had succeeded in finding the grail: the democratic centre, a party that would win the hearts and votes of a majority of the electorate while repudiating the Fascist tendencies of the right and the Communist excesses of the left.

Within five years, the centre had collapsed. Duarte, dying and defeated, was unable to impose unity upon his own party, which lost the legislative elections of March 1988. The economy was kept afloat solely by American aid, and although the guerrillas were clearly unpopular in the cities and in most of the countryside, they still represented a desperate threat to the government's survival. All the efforts of President Reagan's administration had served merely to preserve the crisis, intact and intractable, to be handed over to his successor George Bush.

HISTORY

The roots of the perpetual crisis in El Salvador, as in much of the rest of Latin America, lie in the prolonged refusal of the hereditary élite to share their economic and political power. By the late 19th century, the basis of El Salvador's economy was coffee; in 1931, it was responsible for 95.5 per cent of the country's export earnings, and 14 families owned all the plantations. These families were all-powerful, controlling every aspect of Salvadoran life, including the coffee trade, and they considered every challenge subversive. Their successors still do.

In El Salvador as elsewhere, the Marxist left is equally intransigent. It denounces elections as frauds and considers it a legitimate political act to murder anyone who takes part in an election – candidates, party workers, voters. It insists upon violent revolution and on its right to impose by force its political doctrines upon the country.

These two irreconcilable dogmas first came into conflict in 1932. During the 1920s and early 1930s, as rising expectations among peasants and city dwellers

416

threatened the oligarchs' positions, they formed an alliance with the army. Soldiers were given power, privilege and incomes to which they could not otherwise aspire and, in exchange, maintained the oligarchy's economic domination of the country against all attack.

In 1932, when the Depression had severely affected El Salvador, Communist organizers in the cities allied themselves with disaffected Indian peasants on the coffee plantations and planned a general uprising. The Communist leader was Augustín Farabundo Martí. He and his colleagues were arrested before the demonstrations could begin, and were executed, giving the Salvadoran left its principal martyr. The army suppressed the peasants in what became known as the *Matanza*, or 'massacre'. Between 10,000 and 30,000 people were slaughtered: the army occupied Indian villages, and summarily shot all the men between the ages of 14 and 50. Their thumbs were tied behind their backs, and they were shot in rows behind the village churches. The *Mantanza*'s historian, Thomas Anderson, wrote: 'The extermination was so great that they could not be buried fast enough, and a great stench of rotting flesh permeated the air of western El Salvador.'

A series of military governments ruled the country until the 1980s. There was a certain amount of industrial development in the post-war years but the number of landless peasants increased rapidly. Many of them became economic refugees: in 1965, there were 350,000 Salvadorans living in Honduras.

THE SOCCER WAR

In the late 1960s, Honduras, El Salvador's much larger neighbour to the north and east, went through a period of labour unrest and challenge to the military government. The latter blamed the situation on the illegal Salvadoran immigrants, and in January 1969, Honduras refused to renew the 1967 Bilateral Treaty on Immigration, which was meant to regulate the movement of populations between the two countries. In April, various legal measures were taken against immigrants, and Salvadorans started to return home in large numbers.

As tensions between the two countries increased, their national soccer teams were facing each other in qualifying matches for the following year's World Cup. When the two teams first met in Tegucigalpa, the Honduran capital, there were some disturbances, but at the next match in San Salvador, there were violent anti-Honduran demonstrations: its flag was insulted, and its fans were beaten up. Revenge was taken on Salvadorans in Honduras, and several people were killed; tens of thousands of Salvadorans fled the country. On 27 June, Honduras broke diplomatic relations.

El Salvador moved its troops to the border, the war of words escalated and both nations ignored calls for restraint by the Organization of American States (OAS) and the Central American Mediation Commission. On 14 July 1969, El Salvador's air force attacked Honduran bases, and the army began a general offensive against Honduras. The Salvadoran navy then attacked Honduran islands in the Gulf of Fonseca off its south coast. To begin with, the Salvadorans appeared to be winning, but then the Honduran air force, which was considerably stronger, defeated the Salvadoran air force and then attacked El Salvador's fuel depots. The offensive ground to a halt 5 miles (8 km) over the border because of lack of fuel.

After four days' fighting, the OAS persuaded the two sides to agree to a *de facto* ceasefire. It was formalized on 18 July, and on 29 July, El Salvador agreed to withdraw from Honduran territory by the beginning of August. In all, about 2000 people were killed, mostly Honduran civilians. The two nations finally signed a peace treaty in 1981, and agreed to set up a boundary commission to demarcate disputed areas by 1985 (a provision that was never carried out). Although El Salvador had won the Soccer War on the ground, it had also suffered a major economic defeat: between 60,000 and 130,000 expatriates returned, and the possibility of further emigration to ease the population pressure in El Salvador was ended.

THE CONFLICT

During the 1970s, various popular movements got under way, and opposition political parties developed. The first violent clash in what later developed into a civil war was provoked by a beauty pageant in 1975: students and leftists staged a protest against the government for spending $1.5 million on the Miss Universe pageant in San Salvador: the National Guard fired on student demonstrators: scores were killed; 24 'disappeared', the first of many. Shortly afterwards, the first army and police death squads began operating.

In October 1979, General Carlos Humberto Romero, the current military dictator, was overthrown in a coup by a group of younger, reformist officers. They set up a junta with civilian as well as military members (Guillermo Ungo of the MNR was briefly a member, as were Héctor Dada and Rubén Zamora of the MPSC), and promised reforms, democracy and an end to the killings. They failed on all three counts. The senior officers, while not regretting Romero's departure, and accepting the need to refurbish the country's image, had no intention of loosening the reins of power.

For the next few years, the composition of the junta changed repeatedly as various factions struggled for power; in general, each change brought a more conservative group to the top. The United States actively supported the regime, as an improvement on the previous dictatorship, and urged reforms and new elections. The Christian Democratic party, the country's main centrist party, was split over the issue of whether it should join the junta. Its leader, José Napoleón Duarte, joined on 3 March 1980, and became acting president. Three weeks later, on 24 March, the Archbishop of San Salvador, Oscar Romero was shot by a sniper while saying mass: he had often been threatened for denouncing military repression, and for asking President Carter to suspend military aid to the Salvadoran armed forces.

THE DEATH SQUADS

These first appeared in 1975, following the Miss Universe pageant demonstrations. They had developed out of the National Democratic Organization (ORDEN), formed by the military in 1968, which had up to 50,000 members and operated as a civil defence militia in the countryside. The death squads gave themselves picturesque names: The White Warriors Union, The White Hand, The Falange, The Secret Anti-Communist Army (ESA) and The Maximiliano Hernández Martínez Brigade, named after the general who had perpetrated the *Matanza* in 1932.

Members of the death squads belonged to the army, the national guard and the various police forces. Most feared were the Treasury Police: they were well-organized, with bank balances, salaries and bonuses for good work, all financed by members of the oligarchy. In 1980–2, death squads were responsible for up to 800 deaths a month, perhaps 20,000 people in all. About 8000 trade union organizers and members were murdered or wounded during this period. The death squads' most prominent victim was Archbishop Romero.

In August 1988, the *Washington Post* published a series of articles on the origins of the death squads, based on interviews with two well-placed former members. According to them, one of the first squads was formed by a dentist called Antonio Regalado, who recruited a group of ten teenagers, ostensibly as a Boy Scout troop, and trained them in murder. In May 1980, Regalado and a number of military officers, most notably Major Roberto d'Aubuisson, plotted a coup against the reformist military junta then governing the country. The plot was discovered, and Regalado fled the country. Fearing that his 'boy scouts' might betray him, he had all ten killed by the army.

The country was now spiralling rapidly downwards into chaos. A common front of opposition parties, religious groups and unions was formed – the Democratic Revolutionary Front (FDR) – and the death squads began to slaughter its members and leaders. Others, too, came within their sights: on 2 December 1980, security forces killed four American churchwomen who had been working in El Salvador; and on 3 January 1981, the head of the Salvadoran land reform office and two American officials who had been advising El Salvador on land reform were shot as they took breakfast together in the Sheraton Hotel in San Salvador. The Carter administration, in one of its last acts, suspended all aid to El Salvador. However, when the Reagan administration took over the following month, it resumed aid and tried to persuade the junta that the death squads must be stopped, the government reformed and elections held.

There were elections in March 1982, which were won by Arena whose leader, Roberto d'Aubuisson, believed to be one of the patrons of the death squads, was implicated in both the murder of the archbishop and the Sheraton killings. He had campaigned on a promise to end land reform and crush the opposition: there was a strong element of anti-Americanism in his platform.

D'Aubuisson became president of the National Assembly, but under strong pressure from the Americans, Alvaro Magaña – a conservative civilian and a member of the old coffee-plantation oligarchy – was made provisional president. Duarte left the government. The old regime had by now completely recovered the positions that it had lost in 1979.

The United States did not despair. It continued to support moderate elements within the military as well as centrist politicians. These policies paid off in 1984 when El Salvador enjoyed its first democratic presidential election, and Duarte won by a large majority.

Duarte, who had studied in the United States and spoke English well, proved a genius at public relations. He had been cheated of victory in a presidential election ten years earlier, had been arrested, tortured and sent into exile by the Romero dictatorship. He now went to Washington to present his case as leader of the democratic centre in El Salvador. For the first time in its history, the United   **419**

States devoted sustained, intelligent attention to the problems of Central America. Duarte was embraced by all parties in Washington with more fervour than any other foreign leader since Anwar Sadat. The Americans gave Duarte everything he asked for, with one caveat. Congress stipulated that no more than 55 American advisers should be attached to the Salvadoran military, and they should not take part in any counter-insurgency operation themselves. In other words, there were to be no more Vietnams.

El Salvador's, and Duarte's, tragedy was that his political base was not strong enough, even with unstinting American support, to break the power of the oligarchy and the most conservative elements in the military, or to win over the rebels. Land reform was thwarted, popular organizations were constantly harassed, measures that might have weaned the peasants away from the promises of the guerrillas were blocked.

The only perceptible improvement during Duarte's term of office, at least until the summer of 1988, was that the death squads suspended their work. The war, however, continued.

THE WAR

In January 1981, the guerrillas launched a general offensive, hoping to repeat the Sandinistas' triumph in Nicaragua two years earlier, before Ronald Reagan took office. It was a complete failure. In the aftermath of their victory, the armed forces launched the death squads into a paroxysm of murder and wiped out the leftists, students and labour leaders who might have provided the basis for a new guerrilla campaign – or for a democratic left-of-centre opposition.

The FMLN retreated to the countryside and concentrated on building up its strength among the peasants, particularly in the border provinces. These areas remain their base of operations today. American observers have reached the depressing conclusion that the great majority of guerrillas joined the FMLN during this period, after the overthrow of the Romero dictatorship and during the country's evolution towards a democratic government – that, in fact, the upsurge in guerrilla support was a direct consequence of d'Aubuisson's death squads. In 1983, the guerrillas tried a second general offensive, and were once again defeated. By that time, American advisers had managed to improve the army's level of confidence somewhat, and had succeeded in dissuading the military from massacring peasants.

Since 1980, the Salvadoran army has increased from 12,000 men to 54,000, paid for by the US and trained by American advisers or by Salvadorans who have themselves been trained in the US. There are now thought to be between 4000 and 6000 guerrillas and, of course, far larger numbers of sympathizers. In 1988, the army reported that it was losing about 3000 soldiers dead or wounded a year, and claimed that the rebels were losing 1000 annually.

These are not large numbers, and if that were the whole story, the war might continue indefinitely, with the guerrillas controlling villages in the remoter provinces and the army mounting seasonal offensives against them. However, the rebels have, on occasion, succeeded in bringing the war closer to home. On 31 March 1987, they attacked the headquarters of the 4th Infantry Brigade in a barracks at El Paraiso, 36 miles (58 km) north of San Salvador. It was strikingly successful, especially as the barracks had been designed by officers of the American special forces to be impregnable. The rebels killed 70–80 troops, including an American adviser (Staff Sergeant Gregory Fromius of the Special Forces), losing 11 men themselves. The barracks, including its intelligence centre, was largely destroyed.

More recently, the rebels have concentrated on economic targets, particularly the country's electricity grid (the Shining Path in Peru follows the same tactics). They claim that, since most of the peasantry and urban poor have no electricity, disrupting the electrical grid inconveniences the class enemy alone. They offered the same specious defence for their attacks on coffee plantations.

The United States aid mission to El Salvador calculated in the summer of 1988 that the war, and attacks on the economy by guerrillas, had cost almost $2 billion since 1980. In the same period, the US has provided some $3 billion in aid, but most of it has been either direct military assistance, or has been used for military purposes. Therefore, the war has had a devastating effect on the country's economy. In May 1988, a congressional report in Washington stated that the average Salvadoran income was then 38 per cent lower than in 1980. The report continued: 'El Salvador is approaching the record for dependence on US aid held by South Vietnam at the height of the Vietnam war.' It claimed that 64 per cent of American aid (nearly $2 billion) had gone to fighting the war, rather than to the things, listed in the Kissinger report, that were needed to build a sound economy.

The rebels have been less successful politically. On May Day, 1986, unions sympathetic to the rebels rallied 40,000 people in a march through San Salvador. Encouraged by this success, the rebels stepped up a campaign to bring the country to a halt by shooting up buses and private cars. In the congressional elections of March 1988, the rebels made every effort to prevent people going to the polls: they threatened to kill candidates, polling station officials – even ordinary voters – *pour encourager les autres*. They carried out their threats by attacking a number of polling stations, and, afterwards, by assassinating a number of successful candidates, including several mayors; other mayors were forced to resign.

Despite the threats and murders, the rebels' campaign was a notable failure. Salvadorans voted in record numbers, and a majority turned to the far-right Arena party, in clear repudiation of the left. It was also a repudiation of President Duarte and the Christian Democrats, who had failed to stop the war or revive the economy. Duarte's son was soundly defeated in his bid to be mayor of San Salvador, a post that the party had held since 1964 when the elder Duarte had won it.

Undaunted, the guerrillas tried to repeat their previous May Day success and summoned the faithful to a mass demonstration. A mere 3000 demonstrators turned out, and when some of them started burning cars and building barricades, they were repudiated by the very union leaders whom the rebels had most confidently counted on. In the next few days, in a series of engagements, 29 rebels, 18 soldiers and 12 civilians were killed, by the army's count. The rebels claimed to have killed 228 soldiers, including 100 in an attack on a hydroelectric station. The attack was counted a success: electricity had to be cut off in San Salvador for four hours every day to conserve supplies.

Despite this military achievement, it appeared that the FMLN had lost a good part of its popular support, at least in San Salvador. The rebels were now faced with the task of rebuilding their support in the cities, almost from scratch. Their best hope would be that the new Arena government would revive the death squads and its former policy of generalized massacre, thus losing American support and driving the Salvadoran peasantry and lower classes back into the arms of the FMLN.

There can be no doubt that the guerrilla armies have been supplied by Nicaragua and Cuba and, indirectly, by the Soviet Union. The USSR is thus able, with a small investment, to oblige the United States to lavish enormous sums to prop up the Salvadoran government: the reverse of the Soviets' situation in Angola and Afghanistan. The rebels' arms are smuggled into El Salvador through Honduras, or by sea. It is a small-scale Vietnam: the mountains and forests provide ideal cover for the smugglers. The Central American peace plan, prepared by the Costa Rican president Oscar Arias Sánchez and announced in August 1987, provided that each of the republics should stop helping rebels operating against neighbouring governments. Were it implemented, it would be a severe setback for the FMLN, but not fatal: the guerrillas already manufacture their own landmines and explosives, and can count on a steady supply of weapons captured from the army.

The new, American-trained and much larger Salvadoran army is less brutal than its predecessor in the early days of the war, but there are still frequent incidents of murder and torture. One case caught the attention of the American press in February 1988. Two young peasants, Félix Rivera, aged 25, and Mario Rivera, aged 16, were seized by troops in a village in north-eastern El Salvador, forced to run barefoot through a field of burning crops, and then tortured – their noses, ears and fingers were cut off – before they were killed. Observers feared that such incidents were a sign that the mass terror of the early 1980s was returning. The statistics seemed to indicate this: in 1987, there were 24 death squad murders; in 1988, the rate rose sharply.

Peasants were not the only victims. On the morning of 11 May 1988, Judge Jorge Serrano Panameño was shot outside his house after he returned from taking his four children to school. He had been about to rule on the question of whether two groups of terrorists, one Communist and one closely linked to Roberto d'Aubuisson, were eligible for amnesty under the Central American peace plan.

He had ruled that the Central American Revolutionary Workers' Party – who were accused of murdering 12 people (including four US Marines) at an outdoor café in San Salvador on 19 June 1985 – were covered by the amnesty because their crime was 'political'. (President Duarte, under strong American pressure, refused to release them.) The ruling on the other group involved one of the few cases in which large numbers of death squad members were charged. They had belonged to a kidnapping ring run by military officers who were also directors of the death squads. In 1982–5, they had kidnapped five wealthy Salvadorans and obtained $4 million in ransom. Nine men were charged. Three, including a colonel and a cashiered lieutenant, fled the country. Three others were murdered in police custody, apparently to stop them confessing. Three others were sent to jail to await Judge Serrano's verdict. One of this trio, another cashiered lieutenant and protégé of d'Aubuisson's was also accused of ordering the killings of the two American land reform advisers in the Sheraton hotel in 1981. The case had been broken with the assistance of the FBI and the Venezuelan police.

Judge Serrano was due to rule that week whether the three in jail were eligible under the amnesty. Presumably the death squad concluded that the judge would rule against amnesty, and intended to terrorize the entire Salvadoran judiciary. This ploy had worked before: just after Christmas 1987, three other men accused in the Sheraton case had been released under the amnesty, despite American protests.

AFTER DUARTE

During his five years in office, Duarte managed a degree of reform in banking, commercial practice, taxation and land tenure. He did not, however, manage to strip the oligarchy of its power nor end its control of the economy. At the time of the 1979 coup, 95 per cent of Salvadoran farmers who owned their land farmed plots too small to support their families. At the same time, the '14 families' still owned enormous estates. By the end of Duarte's term of office, the situation had not substantially changed, but the oligarchy still detested him and retained the power to defy him. At the other extreme, the sharp economic decline caused by the war (and also by falling international coffee prices) lost Duarte popularity in the country at large. And, worst of all, he failed to stop the war.

Duarte took office promising negotiations with the rebels. He declared a ceasefire and met the rebel leadership, who presented a joint delegation of the Communist FMLN and the non-Communist FDR. He insisted that the rebels surrender and re-enter the democratic process. They refused, but in 1987, the more moderate of the FDR's political leaders, Ungo and Zamora, returned from seven years' exile and prepared to contest the 1989 elections.

On 10 September 1985, Duarte's daughter, Ines, was kidnapped. After prolonged negotiations, she was released on 24 October, together with a woman friend who had been kidnapped at the same time, 23 mayors and a number of other government officials who had all been prisoners of the FMLN. In exchange, the government released 22 of its own prisoners, including the second-in-command of the Communist party and Nidia Díaz, leader of the Central American Revolutionary Workers' Party. In addition, 101 wounded rebels were allowed to leave the country for medical treatment. This episode did much to undermine the confidence of the army and Salvadoran conservatives in Duarte.

The failure of the Duarte government casts a long shadow over the future of El Salvador. In the legislative elections of 20 March 1988, Arena won a majority of the votes. It won 31 of the 60 seats in the National Assembly, and the Christian Democrats won 22. The National Conciliation Party won seven seats, but as they were allied to Arena, D'Aubuisson and his henchmen had total control of the Assembly.

In June 1988, Duarte, then aged 62, was diagnosed as having stomach cancer. Surgeons in Washington removed two-thirds of his stomach, and on 11 July he returned home to die, although he hoped to survive long enough to hand over to his successor on 1 June 1989. The Christian Democrats were badly split. After an acrimonious dispute, they chose Fidel Chavez Mena, who controlled most of the party machine, as their presidential candidate.

423

The military situation continued to deteriorate throughout 1988, with rebels attacking army posts near San Salvador and in the capital itself, and mounting a campaign of assassination of elected officials in provincial towns. On 1 November, a new army commander was appointed: Colonel René Emílio Ponce, described by one of the American advisers as 'by far and away their last, best hope'. He took over an army that had increased from 12,000 to 54,000 men in the previous six years, had been equipped and trained by Americans and was supposedly far better prepared to fight the rebels. The same adviser said of Ponce: 'If he can't get the army moving again, it might as well get off the playing field.' Ponce, who was then 41, was a leading member of the 1966 graduating class of the Salvadoran military academy: he and his comrades of that class now control virtually the entire military establishment in El Salvador. They are all inclined to push the politicians out of the way in order to get on with the war.

There were some encouraging developments in 1988: the ending of the Contra war in Nicaragua, coupled with Soviet efforts to improve relations with the United States. The left was in retreat internationally, and the guerrillas' support from abroad was weakening. The Salvadoran army might not defeat the rebels, but their own isolation might, in the end, have the same effect.

The future government may be a choice between the FDR and Arena. Many Americans will judge them on a strictly ideological basis. For example, Jeane Kirkpatrick, former American ambassador to the UN, wrote in June 1988, that

Arena is a legitimate political party that espouses market approaches, private ownership, personal initiative and deregulation – the sorts of things Margaret Thatcher and Ronald Reagan have built their careers on. But Arena's international image suffers from the reputation of its last presidential candidate, Roberto d'Aubuisson, whom rumor has long linked to the infamous death squads. Arena's new leader, Alfredo Cristiani, is a prominent civic and business leader of excellent reputation.

D'Aubuisson may have handed over the titular leadership of the party to Cristiani, a coffee producer, but there can be no doubt who really controls Arena.

Cristiani duly won the election, by a large majority, and Duarte formally handed over power in June 1989. The Americans' search for a valid centrist government in El Salvador had failed but they could at least take some consolation from the unusual sight of one democratically elected president handing over to another. For the moment, the Christian Democrats and the FDR together were in total eclipse, and Arena was left to face the guerrillas and the country's intractable economic problems. Duarte had been defeated. Now it was Arena's turn.

FURTHER READING

Baloyra, Enrique, *El Salvador in Transition*, Chapel Hill, University of North Carolina Press, 1982.

Barry, Tom and Preusch, Deb (eds), *The Central American Fact Book*, New York, Grove Press, 1986.

Bonner, Raymond, *Weakness and Deceit: US Policy in El Salvador*, New York, Times Books, 1984.

Duarte, José Napoleón, *My Story*, New York, Putnam's, 1986.
Montgomery, Tommie Sue, *Revolution in El Salvador, Origins and Evolution*, Boulder, Colo., Westview Press, 1986.
Report of the National Bipartisan Commission on Central America, 1984 (Kissinger Report).
Russell, Philip L., *El Salvador in Crisis*, Austin, Texas, Colorado River Press, 1984.

GUATEMALA

Geography	42,042 sq. miles (108,888 sq. km). The size of East Germany.
Population	8.2 million. Half are *ladino* (of Spanish and mixed descent); half are Indian, descendants of the ancient Maya, speaking 22 different languages.
GNP per capita	$930
Refugees	External: 45,500* in Mexico, 380 in Honduras, 400 in Nicaragua, 1200 in Belize. Internal: 500,000 Guatemalans, 1600 from Nicaragua, 500 from El Salvador.
Casualties	About 100,000 people have been killed since 1961, the great majority of them civilians.

If it is necessary to turn the country into a cemetery in order to pacify it, I will not hesitate to do so.

President Carlos Arana Osorio, 1970

We are killing people, we are slaughtering women and children. The problem is, everyone is a guerrilla there.

President Efraín Ríos Montt, 1982

HISTORY

Like the rest of Central America, Guatemala won its independence from Spain in 1821. The landowning oligarchy that had governed the colony under the remote direction of Madrid continued to rule the republic. The governing classes and those living in the cities spoke Spanish, and the mass of the peasants, treated as slaves or serfs since the Spanish conquest, subsisted in the countryside with their own languages and customs.

The United Fruit Company was formed on 30 March 1899. It was a merger of the Boston Fruit Company, which exported bananas from the Caribbean to Boston, and a Central American railway company founded by the Brooklyn entrepreneur Minor Keith, whose interests extended from Costa Rica to Guatemala and who had won the confidence of all the Central American dictators. In 1904, he persuaded the dictator of Guatemala, Manuel Estrada Cabrera, to give United Fruit a 99-year lease on the country's main railway, linking the capital Guatemala City to its only port on the Caribbean, Puerto Barrios. With its transport assured, the company soon took ownership of several hundred thousand acres of banana plantations. In 1936, another dictator, General Jorge Ubico, gave it a 99-year lease on another enormous plantation on the Pacific coast, and reaffirmed its other privileges: it paid few or no Guatemalan taxes, was allowed to import everything it needed without paying duty and paid its labourers 50 cents a day.

425

The United States had no interest in the internal politics of Guatemala, as long as the country was peaceful and American business (meaning United Fruit) was allowed to operate unimpeded. A long succession of dictators were left to their own devices, until World War II. Then General Ubico's political sympathies with Mussolini and Hitler proved an embarrassment. In July 1944, the rising urban middle classes, notably the teachers, took to the streets in protest against Ubico's policies and forced his resignation. He appointed another general, Federico Ponce, to succeed him, but in October, a coup led by two junior officers – Major Francisco Arana and Captain Jacobo Arbenz Guzmán – forced Ponce to resign. About 100 people were killed in the coup. Arana and Arbenz called Guatemala's first free election, which was won with a majority of 85 per cent by the prominent writer and teacher Dr Juan José Arévalo Bermejo, who had lived in exile in Mexico for 14 years. His supporters had to send him the fare before he could return.

Arévalo set about modernizing Guatemala, with policies that were modelled on the New Deal. He introduced a social security programme on the American model, and gave women equal rights for the first time in Guatemalan history. His most radical enactment was a labour reform based on the Wagner Act, the charter of American trade unionism. His policies were strenuously opposed by United Fruit – and by a succession of prominent American liberals. The New Deal Democrats Claude Pepper of Florida, Mike Mansfield of Montana and John McCormack of Massachusetts (later speaker of the House of Representatives), as well as Senator Alexander Wiley of Michigan, a moderate Republican, all denounced Arévalo for proposing policies that were, in fact, based on American legislation. It was a striking example of American ignorance and venality.

Despite this opposition, Arévalo made some progress in social reform. In 1950, abiding by the new constitution, which provided for single-term, six-year presidencies, he stepped down and was succeeded by Jacobo Arbenz Guzmán. The other author of the 1944 coup, Arana, had emerged as the leader of the conservative faction in the armed forces. He was assassinated in July 1949, possibly with Arbenz's connivance.

The new president launched a programme of agrarian reform that United Fruit considered a frontal assault on its position in Guatemala. That position was impressive. The company had investments worth $60 million, including 550,000 acres of land. It employed 40,000 people, owned the country's telephone and telegraph companies and its only port on the Atlantic, as well as 887 miles of railway – almost the entire network. It paid minimal taxes, and its return on investment was 62 cents to every dollar. Between 1942 and 1952, the value of its assets increased by 133.8 per cent.

The company had permitted some social progress since its early days. Workers were provided with housing, medical services and schools. However, unions were banned, and United Fruit – known locally as *la frutera* – fought a bitter strike in the late 1940s over the workers' demand for a basic wage of $1.50 a day. A former United Fruit official, writing his memoirs in the 1970s, commented:

Guatemala was chosen as the site for the company's earliest development activities at the turn of the century because a good portion of the country contained prime banana land and because, at the time we entered Central America, Guatemala's government was the region's weakest, most corrupt and most pliable. In short, the country offered an 'ideal investment climate', and United Fruit's profits there flourished for 50 years. Then something went wrong: a man named Jacobo Arbenz became president.

In March 1953, the Arbenz government proposed its land reform. No cultivated land was touched, but uncultivated land was to be expropriated and divided among the peasants. United Fruit was the prime victim: 83 per cent of its enormous holdings were uncultivated (it claimed that it needed the land as a 'reserve'). In a first measure, it was to lose 210,000 acres (85,000 ha), and subsequently the total was raised to 387,000 acres (156,500 ha). The government proposed to pay the company $2.99 an acre, in government bonds.

The company had paid about $1.50 an acre for the land in the 1930s, and for tax purposes had declared that its value had remained the same. Now that it faced expropriation, it claimed that the land was worth $75 an acre, and an official protest, containing a demand for the larger sum, was presented to the government by the American ambassador.

THE 1954 COUP

The 1954 coup is the key event in modern Guatemalan history, and has continued to play a large role in Latin American perceptions of the United States. The coup was mounted by the CIA at the behest of United Fruit and followed close on the heels of an equally successful operation mounted against the Mossadegh government in Iran at the behest of the international oil companies. Many observers since then, including principals in the two operations, have remarked that, however successful in the short term, the long-term consequences of the coups were disastrous for the countries concerned, for the United States – and also for the CIA.

Following the coups, the agency came to believe that it had a gift for cloak-and-dagger operations, and tried to repeat its successes in Indonesia and Cuba (and, years later, in Nicaragua). American unpopularity in the Third World owes a lot to the CIA. Guatemala was destroyed by the 1954 coup, in a long agonizing sequel that is not yet ended – and when the Iranian students stormed the US embassy in Tehran in 1979, they claimed that they were avenging Mossadegh.

These were the days of the Truman administration, and United Fruit knew it had to rent a few liberals in its campaign to overthrow a democratic regime in Guatemala and replace it with a Fascist dictatorship. To this end, the company recruited the best-known public relations man in the US, Edward Bernays, and Washington's leading lobbyist, Tommy Corcoran, to defend its interests. Corcoran enlisted the assistance of former Senator Robert La Follette of Wisconsin, who had been defeated by Joe McCarthy and was the very paradigm of the American liberal. La Follette and Mansfield, Pepper and McCormack, Bernays and Corcoran were all noted Democrats who had made their names defending trade unions and other worthy causes.

Republicans were involved, too. Senator Henry Cabot Lodge, of Massachusetts, who owned a large quantity of shares in United Fruit, denounced the Guatemalan government as anti-American and probably Communist; later, after the 1954 coup

427

and by then ambassador to the UN, he defended the US action to the Security Council. When Eisenhower won the 1952 election, United Fruit added John Clements to its pack of lobbyists. He was an associate of Senator McCarthy and a leader in that demagogue's anti-Communist crusade.

Bernays knew the power of the press. He invited a succession of reporters down to Guatemala to observe the paternalistic and public-spirited way in which United Fruit conducted its business, and to prove that the company's opponents were all Communists. A long succession of American newspapers and journals – led by the *New York Times*, the *Christian Science Monitor*, *Time*, *Newsweek* and *US News & World Report* – fell for the Bernays touch and repeatedly assured their readers that the Red Menace had reached Central America. In due course, they all welcomed the coup.

Guatemala never stood a chance. If one of the tragedies of Central America has been American ignorance (United Fruit ensured that it was the principal source of information on Guatemala so, of course, La Follette, Lodge, McCormack and the rest were anti-Arbenz), the problem was compounded by Central American provincialism. Democratic politicians there spoke no English, knew nothing of the United States and made no effort to learn, preferring to stay at home and denounce the Yankees from a distance. Their efforts at influencing American opinion were pathetic. All that the Guatemalan ambassador to Washington could do was complain to the US State Department about the anti-Guatemalan bias in American papers. Thirty years later, El Salvador's president, José Napoleon Duarte showed how it should be done: he spoke fluent English, and visited Washington frequently to assure Americans of his sincere democratic principles (*see* El Salvador, pp. 414–25).

The United Fruit Company also approached the CIA. Its director was Bedell Smith, who confided that his ambition was to become president of United Fruit (in due course, after he left the government, he was made a director). The deputy director was Allan Dulles, former member of United Fruit's law firm, Sullivan & Cromwell, which was also the company's chief adviser on foreign affairs. The law firm's senior partner was John Foster Dulles, the CIA deputy director's brother.

The CIA quite understood United Fruit's position, and set about preparing a coup to overthrow the Guatemalan government, giving the plan the codename 'Operation Fortune'. The preparations came to the attention of the secretary of state, Dean Acheson, who promptly stopped them. However, his days were numbered. Eisenhower won the 1952 election, Allan Dulles became director of the CIA, John Foster Dulles became secretary of state, and Bedell Smith moved over to the State Department as his deputy. A new plan, 'Operation Success', was set in motion and approved by the new administration in August 1953.

United Fruit recruited a disaffected Guatemalan colonel, Carlos Castillo Armas. He was living in exile in Nicaragua, under the patronage of President Anastasio Somoza, and immediately agreed to lead the revolution. The plot was not a secret: the CIA was openly recruiting mercenaries to take part in its proposed invasion.

Arbenz prepared to defend himself. However, the Truman administration

had imposed an arms embargo on Guatemala in 1948 because of its supposed leftist leanings (another example of Washington's incorrigible myopia towards Central America). The rest of the world had always accepted that the region was within the United States sphere of influence, and had not sought to replace the US as a supplier of arms. It was a serious difficulty, but in 1954, Arbenz found what he was looking for – in Czechoslovakia. There he bought 2000 tons of arms – rifles, ammunition, anti-tank weapons and light artillery – for $1 million. They were sent through Poland to the Baltic and shipped aboard a Swedish freighter, the *Alfhem*. It reached Puerto Barrios on 15 May, and the arms were taken by rail to Guatemala City.

The CIA plotted the progress of the consignment every step of the way. On 19 May, President Eisenhower asserted that the delivery meant the establishment of 'a Communist dictatorship on this continent'. Meanwhile, Arbenz's military were examining their precious cargo: the anti-tank weapons were superfluous (there were no tanks in Central America); many of the rifles were defective; and the artillery – German war booty – was far too heavy for Guatemala's roads. The Czech arms were of absolutely no help to Arbenz when, on 18 June, Castillo Armas sent his small army across the border to occupy a village on the other side. He had been equipped by Sam Cummings, just starting on a spectacular career as an arms dealer, and had everything he needed.

He also had an air force, supplied by the CIA: three World War II P-47 fighters, which scattered pamphlets over Guatemala City, dropped a few bombs and straffed an army base. One of the aircraft crashed in Mexico, and was found to have a two-man American crew of dubious antecedents. They were CIA men.

The Arbenz government collapsed. The president had lost his nerve, and very few Guatemalans had been ready to fight for him. An Argentinian visitor, Ernesto 'Che' Guevara, had been ready to try, but when Castillo Armas was flown into Guatemala City (on another American plane), Guevara took refuge in a friendly embassy. In due course, he was evacuated to Mexico, where he met Fidel Castro.

By the time Castillo Armas arrived, Arbenz had already given up. He was given asylum in the Mexican embassy and was in due course allowed to go into exile. That was the end of Guatemala's ten years of democratic government. Only one man had been killed in the coup. Sam Cummings bought up the Czech arms, and then won a contract to re-equip the Guatemalan army. It was a highly profitable deal.

THE NEW DICTATORSHIP

United Fruit had won in Guatemala. Then it lost in Washington. The Justice Department started an anti-trust suit against the company, alleging that it monopolized banana production in Guatemala, and the company eventually decided to sell out. The Del Monte Corporation, which did not comport itself with the same flamboyant arrogance as United Fruit, bought most of its holdings.

Castillo Armas set about dismantling all the reforms of the previous decade, including the first steps towards industrialization. Within 18 months, he had driven virtually all the peasants who had obtained land through the Arbenz reforms off the land again. The United States gave large sums in aid, soon amounting to $45 million a year. A great deal of it was embezzled, a great deal wasted, and none of it was used to relieve the peasants of their poverty, though they comprised the great majority of the population. The most useful American contribution was money for roads and the electricity grid.

Castillo Armas was assassinated in July 1957, in the presidential palace. His assailant was found dead nearby, apparently a suicide. (When Benigno Aquino was murdered in Manila in 1983, his 'assassin' was also, most conveniently, found dead on the spot.) The true murderers were never discovered. A junta was hastily formed, which called elections, and to the junta's astonishment, they were won by General Miguel Ydígoras Fuentes, a conservative politician who had lost to Arbenz in the 1950 election, and who had declined a CIA invitation to serve as figurehead for the 1954 coup. The junta tried to annul the result, but were persuaded to call a further presidential election, in January 1958, which Ydígoras once again won. This time he was allowed to take office.

He was supported by the United States because he allowed Guatemala to be used as a base for the attempted invasion of Cuba. When a revolt broke out in some army units on 13 November 1960, the United States provided B-26 bombers, with exiled Cuban pilots, to bomb the rebel bases. The revolt was crushed, but two young lieutenants, Marco Aurelio Yon Sosa and Luis Turcios Lima, were so disgusted by the episode that they started a guerrilla movement of their own. It was the beginning of a long war that, so far, has cost 100,000 lives and shows no sign of ending.

The two rebels joined forces with the illegal Guatemalan Communist party (PGT). In February 1962, they proclaimed a general rebellion against the military regime, calling themselves the Alejandro de Leon November 13 Guerrilla Movement, after a fallen comrade and the date of the abortive army uprising in 1960. They sallied forth from the hills and attacked army posts, and met with inglorious defeat.

Meanwhile, a second revolutionary group – named the October 20 Front after the revolution of 1944, and led by Arbenz's minister of defence, Carlos Paz Tejada – had also issued a call to arms. In March 1962, there were student riots in Guatemala City, costing 20 lives. These various disturbances sufficiently worried the Kennedy administration to set up a counter-insurgency school in Guatemala, staffed by Green Berets. The Americans also approved a 'pacification' programme and supplied the Guatemalan armed forces with aircraft and weapons.

By the summer of 1962, Ydígoras had crushed the students and the guerrillas. The remnants of the various rebel groups formed a new movement: the Rebel Armed Forces (FAR). It was never very successful, but kept up a small-scale insurgency in the hills for the next few years, hoping to repeat Fidel Castro's success in Cuba. However, it never comprised more than 500 guerrillas, and its actions provoked terrible reprisals by the army. By the end of the decade, it had been completely crushed.

Ydígoras had become deeply unpopular, and the Americans feared that he lacked the stamina to fight the Communists. In the summer of 1963, former president Juan José Arévalo Bermejo reappeared and announced his candidacy in the elections which were then due. The army decided that Ydígoras must go and, after consultation with Washington, arranged a coup on 29 March. Ydígoras was replaced by the minister of defence, Enrique Peralta Azurdia.

Apologists for John F. Kennedy deny that the president approved the coup. They also deny that he approved the coup that took place in Saigon the following November. It remains one of the ironies of the times that an ostensibly idealistic administration in Washington, which was intent on establishing democracy, weeding out corruption, promoting land reform and carrying out other admirable objectives in Indochina, should also have promoted military dictatorships in Central America. American Democrats who have accused the Reagan administration of a fondness for authoritarian regimes should remember that their own party was wholly committed to the Fascists 25 years ago.

Guatemala's descent into the pit continued under Peralta Azurdia. His troops pursued the remaining rebels with unremitting zeal. They raided a secret meeting of the Communist party, capturing 28 leaders, who were all murdered (a former Guatemalan congressman was reportedly pushed out of a military aircraft 20,000 feet over the Pacific).

Elections were held in 1966. Anti-militarist factions united behind centrist politician Mario Méndez Montenegro, but he was killed in another of those mysterious murders that had become Guatemala's speciality. Méndez's brother, Julio César, ran in his place, and was elected. The army tried to annul the election, but backed down under American pressure. Méndez was allowed to take office, but not power: he was a complete figurehead.

Command of the counter-insurgency forces was assumed by Colonel Carlos Arana Osorio. American Green Berets were brought in to train his troops and over 30,000 Guatemalan police also received American training; the Johnson administration provided $6 million in military aid and $11 million worth of equipment. Arana then launched a war of unrestricted terrorism on the Indian peasantry. Amnesty International believes that, in the following decade, at least 30,000 people were 'abducted, tortured and assassinated'. American planes, from bases outside the country, were used to drop napalm on suspected rebel bases.

By this time, death squads were operating at every level of Guatemalan life. The regime was not merely fighting peasant guerrillas in the countryside. It believed that its enemies also included union officials, peasant organizers, students, professors, teachers, liberal clerics and every shade of centrist or left-of-centre politician. Leftist terrorists, in retaliation, assassinated military figures and American officials, including the head of the US military mission, Colonel Harold Hauser in 1965 and, in 1968, one of his successors Colonel John Webber and the US ambassador John Gordon Mein.

Colonel Arana was so successful in fighting the rebels that the army decided that he should be elected president. He took office in 1970, and extended to the cities the tactics he had first applied to the Indians. In the first three years of his presidency, the number of people who 'disappeared' increased sharply. Estimates of the numbers of bodies found range from 3500 to 15,000. (As if this were not enough, in 1976 an earthquake killed 25,000 people.)

In 1974, a dissident army general, Efraín Ríos Montt, ran for the presidency against the official candidate – and won. The army promptly annulled the election, and sent Ríos Montt into exile in the Madrid embassy.

Despite the continuing oppression, the guerrilla movements increased. Two new rebel groups had emerged by then, both based on the Indians. The first was the 431

Guerrilla Army of the Poor (EGA), a Marxist organization with a picture of Che Guevara as its logo. The second was the Organization of the People in Arms (ORPA). They both operated in the Indian provinces (though ORPA also had a base in Guatemala City, which was discovered by Argentinian counter-insurgency specialists in 1981). The Rebel Armed Forces (FAR) began to revive in the late 1970s, and in 1981, one section split off and called itself the Leadership Nucleus of the PGT (Guatemalan Communist party). All these four movements formed an alliance in 1982: the Guatemalan National Revolutionary Unity (URNG).

Other opposition groups, which were neither Communist nor violent, were also emerging, despite the state terrorism that oppressed them. The Church, which had supported earlier dictatorships, began to defend Indians and workers against tyranny. One Christian group – the Campesino Unity Committee (CUC) – organized the occupation of the Spanish embassy in Guatemala City on 31 January 1980, to draw attention to the peasants' plight. Troops set fire to the building, burning 39 protesters alive. Shortly afterwards, the CUC organized a two-week strike among cane-cutters and cotton workers, and won a $3.25 daily minimum wage.

By this time, the United States had at last become aware of the sorts of governments it was supporting in Central America. President Carter cut off all aid to Guatemala, but the military regime was not deterred. Guerrilla activity continued in the highlands, and General Romeo Lucas García, who was president from 1978 to 1982, started a scorched earth policy to deal with it. American disapproval, and Lucas García's own corruption, led to a coup in 1982 organized by junior officers, in which General Ríos Montt was finally brought to power. He reined in the death squads in the cities, and allowed a greater freedom of political action there, but accelerated the fight in the countryside.

The war on the peasantry reached its paroxysm under Ríos Montt. He announced that his policy was to be 'beans and rifles'. Loyal peasants were fed, disloyal ones were starved: 'If you're with us, we'll feed you,' said the army. 'If not, we'll kill you.' In the most savage phase of the campaign, loyal peasants were also mobilized into local militias under army officers to hunt down supposedly disloyal peasants. The Washington Office on Latin America, an independent human rights group, estimated that it led to the destruction of 440 villages and the killing of between 50,000 and 75,000 peasants. Amnesty International is more cautious, stating that 'untold numbers died during the administrations of General Lucas García and General Ríos Montt. Estimates vary, but all put the victims in the tens of thousands.' The lowest figure offered by the army itself is 10,000 dead. Tens of thousands of refugees fled to Mexico: the Mexicans say 45,000 are there now; other counts put the number as high as 150,000.

By 1985, the local militias numbered over 900,000 Indian boys and men. The system enabled the army to control the countryside completely, for the first time.

The military government's scorched earth policy was literally that. In December 1982, *Newsweek* magazine reported:

In the far west and far north of the country, large stretches of once green farmland lie ash-black and deserted. And along the Mexico border, refugees huddled in crowded, muddy camps tell harrowing stories of army guerrilla-hunters beheading babies, setting fire to sick old men and driving stakes through the bellies of pregnant women.

The Ríos Montt Campaign sharply reduced guerrilla activity, but at an appalling cost. In October 1983, Ríos Montt was removed in a coup by disgruntled army officers. Among other complaints, they objected to the president's evangelism: he had become a tele-evangelist, and preached regularly on television, calling on Guatemalans to come to Jesus and be saved. Conservative Catholic officers, and younger men who had studied in the United States, did not appreciate the call.

The Reagan administration had approved the 1983 coup (though it did not initiate it). The new president, General Oscar Mejía Víctores, introduced a new pacification plan, to be carried out with American help, called the 'Plan of Assistance to the Areas of Conflict' (PAAC). It involved building model villages, offering food for work, promoting literacy and the Spanish language, and improving sanitation – the slogan was now '*Techo, trabajo y tortilla*' (housing, work and food). The new government also introduced sufficient reforms in democratic practice and human rights to justify a resumption of aid from Washington in 1983. The Americans were now actively supporting democratic politics in Central America, as a counter to Communism. The Kissinger report (*see* El Salvador, pp. 414–25), one of the first comprehensive efforts by the leaders of an American administration to understand Central America, spelled out the close connection between social reform and defeating Communism, and Washington now exerted heavy pressure on the Guatemalan military to stop slaughtering the peasants and, instead, to launch an active rural development programme. American aid to Guatemala increased from $20 million in 1984 to over $100 million in 1985, almost all of it for the highlands.

There were fewer death squad murders under Ríos Montt and Mejía Víctores than under their predecessors, but the improvement was entirely relative. The Parliamentary Human Rights Group, in a 1985 report entitled *Bitter and Cruel*, calculated that: 100,000 people had been killed since 1960; there were 100 political assassinations a month and 10 'disappearances' a week in 1984; and there were 100,000 orphans and 500,000 'internal refugees' in Guatemala. An organization called the Mutual Support Group (GAM) was formed by relatives of the 'disappeared' who met in Guatemala City morgues. The GAM calculated that over 3000 people 'disappeared' during Mejía Víctores's first year in office, and that a further 10,000 children were orphaned. Mejía responded by calling the GAM 'a pressure group that is being manipulated for subversion', and two weeks later, two of the group's leaders were found murdered. One of them was its spokesman, Héctor Gomez, whose body, in frightful symbolism, was found with the tongue ripped out. The group's secretary, a woman of 24, who accused the military of the Gomez murder, was killed four days later, with her son and brother, in what the military described as a 'car accident'.

GUATEMALA NOW

The guerrillas had been defeated: the army conceded that there were no more than 1500 of them left, not nearly enough to be a serious threat to the government. But it was clear that they would return unless major reforms were promptly introduced. Elections to a constituent assembly were held in 1984, and late in 1985, Vinicio

Cerezo Arévalo, a Christian Democrat, was elected president. Cerezo was lucky to have himself survived the terror of the 1970s and early 1980s. At one point, he had sent his family to Washington for safety: his teenage son, who was sick at the time, had to be carried to the plane from hospital on a stretcher, with a nurse holding an IV bottle over his head, surrounded by bodyguards with machine-guns.

Cerezo knew the limits of his power. He did not have the same freedom as President Raúl Alfonsín in Argentina, who was able to purge the army of the officers who had led the 'dirty war' there and put them on trial for murder. Cerezo was obliged to promise that 'the past must be forgotten.' In the last days of the military government, President Mejía Víctores proclaimed a comprehensive amnesty for 'all people implicated in political crimes and related common crimes during the period from 23 March 1982 [when Ríos Montt took power] to 14 January 1986.' The amnesty covered the death squads but, of course, not the Communist rebels. The question, which remains open, is whether the army will allow Cerezo to introduce the other essential reforms.

The army still has a free hand in fighting the guerrillas, and continues to pursue its campaign, including bombing suspected guerrilla bases. One clause of the Central American peace plan prepared by President Oscar Arias of Costa Rica and announced in August 1987, provides that each country will proclaim an amnesty for political adversaries and guerrillas. The Guatemalan army issued its own gloss on the agreement, stating that this clause does not apply to Guatemala. The government held talks with representatives of the guerrillas, in Madrid in October 1987, but did not persuade them to surrender. The army would accept nothing less.

The army high command supports Cerezo in his economic policies, and he has made some progress in tax reform, land redistribution and civil rights. There are fewer murders, but the death squads remain immune from prosecution, and a civil rights commission set up by the Guatemalan congress is completely ineffective. Conservative politicians and military men are bitterly opposed to Cerezo's reform measures, and have launched several attempted coups against him, the most serious in May 1988. It was again led by junior officers, and was put down by the minister of defence, General Héctor Gramajo Morales, who arrested the plotters and charged them with mutiny. The government then charged eight civilians with sedition, alleging that they had incited the coup attempt, and closed down a television station that regularly engaged in far-right propaganda, including continual incitement to mutiny. It was only allowed to resume broadcasting when it agreed to drop the offending programmes.

Cerezo is president, but the army is still the real power in Guatemala, as it is in Honduras. Cerezo, because he has been publicly critical of the Reagan administration's campaign against Nicaragua, has been less popular in Washington than the other democratically elected Central American presidents, and only grudgingly supported against his military critics.

In November 1988, America's Watch (a civil rights group based in New York) reported:

In spite of two-and-a-half years of civilian government, Guatemala remains one of the worst human rights violators in the hemisphere. The improvement has reversed itself in the cities. And in the countryside, there is a *de facto* military dictatorship. Nothing has changed.

Other observers were equally pessimistic, contending that Cerezo was powerless to control the death squads and that he remained in office on sufferance. Indeed, the attempted coup in May 1988 demonstrated the limits of his authority. His position therefore remains exceedingly precarious. The Cerezos have kept their house in Washington: they never know when they might need it again.

THE BELIZE DISPUTE

One of the many irredentist disputes in Latin America concerns Guatemala's claim to Belize. That small country – 8867 square miles (22,965 sq. km), the size of Wales – on the Caribbean coast of Central America is a former British colony. Its population of 170,000 is mostly black and speaks English, but there is also a growing number of Spanish-speaking refugees from El Salvador.

In the 18th century, the British in Jamaica began logging hardwood on the mainland. Spain claimed the entire isthmus, but did not exercise any direct role on the Caribbean coast between Mexico and Panama. As for the British, they periodically recognized Spanish sovereignty but continued logging, and by the end of the century, there were permanent British settlements along the coast. By 1840, the territory that later became Belize had been organized as a regular colony, known as British Honduras. Other British settlements further down the coast were abandoned to Honduras and Nicaragua.

Guatemala claimed British Honduras on the grounds that it had inherited the territory from Spain. Mexico also claimed the northern part of the territory. In 1859, however, Guatemala signed a treaty with Britain, recognizing British sovereignty and agreeing on the border. A subordinate clause in the treaty provided that both parties would continue 'conjointly to use their best efforts' to build a road across the jungles from Guatemala to the Caribbean coast in British Honduras. The road was never built, and on that flimsy basis, Guatemala has since claimed that the 1859 treaty is invalid.

The dispute was forgotten until the 1930s, when it was revived by the Fascist regime of General Ubico. The claim was inherited by the Arévalo government, which, despite all its democratic professions, inserted a clause into the 1945 constitution stating that British Honduras was part of Guatemala. Guatemalan democrats and Fascists alike have continued to assert the claim, like the Argentinians' claim to the Falklands.

In the 1960s, as other British colonies in the Caribbean moved towards self-government and independence, Guatemala stepped up its claims to its '23rd department'. In 1963, troops were massed along the British Honduras/Guatemala border, and Britian had to send a small army of its own to deter an invasion. British troops have been there ever since.

In 1965, President Johnson offered his services to resolve the dispute. He appointed a mediator, Bethuel M. Webster, who concluded that British Honduras should be handed over to Guatemala. Guatemala was then the loyal ally of the United States, so the wishes of the inhabitants of British Honduras were not considered. Britain rejected the proposal.

In 1972, Guatemala again massed troops along the border, and this time, the British sent the aircraft carrier *Ark Royal* and several thousand troops to deter an invasion. (British Honduras also provided excellent training facilities for the British army in tropical warfare.) In 1975, after another threat from across the border, the British called on the R A F, and a squadron of Harriers is now based there.

The colony was by then self-governing (and had assumed the name Belize). Entirely ready for independence, its government finally abandoned the cautious diplomacy of the past, and took its case to the United Nations. To begin with, Belize was supported only by Britain and the Commonwealth, but it rapidly won further adherents including the Non-Aligned Group (Third World members of the UN). The United States, however, continued to support Guatemala by abstaining whenever there was a vote at the UN: there were limits to President Carter's commitment to democracy. Finally, in 1980, the UN voted for Belizean independence: 139 to 0, with 7 abstentions, Guatemala refusing to vote. On that occasion, the US voted for Belize, which at last became independent in 1981.

Guatemala grudgingly agreed to recognize Belize, but only in exchange for its agreement to build the famous road. Even that concession was too much for the Belizeans: there were riots, in which four people were killed, in protest against the treaty. There was also such nationalistic opposition in Guatemala that the treaty was never ratified. Guatemala continues to refuse to recognize Belize, and to veto its application to join the Organization of American States (OAS) and other Western Hemisphere organizations. Britain keeps a small garrison in Belize to ensure its protection.

FURTHER READING

American University, *Guatemala: A Country Study*, Washington D.C., 1983.
Amnesty International, *Guatemala: The Human Rights Record*, London, 1987.
Barry, Tom and Preusch, Deb (eds.), *The Central America Fact Book*, New York, Grove Press, 1986.
Brogan, Patrick, Deadly *Business: Sam Cummings, Interarms and the Arms Trade*, New York, W. W. Norton, 1983.
Fried, Jonathan L. *et al.* (eds), *Guatemala in Rebellion*, New York, Grove Press, 1983.
Schlesinger, Stephen and Kinzer, Stephen, *Bitter Fruit*, Garden City, N.Y., Doubleday, 1982.

NICARAGUA

Geography	57,145 sq. miles (148,005 sq. km). The size of England and Wales.
Population	3.4 million
GNP per capita	$790
Refugees	Internal: 7200 from El Salvador and 400 from Guatemala. External: 29,700 in Costa Rica, 23,060 in Honduras, 1600 in Guatemala.
Casualties	About 10,000 people were killed in the uprising against the Somoza dictatorship, 1978–9. There is no reliable figure for the number killed in the Contra rebellion since 1983, but it has probably not exceeded 10,000 (*see* notes to Appendix I).

Nicaragua was one of the most conspicuous failures of Ronald Reagan's presidency. Through his own inattention, and his susceptibility to right-wing extremism, he allowed himself to be manipulated into a position of demanding the overthrow of the Nicaraguan government even though there was very little popular support in the United States for doing so. He backed a conservative opposition army, the Contras, whose members had connections with the Somoza regime and no hope of victory. By 1982, Reagan had painted himself into a corner, and was too obstinate or unskilful to get out of it. For the rest of his term, he pursued a policy destined to fail. The political consequences in the United States were not severe, because vocal public opposition ensured that he would not send American troops to do the job. However, in Nicaragua, Reagan's policy contributed to bankrupting the country and most of its citizens, and led to the deaths of up to 10,000 people. They were almost all Nicaraguans, killed by other Nicaraguans, but their deaths were a direct result of decisions taken in Washington.

HISTORY

Nicaragua has suffered continuously from American intervention since the middle of the 19th century, as a result of its own political instability. For a century, the country was divided between two competing political parties: the Liberals and the Conservatives. The names did not reflect any political doctrine: they were simply labels attached to rival groups of landowners. From the 1830s onwards, Nicaragua was considered a possible site for a canal through the isthmus, and the two parties vied for the concession. In 1855, the Liberals hired an American adventurer, William Walker, to help them defeat their rivals and take over a profitable trans-isthmus transit company set up by Cornelius Vanderbilt. Walker, who had brought 57 like-minded men with him, succeeded and then he made himself president. He was driven out a year later by another band of mercenaries, financed by Vanderbilt. Walker made two further attempts to set up a private kingdom in Central America but was eventually shot in Honduras.

After the American Civil War, Vanderbilt turned his attention to domestic railways and the idea of a canal lapsed. When it was revived by the French, the site chosen for the canal was the isthmus of Panama. The French failed to complete it, and the project was taken over by the United States, which created a special country, Panama, for the purpose.

Ever since, the United States has considered that a subservient government in Managua is required for complete protection of the canal. This doctrine was first applied in 1909, when the current (Liberal) Nicaraguan dictator started negotiations with European powers for a rival canal. There was a (Conservative) rebellion, and the United States sent the Marines to guarantee its success. In 1912, a more serious intervention was needed to preserve the new government against its rivals. On that occasion, the Marines occupied the country, and they remained, with brief intervals, until 1933.

The purpose of the occupation was to ensure stability, and in the short run, it succeeded. The United States supported a series of presidents, one of whom signed a treaty guaranteeing that Nicaragua would not attempt to build a canal without the consent of the US. However, as the years went by, there was continual agitation against the American presence and their client governments. This agitation usually   **437** took the form of the opposition demanding that the *gringos* should change sides and support them. It is important not to exaggerate American interference in Nicaragua. There were generally very few troops, and they were used to protect foreigners and to dissuade Conservatives and Liberals from carrying on their perpetual civil war.

In 1925, the Marines were withdrawn, and almost immediately there was a Liberal uprising against the Conservative government. The Americans returned in 1926. President Coolidge sent Henry Stimson to mediate, and he imposed a political settlement between the two parties. There was to be a Conservative president and a Liberal vice president – the sort of coalition that well-meaning outsiders have tried to impose on warring factions in Third World countries on frequent occasions since then. Such arrangements are seldom successful.

A small band of Liberals rejected the settlement, refusing to share power with the Conservatives. They were led by a Liberal lieutenant, Augusto César Sandino, who took his guerrilla army of peasants and workers into the remote northern provinces and defied American and government forces. (For a while, Sandino's secretary was Augustin Farabundo Martí, founder of the Salvadoran Communist party; he later deserted Sandino, who was insufficiently Marxist for his taste.) It was not a serious war by later standards, though it was notable for one innovation: the Americans invented the technique of dive-bombing Sandinista camps. The fighting was frequently interrupted for protracted negotiations between Sandino and the Americans. The United States built up the Nicaraguan National Guard as a bipartisan organization – half Conservative, half Liberal – and progressively handed over the fight against the guerrillas to the Guard.

The United States' intervention was deeply unpopular at home and eventually Congress (by then controlled by Democrats) voted to cut off funds, and President Hoover agreed to remove the Marines. Before they left, the Americans organized presidential elections, in 1932, the last free elections Nicaragua was to enjoy until 1984. The Liberal candidate, Juan Bautista Saucasa, won.

He was inaugurated on 1 January 1933, and the Marines left the next day. The commander of the Guard was Anastasio Somoza García, a Liberal and former foreign minister, who was related to the president. They promptly made peace with Sandino for, after all, were they not all Liberals together? Sandino flew to Managua and signed a treaty with Saucasa and Somoza, under which his forces were to surrender their arms in exchange for a 36,000 square kilometre tract of land in the north (a quarter of the country). The terms of the agreement were never completely carried out. In February 1934, Sandino was again in Managua, having talks about the various difficulties, and was invited to a formal dinner with Saucasa in the presidential palace, on the 21st. After what proved to be a particularly amicable evening, Sandino was taken out and shot.

THE SOMOZAS

Somoza founded the longest-lasting of all Latin American dictatorships. He deposed Saucasa in 1936, and the family – in the persons of Anastasio I, Luis and Anastasio II – ruled uninterruptedly until 1979. The third Somoza president was driven out of the country by rebels who named themselves Sandinistas in honor of Augusto César Sandino.

Anastasio I enjoyed a rare advantage that enabled him to gain the Americans' complete confidence and therefore to win command of the National Guard: he had studied at the Pierce School of Business Administration in Philadelphia and spoke fluent English. For all the intimacy of their relations, North Americans, even those most closely concerned with Latin America, have seldom bothered to learn Spanish, and Latin Americans have been equally disinclined to learn English. Somoza not only spoke the language, he understood American ways, and he was able to persuade the US embassy in Managua and a succession of administrations in Washington of his loyalty to the alliance and to American principles of democracy and free enterprise. He even encouraged baseball as the national sport. For over 40 years, the United States government accepted the Somozas without inquiring into the nature of the regime. Roosevelt is alleged to have remarked: 'He's a sonofabitch, but he's ours.' Somoza ensured continuity by sending his sons to school in the United States: it was said of Anastasio II ('Tacho') that he was the only cadet at West Point who was given an army as a graduation present.

Anastasio I ruled as president or through puppets until 1956, when he was assassinated. He was succeeded by his son Luis, who died in 1967 and was in turn succeeded by his brother Anastasio II (who was assassinated in exile, in Paraguay, in 1980). A third generation – Anastasio III – was ready to take over when the 1979 revolution took place. Anastasio III now lives in opulent exile in Miami, hoping for a restoration.

The Somozas plundered Nicaragua as the Pahlevis plundered Iran, the Duvaliers Haiti and Marcos the Philippines. By the 1950s, the family owned one-tenth of the country's cultivable land, its only airline, a television station, a newspaper, a cement plant, sugar refineries, breweries, distilleries and a host of other property. They were cautious, and a great part of their fortune was invested abroad.

The regime based its power upon the American alliance, the old-established oligarchy and the National Guard. Nicaragua gave vociferous support to the United States in all circumstances. It declared war on Germany and Japan immediately after Pearl Harbor, and provided bases for CIA operations against Guatemala in 1954 and Cuba in 1961 and later. Nicaragua's vote could always be relied on in the United Nations or the Organization of American States (OAS). On the home front, the Somozas kept the loyalty of the Liberal section of the oligarchy by granting them commercial favours, and always ensured that a member of the family commanded the National Guard. Guardsmen were well-paid and enjoyed numerous privileges denied to ordinary Nicaraguans. They were detested by the Nicaraguan people and were therefore bound to support the Somozas out of a sense of self-preservation.

The regime was overthrown for a variety of reasons, including the egomania, greed and incompetence of Anastasio II. On 23 December 1972, an earthquake devastated Managua. Howard Hughes, the American billionaire, who was then living in seclusion in a Managuan hotel, took refuge in a carpark just before the building collapsed. Others were not so lucky: 5000 people were killed and 250,000 lost their homes. Very large sums in aid were sent to Nicaragua, and a high proportion was embezzled by the Somozas and their associates. Managua remained a ruin, and little serious attempt to rebuild it was made until after the revolution in 1979. Then American economic sanctions and the Sandinistas' incompetence prevented restoration: Managua is still desolate.

439

THE SANDINISTAS

The Sandinista Front for National Liberation (FSLN) was founded in 1961. Two of its three original leaders were killed during the guerrilla period; the third, Tomás Borge, is now minister of the interior. It developed slowly during the 1960s, carrying out small actions in the countryside (which were always defeated) and in the cities, fomenting strikes, issuing proclamations, trying to build up a political base.

Its effectiveness was hampered by its own divisions. There were three factions: the *Proletarios*, traditional Bolsheviks who sought support among the urban working class; the *Guerra Popular Prolongada* (GPP), which was also dogmatically Marxist and had more influence in the countryside; and the 'Third Force', the *Terceristas*, which, though basically Marxist like the others, recruited non-Communist supporters and advocated mass insurrection. The *Terceristas'* best-known leaders were the brothers Daniel and Humberto Ortego Saavedra. The GPP leaders included Tomás Borge, and the *Proletarios* included Jaime Wheelock Román. In January 1979, in preparation for the final offensive, the three factions united under a nine-man directorate, with three *commandantes* from each of them. It was this politburo that marched into Managua on 20 July 1979.

The guerrilla war from 1961 to 1978 was small in scale and constantly unsuccessful. The FSLN's first major achievement was a raid on a post-Christmas party, on 27 December 1974, when 13 Sandinistas, including three women, took a number of prominent Somocista hostages, including the dictator's brother-in-law and a former foreign minister; they missed the American ambassador by half an hour. In negotiations mediated by Archbishop (later Cardinal) Miguel Obando y Bravo, the regime agreed to release 14 Sandinista prisoners, pay $1 million in ransom, publish long and flamboyant communiqués in the newspapers, and provide a plane to Cuba. It was this episode that split the FSLN: the theoretical Marxists, led by Wheelock, denounced taking hostages as a bourgeois, demagogic error.

Despite that spectacular operation, the Sandinistas were not a serious threat to the regime. The increasing opposition among the middle classes was much more dangerous. The leader of the opposition was Pedro Joaquín Chamorro, publisher of the country's leading newspaper, *La Prensa*. He was a member of a prominent Conservative family: the old division was still going strong. In 1959, he tried to start a guerrilla insurrection himself, and failed. After that, he stuck to politics. The opposition was influential in the cities, where there was much latent hostility to the Somozas, but in the mid-1970s, there were no signs that the regime was nearing its end. Then Chamorro was assassinated on 10 January 1978, and the opposition burst into flames.

It is quite possible that Somoza was not involved in the killing, that it was instead the work of a disgruntled petty crook who had been attacked and exposed in *La Prensa*. It is also possible that Somoza, who was recovering from a heart attack, no longer exercised his former rigorous control over younger and rasher members of his family and government. But the whole country assumed that the dictator was responsible. (The same debate, and the same final outcome, was to take place in Manila in 1986 after Benigno Aquino was murdered.) There were riots and a prolonged general strike in Managua. New opposition leaders emerged, including

440   Alfonso Robelo and Adolfo Calero Portocarrero, who ran a Coca Cola bottling

concession. (They are now leading Contras, as are some members of Chamorro's family.) The first uprisings against the regime took place in a number of cities, and were put down with considerable brutality by the National Guard.

In 1977, 12 prominent citizens had united in opposition to Somoza, and started collaborating with the FSLN. Now they issued a manifesto calling for his resignation and new elections. They formed the nucleus of the non-Marxist opposition, though they were closely allied with the FSLN for tactical purposes. They included several priests and had the blessing of the archbishop. The Nicaraguan situation was now of considerable international concern. However, the Carter administration did not take an active part in organizing opposition to Somoza. That was the task of the governments of Venezuela and Costa Rica, which as democracies both detested Somoza (various members of the Somoza dynasty had also carried out acts of subversion against Costa Rica). Castro, in Cuba, was particularly helpful to the Sandinistas.

Edén Pastora, a noted guerrilla who had fought with the Sandinistas but then left them because they were Communist, now proposed a *coup de théâtre* to galvanize the guerrilla movement. He recruited a band of Sandinistas, 25 strong, and, on 22 August 1978, seized the National Palace (the parliament building and government headquarters in Managua), taking 1500 hostages. Among them were the bulk of the members of the Chamber of Deputies, and Somoza's nephew and a cousin. When reporters asked him to identify himself, Pastora announced that he was '*Commandante Cero*' (Commander Zero). Sandinista cells were strictly anonymous, with the commander taking the designation 'o' and the others numbered after that. On this operation, *Commandante Dos*, the third in command, was Dora María Tellez.

The occupation of the palace lasted two days. Somoza released 50 Sandinista prisoners (including Borge), published Pastora's communiqués, and paid $500,000 in ransom, claiming that that was all there was in the bank. As the guerrillas drove to the airport with their remaining hostages for the flight out of the country, there were large-scale demonstrations of public support. *Commandante Cero* was now a national hero.

THE UPRISING

Somoza's position deteriorated rapidly after that. The Sandinistas staged repeated attacks on provincial towns, particularly in the north. There were strikes, demonstrations and ceaseless political activity in Managua, and after much hesitation, the Carter administration began to look for a centrist opposition to replace the dictator. Venezuela and Costa Rica stepped up their help for the rebels, and considerable quantities of arms were flown from Cuba to FSLN bases in Costa Rica. The Sandinistas and their ally, Pastora, prepared a general offensive from the south, but soon encountered a basic geographical difficulty. In the north, the country is open and access is easy; however, from Costa Rica, the only approach is via a narrow band of territory between the Pacific and Lake Nicaragua, sometimes less than 10 miles (16 km) wide. (Pastora was to face the same problem when he tried to attack the Sandinistas from the same bases four years later.)

The United States had cut off arms deliveries to Somoza, but the regime could still obtain the supplies it needed from the other Central American dictatorships – Guatemala, Honduras and El Salvador – and from Israel. **441**

Somoza's last line of defence was the National Guard, 10,000 strong, which for the most part held its positions against the rebels. Military casualties were light – a few hundred guardsmen and no more than 600 Sandinistas were killed during the uprising – but several thousand civilians, perhaps as many as 7000, died. Many of them were teenagers who died in attacks on the guardsmen.

Somoza's main weakness was political: the business community abandoned him and demanded his departure; the country was in revolt; and the Americans were negotiating with 'The Twelve'. In the summer of 1979, everything was slipping away from Tacho Somoza. A five-member junta was set up in Costa Rica, dominated by non-Marxists. All the various opposition groups, including the Sandinistas, agreed on a 'plan of government' which included guarantees of democratic freedoms. (The Sandinistas' violation of this promise has been held against them ever since.) Finally, Somoza agreed to resign and to hand over to a figurehead successor, who would in turn hand over to the junta. It was hoped that a new director of the National Guard would be found who would hold that institution together to provide a counterweight to the Sandinistas.

On 14 July 1979, the junta announced the names of 12 members of the proposed cabinet, including only one Sandinista, Tomás Borge, who was to be minister of the interior. Somoza resigned three days later and left the country with about 100 relatives and associates. The Sandinistas, and the junta, arrived in Managua on 20 July, and were confronted by the interim president appointed by Somoza and by the remnants of the National Guard. In the course of the following month, the guard disintegrated and the Sandinistas seized power, because theirs was the only military force of any consequence.

THE REVOLUTION

There have been innumerable violent changes of government in Latin America since 1821, but very few revolutions. The word can be used to describe many sorts of events, but in the context of Latin America, it is most usefully applied to the overthrow of one governing class by another. In the 20th century, there have been revolutions in Mexico (in 1911), Guatemala (1944), Cuba (1959) and Nicaragua (1979). There was an attempted revolution in Chile in 1970–3, and both Bolivia and Peru went through partial revolutions: the oligarchies were destroyed, but the army then took over. The Mexican revolution sank into bourgeois, bureaucratic corruption, and the Guatemalan revolution was reversed by the CIA in 1954. The new regime in Cuba has turned into a thoroughgoing Stalinist tyranny that is sustained by the Soviet Union. That leaves Nicaragua.

North America, Western Europe and a few other fortunate corners of the world claim to have escaped all danger of or justification for revolution because they have solidly entrenched systems of representative democracy and because advanced capitalism provides a majority of the population with concrete benefits. The voter who has a secure job and who participates as a consumer in the economic system is not inclined towards revolution. If some classes are excluded – in the black ghettos of the United States, for instance, or disaffected ethnic minorities in various corners of Europe – they are not numerous enough to challenge the social order.

Most of the world is not like that. In Latin America, the free market system that has brought such prosperity to the United States and Europe has so far failed to lift the vast majority of people out of poverty. The peasants of Central America are as wretchedly poor now as they were at the beginning of the century, despite the practice of untramelled capitalism supported by the US Marines. Communism is adjudged a failure in Eastern Europe, the USSR and China because it has manifestly been unable to deliver the prosperity and contentment promised by Marx, Lenin and Mao Tse-tung. But during the same period, capitalism has failed just as completely in the whole of Latin America, a vast continent with every possible natural advantage. If Poland has been kept in poverty by socialism, what are we to say of Honduras, which has never known socialism, or Guatemala, where a mildly socialist government was suppressed in 1954?

The Sandinistas, at any rate, argued that the previous regimes had failed to achieve the political, social and economic ends for which governments are instituted. In the words of the American Declaration of Independence, whenever any form of government becomes destructive of these ends, it is the right of the people to alter or to abolish it. Nicaragua, however, has suffered further misfortunes: its revolution has provoked the bitter enmity of the United States; while the Sandinistas, whatever their revolutionary skills, have proved singularly incompetent at economic management. Measured by its results (and what other criterion is there?), the Nicaraguan revolution has so far been a conspicuous failure.

Immediately after their victory, the Sandinistas set about imposing a socialist revolution on Nicaragua. Although at first their measures were no more extreme than those of the socialist governments of Sweden, or the first Mitterrand government in France, they clearly intended, eventually, to set up a Communist society. They started by expropriating the vast holdings of the Somoza family and its supporters, extending to about a quarter of the country's land and businesses. They nationalized banks and foreign trade and, in the autumn of 1979, took over mining and insurance. The non-Sandinista members of the government protested but never seriously tried to stop the Sandinista take-over. If the collapse of the Somozas was comparable to the February Revolution in Russia that overthrew the tsar, there was nothing comparable to the Bolsheviks' Red October. In Nicaragua, there was a complete vacuum of power, and the Sandinistas filled it and called it revolution.

One after the other, the non-Sandinista members of the government, including Violeta Chamorro, the murdered publisher's widow, resigned. By the first anniversary of the departure of the Somozas, the government was wholly Sandinista.

THE AMERICAN REACTION

In El Salvador, Guatemala and Honduras, the Carter and Reagan administrations have encouraged democratic centrist parties, in the hope that they will reform social and economic conditions sufficiently to permit their peoples to escape from their miserable condition without falling into a Cuban-style tyranny. It remains to be seen whether they succeed. It was too late in Nicaragua. Every American president from Roosevelt to Carter had supported the Somozas, and when the regime had started to collapse, Carter had looked desperately for a democratic alternative – there was none. After the Sandinistas took power with near-universal acclaim, the Carter administration, making the best of a bad job, and deliberately trying to avoid the supposed mistakes of the Eisenhower–Kennedy   443 reaction to the Cuban revolution, tried to establish a working relationship with the new government.

The Sandinistas faced a serious problem of reconstructing the country. About 10,000 people had been killed in 18 months, the damage of the 1972 earthquake had never been properly repaired and Somoza and his friends had emptied the national treasury on the way to the airport. President Carter persuaded Congress to allocate $125 million in aid to Nicaragua.

In Detroit, in July 1980, at the Republican party convention, there was a sign of things to come. During discussions on the Republican party platform, a small group of hardliners inserted a pledge to cancel all further aid to Nicaragua and 'to support the efforts of the Nicaraguan people to establish a free and independent government'. No one of any consequence in the party, least of all Ronald Reagan, ever studied this amendment before it was approved.

Party platforms do not mean very much. Reagan had no very clear views on Nicaragua, except a detestation of Communism and a belief that Carter's policies (and Nixon's and Ford's before him) had allowed a number of countries to be 'lost' to the 'evil empire'. That did not mean that he was committed to supporting an attempt to overthrow the Sandinistas. The hardliners had manoeuvred the Republican party into that position: after Reagan's victory in November, they set about manoeuvring the new administration in the same direction.

They were helped by the Sandinistas. In the months after their triumph, Sandinista leaders, while seeking economic help from Washington, made a series of speeches denouncing the Americans for past and present misdeeds. Then, after Reagan's victory, the Communist rebels in El Salvador decided that they must attempt to win their own victory before the new president could stop them. They therefore launched a general offensive, and the Sandinistas supplied them with the weapons they needed. This connection soon became known, and Carter, before he stepped down, suspended aid to Nicaragua. He also sent emergency aid to El Salvador. The El Salvador rebel offensive was a complete failure, rather to the disgust of the Sandinistas.

Central America was thus at the top of the agenda when Reagan took office on 20 January 1981. He had chosen as secretary of state General Alexander Haig, who knew nothing about the region and who was determined to prove that he was tougher than any of the President's other advisers. He may not have won the prize for machismo, but he easily won the prize for folly. He recommended blockading Cuba as a way to save El Salvador, but the president, wiser than he, vetoed the idea. Reagan's national security adviser was Richard Allen, a man of depressing mediocrity who quickly assembled a team reflecting his talents. Reagan had four national security advisers in his first six years, and in a remarkable example of intellectual regression, each of them was less competent and more ignorant than his predecessor. This downward progression ended with Admiral Poindexter who organized the Iran–Contra fiasco.

The State Department tried to salvage something out of the wreckage, and succeeded. Carter's policy towards El Salvador, Guatemala and Honduras was maintained. But there was a price: the hard right, who became known in Washington as the 'war party', demanded their pound of flesh. They were given

Nicaragua.

The war party, as the writer Roy Gutman put it with careful understatement, 'suffered from the shortage of talent and experience in foreign affairs in the conservative wing of the Republican party'. They insisted on purging the State Department's Bureau of Inter-American Affairs and Carter's ambassadors in Central America. 'A new team would be assembled to manage policy that had one thing in common: all its members lacked Latin American experience.'

THE MISKITO COAST

The Caribbean coast of Nicaragua is wholly different in population and history from its Pacific coast. It was left to its own devices by the Spaniards, though garrisoned with a few forts (Nelson attacked one of them as a young lieutenant). The Miskito coast was settled by British slaves, ex-slaves and runaway slaves from the Caribbean islands. The blacks are Protestant, speak English and have a hereditary distrust of Spanish-speaking rulers from the west. The Indians speak their own languages and are equally hostile to Managua. The British colonized similar territories further north: part were ceded to Honduras, and part eventually turned into Belize, an independent, English-speaking country. The British made no effort to establish permanent rule over the Miskito coast.

When the Sandinistas seized Managua, they set about establishing their control over the Caribbean coastline, and did it brutally. The Miskito Indians and the blacks resisted. Some of the first Contra attacks were in Miskito country, and the Sandinistas responded by relocating tens of thousands of Indians in strategic hamlets well clear of the frontier. The Miskitos responded by fleeing to Honduras, where at least 20,000 refugees are now settled.

THE CONTRAS

Within a year of the revolution, Nicaraguan exiles – both those who had supported the Somozas and those who opposed the Somocistas and Sandinistas equally – set about looking for help. They found their first ally in Honduras, where Colonel Gustavo Alvarez Martínez, who later became chief of staff and *ex officio* ruler of the country, supported them from the beginning. In 1981, the anti-Sandinistas found that the new director of the Central Intelligence Agency, William Casey, could be particularly helpful, and they soon raised enough funds to form the first anti-Sandinista army in Honduras. The Honduran government, or at least Alvarez, planned to provoke the Sandinistas into invading Honduras or Costa Rica, an event he expected would lead to an American intervention in Nicaragua. He set up the first Contra army, 500 strong, to achieve this object. (The Sandinista called them '*Contra-revolutionarios*', or counter-revolutionaries. The term preferred by the Reagan administration – 'freedom fighters' – never stuck.)

The new assistant secretary for Inter-American Affairs was Thomas Enders, a formidable career diplomat who made a last effort to impose a rational Nicaraguan policy. He concluded that the United States' main interest was to stop the further spread of revolution in Central America, and that the way to do that was to support democratic regimes and to persuade the Nicaraguans to stop helping the rebels in other countries. In August 1981, he offered the Sandinistas a deal: if they would stop preaching revolution, stop exporting arms to the rebels in El Salvador and 445

Guatemala, and keep their distance from Cuba and the USSR, the United States would leave them alone.

The Sandinistas agreed to stop arming the Salvadoran rebels (in any event, they had not been impressed by the rebels' 'final offensive'), but refused to adapt their own domestic and foreign policies to Enders' demands: they had not overthrown Somoza to succumb to American bullying. Later, they came to regret their high-principled obstinacy. It had been a good deal, and if it had been consummated in 1981, both sides would have escaped many misfortunes. Enders was repudiated in Washington, where the hardliners had already decided to support the nascent Contra army. He survived, in limbo, excluded from Nicaraguan policy, until he was finally removed in May 1983 and sent off to Madrid as ambassador.

The leading US hardliners were: William Casey; William Clark, Haig's deputy who succeeded Richard Allen as national security adviser late in 1981; Jeane Kirkpatrick, ambassador to the UN who had made her reputation defending right-wing regimes in Latin America; Edwin Meese, counsellor to the president, and Caspar Weinberger, secretary of defence. It was a formidable combination. Their first achievement was a presidential directive, signed in November 1981, committing the United States to support 'political and paramilitary operations against the Cuban presence and the Cuban–Sandinista support infrastructure in Nicaragua and elsewhere in Central America'. Casey proposed three objectives: to get the Sandinistas to 'turn inward', meaning presumably that they should cease and desist from exporting revolution; to 'interdict' (i.e. prevent) the supply of arms to the Salvadoran rebels; and to bring the Sandinistas to negotiate. It was all very vague and hypocritical. Enders' abortive efforts at reaching a settlement had been typical: whenever State Department officials, including George Shultz when he became secretary of state, started negotiating with Managua, the process was always subverted by hardliners in the White House.

Meanwhile, the Contras were getting started. The Nicaraguan Democratic Forces (FDN) were formed in Guatemala on 11 August 1981, and they found a military leader in Colonel Enrique Bermúdez Varela, the most acceptable of the former members of Somaza's National Guard. He had been military attaché in Washington during the Sandinista uprising and thus had no part in the savagery of that conflict. However, many opponents of the Sandinistas refused to work with former National Guardsmen, and the Sandinistas have constantly harped on the allegation that the Contras will bring back the Somocistas.

To train their first troops, the Contras turned to Argentina, whose military government was looking for ways to ingratiate itself with the new American administration. Honduras continued to help, and so did the CIA, to a far greater extent than it ever admitted. By the end of 1982, the Contras had raised 4000 men in Honduras, and by the following spring, the number had reached 7000, including a force in Costa Rica and a contingent of Miskito Indians.

By then, it was public knowledge that the United States was arming the Contras, and Congress became alarmed. As a result, Congressman Edward Boland of Massachusetts, who was chairman of the House Committee on Intelligence, presented the first of his amendments, which was passed in December 1982. It stated that US funds might be used by the Contras only to stop the flow of arms from Nicaragua to El Salvador.

Despite all President Reagan's eloquence, there was always a firm popular majority in the United States against American involvement in Nicaragua, and only tepid support for the Contras: the prevailing view was 'No more Vietnams.' The Democrats in Congress were determined to prevent any use of American troops in Nicaragua, but were less consistent in their opposition to helping the Contras. Sometimes Congress voted funds for them, sometimes it passed laws (the Boland amendments) forbidding the US administration to spend any money on them. Its vacillations have been offered as one of the reasons why Lieutenant Colonel Oliver North and his friends devised the Iran–Contra plan: they claimed that they were showing more consistency than Congress.

In February and March 1983, Bermúdez launched his first offensive into Nicaragua. His troops penetrated into the heart of the country, attacking government posts and carrying out sabotage, and then withdrew to Honduras. The Contras had achieved very little, but considered it just a beginning. They said that they would have achieved much more with greater American assistance, and claimed that the Boland amendment was a stab in the back. The Reagan administration agreed, but that July, for the first time, Congress rejected a Reagan request for Contra aid. The Pentagon then launched the first of a series of large-scale military exercises in Honduras and off both coasts of Nicaragua, with the evident intention of intimidating the Sandinistas.

President Reagan proved quite unable to lay down a coherent policy towards Nicaragua, and as a result, the Contras received constantly changing instructions. In February 1983, they were ordered to invade Nicaragua. Three months later, they were recalled and told that they must improve their performance if they were to persuade Congress to fund them. Then they were sent back into the fight, but without any extra arms. Simultaneously, the CIA launched a series of naval attacks on Nicaragua, for purposes that were never explained, and in October, the Contras were told that their mission was to liberate an area of Nicaragua and to set up a government there which the United States could then recognize. That last scheme was being pushed by General Alvarez in Honduras and some of the wilder men in Washington, including Oliver North who was emerging as one of the leading 'shoot first, ask questions later' operatives on the National Security Council staff. The plan was opposed by the Joint Chiefs of Staff, and also by the Contras, who observed that they were incapable of any such thing.

In the latter half of 1983, as the United States mounted the military exercises in Honduras and off the Nicaraguan coasts – exercises that involved aircraft carriers and even a battleship, and thousands of troops on the ground in Honduras – the CIA station chief in Honduras, Duane Clarridge, sent speedboats to attack ships in Nicaraguan ports, organized sabotage attacks on oil installations and power plants in Managua and, on one occasion, had Managua airport bombed. The following year, he proposed mining the harbours of Nicaragua, and won the approval of the Restricted Interagency Group (RIG), a small claque of middle-level officials in Washington who ran Nicaragua policy.

GRENADA

This, it turned out, was the high point of the Contra offensive, and coincided with a striking exercise of American power: the invasion of Grenada, far to the east in the   447

Caribbean. President Reagan had frequently warned of the dangers of a Communist base in Grenada, a new Cuba in the southern Antilles, citing as proof of its evil intent the construction of a major new airport that was allegedly designed to serve as a Soviet air base. On 19 October 1983, the semi-Marxist government of Grenada was overthrown in a coup by a small group of ambitious soldiers, and the prime minister, Maurice Bishop was killed. A few days after the coup, on 23 October, Lebanese terrorists killed 241 Marines in a car bomb attack in Beirut. Reagan seized the opportunity to divert attention from the Lebanese catastrophe and, at the same time, to eliminate a supposed threat nearer home: US forces landed on Grenada on 25 October.

A group of neighbouring Caribbean governments had requested the intervention for a quite different reason: they had no wish for the Caribbean to fall into the South American and African habit of allowing men with guns to seize power and shoot prime ministers. The official justification offered by the US was that a group of American students in a medical school on Grenada were in danger, and that Grenada was being turned into a Soviet base. This was pure fantasy and another example of the ill-effects of lying to the public. The Reagan administration was constrained to keep up the lie even as the school's officials insisted that the students had never been in any danger. The airport was also found to be quite unsuited for military purposes: it was for tourists only. In addition the large numbers of Cuban and East European 'troops' allegedly on the island all turned out to be construction workers.

The Grenada operation was a complete success. It wiped out the memory of Beirut, and it was very popular in Grenada. Six months later, the US troops went home, leaving a peaceful and democratic island behind them. The operation also put the fear of God into Cuba and Nicaragua. It had been a fearsome show of power, and demonstrated to the Sandinistas that, if the United States ever chose to intervene, neither Cuba nor the Soviet Union would lift a finger to help them.

There was now a brief moment when a deal might have been done. The Sandinistas would have accepted any terms the United States stipulated, short of dissolving their own government, in exchange for a peace agreement. Daniel Ortega visited New York and Washington in an attempt to convey the message. Unfortunately, Washington was distracted by the Middle East. Roy Gutman, for once, blames the State Department, and not the White House hardliners, for the failure to exploit the profound psychological advantage that the US obtained by the Grenada operation. Soon afterwards, it was business as usual.

MINING THE HARBOURS
The CIA's first business was finding a way of dealing with Duane Clarridge's brainwave that mining Nicaragua's harbours would overthrow the Sandinistas. This is an instructive episode for a number of reasons, starting with the complete lunacy of the project itself. The CIA decided that it would be inadvisable to sink too many ships; the mines, therefore, should make a lot of noise but do little damage. It was hoped that the fracas would scare away international shipping, thus cutting off Nicaragua's oil supplies, and bring the government to its knees – or at least cause it severe inconvenience for a month or so. This was what Colonel Khadafy of Libya tried to do in the Red Sea, later that summer, hoping to

inconvenience Egypt (*see* Libya, pp. 39–45). He was severely criticized for this 'terrorism' by many countries, but the United States had to keep quiet.

The first problem was to obtain non-lethal mines – the international arms industry usually produces much more dangerous weapons. In the end, the agency had to manufacture them itself. Non-American CIA agents laid them in January and February 1984, in the harbours at Corinto and Puerto Sandino on the Pacific and El Bluff on the Caribbean. The Nicaraguan government, whose agents were observing all this, denounced the mine-laying when it had barely begun, early in January, and the CIA instructed the Contras to claim the credit.

Nothing more happened until 25 February when the first mines exploded, sinking two small fishing boats at El Bluff. In the next month, a number of other ships were damaged, including a Soviet tanker. In all, ten ships were hit, a number of sailors were wounded and two Nicaraguans were killed. Some cargo ships cancelled visits to Nicaraguan ports. Nicaragua had therefore to transport its exports by road to ports in Costa Rica. However, on the whole, international shipping was not overly impressed. Insurance rates were hardly affected, and Nicaraguan trade continued.

It was not a big story, to begin with. The State Department issued an official denial that the United States had had anything to do with the mining, and the matter might have rested there, as yet another unsuccessful CIA project, but for the sudden intervention of Congress. The political explosion was generated by Senator Barry Goldwater, father-figure of American conservatism, and chairman of the Senate Intelligence Committee. He discovered that the CIA had mined Nicaragua's harbours without telling the committee, and 9 April, he sent a letter of fulminating protest to Casey:

I am pissed off. Bill, this is no way to run a railroad. The President has asked us to back his foreign policy. Bill, how can we back his foreign policy when we don't know what the hell he is doing? Lebanon, yes. We all knew that he sent troops over there. But mine the harbors in Nicaragua? This is an act violating international law. It is an act of war. For the life of me, I don't see how we are going to explain it.

Casey had, in fact, made a reference to the mining in testimony to the committee on 8 March, well after the operation had begun, but Goldwater and his colleagues had missed it. Other senators shared Goldwater's outrage, and his letter was leaked to the press. The full Senate voted 84 to 12 to condemn the mining; the House followed suit; and the Reagan administration was faced with a major political embarrassment. On the day that Goldwater wrote his letter to Casey, Nicaragua took the case to the International Court of Justice at The Hague and asked for a ruling that the mining was illegal and that the US must stop helping the Contras. The United States, which from the time of Woodrow Wilson had defended the rule of law in international affairs, now denounced the International Court and announced that it would not take part in its proceedings. It was a low point in the Reagan presidency. The Court finally ruled against the United States in June 1986: the Reagan administration ignored the ruling.

The mining had even more serious consequences. In yet another Boland amendment, Congress suspended all further aid for the Contras in May 1984, and voted to end all American support the following October. William Casey at the 449

CIA and Robert McFarlane, who was now national security adviser, set about finding alternative, illegal sources of funds. McFarlane applied to Saudi Arabia, which was always ready to oppose Communism and please the US: The Saudis agreed to send $1 million a month.

THE SANDINISTAS

The period from autumn 1983 to spring 1984 was the high-water mark of the Contras' offensive. Bermúdez, based in Honduras, was operating far and wide in northern and central Nicaragua. Edén Pastora, who had broken with his former comrades, accusing them of betraying the revolution, attacked over the border from Costa Rica and for three days held San Juan del Norte, a fishing village on the Caribbean coast. His group, separate from the Contras in Honduras, was known as ARDE (the Democratic Revolutionary Alliance). ARDE's political leader was Alfonso Robelo, a millionaire businessman who had played a prominent part in the revolution against Somoza. The Sandinistas responded to all these attacks in two ways: they announced that they would advance the promised legislative and presidential elections by a year, and they applied to Cuba and the Soviet Union for military help.

The Soviet Union sent arms, ammunition and, above all, Mi-25 helicopter gunships. These fearsome weapons started to arrive in the autumn of 1984 and had a devastating effect on the Contras, who had been operating in large bands of up to 500 men. In the next few years, the Sandinista army was systematically increased and equipped with the latest Soviet weaponry: just as the Reagan administration came to rely upon the Contras, to the exclusion of everything else, to effect its political aims in Nicaragua, the increase in Nicaraguan military strength, particularly the gunships, ensured that the Contras would be defeated.

The elections were held on 4 November, two days before the American elections. For months during the summer and autumn, the Nicaraguan opposition debated whether or not it should participate. The Reagan administration was divided. The hardliners wanted to boycott the elections because they believed that the Sandinista regime was a Communist dictatorship, and they took it as axiomatic that Communists always cheat. The opposition had a presidential candidate, Arturo Cruz, who had been ambassador to Washington after the revolution. But the opposition's divisions and hesitations, and the divisions in Washington, led to endless procrastination until it was too late to register Cruz as a candidate. The Americans then blamed the Sandinistas and claimed that the elections were fraudulent.

Foreign observers judged that the elections were fair and honest. The Sandinistas won 61 of 96 seats in the legislative assembly. In the presidential election, Daniel Ortega won 67 per cent of the vote, on a turn-out of about 75 per cent, against token opposition: Ortega thus won a more sweeping mandate than Ronald Reagan did two days later. With hindsight, Cruz and his supporters concluded that they had made a mistake: they speculated that, if they had taken part in the election, Cruz might have won 40 per cent of the vote and established a permanent political base in Nicaragua.

As it was, the elections were a success for the Sandinistas. However, the economy was heading for collapse. The Soviets had been persuaded to bail them out, to the tune of $500 million to $1 billion a year. On 1 May 1985, Reagan announced a complete embargo on trade with Nicaragua, driving the Sandinistas yet farther into the Soviets' embrace.

By now Ronald Reagan had given up the pretence that his object was to prevent the Sandinistas supplying arms to the El Salvador rebels. He admitted that he wanted the Sandinistas overthrown – all they had to do was 'say uncle'. However, few observers thought the Contras could ever defeat the Sandinistas, and their attacks and the rapidly rising civilian casualties tended to increase popular support for the government, balancing out the unpopularity brought on by the economic disaster. Reagan's policy was inherently self-defeating – and it was driven by a group of tunnel-vision zealots on the National Security Council staff and a few political appointees such as Elliott Abrams who was now head of the State Department's Latin America bureau. They defeated all efforts at negotiation, thwarted the 'Contadora' process (a diplomatic effort at a settlement by the governments of Mexico, Panama, Venezuela and Colombia), and devoted immense effort to supporting the Contras. In the process, they broke the law, which said that no aid should be given to the Contras, and showed astonishing political ineptitude by selling arms to Iran and using the profits for the Contras (*see below*). It was worse than a crime, it was a blunder. It was an amazing victory of ideology over intelligence.

By then the Contras had about 10,000 men under arms, 6000 in Honduras of whom 5000 were operating inside Nicaragua. They looked impressive, but they were never a serious military threat to the government. They concentrated on border areas, within 90 miles (150 km) of the frontier, and achieved some success: they disrupted the coffee harvest in the highlands and won some support among the peasantry. Then the tide turned.

In 1985, the Sandinistas won the upper hand over the Contras. It had taken them that long because, to begin with, they had no regular army at all: Somoza's National Guard had disintegrated, and the new Nicaraguan army had to be developed from scratch. The Sandinistas did not even have many experienced guerrilla fighters who might have been converted to a regular army. The Somoza regime had collapsed as a result of a mass, popular uprising, not after a long guerrilla campaign like the Cuban revolution – and anyway, the *commandantes* all now had desk jobs in Managua.

In the early days of the war against the Contras, the Sandinistas had relied on numbers. They had recruited thousands of peasants and had sent them off to fight the Contras with their shiny new Soviet guns and very little idea of how to use them. The United States had denounced the Nicaraguan army as the largest and most dangerous in Central America when, in fact, it had been no more than a peasant *levée en masse*. By 1985, however, it was reasonably efficient and adequately armed: it had transport helicopters and the Mi-25 gunships and enough pilots to fly them. The regular Sandinista army reached 50,000–60,000 men, and it was at last able to confront the Contras in strength.

Roy Gutman notes that the rule of thumb is that counter-insurgency forces need an advantage of roughly 10:1 to defeat a rebellion. The Contras never had more than 4000–5000 men in Nicaragua and were thus outnumbered by approximately 16:1. By comparison, the Angolan army, together with its Cuban advisers, outnumber Unita by only 7:1, the Mozambique army has only a 4:1 advantage over Renamo, and the Ethiopian army has a roughly 10:1 advantage in Eritrea and Tigray. In El Salvador, where the government's advantage is about 8:1, it has not managed to defeat the guerrillas but has nevertheless fought them to a standstill. In Nicaragua, the army's numerical advantage is enormous.

THE SOUTHERN FRONT

In the spring of 1984, the CIA was sending $400,000 a month to support Edén Pastora and ARDE in the south. It was an untidy arrangement because Pastora insisted repeatedly and vocally that he would have nothing to do with the main Contra organization, the Nicaraguan Democratic Forces (FDN). He claimed that Bermúdez and his closest military associates were former supporters of Somoza, 'people who have tortured us for 45 years'. In May 1984, the CIA demanded that ARDE merge with the FDN. Robelo, seeing that there was no hope for ARDE without American support, agreed to the merger.

On 30 May 1984, Pastora called a press conference at La Penca, his headquarters in the Costa Rican jungle, to denounce Robelo. Just as he began to speak, a bomb exploded. It wounded Pastora and killed four people, one of whom was an American reporter, Linda Frazer, who bled to death in the mud. The many other wounded people were not evacuated for hours: Pastora was rushed away in the one boat available. Tony Avirgan and Martha Honey, a husband-and-wife team of journalists, believe that the bomb was planted by an anti-Khadafy Libyan agent masquerading as a Danish journalist, in the pay of the FDN.

After the attempted assassination, most of ARDE defected from Pastora and joined the FDN. After that, Pastora was a *commandante* without an army, and in 1986, he abandoned the fight. He now spends his time fishing in Costa Rica.

THE IRAN–CONTRA AFFAIR

The Iran–Contra affair is now the subject of litigation, but the congressional hearings in 1987 and the many documents that have been published have revealed the essential details. The guiding spirits of the whole business were William Casey and his assistants at the CIA, and the staff of the National Security Council including Lieutenant Colonel Oliver North. They succeeded in persuading President Reagan that secretly selling arms to Iran would eventually help the United States restore amicable relations with that country after the death of the Ayatollah, and might also lead to the release of American hostages held in Lebanon.

The proposal was vigorously opposed by the secretaries of state and defence, but Reagan ignored their advice. The further development – that the Iranians should be overcharged for the arms they bought, and that the profits should be used for an 'off the shelf', super-secret 'special operations capability' – was Casey's and North's idea. North was able to persuade his superior, Admiral John Poindexter (who had succeeded McFarlane as national security adviser in December 1985), of the wisdom of the proposal. He recruited General Richard Secord to organize the project. Secord had been a special operations specialist, involved in the attempts to rescue the American hostages in Tehran in

Meanwhile, on the diplomatic front, in July 1985, Elliott Abrams took over the Latin American bureau at the State Department. He was one of the superhawks recruited to the government with no first-hand knowledge of foreign affairs but with decided and extreme right-wing opinions. He believed that the Soviet Union is the source of all evil in the world, and that any Third World leader to the left of Torquemada is probably a Soviet stooge. He knew all about power politics in Washington but nothing about the real world in Central America. As a result, he and North won every battle in the capital, while the Contras were losing the fight on the ground and were also losing all political support in the rest of Latin America. All the criticisms of Ronald Reagan's handling of affairs essentially boils down to the fact that he allowed incompetent fanatics such as North and Abrams to run things.

After Congress had voted a complete cut-off of supplies to the Contras in October 1984 and refused to reconsider it, despite Reagan's victory in the presidential election, the Contras' situation became desperate. North hired a British mercenary, David Walker, who was sent into Nicaragua on a sabotage mission. His men attacked a Managua 'military installation' with explosives on 6 March 1985: it turned out to be the maternity wing of the country's major military hospital. Walker also reconnoitred the helicopter base, and concluded that it was too tough a nut to crack. He was asked to supply pilots for Secord's 'enterprise' (*see below*), but the men he sent proved incompetent. Walker was also involved in the most extreme of all North's proposed follies: an attempt at piracy. Walker was to seize a merchant ship, the *Monimbo*, in the China Sea and dispose of its crew. The ship was carrying arms to Nicaragua, and the idea was to divert them to the Contras. Nothing came of this proposed act of criminal lunacy.

On 1 June 1985, North summoned the two principal Contra leaders, Bermúdez and Calero, to a meeting in Miami with Secord. North then decided that Secord should take charge of resupplying the Contras, and that the southern front must be revived. He recruited other members of the NSC staff as well as the new American ambassador to Costa Rica, Lewis Tambs, to set up a secret base in Costa Rica, all this without informing McFarlane or Elliott Abrams.

The Contras were kept going by the $1 million a month provided by the Saudis. By degrees, Secord set up an 'enterprise', to purchase arms and other supplies and ship them to Honduras and, later, Costa Rica. At the same time, the Sandinista forces were showing marked improvement, and despite North's best efforts, Bermúdez was defeated and driven back across the border. In the south, the remnants of ARDE were eliminated.

In June 1985, Congress approved $28 million in 'humanitarian aid' to the Contras, but nothing was delivered until early the following year. General Alvarez of Honduras had been removed from office by his subordinates in March 1984, partly because of his arrogance and dictatorial manner, and partly because he had turned the country over to the Americans and the Contras. (Alvarez Martínez was assassinated on 25 January 1989 by the Popular Liberation Forces, a Honduran guerrilla movement.) The new Honduran chief of staff and the president, Roberto Suazo Córdova, were much less accommodating, and put a ban on all resupply to the Contras. It was not lifted until Suazo's successor, José Azcona Hoyo took office in January 1986.

In June 1986, Reagan finally persuaded the House of Representatives to vote the Contras $100 million, of which $70 million was for arms; the Senate approved in August. Congress, of course, was not informed that North, Poindexter and Casey had started selling arms to Iran in order to finance the Contras and other secret operations, or that the Secord airlift to the Contras had begun on 1 April. The Contra campaign had been won in Washington as a result of an immense public relations effort by the president and his supporters, who accused their opponents of handing over Latin America to the Communists. They were helped by a Nicaraguan attack on Contra bases in Honduras on 23 March. The administration used this comparatively minor incident to drum up support for the Contras in Washington, but first had to overcome a problem in Honduras. The government there had constantly denied that there were any Contra bases in the country, and therefore refused to admit that there had been any Nicaraguan incursion. In the end, the American ambassador in Tegucigalpa, who was suffering from a serious bout of influenza, went in his dressing gown to see President Azcona and told him that he had to ask for help. Azcona reluctantly agreed, and Washington immediately ferried American troops to near the border in a show of force, and approved $20 million in emergency aid to Honduras. Azcona demonstrated his belief in the seriousness of the situation by leaving for the beach, and the ambassador went back to bed.

This American aid and support revived the prospects of Bermúdez and his troops, and by the end of the year, they were ready for a new offensive. However, on 5 October 1986, one of Secord's supply planes was shot down over Nicaragua. It was a C-123, flying from Honduras to make a drop to Contras fighting on the southern front, and it was brought down by a Soviet surface-to-air missile (SAM-7). The two American pilots were killed. A third American, Eugene Hassenfus, whose job had been to push the cargo out of the door over the drop zone, and who had had the wit to wear a parachute, survived and was captured.

American officials, from President Reagan downwards, all denied that they had anything to do with Hassenfus. However, the Sandinistas found a number of incriminating documents in his possession and in the wreckage of the plane, including Secord's phone number. The matter became increasingly embarrassing in the course of October, and in early November news broke of the sale of arms to Iran. On 25 November, the attorney general, Edwin Meese, announced that its profits had been diverted to the Contra supply 'enterprise', and the whole plot started to unravel.

The $100 million agreed by Congress in June was to be the last military funding the Contras were to get. (The aid programme was finally killed in February 1988; they have received only 'humanitarian' aid since then.) The Contras mounted a few last offensives during 1987, doing more damage and killing more people than ever before, but were defeated by the Sandinista army with its Mi-25 gunships.

The military option had failed completely. Its failure had been inevitable from the start: no guerrilla movement can succeed against a well-armed and determined government unless it has a solid base of support inside the country. It cannot be sent across the border to victory. Reagan had been manipulated into supporting a hopeless endeavour, which ended in bankruptcy when the Iran–Contra affair was exposed.

Shultz tried to salvage something by appointing Philip Habib as special ambassador for Central America. He remained in the job for 18 months, achieving nothing.

DIPLOMACY

It was time to revert to diplomacy. Because the Reagan administration's efforts had by then been discredited, and it had exhausted every option, the diplomatic effort was taken out of its hands. In 1987, Washington enjoyed the astonishing spectacle of foreign policy being conducted by the speaker of the House of Representatives, and of Central American presidents ignoring Washington and negotiating among themselves.

Jim Wright, the speaker, became involved in the summer of 1987 when the White House was once again trying to persuade Congress to help the Contras. He told the president the only way to do it was to offer the Sandinistas a peace plan they might accept. Reagan agreed to the idea, perhaps not expecting Wright to succeed, but to general surprise, Wright negotiated directly with the Nicaraguans and announced his plan on 5 August. It was supported by the White House and the State Department though the hardliners detested it. Nicaragua expressed interest.

Two days later, on 7 August, the presidents of the five Central American republics, meeting in Guatemala, announced their own peace plan, which had been prepared by the president of Costa Rica, Oscar Arias Sánchez. It provided for an amnesty, a ceasefire, direct negotiations between the Contras and Sandinistas, an end to the anti-democratic measures in Nicaragua, and an end to all outside interference. The Sandinistas would stop helping the rebels in El Salvador and the Americans would have to stop helping the Contras.

Wright promptly accepted this peace plan, which was very similar to his own. President Reagan was left in a quandary: could he bear to swallow his words and accept a reasonable and straightforward peace plan? Arias won the Nobel Peace Prize, and the Contras reluctantly accepted his proposals. The hardliners were devastated. They managed to prevent Philip Habib travelling to Guatemala City to begin negotiations on implementation, and he promptly resigned. After that, Central America proceeded on its own, with the United States an irritated spectator.

On 5 November 1987, Ortega announced that he would engage in indirect negotiations with the Contras, to be held under the mediation of Cardinal Obando y Bravo, who has consistently opposed the Sandinistas. At a Central American summit on 15–17 January 1988, Nicaragua agreed to direct negotiations with the Contras, and to lift the state of emergency that had lasted since the revolution. On 23 March, the Sandinistas and Contras signed a 60-day ceasefire. When it expired in May, it was extended.

THE PEACE PROCESS

One reason for Nicaragua's readiness to accept the Arias peace plan was the collapse of its economy and the increasing opposition to the government. Half the budget went to defence. The standard of living, already deplorably low under the Somozas, had dropped by one-third after the eight years' of Sandinista mismanagement. For two days every week, water was cut off in Managua to conserve energy. In 1987, inflation was running at 1000 per cent per annum, the   455 country survived on hand-outs from the Soviets, including subsidized oil, there were no currency reserves or credit abroad, and trade was conducted by barter: foreigners would not accept Nicaraguan córdobas. In February 1988, Nicaragua introduced a new currency to replace the old: one new córdoba was worth 1000 old ones. The government tried to fix prices and salaries at the new levels and failed lamentably, and inflation continued unchecked. By the following summer, inflation was running at a rate of 6000 per cent. Banknotes with a face value of 50 córdobas were overprinted with a new denomination, 50,000.

In June, the government announced a new round of reforms, lifting wage and price controls. Socialism was failing, so the Sandinistas were beating a retreat towards a market economy – while still insisting that the eventual goal would be socialism. Another cause for concern was Mikhail Gorbachev. He had agreed to support Nicaragua, but now that was costing at least $500 million a year, and rising rapidly. (Some estimates in 1988 put the Soviet contribution as high as $1 billion.) There appeared to be no political advantage, beyond the pleasure of annoying the United States, in interfering in Central America. In the autumn of 1987, the Soviet Union opened discussions with Costa Rica on eliminating its military role in the region if the Americans stopped helping the Contras. This proposal was anathema to Elliott Abrams and other American hardliners: they needed the Soviet presence in Nicaragua to justify their support of the Contras.

Domestic political opposition in Nicaragua rose sharply as the war came to an end. A group of 14 opposition parties, ranging from the Communists to conservative business groups, formed an anti-Sandinista alliance. In addition, under the terms of the ceasefire, Contra supporters had begun to return from exile. Opposition papers, notably *La Prensa*, which had been suspended in 1986, were reopened after the Arias treaty was signed, and a Catholic radio station was reopened. For the first time since the early days of the revolution, political life was nearly normal in Managua.

Negotiations between the government and the Contras continued sporadically into the summer of 1988, but at the same time, the Contra movement began to break up. The divisions between the civilian leadership, largely the creation of the CIA in Washington, and the military leadership on the ground became acute, and at the same time, factions within the Contra armies opposed to Colonel Bermúdez mutinied, accusing him of corruption, tyranny and incompetence. Meanwhile, the leaders of the Miskito Indians, Brooklyn Rivera and Steadman Fagoth, started their own peace negotiations with the Sandinistas, aiming to reach a settlement that would allow Indian refugees in Honduras to return home. The talks failed.

In June, talks aimed at establishing a permanent ceasefire broke down. Fighting did not resume immediately, and indeed the ceasefire was extended, but sporadic clashes between Contras and government troops became more frequent, and the main Contra armies, which had retreated to Honduras, began to prepare to return to the fight.

In July, as the economic situation continued to deteriorate, the Sandinistas suspended some of the political freedoms that they had restored under the Arias peace plan: *La Prensa* was suspended again, for two weeks; the Catholic radio station went off the air (it resumed broadcasting in mid-August): and an opposition rally was broken up with considerable violence on 10 July. The American ambassador, Richard Melton, and seven other American diplomats were expelled, and four opposition leaders were sentenced to six-month jail terms. After the apparent failure of the new economic measures, the Sandinistas tried a swing back to the left, confiscating Nicaragua's largest private business, the San Antonio sugar plantation. The Contra leadership, meeting in Santo Domingo a few days later, claimed that these events were proof that the Sandinistas had no intention of liberalizing Nicaraguan political life. Colonel Bermúdez was elected a director of the Contras, an event that led a number of Contra rebels to resign. The whole peace process seemed to be collapsing.

However, Ortega announced that the ceasefire would be extended again, until 30 August. It was clearly in the Sandinistas' interest to continue the ceasefire at least until after the American election. Similarly, the Contras could not afford to be seen to break the peace, for fear of losing whatever residual support they might still enjoy in Congress. Ortega accused the United States of trying to provoke a resumption of fighting, and on the past record of the Reagan administration, it was a reasonable accusation.

In August, the US Senate voted $27 million in 'humanitarian' aid for the Contras, to pay for food, clothing and medicine. Administration efforts to persuade Congress to vote military aid failed. By that time, almost all the Contras, and their supporters, had crossed the border into Honduras, where they waited on events, depressed and defeated. Their leaders continued to demand that the Sandinistas share power with them, and various efforts were made to get the peace talks restarted. But it was increasingly apparent that the Contras were no longer major players in the game, if they ever had been. They appeared to have no future, and seem destined to melt away, trying to smuggle themselves back into Nicaragua or joining the hosts of refugees from other revolutions in Latin America.

What counted was the political and economic situation in Nicaragua, where the Sandinistas' position continued to deteriorate. They still had the guns, but that was not enough. They would not willingly share power, let alone give it up. As they said, they did not fight Somoza for a decade to hand over power to the people who had accommodated themselves to the dictatorship for a generation, just because the going gets rough. However, the choice may be taken out of their hands. It is the collapse of the Nicaraguan economy that will pull down the Sandinistas, if anything, not the Contras' incursions across the border. The government claims that it has been the American sanctions and the war that have brought ruin upon the country, but their own incompetence is at least as much to blame. At least 150,000 Nicaraguans – out of a population of 3.4 million – now live in the United States, and the remittances they send home are essential to the country's survival. The only thing that really keeps the country afloat is Soviet aid, and if the Soviet Union decides to abandon its $1 billion a year investment, as part of a wider deal with the United States, the Sandinistas would face immediate disaster, like the Afghan government. Their only salvation would be a political accommodation with the opposition, and with the Americans.

On 22 October 1988, a hurricane devastated the eastern provinces, adding a natural disaster to Nicaragua's man-made calamities. Despite desperate appeals for help, the world community left the country to recover as best it could; other equally poor countries across the world were considered more deserving. According to the   457

Washington Post, one European diplomat in Managua commented, 'The world is beginning to get tired of Nicaragua.'

The regime released the opposition leaders who had been arrested at an anti-Sandinista demonstration in July 1988, but that gesture was not enough. Other governments, including the co-signatories of the Arias plan, no longer trusted Ortega. The currency was rapidly becoming valueless. In 1988, inflation reached 36,000 per cent. By one calculation, the average daily wage, which had bought 30 eggs or 12 litres of milk in 1979 when the Sandinistas took power, by 1988 bought only 2 eggs or 2 litres of milk. Nicaragua faced starvation.

In February 1989, the Sandinistas announced a series of economic reforms amounting to an abandonment of socialism. Private enterprise was to be encouraged, and there were to be sweeping cuts in government programmes and in public investment. The government stated that there would be no more appropriations of private businesses and that land redistribution would be ended.

Then the five Central American presidents met again to consider the failure of the Arias plan. They concluded that it had been too ambitious in its attempt to settle all the wars and conflicts of the region, and decided to concentrate on the Nicaraguan question. They agreed that the Contras would be disbanded, offered an amnesty and allowed to return to Nicaragua. President Ortega promised to restore all civil and political liberties in Nicaragua, and agreed to accept stringent international verification of the process. He said that the next presidential elections would be brought forward to February 1990.

If the Sandinistas were not admitting defeat, they were certainly suing for peace. They could claim that they had survived the Contras and the Reagan administration, while admitting that the economy was in desperate straits. The Nicaraguan opposition, and the new Bush administration, were at first most sceptical, and some of the Contras promised to continue the fight, but it was at least possible that the Central Americans had found a way to end one of their conflicts. The presidents gave themselves three months to work out the details.

FURTHER READING

American University, *Honduras: A Country Study*, Washington, D.C., 1984.
——, *Nicaragua: A Country Study*, Washington, D.C., 1982.
Amnesty International, *Nicaragua: The Human Rights Record*, London, 1986.
Barry, Tom and Preusch, Deb (eds), *The Central America Fact Book*, New York, Grove Press, 1986.
Christian, Shirley, *Nicaragua: Revolution in the Family*, New York, Vintage Books, 1986.
Cockburn, Leslie, *Out of Control: The Story of the Reagan Administration's Secret War in Nicaragua*, New York, Atlantic Monthly Press, 1987.
Gutman, Roy, *Banana Diplomacy: The Making of American Policy in Nicaragua, 1981–1987*, New York, Simon & Schuster, 1988.
Kornbluh, Peter, *Nicaragua: The Price of Intervention, Reagan's Wars against the Sandinistas*, Washington D.C., Institute for Policy Studies, 1987.
Rosset, Peter and Vandermeer, John, *Nicaragua, the Unfinished Revolution*, New York, Grove Press, 1986.
Walker, Thomas (ed.), *Nicaragua: The First Five Years*, New York, Praegar, 1985.

PERU

Geography	496,224 sq. miles (1,285,215 sq. km). The size of France, Spain and West Germany together, or twice the size of Texas. 60% is Amazonian jungle, where 5% of the population live. The rest comprises a narrow coastal strip and the high Andes.
Population	19 million: 50% are white or of mixed race, speaking Spanish; 50% are Indian, speaking Quechua. 6 million live in the capital, Lima.
Resources	Primarily silver. Peru is also the world's largest producer of coca (from which cocaine is derived), producing more than Bolivia and Colombia combined.
GNP per capita	$1130
Casualties	Between 10,000 and 15,000 have been killed since 1980.

The Communist Party of Peru for the Shining Path of José Carlos Mariátegui – or *Sendero Luminoso* (the Shining Path) – is the most secretive and vicious of Latin American terrorist organizations. It is a radical Communist party, named after a phrase used by the founder of the Peruvian Communist party, who died in 1930: 'Marxist–Leninism will open the shining path that will lead to the revolution.' Its heroes are Mao Tse-tung and the Gang of Four, the Chinese extremists, led by Mao's widow, who tried to perpetuate the 'Cultural Revolution' in China after Mao's death in 1976 and were overthrown in a coup a month later. Their nearest parallels in Maoist fanaticism are perhaps Pol Pot's Khmers Rouges in Cambodia.

Sendero's centre of activity is the department of Ayacucho, in south-central Peru in the high Andes, but it has extended its activities to about half of Peru's 25 departments, and has planted bombs in Lima. In the areas that it controls, it enforces a savage regime on the peasants, who frequently fight back in defence of their livelihoods. The army has conducted a reign of terror in the affected areas, in an effort to wipe out the Senderistas, but so far without success. The insurrection that began in 1980 has become a civil war, in which between 10,000 and 15,000 people have been killed.

HISTORY

Ancient Peru under the Incas was the largest of pre-Columbian empires, covering what are now Ecuador, the Andean and coastal areas of Peru and Bolivia, northern Chile and parts of Argentina. Its capital was Cuzco, in the Andes. The empire was conquered by Francisco Pizarro with 180 men in 1531. He moved the capital to Lima on the coast, and ever since, there has been constant tension between the Incas' descendants who speak Quechua, and the Spanish-speaking inhabitants of the cities of the plain.

Peru won its independence from Spain in 1821, along with the rest of Spanish South and Central America. It has been governed by a succession of alternating oligarchies and military dictatorships, often closely related, with occasional attempts at democracy. The most recent military government, which ruled in the 1970s, broke up the oligarchy by attacking its economic domination. One sugar company, for instance, owned by a handful of people, controlled plantations covering an area larger than Belgium. In 1980, suffering from political exhaustion and under intense pressure from the Carter administration in Washington, the military handed over power to a civilian government. Fernando Belaúnde Terry was elected president and was succeeded, in 1985, by Alan García Pérez, then aged 35. He was leader of the American Popular Revolutionary Alliance (APRA), a party that had been the perpetual leftist opposition in Peru since it was founded in 1924. Its earlier electoral victories had been thwarted by the army.

Peru pursues an independent foreign policy, inclined to anti-Americanism but refusing to fall under Soviet influence: President García's relations with Cuba are notably cool. Peru's main problem, apart from the Sendero, is economic. Like most of Latin America, it is having great difficulty modernizing its economy. Though potentially very rich, it remains a Third World country with First World pretensions. Much of its industry and its banking system have been nationalized, with all the inefficiencies that follow such a policy. Its foreign debts are, proportionately, as great as Mexico's: President García in his inaugural address announced that Peru would limit its repayments to 10 per cent of its export earnings. For three years, the economy expanded, inflation was kept to 50 per cent and Peru suffered no painful consequences from its novel approach to its debts. Then, early in 1988, inflation rose to 200 per cent, then 400 per cent, and it continued to accelerate. All the economic chickens came home to roost.

Peru is also the world's chief supplier of coca leaves and is thus in the frontline of the drug wars (*see* The Drug Wars, pp. 466–77). It derives a backhanded advantage from this distinction: by cooperating with the United States government in fighting the drug cartels, it avoids American retaliation against its debt policies.

It is a difficult balancing act. The fundamental political question is whether the country's shaky political system and inadequate economy can survive a Marxist insurrection, pressure from the drug barons and the deep social divisions between Spanish and Indian that go back to the Conquest.

THE WAR

The Sendero insurrection is partly a peasant Indian uprising against an alien and uncaring government, similar to the conflicts in Central America, but its ideology is urban, Spanish and Marxist. A group of extreme Marxists established themselves

460

in the university of Ayacucho on the Andean plateau in the 1960s, in a region that is remote, poor and neglected. The university was intended to educate Indians and to prepare engineers, teachers and other professionals to return to their villages to help them emerge from the night of centuries – a sort of indigenous Peace Corps. By 1968, the Senderistas had won control of the university and its projects.

The Communist party in Peru split after the Sino–Soviet dispute erupted in 1964. In Ayacucho, the pro-Chinese faction, calling itself Sendero Luminoso won the dispute, advocated a policy of Maoist extremism and rejoiced in the Cultural Revolution. The Senderistas detest the Soviets as much as they detest the Americans.

Sendero's leader was Abimael Guzmán Reynoso, known by the *nom de guerre* 'Gonzalo'. He was born in Mollendo, a city on the southern coast of Peru, in 1934, the son of an unmarried woman and her married lover. He studied law and philosophy and, in 1962, was appointed assistant professor of philosophy at the University of Ayacucho. He spent part of the 1960s in China, during the Cultural Revolution. He became the leader of the Marxist theorists at the university, and by 1968, his brand of Communism was dominant and he was himself the most powerful man at the university. For a while, he was director of personnel and was thus able to install his supporters into every available post, from professor to cleaner. Senderista professors taught Marxist dialectics and the philosophy of Mao Tse-tung and recruited a generation of students to the cause. They graduated as both teachers and Senderistas, and returned to spread the gospel in their native villages, though presumably without dwelling on the ideological purity of Chairman Mao and the villany of other Chinese leaders, subjects that would have appeared quite mystifying to the Andean peasantry. Where Lenin used intellectuals and workers as the cadres of Bolshevism, and Mao used Chinese peasants, Guzmán used schoolteachers.

As a result, the Shining Path has spread far into Peruvian society. There are cells in villages throughout the Andean region: the Senderistas can call upon thousands of dedicated militants for their military operations, and are assured of shelter and sustenance. In the mid-1970s, during the upheaval in China following Mao's death, they gave their ideological support to the Gang of Four, and now excoriate the Chinese government as counter-revolutionary, like the Soviet government. (In 1986, they bombed the Soviet embassy in Lima and attacked a shop frequented by Soviet sailors in Callao.) The Senderistas, therefore – unlike the Sandinistas in Nicaragua or the revolutionary parties in El Salvador and Guatemala – have no outside support.

Anti-Sendero forces in the University of Ayacucho fought back, and in 1978, during a period of military government, the Senderistas went underground. Their chief strength remains around Ayacucho, in areas that have been directly subject to Guzmán's influence. His followers describe him as the 'Fourth Sword' of the Communist Revolution (the others being Marx, Lenin and Mao), and revere the 'Guiding Thought of Gonzalo', as once the Chinese revered the 'Thoughts of Chairman Mao'.

A rival Marxist terrorist organization, the Tupac Amaru Revolutionary Movement (MRTA), made its appearance in 1984. It is believed to have 200 or 300 members, mostly university students. Unlike the Senderistas, the MRTA are a typical, urban Latin American revolutionary group, and look for support to Cuba and the USSR. In November 1987, they launched a 'rural column' into the 461 countryside, seizing a number of villages in the Amazonian jungle. The army promptly moved in and suppressed them.

The Senderistas began their military campaign in 1980. On 17 May, during Peru's first free election in years, Sendero attacked a polling station in a village near Ayacucho. It then began attacking police posts and village leaders, and imposing its own government upon isolated villages. The Senderistas follow Mao's exhortation to use the country to strangle the cities. This means that they must occupy and hold territory, which gives the army targets to shoot at.

The police were sent in large numbers to Ayacucho to fight the Senderistas. Their years under a military regime had served the police ill: they were at once brutal and incompetent. There were many cases of torture, rape, mutilation and murder, with the result that hundreds of young people were driven to join Sendero in the mountains.

The Senderistas were equally brutal, and the villagers were caught in the middle. Some of them fought back, killing Senderistas whenever they could. In January 1983, Indians in a village called Huaychao in the high Andes killed seven Senderistas who had marched in and demanded that they join the Shining Path. (Later, it was found that some of the murdered Senderistas were 14- and 15-year-old schoolboys.) A group of eight journalists went to investigate. It was a two-day hike into the mountain, and the villagers, mistaking them for Senderistas come to avenge their fallen comrades, killed them all. The photographer among them had kept his camera working almost until the end, and it was found intact and containing photographs of the crowds of Indians menacing the journalists and the first killings. Peru's most prominent writer, Mario Vargas Llosa, was a member of the commission that examined the incident, and his report was one of the first on Sendero to receive wide publicity. He said that the greatest shock to him and to the other commissioners from Lima was the unbridgeable chasm separating them from the Indians. It was not merely language or income, it was a gap of centuries.

The Senderistas, because they have no foreign support, are poorly armed. What arms they have have been stolen or captured from the police or military, or provided by their supporters. Their chief weapon is dynamite, which is easily obtainable. They blow up buildings, bomb military and civilian targets, and wage a strenuous campaign against the Peruvian electricity grid, regularly blowing up pylons to disrupt power supplies to Lima.

The Senderistas also continue to exhibit their curious political priorities. In December 1980, they hung dogs from the lamp-posts of Lima to show what they thought of 'the running dogs of imperialism', and plastered the walls with posters denouncing Deng Xiao-ping and praising the Gang of Four.

The war in the countryside has been savage and merciless. When the Senderistas seize a village, they shoot any leading citizens who might oppose them. In return, the villagers sometimes revolt and execute all the Senderistas they capture, sometimes waging pitched battles in which scores are killed.

The armed forces are even more brutal, and there are numerous reports of massacres in the Andes. The worst culprits are the Peruvian navy. Amnesty International has prepared detailed reports of the Peruvian 'dirty war'. Mass graves have been found in the 'Emergency zone' and around Ayacucho, and there

are numerous accounts of massacres by the police. In a 1985 report, Amnesty listed

1005 cases of people who had 'disappeared' in 1983 and 1984, but this was clearly no more than a fraction of the real total. Amnesty states:

In most cases of political killings in the Emergency Zone, believed to have been carried out by government forces, the bodies of the victims, when found, are naked, marked by torture, and with single gunshot wounds to the head; in many cases, the victims are found blindfolded and with their hands bound behind their backs. Many victims are unidentifiable: their clothing has been destroyed, features mutilated, and bodies dumped far from the scene of detention, in areas where relatives are unlikely to travel.

The difference between Peru and Chile or Argentina (during their 'dirty wars') is that Peru is a democracy, not a military dictatorship. Protests are therefore possible, and the killings are reported in the press. This scrutiny may inhibit some degree of military terrorism, but not much. In Peru, the victims are Indian peasants, not middle-class Spanish-speaking youths in the cities. The Argentinian mothers of middle-class terrorists, leftists and unlucky students who had been murdered marched around the Plaza de Mayo every Thursday. The mothers and widows of Quechua peasants killed by the Peruvian army or navy have no such opportunity. The Peruvian situation, therefore, is more like Guatemala in the 1960s and 1970s, where a military government, with the aim of suppressing a leftist insurrection, slaughtered tens of thousands of Indian peasants, without arousing much international concern.

In June 1986, Sendero prisoners in Lima's three jails mutinied. They had long enjoyed virtual autonomy within the jails: wardens were not admitted into their cell blocks; the Senderistas maintained their own discipline and carried out military training and ran indoctrination classes. García sent the marines to reoccupy El Fronton, Peru's Alcatraz on an island off the coast. Three marines and one hostage were killed – and so were 135 prisoners. At another prison, this time in Lima, 124 prisoners were killed when an army anti-terrorist squad stormed it. There is no doubt that most of the prisoners were captured alive and shot; some were also taken away and tortured first.

In 1984, Senderistas appeared for the first time in the Huellaga valley north of Lima, one of Peru's main coca-growing areas. They devoted themselves to political work for the next three years, following basic Maoist tactics, and in 1987, having established their base, they started military operations. They fought government troops and competed with the drug traffickers. They took over small towns and imposed 'revolutionary justice'; they have blown bridges and then ambushed and killed workers sent to repair them, and increasingly used the valley's remote jungles as a base.

Sendero has taken up the cause of the coca-growers, protecting them against government attempts to eradicate the drug. They have also started to impose levies on traffickers, and this might, later, prove a serious problem for them. The Senderistas insist that they oppose all use of cocaine in Peru, but have no objection to exporting coca paste. They have always been chronically short of money, and the revenues they can earn from the coca trade would provide all the money they need. It might also corrupt them, as leftists in Colombia and Burma have been corrupted. Every man has his price, and a peasant recruited to fight for social justice and revenge against the class enemy might come cheap.

463

Early in 1988, for the first time, the Senderistas began publishing communiqués, discussion papers and lengthy denunciations of the government. The movement claimed to have held a party congress, and issued a report in February. Some of these documents suggested that Sendero was revising its strategy. It is all very well to encircle the cities in China, but encircling Lima, which contains nearly one-third of the country's population, is a different matter. Sendero, therefore, announced that it planned to extend its operations to the capital. This would mean conflict with the MRTA and other Marxist movements who are opposed to the Senderistas.

In June 1988, security police captured the Senderistas' second in command, Osman Morote, Guzmán's closest associate and the Senderistas' strategist. He was captured in a safe-house, with four comrades, and a haul of documents on the movement's plans. A month later, Guzmán gave a lengthy interview to a sympathetic Lima newspaper, to demonstrate that the movement could survive the loss: it was the first word from 'Gonzalo' himself in a decade. He announced that Sendero was preparing for a general insurrection. 'The crisis conditions into which the outmoded system of Peruvian society has entered indicate that these decisive years will accelerate conditions and develop the revolutionary situation powerfully,' he said. 'Our process of the people's war has led us towards the apex. Consequently, we have to prepare for insurrection, which will be the taking of the cities.'

Peru is not a Latin Lebanon; the Andean provinces have not yet attained the level of anarchy of Uganda; nor have the Senderistas built up a guerrilla army dangerous enough to threaten the government, probably having only 4000 to 5000 fighters and twice that number of supporters (the MRTA, by contrast, probably has only a few hundred militants). Despite this, the Sendero war is going badly for the government: the security forces cannot defend the villages against Senderista attack, and the village militias make their own law.

The human rights group Americas Watch issued a report in November 1988, alleging that violations of human rights by the army and police had increased sharply. A death squad, calling itself the Rodrigo Franco Command (after an assassinated politician), has begun operations. It is rumoured to be linked to the governing party, the APRA.

Meanwhile, the economy was rapidly deteriorating: inflation was running out of control, reaching 1722 per cent in 1988, and unemployment in the slums of Lima approached 60 per cent. President García's popularity collapsed along with his economic policies. In September 1988, in a desperate attempt to redress the situation, the government ordered a massive devaluation of the currency and huge price increases – for example petrol went up by 400 per cent, and in that month, there was inflation of 114 per cent. García continued to refuse to seek help from the International Monetary Fund (IMF), because of the conditions it would impose, or to resume repayments of Peru's foreign debt. He thus was unable to borrow money abroad.

The situation appeared ripe for another military coup – except for the fact that, as far as the security situation was concerned, the military had a free hand already, and their excesses were covered by the democratically elected president. What

would they gain by taking power *and* responsibility?

FURTHER READING

Amnesty International, *Peru Briefing: 'Disappearances' and Political Killings by Government Forces in the Andean Emergency Zone*, London, 1985.
Bonner, Raymond, 'Peru's War', *New Yorker*, 4 January 1988.
Saba, Raul P., *Political Development and Democracy in Peru: Continuity in Change and Crisis*, Boulder, Colo., Westview Press, 1987.
Vargas Llosa, Mario, 'Death in the Andes', *New York Times Magazine*, 31 July 1983.

THE DRUG WARS

The South American drug trade has corrupted government, society and law enforcement in a dozen countries in the Americas. The most seriously affected are Colombia (where the government has virtually surrendered to the drug barons), Panama and the Bahamas (where the governments are allegedly the traffickers' active partners), and the United States. Americans' insatiable hunger for cocaine, heroin and marijuana is one of the great forces of evil in the world: it has induced the enormous corruption of Latin America while poisoning hundreds of thousands of people in the black ghettos, the *barrios* and the affluent white suburbs of the United States. The scale of the problem can be measured by one statistic: the US Treasury believes that drug revenues in the United States are between $60 billion and $120 billion a year. Bolivia, Peru, Mexico, Paraguay, Brazil, Venezuela, Belize, Haiti, Honduras and Nicaragua have also been corrupted to varying degrees, and coca is now grown, refined and sold in Argentina. (*See* Burma, pp. 134–44, for details of drugs emanating from the Golden Triangle.)

COLOMBIA

Geography	439,734 sq. miles (1,138,907 sq. km). The size of Spain, Portugal and France combined.
Population	28,961,000
GNP per capita	$1230
Casualties	Approximately 300,000 were killed in the civil war, 1946–57.
Rebels	• *Revolutionary Armed Forces of Colombia* (FARC): The armed wing of the Colombian Communist party. Has several thousand members, and is heavily armed. On occasion, has hired out troops to the drug cartel. In past three years, its political wing, the Patriotic Union, has lost about 300 men murdered by police or military death squads or by goons employed by drug traffickers.
	• *M-19*: Most flamboyant guerrilla movement. Named after the election of 19 April 1970, which it claims was fraudulent. Leader is Carlos Pizarro.
	• *National Liberation Army* (ELN): concentrates on attacking economic targets.
	• *People's Liberation Army* (EPL): A Maoist group.

- *Jorge Eliecer Gaitan Movement*: Appeared in spring 1988. Kidnapped former governor of Tolima province and announced that it would put him on trial for negligence in connection with deaths of 23,000 people that occurred when Nevada del Ruiz volcano erupted in 1985.

HISTORY

The two dominant strands in Colombian society until very recently were violence and a commitment to a rather ineffective democracy. However, during the past decade, cocaine's corruption has overwhelmed everything else. Apart from those countries engulfed in active warfare, Colombia is the most violent in the world: there were 14,000 murders in 1986, and the numbers have increased steeply since then and reached 18,000–20,000 in 1988. That is proportionately six times the murder rate in the United States – and the US is an exceedingly violent society. As for democracy, Colombia has suffered one brief period of military rule, in the 1960s, but otherwise, it has always had civilian governments, all of which have been notable for their inability to end the killing.

Between 1946 and 1957, the constant fighting between partisans of the country's two traditional political parties – the Conservatives and the Liberals – reached levels approaching civil war. The period came to be known in Colombia as *La Violencia*, and it is said that about 300,000 people were killed. The slaughter was finally suspended when the two parties agreed to divide power between them.

This sharing out of power by two factions of the ruling oligarchy encouraged the Communist opposition, and soon a full-scale guerrilla war was under way. It continued until 1984, when President Belisario Betancur Cuartas signed a peace treaty with the FARC. The guerrillas were left undisturbed in the remote fastnesses of that immense country, and the government promised to institute social reforms to improve the lot of the peasantry. However, prosperity has been a long time coming to the countryside, except in the areas given over to the cultivation of coca, and the considerable prosperity of the cities is due to cocaine and coffee exports, not to government policy.

The ceasefire, in theory, remains in effect, but it is seldom observed. The smaller guerrilla factions, in particular M-19, have resumed open war, and in some parts of the country, notably the wild mountains of the south in Caqueta province, and in the banana-growing provinces of the north, the war has begun again in full force. Paradoxically, the government and the headquarters of the FARC remain in constant communication, with periodic meetings between ministers and guerrilla leaders. There is even a 'hot line' between Bogotá and the FARC base at La Uribe, on a mountain south of the capital.

Both sides recognize that a military victory for either of them is impossible. The country is too big and too wild for the army to win; besides, it cannot find the men for the 10:1 or 15:1 advantage needed for victory in a counter-insurgency. The guerrillas have between 8000 and 10,000 men, and the government cannot send 80,000 to 150,000 troops against them. On the other hand, partly because of its democratic traditions, the Colombian regime is not going to collapse like Batista in Cuba or Somoza in Nicaragua. There is a perpetual stalemate.

467

The same collapse of public order with which the United States is faced in the inner cities now afflicts Colombia, with the same cause: cocaine. There were over 3000 drug-related murders in Medellín alone in 1987. There has also been a series of massacres of villagers in the past two years: at Easter 1988, gunmen slaughtered 34 people at a festival in a village in northern Colombia. Amnesty International has accused the Colombian armed forces of violating human rights, and there are increasing signs that death squads, composed of off-duty military and police, are now operating against the guerrillas or suspected leftists. The break-down in legality that afflicted Colombia during *La Violencia* has now returned.

COCAINE

The Colombian cocaine trade was developed in the 1970s by a group of entrepreneurs in Medellín, a city in central Colombia, north-west of Bogotá. They took what had been essentially a cottage industry and turned it into a major business – with the highest rate of return on investment of any industry in the world. According to the US State Department's Bureau of International Narcotics Matters, Colombia, Bolivia and Peru between them produced approximately 183,000 metric tons of coca leaves in 1988. Were it all converted, and were nothing consumed or lost on the way, it would give about 360 metric tons of pure cocaine.

The entrepreneurs' first problem is to cope with the enormous volume of leaves. Each hectare (2.4 acres) of coca plants produces about one metric ton of leaves. By the State Department's estimate, therefore, 183,000 hectares (440,000 acres) are devoted to growing the plant in those three countries. It takes 200 kilos of leaves to produce 1 kilo of paste. The leaves have to be converted into coca paste on the spot: the sheer volume, not to mention the weight, of the leaves makes it impractical to move them very far. The plantations are scattered in the valleys, and there are thousands of collection points at which the leaves are rendered down. The paste is brought to one of thousands of small dirt airstrips, hidden in the jungles. It is then taken to laboratories in Colombia to be converted first into cocaine base (it takes 2.5 kilos of paste to produce 1 kilo of base), and then into cocaine hydrochloride – pure cocaine. These latter operations require skilled technicians and specialized equipment and supplies.

The entrepreneurs organize all of this, and then handle the smuggling operation to get the cocaine into the United States – and, increasingly, into Europe. It is either concealed in planes or boats or in innocuous exports, or else it is shipped to an entrepôt in Panama, the Bahamas, Mexico or Haiti, whence it is carried into the United States.

Finally, the cocaine entrepreneurs, like oil producers in the Gulf, have set up their own distribution networks inside the US. Unlike the members of OPEC, however, they do not own the land from which their product originates: that remains the domain of peasants and their landlords in the Andes. But they control everything else, from the planes that pick up the loads of coca paste from jungle airstrips, to the runners pushing 'crack', the most deadly form of cocaine, on the Upper West Side of Manhattan. The number of cocaine addicts in New York, almost all of them hooked on crack, has increased from 182,000 in 1986 to 600,000 in 1988. These were 1867 murders in the city in 1988, a 10 per cent increase in one year.

Coca producers have found it as difficult to control cocaine prices as OPEC has found it difficult to control oil prices. In the late 1970s, as the immense expansion of the business began, Peruvian peasants were paid 50 cents for a kilo of coca leaves. Prices rose rapidly at first: Bolivian peasants were being paid $7 a kilo for leaves at the height of the boom, in 1982–4. The laws of supply and demand then came into play. The immense expansion of coca plantations in Peru and Bolivia produced a glut, and prices dropped to $2 a kilo for leaves in 1986, and 40 cents in 1988.

These variations were apparent at the other end. When a kilo of coca leaves cost 50 cents, a kilo of pure cocaine in Colombia (from 500 kilos of leaves) was worth $9750. By the time it reached the user in New York, that kilo was worth $560,000, sold by the gram, and it was no longer pure cocaine, having been 'cut' to 12.5 per cent purity. However, cocaine is now so readily available, despite all the efforts of police and FBI and various task forces, that cocaine on the streets of Miami is sold at 33 per cent purity. A kilo that cost $47,000 to $60,000 wholesale in 1982 now costs only $9000 to $14,000.

In 1983, 6 tons of cocaine were seized in south Florida, and 2.3 tons in Mexico. In 1985, 25 tons were seized in Florida, and in 1986, over 30 tons. In 1987, the federal drug agencies seized 70 tons of cocaine in the US, of varying degrees of purity, 1400 lb of heroin and 20,000 tons of marijuana. In 1988, cocaine seizures reached about 100 tons.

Calculations of the value of these huge quantities of drug are difficult because some of the cocaine seized was 100 per cent pure, some 50 per cent, some merely 12.5 per cent. As we have seen, the State Department estimated that Andean cocaine production reached 360 tons in 1988. Even allowing for losses, local consumption and the seizures, the FBI's estimate of 35 tons of pure cocaine reaching the US market is clearly exceedingly cautious. At $14,000 for a kilo at one-third purity, the suppliers' income from 35 tons would be $1.5 billion. For the full 360 tons, it would be $15 billion. Since the cartel also controls distribution and retail sales, its profits are, in fact, immensely higher, despite the seizures. In a report issued in April 1988, a panel of experts, directed by a former president of Costa Rica and by Sol Linowitz, the former American ambassador who negotiated the Panama canal treaties, stated: 'As long as the profit margin for cocaine is 12,000 per cent from production cost to street value, the lure of trafficking will be irresistible.'

The extent of the problem can be gauged by a short news item, buried inside the 'Metropolitan' section of the New York Times on 22 August 1988. A day earlier, more than 2 tons of cocaine had been seized in an apartment in Queens, New York. Its street value was said by police to be over $400 million. This was an enormous amount of the drug, but nowadays such a discovery is treated as routine by the newspapers.

THE CARTEL

In November 1981, M-19 terrorists tried to kidnap a major drug smuggler, Carlos Lehrer Rivas, and succeeded in kidnapping Marta Ochoa Vasquez, one of the daughters of Don Fabio Ochoa, and sister to Jorge, one of the most important drug traffickers in Colombia. M-19 demanded a $1 million ransom, but instead of   469 paying, the Ochoa family convoked a meeting in Cali, about 200 miles (320 km) south-west of Bogotá, of all the major drug traffickers in the country, and together they declared war on the kidnappers. They issued a leaflet which put the issue bluntly. Describing itself as 'the Mafia', the group announced that it had formed an organization called 'Death to Kidnappers' with a war chest of $4.4 million and 2230 men. They added: 'Kidnappers will be executed in public: they will be hanged from trees in public places or executed by firing squad.' Rewards of $200,000 were offered for information.

The war was short and brutal. Ten leaders of M-19 were captured and tortured, their sympathizers were terrorized and, after three months, M-19 surrendered. Marta Ochoa was released unharmed.

After this success, members of the 'Mafia' who decided to continue to cooperate became known as the Medellín Cartel. Its leading figures are: members of the Ochoa family, of whom Jorge is the most important; Pablo Escobar Gaviria; and Gonzalo Rodríguez Gacha. Rodríguez handles the import of coca paste from Peru and Bolivia. Escobar, who is the principal leader of the Cartel, supervises production and security: he is said to employ 200 full-time killers and to direct two schools for assassins, whose pupils learn such techniques as shooting from motorbikes. The Ochoas handle the export trade. The three are known as *los duenos del cupo* – 'the holders of the quota' – who share out coca paste for refining. The group also supplies smaller enterprises with its product. The most conspicuous of those sub-groups was directed by Carlos Lehrer Rivas who became one of the major cocaine smugglers.

The Cartel is a loose association of drug producers and smugglers, united in self-defence, whose members cooperate to share out the market, beat off rivals and intimidate the government. It is not even a proper cartel, which is classically an association of producers who combine to drive up prices – for example, OPEC is a cartel. On the contrary, the price of cocaine has dropped sharply on the streets of the United States and Europe because the Cartel's suppliers have increased production enormously, and its smugglers have succeeded in flooding the market. The Medellín Cartel describes itself as 'The Company', or the Mafia, but the name, 'Cartel', has stuck.

The Cartel's power, and the progress of its successful war against the Colombian government, can be measured by the history of the 1979 extradition treaty with the United States. The Cartel's leaders saw this as their most serious threat and set about defeating it. In 1985, when the Supreme Court was debating the treaty's constitutionality, the Cartel hired M-19 (allegedly for $5 million) to storm the Palace of Justice, its war with the terrorists in 1981 seemingly forgotten.

The attack took place on 6 November. The commandos drove into the parking garage below the Palace in a bus painted in the colours of the Bogotá Telephone Company. There were 40–45 of them, men and women. They seized the ground floor, and then set about searching the building, floor by floor. They took some 250 hostages, including the members of the Supreme Court, who were holding a meeting to discuss the extradition treaty. The president of the court, Alfonso Reyes Enchandía, was obliged to call President Betancur, and demand that he surrender at once to be tried by a 'people's court'. The president sent in an anti-terrorist assault squad, and the terrorists began slaughtering their hostages, starting with Reyes and ten other judges, taking care to kill all those who supported the treaty. About 60 hostages and 40 terrorists were killed in the final bloodbath. Shortly afterwards, one of the few pro-treaty judges who had escaped was murdered in Bogotá. A year later, the reconstituted Supreme Court annulled the extradition treaty.

Another guerrilla group, the FARC, supplied the guards for the Cartel's major cocaine processing plant, which they named Tranquilandia. It was in the jungle on an island in the Yari river. In March 1984, the newly appointed minister of justice, Rodrigo Lara Bonilla and his chief of the narcotics police, Colonel Jaime Ramírez Gómez, raided the factory. They found $1.2 billion worth of cocaine and laboratories capable of refining 4 tons a week.

That was the high-water mark of the government's war on the Cartel. Lara was murdered a month later, on 30 April, and Ramirez in November the following year. The judge appointed to investigate Lara's murder found evidence of the Cartel's complicity. He, too, was assassinated. Lara's successor as justice minister, Enrique Perejo, was later sent to Budapest as ambassador, for his own safety. The Cartel pursued him there, and shot and seriously wounded him on 13 January 1987.

After Lara's death, there was a brief upsurge of outrage, and the Cartel's leaders found it prudent to leave the country. They moved to Panama with a small army of bodyguards, and paid General Manuel Noriega $5 million for their security. In May 1984, the Cartel met Colombia's attorney-general in a hotel in Panama, and proposed a deal. They would shut down their operations, from production to distribution, in exchange for an amnesty. The government refused. A later, possibly facetious offer by the Cartel to pay off the country's $9 billion national debt in exchange for amnesty was also rejected.

Lehrer, Jorge Luis Ochoa and the leader of the emerging Cali Cartel, Gilberto Rodríguez Orejuela, went to Spain, where the latter two were arrested and sent back to Colombia. They had time to set up a Spanish network, based on Colombian immigrants, which is now rapidly expanding. European narcotics police fear that Europe will catch up with the US in cocaine consumption within five years, with Spain playing the role of Florida as principal importing centre.

Rodríguez Orejuela was put on trial in July 1987, and acquitted. This was partially the fault of the American authorities who had provided the chief witness against him: an agent of the US Drug Enforcement Administration (DEA). The agent could not speak Spanish, and the court provided an interpreter with a very inadequate command of English. However, the trial seemed to American observers to be rigged from the start. Rodríguez was acquitted on all charges – which meant not only that he was free in Colombia, but that he could not be extradited to the United States, even if the extradition treaty were reinstated.

Jorge Ochoa was in prison awaiting trial in August 1986, when a judge released him on bail, and he vanished. When he was finally tracked down in November 1987, he was arrested again. His two brothers and another member of the Cartel, Pablo Escobar, visited the judge in private: Jorge Ochoa was released a few days later.

The attorney general, Carlos Mauro Hoyos Jimenez, ordered an investigation into Ochoa's release, but before it was completed he was murdered in Medellín, his   471 hometown, on 26 January 1988. He had been kidnapped, handcuffed, blindfolded and gagged – and shot ten times in the head. To make sure that the message was clearly understood, a representative of *los extraditables* called the local radio station to inform them: 'The war goes on. I repeat, the war goes on.' President Barca (who had replaced Betancur in August 1986) did not attend the funeral: his security could not be assured in Colombia's second largest city.

A new attorney general was appointed: Alfredo Gutiérrez Márquez. He caused a sensation by suggesting that the only solution to the crisis might be to legalize drugs and negotiate with the traffickers. In March 1988, he was forced to resign when it was found that his brother was involved in trafficking.

Lehrer was not as lucky as Rodríguez Orejuela and Ochoa: he was arrested in February 1987, and extradited to the United States. An informant had told the police where he could be found, and he was picked up at a farm 20 miles (32 km) from Medellín. He was immediately put on a plane to Florida. The Colombian president had signed the extradition order some years earlier, before the extradition treaty with the United States was declared unconstitutional, and he now chose to declare that the order was still valid. In May 1988, Lehrer was convicted of smuggling 3.3 tons of cocaine into the United States through the Bahamas and was sentenced to more than 135 years in jail: a life term, with no parole, and nine consecutive 15-year sentences on other smuggling charges.

It is possible that Lehrer was betrayed by the senior members of the Cartel. He was a psychopathic killer and publicity-seeker, constantly giving interviews and boasting of his achievements: he gave cocaine smuggling a bad name. What is more, his operation in the Bahamas, on Norman's Cay, had been so large, dangerous and conspicuous that even the complaisant government of Sir Lynden Pindling could not overlook it indefinitely. His partner in the Bahamas had reportedly been Robert Vesco, an embezzler on the grand scale who is urgently wanted by American police.

The annulment of the extradition treaty by the Supreme Court in 1987 meant that all proceedings against 100 or more suspects were cancelled.

The new president, Virgilio Barco Vargas, attempted to reverse the tide. In May 1988, he sent the army against the Cartel's drug laboratories in the jungles: it was the first time troops had been used in the drug wars since the mid 1970s. In August, in a severe defeat for the government, the Supreme Court formally suspended the extradition orders against the Cartel's leaders. The favourite to win the 1990 presidential election was Luís Carlos Galán. He vowed to extirpate the drug lords if he won. He was killed at an election meeting on 18 August 1989 and Barco ordered another massive attack on the drug lords, his fourth. He invoked his emergency powers to extradite to the United States Eduardo Martinez Romero, whose role in the Cartel was allegedly to launder money, and confiscated the drug lords' property: all these moves were challenged in the courts, which had proved themselves susceptible to the blandishments of the Cartel, particularly the choice of 'lead or silver' – meaning death or money. President Bush offered to help and sent bullet-proof vests and armoured cars for the judges, but it was clear that the war had to be fought and won by

Colombians, in Colombia.

THE SPREAD OF THE OCTOPUS

After the leaders of the Cartel left the country in 1984, following the murder of the minister of justice, they set about expanding their network of contacts in other Central American countries and in Europe. The rise in cocaine consumption in Europe dates from that year. They had already invested heavily in Panama, according to Ramón Milian Rodríguez, a senior finance official for the Cartel who was caught in the United States and is now serving a 43-year sentence. He testified to a Senate committee that Noriega had been paid about $320 million between 1979 and 1983 for the use of Panamanian airports and the banking system (which was used to launder the enormous amount of money involved). Lynden Pindling in the Bahamas came much cheaper. A witness at the Lehrer trial testified that he had paid Pindling between $3 million and $5 million for the use of Norman's Cay.

The Cartel has also invested in military leaders in Haiti and Honduras, and has backed both the Nicaraguan Contras and at least some members of the Sandinista government. One witness, Barry Seal, implicated Tomás Borge, Nicaraguan minister of the interior. He claimed to have flown at least one load of cocaine from Colombia to Managua, where the transaction was supervised by a man who claimed to be a senior aide to Borge. Seal was the American prosecutor's chief witness against Ochoa. He was assassinated in February 1986 in Baton Rouge, Lousiana: the police had not taken seriously his claim that his life was in danger.

The links between the Cartel and Cuba are discussed on page 477. The Cartel has at times allied itself with the pro-Cuban M-19 guerrilla movement in Colombia. The essential point about the Cartel's politics and its foreign policy is that money is non-ideological. Lenin offered to sell capitalists the rope with which they would hang themselves. The ferocious Medellín capitalists have turned the offer around, and are buying up revolutionaries as freely as they buy old-fashioned military men.

The drug trade is a finely tuned capitalist enterprise. It responds to movements in supply and demand, and the most profitable sectors are refining and distribution. When the US succeeds in enforcing a crackdown in one area – say, eliminating poppy fields in Turkey or coca plants in Peru – production expands somewhere else. When the Medellín Cartel's operations in Colombia were interrupted in 1984, refining and distribution through Mexico expanded.

In a decade, the Medellín traffickers moved from a 'peasant' economy, based on raising marijuana ('Colombian Gold') and smuggling it across the Caribbean, to a modern industrial business with refineries, finance offices and elaborate distribution networks. The Mexicans are no less gifted than the Colombians, the Hondurans no less corruptible. Medellín now faces competition from Culiacan on Mexico's Pacific coast, where the Cartel's business principles have already been introduced: when Mexican police raided a drug depot used by Colombians in Sonora, they found 100 AK-47 assault rifles, 65,000 rounds of ammunition, 92 bayonets and six infra-red night scopes.

In the mid-1980s, as supply exceeded demand in the United States and the price dropped, the Medellín Cartel, which dominated the Miami market, decided to move in on the most lucrative market in the world: New York, which was dominated by the Cali Cartel. There ensued a continuing and violent battle between the two, involving scores of murders, and frequent betrayals. The 2 tons of cocaine found in New York in August 1988 had belonged to the Cali Cartel; the police may have been tipped off by the Medellín Cartel.

The United States has had little success in eliminating coca growing in Bolivia and Peru – but if it did succeed, production would only move to Brazil or further south. The area suitable for coca growing is enormous, and so are the rewards.

HONDURAS

After the murder of the minister of justice in Colombia in 1984, the Medellín Cartel hastily arranged an alternative route for its product into the United States. In 1983, Mexican police had seized 2.3 tons of cocaine, but by 1987, that figure had risen to 9.3 tons. Juan Ramón Matta Ballesteros, a Honduran who had worked in Medellín, had developed a route through Mexico. Accused of murdering a DEA agent there in 1985, he was arrested at his home in Tegucigalpa on 4 April 1988, and immediately extradited to the United States.

Honduran law prohibits Honduran citizens from being extradited, but the military had shipped Matta off anyway. In response, there were riots on 8 April, five people were killed and an annex to the American embassy was burned. It was a striking demonstration of outraged patriotism and resentment at American heavy-handedness. A few days later, protesters were again on the streets, this time demonstrating against the government because of its subservience to the Americans and its tolerance of the drug traffickers. If there was a contradiction in these reactions, it was more apparent to North Americans than to Hondurans.

Matta allegedly had a fortune of $2 billion – quite enough to buy any number of Honduran generals. It is said that he corrupted the military intelligence department and the judicial system: he had returned to Honduras in 1985, after several years in Colombia, and had bought his way out of various legal charges then pending against him. The courts in Honduras are no more capable of convicting billionaire drug traffickers than are those in Colombia.

The Honduran military had apparently decided that unless they acted promptly, Honduras might go the way of Colombia, where the government is terrorized by the traffickers, or Panama, where the traffickers have taken over the government. The latter danger is probably the most serious. On 15 May 1988, a Honduran diplomat was arrested in Miami airport carrying 10 kilos of cocaine in his luggage. He was Rigoberto Regalado Lara, Honduran ambassador to Panama, and the half-brother of General Humberto Regalado Hernandez, the chief of staff.

BOLIVIA

Bolivia is one of the poorest countries in Latin America: its *per capita* GNP is $540 a year, and most of its people are engaged either in peasant agriculture or in the continually declining mining industry. In the mid-1970s, in an attempt to find an alternative to tin mining, the government encouraged the development of cotton growing in the lowlands to the east of the Andes. It did not solve Bolivia's problems: cotton prices collapsed as fast as tin prices. The landowners then replaced cotton with coca.

It was a major investment, and it was made possible with the government's help or, at the very least, its acquiescence. The first stage of cocaine production is the conversion of coca leaves to coca paste, a process that requires huge quantities of acid, diesel fuel and other chemicals, all of which had to be transported over the Andes. Furthermore, coca plants take three years to mature, so the landowners needed bank loans to tide them over.

The president at the time was General Hugo Banzer Suárez from Santa Cruz, the capital of the eastern lowlands. Banzer was an old acquaintance of Roberto Suárez Gómez, the region's principal landowner who was to become cocaine king of the Andes. Suárez formed a syndicate for exporting coca paste, and invited various friends and relatives of the president to join it. Suárez then entered into relations with the enterprising merchants of Medellín.

By the time Banzer retired in 1978, Bolivia's coca crop was developing rapidly, having risen from 11,800 tons in 1976 to 35,000 tons. (It was between 50,000 and 73,000 tons in 1988.) Elections were held, a new president was chosen and, in July 1980, just before he was to be inaugurated, General Luis García Meza seized power.

García was hand in glove with the cocaine traffickers. For a start, he appointed Suárez's cousin as minister of the interior. His job was to lead the campaign against narcotics, and for a year, one of the major coca-producing countries was controlled by the drug traffickers. It was a high point of corruption by drugs in Latin America. The alliance between Suárez and the Ochoas and the other members of the Medellín Cartel flourished. Coca was freely exported from eastern Bolivia, by air, to Colombia and then to the United States, and a great river of money flew back from North to South America.

President Carter exerted himself to have García Meza removed from office, an effort that was continued, after some hesitation, by the Reagan administration. A year after he took power, García was deposed by his fellow-officers. However, by then the pattern of the trade had become well established, and ever since there has been a constant battle between the traffickers and the Americans, with the government in La Paz sometimes leaning to the one side, sometimes to the other.

After the election of Victor Paz Estensorro in May 1985, a vigorous attempt to defeat the drug traffickers was launched, with American assistance. In 1986, in 'Operation Blast Furnace', the United States sent police and special troops to Bolivia in an attempt to round up major traffickers and destroy the jungle laboratories. It was all supposed to be secret, but the sudden arrival of large American planes at the airport was noticed, and soon the papers were full of the news. The operation was a failure and provoked a storm of nationalist outrage in Bolivia.

In 1987, a less ambitious project was started. In 'Operation Snowcap', Americans have been training Bolivian special forces in police work, particularly the techniques of locating field laboratories and destroying them; their chief weapon is the helicopter. They have met with considerable success: over 1500 field laboratories and 10 tons of cocaine (in various stages of production) were destroyed in six months, and over 3000 acres of coca plants were destroyed. This last was accomplished by giving peasants an inducement of $2000 for each hectare they eliminated. In addition, the Bolivian police succeeded in arresting a number of leading drug traffickers and seriously disrupting the Suárez organization – and in July 1988, they arrested Roberto Suárez himself. In August, US Secretary of State   475

George Shultz visited La Paz to congratulate the government on its achievements, and the drug lords made a botched attempt to assassinate him.

In 1985 or 1986, Roberto Suárez had handed over most of his organization to his nephew, Jorge Roca Suárez. Roca was a new generation of Bolivian trafficker. After the Colombians cut the price for coca paste in 1985, from $14,000 a kilo to $9000, he started to examine the possibility of cutting out the Medellín middlemen, and for the first time, laboratories were discovered in the Bolivian jungles that were capable of converting coca paste into coca base and into cocaine hydrochloride (pure cocaine). Roca also started contacting smugglers and distributors who would take his cocaine directly to the market, without the detour through Colombia. His operation was greatly disrupted by the arrest of several of his partners, and his uncle, in 1988.

The steep decline in the price of cocaine had also seriously affected Bolivian production. At 40 cents a kilo for leaves, it was scarcely worth the peasants' time to harvest the crop, particularly in the more remote and difficult districts that had been developed during the great expansion of the late 1970s.

Despite this, in the mid-1980s, cocaine exports brought $500 million a year to Bolivia and provided a livelihood for scores of thousands of peasants. President Paz and his American advisers are now grappling with the problem of finding an alternative. If the peasants can be found a more profitable crop, or at least one as profitable as coca, the programme will succeed and Bolivia will be saved the fate of Colombia. Otherwise, the traffickers will return and there will always be replacements for each drug lord who is arrested. Eradicating Bolivia's coca plants at the present rate of 3000 acres a year would take over 40 years.

PERU

According to the 1988 US State Department report on the drug trade, Peru is the world's leading producer of coca, and produced 109,000 metric tons in 1987. The report notes that the government failed to meet its objective of eradicating 14,825 acres (6000 hectares) of coca plantations in 1987. Even that total would have scarcely made any difference: there are 0.5 million acres (202,000 hectares) of coca plantations in Peru.

The Americans are trying to find an acceptable herbicide to spray on the plants – it simply is not possible to uproot half a million acres – but the problem with herbicides is the ecological damage they do. The coca plantations have already seriously harmed the land: coca plants need direct sun and no competition from other plants, so the growers simply sweep away everything, using the age-old slash-and-burn technique. In a few years, the rain carries away the topsoil, leaving a barren hillside where once the jungle flourished. The American chemicals firm, Eli Lilly & Co, whose herbicide Spike 20P was to be used in Peru, announced in May 1988 that it would no longer supply the product. It was apparently alarmed at the ecological consequences of its widespread use, and also feared its possible legal liability.

The US and Peruvian governments are also looking for alternative crops for the peasants who grow the coca plants. The Peruvian government estimates that 300,000 people make a living in this way, and they would be left destitute if the plants were simply destroyed. Peru, too, has to face the economic consequences: about one-third of its export earnings, $1.5 billion, come from coca.

President García has issued ringing statements of his willingness to pay any price to eradicate coca. The example of Colombia is enough to frighten any government. The Shining Path guerrillas have already allied themselves with the coca traffickers to protect the coca growers, and 32 government workers and six officials have been killed during eradication programmes in the past five years. The numbers are likely to rise rapidly.

BRAZIL

The cocaine trade has now spread to Brazil. In March 1988, the DEA broke up a smugglers' ring that had brought $1.5 billion worth of cocaine from Brazil to the United States via Kennedy airport in New York.

In 1985, the Medellín Cartel had started moving some of its operations, both refining coca paste and smuggling, into Brazil. That vast country's frontiers with Bolivia and Colombia are remote, unpoliced and very long (2000 miles [3200 km] in the case of Bolivia). What is more, western Brazil, in the foothills of the Andes, offers the same advantages of climate, altitude and remoteness enjoyed by coca growers in Bolivia and Peru. Brazil is also a better base for smuggling cocaine to Europe than Colombia itself.

There is now a large and growing market in Rio and other Brazilian cities, and Brazilian police and the military have proved to be just as susceptible to bribery as the Colombians.

CUBA

On 15 June 1989, Fidel Castro announced the arrest of one of Cuba's most senior military officers, General Arnaldo Ochoa Sanchez, on a charge of running drugs into the United States. At his trial two months later, he pleaded guilty to the charge. Drugs had been imported into Cuba on military planes, or to military bases and had then been ferried to the U.S., directly or by way of the Bahamas. The network had run for many years and had made Ochoa and his accomplices hundreds of millions of dollars. Castro denied all involvement by other Cuban officials, a denial received sceptically in America. Ochoa was shot.

FURTHER READING

American University, *Colombia: A Country Study*, Washington D.C., 1977.
Amnesty International, *Colombia Briefing*, London, 1988.
——, *Honduras, Civilian Authority – Military Power: Human Rights Violations in the 1980s*, London, 1988.
Bureau of International Narcotics Matters, US State Department, *International Narcotics Control Strategy Report, 1988*.
Cockburn, Leslie, *Out of Control: The Story of the Reagan Administration's Secret War in Nicaragua*, New York, Atlantic Monthly Press, 1987.
Dolan, Edward A. Jr, *International Drug Traffic*, New York, Franklin Watts, 1985.
Eddy, Paul and Sabogal, Hugo, with Walden, Sara, *The Cocaine Wars*, New York, W. W. Norton, 1988.
Gugliotta, Guy, and Leen, Jeff, *Kings of Cocaine: Inside the Medellín Cartel*, New York, Simon and Schuster, 1989.

SOUTH PACIFIC

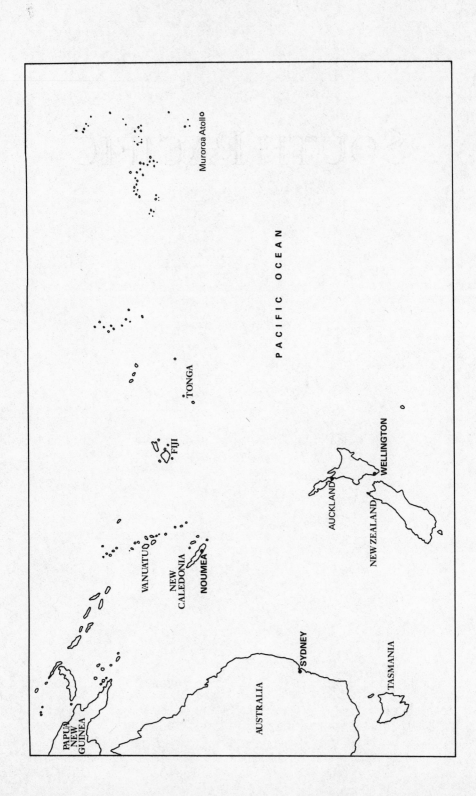

PACIFIC OCEAN

Muroroa Atoll

TONGA

FIJI

VANUATU

NEW
CALEDONIA

NOUMEA

AUCKLAND

NEW ZEALAND

WELLINGTON

PAPUA
NEW
GUINEA

AUSTRALIA

SYDNEY

TASMANIA

FIJI AND NEW CALEDONIA

Fiji and New Caledonia are island groups in the South Pacific, north-east of New Zealand.

Fiji   Consists of two large and about 300 small islands totalling 7055 sq. miles (18,272 sq. km), with a population of 707,000 and a *per capita* GNP of $1810.

New Caledonia (La Nouvelle Calédonie)   Consists of one large island and an archipelago of small ones – the Loyalty Islands (Iles Loyautés) – which cover 7376 sq. miles (19,104 sq. km) with a population of 144,000.

Like the other islands of the South Pacific, Fiji and New Caledonia were inhabited by tribes of Melanesians when they were discovered by European explorers. The tribes are dispersed over an immense area, from New Guinea to the central Pacific. Between them, they make up 0.01 per cent of the world's population, but speak a quarter of its distinct languages. They were visited by Spanish and other navigators in the 16th and 17th centuries, but serious exploration awaited the three voyages of Captain Cook (1768–79). Cook explored the Pacific from Alaska to the Antarctic and named many of the islands (New Caledonia reminded him of Scotland, and he named the archipelago to its east the New Hebrides for the same reason). The accounts of his voyages that he wrote for the Admiralty spread the myth of an earthly paradise in the South Pacific, a myth that remained potent for 200 years.

The Pacific islands were occupied by European powers in the 19th century. In 1874, Cakobau, the senior chief of Fiji, ceded the islands to Britain. France acquired New Caledonia in 1853: it turned out to be the most valuable of the Pacific islands, being enormously rich in minerals, notably nickel. The French and British set up a joint administration in the New Hebrides – now Vanuatu – which lie between the two. The Europeans suppressed tribal warfare, cannibalism and most elements of the Melanesian culture. Western diseases decimated the population, and missionaries converted the survivors to Christianity. Fiji became a stronghold of Wesleyan Methodism.

France used New Caledonia as a penal colony between 1864 and 1894. It was more remote than Devil's Island, the voyage there was yet more atrocious and conditions even worse. (The British had an equally horrible penal colony on Norfolk Island, to the south of New Caledonia.) Freed convicts often remained on New Caledonia, and by the end of the 19th century, 25,000 former convicts and other settlers populated the colony, mostly in the south of the main island around the capital, Nouméa, and owned 90 per cent of the land. Their descendants, who call themselves Caldoches, now comprise a majority of New Caledonia's population. The indigenous inhabitants, the Kanaks, were confined to reservations.

On Fiji, the British at first established cotton plantations, to take advantage of the decline in production in the American South after the Civil War. It was, however, a temporary advantage and the plantations soon failed. Then they tried sugar and imported 60,000 indentured labourers from India to work the cane. This industry flourished. The indenture system was abolished in 1916 but the Indians stayed, and they now form the largest community on Fiji.

Fiji became independent on 10 October 1970. New Caledonia remains a French *Territoire d'Outre-Mer* (TOM), an overseas territory. It is not considered an integral part of France, unlike Martinique and Guadeloupe in the Caribbean or the islands in the Gulf of St Lawrence, which are *Départements d'Outre-Mer* (DOMs) and send deputies to the National Assembly. Otherwise, the TOMs enjoy the same advantages of the DOMs, and suffer the same inconveniences.

The crises that have embroiled both Fiji and New Caledonia are a result of the same problem: the native inhabitants are now outnumbered by immigrants and descendants of immigrants, who speak different languages and have entirely different cultures. Their situations are not unique. In Guyana in South America for instance, the descendants of Indian immigrants are in a majority but descendants of African slaves hold a monopoly of power. There are other, even more notorious examples in Northern Ireland, Malaysia, Sri Lanka, South Africa and Israel. Even though the most recent immigrants in many of these cases arrived hundreds of years ago, the hostility between their descendants and the older communities is virulent and ineradicable. There is not much hope of any better end to the disputes in Fiji and New Caledonia.

FIJI

The population of Fiji is now 48.6 per cent Indian and 46.2 per cent Fijian. The remainder are Europeans, Chinese and a few Polynesians. The Indians occupy most of the administrative posts in the government, and they run virtually all the businesses. As a result, they are better educated and far more prosperous than the Fijians. As the Fijians tell it, the Indians speak Hindi, eat curry and, most serious of all, are Hindus. The Fijians are devout Methodists and speak their own Melanesian language. Both communities also speak English.

The island's economy remains dominated by sugar and tourism: it is on the air route between the United States and Australia, and many travellers interrupt that long and tedious voyage with a night in Fiji. It bills itself as a Pacific paradise with all the modern amenities.

The Fijians retained control of one element of society: the armed forces, which are now 2000 strong. Fijian troops fought for the British in various 20th-century wars, and they have also served in UN peacekeeping forces in Lebanon. One of the more remarkable things about them is that their ceremonial uniform includes the kilt.

The British left behind a parliamentary system in Fiji. The government was directed by a cabinet elected by parliament, while the Queen remained titular head of state, with a Fijian governor general to represent her. At the beginning of the present crisis, this was Ratu Sir Penaia Ganilau, who was also one of the most important chiefs in Fiji (*Ratu* means 'chief'). At independence, Ratu Sir Kamisese Mara became prime minister; his Alliance party is almost exclusively Fijian.

On 12 April 1987, Mara lost a general election, and a parliamentary majority was won by the Indians. The new prime minister was a minor Fijian chief, Timoci Bavadra, but all the other senior ministers in the new government were Indians.

The commander of the Fijian army was on a visit to Australia. On 14 May, the third-ranking officer, Lieutenant Colonel Sitiveni Rabuka, then aged 38, invaded the parliament building with ten soldiers, all wearing gas masks (to conceal their identities) and carrying pistols. They stormed into the parliament chamber and arrested the government. Bavadra and his ministers were marched out, loaded into trucks and driven off to a barracks where they were imprisoned.

Rabuka announced that he had carried out the coup on behalf of the Fijians. He demanded that the government be dissolved and replaced with a Fijian government, and that, in future, Fijian rule be permanently guaranteed. He also claimed to be loyally pro-Western and denounced the non-aligned policies advocated by the new government. (After the coup, some suspicious American leftists claimed that it had been organized by the CIA because the newly elected government had been 'non-aligned' and might have opposed US warships passing through Fijian waters. There is no evidence, so far, to substantiate this allegation, and against it is the evident fanaticism and extreme racial nationalism of Rabuka, who certainly appears to have been quite capable of mounting his coup without any prompting from abroad.)

The former prime minister, Kamisese Mara, issued a statement giving his approval to the coup, which he said he had known about in advance. The governor general, however, disapproved of this change of government by force, and so did the Queen. The governor general refused to appoint a new government, headed by Rabuka, and for several days, there was a stalemate. The coup appeared to be unravelling: Rabuka had the guns but no power. He made an emotional statement that his military career was over and, on 20 May, released the government. Bavadra said that Rabuka was guilty of treason and should be tried, but the governor general issued a general pardon for the men who had carried out the coup. He then announced that new elections would be held, and in the meantime, there would be a transitional government, headed by Mara. On 25 May, a list of new ministers was issued, with Rabuka at the top and Bavadra relegated to 14th place as minister of health.

Evidently, the episode was not over. The Fijians, who had strenuously approved the coup, wanted none of this compromise with the Indians. They now demonstrated against the new government, breaking the windows of Indian businesses in Suva, the capital, and roughing up a few Indians who were out in the streets. The army was called out to maintain order.

Bavadra went to London to protest to the Queen, who refused to see him; in her view, it was up to the Fijians to solve their own problems, without involving the former colonial power. Fiji appeared to return to normal. On 23 September, the

483

governor general announced a new plan for a government, in which the two communities would be equally represented, with himself as its head. Two days later, Rabuka staged his second coup. He once more dissolved the government, announcing that the objectives of the earlier coup were being thwarted by the proposed new government. This time, he stayed in power, and on 15 October, he proclaimed Fiji a republic. The Queen observed wistfully that it was a pity that the people of Fiji had not been consulted. On 5 December, the former governor general, Ratu Penaia Ganilau, was made president and Ratu Kamisese Mara was reappointed prime minister. Rabuka was promoted to brigadier and took the post as home secretary. There was no doubt that the country was and is ruled by the army: three members of the cabinet, besides Rabuka, are colonels. In announcing these appointments in a broadcast, Rabuka added, 'It is my sincere hope that the historic links with the British crown can be re-established.'

There has been no serious opposition to the coup and the new government. However, Rabuka has issued a series of draconian decrees enabling him to arrest and detain people without charge, censor the press and regulate the economy. A country that was once a model for interracial harmony is now beset by fear, according to visiting journalists. Rabuka, like a good Methodist, is a strong sabbatarian and has decreed that the islands must close down completely on Sunday; he has also suggested ominously that the Indians must be converted, or leave.

A further fear in the Indian community, most of whom work on sugar plantations, is that the land will be taken from them. In the 19th century, the British decreed that 90 per cent of the land could not be owned by immigrants (meaning Indians); the remaining 10 per cent could be bought by anyone. While the Fijians could not sell any of the restricted land to them, the Indians could lease it, and eventually much of it was. These leases will mostly expire by the end of the century, and the Indians fear that they will not be renewed and that the Fijians will resume control. Because the coup has had a disastrous effect on tourism and business, many Indians are trying to leave. That, too, may be Rabuka's intention.

NEW CALEDONIA

New Caledonia is a geological phenomenon. Its mineral riches include nickel (first discovered in 1875 and produced ever since), chrome, manganese, cobalt, antimony, mercury, copper, silver and gold, and for its size – 40 miles (65 km) long and 10 miles (16 km) wide – it is one of the richest territories on Earth. New Caledonia declared for De Gaulle's Free French in 1940, and was taken under American protection. It was used as a major American base in the Pacific war and, as a result, acquired roads, harbours and airstrips, all of which greatly helped its development after the war.

The indigenous Kanaks of New Caledonia constitute about 43 per cent of its population. They were in a majority until the 1960s, when the combined totals of Europeans and settlers from Polynesia and Asia overtook their numbers. There are now as many Europeans as Kanaks, and extreme racial tensions between the two communities. Kanaks were not allowed to leave their reservations until 1946, and until that date, they could be used as forced labour.

Things have changed. A long-term plan for New Caledonia, drawn up by
484 President Valéry Giscard d'Estaing in 1979, provided that France would invest

$1500 million in the territory over the following decade, but even that ambitious plan has been exceeded in the 1980s, under the governments of François Mitterrand, a former minister for the DOM-TOMs. The French now spend $250 million a year in New Caledonia, partly to make up for a slump in the mining industry, partly to finance schools and other facilities for the Kanaks. New Caledonia may be exceedingly rich, but it is a net liability to France.

In 1984, the French legislated a new statute for New Caledonia, which provided for a greater degree of self-government and a vote in 1989 on self-determination. The statute was opposed by both the main parties in the territory: the *Rassemblement pour la Calédonie dans la République*, (RPCR; the Alliance for Caledonia in the Republic), which represents the settlers; and the Independent Front, the Kanaks' party, which later changed its name to the *Front de Libération Nationale Kanak Socialiste* (FLNKS). The RPCR thought that the proposal gave too much away to the Kanaks; the Kanaks believed that it was a device to postpone independence indefinitely. The FLNKS boycotted elections held in November 1984, and formed a 'provisional government' of its own. Kanaks started demonstrating their opinions by building barricades in the countryside and setting up 'liberated' enclaves.

The French government responded to this challenge by admitting the failure of the new statute. Mitterrand sent a former Gaullist minister, Edgard Pisani, as a special envoy to investigate and report. In January 1985, he recommended that New Caledonia should become independent and associated with France, like the colonies that had adopted a similar statute in 1958, and which had all later achieved full independence. Pisani also recommended a referendum on the issue. Once again, the two factions rejected the French proposal. The settlers denounced it as a sell-out (they were opposed to any form of independence), and the Kanaks objected to Pisani's proposal to give the right to vote to anyone who had lived for more than three years in New Caledonia, which would give the settlers a veto.

On 12 January 1985, a few days after Pisani issued his report, the FLNKS' 'minister of internal security', Eloi Machoro, was assassinated. He had been one of the most militant of the Kanaks and had taken a band of his followers to Libya for paramilitary training. Fearing trouble, the French flew 3000 troops to the island to keep the peace, and Mitterrand himself flew to New Caledonia on 18 January for 12 hours of meetings with the various factions to 'reopen the dialogue'.

The French made amendments to the Pisani proposals, and complicated matters by insisting that France would keep military bases on the island indefinitely. Regional elections were held on 28 September 1985. The settlers' RPCR won 25 of the 48 seats in the territorial congress, but only one of the four regional councils, Nouméa, where settlers have a huge majority.

By then the socialist government in France had been defeated, and the new Gaullist prime minister, Jacques Chirac, was much less sympathetic to Kanak interests than his predecessor. Conflicts between the French and the Kanaks increased steadily. The situation was not helped when a new law governing New Caledonia was passed in Paris, which led to an executive council, with a settler majority, being established in Nouméa.

On 22 April 1988 – two days before the first round of the French presidential elections in which Chirac was the conservative candidate and Mitterrand was   **485** running for re-election – Kanaks attacked a police barracks on the island of Ouvéa (one of the Loyalty Islands, 110 miles [175 km] from Nouméa), killing three and capturing 27. They released 11, and hid the remaining 16 in a cave. Seven more Frenchmen, including the head of an élite anti-terrorist squad, were kidnapped five days later; they had been negotiating for the release of the police. The French government rushed out 3000 reinforcements to join the 4000 troops already there.

Elsewhere, Kanaks laid siege to a group of about 100 Caldoches who had taken refuge in another police barracks; a number of Kanaks were killed during the rescue. The French troops conducted sweeps through New Caledonia and the larger of the other islands, clearing away roadblocks and breaking up demonstrations. When they discovered the cave where the Kanaks were holding their hostages, they surrounded it, and at dawn on 5 May, French commandos stormed it and rescued the hostages: 19 Kanaks and two French soldiers were killed. The Kanaks accused the French troops of shooting two of their militants after they were captured, and of allowing the group's leader, Alphonse Dianou, who was wounded in the knee, to bleed to death in a truck taking him to hospital. Thirty Kanaks arrested during the operation were sent to France for trial.

Chirac's minister for the DOM-TOMs denounced the FLNKS, and said that it should be banned. Mitterrand accused the Chirac government of provoking the troubles in New Caledonia as part of the election campaign. In the second round of the presidential election, in 8 May, Mitterand won by a comfortable margin.

Six weeks later, on 26 June 1988, the new socialist government reached an agreement with FLNKS leader Jean-Marie Tjibaou and RPCR leader Jacques Lafleur. The local executive council of New Caledonia set up under the Chirac government was suspended, and France temporarily resumed direct rule. A referendum on the territory's future will be held in 1998. Local elections were set for in July 1989, with the territory divided up into three regions, one of which will doubtless be solidly Kanak, one Caldoche (i.e. Nouméa) and the other divided between the two.

Militant settlers and, especially, militant Kanaks opposed the agreement. The Kanaks want to restrict the franchise to those whose parents were born in New Caledonia, and threaten to resume the 'armed struggle'. On 20 August, after further negotiations between the French government, Tjibaou and representatives of the settlers, it was decided that all Kanaks jailed for taking part in the riots would be amnestied, except those specifically accused of murder. The list of those eligible to vote in the 1998 referendum was also further restricted. Some settlers promptly denounced these decisions as a further sell-out.

The settlement was submitted to the French electorate in a referendum on 6 November 1988. The proposal was approved by 80 per cent of those who voted, but the turn-out was only 38 per cent – evidently the French did not take the problems of New Caledonia too seriously. The referendum did not settle the issue: the Gaullist opposition, still led by Chirac, announced that it would not accept the result. On 5 May 1989, Tjibaou was assassinated by a Kanak extremist during a tribal ceremony. The murderer, who had been one of the leaders in the kidnapping of the French police a year earlier, was killed by Tjibaou's bodyguards. The settlement was evidently precarious and the underlying conflicts has not been resolved.

FURTHER READING

American University, *Oceania: A Country Study*, Washington D.C., 1974.
Lal, Brij V. *et al.* (eds), *Politics in Fiji*, Honolulu, Institute for Polynesian Studies, 1986.
Scarr, Deryck, *Fiji: A Short History*, Laie, Hawaii, Institute for Polynesian Studies 1984.

THE NUCLEAR ISSUE

An international aspect of the events of the region concerns the continuing agitation in Australia and New Zealand against nuclear weapons. On 10 July 1985, French frogmen put limpet mines on the Greenpeace ship *Rainbow Warrior*, in Auckland harbour and sank it, killing a Portuguese photographer who was on board. Most of the French terrorist team who had carried out the attack managed to escape, but two, a man and a woman, were arrested and charged with murder.

The French socialist minister of defence, Charles Hernu, was forced to resign, but neither the government nor the French people in general showed the least regret: Greenpeace had planned to sail the *Rainbow Warrior* to Muroroa atoll to protest against French underground nuclear tests there.

The French government soon found a means of exerting pressure on New Zealand: that country's economy depends to a great extent upon exports to the European Community and France systematically set about interfering with the trade. New Zealand reluctantly agreed that the two prisoners should be sent to serve three-year sentences at a French military base on the remote island of Hao in the Pacific. In December 1987, on manifestly spurious grounds of ill-health, the man, Captain Alain Mafart, was sent back to France. The woman, Dominique Prieur, had to wait a little longer: her husband came out to join her and they were sent home on 6 May 1988, just before the French presidential elections (and the day after the French hostages in New Caledonia were rescued) as another proof of Chirac's patriotism; the pretext offered was that she had become pregnant. Mafart and Prieur will both presumably resume their careers in the French secret service.

These developments naturally outraged the New Zealanders, but there was nothing much they could do about it except feel virtuously indignant. They have continued to pursue their opposition to all things nuclear. Among other measures, New Zealand has seceded from ANZUS, the alliance that has united Australia, New Zealand and the United States since 1941, on the grounds that, as long as they are allied, the US can insist on including nuclear-armed or nuclear-powered vessels in visits of the US fleet to New Zealand.

Both New Zealand and Australia consider that they have a special right to object to nuclear tests in the Pacific because they and Muroroa are all neighbours. It is a curious illusion: Wellington is 2500 miles (4000 km) from the test site, and Sydney is as far from Muroroa as New York is from Paris. Perhaps they only look at small-scale maps.

TERRORISM

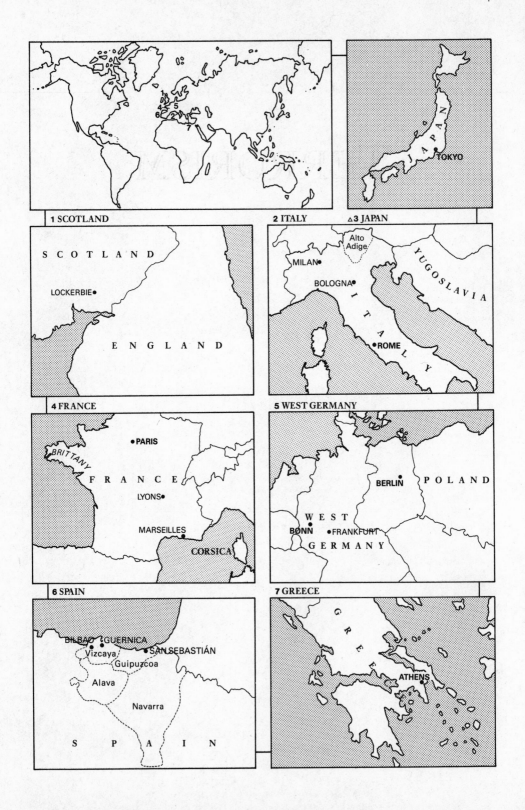

1 SCOTLAND   **2 ITALY**   △**3 JAPAN**

4 FRANCE

5 WEST GERMANY

6 SPAIN

7 GREECE

S C O T L A N D

LOCKERBIE●

E N G L A N D

JAPAN

●TOKYO

Alto Adige

MILAN●

BOLOGNA●

I T A L Y

●ROME

Y U G O S L A V I A

●PARIS

BRITTANY

F R A N C E

LYONS●

MARSEILLES●

CORSICA

BERLIN●

P O L A N D

W E S T

BONN●   ●FRANKFURT

G E R M A N Y

BILBAO●   ●GUERNICA

Vizcaya   ●SAN SEBASTIÁN

Guipuzcoa

Alava

Navarra

S   P   A   I   N

G R E E C E

●ATHENS

MODERN TERRORISM

Terrorism is the cancer of the modern world. No state is immune to it. It is a dynamic organism which attacks the healthy flesh of the surrounding society. It has the essential hallmark of malignant cancer: unless treated, and treated drastically, its growth is inexorable, until it poisons and engulfs the society on which it feeds and drags it down to destruction.

Paul Johnson

Terrorism is frequently denounced as the greatest threat facing the West, as a war to the death between civilization and anarchy and as the latest manifestation of the international Communist conspiracy. The quotation given above, from *Terrorism: How the West Can Win*, edited by Benjamin Netanyahu, is typical of the genre.

Fortunately, in Europe and North America at least, terrorism is none of these things. In Europe, since 1945, only three countries – Northern Ireland since 1968, France in 1961–2 and, to a lesser extent, Italy in the late 1970s – have been seriously afflicted by terrorism. The security measures taken in the United States against imaginary terrorists are the fruits of paranoia and political posturing. The Reagan administration declared that Libyan 'hit squads' were on the loose, and they turned the White House and Capitol into fortresses to prove the point. Nothing happened.

Netanyahu, who has made a career out of stridency, claims that 'the two main antagonists of democracy in the post-war world, Communist totalitarianism and Islamic radicalism, have between them inspired virtually all of contemporary terrorism' and 'Americans account for roughly a third of terrorists' victims since 1968.' These statements are complete nonsense. Most terrorism is inspired by nationalistic or ethnic fervour, not Communist ideology, and there has been a mere handful of American deaths among the tens of thousands who have died as a result of terrorist attacks of every description, including those in Netanyahu's definition: count the dead in Lebanon, Peru or Sri Lanka, just for a start. If the attacks are restricted to those inspired by 'international terrorism', and further limited to attacks on the nationals of countries that are not involved in the dispute that animates the terrorist, the American proportion rises, but terrorism then ceases to be a major international problem, let alone a cancer. As Netanyahu himself admits, 'Terrorism's victims are few, its physical damage limited, its violence sporadic.'

He presumably had international terrorism in mind. This is a real problem, but nothing compared to indigenous terrorism. Terrorists who are a threat to society in various countries have specifically local objectives. The Shining Path in Peru is Communist, but repudiates the Soviet Union. The IRA claims to be Marxist, but no one can take that seriously; its inspiration is entirely nationalistic. The same goes for the Tamil Tigers and their rival Sinhalese terrorists in Sri Lanka, and for the Sikhs. The death squads in El Salvador, the Muslim Brotherhood in Syria, the Kurds in Turkey, Iraq and Iran, and most of the other men of violence in the Middle East are undoubtedly terrorists, without being in any useful sense 'international'.

Least of all is there any apocalyptic threat to 'the West'. A number of countries in the Middle East, Latin America and Asia have suffered seriously from terrorism, among them Lebanon, Syria, Iran, Turkey, El Salvador, Uruguay, Argentina, Guatemala, India and Sri Lanka. Some terrorist organizations have regularly attacked targets in other countries, among them various Palestinian groups, the IRA, and Armenian terrorists, and others have done so occasionally. For the rest, terrorism, though often spectacular, has never been more than a marginal threat. No governments, let alone regimes, have been directly overthrown by terrorism. The civil war in Lebanon is particularly atrocious because the factions use terrorism as their preferred weapon, but terrorism did not cause Lebanon to disintegrate. Rather, it was a sign of disintegration caused by social, religious and political differences. Armies seized power in Turkey, Uruguay and Argentina because the civilian governments, they thought, were not fighting the terrorists fiercely enough. The terrorists were crushed mercilessly. It was not the outcome they had anticipated.

There is no satisfactory definition of terrorism. Netanyahu's Jonathan Institute* has come up with a good but insufficient one: 'Terrorism is the deliberate and systematic murder, maiming and menacing of the innocent to inspire fear for political ends'. That definition, however, would include state terrorism: many governments have used illegal execution, torture or destruction of property against their domestic enemies (or people they have arbitrarily defined as enemies) in order to terrorize the population for political ends. However, to describe Stalin's USSR, Hitler's Germany, Pol Pot's Cambodia, Guatemala after 1954 or Argentina after 1975 as terrorist states, though perfectly justifiable, stretches the net too wide to be useful. The term is best limited to groups acting independently of governments, though they may be financed, armed or encouraged by governments, and to assassins sent abroad illegally by government organizations.

The chief reason for distinguishing between the actions of governments, however reprehensible, and those of self-constituted organizations, is to escape the relativism of the terrorists' apologists who insist that state terrorism is far more serious. They allege that the United States (or Britain, France or Israel) have engaged in state terrorism, and conclude that the terrorists are no more guilty than those governments. It is a transparently dishonest argument, a means of avoiding the issue, and a justification for murder. Governments should be judged by their actions – and so should terrorists.

---

* The Institute was set up in 1976 and is concerned with the study of terrorism. It is named after Lieutenant Colonel Jonathan Netanyahu (Benjamin Netanyahu's brother), who was killed during the Entebbe rescue.

A further problem of definition is distinguishing terrorists from guerrillas. The Jonathan Institute says guerrillas wear recognizable uniforms, attack only military targets and do not use concealed weapons. This immediately leads to difficulties: under this definition, the fanatic who drove a car bomb into the US Marine barracks in Beirut was no terrorist, nor are the Shining Path fighters in Peru, but the Israeli agents who assassinated the PLO leader Abu Jihad in Tunis were terrorists (they hid their weapons and wore no uniforms).

Many legitimate guerrilla movements or popular insurrections have used terrorism as well as conventional acts of war, but to call the Vietcong or the Farabundo Martí Liberation Front in El Salvador or the Contras in Nicaragua terrorists implies that that is all they are.

The term 'terrorist' is most usefully limited to organizations whose principal methods of warfare are terroristic, groups that employ chiefly bombs, murders and ambushes, and whose victims are frequently civilians. This definition most completely covers such groups as the IRA, the Armenian terrorists, the West German Red Army Faction (RAF), the Red Brigades in Italy, *Action Directe* in France and the Japanese Red Army. In an earlier generation, EOKA in Cyprus and the Irgun and the Stern Gang in Palestine fitted this description. It would also include virtually all the Palestinian military organizations because their *modus operandi* is almost exclusively terroristic: they occasionally seek out military targets inside Israel, or Israeli military targets in Lebanon, but the great majority of their attacks have been on civilians.

This definition of terrorism would also exclude counter-terrorist operations, such as the Israeli raid on Tunis in 1988. It leaves to professors of ethics the question of justifying or condemning the secret war of assassination waged between Mossad, the Israeli secret service, and Palestinian terrorists in Lebanon, Cyprus and the four corners of Europe. Those who live by the bomb shall perish by the bomb: it is not possible to feel any sympathy for the Palestinian terrorists who were responsible for the Munich massacre and who were later killed by Mossad, or for the three IRA terrorists who, in the midst of their plan to place a car bomb in a public square, were shot down by the British SAS in Gibraltar. The argument is over the method of their execution. It is easier to justify the actions of the Israelis, who had no alternative, than those of the British, who could have arrested the three. But Mossad has sometimes killed the wrong man, and the car bomb that killed the last of the Munich murderers in Beirut also killed six innocent passers-by.

The usual apologia for terrorism is that 'one man's terrorist is another man's freedom fighter,' which is perfectly true and perfectly irrelevant: murder is not justified by sticking a different label on it. Ramsay Clark, a former attorney general of the United States, defends the IRA on the grounds that they are exactly the same as George Washington and other heroes of the American Revolution. However, Washington never set off a bomb in a restaurant, Thomas Jefferson never advocated machine-gunning a church congregation, Patrick Henry never sent his agents to plant a bomb at a memorial service. If they had, they would have been terrorists.

The 'political justification' – the claim that the end justifies the means – is a debate crucial for fighting terrorism, and it has not been resolved. American courts   **495** have refused to extradite IRA terrorists to Britain on the grounds that their actions were political. So have courts in various European countries, including the Netherlands. France gave asylum to a whole series of terrorists – those from Spain, Ireland and Italy, all the factions of the Arabs, Québécois nationalists and South Americans – and only came to change its policy when terrorists started attacking French targets. The United States was outraged in 1985 when Italy released the mastermind of the *Achille Lauro* piracy, although the Italian courts had been acting exactly as their American counterparts have towards the IRA. There can be no effective international cooperation in the fight against terrorism until democratic countries admit that an attack against one is an attack on all.

There are differences between terrorist groups. Some seek out what they consider 'enemy' targets (usually military): thus ETA concentrates on murdering generals (though it has also killed many civilians). A few take great pains to avoid killing people. The Bretons, for instance, have never killed anyone (though two Bretons killed themselves with their own bomb), and the 'Free Welsh Army' disintegrated when one of its bombs killed two people by mistake; its successors in the 1980s have devoted themselves to arson, protecting Welsh culture by burning down houses belonging to people from England. Other groups, such as the IRA or the Abu Nidal group, deliberately choose civilians. However, they are all terrorists.

Some terrorists, wholly lacking popular support, must always operate in the shadows, though they may have fantasies of rallying the proletariat behind them. Other organizations, enjoying a certain measure of popular support, nevertheless employ only terrorist means because the forces they are fighting are too powerful. That is the case with the IRA, the Shining Path in Peru and ETA in Spain, and was the case with EOKA. An invigorating debate can be carried on concerning the nature of the Turkish, Uruguayan and Argentinian terrorists of the 1970s, turning on the issue of how much real support they enjoyed, but the nub of the matter is that, by defining their methods, not their intentions, they are all to be classified as terrorists.

One of the classic arguments against terrorism was advanced by Lenin in *What Is to Be Done?*, the blueprint for the October Revolution. He insisted that revolution must come through the proletariat, not from the enthusiasm of intellectual terrorists.

The terrorists bow to the spontaneity of the passionate indignation of the intellectuals, who lack the ability or opportunity to connect the revolutionary struggle and the working-class movement into an integral whole. It is difficult indeed for those who have lost their belief, or have never believed that this is possible, to find some outlet for their indignation and revolutionary energy other than terror.

In a later attack on the Social Revolutionary party, which had adopted a policy of terror, he wrote:

In their naïvety, the Social Revolutionaries do not realize that their predilection for terrorism is causally most intimately linked with the fact that, from the very outset, they have always kept and still keep aloof from the working-class movement.

This argument remains as pertinent today as it was 80 years ago, and clearly applies
496 to the romantic European and Latin American terrorists who dream of rousing the

working classes by some dramatic act of violence, but who really have no connection whatever with genuine working-class aspirations.

Trotsky developed the case against terrorism, which he applied in a Communist context but which is just as true for nationalist or religious terrorism:

The capitalist state does not base itself on government ministers and cannot be eliminated with them. The classes it serves will always find new people; the mechanism remains intact and continues to function . . . In our eyes, individual terror is inadmissible precisely because it *belittles the role of the masses in their own consciousness*, reconciles them to their powerlessness, and turns their eyes and hopes towards a great avenger and liberator who some day will come and accomplish his mission.

Communist parties have remained opposed to terrorism, in theory, ever since. The Nicaraguan revolutionaries split on the issue when the doctrinaire Communists, led by Tomás Borge, broke away from Edén Pastora and the Ortega brothers in protest against their policy of spectacular terrorist attacks on the Somoza regime.

Practice and theory, however, are different matters. There is no doubt that terrorists all over the world have obtained their weapons and explosives from the Soviet bloc, directly or indirectly (the Shining Path being one of the few exceptions). For 20 years, the USSR made no effort to distinguish between legitimate 'wars of national liberation' and terrorism. It provided every service possible to the PLO, which it considered the legitimate representative of the Palestinians, without asking itself, or without caring, what the organization did with its weapons and training. The PLO, in turn, financed by the Arab oil states, gave every assistance to Arab terrorists (PFLP, Black September) and to other terrorist groups including the Armenians, the IRA and the Red Army Unit (RAF) in West Germany. (The Entebbe and Mogadishu hijackings were joint Palestinian–RAF operations.) Similarly, the USSR and its allies give Libya everything it asks (and pays) for, turning a blind eye to the uses Khadafy finds for Czech explosives or Soviet weapons.

There are three broad categories of independent terrorist movements in the world today: those inspired by political fervour, usually Communist but including some Fascist movements; those inspired by nationalism or ethnic grievances; and those inspired by Islam. A fourth category is terrorism directed by governments such as Syria or Libya.

The political movements operating in Western industrialized societies are the weakest. They are invariably small bands of fanatics, and once they start a terrorist campaign, they are the subject of relentless police pursuit. Because they have no popular support, they do not recover when their members are arrested: they cannot recruit replacements as nationalist movements can, and by definition, they are not guerrillas (though they call themselves 'urban guerrillas'). They cannot swim like a fish in water, in Mao Tse-tung's famous analogy, because if they were made known to the 'water' (the general population), they would immediately be arrested. The West German police have dismantled two generations of terrorist organizations (the group known as the Baader–Meinhof gang, and the RAF), the Italians have practically wiped out the Red Brigades and the French have all but eliminated *Action Directe*. Only Greece has had no success in breaking up the November 17 group.

These organizations are correctly defined as 'international terrorists' because they cooperate with each other and preach a Europe-wide campaign against 'Nato imperialism'. They have received help and finance from Arab terrorists, who act on the principle that anything that destabilizes Europe is to be encouraged. At one remove, therefore, they are supported by the Soviet Union, which is a fine example of modern cynicism: the RAF and the rest all despise the Soviets for their lack of revolutionary fervour.

It is the collaboration between these groups (RAF, *Action Directe*, Red Brigades) that most nearly meets the conspiracy theorists' notion of a great, Communist-led plot to overthrow democracy with the bomb and the bullet. At its widest, the theory ties in every movement from Japan to Argentina, by way of the PLO, Khadafy and Cuba. Like most other conspiracy theories, however, this one collapses under its own weight. There is collaboration, but there is no conspiracy. Meanwhile, the complete failure of the Euro-terrorists is a striking confirmation of Lenin's and Trotsky's analyses.

Communist-inspired movements enjoy more success in the Third World. The more important ones are in the Philippines, El Salvador and Peru (*see* individual country sections). Apart from those three, nationalist terrorist movements are much more serious than purely 'political' ones, and the most serious of all, for the rest of the world, is the one that has arisen among the Palestinian diaspora. It has a bottomless pool of resentment against Israel and its Western allies, an over-abundance of eager recruits graduating every year from the camps and the small-time militias of Lebanon, and all the money it needs from the oil states.

Outside powers – Syria, Iran, Libya and Iraq – have all availed themselves of the Palestinian terrorist network for their own purposes, and other terrorists have sought training and weapons from and sanctuary with the Palestinians. The Soviet bloc is heavily implicated in at least the arming and training of the Palestinians while rather ostentatiously keeping its distance from Middle Eastern violence. Its involvement is at least as much economic as political: the Czechs and East German arms industries are important foreign exchange earners (as, of course, are those of the Americans, British and French) and their major markets are the Arabs. Western Europe buys oil from Libya, and pays in dollars. The dollars are then used to prop up the decaying economies of Eastern Europe by purchasing weapons that are used against the governments of Western Europe. One of the many unanswered questions of Mikhail Gorbachev's regime is whether it will continue its indirect support for terrorism. The fact that the incidence of terrorism declined in 1987 and 1988 proves nothing.

The Palestinians, unlike the Euro-terrorists, have not directed sustained, systematic campaigns against Western governments. They have mounted spectacular operations against American targets but that is all. Their obsession is fighting Israel – and each other. One terrorist group that put bombs on aircraft was suppressed and its leader, Abu Mahmoud, was executed by Al-Fatah. Abu Nidal and the PLO wage a constant war of assassination, and this incessant fratricide is the clue to Palestinian, and other nationalist, terrorism. Whatever their inclinations towards generalized violence elsewhere, their effectiveness is largely limited to their own concerns. Similarly, the IRA and ETA may exchange weapons or advice, but neither needs the other to mount the operations that really concern it.

498

As for Islamic terrorism, it, too, is largely limited to its home territories, most notably Lebanon, Syria and Iran. Shiite terrorists have hijacked aircraft to extort the release of prisoners from the Israeli and Kuwaiti governments, but despite all the fulminations of the Ayatollah, they have usually stayed in their own countries. The most conspicuous exception to this rule was the attack on France in 1985 and 1986. The limitation is fortunate: a holy warrior certain to attain Paradise if he is killed is the most dangerous of all terrorists. In fact, the word 'assassin' derives from an earlier band of fanatic, and drugged, Shiites.

One form of terrorism – assassination – has occasionally been more successful than others because of its limited objectives, when it is intended to destroy an enemy or frustrate a government or, most crudely, to eliminate a rival. Stalin was never inhibited by Lenin's doubts on the efficacy of terrorism: he had Trotsky murdered in Mexico. Appendix III comprises a depressingly long list of public figures who have been assassinated since 1945, and includes many whose deaths were a severe loss to their countries: Mahatma Gandhi in India, Aung San in Burma, Tom Mboya in Kenya, John and Robert Kennedy in the United States, among many others. The most notorious assassination of the century was the killing of the Archduke Franz Ferdinand of Austria which precipitated World War I. It was one of the few terrorist acts that have changed the face of history.

For some conspiracy theorists, the key event in post-war terrorism was the attempted assassination of Pope John Paul II on 13 May 1981. The would-be assassin, Mehmet Ali Agça, was a member of the far-right Turkish terrorist group, the Grey Wolves, and had some connections with Bulgaria. Those two neighbouring countries have fought a subterranean terrorist war for years past, and the Bulgarians are believed to have carried out at least one assassination abroad, when an exile was stabbed in London with a poisoned umbrella.

The suggestion was that the KGB directed the Bulgarians to kill the Polish pope in order to relieve pressure on the regime in Warsaw, which was then locked in combat with Solidarity. Agça asserted that the attempt had been planned in the Bulgarian embassy in Rome and offered many details that seemed to corroborate his claim; he certainly proved his own Bulgarian connections. However, when the issue was eventually put to trial, he also claimed to be Jesus Christ. The case collapsed, but the conspiracy theorists remain convinced that Bulgaria, and therefore the USSR, were behind the attempt. It is notable that no Western government, not even the Reagan administration, accepted the theory.

The sort of terrorism denounced by Lenin and Trotsky and by politicians of every persuasion since – the secret assault on the state – has never succeeded. Indeed, the most secretive, 'purest' terrorists such as the Red Brigades or the Armenian Secret Army have been the least successful. Their certainty that they alone have the answer to the secret of the utopia to come, and the right to decide their nations' future with the bomb and the gun, verged on dementia (and the Japanese Red Army, clearly, was altogether demented).

Terrorism became a central international preoccupation because of the coincidence of several distinct events and developments in the late 1960s. The first was the defeat of the Arabs in the Six Day War, which led the PLO to terrorism as its only alternative. The second was the series of student revolts in Europe and the United States in 1968, which filled the heads of a number of impressionable youths with revolutionary enthusiasm: if a crowd could gather spontaneously to set fire to the Paris Bourse, what might not a properly organized revolutionary vanguard achieve? At the same time, the civil rights movement in Northern Ireland revived the dormant IRA, and the senility of the Franco regime (and then its passing) permitted the creation of ETA. The accession to power of the 'flaky barbarian' Moammar Khadafy (Ronald Reagan's apt description) in Libya in 1969 might be added to the list.

The 'spirit of '68' is a spent force in Europe, but political extremism still flourishes in Latin America and Asia, Palestinian nationalism is as vigorous and violent as ever, and there is no abatement in the various nationalist struggles. Terrorism will continue for the rest of the century.

National terrorist movements are discussed in the appropriate sections (Northern Ireland, Lebanon, Sri Lanka, El Salvador, etc.). The remaining groups, dealt with in the following sections, fall into various categories: political extremism in Europe and Japan; other nationalist groups (ETA in Spain, Corsican and Breton separatists in France); the forlorn hopes (the South Moluccans in Holland and the Armenians); Palestinian and Islamic terrorism; and, finally, state terrorism. There is, inevitably, some overlapping.

THE EURO-TERRORISTS

WEST GERMANY

The Red Army Unit (*Rote Armee Fraktion*, RAF) was born in 1968, the year of the student upheavals – but before they occurred. On 2 April, a small group of terrorists in Frankfurt set a department store alight – in protest, they said, against the consumer society. Among them were Andreas Baader (age 24) and Gudrun Esslin (age 27). A radical lawyer, Horst Mahler (age 32), defended Baader at his trial, and a radical-chic journalist, Ulrike Meinhof (age 33) wrote admiring articles about them in the magazine *Konkret*.

A few days after the fire, on 12 April, the most prominent of student radical leaders, Rudi Dutschke, was shot and severely wounded in Berlin by a deranged right-wing student. (Dutschke never recovered sufficiently, or never recovered the zeal, to harangue the crowds again; he studied at Cambridge University for a while until he was expelled by a nervous British government.) The event provoked student demonstrations all over the country, the demonstrators claiming that the shooting had been part of a Fascist plot. Extremists mounted a series of attacks in Berlin and elsewhere, aimed particularly at the Springer newspaper chain (which had ceaselessly vilified the students).

These attacks were obscured at the time by the large-scale student demonstrations, sometimes directed against the Vietnam war, sometimes against governments, that were convulsing Japan, West Germany, France, Italy, Mexico and the United States. In every one of those countries, the riots echoed down the years. In the short term, General de Gaulle's authority in France was fatally weakened, Lyndon Johnson abandoned the presidency (and Richard Nixon was elected to succeed him), the massacre in Mexico traumatized the government, and the troubles in Japan, West Germany and Italy appalled their respectable citizens. But in the longer term, in Europe at least, the chief result of the upheavals was the coalescing of various radical groups into violent revolutionary movements that soon developed into full-scale terrorism.

The Frankfurt arsonists were sentenced to three years' imprisonment, but jumped bail. They went underground, and took part in the new rebels' first bombing campaign in the winter of 1969. The targets were judicial offices, judges, the El Al office in Berlin, a US officers' club and an American office block in Berlin, and a lawyers' ball.

Baader was rearrested in Berlin on 4 April 1970. He persuaded the prison authorities to allow him to conduct research at the Social Affairs Institute, and on 14 May, four terrorists – Meinhof and Mahler (who had by then given up journalism and the law in favour of revolutionary terrorism) and two other comrades – shot their way into the building, wounding three people, and rescued him. This episode marked the beginning of the Baader–Meinhof gang. This was before the days of petro-terrorism, and they started robbing banks to raise the necessary funds: on 29 September 1970, three Berlin banks were robbed simultaneously, bringing a combined haul of DM220,000. At least 12 people were involved in the operation.

In the next couple of years, the RAF stole over DM1.5 million, and was therefore able to run an efficient and deadly terrorist organization. Guns and explosives were bought, and members of the gang studied the art of bomb-making. A policeman was killed in one of the robberies. Meinhof stated the gang's political philosophy in an interview: 'We say the person in uniform is a pig – that is, not a human being – and thus we have to settle the matter with him. It is wrong to talk to these people at all, and shooting is taken for granted.' One of their slogans was 'Don't argue, destroy.'

The RAF went over to revolutionary terrorism in 1972, even though by then a dozen of its members had been arrested, including Mahler. There were 15 bomb attacks, in a series that began, on 11 May 1972, with an attack on the US army headquarters in Frankfurt that killed one officer; 38 people were also injured in the bombing of the Springer headquarters in Hamburg. In addition, the RAF began to assassinate individuals, choosing officials whose attitudes were deemed hostile to the 'people's interests'.

The police estimated that there were 17 full-time members of the gang in 1970, and at least 60 people who helped the logistical side of the RAF's campaign, by holding apartments ('safe-houses') available or running errands. The RAF established contact with similar groups in other countries, notably France and the Netherlands. The active members were almost all bourgeois, including several lawyers and two journalists, as were most of their supporters and accomplices. Mahler enunciated the theory that the best leaders of the proletariat were not to be found among workers themselves; they could stand aside and determine the workers' needs objectively, with due appreciation for the modern class struggle. The revolutionaries were occasionally surprised at the workers' reactions to their solicitous concern for their welfare.

The RAF claimed to be disgusted at the crass materialism of the modern West German state. Most of them had been born during or immediately after the war (but not Ulrike Meinhof, who was born in 1934) and, like all Germans, had suffered the privations of the bleak post-war years. As they came to adulthood in the 1960s, however, the West German economic miracle swung into high gear. The older generation that had survived the war and post-war austerity had rebuilt Germany with industry, dedication and self-sacrifice, and were not in the least ashamed of their prosperity. They had earned it the hard way and were astonished and offended by the generation of 1968 when it repudiated it all. They were even more shocked that so many young people rejected 'bourgeois democracy': after all it had been through, the West German establishment was not prepared to have its democratic institutions attacked. Members of the RAF were called 'Hitler's children'. Older Germans remembered the early 1930s, and were afraid of the new anarchists, and therefore repressed them far more vigorously than the French or the Italians did their own youthful terrorists.

The prophet of the West German terrorists was Herbert Marcuse, a German Hegelian who had sensibly moved to California in the 1930s. In a post-war essay, 'Repressive Tolerance', he claimed that 'suppressed and overpowered minorities' had the 'natural right' to resort to violence to achieve liberation. The Baader–Meinhof terrorists claimed that they were part of the same struggle as the Vietnamese, or blacks or Indians in the United States, or Palestinians, or any other oppressed minority. They claimed to be 'urban guerrillas', the comrades of Che Guevara and Mao Tse-tung. Students in West Germany (and also in Britain) marched through the streets waving Mao's Little Red Book and chanting 'Ho, Ho, Ho Chi Minh' and other equally profound philosophical statements.

There were large numbers of women in the RAF, who added the doctrines of women's liberation to their other political teachings. They felt that German society underestimated women. Dr Hans Josef Horchem, a distinguished West German expert on political extremism, wrote of them (in *Contemporary Terrorism*, 1974):

The influence of women accounts for the lack of realism in the overall revolutionary concept, yet they are responsible for day-to-day actions of a practical nature, such as renting a flat under an assumed name and gathering and analysing information.

Dr Horchem would probably expect them also to do the laundry.

The RAF showed its enthusiasm for Third World causes by demonstrating against the shah and against Moise Tshombe (who had tried to set up an independent state with white support in Katanga, in southern Zaïre, in the early 1960s). Those statesmen were doubtless suitably impressed, but the RAF found these causes insufficient to rally the West German proletariat. The RAF studied the techniques of the Tupamaros terrorists in Uruguay and a handbook on 'urban guerrilla warfare' by the Brazilian terrorist Carlos Marighella, who called his book the 'mini-manual for revolutionaries'. It was published in West Germany under the title *Destroy the Islands of Wealth in the Third World*.

The Baader–Meinhof gang chose the name 'Red Army' in emulation of the Japanese Red Army, which first revealed itself by hijacking a JAL plane to North Korea in 1970. They called themselves the Red Army '*Fraktion*', implying that they were a part of a wider, international movement. One of their first manifestos demanded: 'Does any pig truly believe we would talk about the development of class conflicts, or reorganization of the proletariat, without simultaneously arming ourselves?' In 1971, they published *The Urban Guerrilla Concept*, written by Mahler. This is a statement of their objectives and justifications: it claims that the RAF is Marxist–Leninist, calls on the student radicals of 1968 to rally to their call. 'We maintain that without revolutionary initiative, without practical revolutionary intervention (this is our own concept) of the *avant-garde*, without the concrete anti-imperialist campaign, there can be no unifying process.' It says further: 'The class analysis, which we need, cannot be made without revolutionary practice, without revolutionary initiative.' It would be

503

hard to find a better example of the mush-brained, egocentric and élitist nonsense that Lenin and Trotsky had denounced 60 or 70 years earlier. Their other theoretical works had such titles as *Close the Loopholes of the Revolutionary Theory* and, finally, *Red Book 29: RAF Collective – On the Armed Campaign in Western Europe*, also by Mahler.

As RAF terrorists were arrested, the lawyers who were members or sympathizers set up 'Red Help', which became the public face of the RAF, publishing RAF statements that the defence lawyers were able to smuggle out of prison. By the summer of 1972, all but one of the core members of the RAF were in jail, and for a while, they found propaganda easier to achieve and more effective than when they had been on the run.

In the first decade of the RAF campaign in West Germany, 31 people were killed, including nine police, four prosecutors and three diplomats; there were also 25 bombings and 30 bank robberies. Evidently, it was not nearly so serious a business as the IRA in Northern Ireland, but the West Germans over-reacted in a manner that delighted the terrorists: in one anti-terrorist operation in Frankfurt in 1972, the streets were filled with troops, armoured cars, searchlights and enough firepower to blow away half the city. Special legislation was passed to restrict the rights of defence lawyers (because many RAF lawyers had been helping terrorism) and limiting other constitutional freedoms.

It seemed, briefly, to more impressionable observers, that West Germany was about to renounce its hard-earned democracy and revert to the practices of the 1930s. The incompetence of the Bavarian police during the Munich Olympics affair in 1972, which led to the deaths of the Israeli athletes, was another trauma.

However, the police did succeed. They arrested most of the Baader–Meinhof gang, and the first wave of terrorism subsided. Then in February 1975, surviving terrorists kidnapped the leader of the Christian Democratic party in West Berlin, Peter Lorenz. The socialist government capitulated to the terrorists' demands and released five RAF prisoners in exchange for Lorenz, and paid them a ransom of DM20,000.

West German terrorists were by then playing prominent roles in other dramas. On 24 April 1975, six members of the RAF seized the West German embassy in Stockholm, demanding the release of 26 Baader–Meinhof prisoners (including all the leaders). They killed two diplomats (holding one of them up in a window so that the murder would be recorded on television), but their plans went awry. Their explosives expert proved incompetent. He had packed the top floor of the building with dynamite – and it went off with the terrorists inside. One of them was killed, and the 'expert' died of wounds; the four others were briskly extradited to West Germany.

One of the terrorists released in Berlin after the Lorenz kidnapping, Gabriele Kröcher-Tiedemann, was among those who took part in the raid on the OPEC meeting in Vienna in December 1975, led by Carlos (*see* Arab terrorism). She killed two of the three men who were murdered, including an elderly Austrian security guard. 'Are you a policeman?' she asked him. When he admitted it, she shoved him into an elevator, shot him dead, and pushed the down button.

There were also two West German terrorists among the Palestinians who hijacked the Air France jet to Entebbe in June 1976 (*see* Uganda, pp. 108–16). They were both killed in the Israeli rescue.

In May 1976, Ulrike Meinhof hanged herself in her jail cell. A year later, the chief prosecutor of the Federal Republic, Siegfried Buback, was shot in Karlsruhe, in revenge for Meinhof's suicide. Then began the most sanguinary period of the Baader–Meinhof saga – although all the gang's founders were by then in jail. A particularly shocking crime was the murder of a banker, Juergen Ponto. His murderers had been admitted to his house by his god-daughter, Susanne Albrecht, who had joined the RAF.

On 9 September 1977, Hans-Martin Schleyer, a prominent businessman, was kidnapped in Cologne and his three bodyguards killed. A series of letters from his captors, posted in Paris over the next 45 days, demanded that 11 Baader–Meinhof prisoners be released, each of them given $50,000 and flown to a country of his or her choice. The government refused the deal, and Schleyer was murdered. His body was discovered on 19 October, in Mulhouse, just over the border in France.

On 13 October, while Schleyer was still alive and in captivity, a band of Palestinians seized a Lufthansa plane, and, after careening around the Middle East looking for an airport that would take them in, landed in Mogadishu in Somalia. They, too, demanded the release of the Baader–Meinhof terrorists. The West German anti-terrorist force GSG-9, accompanied by two members of the British SAS, stormed the plane and killed three of the terrorists.

On 20 October, the day after Schleyer's body had been found, three of the surviving Baader–Meinhof leaders, Andreas Baader himself, Gudrun Esslin and Jan-Carl Raspe, killed themselves in their cells in Stammheim jail, having lost hope after the failure of the Schleyer and Mogadishu attempts to rescue them. Their supporters claimed that they had been murdered by their jailers, but the police were able to prove that it had been a mass suicide.

That was, abruptly, the end of the Baader–Meinhof gang. It took several years for the RAF and its off-shoot the June 2 Movement to reconstitute itself and resume the fight.

A few survivors picked up the threads and began to rebuild the organization, and to move abroad: cells were set up in the Netherlands, Belgium and France. The first 'operation' of the new RAF was an attempt to assassinate the Nato commander, General Alexander Haig (later US secretary of state), near Brussels in June 1979. It was a sign that the second generation intended to be more 'international' than its predecessor, who had concentrated on purely West German targets. In May 1980, Paris police raided an apartment used by the West German terrorists at 4 rue Flatters, where they discovered large quantities of weapons, ammunition, false papers and money. They picked up two women, old RAF hands, and three more arrived the next day and walked into the arms of the police. All five were shipped back to West Germany.

In August 1981, the new RAF bombed the USAF base at Ramstein and, in September, attempted to kill the commanding officer of the US Army in West Germany, General Frederick Kroesen, using a Soviet rocket-propelled grenade (RPG). This was a new departure. RPGs (the Soviet version is the S-7) are favourite weapons of all the militias of Lebanon and of Irish terrorists, but this was the first to be used by the Euro-terrorists. These two attacks coincided with the big pacifist campaign against the installation of American cruise and Pershing missiles in Europe, and were apparently attempts by the RAF to muscle in on the **505** endeavour. Their friends in Italy responded similarly, kidnapping an American general, James Dozier, in December 1981.

Several of the new RAF leaders were arrested in October 1982. Some mushroom hunters in a wood near Frankfurt noticed suspicious diggings and reported to the police. Investigators concluded that they had stumbled across an RAF arms cache. They set up an ambush and, a week later, arrested two RAF women terrorists who had come to visit the depot. It turned out to contain great quantities of documents, as well as weapons and ammunition. The papers, once they were decoded, led to a further 14 arms dumps, and enabled the police to set a trap for Christian Klar, the RAF's senior terrorist.

The RAF survived these defeats, and by 1985, according to the federal police, the new RAF had about 22 hard-core members (13 of whom were women, who now played a dominant role in the organization), 200 part-time militants and up to 2000 supporters ready to help. Some of the leaders were underground in West Germany, others lived in exile – for example, Susanne Albrecht, who had been involved in the murder of her godfather, lived in Baghdad. From their jail cells, Christian Klar and 29 others tried to assert control and influence by staging a hunger strike.

In the early 1980s, West German terrorism divided into several different tendencies. First of all, the hard-line RAF, in alliance with similar groups abroad, pursued its attacks on Nato and related targets. A separate organization of women terrorists, Red Zora, also played a part in some of these actions, but they were more concerned with social issues. They worried about the expansion of the Frankfurt airport, for instance, and in 1981 assassinated Heinz Karry, the local minister responsible for it; Zora then informed the world that his death had been an accident. Another group, the Revolutionary Cells (*Revolutionare Zellen*, RZ), concentrated on industrial disputes: in 1984, it bombed the miners' union headquarters in the Ruhr as a protest against the export of West German coal to Britain during the British miners' strike. These worthy objectives allowed the mushier representatives of the West German left, notably the Greens, to express their sympathy for the terrorists, and then to extend it to their imprisoned comrades. It was all very encouraging for the RAF, who could claim that they were at last making political progress. Right-wingers claimed that there was an overlap in the membership of the RZ and Red Zora with the Greens.

In all, the RZ and Red Zora carried out over 600 bombings in 1982, mostly aimed at firms thought guilty of 'consumerism'. The police suspected that there were five 'cells', each about 20 strong. The most extreme of these people were probably also members of the RAF, and new recruits to the RAF graduated from the RZ and Zora.

On 11 January 1988, German police arrested the woman whom they suspected of planting the bomb in the La Belle Disco in Berlin in April 1986. It was that episode that had provoked the American air raid on Tripoli. The woman, Christine Endrigkeit, was picked up in a squalid apartment in Lübeck, on the Baltic. It was an empty and cheerless place: she had slept on the floor and hung her clothes on nails. She was caught a few days after police had issued photographs and offered a reward.

However, the prosecutors had difficulty preparing their case against her, despite the fact that her name and phone number had been found in the phone book of

Mansour Hazi, a Palestinian who was sentenced to 14 years' imprisonment for bombing the Arab–German Friendship Society building in West Berlin a week before the disco bombing. Hazi was also suspected of ordering the disco bombing. His brother, Nezar Hindawi, is serving a 45-year term in England for giving his pregnant Irish girlfriend a suitcase containing a bomb to take on an El Al flight to Israel.

Whatever the results of the Endrigkeit case, West German police believe that they have broken up the RAF. Their continuing problem is that the remaining terrorists or would-be terrorists now form autonomous groups (*Autonomen*), modelled on Italian organizations of the same name and which are difficult to penetrate. The police may have dismantled three successive generations of terrorists, but enough of them remain at liberty, underground in West Germany or abroad, to serve as the nucleus of a new Red Army, if the political wind turns.

FRANCE

France has suffered from four of the classic forms of modern terrorism since World War II – nationalist, far left, far right and foreign. It also survived a military *coup d'état* in 1958, which brought General de Gaulle to power, and several further attempted coups. Of the terrorist campaigns, only the *Organisation de l'armée secrète* (OAS) in 1961–2, a group of military dissidents and Algerian settlers who wanted to overthrow De Gaulle and preserve French Algeria, ever presented a serious threat to the state. They nearly killed De Gaulle on two occasions and mounted a major bombing campaign in Paris, which was turned into an armed camp to defeat them.

Earlier, there had been a sanguinary secret war between Algerian factions, and a spate of terrorist incidents connected with the Algerian independence struggle. Compared with the dramatic days of 1958–62, the events of the 1980s are insignificant. The *crise de régime* of 1968 was precipitated by a student uprising and a general strike, and subsided as quickly as it arose.

The nationalist agitations have been the work of Corsican and Breton separatists (*see* Nationalist terrorism, pp. 519–25). A bombing-and-murder campaign by left-wing terrorists, who were closely associated with similar groups in West Germany, Italy and Spain, culminated in the mid-1980s with *Action Directe*, which was eliminated or at least severely hampered when its leaders were arrested in 1987 and 1988 (*see below*).

France has also been the chosen battleground of foreign terrorists and counter-terrorists: Arabs and Israelis have fought their wars of assassination in Paris; Arab factions have attacked each other; Armenians have attacked Turks; the IRA has attacked British targets; and pro- and anti-Khomeini Iranians have settled their accounts on French soil. These battles have often caused French casualties, and in 1986–7 the Armenians, the Syrian and Iranian secret services and an obscure group of Lebanese Christian terrorists together launched a concerted attack on the government (*see* Arab terrorism, pp. 526–47). The campaign coincided with *Action Directe*'s most serious onslaught (a coincidence that can hardly have been accidental), and for a year, Paris was a battleground, temporarily resembling

Belfast. However, the republic was never in any danger, as it had been in 1961, and competent police work soon brought the situation under control.

For many years, France was more tolerant of foreign terrorists than other countries, perhaps remembering that the word 'terror' was first applied in its modern context by Robespierre and St Juste. Furthermore, the French took seriously their reputation as a *terre d'asile* ('land of refuge'). Americans and Israelis frequently reproached France for dealing with terrorists (Israel less so after it emptied its prisons to get three PoWs back from the PLO). There were several notable occasions when the French allowed prominent Arab terrorists to leave the country, but after the Paris bombings and agreements reached in various Western summits, French anti-terrorist police have come to collaborate closely with their foreign colleagues.

France is also the only Western country caught red-handed recently in an act of state-sponsored terrorism: the sinking of the *Rainbow Warrior* in Auckland harbour, New Zealand, in 1985 by French agents (*see* South Pacific: the nuclear issue, pp. 488–9).

ACTION DIRECTE

In the late 1970s, a number of West German terrorists living in France took the lead in reviving the French terrorist movement, *Action Directe*. AD had been founded in 1979 in a merger of other groups. One of these antecedents, which called itself the *Noyaux armés pour l'autonomie populaire* (NAPAP), murdered the Bolivian ambassador in Paris, alleging that he had been involved in the defeat and death of Che Guevara. The Bolivian general who had hunted down Guevara and killed him, was sent to Hamburg as consul, where he, too, was shot in 1971. NAPAP was also responsible for the killing of a night-watchman at the Renault factory in Paris.

Action Directe carried out a number of minor terrorist attacks in its early years. Its leaders were Jean-Marc Rouillan, his girlfriend Nathalie Ménigon, and Régis Schleicher. The first two were arrested in 1981 in a trap set for them in an apartment in the rue Pergolèse. Shortly afterwards, the new socialist government of François Mitterrand released members of the Corsican separatist movement – and at the same time freed Rouillan and 25 other members of AD. Ménigon was not released immediately because she had been charged with resisting arrest by shooting at a policeman, shouting: '*Je suis Action Directe!*' (She had missed.) She then went on a hunger strike to prove that she deserved liberty and, after three weeks, won her freedom. The movement was not considered of any great importance. It was an error.

AD spent the next two years filling its coffers with the proceeds of a number of bank robberies. In the summer of 1982, it resumed 'political' action in a series of attacks on 'international' targets – meaning American and Jewish ones. However, the two worst anti-Jewish atrocities were probably the work of Arab terrorists. The first was the attack on the synagogue in the rue Copernic in Passy in March 1980, which killed four people. A group calling itself European National Fascists claimed responsibility, but police were sceptical. It is much more likely that it had been the work of Abu Mohammed's Palestinian terrorist group, the PFLP-Special Command (*see* Arab terrorism). The second occurred shortly after the

Israeli invasion of Lebanon: an attack on Chez Jo Goldenberg, a Jewish restaurant on the rue des Rosiers in the old Jewish quarter in the Marais, on 9 August 1982, which killed six people. An anonymous caller to a news agency claimed the credit for the restaurant attack for AD. French police were unconvinced, but did discover proof of links between AD and the Abu Nidal gang (*see* Arab terrorism) and the ASALA (*see* Forlorn hopes, pp. 548–54). The bombing was probably the work of Abu Nidal, possibly aided by AD.

These new AD attacks coincided with a wave of Middle Eastern terrorism and prompted the Mitterrand government to order an all-out war on it. In May 1983, AD killed two Paris policemen in a shoot-out in the avenue Trudaine. The two victims had stopped three people, one of whom was carrying a heavy bag of the sort used by gangsters to transport drugs; two other AD terrorists, including Schleicher, had then stepped forward and shot them. All five hijacked a car to escape. Two of the five were Italians and one was Arab, Mohand Hamami.

In June 1984, the new RAF and AD sent delegates to a conference of 'anti-Nato' terrorist groups in Lisbon. There they cemented an alliance with comrades from Belgium, Portugal and Italy and named it the 'Political-Military Front'. That same month, Belgian terrorists calling themselves the Fighting Communist Cells (*Cellules Communistes Combattantes*, CCC) raided a quarry near Brussels and stole nearly a ton of explosives. Over the next few months, bombs from Belgium turned up in numerous places, including the office of the Western European Union (a parliamentary group) in Paris, and a Nato officers' school in the West German Alps. Fortunately, those two bombs failed to explode.

The signal for the new campaign was a hunger strike declared by 30 RAF old-timers in West German prisons, including Christian Klar, who thought they would emulate Bobby Sands and other IRA terrorists who had starved themselves to death in a Belfast jail, and thus revived the IRA during a period of difficulty. The German hunger strike lasted several weeks, but the government refused to meet any of the strikers' demands and, lacking Irish fanaticism, they all eventually capitulated. The struggle would have to be carried on outside the prison.

The terrorist international, directed by the West Germans, aimed at targets all over Europe. Executives of firms involved in defence industries were to be assassinated, and computer companies and firms connected with nuclear energy were also to be attacked. American installations in West Germany and Nato bases in Belgium were prime targets. The RAF and AD issued a long proclamation, announcing the establishment of a 'politico-military network' of 'West European revolutionaries'. They claimed to be acting on behalf of the European proletariat and Third World people who were being crushed and exploited by Western imperialism and neocolonialism.

In 1984, as its contribution to the new offensive, AD attacked the following targets: the Panhard company (which builds tanks and armoured cars); the Atlantic Institute of International Affairs in Paris; the Ministry of Industry; the headquarters of the European Space Agency in Paris; the Western European Union (WEU); Messier–Hispano–Bugatti (another defence contractor); Dassault; the RPR (Gaullist) party headquarters; and the Elf-Aquitaine oil company. Régis Schleicher was arrested in Lyons in March but the campaign proceeded without him.

In 1985, the terrorists moved on to murder. On 25 January, General René Audran, director of French arms sales, was shot as he parked his car outside his house. A few days later, the RAF assassinated Ernst Zimmermann, a German industrialist whose firm made jet engines for fighters. The Euro-terrorists' campaign was now moving into high gear. In June, an AD commando attacked General Henri Blandin, a senior defence official, but he was saved by his chauffeur. Blandin's car had been waiting at a traffic light when the driver had seen in his rear-view mirror a gunman running towards him. The chauffeur took off, zig-zagging, while the gunman opened fire on the car, and missed.

In August 1985, a joint RAF–AD operation planted a bomb at the US air force base at Rhein-Main near Frankfurt, killing two and wounding 16. The terrorists had got on to the base by murdering an American serviceman and stealing his identity card.

In May 1986, AD attacked the Interpol headquarters in Paris with guns and explosives, wounding one man. On 6 July, they bombed the Thomson and Air Liquide chemical companies and, on the 9th, blew up the annex to the police headquarters in Paris, on the corner of the quai de Gesvres and the rue St Martin, killing one policeman and wounding 22. That was also the summer of the FARL and Iranian attacks in Paris (see Arab terrorism). It was evident, at the very least, that the various terrorists were emulating each other, if not actually collaborating.

On 17 November 1986, Nathalie Ménigon and Joëlle Aubron killed Georges Besse, chairman of Renault. The following month, Régis Schleicher and several others went on trial for the avenue Trudaine killings and other acts of terrorism. Schleicher announced from the dock that his friends would wreak vengeance on the court; several jurors asked to be excused, and the trial had to be postponed because of the blatant intimidation. The next day, 15 December, AD tried to kill a former justice minister, Alain Peyrefitte, with a car bomb; his driver died instead. Schleicher was finally tried in June 1987, before a panel of seven judges. He was convicted of murder and sentenced to life imprisonment.

The police were hot on the trail. On 28 March 1986 in Lyons, police arrested one of AD's founders, André Olivier, with two others in a car filled with guns. On 24 September, they arrested nine suspects, including four Lebanese and four French leftists. The next day, a member of AD, Frédéric Oriach tried to give a press conference in the Luxembourg Gardens: as he was introducing himself to the cameras, he was arrested by plainclothes policemen.

On 21 February 1987, the police dealt a body blow to *Action Directe*: they raided an isolated farm at Vitry-aux-Loges (Loiret), 19 miles (30 km) east of Orléans, and arrested four of the five surviving leaders of AD. Nathalie Ménigon and Jean-Marc Rouillan had been living there for three years, raising goats and hamsters. The government had offered a reward worth $180,000 and one of their friends had succumbed to temptation and betrayed them. The police had watched the house for several days, and their patience had been rewarded. On Saturday, the 21st, Joëlle Aubron and Georges Cipriani turned up for the weekend.

The fifth fugitive, Maxime Frerot, was arrested in a parking garage in Lyons on 27 November. He had been seen hanging around the place, and a couple of policemen asked to see his papers, which were obviously forged. He pulled out a gun, there was a shooting in which one policeman was wounded, and after a scuffle in which a passing taxi driver assisted the police, he was arrested.

He had been living in cellars and parking garages for several months, on the run and without hope, After his capture, the French police could legitimately claim that they had eliminated one of the nastiest bands of terrorists in France. Frerot had been AD's bomb specialist, the man who had planted the bomb in the police headquarters annex in July 1986.

The members of *Action Directe* were put on trial early in 1988, charged with a long series of hold-ups, bombings and murders. Before the trials began, they carried out a prolonged hunger strike, in protest against the conditions of their incarceration (they were held in solitary). Rouillan, after 84 days without food, was allowed to lie on a couch during his trial, before a seven-man panel of judges. He, and all the others, were convicted.

GREECE

The last European political terrorist movement capable of violent action is the Greek organization November 17. It is named after a student demonstration against the colonels' regime that was held on 17 November 1973, and in the following 15 years, members of the organization have murdered 12 people, including three American diplomats, and wounded more than 100 in a series of bombing attacks.

Its targets are 'big capitalist sharks and swindlers' and the US bases in Greece. Most of its assassinations have been carried out with the same weapon – a .45 Magnum – but in July 1988, it killed the American defence attaché, Captain William Nordeen of the US Navy, with a car bomb. One of its previous victims, Richard Welch, who was shot in 1975, was the CIA station chief in Athens. His name had been published in a book by a former member of the agency, Philip Agee. Another man named by Agee was Captain George Tsantes, who was shot in November 1983.

November 17 is remarkable in its longevity and seeming immunity from prosecution. Unlike the other European terrorist movements, including the RAF, *Action Directe*, the Red Brigades and ETA, no member has ever accepted the large rewards offered by police for information, and no member has ever been arrested or identified.

On 14 August 1988, a November 17 group of six men seized a local police station in Athens without firing a shot, tied up the police officers there and carried away all their weapons. It seemed to the Greeks that this presaged a new and more violent campaign.

Some anti-terrorist police forces see November 17's continued success as a reflection on the efficiency of the Greek police. Athens has long been a favourite base for Palestinian and other foreign terrorists (including the Armenian terrorist, Hagop Hagopian, who was killed in Athens in 1988). Security at Athens airport was notoriously slack until very recently (after vigorous American protests led to a sharp drop in the tourist trade): a major shooting took place and several hijackings and bombings originated there, including the 1985 TWA incident (*see* Government terrorism *below*). Furthermore, Greece remains one of the last strongholds of the old-fashioned, Marxist, anti-American left, which has gone so conspicuously out of fashion elsewhere. Some Greek newspapers are flagrantly in the pay of the KGB, and openly champion various forms of terrorism – 511 including November 17. There are frequent anti-American demonstrations, usually directed against the bases. Among other things, the Americans are blamed, with some justification, for the occupation of Cyprus by Turkey (*see* Cyprus, pp. 345–50).

ITALY

The Italian Red Brigades followed the same cycle as the RAF in West Germany. Their members are mostly bourgeois drop-outs, prone to anarchistic violence in the name of the suffering proletariat. They were much more numerous than the RAF, and more dangerous. By the mid-1980s, Italian jails held about 2000 terrorists (including Fascists) who had been responsible for 14,000 acts of terrorism over their 15 most active years as well as hundreds of murders. The Red Brigades' most dramatic achievement was the murder of Aldo Moro, leader of the Christian Democratic party and frequent prime minister, in March 1978. Most of the people responsible for that crime, and for other Red Brigade attacks, have now been arrested and convicted. Like the RAF and *Action Directe*, the Red Brigades are now a shadow of their former selves, thanks to successful police work.

The 'first wave' of Red Brigade terrorism grew out of the students' revolt of 1968. The early 'columns' of the brigades were financed and advised by Giangiacomo Feltrinelli, a millionaire radical-chic publisher. His most notable legitimate coup was the first publication of *Dr Zhivago*, but his chief interest in life, possibly in reaction against his family's aristocratic conservatism, was revolutionary politics. He set up a whole organization, the Proletarian Action Group (GAP) in the Milan region, with safe-houses, huge arsenals of weapons, a 'people's prison' to keep captives, and all the paraphernalia of an urban guerrilla army. On 15 March 1972, Feltrinelli killed himself while fixing dynamite to an electrical pylon in a Milan suburb: a stick of dynamite that he had been fastening to the pylon blew up in his hands.

Italians at first found it impossible to take Feltrinelli seriously, and the Italian left wing suspected that he had been the victim of an elaborate plot, despite all the safe-houses, guns and documents. At the time, Fascist terrorism was a much more serious threat to Italian democracy. The students' riots of 1968 had led to a revival of the Fascists' fortunes and, in the decade following Feltrinelli's death, they carried out a series of terrorist atrocities aimed at destabilizing the regime, apparently in the hope of provoking an army *coup d'état*, like the one in Greece in 1974.

The Fascists deliberately hit civilian targets: their first bomb, in the Piazza Fontana, Milan, killed 16 and wounded 90. In 1974, Fascist bombs killed seven people during a demonstration in Brescia, and on 4 August, a bomb on the Rome–Munich express killed 12. On 2 August 1980, an explosion in a restaurant in Bologna railway station killed 85 people and wounded 200: only the blowing up of aircraft has resulted in more deaths in a single incident in Europe. (The mills of Italian justice grind exceeding slow. In July 1988, almost eight years after the incident, at the end of a trial lasting a year and a half, four people were sentenced to life imprisonment for the crime, one got a 12-year term, one six years and two were convicted of slander, including Licio Gelli, former grandmaster of the celebrated P-2 Masonic lodge.) In 1984, a bomb on the Naples–Milan express killed 15 people

and wounded 100.

Left-wing terrorism never resulted in deaths on that scale, but by the mid-1970s, it had become a serious problem in Italy: there was a large number of more or less violent 'guerrilla' groups, 150 by one count. In the late 1970s. there were 2000 terrorist acts a year, including 40 murders. The 'historic founder' of the Red Brigades, Renato Curcio, began by kidnapping a Fiat official and putting him before a 'people's court'; he was convicted, and then released. The brigades soon abandoned such courtesies and began killing. Curcio was arrested in 1976. His wife, another terrorist, had been killed in a shoot-out with police the previous year.

The brigades decided to mount a spectacular operation and, on 16 March 1978, kidnapped Aldo Moro on the streets of Rome, after first killing his five bodyguards. For the next 54 days, all Italy was in suspense as the brigades issued their communiqués, demanded the release of Curcio and other imprisoned terrorists, and delivered a series of letters from Moro to his family and his colleagues. The government refused to negotiate with them, and on 10 May, Moro's captors shot him.

The crime was a turning point, though not in the way the brigades had expected. Because of it, every man's hand was against them, and the Italian police suddenly discovered reserves of competence and sophistication that had been conspicuously absent before. All the political parties, from the Communists to the Christian Democrats, cooperated with the police and supported legislation to suppress terrorism. After all, they might be next. General Carlo dalla Chiesa of the *carabinieri*, the paramilitary police force, was put in charge of the investigation. He succeeded in infiltrating the brigades with informers, and arrested most of their members.

The greatest anti-terrorist successes were scored in 1982, after the brigades tried to recoup their losses, and play a part in a generalized anti-Nato offensive by all the Euro-terrorist groups. To this end, they kidnapped from his Verona apartment Brigadier General James Dozier, the senior American officer in Italy and deputy commander of logistics in Nato's southern command. Four men dressed in overalls had arrived at the apartment, claiming they were plumbers; they had then assaulted Dozier, beaten up his wife and carried him off.

The brigades then issued a communiqué denouncing Nato's threat to the world proletariat, and 'offering an outstretched hand to ETA and the IRA'. It was thought notable that the Italian terrorists should now join the RAF and *Action Directe* in attacking 'international' targets; hitherto, they had been securely local in their interests. The following month, another American officer, Colonel Charles Ray, an attaché in the American embassy in Paris, was murdered by the Middle Eastern terrorist group FARL (*see* Arab terrorism, pp. 526–47). This may have been a coincidence, but it is entirely possible that the two groups had been at the least aware of each other's operations.

Dozier was rescued on 28 January 1982. During his captivity, the brigades had announced that he was being put on trial, and his friends had feared for his life. The Italian police had launched a major search for him, with, thanks to General dalla Chiesa, more determination and efficiency than they had shown for Aldo Moro. On 3 January, they had arrested Giovanni Senzani, a former professor of criminology at the University of Florence. His arrest had been one of many: the police had brought in over 30 members of the Red Brigades and eight of Front Line (another terrorist group). Some of them had confessed, and had given away Dozier's hiding place.

He was being kept in an apartment in Padua, tied up, barefoot, in a pup-tent pitched in the living room. Ten anti-terrorist police broke into the place in mid-morning before the terrorists had time to react. There were no casualties.

That police coup led to the arrest of another 50 *brigadistas* in the following week. One of them later took police to the Rome apartment where Moro had been concealed. It had been occupied at the time by a female terrorist, who was arrested in 1980. Two police officers had lived on the floor above.

After his success against the Red Brigades, General dalla Chiesa was sent against a more formidable enemy – the Mafia. He was assassinated in Palermo, with his wife, on 3 September 1982.

Police action against the brigades reduced them to an inconsequential residuum, but though defeated, they were not destroyed. Like the RAF after the destruction of the Baader–Meinhof gang, the brigades retired to regroup and retrain. In 1985, they reappeared, calling themselves the Fighting Communist party (PCC), and murdered a noted economist, Ezio Tarantelli, who had advised the socialist government to end the sliding scale of automatic wage increases in Italian industry. The brigades calculated that they would win the allegiance of the Italian workers by murdering such a person. They were mistaken.

The brigades managed a number of acts of terrorism over the next three years, despite frequent losses. In February 1986, they attempted to assassinate Antonio da Empoli, an adviser to the prime minister. However, da Empoli's bodyguard killed the assassin, a woman, who was found to be carrying a proclamation signed by the PCC. Later that year, the brigades killed Lando Conti, a former mayor of Florence, and in 1987, they held up a postal van, killing two police guards and stealing 1.2 billion lire ($870,000). On 16 April 1988, they murdered Senator Roberto Ruffilli, a Christian Democrat and a key supporter of the new prime minister, Ciricao de Mita. The killing was clearly intended to upset the new government.

Later that summer, on 7 September, police arrested 21 members of the Red Brigades, 16 men and five women, including the two suspected of the Ruffilli murder. Police, acting on a series of tips from informers, had carried out pre-dawn raids on four terrorist safe-houses and found explosives, pistols, rifles, shotguns and copies of communiqués that the terrorists had issued claiming the credit for previous acts of terrorism. Police said that they had evidence linking those arrested to the Tarantelli and Conti murders, and to the postal raid.

It was a bad year for terrorists: the Red Brigades greatly reduced; the last cells of the RAF and *Action Directe* dismantled; Hagop Hagopian, the leader and chief killer of the Armenian terrorists, himself assassinated. However, the Euro-terrorists, and probably the ASALA (*see* Forlorn hopes, pp. 548–54), have not been destroyed. There is no doubt that scores of accomplices and sympathizers of the Red Brigades and the RAF remain at large, and there are more living in exile. It is entirely possible that they will revive, and stage a 'fourth wave', however unpromising the omens. Curcio and other terrorist leaders were sentenced to 15-year terms in 1978 and will soon be eligible for release. Besides, the *fons et origo* of so much of modern terrorism – the Palestinian dispute – continues as violently as ever.

JAPAN

The Japanese Red Army (JRA) was a pathologically violent organization. In a brief moment in 1972, its demented doctrines horrified the world: half of its members were tortured and murdered by their own leaders, who were subsequently arrested. Then three survivors massacred 28 people at Lod airport in Israel. Since then, every appearance of Japanese terrorists has rung every alarm bell in every police force in the world.

There was a voluble and violent leftist movement in Japan in the 1950s and 1960s, under Communist leadership, which demonstrated against Japan's alliance with the United States. Its greatest success was to force the cancellation of a state visit by President Eisenhower, and later, it succeeded in postponing for several years the opening of a new Tokyo airport. The leftists were also able to mount huge, well-organized demonstrations against the police, the demonstrators wearing crash helmets and armed with staves. Japanese police, too, armed themselves with shields, helmets and staves, and the two 'armies' went to battle like their ancestors in the Middle Ages. The Japanese police were victorious.

The most extraordinary success of the police was their ability to resist the temptation to over-react. They set an example that the South Koreans have followed (most of the time), and that the Israelis conspicuously have not. The Japanese police do not shoot rioters – who, for the most part, later resume their place in society.

In the 1970s, however, a handful of them turned to murder. One group, led by a woman, Hiroka Nagata, was called the 'Tokyo–Yokohama Joint Struggle Committee against the Japan–United States Security Treaty', and another was the Red Army, led by Tsureo Mori, who was a former high school fencing star. The two groups merged in 1970 to form the United Red Army (*Rengo Sekigun*). In its first public act, seven of its members hijacked a JAL internal flight and forced it to fly to North Korea. The hijackers were then armed with Samurai swords, but they later acquired other skills. Some of them travelled to the Bekaa valley in Lebanon, and trained in terrorism and guerrilla warfare with the Palestinians.

In the next two years, the Red Army carried out a number of attacks and murders in Japan. They were not the only fanatics fighting against the new Japan: 515 in November 1970, one of Japan's best-known authors, Yukio Mishima, who was also a militarist of the old school, tried to start a revolution by occupying a barracks with a few followers, and inciting the troops to revolt. They refused, and he committed ritual suicide.

Mori was equally divorced from reality. Late in 1971, he took the 30 or so members of the Red Army into the mountains north of Tokyo to train for the overthrow of the government. In order to start a revolution, they would form three suicide squads who would set out to murder members of the government and other prominent citizens.

After several weeks of this, by later accounts, some members of the band started expressing doubts of the wisdom of their leader's course. Hiroka Nagata, who like Mori was 27 years old, convened a people's court to try the doubters. They were tortured, stripped naked, tied to stakes in the open and beaten with wire – and then left to die of exposure. The guilty women had their heads shaved before they were left to die; one of them was eight months' pregnant. Nagata was described as a singularly unprepossessing woman who considered sexual relations between members of the Red Army to be 'unrevolutionary'.

On 19 February 1972, police encountered a Red Army band, and in the ensuing shoot-out, nine of its members were arrested. Four others, including Mori, escaped and took refuge in a house at Karuizawa, where they took the housekeeper hostage. About 1000 police laid siege to the house for eight days until 27 February, when they stormed the place. Two police were killed, five members of the Red Army (including Mori and Nagata) were arrested, and the hostage was rescued.

The horrors were revealed a few days later, as some of the arrested terrorists described the 'people's trials' and took police to the site in the mountains. Eventually, 14 bodies were recovered. One of the survivors said that Nagata was 'a woman of frail mind and abnormal jealousy'.

Three months later, on 30 May, three members of the Red Army, who had been training in Lebanon, took passage on an Air France airliner from Paris to Lod airport, outside Tel Aviv. Acting perfectly normally, they got off the plane with the other passengers, took the bus to the terminal, and there collected their luggage. Then they opened their bags, pulled out hand grenades and machine-guns, and opened fire on the crowded concourse. They killed 26 people and wounded 76, mostly Costa Ricans who had come on a pilgrimage to the Holy Land. One of the terrorists killed himself with a grenade, possibly a suicide, a second was killed by one of his comrades in the general shooting, and the third – Kozo Okomoto – was captured. (Okomoto was eventually released, in May 1985, along with 1153 other prisoners held in Israel [almost all of them Palestinians], in exchange for three Israeli soldiers who had been captured in Lebanon by one of the Syrian-backed Palestinian organizations.)

The Japanese Red Army was able to survive, mostly in exile: police think that there are now about 40 members left, primarily living in the Middle East. Members hijacked a JAL flight from Amsterdam to Tokyo in 1973. On 31 January 1974, two Japanese and two Palestinians attacked a Shell Oil refinery in Singapore. They took five hostages, and retreated to a boat whence they demanded that the Japanese government release some of their comrades. The government refused. On 6

February, Palestinian terrorists seized the Japanese embassy in Kuwait; the government capitulated.

On 27 July of the same year, a member of the JRA, Yoshiaka Yamada, was arrested at Orly airport in Paris, and was found to be carrying $10,000 in crude counterfeit notes, intended to finance kidnappings in Europe. In September, some of his comrades occupied the French embassy in The Hague, and demanded Yamada's release. The operation was notable because it involved the Euro-Palestinian terrorist Ilich Ramirez ('Carlos'), who also threw a grenade into Le Drugstore on the boulevard St Germain in Paris in support of the Red Army terrorists. The French government complied with their demand, and Yamada was released.

In 1975, Japanese terrorists attacked the Japanese embassy in Kuala Lumpur and, in 1977, hijacked another JAL flight, this time on its way to Dacca. On each occasion, they demanded the release of some of their imprisoned comrades, and their demands were usually met. The Bangladesh incident was resolved when six terrorists were released and the government paid $6 million in ransom.

Now the Red Army has reappeared. One member of the group, said by police to have organized the Lod airport massacre, was arrested trying to re-enter Japan in the autumn of 1987. In May 1988, one of the men who had hijacked the JAL flight to North Korea in 1970 was arrested in Tokyo. There are believed to be five other survivors of that incident living in North Korea.

Another suspected member of the Red Army, Junzo Okudaira, was believed to have placed a bomb outside a US servicemen's club in Naples on 13 April 1988, killing five people and wounding 17. Car rental agents recognized his photograph as the man who had rented the car used in the bombing. Okudaira had been among those released by the Japanese government after the Bangladesh hijacking in 1977. He and a few comrades had apparently been operating in Italy for some time, and were responsible for attacks on the American and British embassies during the Venice summit in 1987. Italian police assume that the Red Army is now working for Libya: the Naples bombing occurred two days before the second anniversary of the American raid on Tripoli, and a group calling itself the Jihad took credit and said it was a reprisal for the air raid.

On the day of the Naples explosion, another suspected member of the Red Army, Yu Kikumura, aroused the suspicions of a highway patrolman on the New Jersey turnpike and was arrested. Three pipe bombs and all the materials to make several more were found hidden in his car. He had been living peacefully in New York for several weeks. In February 1989, he was sentenced to 30 years in prison. Prosecutors claimed that he had planned to bomb a navy recruiting station on the West Side of Manhattan.

The Red Army is the most violent of Japanese left-wing factions, but there are many others. The 'New Left', a radical movement composed of 23 factions, has about 35,000 supporters. Its most extreme section is the Chukaku-Ha, which advocates revolution through mass struggle; it has about 200 full-time members.

Over the past decade, the New Left has frequently attacked Narita airport, Tokyo, the new Kansai airport at Osaka, and railway stations. It has devised some remarkable weapons, including flamethrowers, rockets and mortars. It has launched projectiles at the Imperial Palace in Tokyo, at the building where an economic summit was taking place (May 1986), and at other targets. Its most spectacular attack was carried out against the Liberal Democratic party headquarters in September 1984, when a home-made flamethrower mounted on a truck was used. The building was destroyed. Only a few injuries have been caused by its attacks, but in September 1986, a railway trade union leader was murdered and several others were beaten, possibly by the Chukaku-Ha.

NATIONALIST TERRORISM

BRITTANY

The movement for Breton autonomy or independence is one of the lost causes of Europe. The province has always been different from the rest of France: it is the last survival of ancient Gaul, preserving its Celtic language (which is related to Welsh and, more distantly, to Gaelic) and retaining a consciousness of a distinct, non-French identity to complement its Frenchness.

The independence movement had very little popular support at the height of its campaign in the late-1970s. An ineffectual group called the *Mouvement pour l'organisation de la Bretagne* (MOB) had achieved nothing, and a small group of fanatics then set up a *Front de libération de la Bretagne – Armée républicaine bretonne* (FLB–ARB), which started its campaign in earnest in 1976. The ARB attacked government buildings, including post offices and a TV licence office. In all, there were about 40 bombings. They did not succeed in winning any notable popular support in Brittany; indeed, when the ARB blew up a television mast, cutting off most of Brittany's TV reception for several weeks, there was great public indignation.

The ARB's most spectacular achievement was bombing Versailles on 26 June 1978. The bomb went off in the middle of the night and severely damaged the ground floor of the château's north wing. That part of the building houses a museum dedicated to the glories of the Emperor Napoleon, and a number of huge paintings depicting his victories was destroyed. It was no great loss to art but a severe blow to French equanimity.

The police launched a massive investigation and, by the end of the year, had arrested virtually the entire ARB, all 39 of them, and most were convicted of the bombings. Since they had taken great care not to kill or injure anyone (though two ARB men were killed by their own bomb on one occasion), they escaped with sentences ranging from 2 to 15 years. That was the end of the ARB – though it is always possible that it may reappear at some later date.

By the early 1980s, however, the autoroute had reached Rennes, the provincial capital, as had France's celebrated express trains, and the province's economy benefited accordingly. Furthermore, reversing centuries of linguistic persecution, the state now permits Breton schools, and the language is taught wherever there is a need; it is no longer illegal for children to be given Breton names; and there are Breton programmes on television and bilingual road signs.

It is a grudging concession, and even were it wholehearted, it is probably too late to save the language. There are thought to be about 400,000 people who speak Breton, but the great majority are old, and their language has been lost to their children. The same thing has happened to the patois of different areas of France, to Gaelic in Scotland and to Irish, despite valiant efforts by the Dublin government over the past 60 years.

CORSICA

The Corsican separatists were more violent than their Breton counterparts. The island was annexed to France in 1769 (just in time for Napoleon to be born French), after its inhabitants had fought a famous battle for independence against the city-state of Genoa. The fact that, a generation after the annexation, one of its own became emperor of France was, of course, a source of immense local pride and also reconciled the islanders to their new nationality. This pride has been retained: Bonapartists continued to be elected to local posts in Corsica into the 1960s.

Corsica remains different from the rest of France. Unlike the mainland, where for the most part the local patois have been submerged by French in the past century, the great majority of Corsicans still speak their own language among themselves. It is the poorest region of France, dependent on tourism, handouts from Paris and remittances from expatriates. In the 1970s, the resentment that this situation inevitably produces led to the formation of several more or less violent groups and, in 1975, the first violent action: Dr Edmond Siméoni led 30 men in an armed occupation of a wine cooperative. There was shooting and two policemen were killed. Siméoni did a term in jail and is now leader, with his brother, of a peaceful autonomist party.

His example was followed by more brutal men. The *Front de la libération nationale de la Corse* (FLNC) was founded in May 1976, and there are several other groups that have planted bombs or burned houses, including a group calling itself Francia (the *Front d'action nouvelle contre l'indépendence et l'autonomie*), which attacks FLNC supporters.

There have been hundreds of bombings in Corsica, and a smaller number on the mainland. The Ministry of Finance in the Louvre in Paris was damaged in February 1979, and another bomb in the Palais de Justice in April did extensive damage; in March, 1980, the Hôtel de Ville (town hall) in Paris was also bombed. In Corsica, banks, tourist projects such as Club Méditerranée, Foreign Legion posts, police stations and other government buildings have been blown up. The most costly incident involved a Corsican group that seized a hotel in Ajaccio in 1980: three people were killed in crossfire at a demonstration staged near the hotel. Following the election of François Mitterrand as president in 1981, there was a brief truce, which ended in January the following year. In the run-up to the regional elections in Corsica in August 1982, there were over 300 bombings.

When Mitterrand set up the Corsican assembly, he put the island's destiny in local hands for the first time. There was a turn-out of over 70 per cent in the assembly election, but the only autonomist party to take part won only 7 of the 55 seats – evidently the large majority of Corsicans want to remain in France. The autonomists now hold 6 out of 61 seats, and their percentage of the vote has dropped sharply.

Despite the obvious lack of public support, the struggle continued. Between 1982 and 1984, there were over 1300 bombings on the island, and in 1986, two foreign tourists were killed. On 13 March 1986, the FLNC exploded 13 bombs across the Midi (in Nice, Marseille and Aix). In May 1988, the FLNC announced a six-month truce, in honour of François Mitterrand's re-election as president.

Police claim that they have arrested half the front's leaders and the rest are on the run, but other Corsicans believe that violent opposition can only be countered by a more active language policy (starting with teaching Corsican in schools) and further economic progress.

THE BASQUES

There are about 2 million Basques in Spain and 200,000 in France, living around the western end of the Pyrenees. They like to boast of the antiquity and uniqueness of their language and history. They were there before the Romans conquered Spain and France (and imposed their language upon the rest of those countries), and it was the Basques who ambushed Charlemagne's rearguard, commanded by Roland and Oliver. Their culture and traditions survived the centuries, at least on the Spanish side of the frontier; the assimilationist educational policy of the French republic has almost wiped out the Basque language in France (and it is spoken currently by only a small minority of Basques in Spain). However, the Basques remain as distinct, and as conscious of that distinction, as the Irish, Welsh or Bretons.

There are four ancient Basque provinces in Spain – Alava, Guipúzcoa, Navarra and Vizcaya – which together make up the modern Basque province; and three in France – Soule, Basse Navarre and Labourd – which together make up the ancient province of Béarn (now the Pyrénées-Atlantiques). In Spain before World War II, Guipúzcoa and Vizcaya were industrially more advanced than the rest of the country, and Bilbao, the capital of Vizcaya, was the most advanced industrial city in Spain, and its inhabitants were among the most devoted supporters of the Republic in the 1930s. When Franco's nationalists attacked the Basque country in 1937, they first directed the Condor Legion, the German air squadron that Hitler had sent to Spain, to attack the ancient Basque capital, Guernica. It was one of the great crimes of the century.

After his victory, Franco tried to suppress all traces of Basque nationalism. He failed. The Basque Nationalist Party (PNB), which had governed the province under the Republic, survived in exile and retained the loyalty of the mass of the Basque people. Although it maintained a secret organization, it never sank to terrorism, preferring to wait for better days. Its caution did not satisfy all the Basques, however: in 1953, the first student revolutionary groups were formed, culminating, in 1959, with the formation of *Euzkadi ta Askatasuna* (ETA, 'Basque Homeland and Liberty').

To begin with, ETA was divided ideologically between Basque nationalists and Communist revolutionaries. At one stage, the movement was split into two competing factions, ETA-V and ETA-VI, numbered after its fifth and sixth clandestine assemblies, which adopted different policies on the question.

The first assassination occurred in 1968. ETA's leader in Guipúzcoa was killed in a shoot-out with the police, and in revenge, ETA killed the San Sebastián police chief. This event led to severe police repression, the arrest of many Basque militants, and the trial of 16 ETA men in Burgos in 1970. Six of them were eventually sentenced to death. However, in December, ETA kidnapped Eugene Beihl, honorary West German consul in San Sebastián, and in exchange for his release, Franco commuted the sentences. ETA was then reconstituted, reinforced by new members inspired by the trial.

In 1972, ETA kidnapped a Spanish industrialist. His employees were on strike, and ETA demanded that he accede to their demands – then released him. In 1973, they kidnapped another industrialist, this time for ransom. Then they began serious training in the mountains.

Their most spectacular operation took place on 20 December 1973, when they assassinated the prime minister, Admiral Luis Carrero Blanco in Madrid. He had been Franco's intended successor (Juan Carlos was to be only a figurehead monarch), and there was no one to replace him. The assassins were a group of four amateurs, who had first considered the possibility of kidnapping Carrero; when they had decided that this was impossible, they had turned to murder. The admiral had always driven to Mass every morning at the same time and along the same route. The assassins had dug a tunnel under the road and packed it with explosives, and had taken elaborate precautions to ensure that it had detonated just as the admiral's car had passed over it. The explosion had carried the car over an eight-storey apartment building, and it had lodged on a second-storey balcony on the other side.

Despite that remarkable success, ETA once again split, with the orthodox Marxists setting forth on their own. In all these developments, ETA's history greatly resembles that of the IRA, which also split between Marxists and nationalists. The new division in ETA was between ETA-Militar (ETA-M, the militarists) and ETA-PM (the politico-militarists) – between those who wanted to engage in immediate action and those who preferred to build up the party's political base first.

The leader of ETA-PM, Moreno Bergareche, tried to evolve a doctrine that would combine intense patriotism with Leninist theory; he was murdered by unsympathetic comrades in 1976. In 1978, one of the leaders of ETA-M, José Miguel Beñaran Ordeñana, who had been involved in the assassination of Admiral Carrero, was himself also murdered, in France, on the fifth anniversary of that event.

The French government banished ETA militants from the Pyrénées-Atlantiques. They moved to Paris, to Brussels (where the Belgian Communist party took them in) and to Algiers, where the government provided some weapons and training.

Until Franco's death in 1975, ETA had the outside world's sympathy because it was fighting against a detested regime (the African National Congress enjoys the same status today). Now that it is using the same methods against a democratic government, it has lost its respectability. ETA, once freedom fighters, are now terrorists. However, if we are to be consistent, we must admit that ETA's methods were always reprehensible: they were always terrorists, however odious the regime they were fighting.

After Franco died, Spain immediately set about dismantling the dictatorship. All political prisoners were progressively set free, the last 20 or so E T A members (all convicted of murder or complicity in murder) in 1977. They were released on condition that they leave the country. They did so, and resumed the struggle from abroad.

In due course, the autonomy that the Republic had given to the Basques and Catalans and which Franco had suppressed, was restored. E T A and its political front *Herri Batasuna* ('One People') continue to insist on full independence, but the biggest slice of the vote that it has managed in a free election is 20 per cent.

E T A has greatly accelerated its terrorist campaign since the restoration of democracy. It is responsible for the deaths of hundreds of people (though none so prominent as Carrero Blanco), including not only off-duty policemen but their friends and relatives, their wives and children, and many other civilians. The murder campaign began immediately after Franco's death (19 people were killed in the first year), and has continued ever since. At the same time, Basque exiles, including many E T A veterans, were permitted to return home. One of them was Telesforo Monzón, aged 74, who had been minister of the interior in the Basque government during the civil war. Returning from 40 years' exile, he became a vehement supporter of E T A.

In 1977, 30 people were murdered; in 1978, 66; and in 1979, 130. By the end of 1980, the total had reached 275. The E T A leadership then entered into discussions with the government for a permanent truce and amnesty, but the movement split on the issue, with the result that E T A-M broke away and continued the campaign. They were particularly concerned to defeat the government's plans for Basque autonomy: they wanted the Basques oppressed, so that they would rise in revolt and usher in the new order. They launched a ferocious murder campaign against the Statute of Guernica, which gave the Basques everything they wanted, short of full independence. Subsequent elections have demonstrated clearly that the majority of Basques accept the new constitution, and consider that it meets their demands fully.

Of the two-thirds of Basques who turned out for the referendum in 1979, only 4 per cent voted against the Statute. After the Basque government (called the General Council) was re-established, the president of the Basque government-in-exile, who had lived in Paris since 1939, returned and formally handed his authority over to the newly elected president of the council.

The struggle continues. It needs very few people – only a couple of dozen – to plan a few terrorist actions every year and the occasional major attack. By the end of 1988, the total number of people killed (since 1968) had passed 500. On 6 February 1986, E T A assassinated Vice-Admiral Cristobal Colón (a descendant of Christopher Columbus) merely because of his prominence; he was the 54th senior officer murdered since Admiral Carrero in 1973. On 14 July 1986, a bomb in a Madrid bus killed ten *guardia civil* and wounded 43. A week later, a bomb and rocket attack on the ministry of defence wounded nine people, and on 29 July a bomb at a resort at Marbella wounded a nine-year-old boy.

The Spanish government has not responded as E T A wished – it has not imposed a new military dictatorship in the Basque country. Furthermore, the police have improved their tactics, and many E T A terrorists are now safely jailed. In   523

1982, a general offer of amnesty was issued, and during the next four years, about 250 members of ETA accepted (the most prominent of whom was then murdered by his former comrades). France, which for years had offered asylum to ETA terrorists, now pursues them with as much diligence as the Spanish authorities. In 1979, it revoked the refugee status of Basque exiles and delivered seven of them to Spanish police. In 1985, there were raids on ETA bases and safe-houses in France, and 30 ETA suspects were extradited to Spain – a severe blow to the organization. French police arrested ETA-M's military commander, Santiago Arrospide in October 1987, and in January 1989, they captured the ETA-M commander-in-chief, José Antonio Urrutikoetxea Bengoechea, whose *nom de guerre* is Josu Ternera, near Bayonne. He was allegedly one of the four who killed Admiral Carrero, and directed a number of terrorist acts, including planting a bomb in a parking garage under a supermarket in Barcelona, in June 1987, that killed 21 people. At the same time, French police rounded up a number of other members of ETA, including the only female member of its executive committee.

The French have always treated Spanish Basque separatists cautiously. There is a lurking fear that French Basques might one day be tempted to join the struggle: there is a clandestine organization north of the Pyrenees, known as Iparretarrak, which usually confines its activities to helping ETA. So far, it has not practised terrorism on its own account.

The struggle continues. It needs very few people, a few dozen, to plan a few terrorist actions every year, and the occasional major attack: on 6 February 1986, ETA assassinated Admiral Colon, a descendant of Christopher Columbus, merely for his prominence. He was the 54th senior officer murdered since Admiral Carrero in 1973. On 14 July 1986, a bomb on a bus killed ten Guardia Civil in Madrid, and wounded 43. A week later, a bomb and rocket attack on the ministry of defence wounded nine people and on 29 July a bomb at a resort at Marbella wounded a nine-year-old boy.

There is no doubt that ETA is part of the network known loosely as 'international terrorism'. That is to say, its members have received training from other terrorist groups in Algeria, Libya, Lebanon and Aden, and it has been helped financially and materially by them and perhaps also by certain governments. ETA itself may provide help for visiting terrorists: in May 1986, ten terrorists were arrested in Spain, most of them Lebanese, who had been hired by Libya to attack American and French targets and had carried out a number of bombings. This was at the time of the big bombing campaign in France.

The fact that ETA proclaims itself Marxist–Leninist doubtless wins it friends and supporters. However, like the IRA, it is an indigenous movement, answerable to no one. It is not part of a wider conspiracy, merely an ally of convenience. ETA has been less brutal than the IRA – it has killed fewer civilians – but it is equally implacable, and despite all the concessions granted by Madrid, there is little chance that it will ever completely disappear. Police all over Europe have repeatedly dismantled 'revolutionary' terrorist movements and appear to be winning the fight, but Spain, like Britain in Northern Ireland, has merely held its own in the fight against the far older nationalist movements.

ALTO ADIGE

Early in the morning of 19 May 1988, four large bombs exploded at government offices and housing projects in Bolzano, high in the Italian Alps. No one was hurt, but considerable damage was done, particularly to parked cars. It was the latest episode in a dispute going back over a century.

The province of Alto Adige is known to Austrians as the South Tyrol. Italy annexed it in 1919, as the spoils of war, and part of the German-speaking population has been agitating to return to Austria ever since.

When Italy was united in the middle of the 19th century, its statesmen proclaimed that its natural frontiers were on the line of the Alps. Although this meant the loss of Nice and Savoy to France, Italians obtained everything that they wanted except the hinterland of Trieste and the Alto Adige (even though Garibaldi had mounted his last campaign there). These territories were Italy's price for joining World War I on the side of France, Britain and Russia, and abandoning its alliance with Germany and Austria. In the 1920s and 1930s, Mussolini started agitating for Nice, Savoy and Corsica (formerly under the thrall of the city-state of Genoa), and after Germany defeated France in June 1940, he joined what he thought was the victorious side in order to obtain them. It was a mistake.

Hitler, busy gathering all the scattered Germans into one *Reich*, never claimed the South Tyrol. Despite all his rhetoric about the indivisible *Volk*, he left this pocket of German language and culture to his friend the Duce. After the war, after a prolonged and bitter dispute, the Yugoslavs recovered Istria, behind Trieste, but the Allies let the frontier on the Alps stand.

The first bombing campaign occurred in 1960. A number of Italian police and soldiers were killed before the terrorists were defeated. The Italian government reluctantly granted a measure of autonomy to the province, but were notably dilatory in carrying out their promises. An agreement with Austria was signed in 1969 giving the South Tyroleans the right to use the German language. Eventually, Rome conceded a general statute of autonomy for Italy's many and diverse regions (Sicily, Sardinia, Venetia, etc.), including Alto Adige.

Finally, in May 1988, a new Italian government agreed to further concessions, including the right to German-language courts and bilingual police. The agreement displeased both Tyrolean extremists (because accepting it would mean giving up any hopes of reunification with Austria) and Italian nationalists (who object to favours being granted to German-speaking Italians). The May 1988 bombings, the first of a series, were the work of German extremists: a mysterious group calling itself 'Ein Tirol'.

Over the next six months, there were 23 bombings in the Alto Adige. On 30 October, an Italian school in Bolzano was bombed, and a church in Appiano (known to German-speakers as Eppan), which had been the social centre for the village's Italian-speaking minority, was wrecked by a bomb. A leaflet in German that was scattered in the village said: 'Peaceful coexistence means ethnic commingling and genocide.' It was signed 'Ein Tirol'.

There are about 450,000 people in the province, two-thirds of them German, a reminder of the impermanence of European frontiers.

ARAB TERRORISM

Terrorism, the politics of murder, has always been common in the Arab world: a quite disproportionate number of Arab heads of state have been assassinated. However, mass terrorism, directed at civilians, and especially foreign civilians, is a more recent phenomenon. It was first practised by Palestinians against Israel and its Western supporters after the Six Day War. It reached a crisis in 1970, with a mass hijacking to a desert airstrip in Jordan, which led to the expulsion of the PLO from that country in 'Black September'. Since then, while there has been a number of sanguinary attacks on civilian targets in Israel and abroad, the chief victims of Arab terrorism have been other Arabs: Palestinians attacking Jordanians; dissident Palestinians attacking the PLO; Iraqis and Syrians attacking each other; and, since 1975, all the horrors of Lebanon.

It is often difficult for outsiders to distinguish between the various groups that have taken up terrorism as a means of political expression. They fall into a number of broad categories, but they all frequently overlap. Thus the Palestinians, who are dedicated to fighting Israel and, by extension, its Western allies, were often involved in the activities of outsiders, such as the West German Baader–Meinhof gang, whose objectives had no direct relevance to the Palestinian question. Religious terrorists, inspired by Islamic fervour and the search for martyrdom, may apply themselves to the Palestinian cause or, in support of Iranian objectives, to winning the Lebanese civil war for the Shiites. They may seek to advance the designs of Syria's President Assad, or, in the case of the Muslim Brotherhood, to overthrow him. Some groups, like the Abu Nidal gang, seem no more than pathological killers, hiring themselves out to whichever Arab regime will pay them best.

The victim of a hijacking, or a Western hostage kidnapped in Beirut, may not care very much about which obsession led to his misfortune. In the swirl of events, the Western public has been quite unable to tell the difference between all these groups, a fact that has been greatly to the disadvantage of all the Arabs, who are now automatically lumped together as terrorists.

One of the most significant of Arab terrorist acts was the attempted assassination of the Israeli ambassador to London, Schlomo Argov, in June 1982 by the Abu Nidal gang. The Israeli government used the event as a pretext for the invasion of Lebanon, an operation that had long been in preparation.

It was intended to destroy the PLO, which had taken over southern Lebanon. During the cabinet meeting that authorized the invasion, the chief of intelligence tried to point out that Abu Nidal had been responsible for the attack on the ambassador, and that he was bitterly opposed to the PLO. The chief of staff, General Rafael Eitan, briskly put an end to those quibbles: 'Abu Nidal, Abu Schmidal, they're all the same.'

They are not all the same. There are profound divisions within the Palestinian camp and between all the tribes of Araby. Not only have most of the victims of Arab terrorism been other Arabs, but the chief political victim has been the Palestinian cause, and therefore the PLO. If any demonstration of the counter-productivity of terrorism were ever needed, surely it is provided by the lamentable history of the Palestinians.

THE PALESTINIANS

In July 1968, George Habash, a Palestinian, Christian, Marxist physician, sent his commandos on their first mission to Europe: they hijacked an El Al jet on a flight from Rome to Tel Aviv, and took it to Algiers. It was the first such operation, and Habash considered it a great success.

He had set up the Popular Front for the Liberation of Palestine (PFLP) three months after the Six Day War in order to carry on the struggle by other means. From the start, his operation rivalled Yassir Arafat's Al-Fatah, the mainstay of the PLO. Then, and for another 15 years until its defeat in 1982, the PLO was committed to the fantasy of forming an army to liberate Palestine from the 'Zionist entity'. Habash had a different set of delusions: he would terrorize the Israelis and the world in a series of spectacular operations, and the walls would come tumbling down.

The Palestinians were still shattered by the disasters of 1967, and the first hijacking seemed a glorious victory. Habash was an instant hero, a fact duly noted by Yassir Arafat. The PLO was desperately in need of a new role and a new reputation. Habash was invited to join and, in due course, did so. The history of the PLO has since been one of constant rivalry between Arafat and more violent leaders. Arafat has retained his position as chairman, and nominal leader of the Palestinian people, by following the immortal precept of the 19th-century French revolutionary who exclaimed: 'I am their leader, I *must* follow them!'

After the Algiers incident, hijackings became the chosen *modus operandi* of the Palestinians. Habash's PFLP did the work, and Arafat used the publicity and the enthusiasm that the operations aroused in the Arab world to recruit an army in the camps, extort the money to pay for it from the oil states, and train and equip it in Jordan. By the summer of 1970, he had accumulated what appeared to be a formidable force there, and challenged King Hussein's authority and, eventually, tried to take over the country.

In two years, Habash and his chief of operations, Wadi Haddad (another doctor), organized 14 hijackings, and was probably responsible for the bomb that, in February 1970, destroyed a Swiss airliner on a flight from Zurich to Tel Aviv, causing 47 deaths. The campaign culminated in the Dawson's Field incident.

On 6 September 1970, the PFLP hijacked three airliners in the skies over Europe and attempted unsuccessfully to hijack a fourth. A TWA 707 and a 527

Swissair DC-8 were flown to a disused airstrip in Jordan, Dawson's Field (named after an otherwise forgotten British RAF officer). A Pan American 747 was flown to Cairo. The Egyptian authorities persuaded the terrorists to surrender: they blew up the aircraft after leaving it. The PFLP failed to hijack an El Al flight into London: security guards killed one terrorist – a Nicaraguan-born American serving a greater cause – and arrested the other, Leila Khaled, who had already participated in a hijacking. She was detained in London. On 9 September, the PFLP seized a BOAC VC-10 and took it to Dawson's Field to join the other two planes and their passengers.

The hijackers were met by PLO troops at Dawson's Field, and the Jordanian army surrounded them. The terrorists (Henry Kissinger prefers to call them *fedayeen*) demanded that all Palestinians held in British, Swiss and West German jails be released, in exchange for the hundreds of European hostages they held. They proposed to keep their Israeli and Jewish (mostly American) hostages, and trade them for Palestinian prisoners in Israel. The United States moved the Sixth Fleet to the eastern Mediterranean and prepared for a rescue, and the European governments agreed to release the prisoners – in exchange for all the hostages, including the Israelis. The hijackers released some, but not all, of the hostages.

On 12 September, the PLO moved its remaining hostages to Amman, and blew up the three jets. The event was moving towards crisis, and the American build-up continued. All this was recorded on television. It was the biggest terrorist media event so far, and was not surpassed until the seizure of the American embassy in Tehran, nine years later.

The PLO used the event to threaten the rule of King Hussein. On 17 September, he sent his army into Amman, and soon there was heavy fighting between the Jordanians and the PLO, both in the capital and in PLO bases elsewhere in the country. King Hussein was winning the battle – so on 20 September, Syria invaded Jordan.

It was all a remarkable achievement for the PLO–PFLP: for a few days, it seemed as though Arafat were about to become president of East Palestine, but it all ended in dust and ashes. American-sponsored negotiations between Israel and Jordan collapsed, perhaps the last occasion when Israel was willing to consider giving up most of the West Bank. The Israelis moved tanks into the Golan Heights, threatening the Syrian lines of communication, and the Syrians hastily evacuated Jordan. The Jordanian army completed its occupation of the PLO camps, rescued all the remaining hostages and expelled the PLO. Habash and Wadi Haddad did not renounce terrorism nor did Arafat condemn their adventurism (after all, he had been deeply implicated in the whole episode) but there was no doubt that it had been a serious defeat for them all and a victory for King Hussein. The PLO moved to Lebanon and began building up its forces there, with the result that, five years later, a civil war was provoked that has since destroyed that unfortunate country.

Al-Fatah's next foray into international terrorism was an attack on oil installations in Rotterdam in March 1971. The following summer saw the appearance of a new organization, 'Black September', formed jointly by the PLO and the PFLP and named after the PLO's great defeat in Jordan. It began a series of attacks on Jordanian offices and officials abroad, particularly on Alia, the Jordanian airline, which henceforth was attacked as frequently as El Al. In November, a Black September gunman murdered the Jordanian prime minister in Cairo, and two weeks later, another tried to assassinate the Jordanian ambassador to London.

As for El Al, the PFLP made a number of efforts to plant bombs aboard its flights, using impressionable young women who would be asked to carry a small suitcase to Israel for their Arab boyfriends. All these attempts were detected (although the destruction of a Swissair plane in February 1970 may have been caused by one of these 'carry-on' bombs). There were further hijackings. One of them, a Sabena flight in May 1972, ended spectacularly at Lod airport outside Tel Aviv, when Israeli security men stormed the plane, killed two of the four hijackers, captured the others and rescued the hostages.

There were worse things planned. In May 1972, three Japanese terrorists, members of the Japanese Red Army (*see* Terrorism: Japan), who had been trained at a PFLP base in the Bekaa valley in eastern Lebanon, arrived at Lod, and there opened fire on the crowd in the arrival building. A planeload of Catholic pilgrims from Costa Rica had just arrived for a tour of the Holy Land, and most of the 26 people killed were Costa Ricans. Two of the terrorists were killed and the third arrested. Then in September, there was the massacre at the Munich Olympics.

Seven Black September gunmen stormed the Israeli athletes' dormitory, killing a coach and one athlete. They seized nine other athletes (the rest of the team escaped), and demanded that 200 Palestinians held prisoner in Israel be released. The Israeli government refused. It offered to send a counter-terrorist squad to Munich to rescue the hostages, but the West Germans said they would do the job themselves. It was agreed that a plane would be provided to fly the terrorists and their hostages to Cairo. When the bus arrived at the airport, Bavarian police attacked. It was a botched and clumsy operation: the terrorists had time to throw grenades into the bus that was carrying the hostages, who were tied up in their seats. All the athletes were killed. Four terrorists were shot dead; three were wounded and captured.

The event was given enormous publicity, and for years, Arafat denied that he had been in any way involved. The attack had been a failure on two counts: the terrorists had not intended to get themselves killed (the West Germans had been expected to cooperate, and allow them to fly safely away with their hostages); and an attack on the Olympic Games revolted public opinion everywhere. There was a further unfortunate result for the Palestinians: the Munich attack prompted the West German government to set up an anti-terrorist squad, which later proved its effectiveness at Mogadishu in 1977, and also to pursue Palestinian as well as West German terrorists with great vigour.

As soon as the wounded terrorists were fit to travel, Black September hijacked a Lufthansa flight out of Beirut and demanded their release. The West German government complied immediately. The terrorists flew to Tripoli, where they were given a hero's welcome by Colonel Khadafy.

Then began a deadly war between the Israeli secret service, Mossad, and the PLO. The Israelis set about hunting down and killing all those responsible for the Munich massacre, and also attacked other PLO officials. They were not always successful. In July 1973, a Moroccan waiter in a small town in Norway was assassinated and the murderers caught: they were from Mossad, and had killed the wrong man. They had been looking for Ali Hassan Salameh, who had planned the Munich operation. After that, Mossad was more careful, and over the next few years, they killed the three survivors of the Munich massacre. The most dramatic incident was a commando raid on Beirut in April 1973, in which several PLO leaders were killed, including Mohammed Youssef Najjar, Arafat's deputy and Al-Fatah's chief of staff. In 1979, a car bomb in Beirut finally killed Salameh.

In 1973, a new terrorist organization, the National Arab Youth for the Liberation of Palestine appeared. It was led by a renegade member of Al-Fatah, Ahmad al-Ghafour (Abu Mahmoud), and was financed by Libya, which was then beginning to make its weight felt. The NAYLP's first operation was in August, a machine-gune attack on a TWA plane at Athens airport as it arrived from Israel: five people were killed, 55 wounded. In September, a five-man NAYLP team was arrested in Rome; they had been armed with Soviet SAM-7s, presumably supplied by Colonel Khadafy, and had intended to shoot down El Al airliners approaching Rome airport. In December, the NAYLP returned to Rome and firebombed a Pan Am jet, incinerating 32 passengers; the terrorists escaped by hijacking a Lufthansa plane. In September 1974, the NAYLP put a bomb on a TWA aircraft flying from Israel to the United States via Athens: 88 people were killed. That was too much for Arafat and the PLO. Four days later, Abu Mahmoud was tried, convicted of murder and shot.

By that time, Habash and Arafat had decided to stop the terror campaign outside Israel. Instead of winning the PLO friends and sympathizers around the world and intimidating Israel, it had done huge damage to the Palestinian cause. However, getting the genie back into the bottle proved impossible.

For the next few years, the PLO cooperated secretly with the CIA in thwarting terrorism. That arrangement ended after Arafat was driven out of Lebanon, when some units of the PLO, with Arafat's approval, resumed terrorist attacks. At the end of 1988, Arafat again renounced terrorism and offered his services to track down the people who had destroyed the New York-bound Pan Am jet that had exploded over Scotland in December.

The exploits of Abu Mahmoud showed that Arafat and Habash were not the only commanders of the PLO. Wadi Haddad, Habash's deputy, determined to carry on the terrorist campaign, quarrelled violently with Habash in 1972, and moved his operations to Baghdad. He called his new organization the Special Operations Group and began working with the rising star of the Euro-terrorist movement, Ilich Ramirez Sánchez, known as 'Carlos the Jackal'.

'CARLOS'

'Carlos' is (or was) the son of a millionaire Venezuelan Stalinist who made a fortune out of property speculation and named his three sons Vladimir, Ilich and Lenin. 'Carlos' (he chose his *nom de guerre* from a novel) was born in 1949 and led the life of a pampered, spoiled revolutionary. As an adolescent he studied the violent politics of Latin America, and went to Cuba. He caused so much trouble in Caracas in his late teens that, in 1966, he was sent, with his mother and two brothers, to London to finish his education. Later, he studied at the Lumumba University in Moscow, and visited PFLP camps in Jordan, there becoming converted to the Palestinian cause. He was in Jordan during 'Black September', and fought alongside his Palestinian comrades.

He was picked up by Wadi Haddad in 1972, and given the task of setting up a branch office in London. He lived the life of a Latin playboy and, on 30 December 1973, attempted his first known murder: he was sent to kill prominent Jews, starting with Joseph Sieff, director of Marks & Spencer and a prominent Zionist. He forced his way into Sieff's house, found his target in the bathroom and shot him. Miraculously, the bullet was deflected by Sieff's teeth, and he survived.

Carlos was by then senior PFLP operative in Paris, as well as London. His predecessor in Paris, Mohammed Boudia, had suffered an unfortunate accident with a powerful car bomb in June 1973; he had been on Mossad's list. At Wadi Haddad's direction, and with Iraqi money, Carlos subsidized the Euro-terrorists, notably the Baader–Meinhof gang in West Germany, his theory being that anything he could do to destabilize Western Europe would help the Palestinian cause. Carlos was a Communist, quite possibly working for the KGB or at the very least reporting to it. Thus, it could be said that the Euro-terrorists were allied to the KGB. That, however, is not quite the same thing as saying that Moscow directed their activities.

Carlos set up a network of safe-houses in Paris and began operations. His choice of targets was bizarre. He bombed a small Jewish newspaper, L'Arche, and also two right-wing and faintly anti-Semitic papers, L'Aurore and Minute. In September 1974, the Japanese Red Army occupied the French embassy in The Hague and demanded the release of one of their comrades held in France. Carlos helped out by throwing a hand grenade into Le Drugstore on the boulevard St Germain, killing two people and wounding 20. The French released their prisoner.

In early January 1975, a Carlos team tried to attack an El Al jet at Orly airport with a rocket, but missed. On 15 January, they tried again, but instead got into a fire-fight with police. They took refuge in the airport's toilets with 20 hostages, and were later allowed to leave for the Middle East.

So far, French police had no suspicions of Carlos. However, they were watching a Lebanese interior decorator called Michael Moukharbel, whom they observed visiting Carlos. On 27 June 1975, they arrested Moukharbel and asked him about his Venezuelan friend. He took three officers to meet Carlos at an apartment in the rue Toullier. They were so unsuspecting that they went unarmed.

The apartment belonged to one of Carlos's numerous girlfriends, and the police arrived in the middle of a party. The commissioner had an interesting ten-minute conversation with Carlos and then invited him to come down to the police station. First, however, he confronted him with Moukharbel. Carlos retired to the bathroom – and emerged carrying a gun. He shot and killed Moukharbel and two of the policemen and severely wounded the third before escaping.

The French then exerted themselves to find all Carlos's accomplices and discovered, to their horror, the extent of the terror network that had been operating in Paris. On 21 December 1975, Carlos reappeared. Leading a mixed West German–Palestinian commando, he stormed an OPEC meeting in Vienna and seized

11 oil ministers. The gang killed three men: a Libyan diplomat and two Austrian security guards. They demanded a plane to escape with their hostages, and proposed to tour the world, dropping off each oil minister in his home country, keeping the Saudi and Iranian ministers to the last – when they would be shot. However, one of the terrorists had been severely wounded, so the gang flew directly to Algiers where the hostages were released.

The wounded terrorist, Hans-Joachim Klein, abandoned terrorism as soon as he recovered and has led a precarious existence ever since, hiding from both Carlos and the West German police. He gave an interview in which he described the OPEC raid, and clearly suggested that the operation had been conceived and paid for by Colonel Khadafy, and directed by Wadi Haddad. In that interview, Klein said that Carlos compared himself to the assassin in Frederick Forsyth's thriller *The Day of the Jackal*, and that Carlos had told him, 'The more violent things get, the more people will respect you,' and 'To get anywhere, you have to walk over corpses.'

One of Carlos's comrades was Wilfried Boese, a member of the Baader–Meinhof gang, and together they planned the next, and last, of Carlos's operations. This was the hijacking of a French jet that ended at Entebbe. It was directed by Wadi Haddad: Carlos was chief planner and Boese commanded the operation (for details, *see* Uganda, pp. 108–16). They demanded the release of a long list of prisoners held in various European countries, most of whom were connected to Carlos. Boese was killed in the Israeli rescue. Haddad was lucky to escape: together with other Palestinian terrorist leaders, he had gone to Entebbe, but had left the airport just before the Israelis arrived.

After that defeat, Carlos dropped from sight. He is believed to have lived in Libya for several years, but to have broken with Khadafy in 1981, possibly after quarrelling with Khadafy's own terrorist establishment. He then moved to Syria, and has apparently worked for President Assad ever since, using his surviving European contacts to attack Assad's numerous enemies.

In February 1982, two of Carlos's agents were arrested in Paris, Bruno Breguet, a Swiss, and Magdalena Kaupp, a West German. Two weeks later, Carlos sent a letter to the French embassy in The Hague demanding their release. 'I give you one month to release them,' he wrote. 'If not, I will take up the matter personally with the French government and in particular with Gaston Deferre,' referring to the minister of the interior who was also mayor of Marseille. He signed the letter (which was in Spanish) with his full name, Ilich Ramirez Sánchez, and authenticated it with his thumb prints. A month later, a bomb went off on the Toulouse–Paris express, in the compartment in which the opposition leader, Jacques Chirac, had booked a seat. At the last moment, he had decided to return to Paris by plane, and therefore escaped. However, five other people were killed.

There were two more bombings, both on 31 December 1983: one at the Marseille railway station, and one on the Marseille–Paris express. Between them, they killed another five people. Breguet and Kaupp were released in 1985 – and Kaupp then married Carlos in Damascus. Carlos has since sunk into obscurity.

After Wadi Haddad died of cancer in a hospital in East Berlin in 1979, his organization was taken over by another fanatic, Salim Abu Salim, who had been Haddad's chief of operations. He renamed the gang the PFLP–Special

Command, adopted the *nom de guerre* 'Abu Mohammed' and continued the traditional cooperation with the Euro-terrorists. He is suspected of responsibility for the rue Copernic massacre in Paris in 1980 (*see* The Euro-terrorists: France pp. 507–11), and of bombing a Jewish-owned hotel in Nairobi on New Year's Eve 1980, killing 16 people.

Abu Mohammed, like Carlos, has vanished from sight. They have both been eclipsed by the most deadly of Arab terrorists, Sabri al-Banna, whose uses the *nom de guerre* 'Abu Nidal'.

ABU NIDAL

Yossi Melman's excellent study of Abu Nidal (*see* Further reading p. 563) lists all the atrocities that may be attributed to him from 1973 to 1986: 47 attacks on Arab targets (mainly Syrian in the 1970s, Jordanian in the 1980s), 16 on the PLO, 14 on Israeli or Jewish targets, 14 on Western targets, and one on a Chinese target. In the space of 13 years, the activities of Abu Nidal's group resulted in the deaths of 248 people (by Melman's count). The incidents involving the largest numbers of dead were the 122 killed in a Gulf Air jet blown up in mid-flight in 1983, 59 killed when Egyptian commandos attacked an EgyptAir jet that Abu Nidal's gang had hijacked to Malta in November 1985, 15 people killed by two bombs in cafés in Kuwait in 1985 and 18 people killed in the Christmas 1985 attacks on the El Al counters at Rome and Vienna airports. On 5 September 1986, Abu Nidal's terrorists killed 20 people at Karachi airport on a Pan Am flight that they had hijacked over India, and the next day, two of his terrorists killed 21 worshippers at a synagogue in Istanbul. It is, however, notable how many attempts of Abu Nidal's gang have actually failed: they are not very competent terrorists.

Because the great majority of Abu Nidal's victims are Arabs, some Palestinians claim that a man so dangerous to their cause must be in the pay of Mossad. That, obviously, is a nonsense. At one stage, he worked for the Iraqis, attacking Syrian targets all over Europe and the Middle East. Then he abruptly changed sides: his attacks on Syria stopped in 1977. Evidently, he had been bought. He may also have followed a personal vendetta against King Hussein of Jordan; otherwise, the only other explanation for the number and ferocity of his attacks on Jordanian targets in the 1980s would have to be that he was acting on behalf of the Syrians. He then turned his attentions to the conservative oil states – and Israel. It is, in any event, clear that Abu Nidal is Yassir Arafat's bitterest enemy: Al-Fatah, Arafat's base organization, has sentenced him to death, and Abu Nidal has tried frequently to have Arafat assassinated.

On 11 July 1988, three gunmen attacked passengers on a cruise ship, the *City of Poros*, in the Aegean, killing nine and wounding 98. The terrorists escaped aboard a waiting speedboat, and were not immediately identified. A few days later, the police issued photographs of three suspects, including a woman, who they said had been disguised as French tourists. The people in question, who had returned to France, immediately and indignantly denounced the allegation, and were able to prove that they were entirely innocent.

It seems certain that the terrorists were Palestinians: the attack coincided with the trial of Mohammed Rashid, who was charged and convicted of entering Greece on a forged passport. He claimed that his name was Mohammed Hamdan, but the police had his fingerprints – he had been convicted of smuggling hashish into Greece in 1973.

The United States wanted to extradite Rashid on a series of charges. He was wanted for planting a bomb aboard a Pan Am flight from Tokyo to Hawaii in 1982, which had exploded in mid-air killing one passenger. He was suspected of planning the bombing of the TWA flight from Rome to Athens in April 1986; the explosion had killed four Americans. Rashid was also involved in the murder in Lisbon of Issam Sartawi, a senior official in the PLO; Sartawi was one of several PLO moderates who, over the years, have been murdered for contacting the Israelis. Rashid claimed at his trial that he was a member of the PLO, passing through Greece on a secret mission, and the PLO office in Athens came to his defence. However, police suspected that he was, in fact, a member of the Abu Nidal gang. Greece hesitated to extradite Rashid to the US, partly for political reasons and partly because Abu Nidal threatened to kill any judge who signed the order.

Just before the attack on the cruise ship, a car had exploded near the port where the *City of Poros* was to dock. Its two passengers were killed, apparently the victims of their own bomb. One of them was thought to have been a senior member of Abu Nidal's team, Hejab Jaballah (using the name Samir Kadar), but the bodies were so severely mutilated that positive identification was impossible. Police were not even sure that there were only two bodies: there may have been three.

Jaballah had been one of the world's leading terrorists. He led the commando that murdered an Egyptian journalist in Cyprus (*see* Cyprus, pp. 345–50) in 1978, an episode that ended with a shoot-out between Cypriot and Egyptian troops at Larnaca airport. He is also believed to have organized the shooting of a synagogue in Rome in 1982, and the Rome and Vienna airport massacres at Christmas 1985. Abu Nidal's office in Beirut denied that Jaballah had been in Athens, claiming that he had died three years earlier. However, Greek police were able to match fingerprints left in an apartment used by the terrorists with those taken from Jaballah in Cyprus. A set of keys found there proved to be those of an apartment in Stockholm, where Swedish police found an arms cache and other evidence of the Abu Nidal gang's operations in Europe.

AHMED JIBRIL

Another Palestinian terrorist organization, the PFLP-General Command, was set up in the early 1970s by Ahmed Jibril, a former captain in the Syrian army. Jibril clearly remains under Syrian control; his headquarters are in Damascus. He quarrelled with Habash and Haddad, objecting to their foreign spectaculars, hijackings and the like; the Munich operation and the failure of the hijacking to Entebbe were cases in point. Jibril preferred to send his men directly into Israel. His commandos were usually caught and killed, but he could always find replacements. Some of the targets were legitimate military ones, but from the start, the PFLP-GC also attacked civilians. In April 1974, a three-man PFLP-GC commando infiltrated into northern Israel and, avoiding military targets, took refuge in an apartment building in Qiryat Shemona. They took a large number of hostages, 18 of whom were killed and 16 wounded when the Israeli army stormed the place.

The following month, on 13 May, another PFLP-GC team seized a school in Ma'alot, also in northern Israel. The Israeli army again botched the rescue, and 22 children were killed, together with the three terrorists. The next year, in March 1975, Al-Fatah, not to be outdone, landed a commando from the sea at Tel Aviv, seized the Savoy Hotel and murdered six Israeli civilians and six foreigners before they were themselves killed. In March 1978, a 13-man Al-Fatah commando landed on the coast between Tel Aviv and Haifa. They stopped several vehicles on the highway, commandeered a bus and drove it south, until it was stopped at a road block where, in the ensuing gun battle, most of the hostages were killed (the final death toll included 35 civilians). The ostensible purpose of all these attacks was, first, to hit military targets and, second, when that failed, to take hostages who might be exchanged for Palestinian prisoners – and the terrorists themselves. Al-Fatah's attacks were organized by Khalid Wazir, Arafat's deputy, who was himself assassinated by the Israelis in 1988.

The rivalry between Jibril and Arafat continued into the 1980s. Jibril was closely linked with a Palestinian organization set up by the Syrians to rival the PLO; this was Al-Saiqa, 'The Thunderbolt'. In the 1980s, after the Israelis had driven Arafat and the PLO out of Lebanon, a dissident leader, Abu Mussa, allied himself with the Syrians and challenged Arafat in the PLO camps in the Bekaa valley and in northern Lebanon. It was all part of Assad's rivalry with Arafat: the Syrian president was determined to control all the players in Lebanon, and Arafat was the last to oppose him.

Jibril tried to carry the war to Israel by sending men on hang-gliders to attack army posts, but such suicide missions were difficult and only one succeeded, in November 1987, resulting in the deaths of six soldiers. His tactics were proving no more successful than his rivals', so he changed them. In 1988, he set up a terrorist organization in Europe. West German police arrested several of his operatives in Frankfurt, and discovered a cache of explosives and timing devices. One bomb was concealed in a portable radio.

On 9 December 1988, the first anniversary of the outbreak of the *intifada*, the Israelis bombed Jibril's Lebanon headquarters outside Beirut, killing 20 people. On 14 December, Yassir Arafat formally recognized Israel's right to exist and renounced terrorism. On the 21st, a bomb destroyed a Pan Am jet over Lockerbie, Scotland, killing all 259 people on board and 11 on the ground. The aircraft had been flying from London to New York, a continuation of a flight that had started, with another plane, in Frankfurt. British police established that the bomb had been concealed in a portable radio, and it seemed likely that the suitcase containing it had been among the bags transferred from Frankfurt. Jibril was the chief suspect.

ARAFAT IN TUNIS

Yassir Arafat, driven out of Beirut by the Israelis in 1982, tried to re-establish himself in Tripoli, in north Lebanon. Assad sent the dissident PLO (which now called itself the Palestine National Salvation Front) against Arafat, and in due course, he was once again forced to escape by sea. He set up his new Al-Fatah headquarters in Tunis, and the only other section of the old PLO that remained faithful to him was a training unit on an island off the coast of Aden. His strength was not military, although he ensured that Al-Fatah still maintained all the trappings of a military organization. It was political, and on that field, he was undefeated. His PLO rivals had the guns and Assad. It was not enough.

Arafat remained the most prominent political leader of the Palestinians, dealing with the USSR, King Hussein, President Mubarak and, under the table, with some Israelis. Several members of his staff who were identified with the moderate faction were assassinated, and Arafat's own bodyguard, known as Force 17, was expanded: he was afraid equally of the Israelis and his Arab rivals. Also, the chairman needed to demonstrate that he was still a guerrilla leader, and several groups in the PLO, including Force 17, were given the task of proving the point.

One group, led by Khalid Wazir, who used the *nom de guerre* Abu Jihad, called itself the 'Western Sector' because it was based in Tunis. Its commandos were sent to raid Israel by sea. The first, a 28-man group aboard a small freighter, the *Atavirus*, was intercepted by the Israeli navy on 21 April 1985. The ship was sunk, 20 men were killed and the remainder captured. Despite that unpromising beginning, Force 17 tried the same tactic, sending a motor yacht, the *Casselredit*, south from Lebanon to raid Israel in May 1985. It, too, was intercepted and its eight-man crew, including Force 17's deputy commander, surrendered. The next Force 17 attempt – using another motor yacht, the *Ganda*, sailing from Cyprus – was equally unsuccessful.

After that, events suddenly accelerated. On 25 September, a three-man hit squad from Force 17 seized an Israeli yacht with three people on board, in the marina at Larnaca in Cyprus. First, they murdered a woman passenger, then they demanded various concessions from Israel in exchange for their two remaining hostages. Then they murdered the latter and surrendered. One of the terrorists turned out to be an Englishman, Ian Davison, who had been recruited by the Palestinians while he was travelling around the world. The PLO claimed that the three Israelis had been spying on the movements of ships such as the *Ganda*. Israel denied it.

On 1 October, Israel retaliated with a long-range air raid against Yassir Arafat's headquarters in Tunis. The chairman was lucky to escape: 50 people, mostly PLO men, were killed. On the same day, the Italian cruise liner *Achille Lauro* sailed from Genoa.

The seizure of this ship was carried out by another of Arafat's organizations, a faction led by yet another experienced terrorist leader, Abul Abbas. He booked four young men (the oldest was 20) on the ship and sent a relative to Italy to coordinate the operation. The relative was picked up by Italian police, and the Israeli raid on Tunis destroyed Abbas's communications system. The four young men, who had smuggled large numbers of weapons on board, were left to their own devices.

Abul Abbas claimed later that their mission was to wait until the cruise liner reached Ashdod (the main Mediterranean port in southern Israel) and then storm ashore and attack oil storage tanks. On 7 October, a sailor noticed their weapons, and the terrorists themselves were discovered shortly afterwards. They therefore seized the ship.

The *Achille Lauro* was then sailing along the coast of Egypt. Most of the passengers had left at Alexandria to visit the pyramids; they were to rejoin the ship at Port Said for the trip to Ashdod. However, there were still 427 passengers and a crew of 80 on the ship, and the four pirates threatened them all with death. They demanded the release of 50 Palestinian prisoners in Israel and, when the Israelis refused, murdered a 69-year-old Jewish American tourist from New Jersey, Leon Klinghoffer, who was confined to a wheelchair. First, they shot him, then instructed a sailor to throw his body overboard.

This occurred off the coast of Syria. The Syrians refused to allow the ship to dock, and it therefore returned to Port Said. By then, Abul Abbas had reached Egypt and arranged with the Egyptians that the four pirates would be allowed to go free if they surrendered the ship. The PLO then claimed credit for ending a crisis that it had itself begun.

Abul Abbas and the pirates were put on an Egyptian airliner and flown out: the US Navy intercepted the plane over the Mediterranean and directed it to a Nato base in Sicily. It was the most elegant American riposte to terrorism thus far. As the New York *Daily News* put it: 'WE GOT THE BUMS.' The Italians had not been warned, and insisted on taking charge of the prisoners. In an unpardonable gesture to Arafat, they released Abul Abbas and three of his assistants. The four pirates themselves, however, were tried for murder and piracy and sentenced to terms ranging from 15 to 30 years (the longest sentence was received by the one who had shot Klinghoffer).

After these disastrous efforts at terrorism, Arafat reverted to diplomacy, once again protesting his opposition to attacks on civilians. In November 1985, immediately after the *Achille Lauro* affair, he issued a formal statement condemning 'all outside operations other than in Israel and the occupied territories and all forms of terrorism' – but left himself an escape clause in which he demanded in return that Israel 'halt all acts of terrorism inside and outside'. Israel was not appeased.

When the Palestinian uprising began at the end of 1987 (*see* Israel, pp. 269–95), a new 'war of spooks' erupted. On 14 February 1988, three senior PLO men who had been directing the *intifada* were killed by a car bomb in Cyprus. Three days later, a limpet mine blew in the hull of a small cruise ship, the *Sol Phryne*, at Limassol, also in Cyprus. It had been hired by the PLO who intended to load it with exiled Palestinians and sail it openly to Israel, to recreate the voyage of the *Exodus* in 1947. In March 1988, one of Abu Jihad's commandos captured an Israeli bus in the Negev; three civilians were killed.

On 16 April 1988, Abu Jihad was killed, together with his bodyguards, by an Israeli commando raid on his apartment in Tunis. The most senior PLO leader to be killed for years, Arafat's deputy and last loyalist was also the long-term commander of Al-Fatah, and had founded and commanded Black September in 1970. When he was killed, he had been attempting to coordinate the PLO's reaction to the *intifada*, and had sent several commandos into Israel as a demonstration that the 'military option' was still available to him.

THE LEBANESE

The Palestinians are not the only Arabs to resort to terrorism to further their political objectives. The most violent terrorist campaign waged in Europe since 1945 was the work of Arabs, Armenians and Iranians against France. It reached its climax in September 1986: in two weeks, ten people were killed and 162 wounded in bombs left in public places in Paris. The attacks appeared to be the work of a small gang of fanatic terrorists from the village of Qubayat in north Lebanon. They were Maronite Christians who supported Syria, and most of them were members of the same family: Georges Abdallah and his six brothers. They were closely allied with the Armenian ASALA (*see* Terrorism: 537

Forlorn hopes), which was also an instrument of the Syrian secret services. However, a year later, during a prolonged confrontation with Iran, it emerged that the chief suspects for many of the bombings were not the Lebanese but the Iranians, taking revenge on France for supporting Iraq during the Gulf war.

The *Factions armées révolutionaires libanaises* (FARL; Armed Revolutionary Lebanese Factions), like the ASALA, emerged from the cauldron of the Lebanese civil war. Its first appearance on the scene was in Paris in 1981, when a gunman tried to kill the American chargé d'affaires; he survived. A year later, on 18 January 1982, Lieutenant Colonel Charles Ray, an American military attaché in Paris, was shot. An Israeli diplomat was murdered later that year, by a female assassin. In February 1984 in Rome, FARL killed the head of the American peace-keeping force in Sinai, and made an attempt on the life of the US ambassador.

FARL remained an obscure group, often described as a front for one of the PLO terrorist organizations. Then in the summer of 1984, a 19-year-old Arab, arrested in Trieste, gave many details of FARL's organization. The following October, a tall, bearded man walked into a police station in Lyons and asked for police protection. He said that he was an Algerian engineer and claimed that members of the Israeli secret service were following him and trying to kill him.

The men who had been following him then arrived: they were French police. The bearded man was Georges Ibrahim Abdallah, founder and leader of FARL. He demanded that he be released at once, on the grounds that his organization no longer operated in France. He hinted that the safety of French hostages in Lebanon depended on his release. To prove the point, two of his brothers then kidnapped Gilles Peyrolles, director of the French cultural institute in Tripoli.

The French considered exchanging Abdallah for Peyrolles, but then raided Abdallah's apartment in Paris, where they found the gun that had been used to kill Colonel Ray and the Israeli diplomat. In July 1986, Abdallah was sentenced to four years' imprisonment. It was a ludicrously light sentence, and because he had been held since October 1984, he was due to be released that October. Then came the wave of bomb attacks in Paris, which the government blamed on FARL. Credit for these atrocities was also claimed by the ASALA, and it is certain that the two organizations were working together. Abdallah remained in jail.

An organization calling itself the *Comité de solidarité avec les prisonniers politiques arabes et du Moyen-orient* (Committee for Solidarity with Arab and Middle Eastern Political Prisoners) launched a bombing campaign late in 1985 to win the release of three people held in French jails: Abdallah, a second Arab and Varoujan Garabedian, the Armenian responsible for bombing the Turkish Airlines counter at Orly airport in 1983. The campaign was terrorism in its purest form: the bombs were left in cafés and shops and in the streets, aimed almost exclusively at civilian targets.

The first bombs were left in two large department stores in the centre of Paris – the Galleries Lafayette and Printemps – on 7 December 1985, and wounded 35 people. The next bomb was placed in a shopping arcade at the Hôtel Claridge on the Champs Elysées on 3 February 1986, and wounded three people. The next day,

a bomb in Gibert Jeune, the student bookstore on the boulevard St Michel, wounded four people, and a bomb was found and defused at the Eiffel Tower. Two days later, there was a bombing in the Forum des Halles (an underground shopping mall in the centre of Paris), wounding six people.

It is possible that the bombings were intended to influence the parliamentary elections, which were held in March. The socialists lost their majority, and were replaced by a conservative government, led by Jacques Chirac, the mayor of Paris. His short administration was punctuated by terrorist bombs. On 17 March, an explosion on the Paris–Lyon express wounded ten, and on the 20th, while Chirac was broadcasting to the nation upon assuming office, a bomb exploded at another shop on the Champs Elysées, killing two people and wounding 28. A few days later, the Corsicans set off their bombs in the Midi, and in May, *Action Directe* joined the fray with bombs in Paris (including one at police headquarters on 9 July, which killed two people), followed by selective assassinations.

On 17 August, a car bomb in Toulon exploded prematurely, killing the four Arab terrorists in the car. Then in September occurred the most violent series of attacks, all the work of Arab or Iranian terrorists.

On 5 September, a bomb was found on the Paris Métro and defused safely. Three days later, a bomb in the post office in the Hôtel de Ville (town hall), where Chirac was still mayor, killed one and wounded 18. On the 12th, a bomb in the Caféteria Casino at La Défense, a large office complex in the western suburbs, wounded 41 people. On 14 September, a bomb in the parking garage of Le Pub restaurant on the Champs Elysées killed two people and wounded two others, and the next day, a bomb exploded in a public office in police headquarters in Paris, where driving licences were issued; one person was killed and 51 wounded.

On 17 September, a bomb thrown from a passing car killed five people and wounded 52 outside a store on the rue de Rennes – the most public and horrible of all the attacks. The police claimed that it was the work of two of Abdallah's brothers, who afterwards drove straight to the airport and left the country. They gave a press conference in Lebanon the next day to claim that they had not been in Paris at the time. Simultaneously, the French military attaché in Beirut, Colonel Christian Goutierre, was assassinated.

On 30 September and again on 10 November, *Action Directe* set off a number of small bombs in Paris, and for a time, the city was paralysed. There were hundreds of bomb alerts as nervous citizens reported suspicious packages across the city, and the streets were cleared as police and bomb-disposal squads rushed from place to place.

Meanwhile, the government was trying a different tack, inspired by the theory that, because a small Lebanese gang would not be capable of anything so extensive, Syria and Iran might be behind the bombing campaign. Secret emissaries went to Damascus and the FARL onslaught ceased (though AD continued its work).

Abdallah was put on trial in February 1987. He was accused of various terrorist acts, including the 1984 murder of Robert Home, the American consul-general in Strasbourg. Abdallah was convicted. The prosecutors then suggested that he should receive a 'moderate' sentence. There was a clear impression that Chirac's government had made a deal with Syria that, in return for Abdallah's release, FARL would be brought under control. If this were the case, the French public and the trial judge would have none of it: Abdallah was sentenced to life imprisonment.   539

The bombings ceased, but whether for political reasons or because of police action remains a mystery. The police arrested a Tunisian, Fouad Ali Saleh, and charged him with the Paris bombings, including the one in the rue de Rennes. In March 1987, they arrested a French citizen of Lebanese origin, Mohammed Mouhajer, and claimed that he had been the ideologist of the 'Solidarity Committee'. Meanwhile, the Armenian terrorist, Hagop Hagopian, claimed that his organization, the Armenian Secret Army, had been responsible for the bombings.

The question of responsibility was suddenly revived in July 1987. French police tried to arrest an Iranian, Wahid Gordji, who worked as a translator at the Iranian embassy. He escaped into that building and the Iranians refused to turn him over. The French claimed that he was not a diplomat and therefore did not enjoy any immunity, and they surrounded the embassy, waiting for him to come out. The Iranians promptly put the French embassy in Tehran under guard, holding French diplomats there hostage.

Police now believed that the 1985–6 bombing campaign had been directed by the Iranians, and suspected that Gordji had provided the contacts with the Lebanese and Tunisian terrorists who had planted the explosives. The stand-off between France and Iran continued until the end of November when the French finally agreed that Gordji should be allowed to leave the country unmolested. The sieges of the two embassies were then lifted. A few days later, France expelled 14 anti-Khomeni Iranian refugees and three Turks, and agreed to pay a longstanding debt to Iran. (Evidently, France now found being a *terre d'asile* too much of a strain.) In exchange, two of the five French hostages held in Beirut were released. The following spring, just before the presidential elections, Mohammed Mouhajer was released, ostensibly for lack of evidence, and the last three French hostages in Beirut were freed, evidently through Iran's good offices.

After the Gulf war ended in the summer of 1988, France set about restoring good relations with Iran, and the whole bombing episode was swept under the carpet. However, there remained many unanswered questions, notably concerning the Syrian and Iranian governments' roles in killing French citizens. In April 1986, at the height of the Paris bombing campaign, the Syrian embassy in East Berlin had apparently helped organize the bombing of the La Belle disco, killing two people and provoking the American attack on Libya. A few days later, on 17 April, the Syrian embassy in London was caught *in flagrante* helping a Lebanese terrorist. He had attempted to put a bomb (disguised in a hold-all) on to an El Al flight to Tel Aviv, giving it to his pregnant Irish girlfriend, whom he had told he would meet and marry in Jerusalem. When security men found the bomb, the terrorist immediately fled to the Syrian embassy – which refused to take him. It seems evident that Syria, as a government, was deeply involved in terrorism, attacking Israeli, American and French civilian targets. The British government broke off diplomatic relations with Syria in protest.

LIBYA

The Libyan government's support of terrorism abroad is well documented. Colonel Khadafy formed a whole terrorist apparatus, with a training school in Tripoli, set up by the American terrorist and conman Edwin Wilson. However, Wilson was as much concerned with stealing Khadafy's money as with actual terrorism, and the Libyans he trained were conspicuously inefficient. One group loaded a van with a huge quantity of explosives, and set out for Cairo, where they intended to explode it. They got no further than the border, when their bomb exploded prematurely, killing all of them.

Another unsuccessful plot of Khadafy's was an attempt to murder Abdul-Hamid Bakoush, a former Libyan prime minister living in Egypt. Several British and Maltese were hired for the job. The Egyptian security services faked the murder, and Khadafy triumphantly announced it over the radio. Then the Egyptians produced Bakoush at a press conference.

On an earlier occasion, Khadafy had ordered a submarine in the Libyan navy to sink the *Queen Elizabeth II* which had been hired by a group of American and British Jews for a trip to Israel. The sub's officers were Egyptian, seconded to Libya, and they promptly took it to Alexandria and reported to President Sadat.

Khadafy has sent hit squads to deal with Libyan dissidents living abroad, including one in Denver, Colorado (he was wounded), and a series of bombs were put in places frequented by exiles in Britain in March 1984. The most serious incident occurred on 10 March after a bomb exploded in a nightclub, El Oberge, in Belgravia, injuring 27 people. On 17 April, Libyans in London demonstrated outside the embassy in St James's Square in protest against the execution of a number of students in Libya. A gunman inside fired on them, killing a British policewoman, Yvonne Fletcher, and wounding several other people. As a result, the British government broke diplomatic relations with Libya.

On 8 July, police found the body of a Libyan businessman in his London apartment. Due to stand trial for the bombings, he had presumably been killed by Libyan secret agents to prevent him testifying. A year later, Britain expelled 22 Libyan students, accused of 'revolutionary' activity – that is, terrorism.

In April 1986, the United States bombed Tripoli in retaliation for the Berlin disco bombing. In the event, it turned out that Libya was probably not directly concerned (though it had applauded the deed). In a wider context, the bombing could be seen as justified by all Khadafy's other acts of terrorism.

RELIGIOUS TERRORISM

The Ayatollah Khomeini did not invent religious terrorism. There are plenty of other examples in the modern world – in the Indian subcontinent, in Northern Ireland, in Lebanon and in Syria. Iran was exceptional, however, because there religious terrorism became an instrument of foreign policy. For example, Shiite leaders, who had studied in Iran or in Iraq, played a prominent role in Lebanon's travails, inciting their followers to martyrdom.

One of the periodic revivals in Islam began in the 1960s, among the Shiites of Iraq. It occurred in Najaf, the sect's holiest city, and was led by the Ayatollah Sayyid Mohammed Baqir al-Sadr, who called his movement al-Dawa ('The Call of Islam'). Khomeini, who had directed a similar though more openly political movement in Iran, lived in Najaf after he had been exiled by the shah. Another prominent member of the circle was the Imam Musa Sadr, who established the Amal movement in Lebanon (and was murdered by Khadafy in Libya in 1978). Baqir al-Sadr was executed by Saddam Hussein in 1980. (*See* Iraq, pp. 256–68.)

After the Iranian revolution in 1979, the clerical, Marxist and Kurdish terrorists there fought a vicious war against each other. The clerical authorities, who defeated their domestic enemies, never allowed themselves to be distracted from attacking the Great Satan (the United States), the heretical regime of Saddam Hussein in Iraq, Israel, and Western influences wherever they might be found in the Muslim world. Soon after the revolution, the first units of Revolutionary Guards were sent to Lebanon, where they joined forces with the most extreme of the local Shiites.

In Lebanon, after Musa Sadr's disappearance, his followers split into a variety of contending factions of which the best known were the Amal Militia (led by Nabih Berri) and its most extreme rivals, the Islamic Amal (led by Hussein Mussawi) and the Call of Islam (al-Dawa), also known as the Party of God (Hizbollah), led by Sheikh Mohammed Hussein Fadlallah. All these clerics had studied at Najaf or at least had been heavily influenced by the teachings of Baqir al-Sadr and Khomeini. The dissident Shiite movements are constantly at war with Amal, and with the other factions in Lebanon (*see* pp. 305–22).

Their most remarkable achievement was the invention of the suicide car bomb. Young fanatics, men and women, would be assured of Paradise if they gave their lives for the cause. Scores of them did so, in attacks against Israeli positions, Western embassies (the American embassy was destroyed twice by suicide car bombs) and, most spectacularly, the US Marine and French army barracks in Beirut in October 1983. Islamic Jihad, the group that claimed responsibility for those attacks, and for kidnapping most of the hostages, is composed of members of both Islamic Amal and Hizbollah, with other freelance terrorists recruited for the occasion. In a statement of policy issued two days after the attack on the Marines, Islamic Jihad stated: 'We are the soldiers of God and we crave death. Violence will remain our only path. We are ready to turn Lebanon into another Vietnam.'

Most of these organizations confine their activities to Lebanon, where there is plenty of work for them, but others have been sent abroad to further Iranian or Syrian objectives. It is an exact recreation of the doctrines and practices of the medieval sect founded in 1094 by Hassan ibn al-Sabbah. From his base on Alamut, a remote mountain in Persia, al-Sabbah sent his followers to kill his enemies, with the assurance that, if they did so, they would go straight to Paradise. To prepare them for the ordeal, they were given hashish, from whence they took their name, 'Assassins'. These suicide missions terrorized the Middle East until the sect's base at Alamut was destroyed by the Mongols. Their descendants are the peaceable Ismailis, whose leader is the Aga Khan.

In 1980 in France, one of the Ayatollah's hit squads attempted to kill Shahpour Bakhtiar, the shah's last prime minister. Four years later, Iranian assassins murdered three former officials of the shah's government in Paris, wounding 18 people. The next month, they bombed a Madrid bar favoured by American servicemen. On another occasion, a bomb was thrown into a Madrid office shared by British Airways and TWA, killing one person. This attack coincided with the trial of two Lebanese, who had been caught attempting to assassinate a Libyan diplomat in revenge for the murder of Mussa Sadr.

There was a bomb attack at Frankfurt airport in June 1985; a bomb went off at Rome airport; a bomb was discovered outside the Iraqi embassy in London before it could explode; and a group of Lebanese Shiites planning to attack the US embassy in Rome was arrested. However, despite these atrocities, the main targets of these religious terrorists are in the Arab world. In December 1983, a series of attacks were carried out against targets in Kuwait: one was a suicide car bomb, directed against the American embassy. The group responsible was al-Dawa from Lebanon and it was controlled from Iran. The connection was proved, and reinforced the evidence that Islamic Jihad in Lebanon was working under Iranian direction. It is also clear that the Syrians were deeply involved. Seventeen al-Dawa terrorists were arrested in Kuwait, and three of them were eventually sentenced to death. The sentences were not carried out, but neither were they commuted. They remained suspended over the heads of the imprisoned men.

One Syrian faction, acting on orders from Damascus, was the Syrian People's party (PPS). It was originally a Fascist organization, set up in the 1930s, which during the 1960s and 1970s had fought a long, vicious and losing battle against President Assad, until that worthy abruptly decided to co-opt it and use its brutal fanaticism to his own purposes. It was renamed the Socialist Nationalist Resistance party (SNRP), and allied itself with the various Palestinian terrorist organizations. Its most remarkable achievement was the murder of Bashir Gemayel, president-elect of Lebanon, in September 1982. In April 1986, a woman member of the PPS/SNRP took a TWA flight from Cairo to Athens and left a bomb under her seat. It exploded during a later leg of the flight, killing four people.

Instead of recruiting martyrs for the glory of Islam, the PPS/SNRP found young people ready to kill themselves in the war against Israel. It had the distinction of sending the first female suicide bomber to her death, in April 1985, and broadcasting a video she made in advance. Elegantly dressed, and perfectly composed, she said: 'I am very relaxed as I go to do this operation which I have chosen because I am carrying out my duty to my people. I am from the group that decided on self-sacrifice and martyrdom for the sake of the liberation of land and people.' She then drove a car packed with explosives into an Israeli convoy, killing herself and two Israeli soldiers. This sinister precedent was followed by similar acts of self-destruction by a series of young people, who recorded their last statements on video and then drove off to glory.

In October 1987, three men later identified as members of the PPS/SNRP were arrested entering the United States from Canada. They were convicted of illegal immigration and transporting explosives: they had apparently been on a mission directed against other members of the group in New York.

In 1984, Shiites started hijacking airliners, a tactic that the Palestinians had abandoned. First, a group took a French airliner to Tehran, and demanded the release of the Iranians who had been convicted of trying to assassinate Shahpour Bakhtiar. The French government refused to deal, and the hijackers surrendered to the Iranian authorities. In December, another group of Shiites hijacked a Kuwaiti jet, took it to Tehran, and demanded the release of the 17 al-Dawa prisoners held in Kuwait. During this hijacking, the terrorists murdered two American AID (Agency for International Development) officials who were on the aircraft. Kuwait refused to give in, and after six days on the ground, the Iranian

543

police stormed the airliner and released the hostages. There was widespread suspicion that the 'storming' was a fake, and that the hijackers had been acting on instructions from Iran.

On 14 June 1985, two young Shiites took control of a TWA flight out of Athens, in what turned into the most spectacular hijacking in years. The plane was first taken to Beirut, then to Algiers, then back to Beirut where an American sailor on board was murdered and thrown out on to the runway. The plane then returned to Algiers. By this time, a number of hostages had been released, and now the Greek government did a deal with the hijackers. A third member of the commando had been unable to get a seat on the flight and had been left behind, to be arrested in Athens after the hijacking began. The Greek government flew him to Algiers to exchange him for Greek passengers, including the pop singer Demis Roussos. The hijackers, reinforced by their dilatory comrade, released all the Greeks – except Roussos. Then the plane was taken back to Beirut.

There was a dramatic exchange between the pilot and ground control at Beirut, with the pilot explaining that his plane would crash if it were not permitted to land, and Beirut refusing to allow it; finally, ground control relented. Nabih Berri of Amal controlled the airport, and his troops surrounded the plane. The hostages were taken off, and 30 of them were transported by Amal to precarious safety in Beirut. The hijackers themselves, members of Hizbollah, kept eight others – Jews and American servicemen. Berri supported one of the hijackers' original demands: that Israel release 500 Lebanese Shiite prisoners whom it had taken back to Israel when it had evacuated Lebanon, and 200 Palestinians it had captured during 'Operation Peace in Galilee'. Israel refused, but pointed out that it had already announced that it intended to release its prisoners over the next few months. Since Israel had released 1154 Palestinian and allied prisoners a few months earlier, in exchange for three Israeli PoWs held by Ahmed Jebril's PFLP-General Command, its firm moral opposition to dealing with terrorists was notably weaker than usual.

The hostages were finally released after the United States exerted all the pressure it could manage on President Assad of Syria, who in turn informed Hizbollah that he would cut them off from their bases in Baalbek if they did not turn over the hostages. They were released on 30 June, and sent to Damascus.

Three years later, one of the hijackers, who had been caught in West Germany, was tried there. It was the first major trial involving Islamic hijackers, and it was much simplified when the defendant admitted that he had indeed participated in the crime.

In the next few years, the Iranians were also implicated in the bombing campaign in Paris in 1985–6, and in the Haj riots in Mecca in 1987. There were further attacks in Kuwait, of which the most serious was a suicide car bomb attack on the emir; it failed, though many of his bodyguards were killed. Then in April 1988, a Kuwaiti airliner was hijacked, and after wandering the Middle East and a long stay in Cyprus, during which two hostages were killed and dumped on the tarmac, it finally landed in Algiers. Once again, the demand was for the release of the al-Dawa prisoners, and once again Kuwait refused to give in. After several days' negotiations, the hijackers released their hostages and surrendered, in exchange for permission to leave the country.

These were some of the chief incidents in which Middle Eastern governments authorized terrorism outside the region. The number of attacks in the region itself has been far greater, with constant killings by Iranian, Iraqi and Syrian agents – usually aimed at other Arab or Iranian targets. The two Yemens have also frequently sent assassins against each other. The most blatant examples are provided by Iraq and Syria. In the 1970s, Iraq hired Abu Nidal to attack Syria and the PLO; then, in the 1980s, he worked for Syria, attacking Iraqi targets, and continuing to assassinate PLO officials. In 1980, after the start of the Gulf war, Iraqi agents, masquerading as Iranian Arabs, seized the Iranian embassy in London. The building was stormed by the British SAS when the terrorists started killing their hostages.

AIR TERRORISM

The destruction of a Pan Am flight from London to New York, on 21 December 1988, killing all 259 people on the plane and 11 people on the ground in the small Scottish town of Lockerbie, showed how vulnerable air traffic remained, despite all the precautions developed over the years. Ahmed Jibril's PFLP-GC was suspected of planting the bomb: when West German police had raided a PFLP-GC hideout in Frankfurt in the autumn of 1988, they had discovered a bomb factory and a completed bomb, disguised as a radio. British police established that the Pan Am bomb had been concealed in a radio stowed in a suitcase, most probably in Frankfurt, where the flight had originated.

It was neither the first nor the most deadly plane bomb, and air terrorism was not an Arab monopoly. The first case on record was purely criminal: an American put a bomb in his wife's suitcase, to collect the insurance. The biggest death toll was the Air India explosion in 1985, which killed 329 people.

Attacks on aircraft, either through hijackings, bombings or with guns and rockets, have provoked the most general changes in civilian life in the past 20 years. The scores of hijackings of the 1970s led to elaborate security measures at most airports in the world, including all international airports, and much reduced the threat. There are still hijackings when security is insufficient or when the terrorists have accomplices on the ground, but the greatest danger now is the planting of bombs.

On 2 February 1970, a SwissAir flight from Zurich to Tel Aviv exploded in the air, killing all 47 people on board. George Habash's Popular Front for the Liberation of Palestine was suspected, and it was perhaps the first case of a 'carry-on' bomb. On 28 July 1971, a Dutch girl was stopped by El Al security men: she was found to be carrying a suitcase with a bomb in it that had been given her by a friend to take to Israel. On 1 September, El Al found another 'carry-on' bomb at London's Heathrow airport.

The next recorded bombing attempt was successful: on 9 September 1974, the New Arab Youth for the Liberation of Palestine put a bomb on a TWA flight from Israel to the United States, with a stop at Athens. 84 people were killed when the plane exploded over the Aegean.

Two years later, on 6 October 1976, a Cuban exile terrorist group, calling itself 'El Condor', put a bomb on a Cubana Airways DC-8 flying from Barbados to Kingston, Jamaica, en route to Havana. All 73 people on board were killed when the plane crashed in the Caribbean, including 24 members of the Cuban national fencing team. *El Condor*'s leader, Orlando Bosch, and the two men who had planted the bomb were arrested and sentenced to life terms.

The Nicaraguan Contras are believed to have been responsible for planting a bomb on a Nicaraguan airliner in Mexico City on 12 December 1981; it was discovered in time. On 2 July 1982, the Guatemalan 'Guerrilla Army of the Poor' (EGA) put a bomb on an Eastern Airline jet bound for Miami. It exploded prematurely, killing a baggage-handler at Guatemala City airport. The following month, a new sort of bomb made its appearance, a small device that could be concealed in a luggage rack or under a seat. The first one exploded on a Pan Am flight from Tokyo to Hawaii on 11 August, killing a Japanese teenager. Two weeks later, a similar bomb was found by a Pan Am ground crew in Rio de Janeiro.

There were several bombings and attempted bombings in 1983. A bomb destined for a Turkish airliner, and the work of Armenian terrorists, exploded prematurely at Orly airport in Paris, killing eight people, and a bomb on a Gulf Air jet killed 122 people – an atrocity attributed to Abu Nidal. The Orly bomb, described on pages 551–2, was part of the ASALA attack on Turkey. Abu Nidal's attack was perhaps inspired by Iran, in revenge for the Gulf States' support for Iraq during the Gulf War, or by Syria, working at Iran's behest (Abu Nidal was then employed by Syria).

The other 1983 bombings involved no casualties: a bomb was found on a Pakistani airliner, and three bombs were discovered in December, two on flights to Israel, one on a flight from Rome to New York. In January 1984, a bomb was found on a flight from Tel Aviv to Athens. On 18 January, a bomb exploded in the cargo bay of an Air France flight from Pakistan to Paris. The plane landed safely.

The most serious act of air terrorism occurred in 1985, when an Air India plane was destroyed over the Atlantic, south of Ireland, killing all 329 people on board. It is universally believed that it was the work of Sikh terrorists. According to the US Defense Department report, it had been organized by a Sikh group called the Dashmesh Regiment, which had been founded by General Shabeg Singh under the direction of the Sikh terrorist leader Sant Jarnail Singh Bhindranwale (*see* India, pp. 173–87). There were actually two bombs, both loaded on to aircraft at Toronto on 23 June 1985. One destroyed the Air India flight, the other was put aboard a jet belonging to a different airline, flying to Tokyo. The suitcase with the bomb was ticketed through to India, and should have been transferred to an Air India flight from Tokyo to Delhi. The flight was delayed, however, and the bomb exploded at Tokyo airport, killing two Japanese baggage-handlers.

The next bombings were in April 1986. On 2 April, a bomb on a TWA flight from Rome to Athens exploded as the plane approached Athens. The flight had originated in Cairo, and the bomb had been concealed under a seat occupied on the first leg of the flight by a Syrian Christian woman who lived in Lebanon. She had left the flight in Rome and had flown directly to Beirut. The explosion blew out the side of the plane, killing four passengers. On 17 April, a pregnant Irish girl was detained at Heathrow airport in London. She was booked on an El Al flight to Israel, and her Palestinian boyfriend had given her a suitcase, containing a bomb. He was arrested in London, and the apparent complicity of Syrian security services led the British government to break diplomatic relations with Syria.

On 27 September 1987, a Korean Airlines flight exploded over the Indian Ocean, killing all 115 people on board. It was the work of North Korean terrorists (*see* Korea, pp. 197–203).

Forlorn Hopes

THE ARMENIANS

Early in the morning of 28 April 1988, a respectable Arab businessman left his home in Paleo Faliro, a rich suburb of Athens, intending to go to the airport. He had lived in the apartment near the sea for three years. His neighbours believed that he came from Aden and had noted that he kept strange hours: he would often work all night, and disappear during the day. He and his wife lived a private life, and his visitors came and went discreetly.

On that spring morning, he planned to take an early flight to Belgrade. He never made it. Two masked men were waiting for him in the street, and shot him, point blank, with a sawn-off shotgun. It was an old-fashioned rub-out of an old-fashioned terrorist. The man whom police described as Abu Mohammed Kassim was, in fact, Hagop Hagopian (or Agop Agopian), the 39-year-old leader and chief executioner for the Armenian Secret Army for the Liberation of Armenia (ASALA).

The ASALA was dedicated to redressing an historic injustice, by murder, and intended to force Turkey to cede a large part of its eastern territory to the Armenians. These are the lands from which the Armenian population was driven in 1915, during World War I, with the loss of at least 600,000 lives. It was a great crime, and even though it had occurred more than 60 years before, Hagopian and his friends were determined to avenge it. When they had liberated Turkish Armenia, they planned to federate it with Soviet Armenia, for Hagopian was also a Communist, collaborating with the KGB in destabilizing Turkey. It is not recorded how these exiled fanatics reacted to the Soviet Armenians' suddenly revived nationalism.

Hagopian, like so many modern terrorists, was born in Lebanon, a member of the large Armenian community there. At the beginning of the civil war, he joined one of the first Armenian militias formed to defend the community, and was soon fighting in all the shifting alliances of Lebanon. Although his chief concern was with Turkey, he remained loyal to the Palestinian cause, like George Abdallah of the FARL, who was also a Christian and a Marxist. Both groups had a natural affinity to the Palestinian Christian Marxist George Habash, founder of the PFLP (*see* Arab terrorism, pp. 526–547).

548

Hagopian founded the ASALA in 1975. Eventually it was split by violent disputes, which were settled in the usual manner by execution, sudden murder and car bombs. Hagopian won, but a rival organization – the Justice Commandos of the Armenian Genocide – survived to go its separate and violent way. It is as openly Fascistic as the ASALA is Communist.

Hagopian and his comrades differed from the Arab terrorists, however. While he was perfectly ready to fight the good fight for the Communist revolution, for the Palestinians and against all their enemies, he was a man obsessed with the wrongs done to Armenia. He seems to have spent his life, from his mid-20s, in a hopeless but vicious war against Turkey: within the space of ten years, the ASALA killed 28 Turkish diplomats around the world and 34 other people, in hundreds of shootings, bombings and hostage takings.

Finally, Hagopian's enemies caught up with him. Greek police claimed to have no clues as to their identity. Perhaps they were rival Armenian terrorists, perhaps the murderers were freelance assassins hired for the job, perhaps Turkish, or French counter-terrorist organizations were involved.

HISTORY

There are now about 3 million Armenians in the Soviet Union, engaged in a struggle with Moscow and neighbouring Azerbaijanis over the limits of their autonomy, and control of Nagorno-Karabakh (see Soviet Union, pp. 392–400). There are also between 500,000 and 600,000 people of Armenian descent in the United States, 300,000–350,000 in France, 200,000 in Lebanon and 150,000 in Iran. There are Armenian communities elsewhere including Jerusalem, where the Armenian quarter contains an opulent museum, and Istanbul. In all of Turkey, there are now perhaps 50,000 Armenians where once there were 1.7 million. There are few or none of them in their ancestral home in Eastern Anatolia around Lake Van and Mount Ararat.

The Ottoman empire in its dotage was a cosmopolitan and decadent society. It was also usually tolerant of its many minorities. The sultan was a Turk, but he had Greek, Armenian, Jewish and Arab subjects who, for the most part, coexisted amicably together. Every so often, however, the Turks would suppress revolts among their subjects with wild savagery – for example, the Bulgarian massacres in the 1870s, and a first round of attacks on the Armenians in 1894–6 in which up to 200,000 people were killed.

The nature of the Ottoman empire was abruptly changed as a result of the rise of nationalism in the 19th and 20th centuries. In 1908 – later than the Greeks but earlier than the Arabs – the Turks caught the fever. The old, mad, murderous Sultan Abdulhamid was deposed, and the Young Turks set about establishing a Turkish nation. Up to 1914, they suffered humiliating defeats, losing Libya to Italy and almost all their residual possessions in Europe (including Salonika, Mustapha Kemal's home town). Like that other decaying empire, Austria–Hungary, Turkey allied itself with Germany, and in 1914 these allies forced Turkey into the war. Like the other belligerents, the government appealed to native chauvinism to inspire the troops. In 1915, when the Russians were attacking from the east through Turkish Armenia, and two months after the British had landed at Gallipoli and threatened Constantinople, the government turned on the Armenians, much as Hitler was to turn on the Jews 25 years later. On 24 April 1915, Armenian leaders in Constantinople were rounded up; they were later executed. Armenians in the east were driven from their homes and forced to trek through the wilds of Kurdistan to Syria, Iran and Mesopotamia. The best estimate is that at least 600,000 people were killed or died during the pogrom.

After Turkey's defeat in 1918, there was a brief effort to revive Armenia in its ancestral homelands, but it was swept away by the restored Turkey of Kemal Ataturk. In the process, the Turks expelled the Greek communities of Ionia on the eastern shores of the Aegean, a region that had been Greek since before the Trojan War, 3000 years ago. Anatolia thus became Turkey.

The Armenian Holocaust has been the central national experience for all Armenians ever since, as the Jewish Holocaust is for the Jews. Unlike West Germany, Turkey has never admitted guilt and has never made the least reparation; in fact, it denies that the Holocaust ever happened. Despite the Ataturk revolution, which forcibly remade Turkey into a modern state (it has now applied to join the European Community), there is a strong residuum of chauvinism in Turkey, and a great reluctance to admit error, even after 70 years. It must be added that at the time of the Holocaust, Armenians were actively helping the enemy in the east, and the British were at the gates of the capital. Also, though countless Armenians were massacred by Turkish troops, and the Turkish army was responsible for the deaths of the others who were driven on foot through the mountains, Turkey's object was its own security, not genocide. There were no gas chambers.

TERRORISM

The first act of modern Armenian terrorism occurred in Los Angeles on 27 January 1973. A 78-year-old Armenian immigrant, Gourgen Yanikian – who claimed to remember the massacres of 1915 and to have lost many relatives in them – murdered Mehmet Baydar, the Turkish consul-general in Los Angeles, and Bahadir Demir, the consul. Yanikian was convicted of murder, pleading at his trial that he had been avenging his lost parents, after 58 years.

Three months later, two bombs exploded in Paris, one at the Turkish consulate, another at the Turkish Airlines office. No one was hurt on that occasion, but it soon became evident that a terrorist campaign specifically directed at Turkish diplomats and offices was under way. In October 1973, the Turkish information office in New York received through the mail a package containing a bomb: it was the work of a 'Yanikian commando'.

There were no Armenian terrorist acts in 1974, but the following year, after the official establishment of the ASALA in Beirut, Armenian terrorists in Lebanon began a sustained attack on Turks and Turkish offices there and abroad. In October, ASALA commandos attacked the Turkish embassy in Vienna, killing the ambassador, and assassinated the Turkish ambassador to France, and his driver, in Paris. Attacks on Turks in Lebanon continued, as did bombing attacks on Turkish targets in Europe. In May 1977, five people (including an American) were killed by a bomb planted by an Armenian terrorist at Istanbul airport; the following month, the Turkish ambassador to the Vatican was assassinated.

In 1978, there were attacks on the Turkish ambassador to Madrid (killing his wife and two other people). In October 1979, the son of the Turkish ambassador to the Netherlands was murdered, and a Turkish tourist official was murdered in Paris in December.

There were dozens of bombing attacks in France, West Germany, Switzerland, Britain, Spain, Belgium and the Netherlands. Most of them were the work of the ASALA, but some other Armenian terrorist groups occasionally claimed credit – including the right-wing Justice Commandos of the Armenian Genocide, which has been responsible for many of the attacks in the United States.

A Turkish diplomat in Athens and his 14-year-old daughter were killed in July 1980. The press attaché at the Paris embassy was shot and paralysed in September. In October, two Armenian terrorists were arrested in Switzerland when a bomb they were preparing exploded in their hotel room; one was an American woman, Suzy Mahseredjian from Canoga Park, California. After that, Armenians took to attacking Swiss targets: in October, for instance, the Swiss Centre in central London was bombed. In 1980, a number of bomb attacks were carried out against Turkish targets in New York and Los Angeles. Evidently the Armenian community in the United States had become infected with the same murderous insanity that had already afflicted Armenians in Lebanon.

Terrorism spread to Australia, where the Turkish consul in Sydney was murdered in December 1980 (six years later, a car bomb in the consulate in Melbourne would kill one person) and also to Iran where a commando attacked the Turkish embassy in Tehran in 1981 (two men were captured and executed). There has been a number of other attacks in Tehran since then. In 1981, the terrorists started operations in Denmark, and continued to attack targets in Switzerland and in France. On 24 September 1981, four Armenian terrorists seized the Turkish consulate in Paris, wounding the consul and a guard (who later died). The terrorists later surrendered, were tried and given light jail terms. In October, Armenians attacked Fouquet's, the luxury food shop on the Place de la Madelaine, Paris. The following months saw many other bombings in France.

In January 1982, yet another Turkish consul-general in Los Angeles was assassinated, this time by two men riding a motorcycle, who shot him when his car was stopped at a red light. One of the terrorists was arrested, a 19-year-old immigrant from Lebanon (now serving a life term). The honorary consul in Boston was murdered in May, and the military attaché in Ottawa in August. In December, ASALA added Saudi Arabia to its list of enemies, ostensibly because the Saudis were sympathetic to Turkey. It is also possible that they were acting at the behest of Syria or some other enemy of the Saudis. A pair riding a scooter threw a bomb at the Saudi embassy in Athens; it bounced off a lamp-post, and exploded, killing one of the terrorists. There were other attacks that year in Bulgaria and Yugoslavia and, in 1983, an attack on the British Council in Paris. On 16 June 1983, terrorists carried out an attack with grenades and pistols in the bazaar in Istanbul, killing two (including one of the terrorists) and wounding 21.

In one two-week period in July 1983, 15 people were killed (including five terrorists) and more than 60 wounded. On 14 July, the Turkish ambassador to Brussels was murdered. On the 15th, a bomb in a suitcase at the Turkish Airline counter at Orly airport, south of Paris, exploded, killing eight people and injuring 60. The dead comprised two Turks, one American, one Swede and four French. Varoujan Garabedian, a 19-year-old Syrian Armenian was arrested and confessed to planting the bomb. It had been intended to explode in the air. After that, French police pursued Armenian terrorists unrelentingly, and the terrorists formed a new 'Orly Organization' to fight them.

On the same day, a similar bomb was found in London, but it was defused before it could explode. On the 27th, five terrorists were killed during an attack on the Turkish embassy in Lisbon, four of them by their own explosives. A diplomat's wife and a Portuguese policeman were also killed, and several other people injured.

In March 1985, Armenian terrorists attacked the Turkish embassy in Ottawa, killing a Canadian security guard. They held the place and a number of hostages for several hours before surrendering. Two weeks later, Armenian terrorists threatened to plant bombs on the Toronto underground. However, although the city was seriously disrupted for several days, there were no bombings.

In November 1985, French police arrested an American Armenian terrorist in Paris: Monte Melkonian from Fresno, California. He had been Hagopian's top assistant before splitting with the ASALA to form his own group. By then, Armenian terrorists were regularly putting bombs in shops, offices, bus stations and other public places in France, which was now as much the enemy as Turkey. Terrorists regularly demanded that their comrades in French jails be released.

The new organization, or the new name for the old organization, was the *Comité de solidarité avec les prisonniers politiques arabes et du Moyen-orient* (Committee for Solidarity with Arab and Middle Eastern Political Prisoners). It appears to have been an alliance between the ASALA and FARL (*see* Arab terrorism: The Lebanese), and closely associated with the Iranian and, probably, the Syrian secret services. The ASALA and its allies put bombs in the Galeries Lafayette and Printemps department stores in Paris in December 1985, four more bombs elsewhere in Paris in February 1986, a bomb on a Paris–Lyon train in March, another in a shopping arcade in Paris (which killed two people) on 20 March, and one on the Paris Métro in September. A bomb in the Hôtel de Ville in Paris on 8 September killed a postal worker; three more people were killed in further bombings in the next few days and a bomb in the rue de Rennes on 17 September killed five and wounded 52 people. In October, Hagopian, in Beirut, issued further threats of violence if Garabedian were not released. He said:

ASALA has already declared that all French presence in the world are military targets. We defy Chirac and promise Mitterrand catastrophes in the event that they renege on their promise – that is, the release of political prisoners.

This was presumably a reference to the reputed French agreement to release Georges Abdallah, the leader of the FARL, in the summer of 1986, in exchange for Gilles Peyrolles, a French hostage held in Lebanon. Peyrolles was released, but the French kept Abdallah in jail after discovering evidence that he had murdered an American and an Israeli diplomat. The FARL accused the French of treachery and launched the bombing campaign, with ASALA's assistance. Possibly Hagopian had expected Garabedian to be released at the same time as Abdallah. In February 1987, Hagopian issued a communiqué in Beirut claiming responsibility for all the recent bombings in Paris. It added:

France should start adopting the needed steps and procedures to release Armenian as well as Arab patriots. A truce-like period of calm between us and the French government must have convinced public opinion that we respect the interests and security of the French and other people. The wave of explosions will return to the streets of France; all French economic, air traffic and marine facilities will be subjected to sabotage.

The communiqué finished by again demanding the release of Varoujan Garabedian.

Nothing much was heard of the ASALA in the following 14 months, until Hagopian's death. There were certainly negotiations between the French government and other groups of Lebanese terrorists to achieve the release of French hostages in Beirut, but Garabedian was not released. Hagopian was perhaps the key figure in the Armenian terrorist network, and his death a serious blow. But he had many comrades, and it is not likely that they will give up the struggle.

That will only happen if their supplies are cut off. It is quite evident that the ASALA was supported by other organizations during its most active period: hundreds of bombings and scores of murders obviously required considerable sums and ready access to explosives and arms. The PLO reportedly trained 200 ASALA fighters in 1981, and they joined in the battles against the Israelis the following year. Hagopian and his terrorists had to leave Lebanon with Arafat and the PLO and are believed to have taken temporary refuge in Libya. In the mid-1980s, he was able to return to Lebanon, but apparently continued to live, unsuspected, in Athens. After his murder, his widow informed the police of his identity.

THE MOLUCCANS

The most forlorn of all forlorn hopes is the Republic of South Molucca. There are about 40,000 people of Moluccan descent living in the Netherlands, survivors and descendants of the 12,000 people who fled with the Dutch when they were driven out of Indonesia in 1949 (*see* Indonesia, pp. 188–96). Most of them came from Calvinist Ambon, one of the Spice Islands, and they had fought with the Dutch against Sukarno.

They found their exile in cold and damp Holland not at all to their taste. They did not adapt to the tidy ways of the Dutch and came to form an underclass in their own ghettos in Amsterdam and other cities, together with immigrants from another former Dutch colony, Surinam in South America. The old told tales of their lost paradise, and the young and passionate dreamed of returning there. They all agreed that the Dutch had cheated them twice: first, by betraying their homeland to Sukarno; second, by leaving them to rot in their ghettos. The Dutch, naturally, saw things differently.

On 3 December 1975, one group of Moluccan terrorists seized a train, and another took over the Indonesian consulate in Amsterdam. Six terrorists held the train near Bellen in the north of the country: two passengers and the train driver were killed, and 33 hostages were held captive for three weeks. The five Moluccans who stormed the consultate held 25 hostages, and demanded that their leaders be allowed to hold a televised press conference to air their grievances, that the government apologize for 30 years' mistreatment, and that Indonesia establish an independent republic in the Moluccas. Eventually, they were persuaded to surrender.

553

On 23 May 1977, other Moluccans repeated the same attempt. A seven-man commando seized another train, at Assen, and held 50 hostages, while six other terrorists seized an elementary school, at Bovinsmilde, with 105 children and six teachers. They made the same demands as their predecessors, and once again, the Dutch authorities prepared to wait them out. The terrorists at the school released the children and surrendered after four days, but the siege of the train continued for three weeks. Finally, Dutch marines stormed the train at dawn, distracting and terrifying the Moluccans with thunderflashes. Six of the terrorists and two hostages were killed.

Twenty Years of Terrorism

This list concentrates on 'international terrorism' – that is, operations outside the country of chief concern to the terrorist, or a collaborative effort by more than one group. I have not included the great majority of terrorist incidents that are exclusively limited to one country (Sri Lanka, Peru, India, El Salvador, Guatemala, etc.) which are of no direct international concern. I have also left out most of the acts of terrorism perpetrated by the IRA in Northern Ireland, by various Palestinian groups in Israel and by all the terrorist factions in Lebanon. They are covered elsewhere in this book. I have also followed the practice of Dobson and Payne (*see* Further reading) who list the first appearances of terrorist groups, or the first examples of such terrorist operations as hijackings. Appendix III lists assassinations since 1945.

1968

22 July	PFLP hijacks an El Al flight to Algiers.
26 December	PFLP attacks El Al jet on the ground in Athens. One passenger killed.
28 December	In retaliation, Israel attacks Beirut airport, destroys 13 Middle East Airlines planes.

1969

2 February	El Al plane attacked on the ground in Zurich; copilot and one terrorist killed.
7 February	Marks & Spencer in London bombed.
29 August	First non-Israeli plane hijacked by PFLP, a TWA flight taken to Damascus.
9 September	First diplomatic kidnapping: Charles Elbrick, American ambassador in Brazil, seized and then exchanged for 15 Brazilian terrorists.
12 December	First 3 Baader–Meinhof bombs in Berlin.

1970

2 February	Swissair plane explodes in mid-air: 47 killed, probably by PFLP.
3 March	7 Japanese Red Army terrorists, wielding samurai swords, hijack a JAL flight; take it to North Korea.

31 July	Tupamaros kidnap 2 diplomats in Montevideo; American Dan Mintrone killed.
6 September	3 airliners hijacked by PFLP; 2 taken to Dawson's Field in Jordan, one to Cairo. Terrorists fail to take El Al plane. On 9 September, BOAC jet also hijacked to Dawson's Field. Incident leads to expulsion of PLO from Jordan.
5 October	British trade commissioner in Quebec, James Cross kidnapped, Québecois minister of labour Pierre Laporte kidnapped 10 October. Cross released 3 December, Laporte murdered.
12 December	ETA kidnaps West German honorary consul in San Sebastián, Eugene Beihl. He is released when Franco commutes 6 death sentences passed after Burgos trial.

1971

8 January	Tupamaros kidnap British ambassador to Uruguay, Geoffrey Jackson; keep him in a box for 8 months. They demand the release of 150 prisoners. Government refuses, but 106 escape and Jackson released.
14 March	PLO commando blows up fuel storage tanks in Rotterdam.
5 May	Turkish terrorists murder Israeli consul-general in Istanbul.
20 July	Black September attacks office of Jordanian airline, Alia, in Rome.
28 July	Dutch girl given a 'carry-on' bomb to take on El Al flight; is discovered. Similar plot discovered on 1 September, in London.
28 November	Jordanian prime minister, Wasfi Tal, murdered by Black September in Cairo.

1972

6 February	5 Jordanian workers in Cologne murdered by Black September.
18 February	Factory making parts for Israeli planes bombed in Hamburg.
19 February	Shoot-out between Japanese police and Japanese Red Army is followed by siege of a house in Kauizawa. On 27 February, 1000 police storm house; 2 police killed, JRA leaders arrested. In next few days, 14 bodies of JRA members found buried in woods.
22 February	IRA bombs parachute regiment HQ in Aldershot, killing 9 soldiers and civilians.
	Lufthansa jet hijacked to Aden by PFLP. Plane released after airline pays $5 million in ransom, $1 million to Aden.
8 May	PFLP commandos, 2 men and 2 women, hijack Sabena flight, divert it to Lod in Israel. Israeli security men storm the plane; kill male terrorists and one hostage.
11 May	Baader–Meinhof bombs at US army base in Frankfurt kill Colonel Paul Bloomquist and wound 14.
31 May	3 Japanese Red Army terrorists attack tourists at Lod airport; kill 28. 2 terrorists killed.
8 July	Car bomb planted by Israeli agents kills PFLP official in Beirut.
5 September	Munich Olympics massacre. Black September commandos seize Israeli athletes; kill 11 Israelis, one West German policeman. 4 terrorists killed. 3 survivors released when Lufthansa plane hijacked in October.
9 September	First Israeli killed by letter bomb, a technique later used by Israelis and IRA.

1973

27 January	Armenian immigrant murders Turkish consul-general in Los Angeles and the consul, in Santa Barbara.

1 March	Black September seize Saudi embassy in Khartoum. 2 American and one Belgian diplomats murdered.
28 March	Irish navy intercepts freighter *Claudia* running 5 tons of arms from Libya into Ireland.
4 April	Bombs explode outside Turkish consulate and Turkish Airlines offices in Paris.
10 April	Israeli commando raid on PLO offices in Beirut kills 17 people, including 3 senior PLO officials.
28 June	Leading PFLP terrorist in Europe, Mohammed Boudia, killed by car bomb in Paris.
1 July	Israeli military attaché Yosef Alon shot in Washington.
2 July	Moroccan waiter, mistaken for Black September leader, killed by Israelis in Lillehammer, Norway. Hit men arrested and jailed by Norwegians.
5 August	New Palestine terror group, NAYLP, machine-gun TWA plane arriving in Athens from Tel Aviv; 5 passengers killed.
5 September	Italians arrest NYALP gang armed with SAM-7s, planning to shoot down planes arriving at Rome airport.
28 September	Al-Saiqa (Syrian-backed Palestinian terrorists) seize Austrian train carrying Jewish emigrants from Soviet Union. Austrians close Jewish transit station in Vienna.
17 December	Five NYALP terrorists fire-bomb Pan Am jet at Rome airport, killing 32.
20 December	Spanish prime minister Luis Carerro Blanco killed by ETA car bomb.
30 December	Carlos attempts to assassinate Joseph Sieff, chairman of Marks & Spencer.

1974

31 January	2 Japanese Red Army terrorists and 2 Palestinians attack Shell Oil refinery in Singapore; take 5 hostages.
3 February	IRA bomb in the luggage compartment of a bus on the M62, carrying soldiers and their families, kills 9 soldiers, a woman and her 2 children.
5 February	Patty Hearst kidnapped by Symbionese Liberation Army (SLA).
11 April	PFLP-GC commando infiltrates Israel, takes refuge in apartment building in Qiryat Shemona. 18 killed, 16 wounded.
17 May	6 SLA terrorists killed in gun battle with Los Angeles police.
17 July	IRA bomb at Tower of London kills one, wounds 41.
4 August	Bomb planted by Italian Fascists on Rome–Milan express kills 12, wounds 48.
7 September	TWA flight from Israel blows up over Aegean, after stop in Athens. The man responsible, Ahmed al-Ghafour, leader of the NAYLP, executed by Al-Fatah on 12 September.
13 September	Japanese Red Army seize French embassy in The Hague and demand release of JRA prisoner in France. Carlos bombs Le Drugstore on 15 September, in support, killing 2. French government surrenders its prisoner.
5 October	IRA bomb in pub in Guildford kills 5, wounds 15.
10 November	Baader–Meinhof gang kills West German supreme court judge Guenther von Drenkmann.
21 November	IRA bombs in Birmingham kill 21, wound 168.
13 December	Carlos gang aim rocket at El Al plane at Orly airport, Paris; hit Yugoslav plane.
19 December	Carlos gang returns to Orly, gets into a gun fight with police, takes hostages and hijacks a flight to Iraq.
24 December	Puerto Rican terrorists bomb Fraunces Tavern in New York, killing 4, wounding 21.

557

1975

27 February	Baader–Meinhof gang kidnap Peter Lorenz, conservative Berlin politician. Government frees 5 terrorists in exchange for his release.
27 June	Paris police try to arrest Carlos. He kills 2 policeman and an informant, wounds another policeman, escapes.
22 October	Armenian gunmen attack Turkish embassy in Vienna, killing ambassador. On 24 October, Turkish ambassador to Paris and driver murdered.
3 December	Moluccan terrorists seize Indonesian consulate in Amsterdam and train near Beilen; 4 people killed. They surrender after 4 weeks.
6 December	Siege of Balcombe Street, London: 4 IRA terrorists take refuge in apartment with hostages after a chase through London. They surrender after 6 days.
21 December	Carlos leads West German–Palestinian commando attack on OPEC headquarters in Vienna. 3 guards killed, 11 oil ministers taken hostage; released in Algiers.
23 December	Greek terrorists, of November 17 group, shoot Richard Welch, CIA station chief in Athens.

1976

8 May	Ulrike Meinhof hangs herself in Stammheim jail.
27 June	Palestinian–West German commandos seize Air France jet, take it to Entebbe, Uganda. Israelis rescue hostages, killing 5 terrorists.
31 July	British ambassador to Dublin murdered by IRA.
21 September	Former Chilean minister Orlando Letelier and his secretary killed by a car bomb in Washington D.C.
6 October	Cuban exile organization El Condor plants a bomb on Cubana Airlines DC-8. It explodes over Caribbean, killing 73.
28 October	Protestant terrorists shoot Maire Drumm, IRA leader, in hospital.

1977

4 April	West German chief prosecutor, Siegfried Buback, shot by RAF in Karlsruhe.
23 May	Moluccan terrorists seize school in Bovinsmilde, and a train at Assen, Netherlands. Train stormed by marines after 22 days: 2 hostages, 6 terrorists killed.
29 May	A bomb left by Armenians in Istanbul airport kills 5.
31 July	RAF murders Juergen Ponto, West German banker.
5 September	RAF kidnap Hans-Martin Schleyer, leading businessman, killing 4 bodyguards. He is held in France and murdered on 19 October.
28 September	Japanese Red Army hijack JAL flight to Bangladesh, obtain release of 6 JRA comrades and $6 million ransom.
13 October	PFLP–RAF hijacks Lufthansa plane. Finally land in Mogadishu, Somalia. Plane stormed by West German commandos; 3 terrorists killed.
20 October	Baader and two other RAF leaders commit suicide in Stammheim.
31 December	Two Syrian intelligence agents, posing as diplomats, kill themselves with their own bomb in London.

1978

4 January	Abu Nidal assassin kills PLO representative in London, Said Hammami, who had contacted Israeli liberals.
18 January	Two Abu Nidal gunmen murder Egyptian editor in Cyprus and attempt to hijack Cypriot airliner. Egyptian commandos storm plane, but 15 are killed by Cyprus National Guard.
16 March	Aldo Moro, former Italian prime minister, kidnapped in Rome by Red Brigades; 5 bodyguards killed. He is murdered on 10 May.
15 June	PLO representative in Kuwait murdered by Abu Nidal gunmen.
31 July	Al-Fatah gunmen storm Iraqi embassy in Paris (because of Iraqi support for Abu Nidal). A French policeman and Iraqi diplomat killed.
3 August	Abu Nidal gunmen kill PLO representative in Paris.
7 September	Bulgarian agents kill exiled broadcaster, Georgi Markov, with poisoned umbrella in London.

1979

22 January	Mastermind of Munich massacre, Ali Hassan Salameh, killed by car bomb in Beirut.
22 March	IRA murder British ambassador to Netherlands.
30 March	British Conservative MP, Airey Neave, killed by car bomb at House of Commons garage, by INLA (break-away IRA faction).
29 June	RAF attempt assassination of Nato commander, General Alexander Haig.
8 August	Earl Mountbatten and 3 other people killed by IRA bomb in Co. Sligo, Ireland. 18 British soldiers also killed by bomb at Warrenpoint, Co. Down, Northern Ireland.

1980

January-April	32 summer cottages in Wales burned.
17-19 February	Terrorists seize Dominican embassy in Bogotá, taking 80 hostages, including the US and 12 other ambassadors. After 61 days' seige they are flown to Cuba.
30 April	Iranian embassy in London seized by Iraqi agents posing as Iranian Arabs. SAS storm building on 5 May.
2 August	Fascist bomb in Bologna station kills 84, wounds 186.
26 September	Neo-Nazi bomb at Munich *bierfest* kills 13 (including terrorist), wounds 312.
3 October	Two Armenian terrorists injured in Geneva hotel room while preparing a bomb.
	Bomb in rue Copernic, Paris, kills 4, injures 12.
17 December	Armenians assassinate Turkish consul-general in Sydney.
31 December	Norfolk Hotel in Nairobi, owned by Zionists, bombed by PFLP-GC. 16 people killed.

1981

13 May	Attempted assassination of Pope John Paul II.
31 August	RAF bomb in USAF HQ at Ramstein, West Germany wounds 20.
15 September	RAF attacks US General Frederick Kroesen with rocket-propelled grenade; miss.
24 September	Armenians from Lebanon seize Turkish consulate in Paris, killing 2.
6 October	President Sadat assassinated by fundamentalist terrorists in Cairo.
28 November	Muslim Brotherhood car bomb kills 68 in Damascus.
17 December	US General James Dozier kidnapped by Red Brigades in Verona. Rescued on 28 January.

1982

18 January	Lieutenant Colonel Charles Ray, US military attaché in Paris, shot by FARL.
28 January	Turkish consul-general in Los Angeles shot by 2 Armenians from Lebanon. On 4 May, the honorary consul in Boston is shot.
16 February	Two members of Carlos gang arrested in Paris. Carlos threatens retaliation, and on 30 March, a bomb kills 6 and wounds 15 on Toulouse–Paris express.
3 April	Israeli diplomat shot in Paris by FARL
3 June	Israeli ambassador to London, Schlomo Argov, shot and wounded by Abu Nidal gang. Incident used as pretext for Israeli invasion of Lebanon.
20 July	2 IRA bombs in London (in Hyde Park and Regent's Park) kill 11.
7 August	Two Armenians attack Ankara airport; 9 killed, 82 injured.
3 September	General dalla Chiesa murdered by Mafia in Sicily.
14 September	Lebanese president-elect Bashir Gemayel assassinated by Syrian-sponsored terrorists.
4 November	General Victor Lago killed by ETA in Madrid.

1983

16 June	ASALA attack in bazaar in Istanbul kills 2.
15 July	ASALA bombs Turkish Airlines desk at Orly; kills 7.
27 July	5 Armenian terrorists attack Turkish embassy in Lisbon. Diplomat's wife and Portuguese guard killed, along with all 5 terrorists.
1 October	Bombs at international trade fair in Marseille destroy Algerian, American and Soviet pavilions, killing 1, injuring 26.
9 October	North Korean terrorists try to kill South Korean president in Rangoon; 21 killed.
23 October	Suicide bombers attack US Marines and French troops in Beirut; 241 Americans and 58 French killed.
15 November	Greek November 17 terrorists shoot US naval attaché George Tsantes in Athens.
12 December	Attacks on US and French embassies in Kuwait; 4 killed, 60 injured, al-Dawa terrorists arrested.
17 December	IRA bomb outside Harrods department store in London kills 6, wounds 94.

1984

29 January	*Action Directe* bombing campaign in Paris.
10 March	Libyan secret service bombs exiles in Britain. A bomb at a night club in Belgravia in London injures 27.
17 April	Libyan exiles demonstrate against Khadafy outside embassy in London. Man inside opens fire, killing British policewoman, Yvonne Fletcher.
24 June	Belgian CCC terrorists seize 800 kg of explosives from quarry.
8 July	Libyan agent responsible for March bombings found murdered in London, presumably by other Libyan agents.
31 July	Air France jet hijacked to Tehran; 2 killed.
20 September	Suicide car bomb attack on US embassy in Beirut; 23 killed.
12 October	Bomb in Grand Hotel, Brighton during Conservative party conferences misses prime minister but kills 5.
31 October	Indian Prime Minister Indira Gandhi assassinated by Sikh bodyguard.
3 December	Islamic Jihad gunmen hijack Kuwaiti jet to Tehran; kill 2 US officials on board; demand release of al-Dawa terrorists. Surrender after 6 days.

1985

25 January	*Action Directe* kills French General René Audran.
30 January	French police raid ETA HQ in France; arrest several terrorists; deport them to Spain.
1 February	RAF kills Ernst Zimmermann, president of West German defence association.
10 March	Suicide bomber from Syrian National Resistance party kills 12 Israelis in military convoy. First non-Islamic suicide attack.
26 March	Turkish terrorist bombing campaign in Bulgaria; 7 killed on train.
21 April	Al-Fatah commandos intercepted off coast of Israel; 20 killed, 8 captured.
5 May	Israel releases 1154 prisoners, including Japanese Red Army survivor of Lod massacre, in exchange for 3 Israeli PoWs held by PFLP-GC.
11 June	Jordanian airliner hijacked on flight from Beirut by Shiite terrorists led by Fawaz Younis. Hostages released. Younis kidnapped by American agents 13 September 1987 on a yacht off Cyprus and brought to the US.
14 June	Islamic Jihad hijacks TWA jet out of Athens. American sailor murdered.
23 June	Sikhs put bombs in suitcases on Air India plane out of Toronto and Air Canada flight to Tokyo, intending the latter to be transferred to Air India flight there. First exploded over the Irish Sea, killing 329; second exploded on ground in Tokyo, killing 2.
10 July	French agents sink Greenpeace's *Rainbow Warrior* in Auckland harbour, New Zealand; one passenger killed.
8 August	RAF car bomb kills two American servicemen on air base in Rhein-Main, West Germany.
25 September	Al-Fatah terrorists (Force 17) kill 3 Israeli tourists on yacht off Cyprus. In retaliation, Israel bombs PLO HQ in Tunis on 1 October.
30 September	4 Soviet diplomats kidnapped by Sunni terrorists in Beirut; one killed.
7 October	4 Al-Fatah pirates seize Italian cruise liner, *Achille Lauro*; kill one American tourist before surrendering. Arrested by US Navy.
6 November	M-19 terrorists, in pay of Medellín cocaine cartel, seize Palace of Justice, Bogotá; kill 11 judges and about 100 others.
23 December	ANC bomb in Christmas shopping crowd in Durban kills 5, wounds 48.
27 December	Attacks on El Al airline counters in Rome and Vienna airports by Abu Nidal gang; 19 killed, over 100 wounded.

1986

6 February	ETA assassinates Admiral Cristobal Colón in Madrid.
2 April	Bomb on TWA flight from Rome to Athens kills 4 Americans, including 18-month-old baby. Syrian terrorists suspected.
5 April	Bomb in La Belle disco in Berlin kills US soldier and Turkish woman. Apparently Syrian-inspired operation, carried out by West Germans and Lebanese, with Libyan encouragement. US uses incident as pretext to attack Tripoli on 15 April. 2 British hostages in Lebanon murdered on 17 April in revenge, possibly by Libyans.
17 April	El Al security men find carry-on bomb in luggage of pregnant Irish girl, given to her by Palestinian boyfriend. He was working with Syrians.
19 June	ETA bomb in a Barcelona supermarket kills 21.
26 June	Sendero Luminoso bombs Cuzco–Machu Picchu train, killing 8.

5 September	Abu Nidal gang hijacks Pan Am jet over India; takes it to Karachi. Suspecting attack, hijackers massacre 20 passengers.
6 September	Abu Nidal gunmen massacre 21 people in synagogue in Istanbul; commit suicide.
17 September	Series of FARL/ASALA and Iranian bombs in Paris (beginning on 7 December 1985) climax with bomb in rue de Rennes killing 5, wounding 52.
25 October	ETA car bomb kills governor of Guipúzcon, General Rafaél Garido, his wife and son.
7 November	*Action Directe* kills president of Renault in Paris.

1987

March–April	12 members of the Irish National Liberation Army killed in internecine fighting, including (15 March) Gerard Steenson, known as 'Dr Death', and (21 March) Mary McGlinchy (whose husband had been INLA chief of staff; now jailed).
25 April	Judge Maurice Gibson and wife killed by car bomb in Northern Ireland.
1 June	Rashid Karami, Lebanese prime minister, assassinated.
22 July	Palestinian journalist Ali Naji al-Adhami shot in London; died on 29 August.
30 October	French navy intercepts the *Eksund* off Brittany, carrying 150 tons of Libyan weapons for IRA.
8 November	Bomb at Remembrance Sunday parade at Enniskillen, Co. Tyrone, Northern Ireland, kills 11, injures 60.
25 November	Palestinian hang-glider attacks Israeli army camp; kills 6 soldiers.

1988

13 February	Three PLO officials killed by car bomb in Cyprus, either by Israeli or Abu Nidal agents.
14 April	5 people killed by bomb at US navy club in Naples. Chief suspect is Japanese Red Army member, one of those released by Japanese government after JAL hijacking in 1977.
16 April	Italian senator Roberto Ruffilli murdered by Red Brigades.
17 April	Israeli agents kill PLO leader Khalid Wazir (Abu Jihad) in Tunis.
12 May	Car bomb blows up 200 m from Israeli embassy in Nicosia. Apparent Abu Nidal operation.
19 May	Pro-Austrian secessionists in Alto Adige, Italy, set off series of bombs.
28 June	US naval attaché in Greece killed by November 17 gang.
11 July	2 Abu Nidal killers, one possibly Hejab Jeballah (Samir Kadar), killed by own bomb in Athens. Later that day, terrorists attack cruise ship *City of Poros*, killing 9 and wounding 90. Their weapons came from Libya.
7 September	Italian police arrest 21 Red Brigades terrorists calling themselves the Fighting Communist Party. Believed responsible for series of murders.
9 December	Israel attacks PFLP HQ near Beirut, killing 20.
21 December	Pan American flight from London to New York blown up over Scotland, 270 killed.

FURTHER READING

Becker, Jillian, *Hitler's Children: The Story of the Baader–Meinhof Terrorist Gang,* Philadelphia, Lippincott, 1987.

Cline, Ray and Alexander, Yonah, *Terrorism: The Soviet Connection*, New York, Crane Russak, 1984.

Dempster, Chris, *Fire-Power*, New York, St Martin's Press, 1980.

——, *Terrorism as a State-sponsored Covert Operation*, Fairfax, Va., Hero Books, 1986.

Dobson, Christopher and Payne, Ronald, *The Never-Ending War – Terrorism in the 80s*, New York, Facts on File, 1987.

Gutteridge, William (ed.), *Contemporary Terrorism*, New York, Institute for the Study of Conflict/Facts on File, 1986.

Laqueur, Walter, *The Age of Terrorism*, Boston, Little Brown, 1987. (This work includes a comprehensive bibliography of the subject.)

Martin, David C. and Walcott, John L., *Best-laid Plans: The Inside Story of America's War against Terrorism*, New York, Harper & Row, 1988.

Melman, Yossi, *The Master Terrorist: The True Story behind Abu Nidal*, New York, Adama Books, 1986.

Minority Rights Group, *The Basques and Catalans*, London, 1987.

Netanyahu, Benjamin (ed.), *Terrorism: How the West Can Win*, New York, Farrar Straus & Giroux, 1986.

Rubenstein, Richard, *Alchemists of Revolution: Terrorists in the Modern World*, New York, Basic Books, 1987.

Sterling, Claire, *The Terror Network*, New York, Reader's Digest Press, London, Weidenfeld & Nicolson, 1981.

Taheri Amir, *Holy Terror: Inside the World of Islamic Terrorism*, Bethesda, Md, Adler & Adler, 1987.

U S Department of Defense, *Terrorist Group Profiles*, Washington D.C., Government Printing Office, 1989.

APPENDICES

APPENDIX I: WARS
SINCE 1945

This list is not exhaustive. It includes all the major wars and insurrections since 1945, but leaves out many lesser insurrections and most coups and riots, many of which resulted in the deaths of thousands of people. The casualty figures are usually approximate. There are very few cases (Northern Ireland is one) where an accurate running total can be kept. In others, a precise figure for one side may be added to a rough approximation for the other: for example, the 58,156 Americans killed in Indochina added to the estimate of Vietnamese deaths (2,000,000) gives the spuriously accurate figure of 2,058,156.

Occasionally, high estimates turn out to be far short of the mark. For instance, in June 1988, the Vietnamese announced that they had lost 55,000 men fighting in Cambodia since 1978. Assuming, most conservatively, that Cambodian losses were double that, it means that the Cambodians suffered the deaths of another 100,000 people on top of the horrors of 1970–78.

However, the tendency is more usually to exaggerate casualties. Shirley Christian, in her book on the Nicaraguan revolution, wrote:

The question of how many people died in the insurrection has been tremendously manipulated and twisted in the years since 1979. Although roughly 10,000 was the estimate used by relief workers in the last month of the insurrection, just a month or two later the Sandinista Front began to raise the toll. It first claimed that 30,000 had died, later saying 35,000, then 40,000, then 50,000, sometimes more. The figures were repeated by other organizations and governments and took on the aura of credibility. In fact, there is nothing to substantiate them ... The Sandinista deaths, according to a man who kept what statistics were kept on the Southern Front, were at least 300 and not more than 600. A well-placed official of the Somoza government said that National Guard deaths were likewise no more than a 'few hundred'. ... Finally, Ismael Reyes, the Red Cross leader, thought the civilian deaths fell into the 7000 range, possibly fewer. This means that the total could not have exceeded 10,000.

Despite Christian's research, the figures 35,000 or 50,000 for deaths in the Nicaraguan revolt turn up all the time in books and newspapers. There are equally inflated figures for people killed in the Contra rebellion. Similarly, the figure of 1 million killed in the Iran–Iraq war and another million in Afghanistan have become accepted in most news reports, but should be treated with great suspicion. The Iranians, the Iraqis, the Afghan government and the Mujaheddin have not issued casualty figures (though they all claim an immense slaughter of their enemies).

The figures I give are the best available, and should usually be taken as very approximate and prone to exaggeration. In any event, the totals come to about 20 million people killed in wars, revolutions and massacres since 1945. It would probably be safe to put the figure somewhere between 15 and 20 million, without further precision.

Places, nature and dates of conflict	*Numbers killed*
1945	
Greece: civil war, to 1949	160,000
Indonesia: colonial war, to 1948	5,000
1946	
China: civil war, to 1949	2,000,000
Vietnam: 1st Indochina war, to 1954	600,000
Colombia: civil war, to 1957	300,000
1947	
Israel: war of independence, to 1949	20,000
Madagascar: colonial uprising, to 1948	5,000
1948	
India: partition	800,000
Burma: ethnic insurrections, continuing	40,000
Malaya: Communist insurrection, to 1960	13,000
1950	
Indonesia: insurrection	5,000
Korean war, to 1953	1,500,000
Philippines: Communist revolt, to 1960	9,000
Tibet: Chinese invasion, to 1959	65,000
1952	
Kenya: Mau Mau uprising, to 1956	10,000
1953	
Indonesia: insurrections, to 1960	30,000
1954	
Algeria: colonial insurrection, to 1962	100,000
Cuba: Castro rebellion, to 1959	5,000
1955	
Cyprus: colonial war, to 1960	359
Cameroun: colonial insurrection, to 1960	32,000
1956	
Hungary: insurrection	10,000
Egypt: Suez invasion	10,000

1959
Rwanda: Tutsi massacred by Hatu   20,000

1960
Laos: 2nd Indochina war, to 1973   24,000
Vietnam: 2nd Indochina war, to 1975   2,000,000
Congo (Zaïre): civil wars, to 1965   100,000

1961
Angola: colonial war, to 1975   90,000
Guatemala: peasant uprising, continuing   100,000
Iraq: Kurdish revolt, to 1970   50,000

1962
North Yemen: civil war, to 1969   100,000
India–China border war   4,500
Portuguese Guinea: colonial war, to 1975   15,000

1963
Sudan: civil war, to 1972   400,000

1965
Dominican Republic: civil disturbances   3,000
India–Pakistan border war   20,000
Mozambique: colonial uprising, to 1975   30,000
Namibia: SWAPO insurrection, continuing   40,000
Chad: civil wars, continuing   50,000

1966
Indonesia: insurrection and repression   400,000
Uganda: Baganda massacres   2,000

1967
Nigeria: Biafran secession, to 1970   1,000,000
Middle East: Six Day War   25,000

1968
Israel: war of attrition with Egypt, to 1970   3,000

1969
El Salvador & Honduras: 'Soccer War'   2,000
USSR–China border fighting   1,000
Northern Ireland: IRA terrorism, continuing   2,700
Philippines: NPA insurrection, continuing   100,000

1970
Jordan: 'Black September'   2,000
Cambodia: Indochina war, to 1975   150,000

1971
Pakistan: civil war   300,000
India–Pakistan war   11,000   **569**

Sri Lanka: left-wing insurrection	2,000
Uganda: civil wars/massacres, to 1979	300,000

1972

Rhodesia (Zimbabwe): colonial wars, to 1980	12,000
Burundi: Tutsi massacred by Hutu	2,000
Hutu massacred by Tutsi	200,000

1973

Chile: 'dirty war', continuing	20,000
Middle East: Yom Kippur War	25,000
Pakistan: Baluchi insurrection, to 1977	9,000

1974

Cyprus: civil war/Turkish intervention	5,000
Ethiopia: civil wars, continuing	2,000,000
Iraq: renewed war with Kurds	20,000
Philippines: Muslim insurrection, continuing	60,000

1975

Lebanon: civil war, continuing	150,000
Cambodia: genocide, to 1978	1–2,000,000
Indonesia: war on East Timor, continuing	100,000
Western Sahara: war with Morocco, continuing	10,000
Angola: civil war, to 1976	50,000

1976

Argentina: 'dirty war', to 1982	15,000
Angola: Unita rebellion, continuing	150,000

1977

Turkey: insurrection and repression, to 1979	5,000
Somalia & Ethiopia: Ogaden war, to 1978	9,000

1978

Nicaragua: anti-Somoza insurgency, to 1979	10,000
Iran: revolution	20,000
Afghanistan: civil war, continuing	450,000
Cambodia: Vietnamese invasion, continuing	150,000
Tanzania & Uganda: war, to 1979	4,000

1979

El Salvador: civil war, continuing	65,000
Iran–Iraq war: to ceasefire, 1988	450,000
China & Vietnam: Chinese invasion	20,000
Uganda: civil wars/banditry, continuing	300,000

1981

Nicaragua: Contra insurrection, continuing	10,000
Mozambique: civil war/famine, continuing	400,000

1982
Syria: Muslim Brotherhood insurrection   20,000
Falklands: war between U K and Argentina   1,000
Lebanon: Israeli invasion   50,000

1983
Peru: Communist Shining Path insurrection, continuing   15,000
Sri Lanka: Tamil insurrection, continuing   16,000
Sudan: civil war, continuing   400,000

1984
India: Sikh & other insurrections, continuing   15,000

1986
South Yemen: civil war   13,000

1988
Somalia: civil war   10,000
Burundi: massacres
       Tutsi by Hutu   2,000
       Hutu by Tutsi   30,000

APPENDIX II: COUPS
AND REVOLUTIONS
SINCE 1945

Only successful coups, revolutions or conquests leading to changes of government are listed here. In some countries, such as Bolivia or Syria, only the major incidents are noted: Syria had 15 coups and attempted coups between 1949 and 1970; in 1981, Bolivia had had its 192nd coup since independence in 1825, an average of one every ten months.

1945
19 October   Venezuela

1946
21 July   Bolivia

1947
26 May   Nicaragua

1948
25 February   Czechoslovakia
3 June   Paraguay
23 September   Venezuela
15 December   El Salvador

1949
30 January   Paraguay
26 February   Paraguay
30 March   Syria
14 August   Syria
21 September   China

1951
10 May   Panama
        Syria
10 August   Syria

1952
10 March   Cuba
9 April   Bolivia
26 July   Egypt

1953
13 June   Colombia
16 August   Iran
19 August   Iran counter-revolution

1954
25 February   Syria
28 June   Guatemala

1955
19 September   Argentina
11 November   Brazil

1956
21 October   Honduras
23 October   Hungary
24 November   Soviet occupation of
              Budapest

1957
30 September   San Marino
11 October   San Merino

573

1958
23 January   Venezuela
13 May   France
14 July   Iraq
20 October   Thailand
28 October   Burma
17 November   Sudan

1959
1 January   Cuba

1960
27 April   Turkey
9 August   Laos
14 September   Congo (Leopoldville)
13 December   Ethiopia (reversed 19 December)

1961
25 January   El Salvador
28 January   Ruanda
16 May   South Korea
3 July   South Korea
28 September   Syria

1962
16 January   Dominican Republic
18 January   Dominican Republic
2 March   Burma
28 March   Syria
29 March   Argentina
5 April   Syria
18 June   Peru
27 September   North Yemen

1963
13 January   Togo
8 February   Iraq
8 March   Syria
31 March   Guatemala
3 October   Honduras
1 November   South Vietnam
11 November   Iraq

1964
12 January   Zanzibar
30 January   South Vietnam
18 February   Gabon (French troops reversed it on 19 February)

31 April   Brazil
31 October   Sudan
2 November   Saudi Arabia
3 November   Bolivia
20 December   South Vietnam

1965
27 January   South Vietnam
20 April   Yemen
25 April   Dominican Republic
19 June   Algeria
5 September   Iraq
25 November   Congo (Leopoldville)
29 November   Dahomey

1966
1 January   Central African Republic
4 January   Upper Volta
15 January   Nigeria
22 February   Uganda
23 February   Syria
24 February   Ghana
29 June   Argentina
8 July   Burundi
29 July   Nigeria
26 October   Congo (Kinshasa)
28 November   Burundi

1967
13 January   Togo
22 January   Indonesia
23 March   Sierra Leone
21 April   Greece
5 November   North Yemen
17 December   Dahomey

1968
18 April   Sierra Leone
17 July   Iraq
1 August   Congo (Brazzaville)
4 September   Congo (Brazzaville)
3 October   Peru
11 October   Panama
19 October   Mali
13 December   Brazil

1969
25 May   Sudan
1 September   Libya

26 September   Bolivia
21 October   Somalia
12 December   Dahomey

1970
30 January   Lesotho
22 June   Ecuador
23 July   Oman
6 October   Bolivia
13 November   Syria

1971
25 January   Uganda
23 March   Argentina
22 August   Bolivia
17 November   Thailand
16 December   East Pakistan
20 December   West Pakistan

1972
13 January   Ghana
14 May   Malagasy Republic
22 September   Philippines
17 October   South Korea
26 October   Dahomey
4 December   Honduras

1973
27 June   Uruguay
5 July   Rwanda
17 July   Afghanistan
11 September   Chile
25 November   Greece

1974
8 February   Upper Volta
15 April   Niger
25 April   Portugal
12 September   Ethiopia
15 July   Cyprus
23 July   Greece

1975
22 April   Honduras
17 April   Cambodia
30 April South Vietnam
             Laos
29 July   Nigeria
15 August   Bangladesh
29 August   Peru

3 November   Bangladesh
7 November   Bangladesh

1976
24 March   Argentina
12 June   Uruguay
10 October   Thailand
1 November   Burundi

1977
5 April   Congo
5 June   Seychelles
5 July   Pakistan

1978
27 April   Afghanistan
13 May   Comoro Islands
7 July   Ghana
10 July   Mauritania
21 July   Bolivia
6 August   Honduras

1979
16 January   Iran
6 February   Congo
12 March   Grenada
11 April   Uganda
4 June   Ghana
17 July   Bolivia
             Nicaragua
3 August   Equatorial Guinea
16 September   Afghanistan
20 September   Central African
                 Empire
16 October   El Salvador
27 December   Afghanistan

1980
24 February   Surinam
12 April   Liberia
15 April   Uganda
17 July   Bolivia
12 September   Turkey
14 November   Guinea-Bissau
25 November   Upper Volta

1981
30 July   Gambia (reversed by
             Senegalese troops, 5 August)
4 August   Bolivia

1 September   Central African Republic
31 December   Ghana

1982
23 March   Guatemala
24 March   Bangladesh
7 June   Chad
7 November   Upper Volta
8 December   Surinam

1983
4 August   Upper Volta
8 August   Guatemala
19 October   Grenada
31 December   Nigeria

1984
3 April   Guinea
12 December   Mauritania

1985
4 April   Sudan

27 July   Uganda
27 August   Nigeria

1986
19 January   South Yemen
20 January   Lesotho
29 January   Uganda
7 February   Haiti
25 February   Philippines

1987
14 May   Fiji
3 September   Burundi
25 September   Fiji
16 October   Burkina Faso

1988
17 September   Burma
                 Haiti

1989
3 February   Paraguay
30 June   Sudan

APPENDIX III:
ASSASSINATIONS SINCE
1946

This is a list of the political murders of prominent personages. It includes the names of public officials and the most prominent people murdered in continuing campaigns of terrorism, by such groups as the IRA, ETA and Armenian terrorists, killed during coups or revolutions (the latter are indicated by *). Separate acts of generalized terrorism are mentioned in the relevent chapters. The executions or murders of some prominent opposition figures are also listed, such as Patrice Lumumba, and a few notable rebels, such as Che Guevara, who were killed by security forces. Also listed are prominent politicians overthrown in coups and subsequently executed, such as Kassem, Bhutto and Menderes. A few particularly significant failed assassinations are also noted.

1946
21 July   Gualberto Villaroel, President of Bolivia*

1947
19 July   Aung San, Burmese leader, and seven associates

1948
30 January   Mahatma Gandhi
10 March   Jan Masaryk, foreign minister of Czechoslovakia (officially a suicide)*
9 April   Dr Jorge Gaitan, liberal leader in Colombia
17 September   Count Folke Bernadotte, UN commissioner in Palestine
28 December   Mahamoud Fahmy Nokrashy Pasha, prime minister of Egypt

1949
12 February   Sheikh Hassan al-Banna, head of Muslim Brotherhood, in Cairo
29 April   Widow of President Quezon of the Philippines, her daughter, son-in-law and ten others
18 July   Major Francisco Arana, Guatemalan conservative leader
14 August   Husni Zaim, president of Syria, and Mohsen el-Barazi, the prime minister*

577

1950

1 November	Attempted assassination of President Truman
13 November	Carlos Delgado Chalbaud, president of Venezuela

1951

7 March	Ali Razmara, prime minister of Iran
16 July	Riadh es-Salh, former prime minister of Lebanon
20 July	King Abdullah of Jordan
31 July	General Charles-Marie Chanson and Thai Lap Thanh, governor of South Vietnam
6 October	Sir Henry Gurney, British high commissioner in Malaya
16 October	Liaquat Ali Khan, prime minister of Pakistan

1953

1 July	Prince Azzedine Bey, heir to Bey of Tunis

1955

3 January	Colonel José Antonio Remón, president of Panama

1956

29 September	General Anastasio Somoza García, president of Nicaragua

1957

26 July	Carlos Castillo Armas, president of Guatemala

1958

16 June	Imre Nagy, former Hungarian prime minister, and General Pal Maleter, executed after Soviet invasion (1956)
14 July	King Feisal II of Iraq, Crown Prince Abdul Ilah, Prime Minister General Nuri es-Said and others*

1959

25 September	Solomon West Ridgway Diaz Bandaranike, prime minister of Sri Lanka

1960

29 August	Hazza al-Majali, Jordanian prime minister

1961

12 February	Patrice Lumumba, former Congo (Leopoldville) prime minister
30 May	Generalissimo Rafaél Leonidas Trujillo, president of the Dominican Republic
8 September	Attempted assassination of General de Gaulle
17 September	Adnan Menderes, former Turkish prime minister, executed after 1960 coup
13 October	Prince Louis Rwagasone, prime minister of Burundi

1962

22 August	Attempted assassination of General de Gaulle

1963

13 January	Sylvanus Olympio, president of Togo*

8 February	Abd al-Karim Kassem, president of Iraq*
1 April	Quinim Pholsen, foreign minister of Laos
28 May	Gregory Lambrakis, Greek opposition leader
12 June	Medgar Evers, US civil rights leader
2 November	Ngo Dinh Diem, president of South Vietnam, and his brother Ngo Dinh Nhu*
22 November	John F. Kennedy, president of the United States
24 November	Lee Harvey Oswald, assassin of John F. Kennedy

1964

21 February	Attempted assassination of President Ismet Inonu of Turkey

1965

15 January	Pierre Ngendandumowe, prime minister of Burundi
21 January	Hassan Ali Mansur, prime minister of Iran
21 February	Malcolm X, American Black Muslim leader
24 April	General Humberto Delgardo, Portuguese opposition leader
1 September	Sir Arthur Charles, speaker of Aden legislative Council
1 October	General Achmad Yani, Indonesian chief of staff, and five other generals
29 October	Mehdi Ben Barka, Moroccan opposition leader, in Paris
22 November	Dipa Nusantara Aidit, Indonesian Communist party leader

1966

15 January	Alhaji Sir Abubaker Tafawa Balewa, prime minister of Nigeria; the Sardauna of Sokoto, prime minister of Northern Nigeria; Chief Akintola, prime minister of Western Nigeria, and army leaders*
29 July	General Johnson Aguiyi-Ironsi, Nigerian head of state*
6 September	Dr Hendrik Verwoerd, prime minister of South Africa

1967

25 August	George Lincoln Rockwell, American Fascist
9 October	Che Guevara, Argentinian Communist, in Bolivia

1968

16 January	Colonel John Webber, head of US military mission to Guatemala
4 April	Reverend Martin Luther King
5 June	US Senator Robert F. Kennedy
28 August	John Mein, US ambassador to Guatemala

1969

3 February	Eduardo Mondlane, Mozambique rebel leader
5 July	Tom Mboya, Kenya minister of economic planning
15 October	Abdirashid Ali Shermarke, president of Somalia

1970

5 April	Count Carl von Spreti, West German ambassador to Guatemala, kidnapped and killed
10 June	Major Robert Perry, US military attaché in Jordan
16 July	Pedro Aramburu, former president of Argentina (kidnapped 29 May)
31 July	Dan Mitrione, US diplomat, in Montevideo

22 October	General René Schneider, commander-in-chief of the Chilean army
11 November	Pierre Laporte, minister of labour, Quebec

1971

28 November	Wasfi Tal, Jordanian prime minister, in Cairo

1972

7 April	Abeid Karume, vice president of Tanzania and Zanzibar leader
29 April	Ntare V, ex-king of Burundi
15 May	Attempted assassination of Governor George Wallace of Alabama
16 August	Attempted assassination of King Hassan of Morocco

1973

20 January	Dr Amilcar Cabral, rebel leader in Portuguese Guinea
2 March	Cleo Noel, American ambassador in Sudan; George C. Moore, departing chargé d'affaires; Guy Eid, Belgian chargé d'affaires
11 September	Salvador Allende, president of Chile*
20 December	Admiral Luis Carrero Blanco, prime minister of Spain

1974

15 August	Attempted assassination of President Park Chung Hee of South Korea; his wife killed
19 August	Rodger Davies, American ambassador to Cyprus
30 September	General Carlos Prats, former Chilean defence minister, and his wife, in Buenos Aires
21 November	General Aman Michael Andom, Ethiopian head of state

1975

5 February	Colonel Richard Ratsimandrava, president of Malagasy Republic
25 March	King Feisal ibn Abdul Aziz, of Saudi Arabia
13 April	Ngarta Tombalbaye, president of Chad*
15 August	Sheikh Mujibar Rahman, president of Bangladesh*
22 October	Danis Tunanigil, Turkish ambassador to Austria
24 October	Ismail Erez, Turkish ambassador to France
7 November	General Khalid Musharaf, Bangladesh head of government*
27 November	Ross McWhirter, co-publisher of *Guinness Book of Records* and leading light of the Freedom Association, British right-wing pressure group.
23 December	Richard Welch, C I A station chief in Greece

1976

3 February	General Murtala Ramat Mohammed, president of Nigeria
6 June	Francis Meloy, U S ambassador to Lebanon
21 July	Christopher Ewart-Biggs, U K ambassador to Dublin, and his secretary, Judith Cook
21 September	Orlando Letelier, former Chilean minister of defence, and his secretary, Ronni Moffitt, in Washington

1977

2 February	Kemal Jumblatt, Druse leader in Lebanon; General Teferi Banti, Ethiopian head of state
16 February	Janane Luwum, Anglican archbishop of Uganda
18 March	Marien Ngouabi, president of the Congo
23 March	Cardinal Emile Biayenda of the Congo
10 April	Al-Quadi al-Hajri, former North Yemen prime minister, with his wife, in London
19 April	Mauricio Borgonovo Pohl, foreign minister of El Salvador
5 September	Dr Hans-Martin Schleyer, head of the West German Industries Federation kidnapped; body found in France 19 October
10 October	Ibrahim al-Hamdi, president of North Yemen

1978

4 January	Said Hammami, PLO representative in London
10 January	Pedro Joaquín Chamorro, publisher of *La Prensa*, Nicaragua
27 April	Mohammed Daoud, president of Afghanistan*
9 May	Aldo Moro, former Italian prime minister (kidnapped 16 March)
29 May	Ali Soilih, president of Comoro Islands, shot after coup 13 May*
13 June	Tony Franjieh, Lebanese Christian leader
24 June	Ahmed Hussein al-Ghashmi, president of North Yemen
26 June	Salim Rubai Ali, president of South Yemen*
10 July	General Aboul Razik al-Naif, former prime minister of Iraq, in London
31 August	Imam Musa Sadr, Lebanese Shiite religious leader disappeared in Libya, presumed murdered

1979

14 February	Adolph Dubs, US ambassador to Afghanistan
22 March	Sir Richard Sykes, British ambassador to Netherlands
30 March	Airey Neave, Conservative spokesman on Northern Ireland
4 April	Zulfikar Ali Bhutto, former president of Pakistan, executed after 1977 coup
8 August	Lord Louis Mountbatten and three others, in Ireland
29 September	Francisco Nguema, president of Equatorial Guinea, executed after coup
8 October	Nur Mohammed Taraki, president of Afghanistan
26 October	General Park Chung Hee, president of South Korea
27 December	Hafizullah Amin, president of Afghanistan*

1980

24 March	Archbishop Oscar Romero of San Salvador
12 April	William Tolbert, president of Liberia*
19 July	Nihat Erim, former prime minister of Turkey
21 July	Salah al-Din al-Bitar, former Syrian prime minister
15 August	Imam Sayyid Muhammed Baqir al-Sadr, Iraqi Shiite leader, executed with his sister
17 September	Anastasio Somoza Debayle, former president of Nicaragua

581

1981

21 January	Sir Norman Stronge, former speaker of Stormont parliament in Northern Ireland
30 March	Attempted assassination of President Reagan
13 May	Attempted assassination of Pope John Paul II
24 May	Jaime Roldos Aguilera, president of Ecuador
30 May	Ziaur Rahman, president of Bangladesh
28 June	Mohammed Beheshti, secretary-general of Islamic Republic party of Iran killed with 74 others by a bomb
30 August	Mohammed Rajai, president of Iran, Mohammed Bahonar, prime minister, and 13 others killed by a bomb.
4 September	Louis Delamare, French ambassador to Lebanon
6 October	Anwar Sadat, president of Egypt
14 November	Reverend Robert Radford, M P, Unionist leader in Belfast
18 December	Mehmet Shehu, prime minister of Albania, killed by colleagues

1982

9 March	Galip Balkar, Turkish ambassador to Yugoslavia
14 September	Bashir Gemayel, president-elect of Lebanon

1983

21 August	Benigno Aquino, Philippine opposition leader
9 October	4 South Korean ministers killed by a bomb in Rangoon, Burma

1984

18 January	Malcolm Kerr, dean of the American University in Beirut
30 April	Rodrigo Lara Bonilla, Colombian minister of justice
5 June	Sant Bhindranwale, Sikh terrorist leader, killed by Indian army
20 August	Sant Harchand Singh Longowal, moderate Sikh leader
12 October	Attempted assassination of Margaret Thatcher, British prime minister (4 others killed)
17 October	Father Jerzy Popieluszko, Polish opposition priest
31 October	Indira Gandhi, prime minister of India
27 November	Percy Norris, British deputy high commissioner in India

1985

12 January	Eloi Machoro, New Caledonia separatist leader
4 October	William Buckley, C I A station chief in Beirut (kidnapped 16 March 1984)
6 November	11 justices of the Colombian Supreme Court

1986

2 January	Ignacio Gonzalez Palacíos, head of Guatemalan secret police
6 February	Vice-Admiral Cristobal Colón de Carvajal of Spanish navy
28 February	Olof Palme, prime minister of Sweden
11 August	Indian General Arun Vaidya
7 October	Sheikh Sabhi al-Saleh, Lebanese Sunni leader
25 October	General Rafaél Garricho Gil, governor of Guipúzcoa, Spain, with his wife and son

1987

20 March	General Licio Giogieri, director of Italian space weapons research
25 April	Maurice Gibson, Northern Ireland appeals court judge, with his wife
1 June	Rashid Karami, prime minister of Lebanon
2 August	Jaime Ferrer, minister of local government, Philippines
18 August	Attempted assassination of Junius Jayewardene, president of Sri Lanka
13 October	Yves Volel, Haitian presidential candidate
16 October	Thomas Sankara, president of Burkina Faso*

1988

26 January	Carlos Mauro Hoyos Jimenez, Colombian attorney general
17 February	American Colonel William Higgins serving with UN force in Lebanon, kidnapped. Murder disclosed 1989
16 April	Khalid Wazir (Abu Jihad), PLO leader, in Tunis
28 April	Hagop Hagopian, Armenian terrorist leader, in Athens
18 June	Attempted assassination of Turgut Ozal, prime minister of Turkey
5 August	Allama Arif al-Hussaini, Pakistani Shiite leader
17 August	Mohammed Zia el-Haq, president of Pakistan, US ambassador Arnold Raphel and others in a plane crash, possibly sabotage

1989

25 January	General Gustavo Alvarez Martinez, former Honduran strong man
4 May	Jean-Marie Tjibaou, New Caledonian separatist leader
16 May	Sheikh Hassan Khaled, Lebanese Sunni leader
18 August	Luis Carlos Galan, Colombian presidential candidate
25 September	Pavlos Bakoyannis, Greek member of parliament
13 November	Rohana Nijeweera, Sri Lankan terrorist leader

583

INDEX

585

589

ABOUT THE AUTHOR

Patrick Brogan was born in Oxford and educated at Cambridge University. He has worked for twenty years as a foreign correspondent, and has experienced firsthand many of the war zones of the world. He has written for numerous newspapers and journals, including *The Times* (London), *The Observer*, and the New York *Daily News*. He now lives in Washington, D.C., with his wife and four children.